INTERNATIONAL ACCOUNTING

Peter Walton
Axel Haller
Bernard Raffournier

Second Edition

INTERNATIONAL ACCOUNTING

THOMSON

Australia • Canada • Mexico • Singapore • Spain • United Kingdom • United States

THOMSON

International Accounting – Second Edition

Copyright © 2003 Peter Walton, Axel Haller and Bernard Raffournier

The Thomson logo is a registered trademark used herein under licence.

For more information, contact Thomson Learning, High Holborn House, 50–51 Bedford Row, London WC1R 4LR or visit us on the World Wide Web at: http://www.thomsonlearning.co.uk

British Library Cataloguing-in-Publication-Data
A catalogue record for this book is available from the British Library

ISBN 1–86152–934–1

First edition published 1998 by International Thomson Business Press

Reprinted 2002 by Thomson Learning

This edition published 2003 by Thomson Learning

Typeset by J & L Composition, Filey

Printed by TJ International, Padstow, Cornwall

Contents

Contributors

Kristina Artsberg is professor of accounting at Jönköping International Business School in Sweden. She took her doctorate in 1992 and became docent at Lund University in 2000. She has been a guest teacher at several universities and also in practice. Her research interests are accounting standard-setting, taxation and international accounting, and she publishes regularly in these areas.

Wolf Bay is managing director, finance, of a Taiwanese joint venture within the Daimler-Chrysler group. He took a doctorate at the University of Augsburg, Germany, and an MBA at the University of Chicago, USA. Prior to his current appointment he was a leading member of the team which orchestrated the listing of Daimler Benz shares on the New York Stock Exchange.

Hans-Georg Bruns is a member of the International Accounting Standards Board and serves as liaison member with the German Accounting Standards Board. He took his doctorate at the University of Mannheim, Germany. He is Honorary professor at the University of Stuttgart. He is a former vice-president, corporate control, at Daimler-Chrysler having been vice-president, group accounting and investor relations, at the time of the listing of Daimler Benz in New York.

Begoña Giner Inchausti is professor of accounting and finance at the University of Valencia, Spain. She took an MSc in Accounting and Finance at the London School of Economics. She is an Associate Editor of the *European Accounting Review* and currently sits on the Technical Expert Group of the European Financial Reporting Advisory Group. She has published extensively in the area of financial accounting and her paper 'Disclosure of financial information: an empirical study' won a national prize in 1993.

Axel Haller is professor of accounting and auditing at the Johannes Kepler University, Linz, Austria. His doctoral thesis, which was written at the University of Augsburg, Germany, analysed the social, legal and theoretical framework of US accounting and compared this with Germany. He has also extensively researched the subject of value added accounting and has written a book on the subject. He has been invited to teach at many European universities, for example the London School of Economics, Copenhagen Business School and Lund University, and several US universities. He has authored and co-authored more than 70 articles in books and refereed scientific journals.

Terry Heazlewood is professor of accounting and head, International School of Business, at Charles Sturt University, Wagga Wagga, NSW, Australia. He has authored, co-authored and edited fourteen books and research studies, contributed chapters to a range of books and published numerous articles in refereed and professional journals in Australia, New Zealand, the UK and the USA. He is co-editor of the Australian Company Financial reporting series, which was sponsored by the Australian Accounting Research Foundation. He is a former director, companies branch, of the National Companies and Securities Commission in Australia.

Christian Hoarau has the chair of financial accounting and audit at the Conservatoire National des Arts et Métiers, Paris, France. He is a professionally qualified accountant (*expert-comptable* and *commissaire aux comptes*) and has a doctorate from the University of Paris XII. Author of many books and articles on accounting and finance, he is a member of the Comité de la Réglementation Comptable and the Conseil National de la Comptabilité, the French standard-setters. He is a past president of the Association Française de Comptabilité and a member of the editorial committee of their journal *Comptabilité, Contrôle, Audit*.

Ann Jorissen is Professor of Accounting at the University of Antwerp, Belgium, where she did her doctorate. She is chair of the department of accounting and finance. She was a co-founder of the *European Accounting Review*, was a co-editor from 1992 to 1997 and is a member of its advisory board. She is currently the Belgian representative on the executive committee of the European Accounting Association.

Tatiana Krylova is chief of enterprise internationalization at the UN Conference on Trade and Development. Her responsibilities include coordinating UN activities in promoting international accounting and auditing standards. She did her doctorate at Moscow State University, and taught there, researching in the area of comparative international accounting. She was Raisa Gorbachev visiting fellow at Stanford University in 1991 and in 1997 was International Distinguished Lecturer for the American Accounting Association. She has been a partner in KPMG Moscow, and has worked on an EU TACIS programme to help reform accounting in the Russian Federation. She has worked extensively with the CIS Coordinating Committee on Accounting Methodology.

Gary K. Meek is the Oscar S Gellein/Deloitte & Touche Professor of Accounting at Oklahoma State University, USA and a certified public accountant. He is a past vice-president of the American Accounting Association, and a past chair of its international accounting section. He has written extensively on international accounting, including publication in the relevant major academic journals. His work includes authoritative surveys of current research in the field. He is co-author with Helen Gernon of *Accounting: an international perspective* (Irwin McGraw-Hill, 5th edn, 2001) and with Frederick D S Choi and Carol Ann Frost of *International Accounting* (Prentice Hall, 4th edn, 2002).

Bernard Raffournier is professor of accounting at HEC Management Studies, University of Geneva, Switzerland. He studied his doctorate at Grenoble University, France, and served his internship as an *expert-comptable* in Paris. His main research areas are financial accounting and the application of IASB standards. His publications include *Les Normes Comptables Internationales* (IAS) Economica, Paris 1996. He is a member of the advisory board of *Comptabilité, Contrôle, Audit* and he has been a member of the executive committee of the European Accounting Association.

Jacques Richard is professor of accounting at Paris-Dauphine University, France and a partner in an accounting firm. His doctoral thesis compared eastern and western accounting systems. He is currently involved in training programmes in Bulgaria, Poland, Romania, Russia and Vietnam. His research interests also extend to Schmalenbach and the evolution of charts of accounts. He is a member of the Conseil National de la Comptabilité, the French standard-setter and of the advisory boards of the *European Accounting Review* and *Compabilité, Contrôle, Audit*.

Etsuo Sawa is professor of accounting at Chuo University and previously taught at Keio University, both in Tokyo. He is a qualified certified public accountant under both Japanese and US professional regulations and has practised for 28 years, mainly with Coopers & Lybrand, in both the USA and Japan. He was a senior research fellow at the Japanese Institute of CPAs and was Japan's technical adviser to the IASC Board 1992–99.

Hans R. Schwencke is an associate professor at the Norwegian School of Management, Oslo. He is a lawyer and certified public accountant. He has written books and articles on Norwegian accounting. His primary research interests are international and European accounting issues. He has recently published a book on mergers and acquisitions.

Leo van der Tas is professor of accounting at Erasmus University, Rotterdam, Netherlands. He is a Dutch Registeraccountant and partner with Ernst & Young, The Netherlands, where he is a member of the technical department. He spent two years on secondment to the European Commission in the accountancy section of the DGXV. He is a member of the IASB's International Financial Reporting Interpretations Committee, and is also on the advisory board of the *European Accounting Review*.

Paul A. Taylor lectures in accounting at the Management School, Lancaster University, UK and is a chartered accountant. He specializes in group accounting and consolidated financial reporting. His recent publications include *Consolidated Financial Reporting* (Paul Chapman Publishing, 1996) and a chapter on group accounting in the UK in Ordelheide's *Transnational Accounting* (Palgrave, 2nd edn, 2001). He has published in numerous professional and academic journals. He has also been a visiting lecturer at Melbourne University.

Peter Walton is a professor of accounting at ESSEC Business School, Paris, France, and Reader at the Open University Business School. He qualified as a certified accountant in the UK and worked in industry before taking his doctorate at the London School of Economics. He is a consultant to the UN working group of experts on international standards of accounting and reporting (ISAR) and editor of *World Accounting Report*. He is a former co-editor of the *European Accounting Review* and was given an award in 2002 for his contribution to the European Accounting Association. He is a member of the advisory committee of several scientific journals, and has published extensively.

Stefano Zambon is an associate professor of accounting and business economics at the University of Ferrara, Italy. He studied at the University of Venice and at the University of London (MSc in international accounting and finance at the London School of Economics). He is a dottore Commercialista. He has held visiting posts at London Business School (UK), ESCP, HEC and CNAM (France), and the Universities of Reading, Melbourne, New South Wales, Boston and Metz. He is a member of the executive committee of the European Accounting Association and of the editorial boards of the *European Accounting Review, Comptabilité, Contrôle, Audit* and the *International Journal of Accounting* (he is an associate editor).

Preface

The literature suggests that international accounting courses fall into one of two categories: those that take particular technical issues in accounting as their starting point, and those that take individual jurisdictions as their unit of construction. This book comes from the second tradition, although we have addressed some technical issues separately in the later chapters.

We take the view that accounting in any one country at any one time represents the result of an evolution over many years. This evolution has taken place against a cultural backcloth that imbues each country's rules with many particularities, and institutions have been created which are unique to each country. We think therefore a holistic approach offers a more satisfying way of addressing international accounting differences and one that permits students to gain an understanding of the country's accounting culture.

At the same time, we have provided chapters that address special issues in multinational financial reporting. These include the problems of multi-listed companies, financial statement analysis in a cross-border context, foreign currency translation and hedging, segment reporting and the audit of consolidated accounts.

For the individual country chapters we invited specialists from each of the countries concerned to write us a chapter on their own country. We believe that an essential part of a country's accounting culture is unwritten, and this is therefore best accessed through an author who was educated within that culture but understands something of other accounting cultures. To provide a degree of comparability we have asked authors all to address a number of issues, but we have sought to avoid a checklist approach which assumes that all jurisdictions address the same priorities. At the same time, the book is structured around International Accounting Standards (International Financial Reporting Standards) as a further aid to comparability and as a recognition that these are the standards of reference in international reporting.

The country studies also reflect in their structure the idea that accounting has been much borrowed between jurisdictions. The book is organised on the following basis:

1. Introduction to accounting diversity and change;

2. International Financial Reporting Standards;

3. The major commercial accounting models (France, Germany and the US with the UK added as having influenced the US and to some extent influencing the EU);

4. Individual countries (Japan, Netherlands, Belgium, Spain, Italy, Australia plus a chapter on Nordic countries);

5. Accounting outside Western developed economies.

The second part addresses the multinational reporting environment:

1. Multinational companies and international capital markets;
2. Foreign currency translation;
3. Segmental reporting;
4. The audit of multinationals;
5. Financial statement analysis in an international context.

The book assumes that students will already have acquired a knowledge of the technical issues involved in financial reporting in a national context.

Acknowledgements

Compared with the first edition, original chapters of which started out variously in French, German and English, this new English edition has been a less challenging task, with only one chapter requiring translation (for which I am immensely grateful to students from Mannheim University on an exchange programme at ESSEC Business School).

We should emphasise that the book is a collective enterprise that depends heavily on the goodwill and rigour of colleagues who teach and research in international accounting at different universities around the world. Updating a chapter never occurs at a convenient moment, and the elapse of time usually means that further attention is necessary during the publishing process. In our case this was particularly true of the US material.

We are grateful to the very many people who have contributed to this book in many different ways from its original sketching out in a hotel on Lake Constance in 1995 through to this new English language edition. We thank those people who have used the first edition and commented upon it and we hope that this second edition will prove useful to them. The responsibility for any errors, does, of course, remain ours.

Country differences and harmonization

Axel Haller and Peter Walton

This chapter is intended to set the scene for the rest of the book – to explain why accounting is different from one country to another, and to what extent efforts have been made to reduce differences. The individual country chapters which follow will bring out the special aspects that distinguish one country from another and it will also be possible to see how harmonization has affected some countries. The later chapters of the book are concerned with multinational companies, and specific accounting topics they have to cope with due to the internationalization of their activities.

Accounting differences

The growth and globalization of companies' operations has led to an increase in acquisitions of non-domestic enterprises and to a boost of companies' capital needs which has been a motor of the significant evolution of international capital markets. These international engagements of companies, which are still increasing, have demonstrated the fact that accounting, a major tool of business communication, differs in content and application from country to country around the world. That differences exist is not of itself automatically a problem, but they certainly oblige the business to consider whether they have an economic impact and whether it matters. There is, of course, no easy answer to that question: in some situations accounting differences lead potentially to inefficiencies, missed opportunities and distortions of economic behaviour. In other circumstances, national accounting usually meets its objectives and any attempt to change it to fit some international pattern can also lead to inefficiencies and distortions of existing economic behaviour.

The complexity of the question can be illustrated by the consideration of accounting as a medium for communicating economic information – an economic language. Languages work by encapsulating information or ideas into signs, the meaning of which is understood by those in the same cultural group. So, an anglophone person wanting to convey information about a domestic pet which barks will use the sign 'dog', but if wishing to convey the message to a francophone, he or she must use the sign 'chien' (even then, the anglophone may have a Labrador in mind, and the francophone a poodle). For the message to pass, there must be a pre-existing understanding about the meanings of the signs used. A child learns this from its family and school; accountants learn their much narrower economic sign language at university or during professional training. Having learnt it, they can pass messages to people with the same training.

But this common economic language has been adapted fairly closely to the needs of the individual culture group and is intimately connected, like ordinary language, with other aspects of the same culture. Consequently, the nationally evolved accounting language is adapted for its local purposes, such as talking to the investors, or tax authorities or the bank, but is not intended to be used for communicating across different cultures. Once such communication starts, misunderstandings will almost certainly follow because the reference points of the sender and of the receiver of the information are different. This fact is illustrated in Figure 1.1. It should show this general phenomenon of communication transferred to accounting, and it follows that misunderstandings can occur because of differences in the information sent but also because of differences relating to the perception and interpretation of the information by the receiver.

This is the nub of the international accounting problem. How do companies that want to operate across national (and therefore usually cultural) boundaries convey economic information or receive economic information appropriate for business decisions? In concrete terms, how does the investment manager in Geneva read the accounts of American companies to decide whether an investment is worthwhile? How does a German company present its annual accounts to the investment community in New York? And how are these accounts interpreted by the US investors? Do they interpret the information with an American accounting perception or do they try to be aware that the communicating company is a German one? In fact accounting is a very imperfect economic language which conveys relatively rudimentary information, and this tends to make matters more difficult because there are fewer signs to interpret and therefore a greater chance of significant errors.

Aside from conveying information across national boundaries for communication with institutions outside the company, there are other problems. International companies tend to

Figure 1.1 Reasons for the international accounting problem

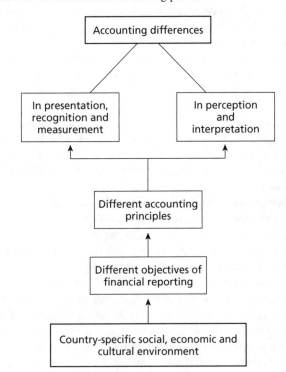

prefer uniform accounting systems throughout their organization, and such systems certainly make the conduct of internal controls and external audit much simpler. They do not, though, get round the problem of needing to present accounts locally for tax and other regulatory purposes. Other problem areas are the conduct of audits of international groups and indeed moving staff from one country to another. For the international company and the international investor, national accounting differences represent a hurdle, at the very least, to understanding.

This is not to say, though, that removal of differences is necessarily a good thing. This phenomenon is explored later in this chapter, but it should be appreciated that if an attempt is made to amend a language for international business reasons, this can disturb the messages which are passed locally and the functioning of the whole national communication system. For example, a different way of measuring profit, which might align with an international approach, is likely to disturb relations with the local investors or the national tax regime. A different valuation approach could change the balance sheet structure and therefore gearing ratios. In this way it unintentionally affects borrowing capacity and costs, because the opinions of what is an appropriate or even ideal balance sheet structure or result of a specific ratio differs from country to country due to national practices in financing and managing a company or different norms of corporate governance.

Curiously enough, the awareness of international accounting differences and the study of these are also culturally biased. In the anglophone literature, the beginnings of study of international accounting can be traced to the late 1960s, more or less reflecting the beginnings of substantial growth in international business. In mainland Europe, there has been a much longer-established consciousness of differences, evidenced by congresses which from the late nineteenth century met to consider national differences and propose steps to reduce these (Forrester 1996).

This links fairly closely with an idea prevalent in the anglophone profession, at least for the first half of the twentieth century, that accounting was a purely technical phenomenon. If other countries had different accounting, this was because they had simply not put enough effort into developing it. The application of a little research and development initiative would result in everyone reaching the same 'best' accounting (which the anglophone literature would suggest was not too far from US generally accepted accounting principles, known as US GAAP).

It was only in the 1970s (e.g. Zeff 1978) that there came to be a growing understanding in the anglophone literature that accounting rules were the result of a political process, in which the economic interests of those concerned were potentially affected, and were not the neutral measuring device which had been previously assumed.

Why national practices differ

The comparison of accounting with language is apt in the sense that accounting is an artificial device, constructed by society, in order to gather and communicate information. It is a 'social construct' which will consequently reflect the society in which it has been developed. Unlike language, accounting is also subject to legislation, as well as unwritten rules developed through usage, and this legislation is often triggered by some economic event or circumstances. If we look at the evolution of the ensemble of accounting rules in a country – that country's GAAP – it is likely to consist of a set of practices evolved by those concerned with accounting to reflect the economic circumstances which they are trying to encapsulate, together with a series of legal requirements which have been established from time to time. These legal requirements are often the response to a financial scandal or other abuse of the system, or are a reflection of economic pressures. For example, the introduction of limited liability, share-issuing companies was usually a response to the economic pressures of the Industrial Revolution, but subsequent legislation was introduced in many countries to curb abuses of this form of vehicle in defrauding investors and creditors (see, for example, the explanations of the evolution of accounting in the USA or Germany in Chapters 3 and 4).

One can imagine, therefore, as a model for the evolution of accounting in any one country a situation where there is an equilibrium state which lasts potentially for years, which is disturbed either by some change in the economic environment or by some unusual event. There is a regulatory response, or at least some change in the rules, and a new equilibrium emerges. This kind of model is known as a 'contingent' model of accounting evolution. Because the same events do not necessarily take place in different economies, or if they do, not necessarily at the same time and/or do not lead to the same effects, it follows that the accounting rules will be different from country to country.

Another variable is determined by the society within which change takes place, and this is the method of regulating change, which can vary in a quite dramatic fashion from one country to another. Some countries work with detailed laws (such as Germany and France), while others prefer to work with a minimum of formal statute supported by rules of best practice (e.g. UK). Equally the attitude to law is different – in some countries it is taken for granted that a law should be obeyed, in others there is a subtle social understanding about which laws are obeyed and in what degree.

Some standard-setters sometimes illustrate the problem with the following joke:

> International understanding on rules is very difficult because the rules have different meanings: in Germany everything is forbidden unless it is explicitly allowed by the law, whereas in England everything is allowed except what is explicitly forbidden in the law. In Iran, on the other hand, everything is forbidden, even though it is allowed by the law, whereas in Italy everything is allowed, especially if it is forbidden.

In all circumstances there is a large element of unwritten code which is part of a society's culture. It follows from this that where accounting is regulated, the means chosen to do so will vary from country to country, thereby providing a different regulatory structure. The means of regulating financial reporting may be seen as an important cultural variable. Because of this, if change is triggered in two countries at the same time by the same event, the means chosen for regulating may well be different.

One should not over-emphasize the differences, since one of the characteristics of accounting regulation is that countries have for many years been quite interested in observing how their neighbours regulate, and borrowing any elements which appear to be useful. Countries have a natural tendency to borrow from their major trading partners who are also likely to be nations with whom there are cultural ties. For example, one can see a tendency for anglophone countries to develop their accounting by reference to what is happening in other anglophone countries, while mainland European countries have borrowed from each other, particularly where there is a clear language link.

An example of this is the share-issuing limited liability company and its annual audit, which were evolved in the nineteenth century by different countries experimenting and observing the results of experiments elsewhere. As a consequence most developed countries by the end of the nineteenth century had a form of share-issuing limited liability company as the medium for large business, even if the importance of this particular vehicle varied, as also did the extent to which companies were quoted on stock exchanges. Those traditional differences can easily be discovered even today.

The audit function that is linked to this went through a series of metamorphoses, which illustrates that even if the same idea starts out in different countries, it can change significantly as it is adapted to local circumstances. In most countries the annual audit was originally intended as an opportunity for shareholders to examine the management of the company in which they had invested. In the UK in the 1850s this was compulsory, but became optional between 1862 and 1900, whereafter the audit was largely entrusted to professional accounting specialists rather than done by shareholders, as was the pattern for the USA and Australia. In France the audit was compulsory from 1867, but was often a mere formality where a member of the family which controlled a business signed the accounts, being replaced in the twentieth century by court officials whose job was to check compliance with the law. In Italy the auditors ('sindaci') came to sit in at board meetings, while in Germany the shareholder audit function was, from the end of the nineteenth century, exercised by the 'supervisory board', which has been the 'watchdog' institution of the German system of corporate governance. The compulsory external audit as it exists today in Germany was introduced by law in 1931 to protect creditors and investors from losses arising from fraud and embezzlement.

How practices differ

The different development of audit is one illustration of how the different circumstances in each country lead to different practices, even when they start from the same point, and these differences will be clear from the chapters which follow. One of the most significant differences is the *general objective* to which accounting should direct itself, which is mainly influenced by the predominance of specific legal forms of enterprises in a country, the way the enterprises are primarily financed and the general attitude in a society towards transparency or secrecy.

Family-owned companies, largely financed by banks or at most by bonds, have remained an important motor of mainland European economies. German companies, such as the car manufacturers Porsche AG and BMW AG or other worldwide operating companies such as Bertelsmann AG (publishing and media), Henkel KGaA (chemicals), Robert Bosch GmbH (electronic equipment), are to a large extent in the hands of only a few investors. Even German public companies often have major banks not only as creditors but as important shareholders: for example, Deutsche Bank owns about 17% of the equity of Daimler-Chrysler. In Japan as well banks play a predominant role as creditors as well as shareholders in the financing of corporations. Those countries where being listed on a stock exchange is not the predominant way of raising capital are usually also characterized by a strong tradition of professional secrecy which leads to relatively light disclosure requirements. The dominant objective of accounting is therefore not the transparency of the real economic situation of a company but much more the calculation of an income which can be distributed to the owners without harming the position of other parties dealing with the company, notably the creditors. This objective of a prudent calculation of income, with the intention of maintaining capital, results in the principle of conservatism as the major accounting principle. This creates a tendency to undervalue assets and overvalue liabilities and therefore to understate the value of a company. Suppliers of, say, a Swiss company do not have much detail about the company's financial situation, but they can rely on its value being understated in the information they do have. They are protected by undervaluation.

This contrasts significantly with the approach in the USA where transparency is deemed to be the best protection of all users but primarily of the investors. While the USA certainly has major private companies, such as Mars, these are not typical and there is a strong tradition of seeking finance through the public markets. This has a major impact on accounting regulation, since it is traditionally seen as important to protect primarily investors in a financial market environment, and market pressures are, in any event, likely to encourage transparency by the company as a means of encouraging investors and reducing the cost of capital. This leads to the objective of financial reporting to provide information which is useful for making economic, and particularly investment, decisions. Income computation is not regarded as an objective per se, but as a component of the information which is assumed to be decision relevant. Therefore accounting is very much oriented round the objective of portraying as far as possible a realistic image of the economic situation of a company, which has created maxims of accounting, such as 'fair presentation' in the USA or 'true and fair view' in the UK, which financial reports should convey. This objective puts a strong weight on notions such as relevance, materiality, comparability, consistency and the accrual principle, which have a significant impact on the measurement practices in the USA and the other anglophone countries.

Very much related to the objective of financial accounting in a country and to the approach to accounting measurement is the *influence of taxation* on financial accounting which arises in all those countries where financial accounting income is the direct base for the computation of income tax. Inevitably companies try to report the minimum income which leads to the minimum tax burden. This tends to reinforce the prudent measurement approach which predominates in some jurisdictions in mainland Europe – an undervaluation of an asset will not only protect creditors but also reduce the taxable profit as a result of the higher depreciation charge. In countries such as Germany or Austria, this is seen as perfectly acceptable and helps to ensure the continuing life of the company as an employer and taxpayer. In other countries, such as the USA and the UK, measurement of profit for tax purposes has been seen as too important to be left to accountants, and computation of taxable profit is a matter of applying legal rules which are not binding for shareholder reporting purposes. This relation of financial accounting to taxation has an impact on asset valuation and the recognition of provisions. In tax-oriented jurisdictions (e.g. Germany, Austria, Italy), assets will probably be depreciated more rapidly than in others, and provisions will be the more readily recognized. This in turn has an effect on gearing since asset write-downs reduce equity, while provisions both reduce equity and increase liabilities, resulting in higher perceived gearing of companies in jurisdictions where taxable profit is closely linked to shareholder profits.

As will be explained in the country studies which follow, it can be seen that most of the continental European countries tend to have a broader focus of financial reporting, which means that they see accounting as a tool serving several users and parties which have an interest in an enterprise (such as creditors, investors, tax authorities, suppliers, customers and general public). Anglophone countries, on the other hand, focus primarily on the information needs of the capital providers with a notable emphasis on investors. It could be said that accounting is traditionally based on a stakeholder view of the firm in mainland Europe and on a shareholder view in anglophone countries.

The *mechanisms of regulation* are a further variable influenced by national culture. As discussed above, this manifests itself in quite different systems in different countries which in turn bear upon the flexibility and adaptability of rules. Because of the general legal approach of 'common law', the Anglo-Saxon jurisdictions have historically preferred a relatively low level of legal constraints in the area of accounting allied to self-regulation by the accounting profession (see Chapters 3 and 6). This is claimed to provide rules which can adapt quickly to circumstances in a rapidly changing economic environment. But it is also criticized as being too flexible and open to abuse, as well as too self-interested.

Other jurisdictions, notably France (see Chapter 5), see accounting regulations as being in the nature of a social contract which results from a compromise negotiated between different interested parties. As such, it is desirable that it should be managed through a state body and it is wholly inappropriate for it to be monopolized by one sector of the economy. Germany (see Chapter 4), on the other hand, sees accounting as the application of the law, as embodied in the Commercial Code (Handelsgesetzbuch), with change taking place through re-interpretation of the founding principles through the arbitration of the courts, or through revisions and amendments of the Code, which happen quite rarely.

Related to the regulatory mechanism is the *nature of the rules*. In the USA, the private sector issues accounting standards, or 'rules' covering individual situations or accounting problems, of which more than 150 are currently in force. France (and other countries) has an accounting plan which includes measurement and disclosure rules but also provides a chart of accounts which is compulsory for the organization of the company's general ledger. Germany has its quite detailed 'Handelsgesetzbuch' (Commercial Code), but also a large quantity of accounting literature, of which special accounting encyclopedias, usually edited by eminent academics and professional accountants, are most important. In these, all the accounting problems a company is expected to face are listed and commented on according to the generally accepted interpretations of the legal rules as well as relevant tax law and court decisions.

Allied to this is the *scope of the rules*. In France accounting rules existed well before limited liability companies and apply to all entities engaged in commercial activities, irrespective of their legal form. In the USA, rules apply automatically only to the 12 000 or so limited liability companies whose reporting is subject to the regulation of the Securities and Exchange Commission (SEC), usually because they are offering securities to the public in one form or another. Many other companies follow these rules, but this is typically because their banks require it, and not because there is any legal mandate for it. In Germany, as in the UK, the rules vary according to the legal form of the business, although there is a size constraint as well. Unlike the UK, where the limited liability, share-issuing company is the only widely used legal vehicle, Germany has a whole range of different forms of enterprise which carry – in some details – different reporting status and different tax status.

There are many interconnections between accounting cultures and it is a mistake to over-simplify comparative accounting analysis by emphasizing the differences and ignoring the similarities. However, there is some sort of loose cultural pattern which can be discerned and which can be quite easily explained by an analysis of history – by shared political and cultural influences which existed on specific countries over a significant period of time in the past. For analytical purposes it is very useful to recognize a degree of family likeness between systems in anglophone countries (referred to as a block as 'Anglo-Saxon' accounting systems), and also a family likeness in countries whose rules were initially influenced by Napoleon's Commercial Code and are characterized by the degree of prudence in measurement (referred to as a block as 'continental European' accounting systems). The major (admittedly generalized) characteristics of those two 'families of accounting approaches' are summarized in Figure 1.2.

There has been much cross-fertilization between countries. For that reason this book is organized by presenting first the accounting of the historically most influential countries (France, Germany, USA and UK) as well as the International Accounting Standards Committee (IASC) and its successor, the International Accounting Standards Board (IASB), which is our central reference, before looking at other countries and asking whether, and if so, how, those have been influenced by the major national accounting models.

Figure 1.2 Fundamental characteristics of continental European and Anglo-Saxon accounting systems. *Source*: Glaum and Mandler 1996, p.28.

	Continental European accounting systems	Anglo-Saxon accounting systems
Social economic environment		
Capital markets	Capital is mainly provided by the banking sector	Capital is mainly raised through stock markets
Culture	State focused	Individualistic
Legal system	Dominated by codified law; law provides detailed accounting rules	Dominated by case law; accounting rules developed by private standard setting bodies
Fiscal system	Financial accounting and taxation is closely connected	Tax rules do not influence financial accounting practice
Accounting objectives		
Decision-useful information		
● primary users of financial statements	Creditors, tax authorities, investors	Notably investors
● accounting principles	The dominance of the prudence principle and the influence of taxation on financial accounting harms the decision usefulness of financial statements	Fair presentation, true and fair view
● scope of disclosure	Tendency towards lower extent of disclosure	Tendency towards higher extent of disclosure
● scope of accounting policy	Considerable amount of recognition and measurement options	Almost no recognition and measurement options
Calculation of distributable income	Prudent calculation of income ● principle of conservatism ● limitation on income distribution ● tendency towards higher hidden reserves	Income calculation is part of decision usefulness ● fair presentation, true and fair view ● dominance of the accrual principle ● no limitation on income distribution ● tendency to lower hidden reserves
Tax base	Mutual influence of taxation and financial accounting	No mutual influence of taxation and financial accounting
Example of countries	Belgium Germany France Greece Italy Japan Portugal Switzerland	Australia Great Britain Ireland Canada New Zealand The Netherlands Singapore USA

How differences are addressed: harmonization

If it is taken as a given that accounting rules and practices are influenced by the environment in which they operate, it is to be expected that the internationalization of the economic and cultural environment which has been taking place with increasing rapidity since the 1960s will have an effect on accounting. Accounting has to address the new problem of how to communicate across national boundaries. Although little formal research has been done in this area (a major exception being Choi and Levich 1990), it is generally taken for granted that accounting diversity hinders the users of financial statements and creates problems for multinational companies. It also provides problems for economic unions such as the European Union. Any idea of a single market probably requires that companies face the same regulatory environment in each constituent part of the market, but this is far from the case in the EU as regards accounting, or taxation for that matter. Having looked briefly at accounting diversity, this next section looks at attempts to produce 'harmony' in accounting. First it will consider the arguments for and against harmonization, and then it will go on to analyse the harmonization initiatives of major institutions such as the IASC and the European Union.

Harmonization is the jargon word used in international accounting to mean the reducing of differences in reporting between countries. *Standardization* is used to mean the application of exactly the same rules. As a result of the fact that accounting is now understood to be embedded in its cultural environment, international standardization of accounting is generally thought to be impossible and not useful, while harmonization is an attempt to set in process a narrowing of differences which will remove the most important obstacles to international comparability. The IASB now uses the term 'convergence' in this context.

The main argument in favour of harmonization is efficiency in trans-border transactions. Multinational companies are presently obliged to keep at least two sets of accounts: group accounts in parent company GAAP for reporting to the home country capital market, and individual accounts for each subsidiary according to local GAAP and destined mostly for tax measurement. If the parent is listed on more than one stock exchange, there would often be a second set of group accounts (or more) destined for the foreign capital market(s). While the audit of multinationals is usually carried out by one of the key multinational audit firms, the need to comply with different local audit requirements and to certify financial statements which are presented according to different accounting principles imposes a high cost on the audit function (which is usually passed on from the auditor to the multinational). Training costs for company and auditor are that much higher. Software is more expensive and transaction costs are higher.

The argument extends persuasively to the capital market. An Austrian (say) pension fund wanting to invest in Spanish securities has difficulty in evaluating the historical performance of the Spanish company over past years when it does not understand the nature of the accounting choices typically made in Spain and the other cultural biases in the accounts. Lack of uniformity and therefore of comparability of accounting information is clearly a barrier to cross-border investment. This leads to inefficiencies in that companies invest on limited information or they stick to their home market, potentially supporting much less efficient local companies which would not survive in open global competition.

In the context of an economic union, lack of uniformity leads to the same inefficiencies within the union, thereby preventing the free flow of capital, goods and services throughout the union. However, this is with the difference that there may be a political structure which makes it possible to attempt to remove or reduce these obstacles, as within the European Union. In addition to the creation of a 'level playing field' for companies within the union, there is a secondary motivation also in the sense that the existence of one or more states within the union which have particularly light or favourable reporting regimes could provide an incentive for companies based elsewhere in the union to move their head offices to the state where the light regime prevails, which would affect competition in a prejudicial way.

The arguments against harmonization are that it upsets social balances which have been worked out over a long period, that it fails to take account of the different role played by financial reporting in each state, and that it is costly and these costs fall most heavily on the small and medium-sized companies, while the benefits from harmonization largely accrue to large companies.

As discussed above, the accounting rules in each country have evolved over time and are a reflection of the needs and social, cultural and economic environment of that country. This balance of interests which has been worked out over many years is set aside by the harmonization process which must by definition be working towards a common set of rules in all major areas.

Another issue that needs to be dealt with is whether accounting of all types of undertakings has to be harmonized or whether harmonization should be limited to specific types of undertakings, such as those listed on the stock exchange, those with limited liability, or those exceeding particular size criteria. Harmonization seems to be clearly necessary for companies that are listed on stock exchanges to ease the transactions of the international capital markets, but whether accounting should be consistent for all kinds of companies all over the world can be argued.

An obvious fact which is an obstacle to this broad and global harmonization is the different priorities and objectives given to financial reporting in general in different countries. As already discussed, in some countries the preparation of the annual accounts has the primary objective of calculating distributable income, and is linked intimately to the taxation process, whereas in others the more important objective is providing information to the capital markets. The former will tend to lead to very prudent accounting and the exercise of choices which would tend to minimize profits, while the latter will encourage companies to make choices which emphasize profitability. These differences cannot be made to disappear overnight, if at all, and will affect comparability deeply. This means that comprehensive harmonization can only be reached if the environments (tax regulations, companies' financing, legal forms, professional education, systems of corporate governance, etc.) are harmonized as well.

The costs of harmonization take different forms. A change in accounting principles which changes a company's apparent profile has a single implementation cost in terms of informing the users of the company's accounts what are the effects of the change. Internally a company has costs in terms of staff training and use of new accounting software. Overall these costs can be quite high, and it is generally true that the costs of accounting are relatively greater for small companies than for large, because of the vastly greater volume of transactions in a large company – economies of scale apply in the unit cost of accounting transactions.

Multinational companies have a range of possible ways of managing the international accounting diversity. As far as external reporting is concerned, they may well produce more than one set of figures. The largest capital market in the world is the USA, and all companies wishing to use that market must register with the SEC. For most funding programmes they will also be required to produce either a set of accounts drawn up using US GAAP, or a reconciliation statement which provides a bridge between net assets and earnings in the company's home principles and net assets and earnings using USA principles. This can be a costly process and also involves showing more than one equity and profit figure. Generally accountants would accept that profit is a theoretical concept whose calculation depends upon valuation rules (depreciation, stock, etc.); once you change the valuation rules, you change the profit. However, financial analysts often find this difficult to accept and ask which is the 'correct' profit figure on which they should base their decisions (see Chapter 17).

Another possibility is to use home country GAAP for individual company accounts (with tax implications in some countries), but use whatever choices are available locally to prepare consolidated accounts which are as near as possible to US GAAP, thereby reducing potential differences. Many companies simply refuse to be listed in the USA or any other market where they are obliged to produce two profit figures, but this is a difficult choice, because it most likely results in considerable finance transaction costs. There is empirical evidence that the different disclosure and accounting requirements of the stock exchanges have an effect on companies' foreign exchange listing decisions (see e.g. Biddle and Saudagaran 1989; Saudagaran and Biddle 1992).

Even if the companies are not formally forced by listing requirements to produce international accounts, they may well have to face international expectations and perceptions of international stakeholders such as investors and their advisors, clients and suppliers. For multinational companies it has become important to respect the information demands of financial statement users of other countries.

Another issue that needs to be mentioned is the internal problem for foreign subsidiaries in that local accounts should reflect local rules and probably are the basis of local taxation, but the consolidated accounts should reflect the accounting principles of the parent (or at least should be on a common basis). There are various ways of dealing with this. Many multinationals apply parent company rules throughout their group, so that accounting records are kept uniformly in all companies of the group (a chart of accounts helps). This makes consolidation easy and ensures comparability of internal management accounts for performance evaluation. Often the foreign subsidiary uses the audit firm to then prepare a local set of accounts using local GAAP for filing, compliance with legal disclosure rules, and taxation purposes. Where there is a compulsory local accounting chart (e.g. Belgium, France and Spain) it may be necessary to keep duplicate accounting records.

The alternative approach is to account locally using local principles and then convert figures for consolidation. This is also done quite often but has the problem that where the figures are also used for management accounting purposes, managers are comparing subsidiary performance based on different valuation rules. It is not certain that multinationals using this approach convert local accounts to home principles very rigorously.

Harmonization and institutions

The demand for harmonization has not passed unnoticed by various institutions with an interest in accounting, and, apart from the efforts made by companies to deal individually with the problem, there have been several initiatives to approach the problem on an international level. The most significant impact has been made by the International Accounting Standards Committee (IASC; now the IASB: International Accounting Standards Board) and the European Union (EU), while the Organization for Economic Cooperation and Development (OECD) and the United Nations Conference on Trade and Development (UNCTAD) have also made contributions in attempting to forge consensus.

International Accounting Standards Board

The IASC, the IASB's predecessor body, came into existence in 1973 and its progress was not uniformly successful during the whole of that period. In its later years it worked with the International Organization of Securities Commissions (IOSCO) towards the objective of having its accounting rules form the basis for admission to secondary listing on all the world's stock exchanges. Endorsement by IOSCO was finally given in May 2000. This gave its work a clear objective and context which it perhaps lacked in its earlier years. In addition its standards are widely used as a benchmark by national standard-setters, even if individual countries usually prefer either to create their own standards or adapt IASB standards on a piecemeal basis. Many individual companies in different countries, though, use IASB standards for their international consolidated accounts. In the following country studies in this book we are using IASB standards as a benchmark for comparison between countries, and readers will find a detailed technical presentation of these in Chapter 2. Individual country chapters will present the accounting rules of their country by comparison with IAS (international accounting standards issued by the IASC).

The IASC was essentially an organization of public accountants and auditors which got together to provide a set of standards for international transactions and commercial organizations. It was formed in 1973, on the initiative of Henry Benson, a partner in Coopers & Lybrand (now part of PricewaterhouseCoopers), by the professional accounting organizations of the USA, UK, France, Germany, Mexico, Canada, Japan, the Netherlands and Australia. While it is typical of an Anglo-Saxon accounting jurisdiction that detailed accounting rules are formulated by the auditing profession, this is not the case in France, Germany and Japan. This is the reason why the IASC input from those countries did not come from national standard-setters and also explains the dominant influence of the Anglo-Saxon accounting approach on the IAS.

As part of the continuing process of evolving into the official standard-setter to the world's stock exchanges, the IASC radically changed its structure at the end of 2000. It broke away from its sponsoring professional accounting associations and became an independent non-governmental organization with a full time Board of standard-setters (International Accounting Standards Board – IASB), many of whom have past experience as standard-setters in different countries. The Board has to raise an estimated $15m a year in voluntary contributions, and the responsibility for this rests with a body of trustees.

The Board liaises formally with eight national standard-setters (Canada, the USA, Australia and New Zealand, France, Germany, Japan and the UK), known as the 'liaison standard-setters'. Individual Board members have responsibility for maintaining the links with these bodies and the standard-setters send representatives three or four times a year for liaison meetings with the full Board. All other standard-setters and other interested governmental and non-governmental bodies liaise with the IASB through its Standards Advisory Committee, which consists of about 50 individuals (rather than organizations) with significant interests in standard-setting. The European Commission has observer status.

Another major part of the IASB's organization is its International Financial Reporting Interpretations Committee (IFRIC – formerly known as the Standing Interpretations Committee). This consists primarily of technical partners from accounting firms who meet regularly to determine issues of the application of IAS in particular circumstances. (Further details of the IASB processes are given in Chapter 2).

The evolution of the IASC has been long and sometimes painful. The reasons for its creation are not entirely clear. Lord Benson's account is that it arose from an initiative of his in the 1960s when he created a joint working group between Canada, the USA and the UK to issue papers on the common ground between the major anglophone accountants. He claimed that other countries later saw the value of this and the IASC was created to widen the scope of the vehicle. Others who were involved agree that its creation was a British initiative (involving Benson and Sir Douglas Morpeth), but observed that the British concern was to create an international technical body, under the control of the accounting profession, which would act as a counterweight to the harmonization programme of the European Union (or European Economic Community as it then was). The 1973 creation of the IASC coincided with the UK, Ireland and Denmark entering the EU.

Initially its pronouncements were greeted with great interest by the financial press, but gradually it became clear that none of the major industrial countries was taking the slightest notice of the standards in their rule-making process. Although the founder professional bodies were in theory committed to supporting the adoption of IAS, in practice they were achieving little in this respect.

The IASC itself was also fairly limited by financial considerations. For various reasons the professional bodies in anglophone countries are much larger, and consequently much richer, than their continental European counterparts (an issue explored in country chapters). Within the IASC, some member associations wished to keep their own contributions low, while also refusing to allow the wealthier bodies to contribute more because they feared this would lead to a diminution of influence.

A related issue was that of the independence of the IASC. It had been created by Benson and Morpeth outside of any international professional structure. However, in 1977 the existing international arrangements for the profession metamorphosed into the International Federation of Accountants (IFAC) which now boasts a membership of more than 150 professional bodies drawn from over 100 countries. Once IFAC was created, some of its members began to think that IASC should be an IFAC committee. This issue was finally resolved with the signing of what were called the 'mutual commitments' in 1982 which involved IFAC members in the IASC without merging the two bodies.

By this time the IASC standards were increasingly being used as a source in teaching and debate, although they were criticized for retaining too many alternative accounting treatments, thereby not providing much harmonization except in name. None the less, a number of developing countries and newly-industrialized countries were also starting to use IAS as an input to their own standard-setting process. In particular countries which had been colonies of Western countries saw no virtue in trying to reinvent accounting but were able to use IAS as an alternative to continuing to draw directly upon their historical links. Clearly, as the only set of accounting rules which have been created outside of a national cultural environment, it is one of the great strengths of IAS that they came as free as possible of political taint and unacceptable associations. In theory any country could have participated in the IASC process, and therefore felt they had some ownership of the resulting rules.

The absence of a clear legal or cultural framework, while a major political advantage, was also a technical problem since the objectives of the process were not clear. A significant step forward in addressing this was taken in 1987 when the IASC, under secretary-general David Cairns, commenced a working relationship with IOSCO. IOSCO was itself at a relatively early stage in its development. It had grown from an association for technical assistance between North and South America to being a fully international organization. Its aims are to improve the quality and efficiency of the world's stock exchanges. One major inefficiency was that if a company listed in one country wished to list on an exchange in a second country, it would very often have to produce completely different information from that produced at home. This introduced costs and uncertainties about accounting measurements (a detailed review of the problems for a multinational is given in Chapter 17). IOSCO launched a project to have a single stock exchange 'passport' – a common set of listing requirements which would be used by all stock exchanges when admitting foreign issuers.

The IASC agreed with IOSCO to provide the necessary accounting standards for this purpose. It then set about tightening up its existing standards through what was called the 'comparability and improvements' project. This lasted until 1993 but IOSCO decided at that point that sufficient progress had not been made, and a new accelerated programme was started in 1995 which culminated in IOSCO's endorsement of IASC standards in May 2000.

At a technical level, IOSCO's endorsement was none the less conditional and still left open the possibility that national regulators could ask for reconciliation to local measures or additional disclosures, etc. This remains the key issue. In effect, all the important stock exchanges except the USA accept IAS accounts without problem. However, the USA is the key market for many multinationals, and therefore the SEC approach to IAS is crucial.

The SEC would probably have preferred that US GAAP were considered in effect the accounting benchmark for international stock exchange listings, and for all of the 1990s many people thought that the IASC was wasting its time, and in the end US GAAP would be adopted as the only practical choice. This was more or less based on the argument that as long as the rules are of a high quality, and as long as everyone uses the same rules, their origin does not matter.

However, this neglects the political aspect. Foreign companies are not much better off if they have to produce one set of figures at home and a different set for foreign stock exchanges. They prefer to produce a single set of consolidated accounts for use worldwide. This means that if the worldwide standard is US GAAP, they will want to use US GAAP at home. This in turn means that national regulators would have to accept that the USA writes accounting standards for them. Because this is not seen to be politically acceptable as a permanent state of affairs at the EU level the EU Commission has decided to intro-duce IAS as compulsory standards for EU companies which are active on EU capital mar-kets from 2005 on. For countries within the EU which do already accept US GAAP as a temporary measure (such as Germany) the compulsory introduction of IAS is delayed until 2007 for companies which actually do apply US GAAP. Furthermore, many consider that the collapse of Enron and the accounting scandals which followed that have robbed US GAAP of their credibility as a superior set of accounting rules.

We are therefore now in a situation of transition, which is likely to last several more years. In effect the new IASB has become the world's dominant standard-setter and many major countries are having to come to terms with the idea that national freedom to set rules is forever going to be constrained by the existence of the IASB. Many countries are now setting out on what is termed 'convergence' – bringing domestic standards into line with the IAS. The US position is also evolving slowly. On the one hand the USA is reviewing some of its own standards which are out of line with developments elsewhere, notably con-cerning business combinations, while on the other it is likely to continue to require some form of reconciliation statement from foreign issuers in the short to medium term. The 'Norwalk Agreement', signed by the IASB and the FASB in 2002, commits the US and IASB to convergence.

The IASB itself has to ensure that its standards continue to evolve. It has a complex relationship with national standard-setters but appears to be trying to work as closely as possible with them so that they are directly involved in the international process.

The European Union

Harmonization of accounting within the European Union is a very different story. Here there existed – and exists – a mechanism for a legally enforceable harmonization: the Council of Ministers approved company law directives which had to be adopted by the individual member states. It is quite probable that you will be able to look back from later in the twenty-first century and see the EU as having conducted a unique experiment in accounting harmonization. The EU (then the EC) conducted this experiment through the 1970s and 1980s and substantially changed the face of accounting in Western Europe, as well as profoundly influencing accounting in states in transition in Central and Eastern Europe. The effects of harmonization will be a recurrent theme in the chapters dealing with European countries. The technical content of the main accounting directives is briefly summarized and analysed in an appendix to this chapter.

The Treaty of Rome (signed 25 March 1957) provides for freedom of movement of labour, capital, goods and services throughout the Union (at the time 'Community'), and the European Commission, the executive institution of the EU, launched a company law harmonization programme with the objective of providing a 'level playing field' for all companies, wherever they were based within the Union. This had the primary objective of removing obstacles to competition and creating a single market, and the secondary objective of preventing the existence of any regulatory havens which could attract corporate headquarters with light nation-specific company regulations.

The harmonization programme was pursued with a great deal of enthusiasm in the 1970s, less in the 1980s and more or less came to a standstill at the time of the Maastricht agreement in 1992, with a number of directives still in process. The essence of the EU process is that the Commission has the exclusive right to initiate draft legislation, while the Council of Ministers has the exclusive right to approve (or not) the draft (although this will be passed in the long run to the European Parliament).

For the company law directives (accounting was most affected by the Fourth and Seventh, and auditing by the Eighth) the process was that the Commission would prepare a draft (in the case of the Fourth Directive, based on a proposal from a European group of accounting experts: the 'Groupe d'Etudes'). The draft would be submitted to the Council of Ministers which would in turn pass it to the European Parliament and the Economic and Social Committee for comment, and there would begin a potentially protracted series of negotiations. As a result there would be re-drafts, and finally a directive which would then be implemented by individual member states. It should be noted that EU directives have to be implemented into national legislation in order to become operational, although there is some jurisprudence which shows that an individual can appeal against national rules where there is a European directive which is relevant.

The Fourth Directive, which was admittedly fairly controversial for many states and therefore perhaps not completely typical, started with a discussion paper produced by the Groupe d'Etudes under the chairmanship of a German auditor named Elmendorff in 1969. The first draft directive was issued by the Commission in 1971, a second draft followed in 1974, and a third version was finally approved by the Council in 1978. Denmark was the first country to implement it, in 1980 (although for precision one should note that Belgium's 1976 accounting law was based on the second draft), while Italy was the last in 1991.

The nature of this process and its length (more than 20 years from initial concept to final implementation in Italy) will already have suggested some of the problems with the EU harmonization process. Firstly, the considerable number of countries and institutions involved means that the initial concepts were very quickly compromised, and the result is a mixture of principles and practices drawn from different countries and different traditions. For example, the 1971 draft, based largely on German company law, said that the accounts should be drawn up according to generally accepted accounting principles (GAAP). The 1974 draft reflected the arrival of the UK and Ireland as new members in the Community and said that the accounts should give 'a true and fair view' (a long-established British approach) and follow GAAP.

Secondly, where it proved impossible to come to an agreement on a single procedure or principle, progress was also made possible by agreeing to options within the directive. That is to say, the directive would in some cases propose only a single approach (e.g. every company must produce an annual profit and loss account, balance sheet and notes), but then allow options (two basic methods of presenting the balance sheet and four variants of profit and loss account) from which each member state could choose, or adopt in full (see appendix of this chapter). Another example is tangible fixed assets, which the directive says must be valued at historical cost less depreciation, but with an option for member states to permit current values. The whole directives can be regarded as historical compromise between the Anglo-Saxon and the continental European accounting systems, which could have only been reached because of the incorporation of a mass of options (e.g. the Fourth Directive contains 76 options in 62 articles).

Thirdly, the adoption of the directive by member states was, in most cases, not a question of rewriting the accounting law, but rather of joining on the new bits to pre-existing law, and using options to align the new bits more comfortably with the old. An example would be that the Fourth Directive required that the accounts give a true and fair view; in France the previous law required that accounts were 'sincere and regular' and 'true and fair' was simply added, so that now French accounts have to be sincere and regular, and give a true and fair view.

Fourthly, the length of time involved means that the directives were potentially out of date before they were implemented. In addition, the length of the process makes it clear that there can never be any rapid response to an evolving economic environment, something which rule-makers in a number of countries have seen as essential. In fact the Commission has evolved a process (known as comitology) for updating existing directives. Under this a directive is issued which creates a committee with a limited mandate to update existing directives. However, while the Commission has looked at this, it has not pursued it to a conclusion for accounting and company law.

The question of just how effective was the EU harmonization initiative is one which is much debated in the research literature. It is certain that it did a great deal to rationalize the approaches to presenting accounting information, and in that sense was extremely useful and effective. It is equally clear, though, that accounting rules in individual countries still have different frameworks and are closely intertwined with other aspects of the economy and society, and these bear upon the recognition and measurement principles as well as the disclosure requirements adopted. Generally one can say that each member state tried to implement the content of the directives in the way that provoked as little change as possible in national accounting principles and rules. Consequently, even today, one cannot compare, say, a set of Spanish accounts directly with a set of Dutch accounts and make an immediately meaningful comparison. However, there is sufficient commonality for someone with information about country-specific recognition and measurement practices (e.g. gained from reading this book!) to be able to arrive at a useful evaluation and sound comparison.

Nevertheless there is a 'mutual recognition' agreement whereby all member countries agree to accept financial statements from companies located anywhere else in the EU as being comparable and consistent with national rules. This acceptance of financial statements through an agreement between countries has long been sought by German multinationals and the German Ministry of Justice from the SEC, to open the door to the American capital market for German corporations. It has always been rejected by the SEC because it is convinced that their GAAP are superior to German rules. The main deficiency of mutual recognition, which is very obvious in the EU, is that although it provides official acceptance, it does not provide comparability.

It may well be argued that a major strategic error was made by the Commission early on, in addressing the harmonization initiative to all companies, without regard to their size. The original Elmendorff recommendations were framed purely for companies listed on stock exchanges, but the first draft of the Fourth Directive applied them to all companies with limited liability, such as public or private companies limited by shares or by guarantee. It is not clear that small and medium-sized companies benefit from harmonization, as we have argued above, and this may have been a considerable obstacle to having a coherent directive. Whatever its relative success or failure, its impact was enormous, causing over two million companies not only to change their methods of presenting their financial information but also to change their bookkeeping and other information systems and to introduce a general obligation for audits throughout the EU. The costs for companies were very great.

The Commission has progressively withdrawn from trying to harmonize all accounts within the EU and instead oriented itself towards international harmonization of consolidated accounts, tacitly leaving single company accounts to national regulators. In 1995 the Commission announced that in its view, future harmonization within the EU should be centred on aligning national rules for consolidated accounts with IAS. This position was considerably reinforced in 2000 when, after IOSCO's endorsement of IAS, the Commission said it was going to introduce rules to make the use of IAS compulsory for the consolidated financial statements of all companies which have securities admitted to trading on a regulated market within the EU. In 2001 the Commission published a Regulation which requires member states to pass legislation to make IAS compulsory for consolidated accounts and optional for single accounts for all companies (depending on the discretion of the member states) from 2005. The Commission approved the Regulation in July 2002, giving member states time to adapt their national legislations. In contrast to its draft, the Regulation allows companies currently using US GAAP to continue to do so until 2007. The same lightening is provided for companies which have only debt securities traded. In addition to this step of the mandatory application of IAS, the Commission has carried out limited revisions of the Fourth and Seventh Directives to permit the use of fair value in line with IAS 39.

The Commission's plan involves a very delicate balancing act, since it wishes to give legal status to IAS within the EU, which means guaranteeing endorsement of rules which, while influenced by Europe, are set outside the control of the EU, while at the same time not creating its own standard-setting body. This difficult political feat is to be achieved by the creation of two committees. One will be a private sector technical group who engage in the IASB's due process, and ultimately express Europe's view at a technical level. A second, political, committee from member states will give standard by standard endorsement to new rules and thus allow them to become in effect part of EU law.

The private sector organization, known as the European Financial Reporting Advisory Group (EFRAG) has been set up by European representative bodies with an interest in accounting, notably the Fédération des Experts-comptables Européens (FEE) and the European employers' lobby group. This has two organs, a supervisory board in which the different sponsoring bodies are represented, and a Technical Expert Group (TEG) which actually does the work on standards. The TEG has a permanent office in Brussels, working under a full-time secretary general. Most members of the TEG are part time and meet for two days every month to debate international standards. The TEG liaises with national standard-setters and with the IASB. It is supposed to respond to IASB exposure drafts and discussion papers on a continuing basis.

The political committee, known as the Accounting Regulation Committee (ARC) is drawn from governments of EU member states. When a new accounting standard (or International Financial Reporting Standard – IFRS – as future standards will be known) is issued by the IASB, the ARC has to decide whether to endorse it for use within the EU. To help it to do this, the ARC will have an expert opinion from the TEG. On the basis of this the ARC must decide whether to accept, reject or modify the IFRS. However, if it does not accept the IFRS, the Commission retains the right to refer the matter to the EU Council of Ministers.

Clearly standard-setters, auditors and preparers fear that the EU endorsement mechanism may be used to provide modifications of IAS, so that Europe develops its own variant of IAS. This phenomenon is typical of the harmonization process, and has to an extent already been seen in the EU's own programme in the 1980s. However, EFRAG has so far been very diplomatic in insisting that it will put its efforts into shaping IFRS upstream, during the formulation process within the IASB, rather than downstream, after approval by the IASB.

There are two potential problems inherent in the structure. Firstly, the ARC may well have problems in approving standards which do not comply with the existing Fourth and Seventh Directives. Looming on the horizon is the question of goodwill. The IASB plans to follow the USA lead and to amend IAS 22 to the effect that goodwill should no longer be subject to systematic amortization. However, the Fourth Directive requires that good-will be amortized, so on the face of it, adoption of the revised IAS 22 by the ARC would involve a breach of the Fourth Directive. To deal with this problem it is more likely that the Commission will revise the directives than object to the IFRS, an approach which has already been practised regarding the topic of fair value accounting of financial instruments.

The second issue is the relationship between EFRAG and the IASB. While EFRAG is the Commission's nominated representative, it does not in fact have any formal liaison arrangements with the IASB. France, Germany and the UK are European countries which have individuals on the IASB acting as 'liaison members' to the national standard-setters but they do not have any mandate to represent the EU as a whole nor any mechanism to do so. No doubt this will be resolved in due course, but many Europeans have expressed concern that Europe, the only geopolitical area to apply IAS directly, and collectively the second largest economy in the world, has no representation on the IASB and no formal liaison link.

United Nations

The early 1970s was a time when a number of institutions became interested in international accounting. Not only was the IASC formed, and the European Commission was evolving the Fourth Directive, but the United Nations (UN) and the OECD also started to take an interest in international standards and form committees to look at these. At that time it looked as though there would be a proliferation of 'international' rules, coming from different sources, and perhaps one of the major successes of that period for the IASC was to persuade these other bodies – over a period of years – that they should stay out of rule-making as such.

In the 1970s the UN's Centre for Transnational Corporations assembled an ad hoc committee to look at segmental reporting by multinational companies. This consisted largely of representatives of developing countries who were keen to force multinationals to provide much more information to host countries where they operated. The committee produced a series of recommendations after several years, but these have been politely ignored by developed countries ever since. Their main effect was to trigger the OECD into producing its own recommendations on the subject (see below) which have been more influential.

The UN remains interested in international accounting matters and it has an accounting policy secretariat in Geneva. This unit, which works under the auspices of the UN Conference on Trade and Development (UNCTAD), has two main lines of activity: technical assistance on a continuing basis, and an annual conference which reviews current issues in accounting. Technical assistance is given to developing countries and countries in transition from a command economy. At the invitation of host countries, the UNCTAD unit will act as an intermediary, or provide directly advice on formulating accounting statutes, creating professional associations, accounting training and similar subjects. It has been very active recently in former communist states, contributing, with the EU, to a coordinating organization for accounting aid, and directly providing help in, for example, Uzbekistan, with a training programme for tax officials, auditors and accountants.

The second arm of its activity is the annual conference of the Intergovernmental Working Group of Experts on International Standards of Accounting and Reporting (ISAR). ISAR identifies accounting issues and commissions research on them. The research reports are presented at the annual conference and are debated by the delegates, normally representing more than 50 countries. The object is to provide technical input to governments on issues where they may be called upon to take a position.

The presentations are published each year after the annual conference and represent a good source of research information in international accounting. ISAR has recently addressed issues such as the accounting needs of small and medium-sized businesses in developing countries, environmental accounting, auditor liability and the adoption in individual countries of IASC standards. It also published (1994) its *Conclusions on Accounting and Reporting by Transnational Corporations* which sets out recommendations for accounting disclosures by multinational companies.

UNCTAD does not aim to set standards. Its main 'clients' are in the developing world whom it helps both with technical assistance and with the provision of technical input on current issues through ISAR. At most it aims to forge consensus, and its input to harmonization is in the form of influencing or informing individual member states.

Organization for Economic Cooperation and Development

The OECD represents the wealthiest thirty or so countries in the world, and, like the UN, started to take an interest in international accounting in the early 1970s. Its main output at that time was its 1976 guidelines on segmental reporting, which recommended that multinational companies should disclose turnover, operating profit and net investment for each significant geographical sector and industrial segment of its business. These guidelines (which were close to the USA accounting standards) have been influential, at least in the Anglo-Saxon accounting world (see Chapter 19).

The OECD has a Committee on Accounting Standards which, like the UN, looks at current issues in accounting and also commissions papers. These papers are, though, issued as OECD staff papers, even though the original may well have been prepared by an outside advisor, and are not widely diffused. It organizes ad hoc conferences which are attended by government representatives and invited representatives of other relevant organizations (e.g. IASC, FEE). These conferences are not open to outside observers and form a private forum where officials can exchange ideas and information about current issues. Again, like ISAR, this is one way in which opinions are formed, but unlike ISAR, the participants are routinely from the developed world. Its recent activity in the accounting area has been the promotion of standards and accounting infrastructure in the former Soviet Union. It has also published guidelines on Corporate Governance.

The OECD is better known for its work in taxation. Its model double tax treaty is widely used as the basis for bilateral treaties between countries, and its papers on transfer pricing (1979, 1994) have also become a standard in international taxation.

International Forum for Accounting Development

IFAD is a new organization, set up in 1999 on the initiative of the International Federation of Accountants (IFAC), and particularly its then president, Frank Harding. Originally the idea was that IFAD should act as a coordinating committee between the different agencies involved in providing accounting aid to developing countries and countries in transition (e.g. the World Bank, UNCTAD) and the different institutions of the profession. It was generally agreed that many institutions may be involved in such aid, and that in the past this has often resulted in both overlap and unnecessary gaps in coverage.

At the same time, the global profession, and the Big Four in particular, were aware that they were increasingly being criticized for accepting the lack of international comparability amongst the financial statements of international companies, and particularly companies based in emerging markets. The Big Four created a global coordinating committee (now extended to include BDO and Grant Thornton) which saw that IFAD presented an opportunity for the large audit firms to demonstrate that they were contributing to improving financial reporting. They therefore offered a programme to IFAD, which has now come to occupy the foreground in that institution.

The programme accepted that the dissemination of international accounting standards is not of itself sufficient to improve financial reporting. IAS as such have been developed out of practices in industrial countries where they are supported by a substantial cultural and technical infrastructure relating to transparency, independence of audit, etc. They proposed therefore, in what was called their 'Vision', that best practice benchmarks should be established in accounting and related areas of professional organization, corporate governance, etc., and then, if regulators in an individual country wish it, a gap analysis could be done to identify areas where development is needed to reach the benchmark.

A number of studies are under way by different organizations with the objective of building the benchmarks. *GAAP 2001*, a survey of the use of IAS in 62 countries by the Big Four plus Two, and published in October 2001 is an example of this (www.ifad.net). Hong Kong has volunteered to be the first territory to launch an analysis of its accounting infrastructure.

While it is certain that some coordinating mechanism between aid agencies is useful in accounting, and early meetings of IFAD did indeed reveal an ignorance of overlapping programmes, there is some danger that IFAD has been 'captured' by the dominant professional firms as part of their own worldwide strategy. The risk here is that their interests are more in bringing newly-industrialized countries, with indigenous multinationals, up to Western standards, and that relatively undeveloped countries, arguably those most needing help, will disappear from the sight of the coordinating body.

The broad and complex field of accounting regulations

As will have been apparent from what has been said, companies generally face compliance with a diverse set of accounting regulations and practices. This set can be categorized on the one hand as compulsory standards and non-compulsory standards and on the other hand as national and international standards. The variety of these standards is shown in Figure 1.3.

It can be seen that a company faces compulsory legal accounting and tax rules and usually accounting is based on an uncodified set of agreed practices. In addition to this, there may well be voluntary accounting rules which derive from industry associations (for example there are voluntary accounting plans used in German industry) and non-compulsory guidelines and proposals issued by professional accounting associations are quite common and influence accounting practice in almost all countries. The last are advice or prescriptions of how special accounting issues not regulated by compulsory regulations should be dealt with, or provide interpretations of promulgated compulsory standards. For example, the German Institute of Auditors (Institut der Wirtschaftsprüfer) has published a wider range of guidelines of this kind which do not have legal force but which are widely respected by auditors and companies.

As far as the international field is concerned, it can be recognized that in competition to the standards and proposals published by the international institutions (IASC, OECD and UN), US GAAP also have a role as being international accounting standards that are used by some multinational non-USA companies for their international consolidated statements. This may be because of the strict listing requirements of the SEC which so far do not accept financial statements unless they comply with US GAAP, but is also because these form a recognizable international benchmark.

Nevertheless the developments in the last few years have made it obvious that IAS will become the international benchmark standards for cross-border publication of financial information. However, as will be discussed in Chapter 2, IAS are already quite consistent with US GAAP and will most likely be so to an even higher degree in the future.

Figure 1.3 Structure of the system of accounting regulations for multinational companies

	National Standards		International Standards
Compulsory Standards	Promulgated accounting standards (by law or standard setting body)	Tax rules	EC Directives*/ EU-Regulations
	General accounting principles		
Non-compulsory Standards	Guidelines and proposals of national associations of the accounting profession		Standards and guidelines of international institutions such as IASB, OECD, UN

*EC Directives relate primarily to EU member states and not to individual companies.

What research tells us about international aspects of accounting

This chapter has attempted to lay out a number of issues that impact upon international accounting, and to describe the major relevant institutions in the international standard-setting scene. The chapters that follow will demonstrate the applicability of these issues to different countries or the different ways in which they impact upon multinational companies. In this final section of the introductory chapter we propose to introduce a classification of the major types of research carried out in this field of accounting, with a view to showing the impact of various issues, and also providing an introduction which may be helpful to those who plan to do some independent research of their own.

Generally speaking, research is published in academic journals, of which there are now a large number in the accounting area. Some journals specialize in the field of international accounting, for example: *International Journal of Accounting*, *Journal of International*

Accounting, Auditing and Taxation, Advances in International Accounting (published once a year and therefore strictly a 'serial' not a journal). Many other journals publish some material which is relevant to international accounting (e.g. the analysis of international accounting research articles in USA-based academic accounting journals by Prather and Rueschhoff 1996). The most common source here are accounting journals which publish in English because of the international acceptance of that language. Such a journal is the *European Accounting Review*, which, because of its international authorship, publishes much relevant material on international accounting research. But also journals such as *Accounting, Organizations and Society, Schmalenbach Business Review* as well as national accounting journals in other languages such as *Comptabilité, Contrôle, Audit* in France and others, occasionally cover international accounting topics.

We would analyse research material as falling into the following types:

1. Analysis of different sets of practices, or country studies

2. Investigation of differences, or comparative studies

3. Analysis of the reasons for differences

4. Classification of different sets of practices

5. Evaluation of accounting harmonization

6. Investigation of the impact of international accounting diversity.

Country studies

Historically there have been very few country studies available, but this has been progressively remedied since the mid 1980s with the appearance of key series such as the Routledge *European Financial Reporting* series, which includes separate volumes on all countries within the European Union, and books such as Alexander and Archer (2001) *The European Accounting Guide*, which consists of contributed chapters on most European countries, or *Transnational Accounting* edited by Ordelheide and KPMG (2001), which has a much broader range of countries and a higher level of detail in its descriptions. However, the literature other than in English is still relatively sparse. Of course, the country chapters in this book fall within this category and the French and German versions are a contribution towards correcting that situation in providing thorough country studies in languages other than English.

Most accounting textbooks written in a country and intended for students within that country tend to deal with detailed applications and make a number of assumptions about prior knowledge. Typically they do not step back and try to present an overall evaluation. It has therefore been left largely to international accounting researchers to prepare or to motivate such studies. These are useful but should be used with care. An inherent problem is that a foreigner viewing another country's accounting will (a) probably view it from the perspective of the researcher's own country (e.g. ask questions which are based on ascertaining whether the foreign accountants follow rules similar to the ones the researcher knows well, rather than trying to evaluate the practices on their own merits), and (b) will have restricted access to implicit cultural understandings which underlie the rules (e.g. are there unwritten rules which have to be followed? Is compliance with formal rules automatic or optional in some cases?).

An example of the sort of mistake it is possible to make (if inexcusable for a professional researcher) was displayed by a North American researcher at a European conference, who was trying to prove that inward investment to Germany increased as a result of companies using harmonized accounting, in line with the Fourth Directive. Unfortunately he chose the approval of the directive by the Council of Ministers (1978) as the pivotal moment, and happily showed that inward investment had grown rapidly in the early 1980s. He was quite unaware that the directives have to be passed into national law, and that this had not happened in Germany until 1985, so no 'harmonized accounts' were available until after the period for which he had investment statistics.

At the same time, someone writing about his or her home country may be inclined to reproduce received wisdoms about that country without questioning them, or may simply not be able to stand sufficiently outside his or her own culture to explain it to someone else. This is one reason why mixed teams of researchers are often the most effective in this area (for example, Scheid and Walton (1992) on accounting in France or Zeff, van der Wel and Camfferman (1992) on the Netherlands), and failing that, researchers who have experience of more than one culture (for example, Haller's 1992 article on the relationship between fiscal and financial accounting in Germany). In all those country studies one should in general avoid putting too much weight behind a single author, and look at several studies of the same area if possible, to assure the soundness of the information that is being offered on a foreign accounting system.

Comparative studies

Here again, comparative studies are a trap for the unwary because of the difficulty in interpreting a different culture, and cross-cultural teams have a better chance of success. An example of the problems would be a comparison of the calculation of depreciation for tangible fixed assets in France and the UK. In both countries the rules say that depreciation should be over the asset's useful life, after taking account of any expected residual value and using either straight line or reducing balance methods. The rules therefore appear to be the same. Only a very careful examination shows that (1) French companies tend to ignore the expected residual value and depreciate to zero; (2) while UK companies nearly all use straight line depreciation, many French companies use declining balance in the early years of the asset's life to benefit from tax relief and later switch to straight line; (3) the UK practice is to include costs such as installation or related legal costs in the depreciable value of the tangible asset, while French practice is to capitalize these separately as deferred charges, showing them in a different part of the balance sheet and depreciating them over a shorter period (Burlaud, Messina and Walton 1996).

Some work has been done with case studies, which throw interesting light on measurement issues, although the extent to which these can be generalized is very limited. Simmonds and Azières (1989) provided a set of data to Touche Ross offices in seven different countries. They asked the respondents to prepare accounts on three different bases: (a) assuming no special instructions, and therefore making choices which would be 'normal' for that country; (b) on the basis of trying to maximize profit, and (c) on the basis of making choices that would minimize profit. The results are summarized in Table 1.1.

These results should not be used to suggest that such wide differences exist between all companies, because the values are a function of the nature of the transactions being accounted for, and in the case study were chosen because they gave rise to significant differences. However, they do show that (a) there may be significant differences in accounting measurements between cultures (e.g. the highest German profit is lower than the lowest UK profit in this example); and (b) measurement rules leave a significant degree of choice within one jurisdiction, so that profit measurement is not necessarily uniform even within a single country.

This latter point is emphasized in a case study (Walton 1992) which asks different accountants in two countries (France and UK) to prepare accounts from the same transactions. This study shows that there is as little uniformity within each jurisdiction as between jurisdictions.

Companies based outside the USA but listed on a US stock exchange have to prepare a reconciliation between earnings and net worth in home country GAAP and the same calculated according to US GAAP. This data is published (and even available on the Internet) and permits a comparison between the rules in different countries. A good example of this kind of study is that by Weetman and Gray (1991).

Table 1.1 Profit measurement. Amounts in millions of ECU

	Maximum possible	Most likely	Minimum possible
Belgium	193	135	90
Germany	140	133	27
Spain	192	131	121
France	160	149	121
Italy	193	174	167
Netherlands	156	140	76
United Kingdom	194	192	171

Analysis of the reasons for differences

It is not clear that it is possible to enumerate in any very precise manner why accounting rules are different in different countries. One can certainly point to particular characteristics that mark choices, notably that companies listed on stock exchanges tend to want to maximize profits because that maximizes the share price, while privately owned companies may prefer to minimize perceived profits to minimize taxes. But these characteristics exist within each jurisdiction and influence choices made by companies, as well as influencing rule-making.

However, there are traditions, such as that German and Swiss law favours the calculation of a relatively low profit (involving, for example, high provisions and depreciation) because this is thought to be better for the continuity of the company, for the protection of those that deal with the company and for the long-term good of the economy. US GAAP, however, prefers disclosure allied to 'economic' measurements and to decision usefulness. Given also that rules are built up over a period of time and therefore represent an accumulation of decisions going back over a period of as much as 200 years and sometimes a response to a particular event, it is not clear that one can take the totality of rules in a country at any one time and deduce from this a coherent picture of attitudes to accounting or influences on it at that time.

The literature, though, does include various attempts to categorize differences. Hofstede (1980) looks at the impact of culture on management approaches, and his work has been taken up by accounting researchers (e.g. Gray 1988, Löning 1995) to apply to accounting and explain or note differences in approach.

Some of the Anglo-Saxon researchers have attempted to categorize countries by relation to a series of criteria which have been developed on a deductive basis. These studies include Mueller (1968), American Accounting Association (1977) and Nobes (1984). Mueller (1968) talked about four significant elements: the stage of economic development; the stage of business complexity; shade of political persuasion and the nature of the legal system. The American Accounting Association (1977) recognized eight critical parameters (P) which shape accounting and which can be regarded as characterizing elements to classify accounting practices:

P1: political system
P2: economic system
P3: stage of economic development
P4: objectives of financial reporting
P5: source of, or authority for, accounting standards
P6: education, training and licensing
P7: application of standards and ethics
P8: client.

Nobes (1984) identified six elements: legal system; business organization and ownership; stock exchanges; taxation; the accounting profession; and unnatural influences (by which he meant the effects of conquest, economic events, etc.).

These studies look at systematic differences, but there is also an issue in terms of the influence of individual thinkers on accounting in particular jurisdictions. It is very difficult to estimate, and no researchers have so far attempted to measure this, the effect of individuals on attitudes and regulation in particular countries. One might wonder where German accounting might have gone without Schmalenbach, how accounting in the Netherlands would have developed without Limberg, and whether there would have been an IASC without Benson. Edwards (1995) brings together material on a number of individuals whose contribution in shaping accounting was extremely significant.

Classification

Some of these Anglo-Saxon analyses of systematic differences (e.g. Nobes 1984) were designed to fit into studies that tried to classify accounting practices into like groups, a research idea that was fashionable primarily at the end of the 1970s and the early 1980s. Our view would be that classification has a major defect from the start in that it assumes that accounting is uniform within each country, which is manifestly not the case. A second problem is that these studies tend to oversimplify the similarities within one grouping, while over-emphasizing the differences between groupings. To illustrate the point, suppose there were only four countries in a study that was attempting to create groupings or clusters of countries, and supposing you could measure differences on a scale based on profit measurement, you might have the following data:

Country	Profit measurement scale
A	100
B	115
C	123
D	136

You could then draw up a spectrum showing the range of profit measurement difference:

$$\text{Minimum profit } A + 15 = B + 8 = C + 13 = D \text{ maximum profit}$$

If you were looking for countries with similar practices, you might decide that B was sufficiently close to A to be part of an AB group, but C was nearer to D and should be part of a CD group, so you would have two clusters, the low profit cluster (AB) and the high profit cluster (CD). However, B and C are actually quite close to each other, and you could more accurately describe the situation as being able to identify the two extremes (A and D), but all other countries fall somewhere in the middle between these. The whole idea of classifying would be creating artificial distinctions where the reality is far less clear cut. Roberts (1995) provides an interesting critique.

The classical statistically, though inductively, derived classification studies are those by DaCosta, Bourgeois and Lawson (1978), Frank (1979), and Nair and Frank (1980), who clustered countries according to their concrete recognition and measurement practices. These are evaluated by Nobes (1984) (further developed in 1992) in advancing his own family tree classification ('morphology'). This uses hierarchies based on the system used in biology/botany (class/subclass/family/species) and gives the result set out in Figure 1.4 (Nobes 1992, p. 89).

Measuring harmonization

Comparative studies may well be framed in terms of demonstrating the need for or lack of success of harmonization. For example, the Walton case study quoted above was carried out after application of European directives in both jurisdictions. However, a relatively new area in international accounting research has been the attempt to provide objective measures of the degree of harmonization. The leading researcher in this area is Leo van der Tas. His 1988 paper proposes a measure of harmonization (which is developed in van der Tas 1992) which he calls a 'C index'. Van der Tas takes observations from published company reports and plots changes in accounting policies over time, demonstrating the dynamic of harmonization as evidenced by how companies report, rather than by what the regulations say. Further research in this field has been carried out by Emenyou and Gray (1992, 1996), Canibano and Mora (2000) and Aisbitt (2001).

Impact of international accounting diversity

Recently researchers, primarily American at first and then European, have started to investigate through empirical studies whether national differences in accounting have measurable influences on accounting-related decisions. In interviewing a sample of market participants, such as institutional investors, issuers of securities, professional raters, from different countries, Choi and Levich (1990) found out that for little more than half of the people interviewed, accounting diversity does not affect their capital market decisions because they have developed tools to cope with the diversity. In another study Choi and Lee (1991) found that (at the time of the study) the different treatment of acquired goodwill in the UK (no obligation to amortize goodwill) and the USA (obligation to amortize goodwill) is associated with the prices paid by UK acquirers compared to USA acquirers. Biddle and Saudagaran (1989) and Saudagaran and Biddle (1992) showed in their studies that the different financial disclosure levels requested by the national listing authorities have an effect on companies' choices among alternative foreign stock exchange listings.

Studies concerning the evaluation of accounting information by reference to market reactions, an area of accounting research that was launched by the Ball and Brown (1968) paper, have also been taken up in this field of international accounting research. These studies try to find out whether different accounting practices and rules in various countries have an impact on the usefulness of the disclosed accounting figures for investors' decisions. This is done by considering the associations between information presented in financial reports and security returns. In addition to pure country studies, which means that only

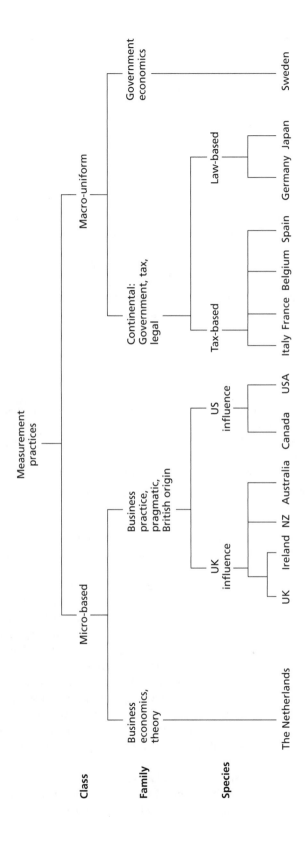

Figure 1.4 Tested hypothetical classification of measurement practices of listed companies in 14 developed countries in 1980. *Source*: Reproduced from Nobes, 1984,

one 'foreign' country is regarded, there are a couple of studies that aim to evaluate and compare the information contents of financial reports in different countries with the market research methodology (e.g. Alford et al. 1993; Harris, Lang and Möller 1994). They suggest that there is also considerable value in financial information in countries other than those like the USA which are oriented more deliberately to this end. Others investigate the relevance of reconciliation information demanded by the SEC from foreign companies listed on a primary USA exchange (e.g. Amir, Harris and Venuti 1993; Barth and Clinch 1996). They reveal that these reconciliations of earnings and equity have significant relevance for investors and are therefore useful.

The value of these studies is ambiguous in international accounting. Firstly they depend on the assumptions of market efficiency which it might be sensible to apply in the US context but which may be questioned in other countries with much smaller domestic financial markets (although some articles have generally found the markets to be efficient also in other countries, see e.g. Choi and Levich 1990). Secondly, as already mentioned above, the role of equity in financing companies is different between countries, which may have an impact on the association between accounting measures and the share returns (share prices). However, there are countries where the association is not as significant as in the US, which is for example pointed out for Japan by a study carried out by Hall, Hamao and Harris (1994). So far there is not enough evidence to enable a definitive judgement to be made.

Conclusion

This chapter is intended to act both as an introduction to the chapters that follow and as a means of posing various questions which need to be addressed by those interested in international accounting, and which inform the examination of accounting in any particular country, or as it affects multinational companies.

The student of international accounting needs to be aware that accounting is different in different countries, of course, but also to ask why this should be the case. Our answer is that accounting is a social construct and therefore varies according to the nature of the society in which it is formed, and to the evolution of that society. It is also influenced by specific events and by interchanges with other jurisdictions. It is not only the rules in themselves that may be different, but also the mechanisms for formulating them, for articulating them and for compliance.

The fact that accounting measurements are dependent upon the rules of the individual country is extremely inconvenient in the context of international business transactions. Investors face an obstacle to cross-border transactions, multinationals face differences in profit concepts and taxation, and governments trying to create trading blocs face unequal opportunities and economic distortions. As a consequence efforts have been made to address and reduce differences, a process known as harmonization.

The most international harmonization is through the medium of International Accounting Standards (IAS). These essentially Anglo-Saxon influenced standards have become a benchmark in the world and are used by non-Anglo-Saxon companies for international purposes, and have evolved into the global norm for multinationals. Consequently they are also used in this book as a benchmark and medium for comparison between countries.

The European Union is a special case in harmonization, representing the only example of a law-based harmonization. The effects of this initiative have been far-reaching and its mark is to be seen in almost any European country. The Fourth Directive introduced key presentation norms and the Seventh Directive ensured the preparation of consolidated accounts on a uniform basis.

The European experiment has shown that harmonization is fraught with difficulties because it disturbs deeply embedded patterns and attitudes. It shows that harmonization is at its most successful when there are clear market benefits for companies involved. This is more obviously the case for multinational companies than for small and medium-sized, owner-managed companies with activities largely in one country.

Research in international accounting is still relatively in its infancy, and is in itself hampered by cultural difficulties, not least that of language. The quality of comparative and individual country studies is somewhat variable, but both quantity and quality of material are improving all the time.

References

Aisbitt, S. (2001) Measurement of harmony of financial reporting within and between countries: the case of the Nordic countries. *European Accounting Review* **10**(1): 51–72.

Alexander, D. and Archer, S. (2001) *The European Accounting Guide*, 4th edn. Aspen Publishers, New York.

Alford, A., Jones, J., Leftwich, R. and Zmijewski, M. (1993) The relative informativeness of accounting disclosures in different countries. *Journal of Accounting Research* **31**(Supplement): 183–223.

American Accounting Association (1977) Report of the AAA Committee on International Accounting Operations and Education 1975–1976. *Accounting Review* **52**(Supplement): 65–101.

Amir, E., Harris, T.S. and Venuti, E. (1993) A comparison of the value-relevance of USA versus non-US GAAP accounting measures using form 20-F reconciliation. *Journal of Accounting Research* **31**(Supplement): 230–263.

Ball, R.J. and Brown, P. (1968) An empirical evolution of accounting income numbers. *Journal of Accounting Research* **6**(Autumn): 159–178.

Barth, M. and Clinch, G (1996) International accounting differences and their relation to share prices: evidence of UK, Australian and Canadian firms. *Contemporary Acccounting Research 1996*: 135–170.

Biddle, G.C. and Saudagaran, S.M. (1989) The effect of financial disclosure levels on firms' choices among alternative foreign stock exchange listings. *Journal of International Financial Management and Accounting* No. 1: 223–239.

Burlaud, A., Messina, M. and Walton, P. (1996) Depreciation: concepts and practices in France and the UK. *European Accounting Review* **5**(2): 299–316.

Canibano, L. and Mora, A. (2000) Evaluating the statistical significance of de facto accounting harmonization: a study of European global players. *European Accounting Review* **9**(3): 349–369.

Choi, F. and Lee, C. (1991) Merger premia and national differences in accounting for goodwill. *Journal of International Financial Management and Accounting* **3**(3): 219–240.

Choi, F. and Levich, R. (1990) *The Capital Market Effects of International Accounting Diversity*. Dow Jones-Irwin, Homewood Ill.

DaCosta, R.C., Bourgeois, J.C. and Lawson, W.M. (1978) A classification of international financial accounting practices. *International Journal of Accounting* Spring: 92–102.

Edwards, J.R. (1995) *Twentieth Century Thinkers in Accounting*. Routledge, London.

Emenyou, E. and Gray, S. (1992) EC accounting: an empirical study of measurement practices in France, Germany and UK. *Accounting and Business Research* **22**: 49–58.

Emenyou, E. and Gray, S. (1996) International harmonization and the major developed stock market countries: an empirical study. *International Journal of Accounting* **31** (3): 269–279.

Forrester, D. (1996) European congresses of accounting: a review of their history. *European Accounting Review* **5**(1): 91–103.

Frank, W.G. (1979) An empirical analysis of international accounting principles. *Journal of Accounting Research* Autumn: 593–605.

Glaum, M. and Mandler, U. (1996) *Rechnungslegung auf globalen Kapitalmärkten*. Gabler, Wiesbaden.

Gray, S.J. (1988) Towards a theory of cultural influence on the development of accounting systems internationally. *Abacus* **24**(1, March): 1–15.

Hall, C., Hamao, Y. and Harris, T.S. (1994) A comparison of relations between security market prices, returns and accounting measures in Japan and the United States. *Journal of International Financial Management and Accounting* **5**(1): 47–73.

Haller, A. (1992) The relationship of financial and tax accounting in Germany: a major reason for accounting disharmony in Europe. *International Journal of Accounting* **27**(4): 310–323.

Haller, A. (2002) Financial accounting developments in the European Union: past events and future prospects. *European Accounting Review* **11**(1): 153–190.

Harris, T.S., Lang, M. and Möller, H.P. (1994) The value relevance of German accounting measures: an empirical analysis. *Journal of Accounting Research* **32**(2, Autumn): 187–208.

Hofstede, G. (1980) *Culture's Consequences*. Sage Publications, London.

Löning, H. (1995) À la recherche d'une culture européenne en comptabilité et contrôle de gestion. *Comptabilité, contrôle, Audit* **1**(1): 81–97.

Mueller, G.G. (1968) Accounting principles generally accepted in the USA versus those generally accepted elsewhere. *International Journal of Accounting* Spring: 91–103.

Nair, R.D. and Frank, W.G. (1980) The impact of disclosure and measurement practices on international accounting classifications. *Accounting Review*, **55**(July): 426–450.

Nobes, C.W. (1984) *International Classification of Financial Reporting*, 1st edn. Croom Helm, London.

Nobes, C.W. (1986) *Financial Reporting in the UK and EEC: Mutual Influences* Research report No. 6, ACCA, London.

Nobes, C.W. (1992) *International Classification of Financial Reporting*, 2nd edn. Routledge, London.

OECD (ed.) (1979) *Transfer Pricing and Multinational Enterprises*. OECD, Paris.

OECD (ed.) (1994) *Transfer Pricing Guidelines for Multinational Enterprises and Tax Administration*. OECD, Paris.

Ordelheide, D. and KPMG (ed.) (2001) *Transnational Accounting* 2nd edn. Palgrave, Basingstoke.

Prather, J. and Rueschhoff, N. (1996) An analysis of international accounting research in USA academic accounting journals, 1980 through 1993. *Accounting Horizons* **10**(1, March): 1–17.

Roberts, A. (1995) The very idea of classification in international accounting. *Accounting, Organizations and Society* **20**(7/8): 638–664.

Saudagaran, S.M. and Biddle, G.C. (1992) Financial disclosure levels and foreign exchange listing decisions. *Journal of International Financial Management and Accounting* **4**(2): 106–148.

Scheid, J.-C. and Walton, P.J. (1992) *European Financial Reporting: France*. Routledge, London.

Simmonds, A. and Azières, O. (1989) *Accounting for Europe: Success by 2000 AD?* Touche Ross, London.

Van der Tas, L. (1988) Measuring harmonization of financial reporting practice. *Accounting and Business Research* **18**: 157–169.

Van der Tas, L. (1992) Evidence of EC financial reporting practice harmonization: the case of deferred taxation. *European Accounting Review* **1**(1): 69–104.

Walton, P.J. (1992) Harmonization of accounting in France and Britain: some evidence. *Abacus* September: 229–254.

Weetman, P. and Gray, S.J. (1991) A comparative international analysis of the impact of accounting principles on profits: the USA versus the UK, Sweden and the Netherlands. *Accounting and Business Research* Autumn: 363–379.

Zeff, S.A. (1978) The rise of 'economic consequences'. *Journal of Accountancy* **106** (December): 56–63.

Zeff, S., van der Wel, F. and Camfferman, K. (1992) *Company Financial Reporting: A Historical and Comparative Study of the Dutch Regulatory Process*. North-Holland, Amsterdam.

Appendix: The European Company Law Directives

The main directives which have been passed and which affect accounting are the Fourth and Seventh, while audit is affected by the Eighth Directive. The Fourth Directive included model presentations of the profit and loss account and balance sheet and established minimum accounting requirements for individual companies with limited liability, such as public and private companies limited by shares or by guarantee. The Seventh Directive extended the requirements of the Fourth Directive to the preparation of consolidated accounts. Variants of these directives have also been issued for use by banks and insurance companies. The directives were modified in 2002 to permit the use of fair value, and a further review may lead to more changes to eradicate any anomolies with IAS.

Fourth Directive

In many ways this is the key piece of European Union harmonization legislation. Its effects have been widespread, not only within the EU but also because other European countries, particularly former Communist ones, have used it as the basis of reforms of their accounting legislation. For an analysis of the evolution of the content of the directive from project to final version, see Nobes (1986).

True and fair view

A key aspect of the directive is its article 2, the objectives of annual accounts. This states that (2.2) the accounts shall be drawn up according to the provisions of the directive, (2.3) that they shall give a true and fair view of the financial situation of the company; (2.4) that if compliance with accounting rules is not sufficient to give a true and fair view, further disclosures should be made in the notes to the accounts; (2.5) and that if further disclosure is not sufficient to provide a true and fair view, then, in such an exceptional case, the rules may be overridden.

Paragraph 2 can be seen as a compromise, typical of the directive-drafting process, between the German approach (accounts drawn up according to proper accounting principles, laid out in the directive) and the British approach (accounts to give a true and fair view). Students should note in the following chapters how this problem has been addressed in the implementation of the directive by individual member states.

Standard formats

The directive introduced standard formats for both the profit and loss account and balance sheet, but here again, the process of compromise means that there are four versions of the profit and loss account, and two of the balance sheet. However, the differences are not great, and the use of standard formats did much to improve the comparability of financial statements within Europe. The degree of detail of the classification in the formats depends on the size of the companies. The directive defines three size categories.

The profit and loss account formats are distinguished on a 2 × 2 matrix: (a) whether expenses are shown by nature or by function, and (b) whether presentation is in the form of a single vertical column, or in a two-column account ('horizontal') format.

The vertical format, with expenses by function (the combination favoured in the UK) is as follows:

Profit and Loss Account for the year ended 20XX

Turnover

Cost of sales

Gross profit

Distribution costs

Administration expenses

Other operating income

Income from participating interests

Interest receivable and similar income

Value adjustments in respect of financial assets

Interest payable

Tax on profit on ordinary activities

Profit or loss on ordinary activities after taxation

Extraordinary income

Extraordinary charges

Tax on extraordinary profit or loss

Other taxes

Profit or loss for the financial year

The horizontal format, with expenses shown by nature (the combination traditionally preferred by many mainland European companies) is:

Charges	Income
Reduction in stocks, work in progress	Net turnover
Raw materials and consumables	Increase in stocks and work in progress
Other external charges	Work capitalized
Staff costs	Other operating income
Value adjustments for non-financial assets	Income from participating interests
Other operating charges	Income from investments and loans
Value adjustments for financial assets	Other interest receivable and similar
Interest payable and similar	Loss on ordinary activities after taxation
Tax on profit or loss on ordinary activities	
Profit or loss on ordinary activities after tax	
Extraordinary charges	Extraordinary income
Tax on extraordinary profit or loss	Loss for the financial year
Profit for the financial year	

As far as the balance sheet is concerned, the main difference is between the layout of the common categories. The UK had traditionally used a vertical format, with liabilities deducted from assets (i.e, assets − liabilities = equity), while mainland Europe had used a two-column account format (assets = liabilities + equity). Both these possibilities were preserved by the directive. The two-column layout was:

Assets	**Liabilities and equity**
Fixed assets	*Capital and reserves*
Intangible assets	Subscribed capital
Tangible assets	Share premium reserve
Financial assets	Revaluation reserve
	Reserves
Current assets	Profit or loss brought forward
Stocks	Profit or loss for the financial year
Debtors	Provisions for liabilities and charges
Investments	Creditors
Cash at bank and in hand	Accruals and deferred income
Prepayments and accrued income	

Valuation and recognition

The Fourth Directive also includes general principles which relate to valuation, such as the accrual principle, the principle of consistency, and conservatism, but leaves much discretion to the member states in implementing those. Although the general valuation basis is historical cost, the national regulatory bodies are allowed to require or admit replacement cost or fair value measures in the national rules. This reluctance in giving precise and strict guidance in the valuation of assets and liabilities is one of the major reasons for the existing accounting disharmony in Europe. The other is the lack of a consistent definition of an asset or a liability, and therefore the lack of consistent recognition criteria. Thus the content of balance sheet items may differ from one member country to another.

Notes to the accounts

Extensive notes to the accounts are more typical of a jurisdiction which believes in transparency as a safeguard rather than a very prudent basis of measurement. The use of the notes has also developed in different ways in that some jurisdictions, notably the UK, try to keep the actual statements very simple, while giving detailed analysis in the notes, which are voluminous. The Fourth Directive introduced a minimum set of disclosures to be put in the notes, which increased the amount of information provided by companies in most jurisdictions.

The directive requires disclosure of: the valuation rules used in preparing the accounts, the extent to which valuation has been affected by application of rules designed to take advantage of special tax relief, the gross cost and accumulated depreciation of assets (if this is not shown on the face of the accounts), the turnover of the company broken down by types of activity and geographical markets, the existence of any financial commitments not included in the balance sheet, the amount of payments to board members, whether by way of salary, pension funding or loans. This last note was the subject of much controversy because it meant revealing information that was regarded in many countries as extremely confidential.

It has to be kept in mind that the Fourth Directive only provides broad guidance and leaves many options available to the member states and/or to individual companies. It also is important to note that it does not cover all major accounting topics. There are gaps in the European legislation concerning, for example, leasing, cash flow statements, long-term contracts, financial instruments, etc.

Seventh Directive

Consolidated accounts are today such a normal form of financial reporting that it is perhaps difficult for the student to realize that in most of the European countries there was a lack of requirements concerning those accounts before the implementation of the European harmonization programme, and that their use was not really widespread in Europe until well into the second half of the twentieth century. While by the 1970s the preparation of consolidated accounts was compulsory for many companies in Germany and the UK, the norm in the Netherlands, and practised voluntarily by many companies in France, there was not a great degree of uniformity in the principles (e.g. different ways of calculating goodwill), and there was no legal requirement in Austria, France, Spain, Italy, Portugal, and others.

The Seventh Directive deals with groups of companies formed by acquisition, not by merger or fusion. It assumes that there is a single 'parent' enterprise and that all other members of the group are subsidiaries of this enterprise. The Seventh Directive is more obviously based in Anglo-Saxon accounting techniques, but includes a number of options that allow its actual implementation in different countries to be different.

A key issue in consolidation rules is which companies are within the consolidated accounts. The Seventh Directive requires that a company is considered to be a subsidiary if another company has control of it. This is deemed to be the case if the parent has a majority of shareholder voting rights, or (where different shares carry different voting rights) the right to appoint the board of directors. This is extended to include situations where a minority shareholder manages a company by agreement with the other shareholders, so there is 'control by agreement'. The directive also allows member states, as an option, to extend consolidation to include companies where the parent has 'de facto control', that is, where the controlled company does not fit any of the legal control definitions, but in practice is in reality managed by another company. This involves the concept of dominant influence, where a company having a minority of shares in another, is still able to dominate it – for example where the dominant shareholder has (say) 30% of the shares, but there is no other major shareholder.

The Seventh Directive provides that banks, insurance companies and other financial institutions may be excluded from consolidation when they are part of a commercial group. It allows that joint ventures may be proportionately consolidated, but that generally associated companies should be accounted for using the equity method.

Under acquisition accounting, it requires that goodwill is fixed by valuing the acquired assets and liabilities at their fair value at the time of acquisition, and deducting this from the purchase consideration. Any difference is accounted for as goodwill. Positive goodwill is carried as an intangible fixed asset and must be amortized to zero, preferably over five years but over the asset's useful life at the option of the member state. An alternative approach, which is available as an option, is that member states may permit goodwill arising on acquisition to be offset against reserves at the time of acquisition.

International Accounting Standards Board

Bernard Raffournier and Peter Walton

The International Accounting Standards Board (IASB), the successor body to the International Accounting Standards Committee (IASC), is the international standard-setting body. This chapter consists of two parts which are different in character: the first is devoted to a description of the institution, and the second provides a summary of the principal elements of the standards so far published.

Part 1: The IASB

Origins and operations

The founding body, the IASC, was created in 1973 by the professional accounting bodies of nine countries: Australia, Canada, France, West Germany, Japan, Mexico, the Netherlands, the United Kingdom and the United States. The history and evolution of the IASC is described in Chapter 1. In 2000 the organization underwent a major restructuring and cut its formal links with the professional accounting bodies who had created it, and became a free-standing non-governmental organization, funded by voluntary contributions and the sale of publications.

The objectives of the IASB, set out in the Preface to *International Financial Reporting Standards* (IFRS)[1] are:

- to develop, in the public interest, a single set of high quality, understandable and enforceable global accounting standards that require high quality, transparent and comparable information in financial statements and other financial reporting to help participants in the various capital markets of the world and other users of the information to make economic decisions;

- to promote the use and rigorous application of those standards; and

- to work actively with national standard-setters to bring about convergence of national accounting standards and IFRS to high quality solutions.

Organization

From 2001, the governance of the IASB is in the hands of the Trustees (known as the 'Trustees of the IASC Foundation'), whose responsibilities include both fund-raising for the IASB and nomination of members of the Board. The members of the Board set accounting standards. There are 19 trustees: six appointed from North America, six from Europe, four from the Asia/Pacific region and three from any area. Aside from the geographical constraint, there should be trustees from international accounting firms, academe and financial executives of institutes as well as 'at large' trustees.

Trustees have a term of office of three years, renewable once. They nominate their successors and also the members of the IASB, SAC and IFRIC.

The International Accounting Standards Board, as of January 2003, consists of fourteen members of whom twelve are full time and the others part-time (see Table 2.1). The Board are appointed for their technical expertise and selection is not based on any geographical

Table 2.1   The members of the International Accounting Standards Board (January 2003)

Chairman – Sir David Tweedie

Vice-Chairman – Thomas E. Jones
Formerly of Citicorp

Board Members
Mary E. Barth (part-time)
Professor, University of California, Stanford

Hans-Georg Bruns (liaison with the German standard setter)
Formerly of Daimler Chrysler

Anthony T. Cope
Former member of FASB

Robert P. Garnett
Financial analyst

Gilbert Gélard (liaison with the French standard setter)
Formerly of KPMG

James J. Leisenring (liaison with the US standard setter)
Former member of FASB

Warren McGregor (liaison for the Australian and New Zealand standard setters)
Former director of Australian Accounting Research Foundation

Patricia O'Malley (liaison with the Canadian standard setter)
Former Chairman, Canadian Accounting Standards Board

Harry K. Schmid
Formerly of Nestlé

John T. Smith (part-time)
Deloitte & Touche

Geoffrey Whittington (liaison with the UK standard setter)
Former member of the UK Accounting Standards Board

Tatsumi Yamada (liaison with the Japanese standard setter)

---

representation. However, the Trustees are supposed to 'ensure that the Board is not dominated by any particular constituency or geographic interest'. The constitution requires that a minimum of five members should have a background as practising auditors, a minimum of three as preparers and a minimum of three as users of financial statements, and at least one an academic background. The Board is run by a full-time Chairman who is also the chief executive. The first chairman is Sir David Tweedie, a former chairman of the UK Accounting Standards Board with a background as an auditor and as an academic.

The IASB also has a Standards Advisory Council (SAC) whose objectives are (a) to give advice to the Board on agenda decisions and priorities; (b) to inform the Board of the views of organizations and individuals on the Council of their views on major standards; and (c) to give other advice to the Board. The Council has about 50 members, appointed by the Trustees, and meets three times a year, in public. The IASC is located in London.

In 1997 the Board formed the Standing Interpretations Committee (SIC). This committee gives authoritative guidance on accounting issues which are likely to receive divergent treatment by preparers. Such issues are either mature issues where practice, based on existing standards, is thought to be unsatisfactory or emerging issues which relate to existing standards but which were not considered when the standards were drawn up. The SIC consists of twelve members, who meet four times a year. The functioning of the SIC was slightly revised in 2002 to take account of the fact that the standard-setting board is now a full-time professional board. The committee's name was changed to the International Financial Reporting Interpretations Committee (IFRIC) and it is now chaired by the Director of Technical Activities at the IASB.

The preparation of standards

The IASB's system of preparing accounting standards is based on that used in Anglo-Saxon countries, known as 'due process'. It is supposed to allow all interested parties (national regulators, preparers and users of financial statements, etc.) to express their point of view and to ensure transparency in the formulation of standards.

The process starts with the creation of a working group, known as an advisory committee, whose members are appointed by the Board. Its task is to study the problems posed by the particular issue and to prepare a summary of the points which need to be considered. After this has been commented on by the Board, the advisory group, in conjunction with the IASB staff, prepares a discussion paper. The purpose of this document is to set out the principles which will serve as the basis of the future draft standard and to describe the possible solutions and the reasons for their adoption or rejection, as well as the preferred solution of the advisory group. This draft is sent for comment to the Board, the SAC and any other interested organizations.

After responses have been received, the staff proceed to preparing a draft standard, known as an exposure draft, which is in turn submitted to the Board. This requires a two-thirds majority of Board members to approve it, after which a period of consultation starts, usually of six months, which should permit all interested parties to give their opinion.

At the end of this period and in the light of the responses received, a draft final standard is submitted to the Board. The final standard is adopted if it is approved by a three-quarters majority of the members of the Board. A list of IASC standards is shown in Table 2.2.

The preparation of interpretations

Draft interpretations are prepared by the IFRIC and submitted to the IASB before being exposed for comment publicly in the same way. Final interpretations are worked out after studying the responses. A list of interpretations is given in Table 2.3.

Table 2.2   IASC Standards

No.	Standard	Date of publication or last revision
	Framework for the preparation and presentation of financial statements	1989
IAS 1	Disclosure of accounting policies Presentation of Financial Statements	1997
IAS 2	Inventories	1993
IAS 3	Consolidated financial statements (superseded by IAS 27 and IAS 28 in 1989)	
IAS 4	Depreciation accounting (superseded by IAS 16 and IAS 38)	1976
IAS 5	Information to be disclosed in financial statements (superseded by IAS 1)	1976
IAS 6	Accounting for Changing Prices (cancelled in 1981 superseded by IAS 15)	
IAS 7	Cash Flow Statements	1992
IAS 8	Net Profit or Loss for the Period, Fundamental Errors and Changes in Accounting Policies	1993
IAS 9	Research and Development Costs (superseded by IAS 38)	1993
IAS 10	Contingencies and Events Occurring after the Balance Sheet Date	1978
IAS 11	Construction Contracts	1993
IAS 12	Accounting for Taxes on Income Taxes	1996
IAS 13	Presentation of Current Assets and Current Liabilities (superseded by IAS 1)	1979
IAS 14	Reporting Financial Information by Segment Reporting	1997
IAS 15	Information Reflecting the Effects of Changing Prices	1981
IAS 16	Property, Plant and Equipment	1998
IAS 17	Accounting for Leases	1997
IAS 18	Revenue	1993
IAS 19	Retirement Benefit Costs (Employee Benefits)	1998
IAS 20	Accounting for Government Grants and Disclosure of Government Assistance	1982
IAS 21	The Effects of Changes in Foreign Exchange Rates	1993
IAS 22	Business Combinations	1998
IAS 23	Borrowing Costs	1993
IAS 24	Related Party Disclosures	1984
IAS 25	Accounting for Investments (superseded by IAS39 and IAS40)	1985
IAS 26	Accounting and Reporting by Retirement Benefit Plans	1986
IAS 27	Consolidated Financial Statements and Accounting for Investments in Subsidiaries	1989
IAS 28	Accounting for Investments in Associates	1998
IAS 29	Financial Reporting in Hyperinflationary Economies	1989
IAS 30	Disclosures in the Financial Statements of Banks and Similar Financial Institutions	1990
IAS 31	Financial Reporting of Interests in Joint Ventures	1998
IAS 32	Financial Instruments: Disclosure and Presentation	1998
IAS 33	Earnings per share	1997

Table 2.2   IASC Standards (*continued*)

No.	Standard	Date of publication or last revision
IAS 34	Interim Financial Reporting	1998
IAS 35	Discontinuing Operations	1998
IAS 36	Impairment of Assets	1998
IAS 37	Provisions, Contingent Liabilities and Contingent Assets	1998
IAS 38	Intangible Assets	1998
IAS 39	Financial Instruments: Recognition and Measurement	1998
IAS 40	Investment Property	2000
IAS 41	Agriculture	2000

Table 2.3   Interpretations

No.	Interpretation
SIC-1	Consistency: different cost formulas for inventories
SIC-2	Consistency: capitalisation of borrowing costs
SIC-3	Elimination of unrealised profits and losses on transactions with associates
SIC-5	Classification of financial instruments: contingent settlement provisions
SIC-6	Costs of modifying existing software
SIC-7	Introduction of the Euro
SIC-8	First time application of IAS as the primary basis of accounting
SIC-9	Business combinations: classification either as acquisitions or unitings of interests
SIC-10	Government assistance: no specific relation to operating activities
SIC-11	Foreign exchange: capitalisation of losses resulting from severe currency devaluations
SIC-12	Consolidation: special purpose entities
SIC-13	Jointly controlled entities: non-monetary contributions by venturers
SIC-14	Property, plant and equipment: compensation for the impairment or loss of items
SIC-15	Operating leases: incentives
SIC-16	Share capital: reacquired own equity instruments (treasury shares)
SIC-17	Equity: costs of an equity transaction
SIC-18	Consistency: alternative methods
SIC-20	Equity accounting method: recognition of losses
SIC-21	Income taxes: recovery of revalued non-depreciable assets
SIC-22	Business combinations: subsequent adjustment of fair values and goodwill initially reported
SIC-23	Property, plant and equipment: major inspection or overhaul costs
SIC-25	Income taxes: changes in the tax status of an enterprise or its shareholders
SIC-27	Evaluating the substance of transactions in the legal form of a lease
SIC-28	Business combinations: date of exchange and fair value of equity investments
SIC-29	Disclosure – service concession arrangements
SIC-30	Reporting currency – translation from measurement currency to presentation currency
SIC-31	Revenue – barter transactions involving advertising services
SIC-32	Intangible assets – website costs

Table 2.3 Interpretations (*continued*)

No.	Interpretation

SIC-33 Consolidation and equity method – potential voting rights and allocation of ownership interests

Up to date information is available on the IASB website: www.iasb.org.uk

Achievements

The work of standardization

By the beginning of 2001, the IASC had produced 40 standards and a conceptual framework (*Framework for the preparation and presentation of financial statements*) intended to serve as a guide in the preparation of new standards and the revision of existing ones.

The standards approved before 1993 are characterized by a fairly substantial range of options. In its early years the IASC was, in effect, essentially attached to the idea of international harmonization and the creation of a body of doctrine which was sufficiently flexible to be acceptable in different countries whose social and economic environments and whose accounting traditions are very diverse.

From 1987, the IASC established that it needed to take a further step to advance the quality of international standards. Its development policy became focused on writing standards which could be used by stock exchange regulators as the common basis for listing worldwide. IASC entered into an understanding with the International Organization of Securities Commissions (IOSCO) who wanted to create a situation where a multinational company listed on its home exchange could list anywhere else in the world with a single international package of disclosures. The reduction of options became a priority for the IASC and was reflected by the adoption in 1989 of E32 on the comparability of financial statements. This document proposed that certain options should be cancelled and that a preferred solution should be clearly indicated where options were still maintained.

Following comments received on this project, the Board adopted a statement of intent in 1990 to serve as the basis for the revision of the existing standards. The introduction of the concepts of the benchmark treatment and the allowed alternative treatment enabled the IASC to show its preferences clearly in cases where more than one method was available in a standard. This work resulted, in 1993, in the approval of a set of ten revised standards which were applicable for the first time for financial periods starting on or after 1 January 1995.

The process of modification accelerated after 1995 when IASC entered into a new understanding with IOSCO, to produce a redefined set of core standards. This process came to an end in 1999 and in May 2000 IOSCO formally endorsed IASC standards as the basis of worldwide listings. The long-awaited endorsement has projected IASC into a new situation, where it moves from being a self-appointed body with no political power base or formal constituency, to being the world's leading standard-setter with a mandate to set standards for listings on the world's stock exchanges. The radical restructuring of the IASC which took place in 2000 reflects this new role.

At the same time, the IOSCO endorsement is not unqualified. IOSCO acknowledges that some of its members have reservations on some of the technical content of IASC standards, and the endorsement contains a detailed annex of items on which individual national regulators may require further information from issuers. While the so-called core set of standards is complete, the IASB has to go forward and refine and extend the standards. In particular its standard on the recognition and measurement of financial instruments is intended as a temporary one. The new IASB's first work was to review and improve the existing range of standards. This has involved a single *Improvements* standard which amends 12 existing standards, a special project to revise and improve IAS 32 *Financial Instruments: Disclosure and Presentation* and IAS 39 *Financial Instruments: Recognition and Measurement*, and a new standard to replace IAS 22 *Business Combinations*. These improvements were still at the exposure stage at the time of writing. Although the issue of IAS 39 was followed by the creation of a Joint Working Group (JWG) of standard-setters to try to find a joint solution to accounting for financial instruments, opposition both to its proposals and to the idea of replacing IAS 39 very quickly by an even more complex standard means that, it is unlikely that IAS 39 will be replaced in the short term.

The influence of the IASC and the IASB

The influence of the IASB is increasing and changing in nature. It can be gauged both at an institutional level, that of national accounting regulatory bodies, and at an individual level, that of businesses.

At the institutional level the international standard-setter's influence is very different depending upon the country. Several countries have adopted IAS as such or with a few minor adjustments. Until recently, these were essentially developing or newly-industrialized countries (e.g. Ghana, Malaysia, Uruguay) which have taken advantage of the opportunity to provide themselves cheaply with a set of rules which are acceptable at an international level and likely to reassure foreign investors. Alignment on IAS is less politically embarrassing for these countries than would be the straightforward adoption of American or British standards.

The same reasons push former Communist countries in transition to a market economy either to adopt IAS as such (Bulgaria) or to base their own rules heavily on them. China, for example, has produced a set of accounting standards based on the IAS.

The influence of the IASC in developed countries has been much less, probably because these countries already have their own accounting regulations and their own established traditions. In Japan and continental European countries the IASC's influence was confronted by the fact that the financing of the economy is done through the banks rather than the stock exchanges, and that their commercial statutes aim to protect creditors rather than to satisfy the information needs of shareholders. The 'financial markets' tradition of the IASC did not therefore correspond well with local tradition.

However, on the other hand, the national regulatory bodies have to take account of the needs of large companies which find the resources for their development in the major financial markets of the world. Accounting regulation therefore began to allow a greater Anglo-Saxon influence, and 2000 witnessed a watershed when the European Union announced that it was adopting IAS as the basis for listing on all EU stock exchanges from 2005. During the late 1990s there was a movement within the EU to accept that companies may, in their consolidated accounts, depart from the rules of the Commercial Code to use, in particular, international accounting principles. This is the case for Germany, Austria, Belgium, France and Italy.

Finally, the influence of the IASC has been at its weakest in Anglo-Saxon countries, probably because there the international standards find themselves almost in direct competition with national accounting principles. The USA in particular has proved virtually impenetrable for the IASC, although Australia has undertaken a programme of aligning its standards with IAS and has now also decided to move to use of IFRS from 2005. In fact the influence of the IASC mostly manifests itself when new standards are being drawn up. For example the IASC's conceptual framework was the basis of the more recent framework published by the Accounting Standards Board in the UK.

How the IASB will fare is very much open to question. Sir David Tweedie, at the inaugural meeting of the Standards Advisory Council in July 2001, told participants that the Board has given itself three years to prove its worth. It is making a major effort to demonstrate its potential by taking the lead in proposing an IFRS (still on the drawing board) for share-based payments, the effect of which will be to cause the issue of stock options to employees to be treated as an expense item. National standard-setters in Europe, not least as a result of the EU decision to adopt IFRS, have to accept that their own role will be somewhat subordinate. The precise way in which European regulators will interact with the IASB is also open to discussion. The EU is setting up an endorsement mechanism (see Chapter 1) which will enable it to take essentially private sector standards from the IASB and give them the force of EU law. But to what extent the EU's endorsement mechanism will seek to amend IFRS as they go through its hands is still to be seen. If the IASB is to work properly, there should not be multiple sets of IFRS in different parts of the world which resemble each other but differ in detail.

In the USA the credibility of US GAAP was damaged by the Enron scandal. Highly prescriptive standards were shown to be ineffective and even the SEC started talking about preferring principles-based standards, in the style of IFRS. A former president of the American Institute of Certified Public Accountants (Chenok and Snyder 2000), accepts that IASB will have a dominant role, but exactly how this will work out in practice remains to be seen.

So far, the SEC has refused to accept accounts based on IFRS as a substitute for US GAAP, and foreign companies using IFRS have to provide reconciliations of earnings and equity (see for example Chapter 17). The most important challenge for the IASC in its struggle for recognition as the premier stock exchange related standard-setter has been to see this reconciliation disappear. This has yet to be achieved although the IASB's 'Norwalk Agreement' with the US standard-setter goes in this direction.

Another issue in this area is the problem of interpretation. IFRS, in particular as opposed to US GAAP, are standards based on the application of principles. Tweedie, in testimony to the US Congress in 2002 explained:

> The IASB has concluded that a body of detailed guidance (sometimes referred to as *bright lines*) encourages a rule-book mentality of "where does it say I can't do this?" We take the view that this is counter-productive and helps those who are intent on finding ways around standards more than it helps those seeking to apply standards in a way that gives meaningful information. Put simply, adding the detailed guidance may obscure, rather than highlight, the underlying principle. The emphasis tends to be on compliance with the letter of the rule rather than the spirit of the accounting standard.

He also said: 'Our approach requires both the company and its auditor to take a step back and consider whether the accounting suggested is consistent with the underlying principle.'

On any particular issue the standards establish what is best practice, but leave it to the preparer and auditor to agree how this is applied in all situations. This leaves room for interpretation, and one criticism voiced by the USA has been that there is a danger that even if different countries use the same rules, national regulators will interpret the principles differently, leading to confusion.

Compliance

Another major concern is compliance with IFRS. For many years voluntary adoption of IAS was often associated, in effect, with only partial adoption – what is known as using 'IAS-lite': adopting IAS except those which the individual issuer finds inconvenient. The IASC ruled, for financial statements for the period beginning on or after July 1998, that this was not acceptable – either preparers follow all IAS or they cannot claim to be using IAS. However the IASC had no means of enforcing its standards, nor does the IASB, nor does it consider that enforcement is the role of the standard-setter.

Most would argue that this is the job of the stock exchange regulators. However, far from all stock exchange regulators have any kind of automatic compliance surveillance mechanism, and this aspect of the use of IAS remains a weak point. The European Commission has said that it will address compliance as part of its initiative to create a single European capital market based on IAS. However, the Federation of European Stock Exchange Commissions (FESCO), the regional equivalent of IOSCO, has pointed out that while it is sympathetic to the surveillance problem, it has no Europe-wide legal framework to carry this out. At national level the regulations and resources for each regulator differ one from another and there is no uniform right of intervention across the EU. The best that can be hoped for in the short term would be a voluntary coordinating committee between national regulators. The Committee of European Securities Regulators (CESR) is addressing this issue.

Audit firms, and particularly the large international networks, have also been criticized for failing to ensure proper compliance with the spirit of international standards. Here too, some progress has been made. The international representative body, the International Federation of Accountants (IFAC) set up a Transnational Audit Committee in 2001 to address these issues, and requires member firms to sign up to compliance with IFAC standards and quality control systems (see Chapter 20), but there is still a long way to go.

Part 2: The Standards

The objectives, assumptions and characteristics of financial statements

Objectives of financial statements

According to the conceptual framework the objective of financial statements is to provide information about the financial position, performance and changes in financial position of an enterprise which is useful to a wide range of users in making economic decisions. These users include actual and potential investors, employees, lenders, suppliers and other creditors, customers, governments and their administrators, as well as the general public.

Unlike the FASB (see Chapter 3), the IASB does not give preference to investors. However this difference is more notional than practical. While recognizing that each category of users has specific information needs, the IASB takes the view that those common to most users are satisfied by financial statements prepared to meet the needs of investors.

More specifically the IASB considers that the financial statements should permit users to evaluate the capacity of the business to generate cash flows, because this capacity is what conditions the potential to pay salaries and suppliers, to meet interest payments and loan reimbursements and to pay dividends.

Accounting principles

The IASB, in its conceptual framework document 'Framework for the preparation and presentation of financial statements', draws a distinction between two types of principles: underlying assumptions and the qualifying characteristics of financial statements.

There are two underlying assumptions:

1. the *accruals basis of accounting*, which signifies that transactions and other economic events are recorded when they take place without waiting for the corresponding inflow or outflow of cash;

2. *going concern*, which supposes, in the absence of special circumstances, that the financial statements will be prepared under the assumption that the entity will continue its activities for the foreseeable future.

Qualitative characteristics are attributes which make the information contained in financial statements useful. The conceptual framework identifies four such characteristics:

1. *understandibility*, which requires that the information is immediately understandable by users who are supposed to have a reasonable knowledge of business and economic activities and accounting, and a willingness to study the information with reasonable diligence;

2. *relevance*, according to which the information given in the financial statements should be of a kind which would influence the economic decisions of users by helping them to evaluate events or to revise previous estimates;

3. *reliability*, which supposes that the statements are free from errors or significant bias;

4. *comparability*, which is the ability to compare financial statements over time or between entities, thanks in particular to consistency of accounting principles.

According to the conceptual framework, reliability requires the exercise of prudence, that is to say the use of a degree of caution in making estimates, in order to ensure that assets and sales are not overstated, nor liabilities and expenses understated. The IASB fixes a limit to prudence in specifying that it should not lead to the creation of secret reserves, contrary to current practice in certain countries (Germany, Switzerland, Japan, etc.).

The other important principle arising from reliability is that of substance over form, which requires that transactions and events should be accounted for and shown in the financial statements in accordance with their economic substance and not only their legal form. This principle reflects the Anglo-Saxon influence at the heart of the IASB. It is not recognized in countries with a more legally-oriented conception of accounting such as Germany or France.

IAS 1 *Presentation of financial statements* was revised in 1997 and amended under the 2002 Improvements project. One of its more contested points was that it has retained the requirement that financial statements should give 'a true and fair view' of the financial position of the business, and that this requirement may, in exceptional circumstances, override compliance with individual standards. This is known as the 'true and fair override' and is one of the issues not accepted by all securities regulators. While in the EU the Fourth Directive (see Chapter 1) includes the override, some EU countries, such as Germany, have difficulties with it. In the USA the equivalent requirement to 'present fairly' does not have an override.

The 2002 revision proposed that the override should operate in rare situations where following IFRS would result in information that was so misleading that it could no longer meet the requirements of the Framework. In countries where there was a statutory override, companies could use alternative rules, but in countries with no statutory override, the company should retain the IFRS solution and provide supplementary information in the notes.

The standard defines a series of 'underlying concepts'. These are:

1. fair presentation: the financial statements should present fairly the financial position, performance and cash flows of an enterprise;
2. going concern;
3. accrual basis of accounting;
4. materiality;
5. prohibition of offsetting;
6. consistency of presentation;
7. comparability through time.

Over time the IASC came increasingly to use the concept of 'fair value' in its standards (Nobes 1994). Fair value is defined as 'the amount for which an asset could be exchanged between a knowledgeable, willing buyer, and a knowledgeable, willing seller in an arm's length transaction', and the IASB seems likely to retain this (Walton 2001).

The elements of financial statements

The conceptual framework defines the basic elements of financial statements and the conditions necessary for their recognition. This collection of general principles constitutes the foundations on which all the IASB standards are constructed.

The elements of financial statements are the assets, liabilities, equity, income and expenses:

1. an *asset* is a resource capable of giving the entity future economic benefits in the form of positive cash flows (receipts or reductions in payments);
2. a *liability* is an existing obligation which will give rise to an outflow of resources which represent economic benefits. The IASB does not distinguish between debts (certain liabilities whose amounts are known) and provisions (uncertain or estimated liabilities);
3. *equity* or owners' capital is defined as the difference between assets and liabilities;
4. *income* refers to increases in equity which do not arise from contributions by the owners. This includes both revenues (arising from ordinary trading activities) and gains (profits from the sale of non-current assets, unrealized increases in the carrying value of assets, etc.);
5. the definition of *expenses* follows that of income. It consists of diminutions of owners' equity other than distributions to owners.

There are two conditions which are necessary for an item to be recognized in the balance sheet or income statement: it must entail a probable increase or decrease in future economic benefits, and its cost or value must be capable of being measured with reliability.

Components and structure of financial statements

According to IAS 1, the financial statements consist of the balance sheet, income statement, a statement showing changes in equity, a cash flow statement and accounting policies and other explanatory notes. The 1997 amendments added a fifth obligatory statement, the statement of changes in equity, which may cover all changes in equity or just non-owner movements in equity (i.e. all the changes in equity other than those which arise from share issues, reductions in capital and dividend payments: these concern mostly revaluation differences and currency conversion differences).

IAS 1 specifies the components of the balance sheet and profit and loss account and how these should be presented. Assets and liabilities should be split between current (likely to be realized within 12 months of the balance sheet date) and non-current, but this distinction is not mandatory. While the detailed analysis of expenses in the profit and loss account is not specified as such, analysis either by function or by nature is encouraged.

In 2001 the IASB launched a project in conjunction with the UK Accounting Standards Board to review the presentation of financial performance. This project is intended to find a replacement for the current profit and loss account or income statement. The intention is to provide a single statement which includes transactions which were traditionally in the income statement but also takes account of unrealized changes in value, or comprehensive income (see also Chapter 3 on the USA and Chapter 6 on the United Kingdom).

IAS 1 interacts with a number of other standards and also incorporates many elements from the conceptual framework (which does not itself have the status of a standard). IAS 7, however, addresses Cash Flow Statements and a number of other presentational issues are referred to incidentally in other standards.

IAS 8 requires that the income statement should show the profit or loss from ordinary activities separately from extraordinary items. Ordinary activities are those which are undertaken as the entity's business or are incidental to it. Extraordinary activities include revenues and expenses arising from events or transactions which are clearly distinct from the ordinary activities and are not expected to occur frequently or regularly. These items are in theory rare (natural disasters, confiscations, etc.). However, the 2002 Improvements project proposes to remove the extraordinary category entirely.

IAS 35, *Discontinuing Operations*, requires that the results of operations which are being discontinued should be clearly distinguished from those which are continuing. Both IAS 8 and IAS 35 incorporate the underlying idea of making clear to the investor or potential investor what part of the year's result is significant in forecasting future results.

Balance sheet items

Tangible fixed assets (*Property, Plant and Equipment* IAS 16)

IAS 16 defines tangible fixed assets as those which are:

1. held by an enterprise for use in the production or supply of goods and services, for rental to others, or for administrative purposes; and

2. expected to be used during more than one accounting period.

When they are acquired by the business, tangible fixed assets are recognized at their cost (of acquisition or of production), including direct expenses necessary to bring the asset into service. Equipment grants which have been received can be deducted from the carrying value of the related asset (IAS 20) or can be shown as a deferred credit and released to the profit and loss account over the asset's useful life. However incidental revenue derived from an asset when under construction cannot be used to reduce its carrying value (SIC-25). Under certain conditions interest costs relating to the period of construction of an asset may be included in the cost (IAS 23).

In the balance sheet, tangible fixed assets should normally be carried at cost, reduced by depreciation and any write-downs necessary (benchmark treatment). Revaluation of these assets is, however, possible subject to their:

1. being carried out regularly;
2. being applied to all assets of the same type;
3. having the revaluation surplus treated as an item of equity.

Tangible fixed assets must be depreciated systematically over their useful life. The depreciation method should reflect the consumption of the economic benefits associated with the use of the asset. The IASB does not define any particular methods. The period of depreciation is the period during which the enterprise plans to use the asset, and does not therefore necessarily correspond to the life of the asset. The amount to be depreciated is the initial cost less the residual value of the asset at the time the enterprise ceases to use it. The methods and periods of depreciation should be reviewed regularly. In the event that a change is necessary, only the depreciation charged in the current period and to be charged in future periods may be changed.

IAS 36, *Impairment of Assets*, requires that the 'recoverable amount' of an asset should be calculated at balance sheet date and compared with the carrying value arrived at by normal methods. If the recoverable value is lower than the carrying value, a write-down should be made. The recoverable amount is the higher of the asset's resale value and its value through its existing use. Its 'value in use' is defined as the 'present value of estimated future cash flows expected to arise from the continuing use of the asset and from its disposal at the end of its life'.

Intangible Fixed Assets (IAS 38)

Taking into account the conditions necessary for recognizing an asset (probability of generating future economic benefits and having a cost or value which can be measured with reliability), IAS 38, *Intangible Assets*, considers that brands and goodwill generated by the business itself cannot, in principle, be recognized in the balance sheet.

Intangible fixed assets are valued:

1. either at their cost as reduced by depreciation and any necessary write-downs (benchmark treatment);
2. or at their fair value, provided that this can be reliably measured (allowed alternative treatment). Reliable measurement depends upon there having recently been a relevant transaction, or there being an active secondary market for this type of asset.

IAS 38 puts forward the principle that all intangible assets should be amortized over their useful life. That should put an end to the arguments over the need to depreciate commercial brands. For purchased intangibles the standard makes a 'rebuttable presumption' of a maximum amortization period of 20 years. If the business does not accept this, it should explain the grounds on which the assumption has been rebutted and review the asset, at least annually, for impairment.

The 2002 changes to accounting for business combinations, and in particular goodwill, involve amending IAS 38 to allow that intangible assets may have an indefinite useful life.

Leased Assets (IAS 17)

The IASB recognizes two kinds of leases: an operating lease and a finance lease. A finance lease is one where the lessee has substantially all the risks and rewards incident to ownership of an asset, whether or not title is eventually transferred. Any lease or long-term rental agreement, with or without a purchase option may enter into this category. This kind of lease is distinguished by the fact that the lease agreement provides for the transfer of title (or gives an option to transfer) of the asset to the lessee at the conclusion of the lease, or by the fact that the lease covers the major part of the useful life of the asset, or by the fact that at the inception of the lease the present value of the minimum lease payments is at least equal to the fair value of the leased asset.

Accounting by lessees

The IASB aligns itself on the practices in Anglo-Saxon countries and requires that assets which are subject to a finance lease should be recognized in the balance sheet of the lessee. This treatment is based on the principle of substance over form, according to which the economic reality should take precedence over the legal form of the transaction. At the inception of the lease, the lessee recognizes both an asset and a liability equal to the 'fair value' of the asset, or at the present value of the lease payments (including the final purchase) if this is less. The discount rate to be used is that on which the lease agreement is based, or if this is not known, then the rate at which the lessee could borrow money.

The lease rentals are broken down into their two components of interest and repayment of principal, using this discount rate. The interest is expensed and the carrying value of the debt is reduced by the amount of repayment. The asset itself is depreciated over its useful life in the same way as if it were owned outright.

Accounting by lessors

The asset does not appear in the balance sheet of the lessor because the lessor does not enjoy the rewards of ownership nor suffer the risks of this. The lessor should be considered as a creditor who lends a sum of money which is reimbursed and rewarded through the lease rentals provided under the lease. At the inception of the contract the lessor records a debt equal to the present value of the future lease rentals. These are then broken down in the same way as for the lessee. Only the portion which represents interest is taken to income.

IAS 17 was slightly revised in 1997, resulting in more guidance on lease classification and further disclosures. The standard was also due for amendment under the Improvements project, with a proposal that long-term leasehold property could be treated as an investment property instead of an operating lease.

The now defunct G4+1 group of Anglophone standard-setters have issued two discussion papers on leasing which suggest that in practice the finance lease/operating lease distinction is difficult to apply and has merely encouraged companies to structure leases differently. It suggests that in principle all leases should be accounted for as finance leases, but no Anglo-Saxon jurisdiction has yet adopted this approach in its domestic standard.

Inventories (IAS 2)

The standard considers inventories to be:

1. assets held for sale or in the process of production for such sale in the ordinary course of business;
2. materials and supplies to be consumed in the production process or in the rendering of services.

Inventories recognized in the balance sheet should be valued at cost, or at net realizable value if this is lower. The cost of inventories should comprise all costs of purchase, costs of conversion and other costs incurred in bringing the inventories to their present location and condition. The costs of conversion includes costs directly related to the units of production as well as a proportion of the indirect costs of production. The allocation of fixed production overheads should be based on the normal capacity of the production facilities (i.e. on the average unit cost basis). Net realizable value is the estimated selling price in the ordinary course of business less the estimated costs of completion and the estimated costs necessary to make the sale.

When items are withdrawn from inventory, those that are not ordinarily interchangeable, or that have been produced for specific projects, should be the subject of an individual identification of their specific costs. Other items should have costs assigned either by the first in first out (FIFO) or the weighted average method (benchmark treatment), or by the last in first out (LIFO) method (allowed alternative treatment). The 2002 Improvements project proposed to remove the LIFO option.

Costs which may be capitalized

Research and Development Costs (IAS 38)

For many years, research and development costs were the subject of a separate standard, IAS 9 which drew a distinction between research costs (to be expensed) and development costs (might be capitalized). IAS 9 has been superseded by IAS 38 which addresses all intangible assets.

IAS 38 similarly suggests that internal projects which generate assets should be divided into a research phase and a development phase. Development is the application of research findings or knowledge to the production of materials, devices, processes, etc. Development costs may be capitalized, but for that to happen the following conditions must be met:

1. the technical feasibility of the product or process can be demonstrated;
2. the enterprise intends to produce and market or use it;
3. the company has the ability to exploit the asset commercially;
4. the asset will generate future cash flows;
5. the company can measure the costs accurately.

Development expenses which satisfy these conditions may, in principle, be capitalized. Any others should, like research costs, be expensed as they are incurred.

Development costs which have been capitalized should be amortized systematically from the time when the product is put on sale or the process is ready for use in line with IAS 38.

Borrowing Costs (IAS 23)

IAS 23 establishes the principle that borrowing costs (interest and ancillary costs) should be recognized as an expense in the period in which they are incurred (benchmark treatment).

Those which are directly attributable to the acquisition, construction or production of qualifying assets can, however, be included in the costs of those assets (allowed alternative treatment). Qualifying assets are those (fixed assets or inventories) that necessarily take a substantial period of time to get ready for their intended use or sale.

The costs to be capitalized are those, by definition, which would have been avoided if the asset concerned had not been acquired. The period for calculating the costs starts with the first costs incurred in relation to the asset and ends when the asset has reached the stage where it can be used or sold. When the asset has not been financed by a specific loan, the amount to be capitalized is obtained by multiplying the costs by the weighted average borrowing cost for the enterprise. The amount of borrowing costs capitalized during a period should not exceed the amount of borrowing costs incurred in that period.

Financial instruments

The IASB undertook a major exercise with the object of producing general principles for the recognition and measurement of all financial instruments in the 1990s. This work has proved controversial, given the basic intention to move towards a system of current value for financial instruments. Banks in particular fear the effect of this on their liquidity ratios and also argue that current values are not necessarily easy to determine. Given the complexity of the subject, the IASC considered that it was better to proceed in stages. A first standard (IAS 32) was published in 1995 and deals only with the presentation of such instruments. IAS 39 which deals with recognition and measurement issues was approved in 1998. The standard-setter was subsequently obliged to issue a set of 200 questions and answers on implementation of the standard. This in turn led to a rationalization of the standard being put forward in 2002. The series of amendments proposed do not fundamentally change the standard, but attempt to clarify and simplify it to deal with operational problems which have arisen. It also offered an opportunity to remove some of the differences with the US approach, although the two sets of standards still differ on a number of points.

Financial Instruments: Recognition and Measurement (IAS 39)

Under IAS 39, all financial assets and financial liabilities, including derivatives, must be recognized on the balance sheet. They are initially measured at cost.

Subsequent to initial recognition, all financial assets are measured at fair value, except for the following, which must be carried at amortized cost:

- loans and receivables originated by the enterprise and not held for trading;
- other fixed maturity investments that the enterprise intends and is able to hold to maturity;
- financial assets whose fair value cannot be reliably measured (e.g. equity instruments with no quoted market price or derivatives linkd to such instruments).

After acquisition, most financial liabilities should be measured at original recorded amount less principal repayments. Only derivatives and liabilities held for trading are remeasured to fair value.

For financial assets and liabilities that are remeasured to fair value, the enterprise can either:

- recognize the entire adjustment in net profit or loss for the period;
- or recognize in the income statement only those changes in fair value relating to financial assets and liabilities held for trading.

The valuation of financial assets and liabilities which are used as hedging instruments are linked to the instrument being hedged. The principle is that any gain or loss on a hedge should be accounted for at the same time as the gain or loss on the item being hedged.

While the essentials of the standard are simple, it is the detail which is extremely complicated, particularly as concerns measurement of the value of financial instruments, derecognition of financial instruments and the designation of hedges.

Presentation of Financial Instruments (IAS 32)

The IASB defines a financial instrument as any contract which gives rise simultaneously to a financial asset in one company and a financial liability or equity instrument in another.

Financial assets include: cash, a contractual right to receive cash or another financial asset (debts payable in cash or in any other fashion), a contractual right to exchange financial instruments under conditions that are potentially favourable (e.g. swaps, warrants, conversion rights, options, etc.), equity instruments of another enterprise.

A financial liability is a contractual obligation to deliver cash or another financial asset to another enterprise or to exchange financial instruments under conditions that are potentially unfavourable. They constitute what would normally be known as debt.

An equity instrument is an instrument that evidences a residual interest in the assets of an enterprise after deducting all of its liabilities. Essentially this means ordinary shares.

In application of the principle of substance over form, a financial instrument should be classified as debt or equity according to the substance of the contractual agreement and not its legal form. If there is any doubt, the essential element to consider is whether there is any obligation to reward or reimburse the issuer. If such an obligation exists, it is an element of debt, if not it is equity.

Certain financial instruments, such as convertible bonds or bonds with warrants attached, constitute both a debt (bond) and an equity instrument (subscription or conversion right). IAS 32 requires that these elements are valued separately and classified separately in the balance sheet of the issuer. Valuation can be done according to two methods. The simplest consists of determining the value of the element which is easiest to calculate (usually the financial debt) and allocating to the other element a value representing the difference between the total value of the instrument and the value of the first element. The other method consists of valuing both elements separately and then adjusting both values to ensure that they add up to the total value of the instrument.

The treatment of receipts from a financial instrument should be consistent with the balance sheet classification. The interest, dividends, gain and losses arising from a financial liability constitute either revenue or expenses of the issuer, while those relating to an equity instrument should be accounted for directly in equity.

Investments in Associates (IAS 28)

The IASB devotes a special standard (IAS 28) to shareholdings which confer 'significant influence'. These requirements are discussed in the section which deals with consolidated accounts.

In the balance sheet of the individual company these investments can be:

1. carried at cost;
2. accounted for using the equity method;
3. or as available-for-sale financial assets, i.e. measured at fair value.

The 2002 Improvements project proposes to remove this option and to make the equity method mandatory.

Pension obligations (*Employee Benefits* IAS 19)

IAS 19, revised in 1998, deals with five areas of accounting for the obligations of employers towards their employees: current benefits, post-employment benefits such as pensions and medical care, other long-term benefits such as those linked to long service awards, termination benefits and equity compensation benefits. For balance sheet purposes, IAS 19 addresses the recognition of long-term liabilities which are some form or other of deferred compensation for employees.

Pension schemes are defined as being either defined contribution plans or defined benefit plans. In a defined contribution plan, the pension ultimately drawn by an employee is a function of the contributions paid during their working life and the investment performance of the fund in which these have been placed. The employer does not assume any responsibility for the final value of the pension, and confines his activities to paying the agreed contributions, which are generally calculated as a proportion of salary. In a defined benefit plan, on the other hand, the pension is fixed in advance, generally in terms of an agreed percentage of the salary at the time of retirement, and the employer is committed to ensuring that the agreed sum will be paid.

Whatever the pension plan being operated, IAS 19 postulates that pension costs should be recognized as an expense at the time that the service is being rendered to the business and not when they are ultimately paid. In a defined contribution plan, the pension expense for a financial period corresponds to the contributions due to be paid for that period. Under a defined benefit plan, the position is more difficult because the annual pension expense should include:

1. the current service cost;
2. amounts recognized in respect of past service costs of current and past employees, experience adjustments and changes in actuarial assumptions;
3. the result of any plan terminations, settlements or curtailments.

Under such a scheme, the pension liability should be estimated using the 'projected unit credit' system. The employer should obtain an actuarial valuation of the pension obligation and provide for the change in this from year to year. However, because this method is sensitive to actuarial assumptions it is likely to provide fluctuations from year to year. Consequently the standard provides a 'corridor' of 10 per cent of actuarial value within which gains and losses need not be recognized.

Other long-term employee benefits such as long service awards or termination benefits should be recognized systematically over the period of related service. IAS 19 takes the view that there is less uncertainty over their valuation and there is therefore no limiting corridor for recognition of costs.

Deferred taxation (*Income Taxes* IAS 12)

The current standard on accounting for taxation (IAS 12) was revised in 1996. The standard advances the principle that the tax expense for an accounting period should be calculated on the basis of tax effect accounting. This gives rise to deferred taxation (either an asset or a liability) every time that tax expense recognized does not correspond to the actual tax paid.

The standard applies an approach based on the balance sheet rather than the profit and loss account. Timing differences are the difference between the accounting value and the tax value of an asset and a liability, a difference which will become taxable when the asset is used or the liability extinguished. The 'temporary differences' defined this way include classic timing differences as between accounting income and income adjusted fror tax purposes, and tax losses which can be carried forward to future accounting periods. But the revised standard also takes in:

1. revaluations of assets;
2. undistributed profits of subsidiaries and associated companies;
3. currency translation differences taken into equity.

Temporary differences are considered to be taxable or deductible according to whether they give rise to an increase or decrease in the taxable profit when the accounting value of an asset is recovered or a liability is repaid. Subject to possible exceptions,[2] any taxable timing difference should give rise to a deferred tax liability. On the other hand deductible temporary differences do not give rise to the recognition of a deferred tax asset unless future taxable profits appear to be sufficient to allow the use of the tax credit which the asset represents.

Any revaluation of an asset, irrespective of whether it takes place in the context of a business combination, will give rise to a recognition of deferred taxation, as also will undistributed profits in subsidiaries and associates.

IAS 12 requires the use of the liability method for calculating deferred tax provisions: the amount is calculated according to tax rates in force at each balance sheet date.

Provisions, Contingent Liabilities and Contingent Assets (IAS 37)

IAS 37 has introduced a tighter definition of provisions than that which is operated in most countries with a strong prudence tradition. For IAS 37 a provision should be created only when (a) there is a present obligation and (b) this will probably result in an outflow of assets. However the standard accepts that an obligation may be 'constructive' rather than necessarily legal. A constructive obligation exists when a company, through established practice or published commitment, has accepted some obligation. The standard does not apply to executory contracts, except where these are likely to be 'onerous'.

If there is a present obligation but little probability that this will result in asset outflows, no provision should be made but disclosure of a contingent liability should be made. If there is a possible obligation but the likelihood of asset outflows is remote, no disclosure is necessary.

Events Occurring after the Balance Sheet Date (IAS 10)

IAS 10 distinguishes two types of event occurring between the date of the balance sheet and the date of signature of the accounts:

1. those which give further information about circumstances which existed at the balance sheet date;
2. those which relate to new circumstances arising after balance sheet date.

Only the former should give rise to any change in the valuation of the company's assets and liabilities, while the latter should be disclosed in the notes. However, any event which indicates that the going concern assumption is not appropriate should be taken into account in the balance sheet.

Income statement items

Revenue (IAS 18)

Revenue is the inflow that arises in the course of the ordinary activities of the enterprise and should be measured at the fair value of the consideration received or receivable, after deducting any trade or volume discounts.

Two conditions are necessary for revenue to be recognized:

1. that it is probable that the enterprise will gain economic benefits from the transaction;
2. the amount can be measured reliably.

For the sale of goods, it is also necessary:

1. that the risks and rewards of ownership have been transferred to the buyer;
2. that the costs incurred or to be incurred can be measured reliably.

Revenue from the rendering of services should be recognized by reference to the stage of completion of the transaction at the balance sheet date. When the outcome of a transaction cannot be estimated reliably, revenue should be recognized only to the extent of the expenses recognized that are recoverable.

Other revenue is recognized on the following bases:

1. *interest*: on a time proportion basis;
2. *royalties*: on an accrual basis;
3. *dividend*: when the shareholder's right to receive payment is established.

Construction Contracts (IAS 11)

A construction contract is one specifically negotiated for the construction of an asset or a combination of assets which are interrelated.

When the outcome of a construction contract can be estimated reliably, contract revenue and contract costs should be recognized as revenue and expenses by reference to the stage of completion of the contract at the balance sheet date. When the outcome cannot be estimated reliably, revenue should only be recognized to the extent of contract costs incurred that it is probable will be recovered. An expected loss on the construction contract should be recognized as an expense immediately.

Accounting for Government Grants (IAS 20)

The standard distinguishes between two types of government subsidy:

1. asset grants, whose primary condition is that the enterprise should purchase, construct or otherwise acquire long-term assets;
2. other grants, known as income grants.

Government grants cannot be recognized directly in equity. They must be recognized as income and matched with the related costs which they are intended to compensate. Asset grants can either be recognized as deferred income or treated as a reduction of the carrying value of the asset to which they relate. Income grants should either be recognized as income or be deducted from the expenses to which they are related.

The Effect of Changes in Foreign Exchange Rates (IAS 21)

Transactions carried out in a foreign currency are recognized on the day of the transaction at the rate ruling on that day; settlements are recognized at the rate ruling on the day of settlement.

At the balance sheet date, items denominated in foreign currencies are valued on the following bases:

1. monetary items (cash, receivables and liabilities): at the closing rate;
2. non-monetary items (inventory and fixed assets) accounted for at historical cost: the rate ruling on the date of acquisition or production;
3. non-monetary items which are carried at fair value (revalued or written down): at the rate ruling when fair value was established.

According to IAS 21 any exchange difference arising on a monetary item, whether realized or not, should be treated as a gain or loss of the period in which it occurred. There is, however, an exception for exchange differences on monetary items which are an integral part of an investment in a foreign entity (long-term receivables and liabilities whose settlement date is not fixed) or which serve as a hedge against such an investment. These exchange differences should be classified as equity. The 2002 Improvement project plans to remove this exception for individual (i.e. non-consolidated) financial statements.

Consolidated financial statements

The preparation of consolidated financial statements is covered principally in IAS 27, IAS 28, and IAS 31, and IAS 21, IAS 22 and IAS 38 also refer to them.

Accounting for Investments in Subsidiaries (IAS 27)

IAS 27 establishes the principle that any company which controls another should prepare consolidated financial statements. Control is defined as the power to govern the financial and operating policies of an enterprise so as to obtain benefits from its activities. Unlike the FASB, the IASB takes the view that ownership of the majority of the voting rights is not a necessary condition. Control can result from:

1. a statute or agreement with the other shareholders;
2. the power to appoint or remove the majority of the members of the board of directors;
3. or the power to cast the majority of votes at meetings of the board of directors.

The scope of the consolidation includes the parent company and all the enterprises which it controls, either directly or indirectly.[3] IAS 27 allows only two exceptions from the need to consolidate:

1. enterprises where control is intended to be temporary;
2. those which operate under severe long-term restrictions (companies in legal administration, subsidiaries subjected to exchange controls, etc.).

These exceptions should probably be modified. According to the 2002 Improvements project, a parent will not need to present consolidated financial statements if and only if:

1. it is a wholly-owned subsidiary or the owners of the minority interests unanimously agree not to present such statements;
2. its securities are not publicly traded;
3. it is not in the process of issuing securities in public securities markets;
4. and the immediate or ultimate parent already publishes consolidated financial statements that comply with IFRS.

The consolidated financial statements should be drawn up using uniform accounting policies. The accounts of individual companies which do not conform to the policies used for the consolidated accounts must be restated. Intragroup balances, intragroup transactions and resulting unrealized profits should be eliminated in full. Only unrealized losses which are incapable of being recovered (i.e. represent a definitive loss of value) should not be eliminated. Minority interests (the investment of external shareholders in the capital of subsidiaries) should be shown separately from liabilities and are not shareholders' equity in the consolidated balance sheet. In the same way, the share of minority interests in the income of the group should be separately presented. These presentation rules should be modified soon. According to the 2002 Improvements project, minority interests will be presented within equity.

Accounting for the assets and liabilities of subsidiaries (*Business Combinations* IAS 22)

IAS 22 is due to be replaced with a new IFRS as a result of the changes which took place in the USA in 2001. The following paragraphs set out the standards in force in 2002, and then there is a section dealing with the proposed changes. Under the current rules, the assets and liabilities of subsidiaries are aggregated with those of the parent company in the consolidated balance sheet. The valuation method depends upon the nature of the transaction which has led to the business combination.

The acquisition method

The aquisition method is applied when one of the enterprises (generally the parent company) is considered to have purchased the other. Under this method the parent company's share of the identifiable assets and liabilities of the subsidiary is carried at their fair value at the time of acquisition. The interest in these of other shareholders (minority interests) can be either accounted for at book value (benchmark treatment), or carried at fair value (allowed alternative treatment).

The difference between acquisition cost and the parent's share of the identifiable assets and liabilities of the subsidiary (at fair value) constitutes goodwill. When this amount is positive, it should be treated as an asset and amortized over its useful life. Unlike the practice which is still often followed in many countries (the UK, Germany, Switzerland, etc.) the IASB no longer allows goodwill to be written off directly against equity. There is a rebuttable presumption that the period of amortization should not be greater than 20 years (IAS 38).

Where the goodwill is negative, it should be presented as a deduction from the assets of the reporting enterprise and, to the extent that it relates to expectations of future losses and expenses, recognized as income when these losses or expenses occur. If negative goodwill is not caused by expected future losses and expenses, it should be recognized as income on a systematic basis over the remaining weighted average useful life of the identifiable acquired depreciable assets, except for the part in excess of the fair values of acquired identifiable non-monetary assets, which should be recognized as income immediately. IAS 22 prefers (benchmark treatment) that this should be deducted from the carrying value of non-monetary assets in the subsidiary. Any balance should be considered as deferred income and be allocated to future income. In line with the treatment of positive goodwill, the maximum amortization period is five years, but may in exceptional cases be extended to 20 years. The allowed alternative treatment is to account for the whole amount of negative goodwill as deferred income and to allocate it to future accounting periods as above.

The 'pooling of interests' method

This method only applies when the subsidiary cannot be considered as having been purchased by the parent. This is a very rare case. In practice it is necessary that:

1. the combination of the two enterprises occurs through the exchange of all or a substantial majority of the shares;
2. the fair value of the one enterprise is not substantially different from the other;

3. the shareholders of each enterprise maintain substantially the same voting rights and interest in the combined entity, relative to each other, after the combination as before.

In effect only mergers and public offers of exchange which are valid for all or nearly all the equity concerned can be accounted for as a pooling of interests.

This method proceeds as though the partners had in fact created a single enterprise. As no transaction is supposed to have taken place, the assets and liabilities of the subsidiary are accounted for at their book value. No goodwill is created and any difference between the value of the net assets and that of the capital issued is accounted for directly within equity.

The new approach

In July 2001 the FASB adopted two new standards, SFAS 141 and SFAS 142, which did away with the possibility of accounting for a business combination as a pooling of interests, and simultaneously allowed that goodwill arising from the acquisition approach should no longer be regarded as a depreciable asset. Instead goodwill became subject to a complex impairment test.

The IASB decided, in the interests of convergence, to go down the same route and replace IAS 22 with a new IFRS which would require all business combinations to be accounted for as an acquisition – this was published as ED3 back in 2002. As in the US standards, the acquisition cost should be allocated over all recognizable assets and liabilities, including intangible assets (a list is provided to encourage companies to recognize intangibles distinct from goodwill). Any unallocated cost left over will be carried in the balance sheet permanently as goodwill arising on consolidation.

This goodwill will not be depreciated, but it will be subject to an impairment test, which is the hidden disadvantage for preparers. The impairment test is difficult to carry out. The IASB version involves preparers 'pushing down' goodwill to individual cash generating units (CGUs) which have been acquired: that is, once a total goodwill figure has been calculated, this should, for impairment purposes, be allocated over all the distinct operational units which have been acquired (and converted to a foreign currency if it is a foreign operation). Thereafter, if the preparer had any reason to think that the goodwill has been impaired, an impairment test must be done, and if necessary, part of the asset must be written off.

Preparers have raised a number of objections, pointing out that often the rationale for an acquisition is the opportunity to combine operations and cut out duplication of costs. Consequently the acquired operation is merged with existing operations and is no longer visible, so calculating the future cash flows becomes a somewhat artificial process. US preparers are apparently finding that the process is also time-consuming and expensive, particularly if outside experts are used to provide reassurance of the accuracy of the valuations.

Financial Reporting of Interests in Joint Ventures (IAS 31)

A joint enterprise is a contractual arrangement whereby two or more parties undertake an economic activity which is subject to joint control. This can be carried out either by the venturers individually or within the framework of a distinct entity. Only the latter is of interest here. Investments in joint ventures can be accounted for either by proportional consolidation (benchmark treatment), or by the equity method (allowed alternative treatment). Proportional consolidation differs from the full consolidation method used for subsidiaries in that only the proportion of the assets, liabilities, revenue and expenses of the joint venture owned by the individual venturer are included in its consolidated statements. It does not give rise to any minority interests.

Unrealized internal profits should be eliminated proportionately to the parent's interest in the venture. As with full consolidation unrealized losses are not eliminated except to the extent that they do not result from a definitive loss of value but are due to the use of transfer prices which are distant from market prices.

The consolidating company's interest in the assets, liabilities, revenues and expenses of the joint venture can be either aggregated with the same items for the parent and subsidiaries or be shown separately. The alternative treatment is the use of the equity method, described below.

Accounting for Investments in Associates (IAS 28)

An associated company is an enterprise on which the parent exercises a 'significant influence', that is to say, has the power to influence its financial and operating decisions without, however, controlling these decisions. There is a presumption of significant influence where an investor controls, directly or indirectly, at least 20 per cent of the voting shares.

In the consolidated accounts these investments should normally be accounted for by the equity method. The only investments carried at cost are:

1. those carried solely with a view to its disposal in the near future;
2. those subject to severe long-term restrictions that significantly impair their ability to transfer funds to the investor (e.g. an enterprise subject to exchange controls).

According to the equity method, the investment is initially recorded at its cost. In line with IAS 22, the difference between this amount and the fair value of the net identifiable assets acquired (i.e. goodwill) is considered as an asset and amortized over its useful life. The investment is then increased or decreased by the amount of the share of the consolidating company in the results of the associate. These are adjusted for goodwill amortization and capital gains on assets recognized at the time the investment was acquired. The value of the investment is also modified as a result of any events which change the equity of the associate (revaluations, exchange differences, etc.). Reflecting the losses made by an associate should not, however, turn the investment into a negative value. The proportion due to the consolidating company is, outside of any special obligation, limited to the accounting value of the investment.

The Effects of Changes in Foreign Exchange Rates (IAS 21)

The method to be applied in converting financial statements prepared in a different currency depends on the degree of independence of the enterprise concerned. IAS 21 distinguishes between:

1. entities whose operations are integral to the operations of the reporting enterprise;
2. foreign entities.

The former carry on business as if they were a simple extension of the reporting enterprise's operations, and have limited freedom of decision. Their financial statements are converted as though their operations had been carried out by the parent company itself. In the balance sheet, the following rates should be used:

1. monetary items (cash, receivables and payables): closing rate;
2. non-monetary items valued at historical cost (inventories and fixed assets which have not been revalued or written down): rate ruling at the time of acquisition or production;
3. non-monetary items which have been revalued or written down: rate ruling at the time of revaluation or write-down.

Revenues and expenses are translated at the rate ruling at the time of the transaction or at an average rate for a period, except for depreciation of assets which is translated at the same rate as that used for the asset. Exchange differences are taken to the income statement. This method is known as the 'temporal method'.

For foreign entities which have more independence, no distinction is made between monetary and non-monetary items. All the assets and liabilities are translated at the closing rate. Revenues and expenses are translated at the rate when the transaction took place or at an average rate for the period. Exchange differences are taken directly to equity. This is known as the 'closing rate method'.

The 2002 Improvements project involves introducing the US notion of 'functional currency' into IAS 21 and also providing rules to permit a company to provide consolidated accounts in a currency other than that of the parent – it introduces the notion of 'presentation currency'.

Cash Flow Statement (IAS 7)

The IASB conceptual framework makes a statement of financial flows an integral part of the financial statements. IAS 7 regulates the nature and method of presentation of this in requiring the preparation of a cash flow statement.

Analysis of cash flows

The cash flow statement should show inflows and outflows relating to:

1. operating activities;
2. investing activities;
3. inancing activities.

Investing activities are the acquisition and disposal of long-term assets and other investments not included in cash equivalents:

1. acquisitions and disposals of fixed assets or investments;
2. advances, loans and refunds of these.

Financing activities are those that result in changes in the size and composition of the equity capital and borrowings of the enterprise. They include in particular:

1. the issue and re-purchase of shares in the enterprise;
2. the issue of debentures, loans, notes and other borrowings and their refund.

All other activities are operating activities.

Interest and dividends paid can be considered either as financing flows or as operating flows. Interest and dividends received can be considered as investing flows or operating flows. Taxes on profits should be considered as operating flows except if they can be identified as deriving from investing or financing activities.

Presentation of the cash flow statement

Operating cash flows may be shown using either the direct method or the indirect method. The direct method involves showing the actual inflows and outflows of cash during the financial period, aggregated by category (receipts from customers, payments to suppliers, etc.). The indirect method reconstitutes the net operating cash flow from net income. It consists of adding to net income:

1. transactions which do not involve cash flows (depreciation and provisions, unrealized exchange differences, etc.);

2. any difference which relates to timing differences for operating cash inflows and outflows (in particular changes in trade payables and receivables);

3. revenues and expenses which relate to financing or investing operations.

IAS 7 encourages the use of the direct method, though without going so far as to make it the benchmark treatment. Financing and investing flows must be shown according to the direct method. Flows relating to extraordinary items should be shown separately within each section of the cash flow statement.

Treasury

The concept of treasury is not defined by IAS 7. It seems to apply to cash and cash equivalents. Cash equivalents are short-term investments which are very liquid, easily convertible to a known amount of cash and whose value is unlikely to change significantly.

The enterprise must provide a reconciliation statement between the amounts appearing in the cash flow statement and the corresponding amounts in the balance sheet. It should therefore be possible, starting from the treasury balance at the beginning of the year, to add the cash flows and come back to the balance of cash and cash equivalents at the end of the year.

Other information

Fundamental Errors and Changes in Accounting Policies (IAS 8)

Earlier financial statements may be affected by the discovery of errors which relate to them or as a result of a change in estimates or in accounting policies. IAS 8 shows the manner in which these events should be dealt with.

The discovery of errors does not automatically call into question the validity of earlier financial statements. In most cases corrections are included in income for the period in which the error was discovered. Only 'fundamental errors', that is those which are of such significance that the financial statements of a prior period can no longer be considered to have been reliable, call for special measures. According to the benchmark treatment in IAS 8, these errors should be corrected by adjusting the opening balance of retained earnings. Comparative information must be restated.

At the same time IAS 8 provides an allowed alternative treatment whereby such differences are taken to income for the period when the error was discovered, which meets the needs of countries where no change is permitted in the opening balance sheet. Where this treatment is followed, the enterprise should provide information as to what the net income would have been in current and prior periods, had the errors not been committed.

The 2002 Improvements project involves major changes in these rules. According to this exposure-draft, the distinction between fundamental errors and other material errors will be removed, and all errors will have to be corrected retrospectively.

IAS 8 makes a clear distinction between changes in estimates and changes in accounting policies. A change in an accounting estimate (modification of a provision, change in the estimated life of an asset, etc.) do not have any impact upon prior period financial statements. Only net income for the current period, and conceivably of future periods, is affected by the change.

However, a change in accounting policies involves a retrospective modification of prior period statements. The effect of the change on prior periods should, in principle, be taken to opening retained earnings (benchmark treatment). The allowed alternative treatment, which recognizes the inviolability of the opening balance sheet, allows for the effects of the change to appear in the income of the current period. In this case the enterprise must provide pro forma financial statements for the prior period. The 2002 Improvements project plans to remove this allowed alternative treatment.

Segment Information (IAS 14)

IAS 14 was revised in 1997 and is reasonably similar to US and Canadian standards alongside which it was developed. The objective of the standard is to provide information which will help users understand the different elements of business which are brought together in the consolidated statements. IAS 14 assumes that the analysis which is used for the external disclosure will correspond to the analysis which is used internally within the entity for management decisions and performance evaluation.

The standard recognizes that segments may be defined either by line of business or by geographical area (either where products are manufactured or where they are sold). It requires the entity to determine which form of analysis is the primary one for understanding the business. While disclosures are required for both forms, greater detail is required for the primary segments. These include segment turnover, result and assets employed, as well as capital expenditure in the period on new assets and aggregate depreciation and amortisation charges. For the secondary segments, IAS 14 requires disclosure of segment turnover, carrying amount of assets and new capital expenditure.

Related Party Disclosures (IAS 24)

IAS 24 deals with information concerning physical or legal persons over which the enterprise may have an influence, or which may have an influence over the enterprise. It concerns not only subsidiaries, joint ventures and associated entities but also shareholders, directors and any entity in which these individuals may exercise a significant influence. The enterprise must disclose the nature of any transactions undertaken with related parties as well as any further information necessary for an understanding of the financial statements.

The Effects of Changes in Prices (IAS 15)

In 1981 the IASC published a standard (IAS 15) requiring large enterprises to calculate and publish certain adjustments necessary to take inflation into account. The enterprises concerned should, in theory, disclose:

1. the amount of the adjustment to, or the adjusted amount of, depreciation of property, plant and equipment;
2. the adjustments relating to monetary items as well as the effect on borrowing or equity interests of these;
3. the effect of these adjustments on results.

The method or methods used to calculate these should also be disclosed. Enterprises using current costs (replacement costs) should in addition disclose the cost of property, plant and equipment and inventories.

Given that this standard has rarely been complied with, and that the rate of inflation in the industrialized countries has slowed down, the IASC removed the requirement to follow this standard in 1989. The withdrawal of IAS 15 is included in the 2002 Improvements project.

Earnings Per Share (IAS 33)

Taking account of the fact that earnings per share is one of the performance measures most frequently used by investors and that information published on the subject is extremely varied, the IASB includes a definition within its core set of standards. The standard requires that any enterprise whose shares are listed on a stock exchange should disclose:

1. basic earnings per share
2. fully diluted earnings per share.

Basic earnings per share is obtained by dividing the net profit distributable to ordinary shareholders by the number of shares outstanding during the year. The expression 'ordinary share' covers any share whose return is subordinate to that of other financial instruments within equity capital. This category differs, for example, from certain privileged shares which give a priority right to a dividend. Where the number in issue has varied during the year, the weighted average is used. For the purposes of this calculation any free issue of shares and reductions of capital caused by losses are deemed to have taken place at the beginning of the year. Where there are several classes of shares, the enterprise should calculate earnings per share for each category.

Fully diluted earnings per share takes account of the potential dilution which is represented by conversion rights or warrants issued by the enterprise. It is obtained by adding to the ordinary shares all those which would have been created if all these rights had been exercised at the date of their issue. Only rights which would have a diluting effect should be taken into account, that is those which would reduce earnings per share.

First time application of IFRS

In 2002, the IASB started work on a new standard whose object is to provide rules dealing with the transition when companies change from national GAAP to using IFRS. This standard will be critical, of course, for listed companies in the EU who are switching to IFRS in 2005. The standard is being developed in conjunction with the French standard-setter, the Conseil National de la Comptabilité. IFRS require that one year's comparative figures are supplied in the financial statements. So a company which uses IFRS as its primary reporting base in year N, needs also to calculate its figures for year N − 1 according to IFRS in order to publish comparatives. This means that a first time adopter will ultimately prepare two sets of figures for the year N − 1, the local GAAP figures published in the normal way at the end of N − 1, and then the comparatives published alongside the IFRS figures for year N.

The draft standard proposes that the company prepares an opening IFRS balance sheet at the start of N − 1. This balance sheet should recognize all assets and liabilities according to IFRS, even if these were not previously recognized. Normally these assets will be at historical cost, but if reconstructing the historical cost causes 'undue cost and effort', they should be valued at fair value. If the company previously recognized intangibles which are not recognized under IFRS, these should be added to goodwill. Any other differences are taken to equity within a special, one-time adjusting entry. Past business combinations, however, do not have to be restated.

In the financial statements for year N the company should provide a note in which it reconciles its year N − 1 local GAAP figures with its year N − 1 IFRS figures, and provides explanations of the differences.

Requirements relating to particular enterprises

Financial Reporting in Hyperinflationary Economies (IAS 29)

IAS 29 requires that financial statements prepared in the currency of a hyperinflationary economy should be restated in terms of the measuring unit current at the balance sheet date. The standard does not indicate at what level of increase in prices an economy should be considered as hyperinflationary. It does, however, provide a list of characteristics of such an economy:

1. the general population prefers to keep its money in non-monetary assets or in a relatively stable foreign currency;

2. receivables and payables are not measured in local currency but in a relatively stable foreign currency;

3. sales and purchases on credit take place at prices that compensate for the expected loss of purchasing power during the credit period, even if this is short;

4. interest rates, wages and prices are linked to a price index;

5. the cumulative inflation rate over three years is approaching or exceeds 100 per cent.

The restatement consists of adjusting the carrying value of non-monetary assets by a co-efficient representing the general increase in prices since the assets entered the balance sheet or were last revalued. The gain or loss on the net monetary position at the beginning of the period when these restatements are applied is taken to equity. However, subsequent gains and losses are considered as income or expenses of the period in which they are recognized.

Accounting and Reporting by Retirement Benefit Plans (IAS 26)

IAS 26 regulates the financial statements of pension schemes. The financial report of any pension plan should include:

1. a report showing the net assets destined to meet pension claims and their development during the current period;

2. a summary of the principal accounting policies followed;

3. a description of the pension scheme and, if relevant, the effects of any change which has occurred during the year.

Defined contribution plans must also describe their investment policy. Defined benefit plans should disclose the actuarial value of promised retirement benefits, distinguishing between those where the right has vested and those where it has not. The calculation can be made on the basis of either current salary levels or projected salary levels on retirement. IAS 26 also requires that the investments of retirement funds should be valued at market value.

Disclosures in the Financial Statements of Banks and Similar Financial Institutions (IAS 30)

IAS 30 deals with disclosures relating specifically to banks and similar financial institutions. Revenues and expenses in the income statement should be classified according to their nature, as also should be assets and liabilities, which should appear in the balance sheet in an order which reflects their relative liquidity. Any offsetting of assets and liabilities is prohibited except where a statute authorizes it and if the resulting balance corresponds to the actual amount which will be paid or received. In the same way revenues and expenses should not be offset, except if they concern hedging operations or revenues and expenses relating to balance sheet items for which offset is permitted.

IAS 30 sets out certain contingencies and commitments which banks and financial institutions must disclose. It also requires a detailed analysis of the provisions for losses on loans and advances. Any significant concentrations of assets, liabilities and off-balance sheet items should be disclosed, as well as the amount of significant net foreign exchange exposures.

Investment Property (IAS 40)

This concerns property which is 'held to earn rentals or for capital appreciation or both' and is not used for production or the supply of services or for administrative purposes, and is not held for sale in the normal course of business. Companies may choose between valuing their properties at fair value or at depreciated historical cost. Where the fair value basis is used, all changes in fair value should be recognized in the profit and loss account.

Agriculture (IAS 41)

The standard on agriculture was produced at the request of the World Bank, but was much delayed by the pressure to finalize the IOSCO core set of standards. It has been developed from an Australian model, and in effect requires that 'biological assets' should be valued at fair value and that changes in fair value should flow through the profit and loss account. Assets which are harvested should be valued at fair value at the time of harvest and then be treated as inventory thereafter. Non-biological assets should be valued in line with normal IAS. As with other fair value standards, businesses object that the fair values of many assets at an incomplete stage of development are difficult to calculate.

Notes

1. The restructuring of the IASC was accompanied by a number of changes in nomenclature. The standards issued by the IASC are known as International Accounting Standards (IAS), whereas those issued by the IASB are known as International Financial Reporting Standards (IFRS). The official generic term is now IFRS – a company saying it complies with International Standards should describe itself as complying with IFRS, and that is understood to mean IAS and IFRS together.

2. These concern goodwill whose amortization is not deductible for tax purposes as well as assets and liabilities whose initial accounting and tax values were not the same.

3. Indirect control is exercised through votes held through another subsidiary.

References

Alexander, D. and Archer, S. (2000) *Miller's International Accounting Standards Guide*. Harcourt Professional Publishing, San Diego.

Cairns, D. (1996) *A Guide to Applying International Accounting Standards*. Accountancy Books, London.

Chenok, P. B. and Snyder, A. (2000) *Foundation for the Future*: The AICPA 1980–1995. JAI Press, Stamford, CT.

Coopers & Lybrand (1996) *Understanding IAS: Analysis and interpretation*. Coopers & Lybrand, London.

IASC (1997) *International Accounting Standards 1997*. IASC, London.

Nobes, C. (1994) *A Study of the International Accounting Standards Committee*. Coopers & Lybrand, London.

Price Waterhouse (1996) *An Introduction to International Accounting Standards*. Price Waterhouse, London.

Raffournier, B. (1996) *Les normes comptables internationales (IAS)*. Economica, Paris.

Walton, P. (2001) Oh no, not that value thing again. *Accounting and Business*. July.

Accounting in the United States

Gary K. Meek

Financial accounting and reporting in the United States represents a dominant influence on accounting in the world today. It is in the Anglo-Saxon model and hence has many similarities to accounting in such countries as the United Kingdom and Australia, and it is largely consistent with standards promulgated by the International Accounting Standards Committee (now International Accounting Standards Board, or IASB). Financial statements are supposed to *present fairly* the financial position and results of the company *in conformity with generally accepted accounting principles*. Accounting is regulated by a private sector body, the Financial Accounting Standards Board, but a government agency, the Securities and Exchange Commission, underpins the authority of the standards. Standards are quite voluminous and detailed because of the litigiousness of US society and the intense competition among accounting firms for business.

Legal and institutional basis of accounting regulation

US Securities and Exchange Commission

To understand standard-setting in the United States, one must begin with the US Securities and Exchange Commission (SEC), a federal regulatory agency established by Congress in 1934. The stock market crash of 1929 understandably damaged investor confidence and the credibility of US capital markets. As the events leading up to the crash were analysed, one of the causes seemed to be that complete and understandable information was not being disseminated to shareholders. Moreover, it also became obvious that companies were following many different accounting methods in their financial statements. Companies, accountants and the stock exchanges came under severe criticism. In the United States, corporations are formed under state law, not federal law. At the time, there were no national regulations governing the flow of communication to investors. Each state had its own set of regulations and the resulting hodge-podge was viewed as ineffective in adequately informing investors about publicly traded companies.[1]

The Securities Act of 1933 sets forth accounting and disclosure requirements for initial public offerings of securities, while the Securities Exchange Act of 1934 applies to subsequent trading of these securities, prescribing periodic reporting requirements for companies listed on organized stock exchanges or whose securities are traded in over-the-counter markets. The SEC was established to administer the 1933, 1934 and several other federal acts. These acts supplemented and superseded existing state laws referred to above.

The SEC is an independent government agency, rather than a department of the US government, which means that the White House and Congress have no direct influence over SEC policies. Nevertheless, the five full-time Commissioners are appointed by the President (to five year terms of office) and confirmed by the Senate. Additionally, Congress exercises supervision over the SEC by, among other things, controlling its budget. The SEC has four principal operating divisions. The Division of Corporation Finance, which is the largest, reviews disclosure documents for compliance with SEC requirements. The Chief Accountant is the principal advisor to the Commissioners on accounting and auditing issues. The SEC has a full-time staff of over 2600.

As noted above, the SEC has jurisdiction over companies listed on stock exchanges (such as the New York and American Stock Exchanges) and traded in the over-the-counter markets, commonly referred to as *public* companies. Approximately 12 000 companies are subject to the SEC's jurisdiction, out of some 3.7 million US corporations altogether. While the SEC has the legal authority to prescribe accounting and reporting standards for public companies, its policy since the late 1930s has been to rely on the private sector to develop *generally accepted accounting principles* (GAAP). However, it was not until 1973 that the SEC's policy was officially affirmed, in *Accounting Series Release (ASR) No. 150.* ASR No. 150 states that

> principles, standards and practices promulgated by the FASB will be considered by the Commission as having substantial authoritative support, and those contrary to such FASB promulgations will be considered to have no such support.

The Financial Accounting Standards Board (FASB) referred to in ASR No. 150 and predecessor private sector standard-setting bodies are discussed below.

While the SEC collaborates with the private sector in establishing accounting standards, it has not relinquished its authority. Indeed, the threat of SEC (or, 'government') intervention hangs over the private sector's head. On those occasions when the SEC has felt that the private sector is moving too slowly or in the wrong direction, it has not hesitated to impose its own requirements, delay or even overrule a private sector pronouncement. At times, the SEC has placed considerable pressure on the FASB and earlier bodies in exercising its assumed oversight role. However, since the 1970s the SEC reporting requirements have generally focused more on disclosure issues than measurement issues. For example, it is an SEC requirement for a management's discussion and analysis (MD&A) of the company's results and financial condition and for disclosure of the compensation of a company's top executives. Arguably, the SEC's oversight role in standard-setting means that US GAAP are often biased toward large, listed firms.

SEC disclosure requirements are contained in *Regulation S-X*, 'Form and Content of Financial Statements' and *Regulation S-K*, 'Integrated Disclosure Rules.' *Financial Reporting Releases* provide the SEC's position on accounting, reporting and auditing issues. Some of these are unique to SEC requirements, such as reporting quarterly financial data, while others address accounting practices unacceptable to the SEC. *Staff Accounting Bulletins* are administrative interpretations and views about accounting matters.

SEC policy is designed to protect individual investors and to ensure the integrity of the securities trading system. Investor protection is achieved through full public disclosure of all information needed to make an informed investment decision. Extensive requirements for information disclosure are seen as necessary to permit individual investors to compare investment opportunities meaningfully. Comparability of financial information has always been one of the driving forces of the SEC.

Financial Accounting Standards Board

The FASB, established in 1973, is the private sector body authorized to establish generally accepted accounting principles in the United States. It was preceded by the Committee on Accounting Procedure (1938–59) and the Accounting Principles Board (1959–73). As noted above, the SEC embarked on its policy of reliance on the private sector for developing GAAP soon after it was created in the 1930s. The profession responded with the Committee on Accounting Procedure (CAP), a part-time, 21 member committee of the American Institute of Certified Public Accountants (AICPA),[2] drawn from public accounting and academe. Altogether the CAP issued 51 *Accounting Research Bulletins (ARBs)* which dealt mostly with specific accounting and reporting problems rather than general principles or a theoretical framework. Nevertheless, the 51 ARBs established some general principles, either explicitly or by implication (Mutchler and Smith 1984):

1. Historical cost was established as the appropriate valuation basis for accounting.
2. Revenue realization at the time of sale, with only a few exceptions, was accepted as the basic standard for recognizing revenue.
3. Matching expenses to the period when benefits are realized was established.

Additionally, the CAP did manage to halt many of the abuses of earlier days. Perhaps most importantly, the CAP established the private sector as a viable force for developing accounting standards.

In 1959, the CAP was replaced by the Accounting Principles Board (APB). It was also a committee of the AICPA, but with broader representation. Members were drawn primarily from public accounting, but also from industry, the financial community, academe and government. However, like the CAP, it was part-time; membership ranged from 18 to 21. The APB issued 31 *Opinions* and four *Statements*. The former are authoritative pronouncements of GAAP, while the latter are advisory only.

The APB was criticized almost from its beginning. One of its objectives was to establish broad accounting principles, but too many of its decisions were ad hoc in nature and, similar to the CAP, focused on specific problems. The APB had trouble producing *Opinions* that were consistent internally and across one another. The APB was also charged with failing to act promptly to correct alleged accounting abuses and for a lack of productivity. Moreover, its structure was criticized as ineffective; it was large, its members had part-time status and were unpaid, and it met only a few days each month. The APB was also criticized for being so closely tied to the AICPA and for being dominated by practising certified public accountants (CPAs) who, by way of concern for their clients, might have a vested interest in various agenda items. In the end, the APB was not only similar in form to the CAP but also operating in very much the same manner. The shortcomings of a part-time standard-setting body once again became apparent. The APB was unable to solve expeditiously an increasing number of complex problems.

Responding to the growing dissatisfaction with APB, in 1971 the AICPA formed the Study Group on Establishment of Accounting Principles, known as the Wheat Committee. The Wheat Committee recommended that the APB be abolished and that it be replaced by an autonomous, Financial Accounting Standards Board with seven, full-time paid members responsible for setting financial accounting and reporting standards. The AICPA accepted these and supporting recommendations, and in July 1973 the FASB began operations.

The operations of the FASB are overseen by the Financial Accounting Foundation (FAF) whose trustees are drawn from several groups including the Financial Executives

International, Institute of Management Accountants, American Accounting Association, Association for Investment Managment and Research, as well as the AICPA. FAF is responsible for raising and managing the FASB's funds and for selecting its seven members. In addition, the FAF appoints members to the Financial Accounting Standards Advisory Council (FASAC). FASAC has 33 members who are broadly representative of preparers, auditors and users of financial information. FASAC advises the FASB on policy matters, agenda items, priorities and technical issues. The FASB also has an Emerging Issues Task Force (EITF) concerned with identifying emerging issues and resolving technical issues amenable to quick resolution but which are of limited importance or scope.

There are several key differences between the FASB and APB which are designed to make it more effective and garner greater support. These differences are:

1. *Smaller size*. The FASB has seven members whereas the APB had 18.

2. *Full-time, paid members*. FASB members sever all ties with their employers, work full-time for the FASB, and are well paid. They are appointed for renewable five-year terms. APB membership was part-time and unpaid, since members continued to work for their respective accounting firms, companies or institutions.

3. *Financial independence and greater autonomy*. The FASB is financed by a wide cross-section of organizations, none of which contributes a large percentage of its budget. It is also answerable only to the FAF. The APB had no separate funding and was a committee of the AICPA.

4. *Broader representation*. FASB members are not required to be CPAs. APB members had to be CPAs and members of the AICPA.

In addition, the FASB is assisted by a staff of approximately 40 professionals plus support personnel, and as noted above, enjoys a wide array of advisory support including FASAC and EITF.

The FASB issues two primary types of pronouncements. *Statements of Financial Accounting Concepts (SFACs)* are the fundamental concepts upon which financial accounting and reporting standards are based. Aspects of the FASB's conceptual framework are discussed in the next section. SFACs do not establish GAAP. *Statements of Financial Accounting Standards (SFASs)* establish accounting procedures and principles for financial reporting, and are considered GAAP. Note also that the ARBs and Opinions of the CAP and APB, respectively, remain in force (i.e. are still GAAP) unless amended or superseded by the FASB.

In an attempt to be responsive to public opinion, the FASB goes through a lengthy *due process procedure* before issuing a SFAS.[3] Once a topic is added to the FASB's agenda, research and analysis is conducted by the FASB technical staff and an advisory task force of experts is appointed. The FASB even commissions outsiders to conduct research when necessary. A *Discussion Memorandum* or other discussion document presenting the issues and possible solutions is prepared and disseminated for public comment. Public hearings are held and oral and written comments are carefully analysed. The seven members of the FASB then begin formal discussions in meetings open to the public. Next, an *Exposure Draft* is issued which sets forth the proposed standard as well as an explanation of the basis for conclusions. Four of the seven members must approve an Exposure Draft for issuance. After reviewing comments on the Exposure Draft, the FASB may revise it for additional public comment. However, when it is satisfied that all reasonable alternatives have been considered, a vote on the final SFAS is taken and must be approved by four of the seven members.

The due process, 'in the sunshine' procedures of the FASB ensure that standard-setting in the United States is a political as well as technical process. For one thing, the SEC has delegated responsibility for determining GAAP to the FASB, and the FASB always has the SEC looking over its shoulders. The FASB also depends on general constituency support for its authority to develop reporting standards. However, it must also remain independent of any particular constituent. Pressure is exerted on the FASB whenever it deliberates new standards and the resulting balancing act means that compromises are often necessary. The open process also ensures that the FASB considers the economic consequences of its pronouncements.

To date, approximately 150 SFASs have been issued, of which about one-third are amendments or supplements to earlier statements. They are thus numerous and they are also quite detailed. Zeff (1995, p. 65) explains both the volume and rule-oriented nature of SFASs as attributable to the litigiousness of American society and the feverish competition among public accounting firms for clients. Regarding litigation, auditors want to be able to cite express provisions of GAAP as a defence in potential lawsuits. As to competition among firms, 'opinion shopping' is quite common whereby companies claim to their auditors that other public accounting firms would be more flexible on certain accounting treatments. More detailed rules alleviate auditors from being individually responsible for making judgements based on existing rules.

Financial statements are supposed to 'present fairly' the financial position of the company and the results of its operations 'in conformity with generally accepted accounting principles'. Compliance with GAAP is the test for a fair presentation and there is no subjective override, such as the 'true and fair' override in the United Kingdom. In 1964, the AICPA adopted a general requirement (now Rule 203 of the AICPA's *Code of Professional Ethics*) that auditors may not express an opinion about conformity with GAAP when financial statements contain a material deviation from it. Rare exceptions are allowed when it can be shown that financial statements would be misleading by following GAAP. However, in these cases, the departure is disclosed along with the reason for it. The SEC also expects compliance with GAAP and will not accept auditors' reports with an 'adverse' opinion.[4]

International initiatives

Until recently, international developments have felt the benign neglect of both the SEC and the FASB. Attitudes were parochial, largely reflecting the belief that US standards were the best in the world and that it was only necessary for the rest of the world to rise to US quality. Things have now changed. The globalization of capital markets has intensified competition among the world's capital markets and has especially affected the competitiveness of US markets. Foreign[5] markets are often more attractive than US markets because of stringent filing and disclosure requirements imposed by the SEC. Indeed, there is evidence that companies avoid US capital markets because of them. Diversity in reporting requirements worldwide especially hurts the United States since US requirements are generally the most stringent in the world. While the SEC has relaxed reporting requirements somewhat for foreign companies, they are still viewed as onerous by many companies. This is especially the case regarding the SEC requirement for compliance with US GAAP. Foreign companies may use US GAAP in preparing their primary financial statements or they may reconcile net income and stockholders' equity from their respective home GAAP to US GAAP.

US stock exchanges have been pressuring the SEC to do something so that they can stop losing business to foreign exchanges. Of course, the SEC is charged with investor protection via adequate disclosure of information. Long term, the SEC is committed to the objective of the International Organization of Securities Commissions (IOSCO) for comprehensive international accounting standards for securities trading. Indeed, the SEC is a member and active participant in IOSCO. In May 2000, IOSCO formally endorsed IASC standards as the basis for worldwide listings (see Chapter 2). The SEC is now considering whether to accept IASs in lieu of US GAAP for non-US companies. One of the SEC's primary concerns is enforcing compliance with IASs. The SEC has said that it will not endorse IASs without the creation of a global stock market regulator (*Accountancy*, April 2000, p. 10).

As far as the FASB is concerned, it was not until 1991 that it developed its first strategic plan for international activities. It was revised in 1994, adding as a new objective encouraging the equality of financial statement requirements for foreign and domestic companies in their utilization of US capital markets.

The FASB has quickly engaged itself internationally. For example, SFAS 131 on segment disclosures was a joint project with Canada, and SFAS 128 on earnings per share and SFAS 133 on financial instruments were developed parallel to the comparable International Accounting Standards. The FASB is also participating with standard-setters in Canada, Mexico and Chile to explore areas in which the four countries can more fully cooperate on minimizing differences in their accounting standards. It works with standard-setting bodies in other countries and now focuses much attention on its relationship with the IASB. The FASB believes that the IASB currently is the logical focal point for internationalization efforts.

American Institute of Certified Public Accountants

Until the FASB was established in 1973, the AICPA provided the private sector leadership in developing financial accounting standards and practices. As discussed above, the AICPA acted through its Committee on Accounting Procedure from 1938 to 1959, and through the Accounting Principles Board from 1959 to 1973. After the FASB was established, the AICPA formed the Accounting Standards Executive Committee (AcSEC) to speak for the AICPA on behalf of financial reporting matters. Besides advising the FASB on agenda items, AcSEC also provides guidance to AICPA members on reporting issues that are not covered by existing standards and other accounting matters that usually apply to specific industries.

The primary responsibility of the AICPA today concerns the independent audit of financial statements by certified public accountants (CPAs). Ten *generally accepted auditing standards* (GAAS) provide a general framework. They deal with the personal qualities an auditor should possess (e.g. competence and independence), the performance of the audit in the field (e.g. understanding the internal controls and gathering sufficient evidence), and reporting the results of the audit (e.g. whether the financial statements conform to GAAP). Specific auditing pronouncements, called *Statements on Auditing Standards (SASs)*, are issued through the AICPA's Auditing Standards Board. GAAS and SASs are the authoritative guidelines that auditors are required to follow.

The AICPA is also responsible for the *Code of Professional Ethics* which provides a standard of conduct for CPAs. For example, Rule 101 requires independence for attestation engagements. Rule 203, discussed earlier, concerns GAAP as the basis for a fair representation of financial statements. Another major function of AICPA is writing and grading the Uniform CPA Examination.[6]

Congress passed the Sarbanes-Oxley Act in 2002 in reaction to the US accounting scandals that began with the collapse of Enron, the energy trading giant. One provision is the establishment of the Public Company Accounting Oversight Board to oversee the audits of public companies and more closely regulate the accounting profession.

Internal Revenue Service

The federal income tax law dates back to 1913 and has been revised, amended and over-hauled many times since then. The current statutory law is the Internal Revenue Code of 1986 (as amended to date), a legal document approximately 2800 pages in length. The Internal Revenue Service (IRS) is the branch of the Treasury Department responsible for interpreting and administering the tax law. Overall interpretive guidance on 'the Code' (as it is called), is issued by the Treasury Department as Treasury regulations. In addition, the IRS issues revenue rulings, revenue procedures, and a variety of other interpretive pronouncements in carrying out its administrative responsibility. Court decisions also establish precedent in the interpretation of the tax law.

In the United States, as with other countries of the Anglo-Saxon model, financial accounting and reporting is distinct from tax accounting. Nevertheless, many of the income determination rules are the same, and the determination of taxable income begins with the determination of financial accounting income. Thus, in general tax law does not establish generally accepted accounting principles. The major exception is the use of LIFO (last in first out) for inventory valuation. The Code allows LIFO for tax purposes, and the IRS has imposed a LIFO conformity rule, requiring LIFO for financial reporting if a company uses it to determine taxable income. The most important difference between taxable and financial incomes has to do with the depreciation deduction.

Objectives, assumptions and qualitative characteristics

The objectives, assumptions and qualitative characteristics of financial statements in the United States are contained in the Statements of Financial Accounting Concepts (SFACs) issued by the FASB between 1978 and 2000. The so-called Conceptual Framework Project began shortly after the FASB was formed in 1973. SFACs set forth fundamentals on which financial accounting and reporting standards are based.

The relevant SFACs are:[7]

1. *SFAC No. 1*, 'Objectives of Financial Reporting by Business Enterprises', presenting the goals and purposes of financial reporting.
2. *SFAC No. 2*, 'Qualitative Characteristics of Accounting Information', identifying the characteristics that make accounting information useful.
3. *SFAC No. 5*, 'Recognition and Measurement in Financial Statements of Business Enterprises', specifying the fundamental criteria for recognition and measurement in financial statements.
4. *SFAC No. 6*, 'Elements of Financial Statements', defining the items in financial statements, such as assets, liabilities, revenues and expenses.
5. *SFAC No. 7*, 'Using Cash Flow Information and Present Value in Accounting Measurements,' providing general principles governing the use of present value techniques when the amount of future cash flows, the timing, or both are uncertain.

The lack of a conceptual framework to serve as a foundation for more specific accounting standards had dogged the profession since the 1930s. As discussed above, both the CAP and APB were criticized for failure to develop a statement of basic accounting principles to guide standard-setting. However, both organizations attempted to do so. For example, in 1949 the CAP appointed a subcommittee to develop such a statement, but the results were unsatisfactory. In the end, the CAP merely issued ARB 43, which is a revision and restatement of previous *ARBs*. Early in its life, the APB commissioned two projects on accounting postulates and principles, published as Moonitz (1961) and Sprouse and Moonitz (1962). The APB rejected both as too radically different from existing GAAP. In 1965, the AICPA published *Accounting Research Study No. 7* (Grady 1965), which drew on current practices and pronouncements in an attempt to piece together a hierarchy of basic concepts and principles. This work was essentially ignored. Finally, in 1970 the APB issued Statement No. 4, *Basic Concepts and Accounting Principles Underlying Financial Statements of Business Enterprises*. Overall, it added little to what had already been covered in Grady (1965) and was never accepted as a foundation for building accounting standards. With so many failed attempts by the profession littering the landscape, it was a matter of some importance to the FASB to develop a conceptual framework of accounting.

Objectives

The objectives of financial statements[8] outlined in SFAC No. 1 are developed in the context of the role of financial accounting and reporting in the US economy – to provide even-handed financial and other information that facilitates the efficient functioning of capital and other markets and which assists in promoting the efficient allocation of scarce resources in the economy. Investors and creditors and their advisors are identified as the primary users of financial statements.[9] Accordingly, the objectives of financial statements are:

1. To provide information that is useful to present and potential investors and creditors and other users in making rational investment, credit and similar decisions.

2. To provide information to help investors, creditors, and others assess the amounts, timing and uncertainty of prospective net cash inflows to the related enterprise.

3. To provide information about the economic resources of an enterprise, the claims to those resources, and the effects of transactions, events, and circumstances that change resources and claims to those resources.

While the objectives focus on helping users assess prospective cash flows, SFAC No. 1 goes on to state that information based on accrual accounting generally provides a better indication of an enterprise's ability to generate cash flows than does strict cash flow information.

Assumptions

Four basic assumptions underlie the structure of US financial accounting. Though not explicitly covered in SFACs, they are implicit in the recognition and measurement criteria of SFAC No. 5. (1) The *entity assumption* means that the activities of an enterprise can be kept separate and distinct from those of its owners and other enterprises. It establishes the unit of accountability and thus the boundaries of what information to include in the financial statements of that entity. (2) The *going concern assumption* means that, unless there is evidence to the contrary, the entity can be expected to be in business in the foreseeable future, long enough to carry out existing plans, contracts and commitments. (3) The *periodicity (or, time period) assumption* means that the life of the enterprise can be divided into artificial time periods for purposes of financial reporting. In this way, investors and others can be supplied with accounting information on a timely basis. (4) Finally, the *monetary unit assumption* means that money amounts are the appropriate common unit for measuring the economic activity of an enterprise. In the United States, it also implies that the monetary unit (i.e. the US dollar) remains stable over time.

Qualitative characteristics

SFAC No. 2 presents a hierarchy of the qualities that make accounting information useful. The hierarchy is presented in Figure 3.1.

According to SFAC No. 2, the two most important characteristics that make accounting information useful to decision-makers are relevance and reliability. *Relevance* means that the information is capable of making a difference in a decision. If it improves a decision-maker's ability to predict, it has *predictive value*. If it confirms or corrects earlier expectations, it has *feedback value*. Relevant accounting information often does both at once, since knowledge about the outcome of actions already taken can improve the decision-maker's ability to predict the results of similar future actions. *Timeliness* means that information is available when needed. Information that is not timely loses its capacity to influence decisions. Thus, a lack of timeliness can rob information of relevance that it might otherwise have had. Predictive value, feedback value and timeliness are viewed as ingredients of relevant accounting information.

Reliability assures decision-makers that they can depend on the accounting information to be effective in doing what it is expected to do. Reliable information is free from bias. *Verifiability*, sometimes referred to as objectivity, minimizes measurer bias. It refers to a consensus among measurers as to results of what is being measured. In other words, verifiable information can be replicated by different measurers using the same measurement methods. *Representational faithfulness*, sometimes called validity, refers to an agreement between a measurement or description and the phenomenon it purports to represent. In essence, accounting numbers and descriptions should picture what really happened or existed. *Neutrality* means that accounting information is not designed to cause a predetermined outcome or type of behaviour.

Comparability and *consistency* are viewed as secondary qualitative characteristics. If accounting information is measured and reported similarly for different enterprises, it is

Figure 3.1   A hierarchy of qualitative characteristics of accounting information

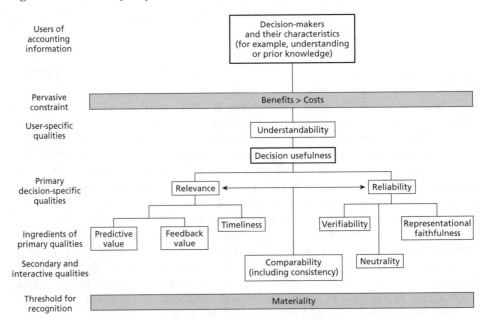

comparable. When it is measured and reported similarly for the same enterprise from one year to the next, it is consistent.

Materiality is described as a threshold for recognition, while *benefits > costs* is a pervasive constraint for financial reporting. An item of information is material if it is likely that users will be influenced by it. Materiality depends both on the amount of an item and its nature. Materiality and relevance have much in common in that they are both defined in terms of what influences an investor or other decision-maker. However, they can be distinguished. Certain information may not be reported because investors have no interest in it (it is not relevant) or because it is too inconsequential to make a difference (it is immaterial). Materiality is a judgement call.

Benefits > costs overrides all aspects of financial reporting. Given that the burden of the costs and the incidence of benefits fall unevenly throughout the economy, this becomes an extremely difficult judgement to make.

Conservatism, meaning prudence, is not considered a quality of accounting information that makes it useful. According to SFAC No. 2, conservatism has a place in financial reporting as long as it ensures that uncertainties and risks inherent in business situations are adequately considered. However, the concept needs to be applied with care. It should not connote deliberate, consistent understatement of net assets and profits, since this introduces bias in financial reporting and conflicts with such characteristics as representational faithfulness, neutrality and comparability.

SFAC No. 2 differs in detail, though not in spirit, from the International Accounting Standards Board's (IASB's) Framework for the Preparation and Presentation of Financial Statements (Framework). Most of the same concepts are discussed, for example, relevance and reliability. However, comparability is considered equally important to relevance and reliability in the Framework. Of course, improving international comparability is a main objective of the IASB, so it is not surprising that comparability figures more prominently in the Framework than it does in SFAC No. 2. Framework also discusses 'substance over form' and 'completeness' which SFAC No. 2 does not. Nevertheless, substance over form underlies US GAAP, while completeness (i.e. nothing is left out) is subsumed in SFAC No. 2's notion of reliability.

Requirements to publish accounts and have them audited

The United States has no national statutory requirements for the publication of audited accounts like those contained in the Companies Acts of, for example, the United Kingdom. As noted earlier, the SEC was formed in part because the laws of the various states were viewed as ineffective in regulating the control of information to investors and other interested parties. And it is still the case that the laws of the 50 states have no accounting or auditing regulations of any great consequence. Only the some 12 000 public companies subject to SEC jurisdiction and certain large corporations (those with more than 500 shareholders and assets over $5 million) are required to have their annual financial statements audited. Unless forced to do so by their shareholders or lenders, other limited companies have no such compulsory requirements. In this regard, the United States is rather unusual by international norms.

Audited financial statements and supplementary notes are included in the annual report sent to shareholders and the stock exchanges on which public companies' shares are listed. The annual report is also filed with the SEC as a part of Form 10-K within 90 days after fiscal year-end. In addition, selected non-audited financial statement information is filed in Form 10-Q within 45 days after the end of the first three fiscal quarters.

As noted earlier, ten generally accepted auditing standards (see Figure 3.2) provide the framework for the conduct of an audit. Adopted by the AICPA in the late 1940s, they have, with only minor changes, remained the same.

The requirements for issuing audit reports are contained in the four standards for reporting, and roughly half of the *SASs* deal with reporting requirements. The auditor's report (also referred to as the auditor's 'opinion') indicates whether *generally accepted auditing standards* have been followed. It also states whether the financial statements (including notes) *present fairly* the company's financial position, results of operations, and cash flows *in conformity with generally accepted accounting principles*. The most common type of audit report is the *standard unqualified report*, used for more than 90 per cent of all audit reports. In some circumstances, an *unqualified report with explanatory paragraph* is issued. These circumstances include the lack of consistent application of (i.e. a change in) GAAP, material uncertainties and substantial doubts about going concern. Figure 3.3 is the audit report from the 1999 annual report of Colgate-Palmolive Company. When the auditor concludes that financial statements are presented fairly overall, except for specified departures from GAAP, a *qualified* opinion is issued. If departures from GAAP are so material or pervasive that the overall fairness of financial statements is in question, an *adverse* opinion is issued.[10]

To say that American society is litigious is probably an understatement. Many accountants believe that the most serious problem facing the profession in the United States today is legal liability and its repercussions. Arens and Loebbecke (2000, p. 112) put the situation in perspective as follows:

Figure 3.2 The ten generally accepted auditing standards

GENERAL STANDARDS
1. The audit is to be performed by a person or persons having adequate technical training and proficiency as an auditor.
2. In all matters relating to the assignment, an independence in mental attitude is to be maintained by the auditor or auditors.
3. Due professional care is to be exercised in the performance of the audit and the preparation of the report.

STANDARDS OF FIELD WORK
1. The work is to be adequately planned and assistants, if any, are to be properly supervised.
2. A sufficient understanding of the internal control structure is to be obtained to plan the audit and to determine the nature, timing, and extent of tests to be performed.
3. Sufficient competent evidential matter is to be obtained through inspection, observation, inquiries, and confirmations to afford a reasonable basis for an opinion regarding the financial statements under audit.

STANDARDS OF REPORTING
1. The report shall state whether the financial statements are presented in accordance with generally accepted accounting principles.
2. The report shall identify those circumstances in which such principles have not been consistently observed in the current period in relation to the preceding period.
3. Informative disclosures in the financial statements are to be regarded as reasonably adequate unless otherwise stated in the report.
4. The report shall either contain an expression of opinion regarding the financial statements, taken as a whole, or an assertion to the effect that an opinion cannot be expressed. When an overall opinion cannot be expressed, the reasons therefor should be stated. In all cases where an auditor's name is associated with financial statements, the report should contain a clear-cut indication of the character of the auditor's work, if any, and the degree of responsibility the auditor is taking.

Legal liability and its consequences are significant for CPAs. It is estimated that the profession's aggregate liability exposure exceeds $30 billion. Although firms have insurance to help alleviate the impact of assessed damages, the premiums are high and the policies available to the firms have large deductible amounts. The deductibles are such that the large firms are essentially self-insured for losses of many millions of dollars.

Legal liability can have serious consequences. One large national accounting firm, Laventhol & Horwath, filed for bankruptcy because of a large number of malpractice suits with large damage amounts facing the firm. Another large national firm, Panell Kerr Forster, closed or sold about 90 percent of its offices and reorganized its remaining offices as individual professional corporations partially because of litigation it faced.

Accountants' liability also affects the profession in human terms. For example, a study completed in 1994 indicated that of partners and managers leaving the six largest auditing firms in recent years, 29 percent were influenced by the threat of litigation, and 46 percent were influenced by the effect of ongoing litigation costs on future profits.

Several factors contribute to the legal environment in the United States. One is the doctrine of joint and several liability (often referred to as the 'deep-pocket' concept) whereby liability is apportioned on the basis of ability to pay rather than degree of responsibility or fault. Another is the contingent-fee basis for attorney compensation. This encourages actions against accountants by providing claimants the potential for gains when a lawsuit is successful, but without corresponding potential for loss when a lawsuit is unsuccessful. Further, 'class action' lawsuits can be filed to include the plaintiffs and all other persons with an identical interest in the alleged wrong.

Figure 3.3 Auditor's report – Colgate-Palmolive Company

Report of Independent Public Accountants

To the Board of Directors and Shareholders of Colgate-Palmolive Company:

We have audited the accompanying consolidated balance sheets of Colgate-Palmolive Company (a Delaware corporation) and subsidiaries as of December 31, 1999 and 1998, and the related consolidated statements of income, retained earnings, changes in capital accounts and cash flows for each of the three years in the period ended December 31, 1999. These financial statements are the responsibility of the Company's management. Our responsibility is to express an opinion on these financial statements based on our audits.

We conducted our audits in accordance with generally accepted auditing standards. Those standards require that we plan and perform the audit to obtain reasonable assurance about whether the financial statements are free of material misstatement. An audit includes examining, on a test basis, evidence supporting the amounts and disclosures in the financial statements. An audit also includes assessing the accounting principles used and significant estimates made by management, as well as evaluating the overall financial statement presentation. We believe that our audits provide a reasonable basis for our opinion.

In our opinion, the financial statements referred to above present fairly, in all material respects, the financial position of Colgate-Palmolive Company and subsidiaries as of December 31, 1999 and 1998, and the results of their operations and their cash flows for each of the three years in the period ended December 31, 1999, in conformity with generally accepted accounting principles.

Arthur Andersen LLP

New York, New York
February 1, 2000

Auditors are liable to their clients under common law for negligence and/or breach of contract. They are also liable under common law to third parties who rely on the results of their work. Both the Securities Act of 1933 and the Securities and Exchange Act of 1934 are a source of civil liability to third parties under federal securities laws, and are the basis for the greatest growth in liability litigation against accountants.

The AICPA and the profession as a whole have taken a number of steps to counter the legal liability environment in the United States. One step was revising the auditor's report in 1988 clarifying the nature of an audit and that a company's management is primarily responsible for the financial statements. New SASs have been issued requiring additional audit procedures designed to protect the auditor. Peer review requirements have also been enacted. Finally, the AICPA has been active in lobbying the US Congress for changes in federal statutes governing professional malpractice and securities fraud litigation. The profession also organized similar efforts. In 1992 the (then) Big Six accounting firms, along with nearly 200 corporations, organized the Coalition to Eliminate Abusive Securities Suits (CEASS). Targets included joint and several liability and contingent fees, discussed above. CEASS was instrumental in backing the *Private Securities Litigation Reform Act of 1995* which became law in December 1995. It is aimed at deterring frivolous class-action lawsuits against public companies by disappointed investors. Among its provisions are the introduction of proportionate liability for defendants in a fraud action, based on their level of responsibility (thereby eliminating joint and several liability, except for defendants who engage in knowing fraud), limits on attorney's fees, and sanctions for parties and attorneys for initiating suits that are frivolous or groundless. The *Securities Litigation Uniform Standards Act* of 1998 extended this relief to lawsuits brought in state courts.

These efforts are overshadowed by recent events that have rocked the US accounting scene, including the Enron and WorldCom scandals and the demise of Andersen, a Big Five audit firm. It is unclear at the time of writing how the previously mentioned 2002 Sarbanes-Oxley Act will affect legal liablity.

Components of annual reports

The financial statements in annual reports consist of an *income statement, balance sheet, statement of cash flows, statement of stockholders' equity* and *statement of comprehensive income*, together with a summary of the company's significant accounting policies and other footnote disclosures. Comparative balance sheets for the last two fiscal years are normally prepared, while the statements of income, cash flows, stockholders' equity and comprehensive income are normally prepared for the last three fiscal years.

The income statement contains, with some exceptions, all items of profit and loss during the period, including extraordinary gains and losses, discontinued operations and the effects of most changes in accounting principle. It is normally presented first. The balance sheet is classified into current and noncurrent items. Current items are listed before noncurrent items and in order of liquidity. Thus, current assets precede non-current assets, with cash listed first, receivables before inventory, and so on. Current liabilities are listed before non-current liabilities. Assets are totalled and this amount equals the total of liabilities and stockholders' equity. The statement of cash flows summarizes the company's cash receipts and disbursements during the period and classifies them as resulting from investing, financing or operating activities. The statement of comprehensive income summarizes non-owner changes in equity that are not included in net income. These include foreign currency translation adjustments, unrealized gains and losses on certain debt and equity securities, and minimum pension liability adjustments. The financial statements are presented on a consolidated basis; unlike a number of other countries, separate parent company financial statements are not required and are very rarely provided.

The *notes* are an integral part of the financial statements and are audited. They include a summary of significant accounting policies and additional information relating to specific accounts and transactions, such as income tax expense, long-term leases, contingent liabilities, and pension and stock option plans. Under Rule 14a-3 of the Securities and Exchange Act of 1934, public companies must also include the following in their annual reports, either in the notes or elsewhere:

1. Selected quarterly financial data.
2. Disagreements with accountants on accounting and financial disclosure.
3. Summary of selected financial data for the last five years.
4. Description of business activities.
5. Segment information.
6. Listing of company directors and executive officers.
7. Market price of company's common stock for each quarterly period within the two most recent fiscal years.
8. Management's discussion and analysis of financial condition and results of operations.

Table 3.1 International Accounting Standards checklist

IAS	US practice
1	Prudence and substance over form, though consistent with US GAAP, are not explicit. Basic principles are contained in SFACs. APB Opinion No. 22 requires disclosure of accounting policies.
2	Dealt with in ARB 43, Chapter 4. Inventory is valued at lower-of-cost-or-market, where market is the lower of replacement cost or net realizable value. FIFO, LIFO and average are all acceptable.
4	ARB 43, Chapter 9A is consistent.
7	SFAS 95 is similar.
8	Covered by APB Opinion No. 9 and 20; and SFAS 16. Extraordinary items must be both unusual and infrequent. Discontinued operations are separately reported after income from operations. Errors are corrected by adjusting the opening balance in retained earnings. Most changes in accounting policy are included in current period income.
9	SFAS 2 is similar, except that all development costs are expensed.
10	SFAS 5 is similar.
11	ARB 45 is consistent.
12	SFAS 109 requires comprehensive tax allocation using the liability method.
13	ARB 43, Chapter 9A is consistent.
14	SFAS 131 is similar, but bases reportable segments on the company's internal reporting system (the so-called 'management approach') rather than a risk and return

Table 3.1 International Accounting Standards checklist (*continued*)

IAS	US practice

approach. SFAS 131 also requires the use of the accounting policies used for internal reporting purposes, which are not necessarily the same ones used in the consolidated statements.

16 ARB 43, Chapter 3A is consistent.

17 SFAS 13, as modified or amended by several subsequent SFASs, provide similar accounting treatment.

18 No US standard, though US practice in line with IAS. Revenue included in SFAC No. 6 and recognition principles are in SFAC No. 5.

19 SFAS 87 (pension plans) and SFAS 106 (other post-employment benefits) provide similar accounting treatment. Projected benefit valuation method is used if the plan incorporates future salary levels.

20 No US standard, though predominant practice complies with IAS.

21 SFAS 52 is similar, except that the temporal method is used for foreign entities operating in hyperinflationary economies.

22 All business combinations are now accounted for as a purchase and goodwill is reviewed for impairment rather than systematically amortized.

23 SFAS 34 requires interest capitalization during construction of qualifying assets.

24 SFAS 57 is similar, though the definition of related parties and disclosure requirements are more restrictive under US GAAP.

25 Accounting treatment is no longer based on current versus long-term classification. SFAS 115 specifies different treatments for certain debt and equity security investments classified as held-to-maturity, trading, or available-for-sale.

26 SFAS 35 is similar.

27 ARB 51 and SFAS 94 provide similar accounting treatment. Control is defined as owning more than half of a subsidiary's voting interest but the FASB has proposed expanding the definition of control. Separate financial statements for the parent are not required.

28 APB Opinion No. 18 provides similar treatment.

29 No US standard.

31 The equity method is used for investments in jointly controlled entities.

32 SFAS 107 and 113 are consistent.

33 SFAS 128 is comparable.

34 Practice is generally in line.

35 FAS 144 requires separate reporting of a discontinued operation when management accepts a plan for discontinuance. The gain or loss on discontinued operation includes actual and estimated effects of the discontinued operation.

36 SFAS 121 uses an undiscounted amount to trigger an impairments test and prohibits the reversal of impairment losses.

37 SFAS 5 is similar.

38 No development costs may be capitalized under SFAS 5. US GAAP does not permit revaluation accounting for intangible assets.

39 SFAS 133 is similar.

40 Investment properties must be valued at depreciated historical cost.

41 No US standard.

Measurement and recognition practices

An overview of predominant US practice is provided in this section.[11] It begins with a comparison to International Accounting Standards (IASs). As already noted, US GAAP is largely consistent with IASs. As Table 3.1 shows, the differences are few.

Profit and loss account

The profit and loss account is referred to as the income statement, or sometimes, the statement of earnings. It includes all items of profit and loss during the period, including gains and losses that are unusual or non-recurring. The most popular format is the multiple-step form in which cost of goods sold is deducted from sales revenue to show gross margin, and other costs and expenses are subtracted to derive operating income. Also, non-operating revenues, expenses, gains and losses are reported separately from operating items, and income tax expense typically is deducted as the last item before income from continuing operations.

The following, as applicable, are required to be shown net of tax, after income from continuing operations: discontinued operations, extraordinary gains and losses, and the cumulative effect of a change in accounting principle. Net income is the 'bottom line'. *Discontinued operations* are the disposal of a separate operational component of the company, including both actual and planned dispositions. Generally, the actual and estimated income effects are reported in the year in which management commits itself to the plan of disposal. *Extraordinary* gains and losses relate to events that are both unusual (highly abnormal) and infrequent (unlikely to recur). Gains and losses that meet one but not both criteria are included in income from continuing operations. The effects of most *changes in accounting principle* are also included in the current period's net income. However, sometimes new SFASs allow or require these to be accounted for retroactively through adjustments to beginning retained earnings.

Earnings per share (EPS) information is required to be shown on the face of the income statement, reflecting the investor focus of US accounting. Both income from continuing operations and net income must be shown on a per share basis, and the per share effect of a change in accounting principle must also be shown. SFAS 128 requires showing *basic earnings per share* and, if a company has a complex capital structure, *diluted earning per share*.

Balance sheet

The most popular format for the balance sheet is the report form which shows a downward sequence of total assets equal to total liabilities plus stockholders' equity. Balance sheets are also normally classified: current assets are shown in their order of liquidity, followed by non-current assets; and current and non-current liabilities are shown separately. Such classification draws attention to a company's short-term liquidity. *Current assets* are cash and other assets that are likely to be converted to cash or consumed during one year or the normal operating cycle of the business, whichever is longer. *Current liabilities* are obligations that will be eliminated through the use of existing current assets or the creation of other current liabilities.

Current assets

Cash and cash equivalents are shown first, followed by short-term investments. *Trading securities*, those bought and held principally for the purpose of selling them in the near term, are always included in short-term investments. They are valued at fair value and unrealized holding gains and losses are included in earnings. *Available-for-sale securities* that are expected to be sold in the next year or operating cycle and *held-to-maturity securities* (which are debt instruments) that will mature within the year or operating cycle are also classified as current. Fair value is used for available-for-sale securities if determinable and unrealized holding gains and losses are reported as a separate component of stockholders' equity. Held-to-maturity securities are reported at amortized cost. Other current assets are trade and non-trade receivables (debtors) less an allowance for uncollectible accounts, inventories (stocks), and prepaid expenses. Inventories are usually valued at the lower of cost or market, where market is defined as replacement cost. However, net realizable value is used when replacement cost is higher. According to the AICPA's *Accounting Trends and Techniques* (2000, p. 201), first in first out (FIFO) is the most popular inventory cost determination method among the companies surveyed, followed closely by last in first out (LIFO). A significant minority of companies also use the average cost method. It is also not uncommon for a company to use more than one method to determine the total cost of inventory.

Noncurrent assets

Property, plant and equipment (also called fixed assets or plant assets) includes land, buildings and improvements, and machinery and equipment. Historical cost is used and revaluation to current market value is not allowed. Interest costs are also capitalized as a part of the cost of acquiring certain assets that require a period of time to be constructed or readied for their intended use. The straight-line method is the most popular depreciation method, though accelerated methods are also allowed, as is the units-of-production method.

Investments in debt and equity securities are accounted for in a variety of ways. If an equity investment enables the company to exercise significant influence (but not control, i.e. normally an investment between 20 and 50 per cent), the equity method must be used. Non-current investments in available-for-sale and held-to-maturity securities are valued as described above in the current assets discussion.

Intangible assets include patents, trademarks, brand names and copyrights. They are initially recorded at cost and amortized over the shorter of economic or legal life. Goodwill from a business combination (purchase) must be capitalized. It is impairments tested rather than amortized. Only intangibles acquired through purchase may be capitalized. In other words, the value of internally generated intangibles may not be capitalized.

Most companies also have a catch-all category, 'other' noncurrent assets. Included here are such items as deferred tax assets, prepaid pension costs and property held for sale.

Liabilities

Current liabilities include short-term notes, accounts payable, accrued expenses and the currently payable portion of long-term debt. The most common non-current liabilities are long-term notes, bonds, deferred taxes, pension and other post-retirement obligations and lease obligations. Other than deferred taxes, noncurrent liabilities are generally reported at the present value of future cash payments.

Deferred tax liabilities[12]

Income taxes are accounted for under the liability method (called the asset/liability method in the United States). Deferred tax liabilities are accrued for the tax effects of temporary differences and carryforwards. Comprehensive income tax allocation is required, as opposed to partial allocation. The measurement of deferred tax liabilities is based on the future tax rates that will apply when they are expected to be settled. Future tax rates are based on enacted tax laws; the effects of anticipated changes in the tax laws or rates are not considered. This method takes a 'balance sheet' approach to measurement instead of an 'income statement' approach in that it uses expected future tax rates, not current tax rates. Deferred tax liability balances are adjusted whenever new tax rates are enacted into law.

An important temporary difference that gives rise to deferred tax liabilities is depreciation. Most US companies used straight-line depreciation for financial reporting purposes. The tax law allows the so-called modified accelerated cost recovery system (MACRS).

Liabilities for pension and other post-retirement benefits

Private (employer-sponsored) pension plans are an important source of economic security for most US retirees. Many employers also provide other post-retirement benefits, the most common being payments for health care. They are an important element in the total compensation package of many American workers. Bear in mind that, unlike most industrialized societies, the United States does not have universal, government-provided health care. Pension plans and other post-retirement benefits represent a significant cost to American business.

Employers' accounting for pensions is governed by SFAS 87, while accounting for other post-retirement benefits is contained in SFAS 106. The theory behind both standards is that the benefits are a form of deferred compensation to employees in return for their current services. As such, accrual accounting requires that the costs be recognized over the periods in which employees earn their benefits; unfunded obligations should be reported as a liability on the balance sheet. US GAAP has actually required accrual accounting for pension plans since the mid 1960s. However, to improve comparability, SFAS 87 (issued in 1985) standardized the way periodic pension expense is measured and it expanded disclosures. It also began requiring the immediate recognition of a liability whenever the accumulated pension benefit obligation exceeds the value of pension plan assets.

Until the issuance of SFAS 106, most companies used pay-as-you-go, or cash basis, accounting for other post-retirement benefits. However, the 1980s witnessed an explosion in health care costs and with it, a huge unfunded obligation for corporate America – as much as $500 billion by one reckoning at the time.[13] The issuance of SFAS 106 was controversial. Not surprisingly, it had a significant impact on the income of many US companies in the year of adoption. Hardest hit among Fortune 500 companies was General Motors, which took a $20.8 billion charge when the company implemented SFAS 106 in 1992.[14]

Contingencies

Contingent losses/liabilities are accrued and disclosed when they are both probable (likely) and the amount can be reasonably estimated. If both criteria are not met, but the contingency is at least reasonably possible, only disclosure is required. Certain commitments, typically those in the form of guarantees, must also be disclosed even if the possibility of loss is remote. As discussed later, disclosure of information about financial instruments with off-balance sheet risk is also required.

Stockholders' equity

This is also called shareholders' equity, consisting of the company's capital stock, additional paid in capital, and retained earnings. Depending on the situation, capital stock may be further divided into common and preferred stock. Companies may issue capital stock with or without par values. Par values are normally set low and so the amounts in capital stock and additional paid in capital are distinguished for legal reasons rather than reasons of economic interpretation.

Retained earnings accumulates net income or loss, and dividend distributions. Prior period adjustments for error corrections and some accounting changes are also made to retained earnings. The accounting profession recommends that the word *reserves* be used only for appropriations of retained earnings. Unfortunately, it is most commonly used for amounts designated as valuation allowances deducted from assets or as accruals for estimated liabilities. Hence the use of the word in the United States is rather confusing. Nevertheless, US GAAP does not allow reserves for such purposes as income smoothing or asset revaluations, as seen in some other countries.

Stockholders' equity may also contain cumulative translation adjustment amounts, discussed later, and unrealized gains or losses on investments in available-for-sale securities, discussed earlier. Finally, the cost of treasury stock, a company's own reacquired shares, is deducted from total stockholders' equity.

Statement of cash flows

The United States became the first country to require a statement of cash flows with the issuance of SFAS 95 in 1987. This requirement probably accelerated the already existing international trend toward focusing on cash flows instead of 'funds', normally defined as working capital. Prior to SFAS 95, US companies prepared a statement of changes in financial position based on working capital (i.e. current assets minus current liabilities).

'Cash' is defined as cash and cash equivalents. The statement of cash flows is organized on an activity format, meaning that cash flows are classified in terms of operating, investing and financing activities. Cash flows from operating activities may be shown using either the direct or indirect approach. While the FASB encourages the direct approach, nearly every company surveyed in the AICPA's *Accounting Trends and Techniques* (2000, p. 523) uses the indirect method. This may be because, regardless of which method is used, SFAS 95 requires that a reconciliation of net income to cash flows from operating activities be presented. This is accomplished by using the indirect method in the statement itself. However, when the indirect method is used, footnote disclosure of the amounts of interest and income taxes paid is required.

Note that under US GAAP interest paid is reported under operating activities, even though interest expense arises because of a company's financing activities and dividends paid are shown under financing activities. Also, cash inflows from sales of property, plant and equipment are shown as an investing activity, not as an operating activity. Investing and financing activities not affecting cash must also be reported either in a supplementary schedule or in a narrative footnote.

Statements of stockholders' equity and comprehensive income

The statement of stockholders' equity reconciles the changes in the various stockholders' equity accounts during the period. The components of stockholders' equity were discussed above, in connection with the balance sheet. Thus the statement of stockholders' equity enumerates, as applicable, additions to capital stock and additional paid in capital from the issuance of new shares; changes in retained earnings resulting from net income or loss, dividends, prior period adjustments, and some accounting changes; changes in the valuation allowances arising from foreign currency translation and valuing investments in available-for-sale securities; and changes due to treasury stock transactions.

Several accounting standards require that certain items be included in stockholders' equity rather than net income. These items are foreign currency translation adjustments (SFAS 52) minimum pension liability adjustment (SFAS 87), unrealized holding gains and losses on available-for-sale securities (SFAS 115), and changes in the fair value of cash flow and foreign currency hedges (SFAS 133). They are considered part of comprehensive income, but not net income. SFAS 130 requires a statement of comprehensive income in one of three ways: (1) as a single statement of net and comprehensive income; (2) as separate statements of net income and comprehensive income; or (3) in another financial statement, such as the statement of stockholders' equity. According to *Accounting Trends & Techniques* (2000, p. 429), most companies combine the statement of comprehensive income with the statement of stockholders' equity.

Consolidation practices

Consolidation is required in substantially all cases where an entity owns, directly or indirectly, a majority of the voting shares of another entity.[15] Exceptions are made when control is temporary or when there is significant doubt about the ability to control the other entity. Entities with 'nonhomogeneous operations' are required to be consolidated. For example, General Motors includes its finance subsidiary, General Motors Acceptance Corporation (GMAC), in its consolidated financial statements.

Before 2001, US GAAP specified two methods of accounting for business combinations: the purchase (acquisition) method and the pooling of interests (merger) method. However, the pooling of interests method was eliminated in 2001. All business combinations initiated after 30 June 2001 must be accounted for as a purchase. Goodwill is capitalized as the difference between the fair value of the consideration given in the exchange and the fair values of the underlying net assets acquired. Thus, the 'purchase price' is first allocated to the acquired assets based on their fair values, less liabilities, and any remainder is goodwill. Acquired intangible assets that arise from contractual or other legal rights or that are capable of being sold or separated from an entity are not recognized as a part of goodwill. Goodwill is now reviewed for impairment rather than systematically amortized to income. Under the impairment approach, goodwill is only written down and expensed to earnings in periods when its book value exceeds its fair value.

The equity method is used for investments in joint ventures and companies owned 50 per cent or less over which the investor can exert 'significant influence'. Normally, owning more than 20 per cent is presumed to result in significant influence. In terms of joint venture accounting, US GAAP gives little guidance.

Foreign currency translation

SFAS 52 established the *functional currency* notion as the basis for translating the financial statements of foreign subsidiaries. A subsidiary's functional currency is the currency of the primary economic environment in which it operates. Normally, the functional currency is either the foreign subsidiary's own local currency or the US dollar. The functional currency is based on the operational relationship that exists between the parent and subsidiary. Specifically, a foreign subsidiary is classified as either *autonomous (self-sustaining)* or *integral* to the activities of the parent company. Autonomous subsidiaries operate relatively independently from the parent and cash flows and other transactions between parent and subsidiary are few. For these subsidiaries, the local (foreign) currency is the *functional currency*. These subsidiaries are translated using a modified current rate method. The year-end exchange rate is used for the balance sheet and the average-for-the-year exchange rate is used for the income statement. Translation differences bypass the income statement and are deferred in the cumulative translation adjustment account in stockholders' equity.

Integral foreign subsidiaries operate as extensions of the parent. Cash flows and inter-company transactions between the parent and subsidiary are numerous. The functional currency for integral foreign subsidiaries is the US dollar and the temporal method of translation is used. Generally, assets and liabilities valued at historical cost, along with their related expenses and revenues, are translated at various historical exchange rates. Everything else on the balance sheet is translated at the year-end exchange rate and other items on the income statement are translated at the average-for-the-year rate. Translation differences are reported as gains or losses in consolidated income for the period. Revsine (1984) shows that the temporal method has the effect of translating subsidiaries' financial statements as if their transactions originally occurred as the parent's in US dollars, consistent with notion that the dollar is the foreign subsidiary's functional currency.

The financial statements of autonomous subsidiaries operating in hyperinflationary environments also use the temporal method. (A hyperinflationary environment is one in which cumulative three-year inflation is approximately 100 per cent or more.) This approach is inconsistent with IAS 21, which requires the subsidiary's financial statements to be first restated for changes in general price levels, then use of the current rate method. The restate–translate approach was considered by the FASB but rejected largely because general price level accounting is not acceptable under US GAAP. With the foregoing exception, the SFAS 52 approach to foreign currency translation has subsequently become the basis for GAAP in other countries as well.

Management's discussion and analysis

Under SEC requirements, public companies are required to include in their annual reports management's discussion and analysis (MD&A) of the financial condition and results of operations. The MD&A gives management an opportunity to amplify the financial statements with its own insights into what has happened to the company and what lies ahead. The MD&A focuses on three broad areas: liquidity, capital resources and results of operations. The impacts of significant events, transactions, commitments or uncertainties, as well as favourable and unfavourable trends, in these areas are discussed over a three-year period. The SEC encourages companies to provide forward-looking information, but it is not required. However, presently known information that will affect the future should be provided. The effects of inflation and other changes in prices need only be discussed when considered material. In practice, many US companies incorporate the required MD&A disclosure with a wide variety of other voluntary financial data in a financial review section of the annual report. In addition, there is ordinarily a review of operations for each line of business, apart from the segments disclosure required under SFAS 131, discussed next.

Notes to the accounts

Segment reporting

SFAS 131 replaced SFAS 14 on segment disclosures. SFAS 131 requires a 'management approach' in determining reportable operating segments. The idea is to provide financial statement users with insights into how management views the business. Hence, segment information reported to users is prepared using the information from the company's internal financial reporting system, that is that seen by management and based on the company's organizational structure. Most companies are organized either by products and services or geographic area. The accounting principles used for segment disclosures need not be the same ones used in the consolidated statements.

Extensive information is required for each reportable segment, including general information about their activities, and the amounts of profit or loss and assets. Other items must also be reported if they are included in determining segment profit or loss. These include revenues from external customers and other operating segments; interest expense and revenue; depreciation, depletion, and amortization expense; unusual and extraordinary items; and income tax expense. In addition, segment revenues, profit or loss, and assets must be reconciled to their corresponding consolidated totals. Limited other information is required by geographic area if reportable segments are based on products and services.

Derivative financial instruments

Financial instruments were on the FASB's agenda for over 10 years. Given the complexity of the subject and the continuing emergence of new and creative financial instruments, it is easy to see why it is took so long for the FASB to reach conclusions about the issues. The first reporting standards (primarily SFASs 105, 107 and 119) focused on disclosures, leaving the more vexing recognition and measurement questions until later. Recognition and measurement were addressed in SFAS 133, which supersedes SFASs 105 and 119 and amends SFAS 107.

SFAS 133 requires all derivatives to be recorded on the balance sheet at fair value. If the derivative does not qualify as a hedging instrument, changes in fair value (i.e. gains and losses) are recognized in earnings in the period of change. SFAS 133 establishes accounting for three different types of hedges: hedges of changes in the fair value of assets, liabilities, or firm commitments ('fair value hedges'), hedges of the variable cash flows of forecasted transactions ('cash flow hedges'), and hedges of foreign currency exposures of net investments in foreign operations ('foreign currency hedges'). Gains and losses on fair value hedges are recognized in current income as an offset to the loss or gain on the fair value of the item hedged. Gains and losses on cash flow hedges are reported initially in comprehensive income and subsequently reclassified into earnings when the forecasted transaction affects earnings. Gains and losses in foreign currency hedges are reported in comprehensive income as a part of the cumulative translation adjustment. Companies must disclose their objectives for holding derivative instruments and strategies for achieving those objectives along with details of their hedging instruments.

Conclusion

Until recently, one could argue that US accounting policy-making bodies operated in almost 'splendid isolation' from the rest of the world. International issues took a back seat to domestic ones, or were ignored altogether. However, it is clear that domestic US accounting issues are now so intertwined with international accounting issues that it is no longer possible to separate the two. Understandably, domestic financial reporting needs will continue to be the FASB's first priority.[16] Nevertheless, the FASB is genuinely engaged in cooperative efforts with not only the IASB but also standard-setters in other countries to converge the differences in accounting and reporting standards worldwide. It seems likely that the FASB will continue to work within an international framework in developing US accounting standards. The SEC has worked closely with IOSCO and is now considering whether to accept International Accounting Standards in filing by non-US companies. The SEC has spelled out three criteria for accepting IASs: they (a) constitute a comprehensive, generally accepted basis of accounting; (b) are of high quality; and (c) can be rigorously interpreted and applied. The regulatory infrastructure for enforcing compliance with IASs is a primary concern, but the SEC is also concerned that there be a 'level playing field' for US domestic companies should non-US companies be allowed to use IASs. The deliberations are ongoing at the time of writing and the outcome is uncertain.

Notes

1. However, the New York Stock Exchange did have requirements (prior to the establishment of the SEC) for the annual disclosure of an income statement and balance sheet, along with interim reports and disclosure of material information.

2. The American Institute of Certified Public Accountants (AICPA) was known as the American Institute of Accountants (AIA) at the time. The AIA was renamed the AICPA in 1957.

3. The same due process procedure was followed in issuing the SFACs, discussed in the next section.

4. Generally, the GAAP followed for consolidated and separate company statements are the same, and with a few exceptions, GAAP are the same for companies of all sizes.

5. In this context, the word 'foreign' means 'non-US'.

6. Each of the 50 states sets its own education and experience requirements for becoming a CPA and for retaining the licence to practise. However, the Uniform CPA Examination is administered nationwide.

7. Altogether seven SFACs were issued. However, SFAC No. 3 was replaced by SFAC 6 and SFAC 4 is for nonbusiness organizations.

8. SFAC No. 1 distinguishes financial *reporting* from financial *statements* in that financial reporting is not restricted to information communicated in financial statements; some useful information can be better (or only) provided by means of financial reporting other than financial statements. Hence, financial reporting is a broader concept than financial statements. However, they have essentially the same objectives.

9. The investor focus of US accounting may be contrasted to a wider, stakeholder orientation found in Europe and elsewhere.

10. If the scope of the audit has been restricted, a qualified or *disclaimer* of opinion is issued, depending on the materiality of the scope restriction. A disclaimer is also issued whenever the auditor is not independent, as determined by Rule 101 of the *Code of Professional Ethics*.

11. For details, consult the *Miller GAAP Guide* (Williams 1999).

12. Deferred tax assets also arise when there are estimated future refunds resulting from deductible temporary differences or operating loss carryforwards. They are basically measured the same way as deferred tax liabilities, but require additional consideration of future taxable income, including the company's tax planning strategies to make income available at appropriate times in the future that would not otherwise be available. Deferred tax assets are reduced by a valuation allowance if it seems likely that some or all of the asset will not be realized.

13. 'New FASB rules on accounting for other postretirement benefits'. *Deloitte & Touche Review*, 31 December 1990.

14. Doron P. Levin, '$20.8 billion G.M. charge for benefits'. *New York Times*, 2 February 1993; and 'Fortune 500 profits plummet due to accounting rule'. *Tulsa World*, 31 March 1993.

15. The FASB has proposed extending the consolidation requirement to other entities that a company controls based on its ability to direct the entity's policies and management.

16. Financial Accounting Standards Board, 'FASB's plan for international activities'. *Financial Accounting Series Status Report No. 262*, 31 March 1995.

Websites

US Securities and Exhange Commission
   www.sec.gov
Financial Accounting Standards Board
   www.fasb.org
American Institute of Certified Public Accountants
   www.aicpa.org
Internal Revenue Service
   www.irs.treas.gov

References and further reading

Accountancy (2000) SEC demands regulator. *Accountancy* (April): 10.

American Institute of Certified Public Accountants (2000) *Accounting Trends and Techniques* AICPA, New York.

Arens, A.A. and Loebbecke, J.K. (2000) *Auditing: An Integrated Approach*, 8th edn. Prentice-Hall, Englewood Cliffs.

Cairns, D. (2000) Waving a different flag. *Accountancy* (September): 104–106.

Chasteen, L.G., Flaherty, R.E. and O'Connor, M.C. (1998) *Intermediate Accounting*, 6th edn. McGraw-Hill, New York.

Coopers & Lybrand (1993) *International Accounting Summaries: A Guide for Interpretation and Comparison*, 2nd edn. Wiley, New York.

Ernst & Young (1991) *Doing Business in the United States*. Ernst & Young International, New York.

Financial Accounting Standards Board (1994) *Statements of Financial Accounting Concepts*. FASB, Norwalk.

Grady, P. (1965) *Inventory of Generally Accepted Accounting Principles for Business Enterprises* (Accounting Research Study No. 7). American Institute of Certified Public Accountants, New York.

Hendricksen, E.S. (1977) *Accounting Theory*. Irwin, Homewood.

Kieso, D.E., Weygandt, J.J. and Warfield, T.D. (2001) *Intermediate Accounting*, 10th edn. John Wiley, New York.

Moonitz, M. (1961) *The Basic Postulates of Accounting* (Accounting Research Study No. 1). American Institute of Certified Public Accountants, New York.

Murphy, K.E. and Higgins, M. (2001) *Concepts in Federal Taxation*, 2001 edition. South-Western, Cincinnati.

Mutchler, J.F. and Smith, C.H. (1984) The development of financial accounting standards in the United States: past and present. In H.P. Holzer, *International Accounting*. Harper & Row, New York.

Pacter, P. (1999) Side by side. *Accountancy International* (June): 74–76.

Revsine, L. (1984) The rationale underlying the functional currency choice. *Accounting Review* (July): 505–514.

Skousen, K.F. (1991) *An Introduction to the SEC*, 5th edn. South-Western, Cincinnati.

Sommerfeld, R.M. and Jones, S.M. (1991) *Federal Taxes and Management Decisions*. Irwin, Homewood.

Sprouse, R.T. and Moonitz, M. (1962) *A Tentative Set of Broad Accounting Principles for Business Enterprises* (Accounting Research Study No. 3). American Institute of Certified Public Accountants, New York.

Williams, J.R. (1999) *Miller GAAP Guide*. Harcourt Brace, San Diego.

Zeff, S.A. (1995) A perspective on the US public/private-sector approach to the regulation of financial reporting. *Accounting Horizons* (March): 52–70.

Accounting in Germany

Axel Haller

Introduction and historical background

The major characteristics of German accounting as regards the institutional basis of its regulation, the function of accounting and the basic principles derived from this, can be traced back to the seventeenth, eighteenth and nineteenth centuries. Although book-keeping had already become a fairly well developed technique for German merchants and traders, as in many other European countries, the French Ordonnance de Commerce of 1673, and the 1807 Code de Commerce can be regarded as the roots of accounting principles and regulation in Germany. The first General German Commercial Code, enacted in 1861, has a lot in common with its French counterpart in terms of accounting. Most of the major accounting principles and assumptions which are still part of the 'German accounting model' today were developed in the nineteenth century (for a more detailed consideration of German accounting history see, for example, Schröer 1993; Schneider 1995). From that time until the 1920s the development of accounting principles was dominated by lawyers – from the beginning accounting was regarded as a matter of law. In formal but also material respects the underlying legal approach in accounting is, as in all other legal areas in Germany, that of Roman law.

The predominant purpose of accounting in those early days was to show the wealth of an entity, primarily to enable creditors to evaluate their risks. Since that time the principle of creditor protection has been the central concern of accounting in Germany and has had a major impact on accounting. Because of this, financial reporting in Germany has always been focused on the complete presentation of all assets and liabilities. The balance sheet has therefore been, up to now, the predominant financial statement. The official definition of income is not revenues minus expenses, but the difference between the opening amount and the closing amount of net assets for a period (after adjustment of drawings and contributions of equity capital). The income statement has had (until recently) a subordinate function, that of showing which transactions have led to an increase or decrease in net assets.

Another effect of this focus on protecting creditors is the overall *principle of conservatism* which impacts particularly on the interpretation of the realization and matching principles and therefore the valuation of assets and liabilities. Commercial asset valuation recognizes that the company must fulfil its obligations (liabilities) on the one hand and still remain a going concern on the other. This means a conservative, understood as prudent, valuation that recognizes risks, and results in a tendency to undervaluation of assets and overvaluation of liabilities. The conservative interpretation of principles of realization and of lower of cost or market in Germany can be traced back to the Common Prussian Law (Allgemeines Preussisches Landrecht) of 1794.

Conservative valuation leads to a prudent calculation of income. In consequence, the commercial balance sheet (*Handelsbilanz* – the published balance sheet, so called to distinguish it from the tax balance sheet, or *Steuerbilanz*, see below) is seen as a means of arriving at a prudent computation of the distributable income which can be given to the owners (as dividends) without harming the position of the creditors. Thus historically the main function of the balance sheet in Germany is the computation of the distributable income of the company, through a prudent valuation of the increase in the company's net assets. The idea of providing relevant economic information and the application of the matching convention are subordinated to the prudent determination of net assets. Thus the principle of conservatism is not understood as a sub-characteristic as in the USA or the UK but rather as the central principle of accounting which follows logically from the objective of creditor protection. It is, therefore, one of the major causes of differences between the German accounting model and the Anglo-Saxon one.

The vigour of the *creditor protection* approach was increased as a result of the large number of companies which went bankrupt during the worldwide economic crisis of the late 1920s and early 1930s. The legislator took the scale of corporate failure as proof that existing acounting practices were unable to protect creditors adequately in cases of bankruptcy. Consequently the principle of prudence was explicitly incorporated in the *Stock Corporation Law (Aktiengesetz)* of 1937 (the first stock corporation law was passed in 1870 with a revision in 1884) as the predominant parameter. Clearly the economic crash at the end of the 1920s provoked different consequences in Germany than in the USA. Whereas in the latter the dominant reaction was to protect the shareholders, which led to the Securities Act (1933) and the Securities Exchange Act (1934), in Germany, due to tradition, creditor protection was emphasized rather than the protection of the interests of the shareholders.

It was not until its next revision in 1965 that the Stock Corporation Law considered the interests of the shareholders. In particular, the opportunities for undervaluation of assets were limited at that time. However, the principle of prudence and the idea of creditor protection have remained very important. None the less, this revision marks the first time that the information function of accounting was taken into account in some regulations. Prior to that only the stewardship function and the objective of computing income prudently were regarded as relevant for financial reporting.

Another cornerstone of German accounting is the principle that the treatment of transactions in the financial statements drawn up for tax purposes should be consistent with that in the commercial balance sheet. This principle, called the *Massgeblichkeitsprinzip*, can also be traced back to the nineteenth century. At that time the states (*Länder*) had the authority to impose taxes, and it was in 1874 in Bremen and Sachsen that the first tax law of a state referred to the income computed in the commercial accounts as a tax computation base. In 1934 this principle was asserted in the German Tax Code (*Einkommensteuergesetz*, EStG) in nearly the same manner as today. This principle is of primary importance for tax purposes, but it also influences the commercial accounts, because an optimized tax strategy affects the commercial financial statements and the carrying values of assets (for the explanation of this principle see below).

The latest substantial changes in German accounting were made in 1998 with two Revision Acts, the KonTraG ('*Gesetz zur Kontrolle und Transparenz im Unternehmensbereich*') and the KapAEG ('*Kapitalaufnahmeerleichterungsgesetz*'), as well as with the TransPuG ('*Transparenz-und Publizitätsgesetz*') in 2002. Those Acts introduced several rules in the Commercial Code and the Stock Corporation Law to improve financial reporting and corporate governance of companies and to adapt it to international standards. Based on the KonTraG, German groups are now obliged to add a cash flow statement as well as a segment report to their annual consolidated financial statements. The KonTraG also gave a legal basis for the establishment of the first private standard-setting body in Germany (explained in detail below).

The main feature of the KapAEG is an option for German groups to publish their financial statements either based on German accounting rules or on internationally acknowledged standards, namely IAS or US GAAP, as long as the parent companies or subsidiaries are listed on a stock exchange or otherwise make use of international capital markets. This option to use other than national standards is restricted to group accounts, because their only purpose is to provide useful information without being subject to the direct impact of the *Massgeblichkeitsprinzip*.

The TransPuG introduced some major adaptations to IAS with regard to the presentation of consolidated accounts, such as the obligation to present a statement of changes in owners' equity (only for groups which have securities admitted for trading), the obligation to have identical balance sheet dates within a group, and the prohibition to use values which are influenced by tax considerations.

Legal and institutional basis of accounting regulation

Sources of accounting regulation

As a result of its historical roots, accounting in Germany is still dominated by a *legalistic approach*. The accounting system is part of the legal framework, and the process of accounting regulation is still predominantly the duty of government and parliament.

Because the creation or revision of legal requirements is a long-lasting and inflexible process, regulation has been discontinuous and slow in Germany. However, in addition to the codified law which has the predominant role in shaping accounting in Germany, there is a set of uncodified rules and principles, known as the *Grundsätze ordnungsmäßiger Buchführung* (GoB) which could be translated as 'principles of proper accounting'. These principles have special functions and arise from different sources, such as court decisions, accounting practice and the professional institution of the auditors (in Germany there is no accounting profession comparable to those in the UK or the USA, as is discussed below).

Due to the increasing importance of international capital markets, particularly as regards international harmonization of accounting standards, the German legislator in 1998 allowed the establishment of a private standard-setting body, namely the *Deutsches Rechnungslegungs Standards Committee (DRSC)* (German Accounting Standards Committee, GASC), with its standard-setting board, the *Deutsche Standardisierungsrat (DSR)* (German Accounting Standards Board, GASB), which has been tailored according to its American counterpart, the *Financial Accounting Standards Board* (FASB). The main task of this committee, which was founded by retired representatives of leading German industrial and accounting firms as well as financial institutions, is to elaborate *Deutsche Rechnungslegungs Standards (DRS)* (German Accounting Standards, GAS), which are to be presumed to represent principles of proper accounting and which should harmonize German group accounting with international standards, and to participate actively and represent German interests in the convergence process of national and international accounting standards.

Consequently the current sources of accounting regulation in Germany can be portrayed as being structured as illustrated in Figure 4.1. In the following sections these two sources of accounting regulations will be explained (for the GASC and its authority, see below).

Figure 4.1 Structure of accounting regulation in Germany

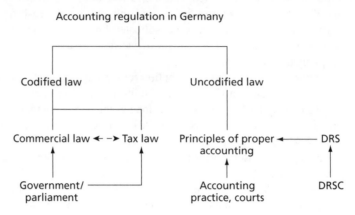

Codified law

Commercial law

Until 1985 the *Stock Corporation Law of 1965* (AktG) was the sole codified source of detailed accounting regulation in Germany. Legally these regulations had no impact, however, on entities which were not share-issuing public companies (AG). Therefore legal forms other than AGs could be highly flexible in their accounting practices. However a lot of other corporations applied the rules of the AktG in their financial statements without any legal obligation to do so.

In 1985 the Fourth, Seventh and Eighth Directives were implemented into German accounting law. In contrast to most of the other European countries all three directives were implemented at the same time. This provided an opportunity to create a new structure and scope for codified accounting rules and brought about changes in a number of separate Codes. Although the directives only covered entities with limited liability, the opportunity was taken to totally reform German accounting regulation. The most important change was the unification of almost all relevant accounting rules for all types of entities and their incorporation in the third book of the *Handelsgesetzbuch* (HGB, German Commercial Code). Since this comprehensive restructuring of accounting regulations, which became effective on 1 January 1986, the HGB has become the predominant source of codified accounting rules.

However this reform was very much a formal one. The European harmonization endeavour has not led to material changes in German accounting principles or practices concerning recognition or valuation. This is mainly as a result of the impact of the *Massgeblichkeitsprinzip* and the potential tax implications of accounting changes. The reform arising from the implementation of the directives consisted primarily in a codification of existing non-codified principles (GoB), a concrete structuring of the relevance of specific regulations for specific types of entities and the expansion of regulations for consolidated financial statements in detail and in scope.

The third book of the HGB contains:

1. general accounting rules for all types of business entities (Art. 238–263 HGB);

2. additional rules for entities with limited liability (including consolidation requirements) (Art. 264–335b HGB);

3. additional rules for registered cooperatives (Art. 336–339 HGB);

4. additional rules for banks and insurance companies (Art. 340–341o HGB);

5. the foundation of a private or state-governed standard setting body (Art. 342–342a HGB).

Subsequent to the reform of accounting regulations, the special acts for the different legal forms (e.g. Stock Corporations Act, Act for Corporations with Limited Liability, Cooperatives Act) contain very few accounting relevant rules. Those special rules generally cover the presentation of income appropriation specific to the different legal forms.

As a result of the long-established predominant objective of creditor protection, and the legal approach of German accounting, the accounting requirements depend in their scope and degree of detail on the legal form of the company. This in turn is related to the scope of the liability of the owners to the creditors and to some extent to the size of the company, the amount of owners and the degree of their involvement in management.

In the context of German accounting it is important to distinguish between the following different major types of business vehicles.

1. *Entities with unlimited liability* (the owners have unlimited liability with regard to creditors):

   – sole proprietorship (*Einzelkaufleute*);
   – general partnership (*Offene Handelsgesellschaft*) (Art. 105–160 HGB).

2. *Entities with limited liability* (the liability of the owners is limited to payment for their capital contributions as laid down in the company's statutes; there is no unlimited personal liability for any owner):

   – stock corporation (*Aktiengesellschaft*, AG) (Art. 1–277 AktG), which is a share-issuing limited liability company and is similar to a stock corporation in the USA, a Public Limited Company (PLC) in the UK and a Societé Anonyme (SA) in France;
   – limited liability company (*Gesellschaft mit beschränkter Haftung*, GmbH) (*Gesetz betreffend die Gesellschaften mit beschränkter Haftung*, GmbHG), which does not issue publicly traded shares and which is usually closely held. It is permissible for GmbH companies to be founded and held by only one person (similar to the Sàrl in France);
   – partnership with at least one limited liability company serving as partner with limited liability (GmbH & Co). This is basically a limited partnership, but with a limited liability company as the general partner. Although it is a partnership there is no unlimited liability for any physical person, only for the entity (legal person) which is a limited liability company;
   – registered cooperative association (*eingetragene Genossenschaft*, eG) (*Gesetz betreffend die Erwerbs- und Wirtschaftsgenossenschaften*, GenG): unlike other legal forms, this is a non-profit-making organization with no fixed capital which promotes the economic interests of its members.

3. *Entities with partly limited liability* (the liability of one or more partners (Kommanditist) vis-à-vis the partnership's creditors is limited to the amount of their capital contribution (limited partners) whereas the general partner(s) (Komplimentär(e)) has(ve) unlimited personal liability):

   – limited partnership (*Kommanditgesellschaft*, KG) (Art. 161–177a HGB);
   – partnership partly limited by shares (*Kommanditgesellschaft auf Aktien,* KGaA) (Art. 278–290 AktG), which is a mixture between a stock corporation and a limited partnership, in which at least one shareholder, the general partner, is personally

liable for the company's obligations to its creditors, whereas the other shareholders are liable only to the extent of their interest in the company.

The major large companies in Germany are stock corporations (minimum capital Euro 50 000). Middle sized enterprises are very often GmbHs because of the relatively low capital requirements (minimum capital: Euro 25 000) and the limited liability of the shareholders. Partnerships and sole proprietorships are used for small companies or family-held businesses.

Although they are significantly fewer in number than limited liability companies, partnerships or sole proprieterships, the stock corporations (approx 3600) in total have considerable economic importance.

Entities with limited liability have a much higher regulation load than entities with unlimited liabilities, both in scope and in degree of detail. As mentioned above, before the implementation of the EC directives into German law, special codified accounting regulation existed only for AGs; thus for the smallest number of companies. For all other companies the legal basis comprised some very general requirements in the Commercial Code which referred to the GoB. At that time an intensive discussion was going on as to whether the requirements for AGs should also be relevant for other vehicles. Due to the legal approach the predominant opinion was against this general extension of the authority of the rules of the AktG. But, nevertheless, the rules became a basis of reference for proper accounting and have influenced general accounting practice to a noticeable extent. This applies especially to the rules regarding the format and content of the balance sheet and the income statement. Furthermore, certain valuation rules specified in the AktG had been broadly accepted for companies using other legal forms as well.

Even before the implementation of the Fourth and Seventh Directives and the size criteria they included, the application of accounting requirements in Germany had depended on the size of an entity. The Publicity Act (*Publizitätsgesetz*) of 1969, which is still in force, obliges all types of businesses which exceed two of the three following criteria on three successive balance sheet dates (balance sheet total greater than Euro 65 m; sales greater than Euro 130 m; employees more than 5000) to publish accounts which comply with the regulations (a few are excluded) for AGs.

The size criteria for companies with limited liability which were introduced into German law as a result of the Fourth Directive and which were reformed according to the Revision Act KapCoRiLiG (Kapitalgesellschaften- und Co. Richtlinie – Gesetz) in 1999 are shown in Table 4.1.

The fact that the legal form and/or the size of an entity is relevant for the application of special accounting requirements is one of the most particular characteristics of German accounting regulation which makes it completely different, for example, from the USA, where the participation of a company on the capital market is the crucial point. The question of whether or not a company is listed on a stock exchange has, until recently, had

Table 4.1 Size criteria for companies with limited liability

Companies	Total assets in euro (millions)	Total sales in euro (millions)	Total number of employees
Small	Under 3.438	6.875	50
Medium	Under 13.750	27.500	250
Large	Over 13.750	27.500	250

no impact on the accounting rules with which it has to comply. However, since 1998, the trading of its securities is the crucial factor for a company which wishes to be allowed to apply IAS or US GAAP for its consolidated statements and also determines the extent of consolidated financial statements which have to be prepared (additional preparation of a cash flow statement, a segmental report and a statement of changes in owners' equity).

Tax law

German tax law requires that taxable income be determined by comparing the net assets of a firm at the beginning and the end of the fiscal year. For this reason companies (except very small ones) must prepare a special balance sheet (*Steuerbilanz*) to compute taxable income. In accordance with the traditional German focus on the balance sheet, German tax authorities are more concerned with the balance sheet than with the income statement. One of the basic articles (Art. 5) of the German Income Tax Code (*Einkommensteuergesetz,* EStG) states that for the computation of taxable income the accounting regulations and principles (GoB) are binding. This section is usually interpreted to mean that the recognition and the valuation of the assets and liabilities in the tax balance sheet must be in accordance not only with the regulations of German commercial law but also with what is reported in the commercial accounts of a specific firm. In other words, the recognition and measurement policies of the commercial accounts must, in general, be incorporated into the tax balance sheet. This dominant principle for taxable income is called the *Massgeblichkeitsprinzip* which is variously translated in the English accounting literature as 'principle of congruency' or 'authoritative principle' (see, e.g., Haller 1992; Machartina and Langer 2000, p.235).

However, specific accounting treatments which differ from the commercial accounting rules are required by the tax law for some specific items and in some circumstances. The main departures from commercial accounting are in the areas of recognition options, depreciation and revaluation. In general, all commercial accounting recognition options relating to assets are recognition requirements in the tax balance sheet, and all recognition options which refer to liabilities are not allowed for tax purposes. There is only one main exception to this general rule, which is the commercial recognition option of 'organizational start up and business expansion expenses' (Art. 269 HGB). As a so-called 'accounting convenience' (Bilanzierungshilfe; for an explanation of this term see below) their deferral as an asset is not allowed in the tax accounts. In essence there are no recognition options in the tax balance sheet.

In addition to these differences, German tax law differs from commercial law in that it contains a number of strict depreciation requirements. For example the depreciation period of goodwill acquired in an asset transaction must be 15 years and the maximum percentage of the declining balance depreciation method is 20 per cent. Other major differences are the prohibition to revalue assets and to recognize provisions for expected future losses from uncompleted transactions.

All these requirements in the tax law which are stricter than commercial rules are designed to minimize opportunities for income manipulation in the tax accounts. In all areas where there are strict and specific tax requirements, the *Massgeblichkeitsprinzip* has no effect and, therefore, the tax accounts can or must differ from the commercial accounts.

However, the *Massgeblichkeitsprinzip* embodies not only the influence of commercial law and financial accounting practice on income tax computation but also involves a converse effect, so that special tax accounting rules have an impact on commercial accounting. Tax benefits in the form of special tax depreciation allowances (*steuerliche Sonderabschreibungen*), and tax-free reserves (*steuerfreie Rücklagen*) must be applied equally in the commercial acounts to be allowed for tax computation. Because these valuations do not refer to the 'real' carrying amount of the assets, which should be included in the commercial accounts, there are special provisions in German commercial law which allow these (economically unrealistic) values to be included in the commercial accounts. This direct impact of tax law on financial accounting is called the principle of converse congruency (*umgekehrtes Massgeblichkeitsprinzip*). It is a logical consequence of the tax authorities' aim of achieving a consistent and close relationship between tax and commercial income computation.

In conclusion, the congruency principle can be summarized as having three characteristics:

1. Basically, the recognition and measurement of assets and liabilities in the commercial financial statements is also the legal basis for the computation of taxable income.

2. For some items, specific and strict tax regulations require a potentially different treatment in the tax accounts.

3. Tax benefits in the form of special depreciation allowances and tax-free reserves are only granted if they are also exercised in the commercial financial accounts (principle of converse congruency).

The basic objective of the principle of congruency and its converse effect is to represent economic items, as far as possible, in the same way in the tax balance sheet and the commercial balance sheet. The main reasons for this are simplification for the tax legislator and the practical and economic advantage for the companies of being able to prepare only one set of financial statements for both purposes. This last argument is supported by observed practice. Statistics show that most businesses prepare only one set of financial statements, called the 'unified blance sheet' (*Einheitsbilanz*). Generally, only listed companies prepare two sets of statements. These companies try to achieve different accounting policies in the different types of accounts and to publish commercial accounts which are, as far as possible, within the constraints of tax law, while not being totally distorted by tax-driven values.

The *Massgeblichkeitsprinzip* has long been the subject of debate in Germany and subject to criticism by outside observers, without having been modified or abolished. It has managed to be, like creditor protection, a 'sacred cow' of German accounting. It has had a number of direct effects on the development of financial accounting rules and their interpretation as well as on accounting practice, particularly for those companies which prepare only a unified balance sheet. They have to deal with conflicting aims, because a high income – which might be desirable in the commercial accounts – leads to higher tax payments, while minimizing taxable income – to keep the tax burden low – decreases commercial income. Tax minimization is usually found to be the primary goal and therefore the more compelling argument in German companies' decision-making. So, for most companies, and for small and medium-sized ones in particular, it can be said that tax accounting generally dominates commercial accounting. The principle of congruency stimulates a desire to create hidden reserves. The undervaluation of assets for tax reasons tends to lead to an even more pessimistic presentation of the financial position of a company than the very strong principle of prudence already does.

It is also quite obvious that the principle of congruency was one of the main reasons for the very conservative transformation of the Fourth Directive into German law. All interest groups concerned agreed that an increase in the tax burden on firms must be avoided in all circumstances when implementing the directive. Consequently, there was a strong desire to change accounting principles as little as possible in implementing the directive, because nearly all the proposed changes would have had an influence on the tax computation (see Haller 1992).

Due to the increasing impact of the Anglo-American accounting approach on German accounting, through the expectations and demands of international actors on capital markets, the critics of the congruency principle have become louder in recent years. Additionally, for the national budget reasons the tax legislator has introduced since the end of the 1990s several new tax accounting rules, which are in conflict with the commercial rules and therefore hinder a congruent treatment in tax and financial accounting. The predominant position of the principle of congruency has subsequently become weaker and, in the process to converge German accounting rules with international ones, the continuing erosion of this principle becomes more and more likely.

The computation of corporate income tax on the basis of prudently calculated commercial income had to be considered alongside the relatively high rates of income tax that German companies had to face. All entities with limited liability are subject to corporation tax (*Körperschaftsteuer*). The basic rate was 45 per cent, but income which was distributed by way of dividends to shareholders was charged at the reduced distribution rate of 30 per cent. From 2001, the changes resulting from the recent tax reform in Germany came into effect and the basic tax rate is now a uniform 25 per cent. Income distributed to shareholders by dividend payment is additionally charged on the investors' level with half of the individual income tax rate of each investor (*half-dividend-income approach*).

Entities with unlimited or partly limited liability are not subject to federal income taxes because they are not regarded as having a legal personality. Instead, the income of the entity is allocated proportionally to the owners and is subject to personal income tax (*Einkommensteuer*). This is a progressive tax which starts at 19.9 per cent and rises to a maximum of 48.5 per cent. In accordance with the tax reform regulations, these rates will decline until 2005 to 15 per cent and 42 per cent respectively. For both types of income tax, losses may be carried forward or may be carried back for two years.

All commercial enterprises are also liable for municipal trade tax on income (*Gewerbeertragsteuer*). The effective rate depends on the municipality. It generally ranges (related to income) between 10 per cent and 19 per cent. However, the municipal trade tax is deductible as an expense in calculating the trade tax itself and also in calculating corporate or personal income tax.

Uncodified law

All those principles and rules of accounting which are not included in codified law form the system of *Grundsätze ordnungsmäßiger Buchführung* (GoB – principles of proper accounting). This expression is often translated into English as 'Generally Accepted Accounting Principles' and interpreted similarly to the US GAAP. Such an interpretation is a misunderstanding of German accounting. Whereas US GAAP comprises all rules and principles of accounting (promulgated or not) German GoB generally embraces only non-codified rules and principles which have developed in accounting practice. The scope of GoB is undefined because, in contrast to the codified rules, they are not a static set of principles but are subject to continuous development and they guarantee a dynamic evolution of German accounting. They derive their legal authority in as much as the law refers to them in all areas where there are no legal regulations in existence. While GoB may supplement the written law, they do not replace it.

GoB covers the principles of regular bookkeeping, of regular stocktaking and of financial reporting. They can be divided into three categories.

1. First, basic accounting principles and assumptions which are referred to in most conceptual frameworks as 'qualitative characteristics' and which can be deduced from

the objectives of accounting. As a result of the Fourth Directive, these GoB have now been included in the general accounting regulations of the HGB; therefore what had been previously non-codified principles became codified.

2. Secondly, there are detailed principles for solving specific accounting problems which are not covered by codified rules. These would include issues such as foreign currency translation, accounting for leases, accounting for government subsidies and grants, accounting for financial instruments.

3. Thirdly, principles developed through the interpretation of codified regulations. As accounting is regarded as a legal matter, the interpretation of law allows the legal requirements to be put into practice. Quite often, codified regulations are relatively inflexible and unspecific and have to be interpreted.

The continuing process of interpretation of existing codified and non-codified rules, which takes place on different levels, is the main source for the development of new and the improvement of existing GoB. It is not a formalized process and is not limited to particular organizations or institutions, it is more or less, a political process, which is influenced by many differing and conflicting interests. The main factors in this process, which are very much interrelated, are described under the following sub-headings.

Accounting practice by large companies

The financial reporting practice of large companies works indirectly and informally by furnishing appropriate examples of adequate interpretation of what can be regarded as 'proper accounting' and is quite often a dynamic force in the development of accounting in Germany. An obvious example of this is the case of the Daimler-Benz listing on the New York Stock Exchange (see Chapter 17) and the related change of the reporting policies of the group. This event instigated the internationalization of the German accounting debate and has provoked an avalanche of changes in the annual reports of other large corporations and has even triggered revisions of the codified law (see Haller 2002).

A considerable role in what might be called the 'interpretation business' is played by the large accounting firms which, during the last 20 years, have become affiliates of the Big Four international firms. It shows that the internationalization of accounting firms in Germany have had an impact on the internationalization of German accounting, not only through auditing but also through the interpretation of German accounting rules.

Published opinions in commentaries and journals

There is a vital market for published bound commentaries on the whole set of codified and uncodified accounting principles as well as new accounting issues. These voluminous commentaries, books devoted to special accounting topics, and articles in practitioner oriented journals, are the sources which form opinion in accounting. These publications are written by practising accountants, auditors and often academics, and draw their arguments partly from the law and partly from business administration. They provoke sometimes heated debates, and help to ensure that accounting, despite the quite inflexible process of formal regulation, is a continuously evolving and dynamic field in Germany as in other countries.

Accounting profession

Another logical consequence of the legalisitic approach to accounting in Germany is the fact that there is no accounting profession comparable to that in the UK or the USA. Quite often the two organizations of auditors in Germany are referred to as being the German accounting profession which is – in terms of the Anglo-American meaning of this expression – not true. As compared with, for example, the UK, the German auditing profession has a rather short tradition. Although some auditing firms had their foundation in the early 1900s, they acted more as consultants than as auditors, and the development of the profession was very much linked with the legal requirement for corporate audits. The statutory annual audit for stock corporations was introduced in the Stock Corporation Act (AktG) of 1931. For large non-stock corporations the annual audit became obligatory with the Publicity Act of 1969. The audit of all but small limited liability companies became compulsory as a result of the Fourth Directive. This continual enlargement of the audit requirement has caused a significant growth of the audit profession, especially in the 1980s, because of the considerable increase of statutory audits caused by the implementation of the Fourth Directive.

Every auditor must be a member of the *chamber of certified auditors (Wirtschaftsprüferkammer)* which was created in 1971 by a special law which regulates the auditing profession. So it is a statutory body, which is supervised by the Federal Minister of Economic Affairs, which represents the interests of the profession. Every *Wirtschaftsprüfer* (auditor) who passes the professional examination and is accredited has to become a member of the *Wirtschaftsprüferkammer*. The educational standards required to achieve this are very high compared to other countries. In general, it is necessary to have a university degree in business administration, law, general economics or similar subjects, and five years of practical experience (including at least four years as an auditor). There is then a written and oral professional examination before somebody can become a *Wirtschaftsprüfer* (WP). If an auditor leaves the profession and takes a post in industry or anywhere else outside professional practice, even if he deals with accounting or internal auditing, he loses his accreditation and his membership of the *Wirtschaftsprüferkammer*.

In addition to the *Wirtschaftsprüfer* there is another group of external auditors, who are called *Vereidigte Buchprüfer* (vBP), who can be regarded as second tier certified auditors. They have lower professional qualifications and are only allowed to audit medium-sized limited liability companies (GmbH). They are also members of the *Wirtschaftsprüferkammer*.

The tasks of the *Wirtschaftsprüferkammer* (which at January 2002 had 10 881 WP and 4068 vBP on its roll) range from the supervision of its members to the representation of the profession to other parties. A lot of tasks which might be fulfilled by the *Wirtschaftsprüferkammer*, such as development of rules of conduct, professional standards and continuing education of auditors, are actually performed by the *Institute der Wirtschaftsprüfer in Deutschland e.V.* (IdW) which was formed as a private institution in 1932 following the provisions of the Stock Corporations Act of 1931. Membership of this institution is voluntary. This body is also restricted to audit practitioners. Its main body, the *Hauptfachausschuß* (HFA), has published many statements on particular auditing and accounting topics by way of guidance to its members. The IdW and the *Wirtschaftsprüferkammer* work closely together.

Neither the recommendations and opinions of the IdW on auditing matters nor those on accounting matters are legally binding, not even for the members of the IdW or the *Wirtschaftsprüferkammer*. These two auditing professional bodies have no direct way to develop mandatory accounting rules but they have an indirect influence. The IdW in particular makes recommendations and guidance not only for its members but also as a proposition for general accounting practice. Each member has to take notice of these recommendations and should not depart from them without good reason. These recommendations also acquire authority by court decisions. They may be used as references by the courts as to good accounting or auditing practice. So for the auditor and also the preparer of the accounts it may be quite difficult to defend in court their reasons for not following the IdW's recommendations. In addition the IdW is consulted by the government as a group of experts for accounting topics in the law making process, which also provides it and its pronouncements indirectly with a considerable amount of authority.

There is no special professional organization for people who deal with accounting and are not professional auditors. This is a crucial difference between the German accounting model and the British or American one, where there are several accounting professional bodies. The only body which brings together people from different areas of accounting is the Working Group on External Financial Reporting (*Arbeitskreis Externe Unternehmens-rechnung*) of the *Schmalenbach Gesellschaft für Betriebswirtschaft e.V.* The *Schmalenbach Gesellschaft* is the leading scientific society in the area of business administration in Germany. In numerous working groups an active debate between theory and practice is encouraged in order to develop solutions for common problems. The Working Group on External Financial Reporting consists of accountants from industry, auditors and accounting academics. Its recommendations have been of great practical importance in recent years. However, after the Deutsche Standardisierungsrat (DSR) published the first standards in 1999 the recommendation regarding the Cash Flow Statement in particular was reduced in importance. So far, besides others, the following major issues have been covered:

- Earnings per Share (1988);
- Preparation of Consolidated Accounts (1989);
- Interim Reports under the new law relating to quoted businesses (1989);
- Cash Flow Statement (joint recommendation with the HFA of the IdW) (1995);
- Application of IAS and US GAAP (1997 and 1999);
- Earnings according to the DVFA/SG Method (revised) (joint recommendation with the German Society of Investment Analysis and Asset Management (DVFA) (2000);
- Differentiation and Development of Accounting Regulation in the Future (2001);
- Enforcement of Accounting Regulation (2002).

In a similar way to the professional side of accounting, there is no association for accounting academics, such as the American Accounting Association (AAA) in the USA or the Association Française de Comptabilité (AFC) in France. There is an academic organization for business administration in general, within which there is a special accounting committee, the *Kommission Rechnungswesen im Verband der Hochschullehrer für Betriebswirtschaft e.V.* which tries to provide academic input into the legal process of regulation although, so far, the influence of this institution has been quite modest.

Court decisions

The decisions of judges are always based on the interpretation of legal rules and have authoritative weight. Whereas lawsuits concerning accounting are quite rare in the civil courts, judgments in the tax courts (*Finanzgerichte*) and the supreme tax court (*Bundesfi-nanzhof*, BFH) are much more frequent and considerably more important. The importance of these judgments is derived from the close relationship between taxable and financial accounting in Germany (the principle of congruency). On the one hand this means that almost all small and medium-sized companies prepare only one set of accounts for financial reporting as well as taxation purposes. On the other hand, GoB are relevant for the computation of income, so in determining whether a treatment in the tax accounts of a company is correct or not the court has to decide whether it complies with the GoB, which means the tax court has to interpret those basically commercial accounting principles.

Standards released by the *Deutscher Standardisierungsrat*

The German Accounting Standards Committee (GASC), the so called *Deutsches Rech-nungslegungsstandards Committee* (DRSC), was founded by a private initiative with the aim of acting as a recognized source of independent advice to the Government, without the sovereignty of the legislature and courts being adversely affected. Its foundation became possible due to the Revision Act 'KonTraG' in 1998. The DRSC's main tasks are:

- to develop accounting standards for application in the area of consolidated financial reporting;
- to cooperate with the International Accounting Standards Board (IASB) and other standard-setting committees;
- to act in a consultative role in relation to the development of legislation at national and intergovernmental level, particularly with regard to accounting regulations;
- to represent Germany on international standard-setting committees and in organizations promoting harmonization;
- to promote research in these areas.

The governing bodies of the DRSC are: (1) the Management Board, (2) the Administrative Board, and (3) the General Meeting. An Administrative Board is formed, comprising the Management Board as a committee and 14 other members who are elected by the General Meeting every three years. One of the Administrative Board's main tasks is the selection and appointment of the members to the Deutscher Standardisierungrat (DSR), which is the German Accounting Standards Board (GASB).

The DSR was established for the development, determination and interpretation of the Accounting Standards. Furthermore, the DSR shall promote international standards committees, appoint German representatives and give instructions to these persons. The DSR consists of the President, a Vice President and five further persons, all experts in accounting, who are elected for a period of four years. The members of the DSR work independently.

In addition, the DRSC has also set up a Consultative Council to give interested parties the opportunity to have their views on important decisions directly expressed to the DSR. As with private standard setters in other countries, the standards of the DSR (called *Deutsche Rechnungslegungsstandards*, DRS) are elaborated with the participation of steering committees and after passing through a due process.

Although the foundation of the DRSC, as a private standard setting body, is a milestone in German accounting tradition, its novelty and legal construction does not supply the DSR (unlike, for example, the French Conseil National de la Comptabilité) with the authority to go beyond its present purpose in order to release any binding regulations of its own.

The legal weight of the standards published by the DRSC is still ambiguous. The German Accounting Standards need the approval of the *Federal Ministry of Justice* (BMJ) to become effective. Once approved they do not have the authority of codified law but they are to be presumed to represent principles of proper accounting (Art. 342 Para. 2 HGB). So far such approval is withheld if the content of a standard violates codified law. This results in the curious fact that the DRSC is tasked to revise the law but that its standards are only approved if they do not conflict with existing rules. It is also not clear whether the standards have any legal relevance in the courts and what will happen if a court decides against a ruling of a standard. This is the reason why the DSR in the early days of its existence has only published standards on topics which just clarify codified rules and which do not conflict with existing law. Those standards are (at the end of 2002):

- DRS 1: Exempting consolidated financial statements
- DRS 2: Cash flow statements
- DRS 3: Segment reporting
- DRS 4: Acquisition Accounting in consolidated financial statements
- DRS 5: Risk reporting
- DRS 6: Interim Financial Reporting
- DRS 7: Group Equity and Total Recognised Results
- DRS 8: Accounting for Investments in Associated Enterprises in Consolidated Financial Statements
- DRS 9: Accounting for Investments in Joint Ventures in Consolidated Financial Statements
- DRS 1a: Consolidated Financial Statements in Accordance with US GAAP: goodwill and other non-current intangible assets
- DRS 10: Deferred Taxes in Consolidated Financial Statements
- DRS 11: Related Part Disclosures.
- DRS 12: Non-current Intangible Assets
- DRS 13: Consistency Principle and Correction of Errors

As a diplomatic solution to the conflict-provoking duty of the DSR to create standards which should enable German group accounting to converge with international standards without violating German codified rules, the published standards regularly consists of two parts: the 'official' part which includes the norms which are deemed to be the binding rules and which conform with the current law and an annex which includes propositions for future revisions of the law.

Objectives and major qualitative characteristics of financial accounting in Germany

Given the legalistic system of regulation, no explicit conceptual framework of accounting such as exists in countries with a common law tradition and private standard setters, such as the USA, Australia and the UK, has been developed. Nevertheless, accounting academics have been very active in building up adequate deductive explanatory models which try to fit German accounting rules into a logical structure. These academic rationales have had quite an influence on the content of accounting regulations in Germany and also on their interpretation and their development.

Objectives of accounting

In order to understand the rationale of the German accounting model, it is necessary to consider not only the historical evolution of the law discussed above, but also factors such as the predominant method of financing business and the general concept of the firm in Germany.

As regards financing, it is significant that equity financing plays a relatively minor role, and that banks are quite often creditors of and investors in a stock corporation at the same time. An indicator of the minor role of equity investment is the low rate of private share-ownership in Germany. Due to some large Initial Public Offerings (IPOs), such as the one of the Deutsche Telekom in 1996, the tremendous hausse (rise in share prices) on the capital markets at the end of the 1990s and the creation of a new segment of the German capital market (the so-called *Neuer Markt*) the role of equity investment has increased but it is still much smaller than in countries like the USA, Canada or the UK, where it has risen to more than 25 per cent.

Another indicator is also the comparatively low equity ratios of German corporations (under 27 per cent on average for stock corporations). However, looking at this fact, it should be borne in mind that this low figure can be explained to some extent by the conservative accounting approach and the fact that, as well as debt, the establishment of accrued liabilities, provisions and deferred credits are also important instruments of financing. Special attention needs to be given to pensions in this context. Very often German companies accrue a pension liability in the balance sheet rather than make payments to an independent pension fund and remain directly responsible for paying pensions to retired employees. This means that they accumulate a substantial pension provision as part of their overall liability structure, something which to a large extent does not exist in many other countries.

The German banking system is such that most (more than 90 per cent) of the banks are universal banks, which provide a wide range of banking services. A portion of bank deposits is usually invested in extensive holdings in commercial and industrial corporations in various industries. As a result, bank representatives are quite often members of the supervisory boards of large corporations. The role of the banks is further emphasized by proxy rights. As many individual investors have little interest in attending or voting at shareholders' meetings, they assign proxies to their banks. For example, 95 per cent of the voting rights at the general meeting of Siemens in 1992 were exercised in the form of proxies held by leading German banks (Baums 1996).

Although debt financing is still playing an important role in corporate financing, the equity markets are increasingly gaining importance due to the capital needs of large globalized companies which exceed the capacities even of large banks.

In addition to the German approach to financing, the general concept of the firm is much more a stakeholder-oriented one than a shareholder-oriented one. German financial reporting primarily serves the interests of the capital providers but also has the function of reflecting the responsibility of a company to its employees, the government, society and the environment. The concern for the employees in the German cooperation model has led to a comparatively major participation of employees and their representatives in the decision-making of corporations. This participation takes place at branch and headquarters levels, as well as in the workplace. As one would expect in Germany's legally oriented culture, three laws regulate the participation of employee representatives on the supervisory board of a corporation. These are the *Montan-Mitbestimmungsgesetz* (Montan Participation Act) of 1951, the *Mitbestimmungsgesetz* (Participation Act) of 1976 and the *Betriebsverfassungsgesetz* (Industrial Constitution Act) of 1952. These provide, for instance, that up to 50 per cent of supervisory board members are elected by the employees. This fact of significant employee participation in corporate governance is also often used as a justification for the conservative income calculation policy of German corporations (Working Group on External Financial Reporting of the *Schmalenbach-Gesellschaft-Deutsche Gesellschaft für Betriebswirtschaft*, 1995).

In addition to the creditor protection principle, which is a very visible sign of a stakeholder-oriented approach, there are also special accounting rules (e.g. minimum values for fixed assets, inventories and other assets) which focus on the protection of minority shareholders and their interests and prevent a total undervaluation of assets by management through an over-enthusiastic application of the conservative principle as well as safeguarding an appropriate level of reported income.

The reverse congruency principle (*umgekehrte Massgeblichkeit*) (see above) can also be interpreted as providing evidence of an underlying stakeholder concept of the firm in Germany. The justification for the German tax authorities requiring the two-way effect of undervaluation, both for tax and commercial accounts, is the reduction of distributable income. As a result of conservative valuation rules, the tax authorities receive a smaller portion of companies' income in the form of income taxes. Following on from this renunciation by the tax authorities, the shareholders should also – in a sense of fair play – renounce a part of their income. Therefore distributable income in the commercial accounts must be reduced.

Overall, the German financial accounting model is not focused exclusively on one interest group but has to serve for a range of stakeholder groups. In this context the general objectives of financial accounting in Germany can be identified as:

- stewardship;
- income calculation;
- providing information.

Although providing information has become more and more important during recent years, and is going to continue to do so in the future, so far it cannot be regarded – as in the UK or the USA – as the dominant objective of financial reporting in Germany. It follows automatically that the requirement to give a 'true and fair view' as an overriding principle does not exist in a comparable manner. The implementation of the European Directives into German law confronted the German accounting landscape with the notion of the '*true and fair view principle*' and its overriding function in UK accounting. There was an overwhelming consensus at that time that this concept had to be transformed in such a way that it would change German accounting practice as little as possible.

Due to the legalistic view of accounting, where objectivity and verifiability play a dominant role, a vague, undefined concept such as the true and fair view, is not regarded as an appropriate basis for income measurement. The overriding requirement in German accounting is to be in conformity with the regulations and the GoB (Art. 243 Para. 1 HGB). This principle applies to all types of entity. As a result of the Fourth Directive, this has been transformed for companies with limited liability in such a way that their financial statements have to give a 'realistic' view of the wealth, the financial position and the earnings of the company while at the same time complying with the regulations (Art. 264 Para. 2 HGB). This wording represents the transformation of the true and fair view principle into German accounting law. According to the German legislator and the general opinion of accountants, the true and fair view requirement does not influence the computation of income but rather the information given in the notes to the financial statements. The notes should comply with the principle of a true and fair view in giving information in addition to what is in the balance sheet and profit and loss account. According to the legislator, this perception of the true and fair view principle has the advantage of providing greater reliability and objectivity in commercial accounting (and as a result of the congruence principle also in tax accounting) because the presentation of an item in the balance sheet does not depend so much on individual judgement and interpretation.

Furthermore, a transformation of the principle of a true and fair view in the British sense into German law would have meant the end of the strict *Massgeblichkeitsprinzip* because the two prinicples are in conflict. This conflict arises because, due to the converse effect of the congruency principle, values enter the commercial accounts which are motivated purely by tax considerations and do not give a 'fair' presentation of the economic situation of the business. For example the application of tax-driven accelerated depreciation charges against profit is not 'fair', but it is certainly 'correct' or 'legal'.

In sum it can be said that the implementation of the 'true and fair view principle', required by the Fourth Directive, has not led to a change of valuation or recognition principles in Germany. The notes have the function of giving adequate information so that the financial statements taken as a whole (balance sheet, income statement and notes) give a true and fair view. The true and fair view principle is not applied to each individual statement but to the financial statements as a composite whole. Clearly this weak interpretation of the true and fair principle in Art. 264 Para. 2 S. 2 HGB results in a situation where in the (few) cases where compliance with the GoB does not lead to a realistic view of the economic situation of an entity, the entity has to stick to the rules and just give adequate additional information in the notes. The interpretation of the true and fair view principle in the accounts of individual companies in Germany is weaker than, for example, that in France because in Germany no relaxation of concrete accounting rules is permitted in order to fulfil the true and fair view objective. This specifically German interpretation takes the position that compliance with the GoB generally provides a true and fair view of the economic situation of a company.

As has been mentioned above, no explicit conceptual framework has been constructed for financial accounting in Germany. Nevertheless the system of GoB is based on an undefined implicit framework. As far as the qualitative characteristics of accounting are concerned, the different perception of the accounting function in Germany as compared to that in the USA, the UK and the IASB give rise to a different weighting and a different interpretation. It can be seen from the discussion above that *reliability* and its sub-characteristics are the predominant principles. Whereas *faithful representation* and *completeness* are interpreted in similar ways to other countries, German accounting is characterized by the dominant role of *prudence* and *objectivity*, due to the importance of income calculation. These are regarded as the most important aspects of reliability.

The wide range of possible accounting policies (i.e. the existence of many accounting options) is evidence that the *principle of neutrality* is interpreted in Germany differently from the way it is interpreted in Anglo-Saxon models. Despite the fact that the informational aspect of accounting has been increasingly emphasized in Germany over the last few years, the characteristic of *relevance* has never been dealt with explicitly. Nevertheless the principles of *comparability*, *consistency* and *understandability* are major GoB and are interpreted almost in the same way as they are by the IASB. However, there are in Germany many more ways of deviating from the consistency principle than in the British and American accounting models. In addition, timeliness and an excess of benefit over cost, the two pervasive constraints of the explicit conceptual frameworks, are absent from GoB because of the absence of a decision usefulness principle.

The principles of *materiality* and *substance over form* do exist in German accounting, but not explicitly and they are not regarded as basic principles. *Materiality* is primarily taken into account in the notes, where the presentation of additional information is usually only required if it is material. Some explicit references to this principle are made in the HGB in the context of consolidated financial statements. Nevertheless, the principle of completeness is generally regarded as superior to materiality in the balance sheet and the profit and loss account.

The principle of *substance over form* has only one important application in German accounting, which is in cases where legal ownership is separated from economic ownership of an asset. Generally it is the economic owner of an asset who has to recognize it in his accounts and not the legal owner. The economic owner is the person who has the right of usage and who is liable to the legal owner in the event of the destruction of the asset. In other areas of accounting, substance over form is not a principle which influences recognition and measurement decisions in German accounting. On the contrary, due to the legally-oriented approach, it could be said that in accounting issues which impact upon the shape and content of the balance sheet and income statement there is a greater tendency towards an implicit approach of form over substance. Like the true and fair view and the materiality principle, the characteristic of substance over form has an impact – if at all – primarily on the notes to the financial statements.

Given the objective of meeting the interests of the various stakeholders which traditionally shapes German accounting, the *going concern assumption* is very dominant. The idea of safeguarding the company as a source of income generation, combined with the function of the balance sheet in calculating taxable income, leads to an emphasis on capital preservation which influences the definition of assets and liabilities as well as the interpretation of the accrual principle (see below). The concept of the preservation of capital, which is concretely interpreted as financial capital maintenance (preservation of nominal equity), is also the reason for the importance of the principle of prudence which leads to the use of so-called hidden (or secret) reserves, the feature of German accounting which has long been criticized internationally. Such reserves are counterproductive in an accounting model whose only objective is to give information, because secrecy is the opposite of information. In a model which stresses prudent income calculation with the objective of the preservation of capital and an underlying concept of creditor protection, however, it is a very logical approach. For stock corporations (AGs), the calculation of distributable income is influenced by the fact that decisions regarding income distribution are not solely a management prerogative in Germany: in general, shareholders are entitled to 50 per cent of the reported profit according to Art. 58 AktG.

Financial statements for groups of companies have to be based on essentially the same accounting principles as the ones in effect for individual companies operating on a stand-alone basis. This means that the legal requirements for individual companies must also be applied for consolidated financial statements. The entity concept of consolidated accounts makes it necessary that all accounting methods are applied identically in all the individual companies before the process of consolidation. However, where accounting options exist, those chosen for the group accounts can differ from those used in the accounts of the individual companies. As mentioned above, one of the major differences between group accounting and that applied in the single accounts has been the possibility of avoiding any impact of tax regulations in the group accounts. Since the adoption of the revision act 'TransPuG' in 2002 companies are no longer allowed to present any values which are influenced by tax rules or considerations in their consolidated statements (see above).

This possibility of having accounting policies in the consolidated accounts which are independent of those in the individual accounts is a logical result of the single objective which consolidated financial statements have in the German accounting model. This objective is simply to provide useful information on the economic situation of the group. The profit calculated in the group accounts does not have any distribution consequences in law. In fact companies do, nevertheless, always try to ensure that the profit disclosed in the group accounts does not show a totally different situation from that in the accounts of the parent company, in order not to provoke questions from the shareholders.

As mentioned above, since 1998, the parent company of a group which has securities traded on a regulated market is allowed (according to Art. 292a HGB) to prepare the group accounts on the basis of IAS or US GAAP instead of German rules if those accounts are still in conformity with the Seventh EC Directive. All the companies listed on the major German stock market segment, the DAX, have opted for this alternative. Companies listed on the SDAX (for smaller companies) and 'Neuer Markt' (for technological companies) are obliged to apply IAS or US GAAP according to the rules of the Frankfurt stock exchange (Deutsche Börse AG) (see later).

Components of Annual Reports

All types of commercial entities have to prepare financial statements. For companies with unlimited or only partly limited liability (even large ones as defined in the Publicity Law of 1969) these consist only of a balance sheet (*Bilanz*) and an income statement (*Gewinn- und Verlustrechnung*). Companies with limited liability (GmbH and AG) must – following the Fourth Directive – add notes (*Anhang*) to these two financial statements as well as a management report (*Lagebericht* – sometimes also called a directors' report). The legal requirements for the management report (which is not compulsory for small corporations) comply entirely with the Fourth Directive: in addition to an explanation of the general situation of the company and the development of the business during the financial year, it should also contain information concerning post balance sheet events of significance, anticipated future developments and research and development activities, as well as explanations of the major risks the company is confronted with. This report has to provide information which contributes to the presentation of a true and fair view of the company, but it is not regarded as a component of the financial statements. Large companies quite often use this management report as a public relations tool and include analyses of the accounts, comments on material variations of particular figures compared with previous years, details of new products and markets, and reports on social issues.

In contrast to many other countries a cash flow statement or statement of change in financial position was, until recently, not mandatory for German companies. As pointed out above, since the KonTraG was transformed into the HGB (Art. 297 Para. 1 HGB), groups which have securities admitted for trading are required to include a cash flow statement in the their group accounts. DRS 2 was published by the DSR to set out the shape and content of such a statement in concrete terms. The standard is very much comparable to IAS 7.

A statement of stockholders' equity had not been mandatory in Germany until 2002, although stock corporations (AGs) have to show their income appropriation on the face of the income statement (Art. 158 AktG). Since the revision act 'TransPuG' (see above) parent companies which have securities admitted for trading are required to present a statement of stockholders' equity in their group accounts. In addition to that, DRS 7 proposes that consolidated financial statements should include a statement of 'group equity and total recognized results' similar to the equity statement under IAS 1.

The preparation of the financial statements has to take place within three months of the balance sheet date for large and medium-sized corporations as well as for other large entities (covered by the Publicity Law), and within six months for small corporations. There is no time limit for other entities.

The precise format of the financial statements is regulated only for companies with limited liability. All others are only subject to the requirement that the balance sheet should show fixed and current assets and the owners' equity as well as the liabilities. For entities with limited liability the *balance sheet format* complies with the requirements of the Fourth Directive and therefore embraces a more detailed structure for large corporations than it does for small ones. In contrast to the American style of structuring the balance sheet, an accounts format is prescribed and the asset side starts with fixed assets and then current assets, while the financing side of the balance shows equity first, then provisions, debt and finally short-term liabilities. It may be seen as an upside-down version of the most common US format.

The structure of the different items does not follow an overriding general principle. The primary characteristics of structure are maturity or duration of usage, but, for example, debtors and liabilities are structured according to type rather than maturity. Supplementary information about the maturity of these items has to be given (either in the balance sheet or in the notes). There is a growing tendency to put as many disclosures as possible into the notes, where this is an option, and also to use such opportunities as the law allows to combine headings in the balance sheet, while providing additional analyses in the notes. Previous year comparative figures also have to be provided.

The *format of the income statement* is also regulated for entities with limited liability and has to be in a vertical form. There is an option allowing expenses to be presented either according to the nature of expenditure format or the functional format (see appendix to Chapter 1). The format using expenses by nature was the only one allowed before the implementation of the Fourth Directive in 1985 and it is still more popular with German companies. Nevertheless, recently, more and more large, globally active companies have switched to the expenses by function format which is the internationally preferred approach. In compliance with the Fourth Directive, the income statement is split into three subsections: operating income (*Betriebsergebnis*), non-operating income (*betriebsfremdes Ergebnis*) and extraordinary gains and losses (*außerordentliches Ergebnis*).

The general structure of an income statement is:

Operating results
+   Financial results
=   Results from ordinary activities
+   Extraordinary results
−   Taxation
=   Net income/net loss of the year

As in other countries, there is a considerable amount of subjectivity in the perceptions of *ordinary and extraordinary*. On the whole, the interpretation of what is regarded as extraordinary has become very narrow since the implementation of the Fourth Directive. Only events that are both unusual (highly abnormal) and infrequent (unlikely to occur), such as disasters, expropriations or discontinued operations and comparable items, are treated as extraordinary. Unlike France, disposals of assets are not treated as extraordinary. Explanations of specific income statement items should be given in the notes if this is necessary to give a better insight into their treatment.

Earnings per share information is not required by the regulations or GoB but has increasingly been disclosed by large stock corporations as part of the financial statements or in other parts of the annual report. If companies do disclose this information they tend to refer to a particular earnings per share definition developed by the Society of Investment Analysis and Asset Management (*Deutsche Vereinigung für Finanzanalyse und Asset Management eV, DVFA*) and the Working Group of the *Schmalenbach-Gesellschaft* on 'External Financial Reporting' (see above) which adjusts the published net income figure for major items which are influenced by accounting policy choices (such as depreciation, special types of provisions and other accruals) and intends to adapt the figure to the application of IAS to provide more comparable figures (see Busse von Colbe, W. *et al.*, 2000).

The requirement to publish *notes* to the accounts, and the detailed prescription of information which should be incorporated in these is one of the most important changes brought about by the implementation of the EC Directives. As has been discussed, the notes in Germany have a special extra function in addition to the British and American practice of providing supplementary information for the interpretation of the financial statement figures. Due to the fact that the true and fair view principle is not applied to each financial statement but to the set of statements as a whole, the notes are seen as the instrument to correct any potentially misleading information in the balance sheet or income statement.

The information given in the notes to the accounts which is generally required by law is very similar to the requirements of Art. 43 and 34 in the Fourth and Seventh Directives. It can be divided into four major subsections (for detail see Ordelheide and Pfaff 1994, pp. 162–3 and Ballwieser 2001, pp. 1326–31): (1) general information on the annual accounts (e.g. breach of the principle of consistent presentation); (2) basic principles of accounting and valuation (e.g. general information on the accounting and valuation methods used, basis for foreign currency translation, definition of production cost, profit impacts of tax-based depreciation, extraordinary depreciation of fixed assets, write-downs and revaluations); (3) explanations concerning items in the balance sheet and the income statement (e.g. schedule of fixed assets, breakdown of aggregated balance sheet items, provisions, special items with a reserve component, deferred taxes); and (4) supplementary information (e.g. contingent financial commitments, number of employees, total remuneration of members of the executive and supervisory boards).

Publication and auditing requirements

The requirements for publication and auditing depend on the legal form and size of the company. Thus only entities with limited liabilites except small ones and groups have to publish financial statements and have them audited by an external auditor, which proves that the limitation of liability and the general economic responsibility of a company, which increases with its size, are traditionally the driving forces for financial reporting in Germany. Consequently entities with unlimited or partly limited liability (with the exception of KGaA) need neither to publish their accounts nor to have an auditor's opinion on them. Only partnerships and single proprietorships – which on account of their size fall under the Publicity Law – are generally treated as large corporations and therefore have a publication obligation (limited to the balance sheet, income statement data and some supplementary information) and an audit requirement.

In contrast to Anglo-Saxon countries the predominant set of financial statements in Germany has been that of the single entity, the corporation, and not that of the group. Only under very strict conditions is a subsidiary relieved from the presentation and publication of single financial statements under German law (Art. 264 Para. 3 HGB). The publication requirements consist, for large and medium-sized companies, of filing in the commercial register (*Handelsregister*) and (for large corporations only) publication in the federal gazette (*Bundesanzeiger*) which is the official medium of the Federal Ministry of Justice for official announcements. The extent of the information published in the Handelsregister depends on the size of the corporation (Art. 325–328 HGB).

The publication of group accounts does not release management from the obligation to disclose the accounts of the individual member companies. Since the two sets of financial statements have different functions (individual accounts: income determination and information; group accounts: only information) each is subject to disclosure requirements. A group has, in principle, the same publication obligations as a single corporation (Art. 325 Para. 3 HGB).

In reviewing the annual reports which are prepared for the shareholders and other interested stakeholders of a corporation, a very obvious change in publication policy can be seen to be taking place. While a few years ago published annual reports were based on the financial statements of the parent company of the group with very abbreviated group financial statements as a kind of appendix, large multinational groups now base their annual report on the group and its accounts and disclose just very condensed versions of the statements of the parent company at the end of the report. This is a clear sign of the increased importance of consolidated statements which has been provoked by the implementation of the Seventh Directive and by the internationalization process of financial reporting in Germany. Consolidated financial statements are nowadays regarded as being more useful for economic decision-making than those of an individual company, as in countries with a British or American accounting approach. A particular advantage in Germany is the fact that the influence of the *Massgeblichkeitsprinzip* on the consolidated accounts is much less, as discussed above.

In terms of the underlying rules for the preparation of the group financial statements, IAS and US GAAP are gaining increasing importance. On the one hand, companies that choose to be listed at the now defunct 'Neue Markt' or the market segment for small companies (the so-called SDAX) needed to prepare financial statements according to either IAS or US GAAP due to listing requirements of the Frankfurt Stock Exchange (*Deutsche Börse AG*). In order to prevent companies having to prepare two statements, one based on international accounting standards and one based on German rules, as well as comply with the increasing need in capital markets for financial data which can be understood worldwide, the German legislator introduced §292a HGB into German accounting law. According to this rule, parent companies, which are listed on a capital market or intend to be, are not obliged to prepare consolidated financial statements based on German rules, as long as they prepare statements based on either IAS or US GAAP which comply with the Seventh Directive.

Figure 4.2 shows the development of the underlying accounting standards for the preparation of consolidated financial statements by the largest listed German companies (share

Figure 4.2 Accounting standards applied by the German DAX 30 companies for consolidated financial statements

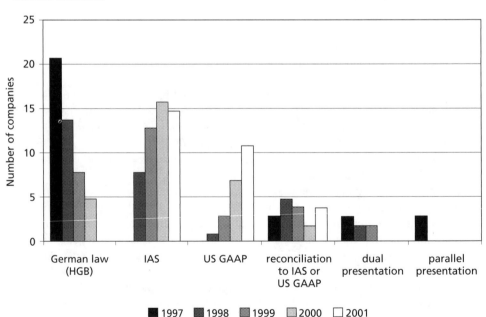

Source: based on Spanheimer and Koch (2000) and author's own studies.

market index DAX which comprises 30 companies). It shows that since 2001 there are no more companies included in the DAX, which present their statements according to HGB. Also, therefore, the former practice of presenting accounts which comply with HGB and IAS at the same time ('dual accounts') or presenting two complete sets of accounts (according to HGB and IAS or US GAAP) in parallel has ceased to exist.

In addition to the mandatory financial statements, the published annual reports of large corporations or groups include further sections which give general information about the enterprise, its products, markets and employees. These are aimed primarily at investors and stakeholders; their provision is subject to no restrictions and they are not audited.

A German *auditor* certifies, in contrast to his British or American colleagues, primarily that the financial statements comply with legal requirements and only secondarily that they give a true and fair view. The management report must be audited as well. It must be certified that it is consistent with the financial statements. Half-yearly reports, which have to be published by companies that issue listed securities due to the requirements of the Stock Exchange Act (Art. 44b. Börsengesetz), do not have to be audited. The standard of the DSR on interim financial reporting (DRS 6) proposes that a quarterly report be published which is very similar to IAS 34 but also does not require an audit.

Until 1998, the text of an unqualified auditors' opinion (*uneingeschränkter Bestätigungsvermerk*) of a company or group, which had to be published together with the financial statements, was explicitly stated in German accounting rules. With the introduction of the KonTraG in German law, this regulation was abandoned. Auditors now are required to formulate the auditors' opinion individually for every audit. Nevertheless, Art. 322 HGB addresses several general issues which have to be included in the auditors' opinion. In addition to the presentation and assessment of the results of the audit, the auditor's opinion has to contain a description of the subject, the type and the scope of the audit. If there are no objections, the auditor finally confirms that the financial statements give a true and fair view of the net worth, financial position and earnings of the (company or group).

As well as the above mentioned features of the KonTraG, a core element of this law is the obligation for a company's management to implement a *risk management system* in order to guarantee that the company continues to be a going concern. The KonTraG requires auditors to verify whether management has implemented such a system and whether this system is appropriate for the company's specific risks (Art. 317 Para. 4 HGB). The result of this particular audit must be mentioned in the auditors' opinion.

The auditor presents a voluminous and detailed report of the audit and its results to the supervisory and the management boards. This report is not published. As in other countries, the auditors' opinion has to be qualified or disclaimed if there are any objections, which in practice is quite rare.

Auditors do not have a duty to search for fraud or other criminal acts by management. Only if violations are found by chance during the conduct of the audit do they have to report them to the supervisory board. The KonTraG has expanded the legal liability of the auditor. This might serve to reduce the *expectation gap* (the difference between the general public's opinion about the duties of an auditor and his actual legal duty) which 'historically' has been even larger in Germany than in Britain or the USA, due to the reduced legal liability of German auditors. To further improve the quality of German audits a peer review comparable to US practice was implemented in 2001.

Additionally there is a lively discussion going on at the moment over whether to introduce a body to enforce the compliance with the rules, such as the *Financial Reporting Review Panel* (FRRP) in the UK or the SEC in the USA, to improve the quality of the financial reporting of listed companies (see Evans, Eierle and Haller 2002).

Measurement and recognition concepts and practices

The influence of the idea of creditor protection in German accounting is mainly seen in the specific definitions of assets and liabilities as well as in the conservative interpretation of the accrual principle.

General definition of assets and liabilities

Curiously, there is no statutory definition of the elements of financial statements such as assets, liabilities or revenues and expenses, but definitions have developed as GoB. An *asset* (*Vermögensgegenstand*) is defined by three major characteristics. It must be (1) an economic value, (2) which can be separated from the enterprise (i.e. transferred or sold independently of other assets) and (3) can be valued independently. The element of the asset definition of the IASC of 'having future economic benefits' is not mentioned explicitly in the German definition. However, it is to some extent incorporated implicitly in the idea of having an economic value: arguably if an enterprise cannot derive a benefit from an item, this item usually has no economic value.

This definition reflects the idea of creditor protection in that creditors can only have direct recourse to saleable goods. According to this definition self-generated intangible items are not regarded as assets which can be recognized in the balance sheet. However, those which have been purchased and have therefore proven to be saleable must be recognized as assets in the accounts. The major reason for this is that those items can be measured objectively as a result of the purchase transaction. Thus objectivity in measuring the value of an item is the crucial element of German asset definition.

Some items which do not meet the definition of an asset are nevertheless explicitly allowed to be recognized as an asset by the Commercial Code. These are goodwill (arising from consolidation), deferred tax assets and business start-up and expansion costs (not including formation expenses and the costs of raising equity capital). These items (they are called *Bilanzierungshilfen* which might literally be translated as *accounting conveniences*) may be capitalized even though they cannot be separated from the business. If capitalized, they have to be amortized over periods which are also laid down in the Commercial Code. This recognition option widens the range of accounting policies open to German companies. Their introduction into German accounting can be explained by the impact of the accrual principle which has begun to be more rigorously applied as a result of the Fourth Directive. In order not to damage the function of prudent calculation of income, companies which capitalize such items have to apply an equivalent limitation on distributions.

In addition to the economic assets and the deferrals, there is a third kind of item which is included in a German balance sheet: prepayments for timely fixed received services, such as insurances, public fees and charges, which must – according to the accrual principle – be split up and proportionally allocated to the periods of their economic cause. They are regarded as purely technical accounting items.

It becomes obvious that the definition of assets is narrower and less dynamic than in the IASB accounting model because all types of deferred items are not regarded as assets as such but rather as a kind of technical accounting adjustment. Figure 4.3 illustrates this difference.

The German definition of *liabilities* (*Verbindlichkeiten*) is narrow in comparison with other accounting models. It embraces only present obligations to third parties which are certain. Of course, companies also have to recognize provisions (*Rückstellungen*) for probable future obligations which result from past transactions or other past events as well as

Figure 4.3 Asset definition in the German accounting model compared with the British and American accounting models

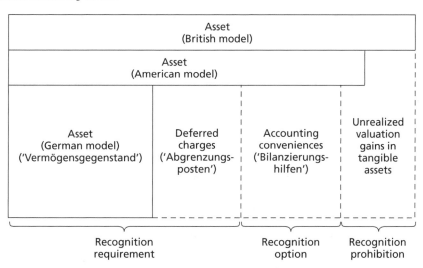

for obligations which might possibly arise in the future. These provisions must be disclosed separately. German balance sheets typically show a much higher proportion of provisions than do American or British ones because German accounting principles prescribe that such items have to be recognized even if there are only slight indications that obligations or specific losses could occur in the future due to past events or transactions. The underlying conservatism is also shown clearly in the option which is open to companies to recognize provisions for particular future expenditures which have their economic cause in the period under review (or previous ones) and are not provoked by obligations to third parties but by the economic circumstances of the company (e.g. future overhauls of plant). Figure 4.4 illustrates that the American definition of liabilities embraces German liabilities and provisions as well as particular accruals (in the same way as occurs on the asset side of the balance sheet).

As in other countries *equity* (*Eigenkapital*) is defined as the difference between assets and liabilities.

Interpretation of the accruals principle

In the same way as the definition of assets and liabilities, the accruals principle is interpreted on a very conservative basis in comparison with the British and American models.

Realization principle

In order to preserve the capital which is invested in a company only those profits which have been realized can be distributed. This principle is very conservatively interpreted, which means that an increase in net equity (i.e. net income) is only recognized if the underlying economic transaction has been completed, that means at the moment when, objectively, the income is sufficiently certain. For example, holding gains not realized through a concrete sale of the particular item are, therefore, not allowed to be recognized. The major effects of this are as follows:

- Historical acquisition or production cost represents the maximum value for accounting purposes. A revaluation to a higher value is not allowed. An exception to this will be

Figure 4.4 The scope of liabilities in the German accounting model compared with the British and American models

	Deferrals of received prepayments	Obligations					
		Certain	Uncertain				
			To third parties		To the company itself	Possible but unlikely
			Probable	Possible	Probable or possible	
German	Credit accruals ('Rechnungs-abrenzungs-posten')	Liabilities ('Verbindlichkeiten')	Provisions ('Rückstellungen')			*No recognition
			Prescribed recognition		Optional recognition	
British	Credit accruals	Liabilities	Provisions		No recognition	
American	Liabilities				No recognition	

* These items have to be shown on the face of the balance sheet.

incorporated in the Commercial Code in due course through an implementation of the amendment of the Fourth and Seventh Directives which introduce fair value accounting for particular securities into EU law.

- The percentage-of-completion method for long-term contracts is not allowed.

Matching principle

Germany has a 'principle of imparity' (*Imparitätsprinzip*) whereby losses concerning particular items or transactions which have not yet occurred but are likely to occur in the near future have to be anticipated and should be regarded as expenses of the current year. The name of this principle reflects the fact that future losses of specific transactions are treated in the opposite way (do not have parity) from gains or income. This very broad concept of anticipating losses on transactions or write-downs of assets has the following major effects:

- principle of lower of cost or market value for all current assets, even if the diminution in value is only temporary;
- the possibility of write-downs of current assets due to expected decreases of value in the near future;
- formation of deferred credits for future expenses which are not caused by obligations to third parties;
- self-produced assets need only be valued at direct cost, and all overheads can be treated as expenses of the current year;
- recognition of accrued and contingent liabilities in a much wider manner than in the American or British models. The possibility of the loss, not the degree of likelihood is the predominant factor which triggers recognition. If there are several, equally likely estimates of value, the highest amount has generally to be provided for.

Major measurement concepts

By way of summarizing some of the above issues and also to stress the major measurement issues before proceeding to a direct comparison with the IAS, it is worth noting that for all items on the asset side of the balance sheet *historical cost* (acquisition or production cost) is the maximum value which can be capitalized (the implementation of the 'fair value directive' will provide a change in this respect for particular financial instruments). In calculating production cost, companies have the option of valuing at direct cost only or including indirect costs. Contrary to US GAAP and IAS, general administration costs can also be allocated to the production cost. All assets with a useful life have to be depreciated systematically over this period. The declining balance method is accepted as an alternative to the straight-line method and is quite popular in practice.

Owing to the principle of lower of cost or market, *non-current assets* must be written down if the fair value of the asset drops under the carrying amount and this is expected to be permanent. *Current assets* must be written down for any drop of fair value under the carrying amount, no matter whether it is permanent or not. They may also be written down if there is a reliable estimate that the market value will fall below the book value in the near future. There is a general obligation to revalue an asset because of an increase in market value after a devaluation up to its historical cost net of depreciation or amortization. The revaluation may be refrained if the revaluation in the financial balance sheet provokes a revaluation in the tax balance sheet due to the congruency principle (Art. 280 Para. 2 HGB). Since a revision of the tax law in 2000, which has brought a general obligation to revalue assets in the tax accounts if the reason for write-down has ceased to exist, this option to refrain from the write up can no longer be applied.

Accelerated depreciation or special write-downs for *tax purposes* can be introduced in the commercial financial statements (since 2002 this has been restricted to single accounts). If a company makes a special write-down there are two possible ways to account for it. The company can either depreciate the asset and reduce the book value disclosed in the balance sheet, which leads to an economically false and misleading valuation in the financial statements, or it can leave the book value alone and treat the allowance for tax reasons in an indirect way by showing it as a kind of correcting item on the liability side of the balance sheet. This item is called special item with an equity portion (*Sonderposten mit Rücklageanteil*) and can be regarded as nothing other than an untaxed reserve. In subsequently depreciating the asset in the regular way or when the asset is sold, this special item has to be written back.

Another proof of the predominance of the prudence principle and the little regard accorded to the idea of substance over form is the valuation of *liabilities*. These must be valued at their net settlement value (redemption amount) and even if they are of long maturity not at the present value. If the current value of a liability reduces (e.g. due to foreign currency translation), there is no possibility of devaluing the liability. Provisions or contingent liabilities have to be valued on a very prudent basis and with a worst case perspective.

Major differences between German accounting principles and IAS

Before going into a more detailed discussion of the major differences between the financial reporting requirements of the IAS and those in Germany, the following checklist gives a brief overview.

To begin with, it is worth noting that in general the *disclosure requirements* included in the IAS exceed the comparable requirements in Germany in most topics. This is logical because of the relative lack of impact that principles like relevance and substance over form have in German accounting and the traditional focus on the presentation of net asset and its change, which is net income. The major differences between IAS and German accounting can be found in the following areas:

Table 4.2 International Accounting Standards checklist

IAS	German practice
1	Differences regarding the amount and the structure of the financial statements.
2	Option to measure only at direct costs; LIFO, FIFO and average method are equally allowed, as well as the 'method of fixed value'.
7	Requirement to prepare a cash flow statement for group financial statements only. DRS 2 contains details.
8	Much lower disclosure level, more possibilities for changing policies.
10	Disclosure of events occurring after the balance sheet date in the management report.
11	Only completed contract method is allowed.
12	Liability method is used; recognition option for deferred tax assets; recognition obligation for deferred tax liabilities and deferred tax assets arising from consolidation. Timing differences are the basis for recognition.
14	Segmentation only of sales, on line of business and geographical region basis; segment reports required for group accounts are more detailed according to DRS 3.
15	No explicit rules; valuation is based on nominal values.
16	Revaluation above historical cost is not allowed; tax related depreciation is often used.
17	No legal rules; accounting practice is quite similar to IAS17; sale and leaseback transactions are treated as sale transactions.
18	No major differences, percentage of completion method is not allowed.
19	Projected benefit valuation method; trends of future changes in salary or inflation are not usually taken into account.
20	Deduction of grants from related expenses is not allowed.
21	Unrealized currency gains from transactions may not be recognized, but unrealized currency losses have to be recognized; there is no legal rule for the treatment of translation differences.
22	The use of the purchase and the pooling of interests method is quite comparable; wide range of options in the treatment of goodwill; a negative goodwill can only be released in very restricted circumstances, amortization over the average useful life of non-monetary assets is not allowed.
23	Capitalization of borrowing costs of a purchased asset only under very rare circumstance; under specific conditions related interest can be added to the production costs of an asset.
24	Separate disclosure of investments in and receivables and payables with related parties in the balance sheet; additional information has to be given.
26	See IAS 19.
27	In detail different preconditions for the preparation of group accounts; notable amount of possibilities to exclude a subsidiary from the group accounts.
28	Equity method is only allowed in group accounts; there are some differences in detail in the application of the equity method.
29	No special rules; valuation above historical cost is not allowed.
30	There are special accounting rules for banks and insurance companies.
31	Option to use either the equity approach or a proportional consolidation.

Table 4.2 International Accounting Standards checklist (*continued*)

IAS	German practice
32	No legal rules; only requirement to disclose future commitments in notes.
33	No legal rules to publish earnings per share; published voluntarily by many companies.
34	Only listed companies are obliged to present interim reports according to listing requirements; only a few figures have to be reported.
35	No legal rules.
36	Different regulations for current and non-current assets; regulations are based on the principle of prudence.
37	Broader possibilities for making use of provisions; estimation of the amount follows a worst case scenario.
38	Internally generated intangible assets may not be recognized.
39	Differentiation of current and non-current assets; subsequent measurement follows the principle of lower of cost or market. Valuation higher than acquisition costs is not allowed.
40	Assets may not be valued higher than acquisition costs; realization principle as basis.
41	No legal rules; fair value accounting is generally not allowed.

Presentation of Financial Statements (IAS 1)

According to German regulations, there is no general obligation to expand the financial statement by a *statement of changes in equity* or a *cash flow statement*; only groups which have securities admitted for trading have to present a *cash flow statement* and a statement of changes in owners' equity in their consolidated accounts (Art. 297 Para. 1 HGB). For both types of statement the DRS has published standards which are in line with the international standards (DRS 2; Cash Flow Statement; DRS 7: Statement of Changes in Owners' Equity).

In opposition to IAS, German accounting rules, in accordance with the Fourth Directive, do contain detailed regulations concerning the structure and classification of the *balance sheet* as well as the *profit and loss account*.

The principles of accounting according to IAS 1 differ in terms of their level of importance compared to their use in Germany.

Inventories (IAS 2)

There is an option to value self-produced inventories only at their direct costs (option in the definition of production costs). General administration overheads can be included, but not selling expenses. Also the carrying amount can be written down by anticipating decreases in the market values of inventories which might occur in the near future (Art. 253 Para. 3 HGB).

FIFO, LIFO and weighted average valuation method are all allowed in commercial accounts. There are no special disclosure requirements when using LIFO. However, since LIFO has been excluded from tax accounts, its popularity has decreased in Germany. In contrast to IAS a method known as fixed value (*Festwertverfahren*) is allowed for inventories and particular non-current assets which do not change significantly in amount and value.

Cash Flow Statement (IAS 7)

An obligation to present a *cash flow statement* exists only for parent companies for the group accounts (Art. 297 Para. 1 HGB). As the HGB is silent about the form and content of the statement, companies are encouraged to apply DRS 2, which includes comparable rules to IAS 7.

Profit or Loss for the Period, Fundamental Errors and Changes in Accounting Policies (IAS 8)

The information which has to be given in the notes on such items is generally less than that required in IAS 8. The principle of consistency is legally not generally interpreted as strictly as by the IASB. Usually the effects of changes are part of the periodic income figure. German companies are quite reluctant to provide quantitative information about the effects of changes in accounting methods in the notes. The definition of extraordinary items is almost the same except that effects from discontinued operations are usually included in Germany. According to DRS 13 all effects of changes in accounting policies should be recognized in the income statement of the current year. The interpretation of the principle of consistency in DRS 13 is similar to the one in IAS.

Events after the Balance Sheet Date (IAS 10)

According to the GoB non-adjusting events after the balance sheet date may not be recognized in the financial statements. However, if regarded as important and material, they should be disclosed in the management report (*Lagebericht*).

Construction Contracts (IAS 11)

Only the completed contract method is allowed in Germany. Contingent losses on long-term contracts must be accrued.

Income Taxes (IAS 12)

Due to the close relationship between commercial accounting and the computation of taxable income deferred taxes are traditionally not an accounting issue in Germany. Deferred taxation was introduced (only for entities with limited liability) by the EC directives in the 1980s. Without being explicitly codified, the liability method is regarded as the appropriate way to account for deferred taxes. They are recognized in the event of timing differences and not temporary differences. Generally only the net balance between deferred tax assets and liabilities is recognized. If it is a debit balance it may be recognized but if it is a credit balance (liability) it has to be recognized. Deferred tax assets are not regarded as *Vermögensgegenstände* (assets) but as *Bilanzierungshilfen* (accounting conveniences). Deferred taxes arising from consolidation have to be recognized irrespective of whether they are tax assets or tax liabilities. DRS 10 regulates the treatment of deferred taxes arising in consolidated accounts and is similar to IAS 12. However, it does not apply the temporary concept but the timing concept and does not require disclosure of tax assets and liabilities under non-current items.

Segment Reporting (IAS 14)

As a result of the very limited requirements of the Fourth and Seventh Directives, German law for single financial statements of companies with limited liability only requires a segmentation of sales by business segments and geographically defined markets, according to the sales organization of the company's goods and services. The company can omit this disclosure if it is regarded as likely to significantly harm the company or an enterprise in which the company holds at least one-fifth of the shares. Since 1998, listed parent companies are required to add a segment report to their group financial statements. Since the design of this report is not specified by law, the groups are expected to apply DRS 3, which intends to combine the contents of IAS 14 and SFAS 131 and therefore represents a mixture of those standards.

Information Reflecting the Effects of Changing Prices (IAS 15)

There is no such requirement in Germany. German accounting is based on the maintenance of nominal capital and therefore an approach which publishes specific statements or other information on the effects of changes in the value of money is not at all popular.

Property, Plant and Equipment (IAS 16)

Revaluation above the historical acquisition or production cost is not allowed in Germany. Extending the useful life is only possible under restrictive conditions. The carrying amount may be increased only as a write-back of a previous write-down, which is generally required for entities with limited liability (Art. 280 HGB).

Depreciation may be calculated according to tax considerations (with additional information on the differences between commercial and tax depreciation rates in the notes). There is an option to use either the straight-line method or the declining balance method. Both are seen in practice. The amount of additional information required in the notes is smaller according to German rules.

Leases (IAS 17)

Due to the lack of statutory rules, the treatment of leasing usually follows the tax rules. Operating leases are treated in a similar way to IAS 17; lease rentals are expensed by the lessee and recorded as income by the lessor in the periods to which they relate. The treatment of finance leases is in general not dissimilar to IAS. The general rule is that assets under a finance lease contract are recognized in the balance sheet of the lessee as assets and an equivalent amount as liabilities. The lessor shows an equivalent receivable for the lease rentals.

The treatment of leases is a very good example of the existence of the principle of substance over form in the German accounting model, albeit with a much narrower scope than in the British and American models. There are some differences in the accounting treatment of leases as compared with the IAS. This is clearly the case for sale and leaseback transactions which are treated as normal sales in German accounts, whereas IAS tries to portray the economic reality more clearly.

Revenue (IAS 18)

There is no difference concerning revenues from interest, royalties and dividends but there are minor differences in the treatment of revenues from the sale of goods – for instance the percentage of completion method in accounting for long-term contracts is not allowed in Germany.

Employee Benefits (IAS 19)

In Germany – in contrast to the USA – retirement benefits are not regarded so much as a form of deferred compensation to employees in return for their current services but more as an extra bonus for their fidelity to the enterprise. Direct commitments by companies to grant a pension to their employees are very popular. For these a provision must be created to cover the liability (there is an option for commitments which were made before 1 January 1987) and this is revalued each year on an actuarial basis. There are also some indirect arrangements, such as funding external pension funds through insurance companies.

Payments by a company to an external pension fund are treated as expenses in the income statement. A provision is usually not necessary in such cases.

The basis for the valuation of pension provision relating to direct contracts is a single employer defined benefit pension plan which is measured using a projected benefit valuation approach. There is an uncodified rule in German accounting that the discount rate should be between 3 and 6 per cent (the latter rate is mandatory for tax purposes). There is consequently much less fluctuation in the discount rate used than is the case when using the market rates as the IAS requires. Trends of future changes in salary, inflation or interest rates are not usually taken into account in German accounting. The treatment laid out in IAS 19 is presumed to be in accordance with German principles.

Accounting for Government Grants and Disclosure of Government Assistance (IAS 20)

In general there is no difference. The deduction of revenue grants from the related expense is not allowed under German law and the disclosure requirements of IAS are much wider than those in Germany.

The Effects of Changes in Foreign Exchange Rates (IAS 21)

Traditionally unrealized foreign currency gains are neither taken into the profit and loss account or transferred directly to reserves. Unrealized currency losses have to be treated as expenses. This is a typical consequence of the application of the prudence principle and its influence on the German interpretation of the accrual principle. In recent times – due to the internationalization process – there has been a tendency in accounting opinion that currency gains should also be recognized.

There is no statutory rule for translating the statements of foreign subsidiaries and so all established methods are possible. However, the closing rate method or the temporal principle method are the ones primarily recommended (e.g. by the IdW 1986) with a conceptual preference for the temporal principle (recommendation of a special working group of the Schmalenbach-Gesellschaft 1989; see Busse von Colbe, Müller and Reinhart 1989). In practice all the different types of translation can be found as well as mixtures of different methods. There are also different treatments of the translation differences (as gains/losses or as reserves). In the last years the functional currency method has become increasingly popular in German accounting practice. Most of the companies apply the closing rate method. Changes in the equity of subsidiaries and affiliates originating from foreign currency translation should be reported as a separate component of equity.

Business Combinations (IAS 22)

The perception of goodwill in Germany is different from that of the IAS because it is regarded more as a technical item (consolidation difference) than as an asset. It is therefore classified as an accounting convenience (*Bilanzierungshilfe*). In individual company accounts, goodwill resulting from a fusion (a merger where two companies combine into a single legal entity) can be capitalized. The law requires goodwill to be amortized on a straight-line basis over four years (starting with the year after the acquisition) or over its useful life. There is no definition of useful life and in practice 15 years are quite often taken as appropriate because of a tax rule which states that the useful life of a goodwill has to be 15 years.

There is a wide range of treatments for goodwill resulting from consolidation under the acquisition method. It can be set off directly against reserves (as it also used to be in the UK), but the popularity of this treatment amongst large companies has decreased in recent years, due to the increasing impact of the American or IAS accounting model on German accounting. It can even be split into one part which is capitalized and amortized and another which is set off against reserves. The possibilities of amortization are the same as in single financial statements. Obviously goodwill accounting is a very fruitful area of accounting policy in German group accounts.

Negative goodwill may only be released in very restricted cases. There are minor differences in the use of the pooling of interest method between the HGB and IAS 22. According to HGB there is only an option to apply the pooling of interest method if the requirements are met (Art. 302 HGB).

DRS 4 'Acquisition accounting in consolidated financial statements' published in December 2000 handles issues of business combination in a very similar way to IAS 22. In limiting the legal option it prohibits the direct offsetting of goodwill against reserves and fixes the useful life at a maximum of 20 years. Negative goodwill is also treated similarly to IAS 22. As a reaction of the introduction of the 'impairment only approach' in the USA (SFAS 141 and 142) the DSR has stated that this approach does not conflict with German rules or the Seventh Directive (see DRS 1a).

Borrowing Costs (IAS 23)

Related interest can be added to the production cost of an asset for the period of its production. No borrowing costs other than the interest may be capitalized into the value of a self-produced asset. Borrowing costs may only under very rare preconditions be added to the acquisition cost of an acquired asset.

Related Party Disclosures (IAS 24)

German enterprises have to disclose as separate items in the balance sheet investments in as well as receivables and payables concerning related parties. Other specific information about the relation with other companies has to be given in the management report (not the financial statements as such). Only enterprises are considered to be related parties under German accounting law and not individuals as in IAS 24. DRS 11 contains rules comparable to IAS.

Accounting and Reporting by Retirement Benefit Plans (IAS 26)

Usually there are no retirement benefit plans other than pensions in German practice.

Consolidated Financial Statements and Accounting for Investments in Subsidiaries (IAS 27)

The German accounting principles are quite similar to the IAS. However, under IAS there is no need to prepare consolidated accounts if a company does not exercise control over another company even if it holds more than 50 per cent of the voting rights in that company. In Germany, by contrast, a majority of votes creates an obligation to prepare consolidated accounts, subject to specific exclusions which go beyond those in paragraphs 13 and 14 of IAS 27. This is again evidence of the weak importance of the principle of substance over form in Germany.

If a subsidiary carries out a substantially different activity than the other enterprises of the group, this is accepted as one of the possible reasons for its exclusion from the group accounts. Such companies should be incorporated in the group accounts using the equity method. The number of explicitly cited requirements or options to exclude subsidiaries from consolidation is much higher in Germany than in IAS 27 (see Art. 295 and 296 HGB). There are even size criteria, below which the preparation of consolidated accounts is not required at all (Art. 293 HGB). Nevertheless it could be argued that some of the explicit cases in the HGB would correspond with the normal application under IASB rules of the general principles of relevance, substance over form and materiality.

Accounting for Investments in Associates (IAS 28)

The equity method is only allowed in consolidated accounts and not in individual accounts; at the time of its first application, the acquisition cost of the investment is the ceiling. The equity method is used for investments in associates (ownership of more than 20 per cent of the voting rights is regarded as an indicator of a company being able to exert 'significant influence' on another), joint ventures that are not proporionately consolidated and those subsidiary enterprises that are not fully consolidated, as mentioned above. There is no provision that the equity method should not be applied when the associate operates under severe long-term restrictions that significantly impair its ability to transfer funds to the investor.

In Germany enterprises may choose between the book value method and the share capital method (Art. 312 HGB), whereas IAS 28 only allows the book value method. German enterprises should eliminate inter-company profits using the equity method, if they have access to the information necessary to do this.

Comparable to DRS 4 with accounting for business combination, DRS 8 limits the legal options and states more precisely the treatment of investments in associates comparable to IAS 28.

Financial Reporting in Hyperinflationary Economies (IAS 29)

There is no special rule which deals with this issue. In general the valuation of assets above historical cost is not allowed.

Disclosures in the Financial Statements of Banks and Similar Financial Institutions (IAS 30)

Specific regulations for banks and insurance companies are incorporated in the HGB. There are also special DRSs (e.g. concerning cash flow statements, segment reporting, risk reporting) for such institutions. The discussion of these special rules is beyond the scope of this book.

Financial Reporting of Interests in Joint Ventures (IAS 31)

To account for joint ventures, German accounting rules provide an option to either make use of the equity approach or the proportional consolidation (Art. 310 HGB). DRS 9 gives concrete advice on how to account for jointly controlled entities, which is comparable to IAS 31. It is silent about jointly controlled operations and jointly controlled assets.

Financial Instruments (IAS 32)

There are so far no specific rules concerning the disclosure of information about financial instruments in Germany which go beyond the general requirements for disclosure of financial commitments in the notes which are derived from the Fourth Directive. Contingent losses which are likely to occur should be provided against. Treasury shares have to be recognized as assets while a special item has to be included with the same value under equity.

Earnings per Share (IAS 33)

German accounting does not require that this information be considered in the financial statements. Nevertheless, many companies publish this figure, given its importance for capital markets. The relevant earnings figure is usually calculated according to the scheme, which was developed by the *Deutsche Vereinigung für Finanzanalyse und Anlageberatung e.V.* (DVFA) in cooperation with the *Schmalenbach Gesellschaft* (see above, Busse von Colbe *et al.* 2000). The definition of this specific earnings figure tries to eliminate all exceptional, extraordinary items and holding gains and losses. It also is designed to be comparable to IAS income.

Interim Financial Reporting (IAS 34)

So far, interim financial reports are only to be published on a half-yearly basis by listed companies according to the securities and exchange law and the rules of the German stock exchanges (*Börsengesetz*; admission regulations for the segment *Neuer Markt* of the German Stock Exchange, *Deutsche Börse AG*). This report needs to contain information about sales, earnings and comparable figures for the previous year; it also has to contain explanatory notes. Those regulations are much less comprehensive than IAS 34. However DRS 6 requires parent companies that are obliged to publish interim financial reports according to other regulations (especially listing requirements) to present interim reports on a quarterly basis. Similar to IAS 34, those reports should be quite detailed and include condensed financial statements and extensive notes. Interim reports do not have to be audited.

Discontinuing Operations (IAS 35)

There is no special rule which deals with this issue. Revenues and expenses from such operations are usually treated as extraordinary items.

Impairment of Assets (IAS 36)

The treatment of the devaluation of current and non-current assets is differently regulated. Entities with a limited liability may not write down property, plants and equipment due to a temporary decline in market value; however, there is an obligation if the devaluation is likely to be permanent. On the other hand, current assets always have to be valued at the lower of book or market value, even if the decline in value is only temporary. If the reason for a past write-down no longer exists, the company is obliged to write-up the asset (Art. 280 HGB; there is an option to write-up for entities with unlimited liability). The valuation of cash generating units is not possible.

Provisions, Contingent Liabilities and Contingent Assets (IAS 37)

Provisions are another example of the conservative character of German accounting. On one hand, German accounting rules provide more situations which lead to the recognition of provisions; especially provisions for expenses without a legal obligation. On the other hand, the required probability of a decrease in economic benefits is below 50 per cent. Additionally, the valuation of the provision follows a worst case consideration.

According to the so-called *Imparitätsprinzip* the voluminous necessity to recognize provisions is an instrument for anticipating future economic risks.

Intangible Assets (IAS 38)

Internally generated intangible assets as well as research and development costs may not be recognized. Also a revaluation of intangible assets exceeding historical costs is not possible.

Due to legal rules DRS 12 may not provide the option or requirement to recognize internally generated intangible assets and is therefore not in accordance with IAS 38.

Financial Instruments: Recognition and Measurement (IAS 39)

German accounting standards differentiate between current financial assets and non-current financial assets. As for all assets, the principle of the lower of cost or market value has to be applied. For current financial assets even prospective declines in market value likely to occur in the near future may be provided for. For non-current investments the requirement to write down the asset is restricted to losses which are expected to be permanent. Write-downs in respect of temporary reductions in value are optional. A subsequent release of a write-down following a rise in value is mandatory for either current and non-current investments. Due to German accounting's conservative interpretation of the realization principle, a valuation at a fair value higher than the acquisition cost has so far not been allowed. Disclosure of current market values is not required. There exist no special regulations for derivatives. The fair value directive of the EU will most likely not be incorporated into German law before the year 2004.

Investment Property (IAS 40)

German accounting does not have separate regulations for investment properties. They are treated the same way as other fixed assets. Furthermore, a valuation of assets, based on the fair value higher than the acquisition costs, contrasts with the conservative interpretation of the realization principle, particularly if it affects the profit or loss of the period.

Agriculture (IAS 41)

There are no special rules for agricultural activities. Fair value accounting is generally not allowed.

Conclusion

The rationale behind the German accounting model (which is reflected almost identically in accounting practice in Austria) is to safeguard creditors' interests by a conservative measurement which preserves nominal capital; this has priority over the objective of providing open, unbiased information about profitability. The focus on a prudent determination of profit leads to silent reserves, a characteristic for which German accounting is known and criticized, and which often impairs the information function of financial reporting. Compared to US and British rules, German accounting rules provide a much wider range of explicit recognition, measurement and disclosure options which gives greater opportunity for companies to exercise accounting policy choices.

Because of the increasing need of German multinationals for capital to finance investment and strong pressure from international capital markets, German accounting practice has started to change and to adopt more international principles. The major starting point for this internationalization initiative was the listing of Daimler Benz on the NYSE which forced the company to comply with the strict SEC disclosure requirements (for more detail of this revolutionary event see Chapter 17). Subsequently, German accounting has been continuously adapting to the requirements of capital markets. On one hand, since the revision of the Commercial Code in 1998 due to the KapAEG, German groups which have securities traded on a stock exchange are now allowed to publish financial statements which are not in accordance with German rules as long as they publish statements that are in line with either IAS or US GAAP and that do not conflict with the Seventh Directive. Groups which have securities admitted for trading and which decide to continue to publish financial statements based on German rules are, following the introduction of the KonTraG and TransPuG, obliged to present a cash flow statement, a segment report and a statement of changes in owners' equity. In addition, the standards published by the DRSC are to a high degree comparable to the equivalent international standards. Therefore, the developments during the later 1990s are clearly moving German accounting towards the provision of internationally required information that is useful for investment decisions, even to the extent of neglecting German accounting traditions (for more explanation, see Haller 2002).

This development is in accordance with and gets an additional impetus from the intention of the EU Commission, presented in 2000, that from 2005 onwards consolidated financial statements of groups listed on an European stock exchange should be published in conformity with IAS. Although this intention will increase the international comparability of financial statements on the consolidated level, it jeopardizes national comparability between single financial and consolidated financial statements. That is the reason why the German legislator intends to continue to revise the German accounting system (at least the rules for group accounts) until 2005.

For the time being there is great uncertainty about the future development of financial reporting in Germany. It is very obvious that all companies active on capital markets or with a high degree of global operation will adopt IAS (or US-GAAP if they are, or intend to be listed in the USA). Additionally the so far published standards of the DRSC illustrate that the principles for preparing consolidated financial statements will become closely comparable to IAS. However, it is questionable whether this wave of internationalization will also impact on the rules for single accounts and all types of business entities, without regard to their size and/or legal form. If this happens to be the case, the traditionally close relationship between financial accounting and tax computation will also cease to exist. Whatever the outcome, the German accounting system faces its most challenging period ever.

References

Ballwieser, W. (2001) Germany: Individual accounts, in D. Ordelheide and KPMG (eds), *Transnational Accounting, Vol. 2*, 2nd edn, Palgrave, Basingstoke, pp. 1217–1351.

Baums, T. (1996) Vollmachtstimmrecht der Banken – Ja oder Nein? *Die Aktiengesellschaft*, **41**(1): 11–26.

Busse von Colbe, W., Müller, E. and Reinhard, H. (eds) (1989) Aufstellung von Konzernabschlüssen, *ZfbF-Sonderheft 21/87*, 2nd edn.

Busse von Colbe, W., Geiger, K., Haase, H., Reinhard, H. and Schmitt, G. (eds) (2000) *Ergebnis je Aktie nach DVFA/SG*, 3rd edn, Schäffer/Poeschel, Stuttgart.

Evans, E., Eierle, B. and Haller, A. (2002) The Enforcer, *Accountancy*, **129** (January): 106–107.

Haller, A. (1992) The relationship of financial and tax accounting in Germany: A major reason for accounting disharmony in Europe. *International Journal of Accounting*, **27**(4): 310–323.

Haller, A. (2002) Financial accounting developments in the European Union: past events and future prospects. *European Accounting Review*, **11** (1); 153–190.

IdW (1986) Geänderter Entwurf einer Verlautbarung zur Währungsumrechnung im Jahres- und Konzernabschluß. *Die Wirtschaftsprüfung*, **39**: 664.

Machartina, K. and Langer, K. (2000) Financial reporting in Germany, in C. Nobes and R. Parker (eds), *Comparative International Accounting*, 6th edn, Prentice Hall, London, pp. 228–249.

Ordelheide, D. and Pfaff, D. (1994) *European Financial Reporting: Germany*, Routledge, London.

Schneider, D. (1995) The history of financial reporting in Germany, in P. Walton (ed.), *European Financial Reporting*, Academic Press, London, pp. 123–155.

Schröer, T. (1993) Company law and accounting in nineteenth-century Europe – Germany. *European Accounting Review*, **2**(2): 335–345.

Spanheimer, J. and Koch, Ch. (2000) Internationale Bilanzierungpraxis in Deutschland (Ergebnisse einer empirischen Untersuchung der Unternehmen des DAX und MDAX sowie des Neuen Marktes). *Die Wirtschaftsprüfung*, **53**: 301–310.

Working Group on External Financial Reporting of the Schmalenbach-Gesellschaft-Deutsche Gesellschaft für Betriebswirtschaft (1995) German Accounting Principles: An Institutionalized Framework. *Accounting Horizons*, **9**(3, September): 92–99.

Further Reading

Adler, Düring and Schmaltz (1995) Rechnungslegung und Prüfung der Unternehmen, in K. Forster, R. Goerdeler, J. Lanfermann and H. Müller *et al.* (eds), 6th edn, Poeschel, Stuttgart.

Baetge, J. (1990) Principles of proper bookkeeping and accounting, in E. Grochla *et al.* (eds), *Handbook of German Business Management*, Poeschel, Stuttgart, pp. 1815–1834.

Busse von Colbe, W. (1990) Consolidated accounts, in E. Grochla *et al.* (eds), *Handbook of German Business Management*, Poeschel, Stuttgart, pp. 474–493.

Busse von Colbe, W. (1992) Relationship between financial accounting, standards setting and practice in Germany. *European Accounting Review*, **1**(1): 27–38.

Coenenberg, A.G. (2000) *Jahresabschluß und Jahresabschlußanalyse*, 17th edn, miVerlag, Landsberg a. L.

Flower, J. (2002) *Global Financial Reporting*, Palgrave, Basingstoke, pp. 158–174.

Haller, A. (1995) International accounting harmonization – American hegemony or mutual recognition with benchmarks? Comments and additional notes from a German perspective. *European Accounting Review*, **4**(2): 235–247.

Layer, M. (1990) Business accounting principles and standards, in E. Grochla *et al.* (eds), *Handbook of German Business Management*, Poeschel, Stuttgart, pp. 240–246.

Moxter, A. (1990) Valuation of a going concern, in E. Grochla *et al.* (eds), *Handbook of German Business Management*, Poeschel, Stuttgart, pp. 2433–2444.

Ordelheide, D. (1993) True and fair view: A European and a German perspective. A commentary on *A European True and Fair View?* by David Alexander. *European Accounting Review*, **2**(1): pp. 81–90.

Ordelheide, D. (2001) Germany: Group Accounts, in D. Ordelheide and KPMG (eds), *Transnational Accounting, Vol. 2*, 2nd edn, Palgrave, Basingstoke, pp. 1353–1449.

Peltzer, M., Doyle, J. and Allen, M.-T. (2000) *Handelsgesetzbuch (deutsch/englische Textausgabe)*, 4th edn, Köln, Schmidt.

von Wysocki, K. (1993) Group accounting in Germany, in S.J. Gray, A.G. Coenenberg, and P.D. Gordon (eds), *International Group Accounting*, 2nd edn, Routledge, London, pp. 97–109.

Accounting in France

Christian Hoarau

For a long time, the main characteristic of the institutional structure of accounting in France, by comparison with the anglophone world, was the role of the state in accounting regulation. The particularly original feature of this is the Plan Comptable Général (PCG – general accounting plan). Supervision by the state, does not, however, prevent actors in the private sector, particularly from the profession, from exercising a significant influence, thanks to the practice of involving interested parties and a search for the widest possible consensus. But as a result of the development of international standard-setting, the large, listed companies and the major audit firms now play a more important role than they did in the past. France has also been one of the first countries to allow a divergence between the regulation of consolidated accounts and that of individual companies.

The legal framework of accounting consists of a series of fundamental laws and other statutory instruments which have been adopted since the introduction of the Fourth Directive in 1983. The objectives attributed both explicitly and implicitly to the French accounting system show that, as far as the accounting of individual companies is concerned, the function of providing a summary of transactions, particularly in relation to fiscal and social obligations, has priority over the decision usefulness of accounting information. Consolidated accounts, on the other hand, are disconnected from taxation, and to a certain extent from the rules applicable to individual accounts, and have, in contrast, an implicit objective of satisfying the information needs of the financial markets. They also represent the effects of internationalization on French accounting.

The development of international harmonization is likely to lead in time to a legal formalization of the duality of the French system and thus institutionalize a complete rupture between the accounts of individual companies prepared according to national rules, and the consolidated accounts, freed from the French framework in favour of international standards.

The institutional and legal framework

The term accounting regulation is used here to refer to the totality of rules applied to companies in the preparation and presentation of their financial statements. Contrary to the situation in Anglo-Saxon countries, accounting regulation in France is the prerogative of the public authorities, even though representatives of the private sector, and particularly accounting professionals, are closely associated with the creation of rules.

The process of establishing accounting regulation involves several institutions as sources of rules: the parliament, the government, the Comité de la Réglementation Comptable (CRC – Accounting Regulation Committee), and the Conseil National de la Comptabilité (CNC – National Accounting Council). The last two comprise the standard-setting organization in the strict sense. The Commission des Opérations de Bourse (COB – Stock market operations commission) has regulatory authority as regards listed companies.

Legislative and executive authorities

French accounting had very few statutory rules or government orders before parliament passed the law of 30 April 1983, known as the accounting law, which dealt with the har-monization of the accounting requirements of commercial businesses and certain other companies with the Fourth Directive. Since then, such statutes have provided an important means of defining the accounting framework. They include the following:

- Laws passed by parliament: the accounting law of 30 April 1983 and the law of 3 January 1985 on consolidated accounts which permitted the transposition of the Seventh European Directive into French law. The content of these laws is taken up in the Commercial Code (Code de Commerce).

- Decrees for the application of these laws issued by the government: accounting decree of 29 November 1983 and decree of 17 February 1986 relating to consolidated accounts.

- Two statutory orders ('arrêtés') issued by the Ministry of Finance: the first dated 22 June 1999 which endorsed ruling 99-03 of 29 April issued by the CRC, and substituted the 1999 PCG for the 1986 version. The second, also of 22 June 1999, which endorsed ruling 99-02 of 29 April 1999 issued by the CRC, which addresses accounting principles and methods to be used in the preparation of the consolidated accounts of commercial companies and public sector enterprises.

In parallel to the fundamental accounting statutes which modified the existing basic laws such as the Code de Commerce (articles 8 to 17) or the main statute on commercial com-panies, the law of 24 July 1966, there are many individual laws which may also have an accounting effect, such as fiscal laws, social laws or those relating to the economy. In the face of this dispersion of accounting rules in several laws, decrees and statutory orders, parliament authorized the government in 1999 to restructure the legislative part of the Commercial Code, thereby allowing the various statutes affecting accounting to be brought together in one place. The new Commercial Code came into force on 22 September 2000.

The re-writing of the old code was done on the basis of not changing any of the exist-ing regulations, but the code itself changed completely. The new code now has more than 1800 articles concerning private business which were not in the old one. In particular the 1966 companies law was essentially abolished and put into the code, as well as the law of 1 March 1984 and its decree of 1 March 1985 concerning the prevention and settlement of difficulties in companies.

The articles which were in the previous code (8 to 17-4) have become articles L 123-12 to L123-28 of the new code. The 1966 companies law has been taken up in the following articles: annual accounts are in articles L 232-1 to L232-20; subsidiaries, associates and controlled companies are to be found in L 233-1 to L233-15; and finally consolidated accounts are in L 233-16 to L233-27.

The hierarchy of statutes which form the accounting law is the same as that of common law: European directive, law, decree, ministerial order.

We shall first examine briefly the content of the fundamental laws, which are the source of accounting rules, and then examine the links between accounting rules and tax rules.

The fundamental statutes

The accounting law of 30 April 1983 and its decree determine the accounting obligations of commercial businesses, commercial companies and civil companies that are authorized to issue public securities. They provide the legal basis for a body of accounting doctrine which includes the compulsory financial statements, the conventions for keeping accounts and the valuation rules.

The law of 3 January 1985 and the decree of 17 February 1986 together with the ministerial order of 9 December 1986 prescribe the accounting rules for consolidated financial statements. The principal articles of the law and decree amend and amplify the law of 24 July 1966 on commercial companies and its decree of 23 March 1967.

The Plan Comptable Général (PCG – general accounting plan), which was for many years the main instrument of French standard-setting, is now used only for the individual accounts of companies. It is a publication which brings together general principles, terminology, valuation rules, official titles for accounts and model financial statements. It is created and kept up to date by the CNC.

The cornerstone of regulation and the French accounting model, the PCG is a product of history. A German concept initially, the chart of accounts was introduced into France during the years of Occupation when the Vichy regime created, by a decree of 22 April 1941, an Inter-ministry Commission with the task of preparing and introducing a national accounting plan for different sectors of industry. This plan was finished in 1941–42 and published in 1943, but it was never officially promulgated and its application was limited to certain businesses in the aeronautical sector. The 1942 plan was inspired by a German accounting plan, known as the Goering Plan, which had been adopted by the Nazi regime in 1937 and used the methods for calculating costs that had been developed by CEGOS.[1]

After liberation, the public authorities, and in particular those responsible for the state's five-year economic plans, took up again the idea of a national accounting chart, in particular to use it as an instrument of macroeconomic management. A Commission was set up by a decree of 4 April 1946 with the task of preparing a new accounting plan. Adopted in 1947 the PCG, while retaining some relationship with the 1942 plan, marked an important development from there: it clearly separated accounts relating to financial accounting from those concerned with management accounting, rather than integrating them. In the context of the reconstruction of the economy and the installation of a planning system, the PCG offers a macroeconomic view of the business, while facilitating external checking by the tax authorities or banks.

The PCG has since been revised three times. The first change was in 1957. It had been worked on by the Conseil Supérieur de la Comptabilité, which had been formed in 1947 to replace the Commission de Normalisation des Comptabilités, and which itself became the Conseil National de la Comptabilité (CNC) in 1957.

Given the responsibility for the application and adaptation of the PCG, the CNC started the second revision in 1971. This work was finished in 1982, having substantially modified the PCG to take account of the economic, social and technical evolution of the business environment and above all the obligations conveyed by European accounting harmonization.

By comparison with the previous plans, the 1982 PCG retained its major characteristics while introducing substantial improvements in two areas. It set out general principles that should guide the search for a true and fair view (image fidèle), which although somewhat brief, more clearly reflected the needs of financial analysis and management. The PCG preserved from its predecessors a terminology, a chart of accounts using a decimal code system, an allocation of entries to classes of accounts organized as either balance sheet classes or profit and loss classes, a detailed description of the functioning of the accounts, and standard formats for the balance sheet and profit and loss account. Conceived as a complete and coherent accounting system, the PCG allows regulation to extend right across the field from prime entry through to published financial statements.

The PCG was once again revised in 1999 (CRC ruling 99-03). The new version was done without changing the legal framework and did not introduce any major changes for individual company accounts. The new framework, which has numbered articles, makes it easier to insert later modifications. Subsequent changes have concerned the rules for long-term contracts, changes of accounting policy and the definition of liabilities. These were changed in CRC rulings 99-08 and 99-09 (endorsed by ministerial order on 20 December 1999) and ruling 2000-06 (ministerial order of 17 January 2001).

In its current form the PCG has five parts: the objectives and principles of accounting are in Section I, the definitions of assets, liabilities, equity, revenues and expenses are in Section II, accounting and valuation rules Section III, bookkeeping and the structure of the ledger in Section IV and financial statements in Section V.

Since 1947 the field of application of the plan has widened. Today it covers the following sectors: industrial and commercial businesses in both private and public sector, agricultural businesses, public administrative establishments, local authorities, legal entities constituted under non-commercial private law with an economic activity, banks and insurance companies. But regulation does not mean standardization. The PCG can be adapted in the form of specialized industry modifications or individual plans, if the needs of an industry sector or kind of activity justify it. Adaptations for special sectors need formal approval from the CNC.

The influence of taxation on the accounting rules

This influence is exercised primarily on the individual company accounts. The accounting rules relating to individual companies must be followed, even if the tax law does not require it, or indeed imposes different requirements. But this independence of the accounting rules from taxation is relative. In general terms a desire to reduce taxation motivates businesses to make accounting choices that are the most advantageous from a tax perspective. Exceptions to the principle of separation equally spring from the tax authorities who make it a condition of enjoying tax advantages in the area of depreciation and provisions that the charges are reflected in the company's accounts. Businesses are therefore obliged to recognize in their accounts all the depreciation and provisions which they wish to claim as tax deductions, even when these do not reflect an economically realistic write-down or liability. The regulators have provided special profit and loss account and balance sheet items (account 14, 'provisions réglementées' regulated provisions) to enable accounts users to identify the effect of tax derogations on the accounting rules.

In determining the taxable profit, which is the basis of assessment for company taxation, companies are required to follow the rules of the PCG, unless these are incompatible with the tax rules in the Code Général des Impôts (CGI – General Tax Code). The tax form for the declaration of profits consists essentially of the individual company accounts (balance sheet, profit and loss account and notes) prepared according to the accounting rules and a special reconciliation schedule for the calculation of the taxable profit according to the CGI rules, starting from the accounting profit. As a consequence, when there is a conflict between the tax rules and the accounting ones, the differences are reflected in a deduction or an addition in the schedule for determining taxable profit.

In the consolidated accounts, the connection between taxation and accounting is neutralized. Companies are supposed to eliminate from the individual accounts included in the consolidation those entries that have been made purely to comply with fiscal rules (in particular investment subsidies, depreciation and provisions). In addition, consolidated financial statements report deferred taxation, whereas single company statements show only tax immediately payable.

The consolidated accounts are not, in principle, constrained by fiscal considerations. Furthermore, their preparation involves no fiscal consequences except for a very limited number of companies which have chosen to have their company profits assessed under either the system for fiscal integration of companies where more than 95% of shares are held, or the global profit system, or the system of consolidated profits.

Conseil National de la Comptabilité (CNC)

The CNC currently has 58 members. These can be split into three groups:

1. A president and six vice-presidents. The vice presidents are the director of public accounting, the president of the Ordre des Experts Comptables, the president of the Compagnie Nationale des Commissaires aux Comptes, two representatives of corporations and one representative of non-governmental associations.

2. Forty individuals who are competent in accounting matters and represent the economic world (practising accountants, company accountants, financial analysts, employee representatives, etc.)

3. Eleven representatives of the government and its agencies (different ministries, Cour des Comptes, COB, Banking Commission etc.)

The members of the CNC are organized for working purposes into five specialist sections:

1. company accounting;
2. international standards;
3. other organizations (voluntary associations, public establishments, etc.);
4. organizations which come under the authority of the banking and finance regulatory committee;
5. organizations regulated by the insurance code, mutual organizations and pension organizations regulated by the social security code.

Apart from these sections, there is a commission for management accounting and there are working groups.

The CNC was last re-organized under Decree 96-749 of 26 April 1996. Under article 2 of that decree, the CNC's mission is to issue opinions (*avis*) and recommendations on accounting for all economic sectors. In cooperation with the competent services, associations and organizations, it is specifically mandated with

- giving a preliminary view on all dispositions of an accounting nature, where they originate in France or within the European Union;
- giving an opinion on standards issued by international or foreign standard-setting bodies;

- putting forward all measures relating to the exploitation of accounts, either in the interests of companies and professional associations, or for the purposes of establishing national statistics or budgets and national accounts.

The CNC has its own 'due process' by which it issues its *avis* and recommendations. The first stage is the choice of a subject and the appointment of the chairman of a working group. This is normally done by the president of the CNC with the help of the staff. The chairman of a working group would normally be a member of the CNC. After this, a working group is formed and starts work.

In the second stage, the working group prepares a technical document which is submitted to whichever of the five sections is responsible for the group's work. The technical document is discussed by the section and work moves forward to drafting a preliminary recommendation. Generally speaking there is an iterative process during which the drafts are commented on by the section and then re-drafted, etc.

In the third stage, the proposed *avis* or regulation is approved by the section and passes on to a full meeting of the CNC. At this fourth stage, a simple majority of the CNC members present has to approve the draft and expresses the wish that the obligatory parts of the draft should be endorsed by the CRC. There is a full meeting of the CNC once a quarter and the quorum consists of half of the appointed members.

In the fifth stage, the document is published on the CNC's website (www.finances.gouv.fr/CNCompta) and in the quarterly journal of the CNC and the proposed regulation is passed over to the CRC.

Since 1996 the CNC also has an urgent issues task force, the *comité d'urgence*. This consists of the president of the CNC and the six vice-presidents, together with representatives of the ministry of the economy, of Justice and of the Budget, and a representative of the COB. This committee can be asked to take a position on any accounting matter requiring an urgent decision. It is obliged to publish its views within three months.

Comité de la Réglementation Comptable (CRC)

Created in 1998, the CRC is the ultimate authority in French standard-setting. It sets no standards itself, but gives statutory force to standards which have been drafted by others. It has 15 members. It is chaired by the Minister for Economy and Finance (or a representative of the minister). It includes the Minister of Justice and the Minister of the Budget (or their representatives), a member of the Conseil d'Etat (constitutional body), a member of the Cour des Comptes (supreme authority on government accounting), a member of the appeal court, the president of the COB, the president of the CNC, the president of the Ordre des Experts Comptables, the president of the Compagnie Nationale des Commissaires aux Comptes, three representatives of business and two representatives of organized labour (all of whom must be members of the CNC).

The CRC has the right, under law 98-261 of 6 April 1998, to establish both general and industry-specific rules which apply to all moral or physical persons who are obliged to maintain accounts. Only legal entities which are constituted under public law and subject to the rules of public accounting are excluded from this. The CRC makes decisions on a simple majority, and the chairman has a casting vote. In order to gain statutory force, its rulings have to be endorsed by ministerial orders, signed by the Ministers of the Economy, Justice, the Budget, and, in the case of any sector-specific rule, the ministry responsible for the relevant sector. These are published in the official journal.

Commission des Opérations de Bourse (COB)

The COB is an autonomous public institution created by a government order in 1967, which has since had its powers reinforced by several laws. Its functions are to oversee the protection of investment, information for investors and the proper functioning of the markets. To meet its duties the COB has regulatory power, power to refer matters to the courts and power of enquiry. Its decisions, which have a general application, can take the form of regulations, instructions, recommendations, opinions and proposals for the modification of statutes to regulations.

The COB's regulations can be issued in the field of the functioning of the financial markets, or may prescribe rules of professional practice, in particular in the area of publication of financial information, which are binding upon issuers of public securities. These rules are endorsed by the Ministry of Finance before being published in the Journal Officiel. The COB also contributes to accounting doctrine both through its annual report – destined for the President of the Republic – and through its instructions and recommendations published in its monthly bulletin. Its opinions, on the other hand, are considered simply as interpretations.

The accounting profession

If the accounting profession is not responsible for regulation, unlike its Anglo-Saxon counterparts, it does none the less play an essential role before, during and after the creation of standards. A particular feature of the profession is the existence of two separate professional bodies, one for those offering accounting services (expert-comptables – expert accountants) and the other for auditors (albeit most professionals are members of both bodies), and the fact that those members who move to work in industry and commerce automatically lose their membership.

Ordre des Experts Comptables (OEC)

The OEC's object is the defence of the honour and independence of the profession which it represents. It has delegated to it from the state a power of control over the competence and morality of its members (some 16 320 in 2001) granted to protect the public. Originally created under the Vichy regime in 1942, as were many other professional orders, the OEC is a reflection of the corporatist thinking of the time, and the desire, already apparent towards the end of the 1930s, to impose ethical standards on the professions. After liberation and the re-establishment of republican law, the OEC's existence was legitimized by a government order of 19 September 1945, issued by the provisional government of the French Republic. It has since been modified a number of times – 1968, 1994 and 1995.

An organization formed under private law but with a civil personality, the OEC is under the supervision of the Ministry of Finance. At its head is the Conseil Supérieur, which represents the profession in its dealings with the state. The president of the Conseil Supérieur (who is *ex officio* a vice-president of the CNC and a member of the CRC) and those other accountants who are members of the CNC exercise a significant influence in the preparation of accounting standards.

In addition to this, the Conseil Supérieur plays an important role as concerns accounting principle and practice through the medium of the opinions published by its Comité Professionel de Doctrine Comptable (professional committee on accounting doctrine) for the use of its members. These opinions, which are not binding upon business, concern accounting principles, the role of the expert-accountant and professional behaviour. The opinions of accounting principle generally serve to amplify official regulations or detail applications.

Compagnie Nationale des Commissaires aux Comptes (CNCC)

In its present form,[2] this was created by a decree of 12 August 1969, which gave it legal form and placed it under the supervision of the Ministry of Justice. The CNCC is responsible for all commissaires aux comptes (auditors), of which there were 16 400 in 2001, of whom about 90% are also expert-accountants, and defends their material and moral interests. It is run by a Conseil Supérieur which represents the CNCC vis-á-vis the public authorities and proposes measures for the organization of the profession and for the conduct of audit engagements. In application of legal and regulatory requirements, it prepares auditing standards and commentaries relating to ethical issues and the conduct of audits, and publishes technical information.

The secretariat has standing committees to prepare its assessments, opinions and recommendations. Within this, its Commission des Etudes Comptables (accounting studies committee) has a particular duty to identify problems arising from the application of accounting rules, and to offer answers to technical problems referred to it by auditors. When their content has a general application, the responses and opinions of the Commission are published in the bulletin of the CNCC's Conseil National. Aside from its participation in the CRC and CNC, the CNCC contributes to accounting doctrine through its opinions, although perhaps more through necessity than desire.

International accounting standards

The IASB's standards exert a certain influence on accounting regulation, in particular as far as consolidated accounts are concerned. Aimed primarily at the financial markets, the consolidated statements are prepared using valuation and presentation rules which are sometimes not in line with the Code de Commerce and are not accepted for the preparation of individual company accounts, but which allow an alignment with international practices. This situation leads to a separation of the consolidated accounts from the underlying company accounts.

According to the annual survey of published accounts carried out by Deloitte & Touche, KPMG, Ernst &Young and Mazars & Guérard,[3] the largest French groups refer unanimously to French accounting principles in the notes to their accounts, since the publication of CRC regulation 99-02 on consolidated accounts. There has been little evolution in the choice of foreign accounting principles in the last two years. In 2000, from a sample of 34 of the 40 members of CAC40 index, 10 also referred to US GAAP and 3 to IAS (against 10 and 2 in 1999, and 8 and 7 in 1998).

Evidently the situation in France will change in due course as a result of the EU decision to make the use of IAS (or IFRS) compulsory for listed groups from 2005. It is expected that the CNC will allow unlisted companies which have to prepare consolidated accounts a free choice as between IFRS and national rules.

The objectives, underlying hypotheses and qualitative characteristics of financial statements

The financial statements comprise the annual accounts and the cash flow statement, although preparation of the latter is obligatory only in the notes to consolidated accounts. Individual company accounts or consolidated accounts comprise the balance sheet, profit and loss account and notes, which form an indivisible whole. While a cash flow statement is not generally required for individual company accounts, it is obligatory for certain companies under the law on the prevention of business difficulties (see below).

Individual accounts or consolidated accounts must be prepared in accordance with the requirements of the Commercial Code the regulations of the CRC and the PCG. The latter, which was the only instrument of accounting regulation until 1983 and remains the cornerstone today for individual accounts, does not give, in any explicit way, a predominant place to the question of the users of financial statements and the satisfaction of their needs.

In its introduction, the PCG 1999 says that accounting is a system for organizing financial information which enables the collection, classification and recording of basic figures and permits the preparation of statements which give a true and fair view of the capital, the financial position and the results of the entity at the balance sheet date. It does not at any point indicate explicitly who are the users concerned, what needs are to be met, and to what degree these should be satisfied. An analysis of the representations of the firm which are implicit in the PCG shows in fact that this tries to satisfy, without always doing so, many needs which are either indeterminate or not well understood, of a range of users who are never explicitly identified (Hoarau 1992).

It is generally agreed that the consolidated financial statements, which are for the most part prepared by listed companies, have the implicit objective of meeting the information needs of stock exchange investors. But this objective is not clearly stated in any rule. The compromising or transactional nature of French regulation, and the wish of the CNC to seek the widest consensus amongst its members, implies the retention, up to a point, of a certain fluidity in the objectives assigned to financial information, and in particular a need to avoid identifying privileged users and needs to be met (Colasse 1991). This characteristic of the French process of regulation is called into question by the pressure of international harmonization, just as the unity of the French accounting system has already been damaged by the Seventh Directive and the CRC Regulation 99-02. This could develop into a total disconnection between the rules for individual company accounts and those for consolidated accounts, whose objective of providing information useful for investment decisions could then be clearly identified.

Objectives of financial statements

Prior to the introduction of the true and fair view into French regulations by the law of 30 April 1983, the PCG only fixed requirements relating to the preparation of statements: regularity and sincerity were to be observed. Subsequently, if financial statements are not aimed at meeting precise and explicit information needs, they must none the less meet a triple requirement of regularity, sincerity and a true and fair view. Companies have a certain flexibility in the presentation of their accounts, depending on their size, and groups of companies benefit from some exemptions from the normal rules.

The 1983 accounting law, following the Fourth Directive, has added to the old requirements of regularity and sincerity an obligation for the preparer of financial statements which bears truly upon the effect: a true and fair view of the information communicated to the readers of the accounts. Indisputably a quality attaching to the end-product, the provision of a true and fair view presupposes a regular and sincere application of accounting principles. However, in the case of a conflict between the true and fair view and regularity, which should be an exceptional event, the law provides for a relaxation of accounting rules. All the same, the use of valuation or presentation rules for the consolidated accounts which are different from those used for the individual accounts can lead perfectly legally to two different true and fair views.

Regularity and sincerity correspond respectively to an obligation regarding the means of accounting and a moral obligation (Alexander and Burlaud 1993). Regularity is defined by the PCG as 'conformity with the rules and procedures in force'. Annual accounts will be regular if they satisfy the requirements of the accounting regulations, particularly by respecting the fundamental principles such as those imposed by the Commercial Code. Regularity assumes that the business has put in hand the means of confirming, for example through the organization of its accounting systems and its control procedures, that the legal obligations are systematically observed. Regularity is a necessary but not a sufficient condition of good information.

It is augmented by sincerity. The PCG defines this 'as the application in good faith of the rules and procedures in the light of the knowledge which those responsible for the accounts should normally have of the realities and size of the operations, events and situations'. Sincerity implies the good faith of the person who is preparing the accounts, but equally their concern to describe the operations and events in a way that is adequate, faithful, clear, precise and complete. Objective sincerity supposes some degree of fair representation.

A major principle of the Fourth Directive, the idea of the true and fair view, is a French translation (image fidèle) of the British accounting concept. Introduced into national law by the 1983 accounting law (which modified the Commercial Code), it also appears in the general principles, and in the rules for the preparation of the financial statements in the PCG. It is often mentioned but never defined, either by the accounting law, or by the PCG. It applies to the net worth, the financial position and the results of the business.

The absence of a rigorous definition reinforces the link between a true and fair view of the annual accounts and following the obligations for regularity, notably in applying accounting principles, and for sincerity. If these conditions seem necessary in order to presume that a true and fair view is given, they are also insufficient. Regularity may even be an obstacle to the presentation of a true and fair view. Article 123-14 of the Commercial Code specifies 'when the application of an accounting requirement is not sufficient to give a true and fair view, supplementary information should be given in the notes'. Furthermore, it adds that

> If, in an exceptional case, an accounting rule makes it impossible to obtain a true and fair view of the net worth, financial position or results, it should not be followed. This relaxation should be mentioned in the notes together with the explanation for it and an indication of its effect on the net worth, financial position and results of the business.

This possibility of a relaxation of the rules is also provided in the PCG. In the end, if accounting rules do not permit the achievement of a true and fair view, further information should be given. And in the possible case of a contradiction between regularity and fairness, the right to deviate from the rules in exceptional cases gives the true and fair view primacy. The notion of a true and fair view appears therefore as the true object to be attained.

The qualitative characteristics of accounting information

Table 5.1 has been drawn up to provide a comparison between the characteristics mentioned in the frameworks of the IASC and those that are explicit or implicit in French regulation relating to individual accounts or consolidated accounts.

Publication and audit of financial statements

Since the law of 24 July 1966, commercial companies have been obliged to publish their financial statements. For listed companies, their quarterly, six-monthly and annual statements must be submitted to the COB. The financial statements are subject to audit by *commissaires aux comptes* before being distributed to shareholders and published. From 1935 to the present, the development of audit has been characterized by three major preoccupations in terms of legislation: the reinforcement of the independence of auditors, the raising of their standards of technical competence and the widening of the scope and application of audit checks.

Public limited companies (sociétés anonymes), private limited companies (sociétés à responsabilité limitée) and partnerships controlled by limited companies must, in the month following the annual shareholders' meeting, file at the local commercial court a copy of the annual accounts, the management report, the auditors' report, the proposal for dividend and the minutes of the annual meeting. If the company is required to prepare consolidated accounts, it must also provide two copies of its consolidated accounts. Listed companies must also file with these documents two copies of a list of financial investments with valuations as at balance sheet date.

Table 5.1 Qualitative characteristics of financial statements

Qualities	IASB	Individual	Group
Intelligibility/Comprehension	x	Not explicit	Not explicit
Decision-useful	x	x	x
Materiality	x	x	x
Reliability	x	Regularity sincerity	Regularity sincerity
True and fair	x	x undefined	x undefined
Substance over form	x	Not recognized	x
Objectivity/neutrality	x	Linked to taxation	x
Prudence	x	x	x
Completeness	x	x	x
Comparability	x	x	x
Consistency	x	x	x
Timeliness	x	Unknown	Unknown
Cost/benefit	x	Unknown	Implicit
Verifiability	–	Implicit (regularity)	Implicit (regularity)
Regularity	–	x	x
Accounting choice	–	Unknown (contrary to regularity)	x

These documents can be consulted by anyone asking at the Commercial Court to see them (and are available via the Minitel data system). However, it should be emphasized that some companies prefer to pay the €2000 fine and not file their accounts.

In addition to these formalities, which are intended to ensure public information, listed companies (about 730 in total in the main and second markets) are obliged, under the control of the COB to publish information about their financial position periodically in the *Bulletin des Annonces Légales Obligatoires* (BALO).

The annual data appear both before and after the annual meeting. Within four months of the balance sheet date, and at least two weeks before the annual meeting, the company must publish the annual accounts, the dividend proposal, and, if relevant, the consolidated accounts in the BALO, mentioning specifically that these are unaudited draft figures. In the 45 days following the annual meeting the company must publish its figures in the BALO again: annual accounts approved by the shareholders, accompanied by the audit report and the dividend decision approved by the shareholders, the consolidated accounts and the audit report on those. If there has been no change to the drafts which were initially published, the company may simply make a reference to the original publication while publishing the audit report.

Six-monthly figures must be published within four months of the end of the first half year. Within this period the company must publish in the BALO a profit and loss account, and a report for the six months. These must be accompanied by a report from the auditors confirming the sincerity of the information. If the company prepares consolidated figures, it must publish consolidated data instead of individual company figures, but also the turnover and net profit of the parent company.

The quarterly figures, which are much more modest, should be provided within 45 days of the end of each quarter. These should be simply the turnover for the quarter, together with figures for the previous quarters in the same year and the same quarter in the previous year. If the company is obliged to prepare consolidated accounts, then consolidated turnover must also be given, as well as an analysis by industry segment, unless the company considers that such information would be prejudicial to its interests.

Audit of financial statements

First introduced into France by the law on companies of 24 July 1867, statutory audit is nowadays carried out under the requirements of the law on companies of 24 July 1966, amended principally by the law of 1 March 1984 on the prevention of business difficulties.

The profession of auditor (*commissaire aux comptes*) is regulated by the decree of 12 August 1969, which provides in particular that no one may operate as an auditor unless they are entered, either as an individual or a firm, on a register held for that purpose by regional commissions based in the same town as the regional court of appeal. Inclusion on this register depends upon being able to provide appropriate guarantees of integrity and having a recognized professional qualification. The audit profession has 16 400 members, of which 90% are also expert-accountants, and nearly 87% are individuals. The industry's turnover in 2000 was of the order of €1.5bn.

Many organizations are required to have an audit. The appointment of at least one auditor is required of all companies which issue shares (sociétés anonymes, sociétés en commandite) and economic interest groupings which have more than 100 employees or issue bonds. Certain other types of legal entity are required to appoint an auditor when they exceed two of the three following size limits: total assets €1.55 mn, turnover €3.1 mn or 50 employees. The entities concerned are private limited companies (sociétés à responsabilité limitée), partnerships or similar collective organizations and non-commercial legal entities formed under private law but having an economic activity (for example some associations with social or medical objectives).

The widening of the application of statutory audit is an expression of the fact that the regularity of the entity's operations and the viability of its financial information are of interest not only to its members or direct partners but also to a wider public. In this spirit compulsory audit has been extended in recent years to sports associations and political parties.

The appointment of the auditor is made by the annual general meeting, or similar authority. The auditor is given a mandate for six years, which can be renewed indefinitely. The audit fees are paid by the entity being audited. The auditor has extensive powers to demand information and to conduct enquiries, and may perform at any time whatever checks and tests are thought necessary.

The audit objectives are defined by the law. These include both general and specific checks. The general audit missions fall into four principal categories: the conduct of the annual audit leading to the annual report, the extension of the annual audit to cover the legality and sincerity of specific items, a mission related to the prevention of business difficulties, a mission to provide information for certain organizations and individuals identified by the law (the managing body of the enterprise, the public prosecutor, the employee committee, etc.). The specific checks are numerous and consist basically in certifying the regularity or reality of certain transactions made by the business, such as modifications in its share capital or merger with another company.

The principal mission, that of the statutory audit, consists of reporting that the financial statements prepared by the company meet the legal requirements of regularity, sincerity and giving a true and fair view (art. 228, para 1 of the law of 24 July 1966). The auditor supplies a general report composed of two parts: a first part, which gives the opinion concerning the annual accounts, and a second part, which gives details of the additional specific verifications required by the law which have no consequence on the overall opinion. There are three forms of certificate: an unreserved opinion, an opinion subject to reservation, and a refusal to certify.

A particular feature of the French system is the link between the auditor and the justice system. At one time the auditor was almost a court official (Mikol 1993). The special duties of the auditor include an obligation to report to the public prosecutor details of any crime encountered in the course of the audit. Since 1984 the auditor has also had a role to play in providing an early warning of business difficulty. If the auditor, in the course of the audit, comes to the conclusion that the business is heading into difficulties and potentially faces liquidation, he or she must so advise the managing director, who should in turn produce a plan for remedial action. In the event that the managing director does not do this, or fails to satisfy the auditor, the next step is to convene the board of directors, and if that fails to yield results, eventually the auditor must appeal to the commercial court to intervene (Collins 1992).

The components of financial statements

The annual report of a company consists generally of the annual accounts, the cash flow or financing statement, the auditors' report and the management report. The annual accounts consist of the balance sheet, profit and loss account and notes to the accounts. These documents form, according to the law, an indissoluble whole. As far as *individual accounts* are concerned, the accounting decree of 29 November 1983 fixes, in conformity with the Fourth Directive, the elements that must appear in the balance sheet, profit and loss account and notes.

As far as *group accounts* are concerned, the statutes are the Commercial Code, the law of 3 January 1985 and its decree of 17 February 1986 (which provided for the adoption of the Seventh Directive in French law) and subsequently the CRC ruling 99-02.

This last constituted a profound change for French companies, particularly as regards the rules of consolidation and valuation and the disclosure of financial information. The regulation made it obligatory for companies to include in their consolidated accounts a cash flow statement (in the notes), a statement of changes in equity, segment information by business sector or geographical area, and a calculation of earnings per share (basic and diluted). Companies must indicate if they have deviated from recommended accounting principles and provide full information on any special purpose entities excluded from consolidation. The principle changes introduced by the CRC 99-02 ruling could be seen as introducing greater convergence with international standards (IFRS).

Individual company accounts

The PCG provides three systems for the presentation of the financial statements of individual companies, whose use depends upon the size of the company: the basic system, the abbreviated system and the extended system. Operating from a common base, these systems differ in terms of the quantity and detail of the information provided.

The basic system comprises the minimum accounting requirements which must be observed by medium-sized and large companies. The abbreviated system is intended for companies whose size does not justify use of the basic system. The extended system offers, in addition to the requirements of the basic system, further documents which provide analysis of the figures with a view to explaining more fully the company's management. It includes: a model balance sheet, profit and loss account, notes, a table which analyses margins and other aspects of the profit and loss account, a schedule showing the company's internally generated cash flow, and a cash flow statement. This system is voluntary. Companies can adopt it completely, or only in part.

As already indicated, consolidated financial statements are prepared according to rules that in certain cases deviate from the Commercial Code. Companies can then use valuation methods for their consolidated accounts that are not authorized for individual company accounts.

The balance sheet should include as many headings as are necessary to give a true and fair view of the net worth, financial situation and profit or loss. The standardized format used for the PCG establishes as close as possible a relationship between the balance sheet headings on the one hand and the situations and economic and financial operations in which the company engages, classified according to their function, on the other hand. The assets are classified according to their use or objective (fixed assets, current assets linked to operations, non-operating current assets, bank and treasury items, deferred items). The liabilities and equity items are classified according to their origin and not according to their maturity date (shareholders' capital, other components of equity, provisions for liabilities, loans, trade creditors, non-trade creditors).

The profit and loss account summarizes the revenues and expenses, and shows the profit or loss for the period as a difference after deduction of depreciation and provisions. The standard presentation of the profit and loss account, in either horizontal or vertical form, is based on classifying revenues and expenses according to their nature, thereby totally dissociating financial accounting and management accounting perspectives.

The revenues and expenses, classified according to their nature, are presented in such an order that the final result can be broken down into: the operating result (operating revenues less ordinary operating expenses); the financial result (financial revenue less financial expenses); and the extraordinary result (extraordinary income less extraordinary expenses). The ordinary result is the sum of the operating and financial results. The net profit or loss is the sum of the ordinary and extraordinary results, after deduction of corporate income tax, and the share of profit attributable to employees. The structure that has been used makes it possible to distinguish between items involving cash flow and others (depreciation and provisions), as well as to calculate directly the value added, the gross operating margin and the net operating cash flow of the business. It is, however, often criticized by those who prefer a classification of expenses by function.

The legal framework provides two essential criteria for determining what information should be given in the notes to the accounts: their contribution to a true and fair view, and their materiality. The quantity of information varies according to the size of the business, but its presentation is organized round three headings: accounting principles and methods, information that supplements the figures in the balance sheet and profit and loss account, and other information. The accounting decree provides a minimum list of items to appear in the notes.

Consolidated accounts

The consolidated balance sheet is presented in the horizontal format (albeit companies which used the vertical format prior to the CRC ruling 99-02 may continue to do so). It is based on a shareholder approach: equity includes only the interests of the shareholders in the parent company. Minority interests, considered as quasi-debt, is displayed between shareholders' equity and provisions.

The profit and loss account is presented in vertical format (or potentially in horizontal format) with revenues and expenses classified either by nature or by function. Whichever form is used, the statement should include the following lines: net consolidated turnover, profit or loss after tax for all companies that are fully consolidated and proportion of profit or loss for companies accounted for by the equity method. Drawn from Anglo-Saxon accounting, the profit and loss account organized by function has been adopted by the largest groups.

As far as the notes are concerned, the information is to be given under the following main headings: general principles, basic system of GAAP applied, consolidation method, valuation rules, details of scope of consolidation, comparability of the accounts, detailed notes on the balance sheet and income statement and changes in these, other information (in particular segment information and cash flow statement).

Cash flow statement

The publication of a cash flow statement is obligatory, in consolidated accounts. It is not compulsory for individual accounts even though its preparation may be required under the law of 1 March 1984 concerning the prevention of business difficulties. In practice about two-thirds of listed companies publish a cash flow statement in their annual report. The model used is similar to IAS7.

Management report

A management report (Rapport de Gestion) is obligatory for all commercial companies and credit institutions. It includes three broad types of information: (1) compulsory information dealing with the economic situation of the company or group, including in particular a review of its business operations and operating result; (2) compulsory information dealing with the legal life of the group, and in particular any significant shareholdings, the body of shareholders and any cross-shareholdings; (3) compulsory information concerning the social affairs of the group, and particularly the personnel and the management.

Valuation methods and accounting principles

Table 5.2 shows the principal differences between French accounting rules and IAS.

Table 5.2 Comparison of French principles with IAS

IAS	French rules
1	The principle of substance over form, discussed in the Framework and also in IAS 1 is not recognized except for consolidated accounts. Its practical application in France gives rise to two significant differences with IAS as far as concerns special purpose entities and in-substance defeasance. In the first case the CRC Regulation 99-02 has maintained legal ownership as a condition for consolidation of an SPE. This condition, provided by art. L233-18 of the Commercial Code, is a derogation from substance over form. In the second case French standards, unlike IAS 39, do not prohibit the derecognition of assets and liabilities linked to defeasance. According to French rules (CRC 99-02 §40) goodwill should appear in the consolidated balance sheet on a separate line after intangible assets. According to IAS 1 this item should be included in intangibles.
2	LIFO is forbidden for individual accounts.
8	A French profit and loss account routinely includes both ordinary and extraordinary items. According to IAS 8 many of the things included in the French extraordinary result should be in the ordinary section.
11	Regulation CRC 99-02 proposes the percentage of completion method for long term contracts as a preferred method (see below) whereas it is obligatory for IAS 11 if the outcome of the contract can be predicted with reasonable certainty.
12	CRC 99-02 allows discounting of deferred tax assets and liabilities while IAS 12 forbids it. The French rules do not permit the creation of a deferred tax provision for intangible assets which are not amortized which cannot be sold separately from the business (particularly brands and market share). IAS 12 does not make any exception to the recognition of deferred tax on all valuation differences.
14	In general the amount of information to be provided in the notes is less detailed than that required by IAS. In particular segment reporting is less demanding in the following areas: no primary and secondary reporting format, less precise definition of segments, no requirement to create a new segment when the company organization does not correspond with the standard.
16&18	The French rules do not provide for any discounting of values in the event of deferred payment, while IAS 16 on property plant and equipment and IAS 18 *Revenue Recognition* require it. Discounting is recommended however by the COB and the OEC.
17	The recognition of assets obtained under a finance lease is a preferred method under CRC 99-02 while it is obligatory under IAS 17.
19	Accounting for pension provisions is not obligatory in individual accounts. Nevertheless the PCG 1999 considers it a desirable method which gives better financial information. In the consolidated accounts CRC 99-02 recognizes the creation of provisions for pensions and post-employment benefits as a preferred method, without giving any indication of what actuarial methods to use.

Table 5.2 Comparison of French principles with IAS (*continued*)

IAS	French rules
20	In individual company accounts, government grants can either be treated as deferred credits and be amortized over time to the income statement, or can be recognized in full in the period when made. In group accounts CRC 99-02 does not allow grants to be taken up in the income statement. Certain groups have therefore taken them directly to equity. IAS 20 forbids their treatment as an equity item.
21	IAS 21 makes no distinction between realized exchange differences and translation differences on individual transactions. All of these must be taken to the profit and loss account, whether gain or loss. In individual accounts in France only potential losses cause a provision to be made. Unrealized gains are not recognized. For group accounts, CRC 99-02 says that recognition of all differences in the profit and loss account is the preferred treatment.
22	CRC 99-02 includes a derogation which allows a kind of pooling of interests to take place under certain conditions (see text). Otherwise the acquisition method as in IAS 22 is followed. In calculating goodwill, CRC 99-02 allows for the recognition of patents, brands, client lists and market share and there are no rules for amortization. The latter two are generally included in goodwill under IAS 22, although not in its replacement. Goodwill has to be amortized over its useful life, with no limits specified in the French rules.
31	According to CRC 99-02, the transfer of assets to another entity should give rise to an asset disposal. However, Avis 99-14 of the CNC says that where an asset is transferred to an entity where the original owner has joint control, the pooling of interests method can be applied. Changes in the value of the owner's share of the equity of the joint venture are recognized in the owner's accounts.
36	The Commercial Code provides that the value of assets should be checked at balance sheet date for impairment. However, the methods for dealing with this are not specified, unlike IAS 36.
37	CRC Regulation 2000-06 aims to converge with IAS 37 for provisions. There remains, however, a major difference in the area of provisions for major repairs. According to the French rules, such provisions are obligatory, whereas in IAS 37 expenses for major repairs cannot be the subject of a provision if the enterprise would only incur the costs if it decided to continue using the asset, and it has no obligation to do so. Inspection costs and regular maintenance charges during the normal economic life of the asset, necessary for its continued use, are expensed in the period in which they are incurred.
38	Aside from differences in the approach to intangibles acquired as part of another company, discussed above and in the text, there are three basic differences in the French approach. The amortization rules are more precise in IAS 38 than in France. IAS 38 also allows that intangibles can be revalued to fair value subsequent to their recognition, while in France any revaluation of intangibles is forbidden. Certain costs are treated as intangible assets in France (company set-up costs, pre-opening expenses or start-up costs) but are taken as a period expense under IAS.
39	Premiums and discounts from issuing bonds, and the cost of debt issuance generally should be amortized over the life of the liability in group accounts, according to CRC 99-02's preferred method. De-recognition of assets and liabilities can be done where in-substance defeasance has taken place, whereas IAS 39 has stringent 'continuing involvement' rules. The French rules say little about financial instruments. But no unrealized gains may be recognized. As far as hedging is concerned, French rules do not allow the recognition of losses on a hedging instrument when they are counter-balanced by gains in the hedged item.
40	Although there is a PCG specifically adapted for agriculture (Plan comptable general agricole) there are no special accounting rules for agriculture as such.

Framework: There is no explicit conceptual framework at the moment, although since 1999 French accounting has been influenced by the IASB Framework.

Hypotheses and conventions relating to financial statements

If the preparer of financial statements complies with accounting principles, which include assumptions and conventions, this should permit the attainment of the principal objective indicated by the law: a true and fair view of the net worth, financial situation and the result of the company's operations. As we have already stressed, the link between the application of the rules and the fairness of the accounts is all the more important because the true and fair view is not defined.

Among the principles applied in France, it is useful to distinguish between those that are explicitly mentioned in the law, and those that are implied by the law. There are three assumptions underlying the preparation of annual accounts and four accounting conventions that are specified by the law. The regulations recognize the going concern assumption, accruals and matching, and consistency. Substance over form is also recognized for group accounts.

Going concern: the business is considered as being likely to continue to operate for the foreseeable future without any noticeable reduction in the level and scope of its activities (Commercial Code L123-20). When the going concern principle seems to be valid, then the financial statements can be prepared following the other principles. If it is not valid, the business should prepare a balance sheet on the basis of liquidation values.

Accruals and matching: the profit and loss account takes in the revenue and expenses for the period without regard to their date of payment or receipt (Commercial Code L123-13). The principle of separate reporting periods is reinforced by the legal obligation for anyone, whether incorporated or not, who operates as a trader, to measure their inventory at least once every 12 months and establish a balance sheet (this obligation dates back to the first accounting rules established in 1673). The company must prepare annual accounts based on its accounting records and the inventory values (Commercial Code L123-12). Linked to the time period, the matching and accruals principles are made operational through the medium of balance sheet 'comptes de régularisation' (accruals and prepayments accounts) which are defined as: 'used for allocating expenses and revenue over time in order to attach to each accounting period those expenses and revenues which relate to it, and only those'.

Consistency: the presentation of the annual accounts and the valuation methods used may not be changed from one year to another, unless there has been some change in the situation of the business. If changes do take place, they must be described and justified in the notes to the accounts (Commercial Code L123-14). They should also be mentioned in the management report, and, as necessary, in the auditors' report (law on commercial companies, 1966). The consistency principle is also specified by the PCG.

In a general sense a departure from the consistency principle can only be justified by enabling better information to be provided or in the search for a true and fair view of the net worth, financial position or results of the business. Unjustified changes are modifications made other than for these reasons and constitute irregularities.

Justified departures can concern five categories of change: change in accounting method, change in the application of the rules, change in accounting regulations, other regulatory changes. Two other types of change are not in a strict sense changes in accounting method: modifications relating to tax opportunities and the correction of errors.

Changes in accounting method are the choice of the business. They may concern either the presentation of the accounts or the valuation methods, and are subject to two conditions: that there should have been a substantial change in the operating circumstances of the company, and they should lead to a better true and fair view. Changes in the application of accounting methods consist of a change in the basis of calculation used within an unchanged accounting rule, as a consequence of events that have occurred subsequent to the initial application or of recognition that they do not reflect reality.

Changes in accounting regulation concern a change of method that is imposed on the business as a result of a new rule (or establishment of additional doctrine) or a new set of rules. An example of this occurred in 1984 when firms had to apply the PCG 1982 for the first time; another will be the first time application of IFRS. Other regulatory changes might involve the application of new methods following tax changes, or changes in the Labour Code or government policy. They are independent of accounting rules and methods.

The conventions explicitly recognized in accounting law are: historical cost, fair value, prudence, non-compensation, the inviolability of the opening balance sheet. The historical cost convention is applied for the valuation of goods at the moment they enter the company. This is operationalized by using the cost of acquisition for purchased items and the cost of production for items created by the company (Commercial Code L123-18).

French accounting law provides for several departures from the application of historical cost. The most recent is the application of 'fair value' to financial instruments (IAS 39), while the earliest appeared in the 1985 accounting law and its 1986 decree. The law also allows, for consolidated accounts only, the use of values which take into account changing prices or replacement values. Companies can use constant purchasing power values or replacement costs for depreciable tangible assets and stocks in their group accounts. In practice these departures are rarely used. The other departures from the general rule are: the right to value shareholdings according to the equity method in the accounts of individual companies (art. 340, law of 24 July 1966 included in the Commercial Code); and finally the revaluation of the whole of the tangible fixed assets, which is provided by the Commercial Code (L123-18).

Prudence is defined by the PCG as: 'a reasonable appreciation of facts in order to avoid the risk of transferring to future periods present uncertainties which are likely to damage the net worth of results of the business'. It also appears in the general rules for preparing accounts: 'in order to provide financial statements which reflect a true and fair view of the situation and activities of the business, the accounting must satisfy the obligations of regularity and sincerity while respecting the rule of prudence'. In applying this convention, revenues may not be taken into account until they have been realized, while expenses should be recognized once their realization is probable or even likely. This results in an asymmetric treatment of unrealized gains and losses. The latter are recognized while the former are not. There are numerous exceptions to the rule of prudence, such as those relating to the use of exceptions to the historical cost rules, or to the method of recognition of profits on long-term contracts by percentage of completion.

The non-compensation rule expressly provides that no asset accounts may be offset against liability or equity accounts, and no expenses against revenues (Commercial Code L123-19).

As regards the inviolability of the opening balance sheet, accounting law says that 'the opening balance sheet for the year must correspond to the closing balance sheet for the preceding year' (Commercial Code L123-19). It is this principle which makes it impossible to modify equity directly in the opening balance sheet to take account of retroactive changes in accounting method, or omissions or the correction of errors in recording revenues or expenses of past periods. These must be recorded in the current profit and loss account. At the same time, the regulations and accounting doctrine accept that the effects of changes in accounting regulations in the legal sense of the term may be passed directly into equity. The impact of changes brought about by the first application of revised IASC standards, may not, therefore, be taken directly against equity.

As far as consolidated financial statements are concerned, the application of the principle of the inviolability of the opening balance sheet presents some specific implications. It presumes in particular that it has been followed in the accounts of the individual companies, specifically in the case of intermediate accounts and the systematic take-up in one period of the balance sheet accounts used in the previous period's consolidation.

The concept of substance over form is only recognized explicitly as far as concerns consolidated accounts. On the contrary, it is not recognized in individual accounts which remain marked by an ownership approach to the business and accounting.

Valuation principles in the consolidated accounts

Intangible assets do not have a special definition. The principles used in accounting for them can be split into three areas: identifiable intangible assets, non-identifiable intangibles (goodwill) and research and development costs. The recognition in the consolidated balance sheet of identifiable intangible assets, such as patents, licenses, software, market share, brands, client lists, concessions and similar rights, which do not appear in the accounts of individual companies, is conditional. The CRC 99-02 regulation allows recognition, in the context of an acquisition, of intangible assets such as patents, brands, market share and client lists, provided that the conditions for recognition are satisfied. These are that their valuation must be regularly reviewed, and carried out using objective and relevant criteria based on future economic advantage or market value, if there is a market for similar assets. If these methods are not possible, other methods used in the industry sector may be used (for example a valuation by an independent expert may be necessary).

Consequently, in France brands, market share and client lists can be recognized as intangible assets in consolidated accounts. They are not systematically amortized as there is no rule covering this.

Goodwill, or consolidation difference, corresponds to the price of acquisition of a business and the proportion of its assets and liabilities which have been acquired. Positive goodwill is included in intangible assets and amortized over its useful life, for which the regulations prescribe no maximum. It cannot be charged directly against equity, except if the company can demonstrate that this is necessary to give a true and fair view (Commercial Code L123-13, L123-14). Negative goodwill is recognized as a liability and released systematically to the profit and loss account.

Article 215 of the CRC Regulation 99-02 allows a derogation which results in a method similar to pooling of interests. Instead of using the cost of acquisition, the company may recognize the book value of the assets and liabilities of the acquired company, subject to four conditions being met. These are that at least 90% of the shares were acquired at one time; that the shares were acquired in exchange for those of the acquiring group; any cash element should be no more than 10% of the price paid; and that the nature of the operation is not called into question during the following two years by transactions such as the re-purchase of shares, exceptional dividends, etc.

Tangible assets are valued at historical cost. In the consolidated balance sheet they may also be valued at replacement cost or historical cost adjusted for general price inflation. In practice, French companies do not use these alternative valuation options.

Stocks, like all other assets in the balance sheet, should be valued at the lower of original (purchase or production) cost and the 'inventory value', defined by the Commercial Code as the current price or the market value. This value is in practice close to net realizable value. The idea of inventory value dates back to the seventeenth century (see above) when the original accounting rules required the preparation of an annual inventory of assets and liabilities, and the trader's income was the difference between two annual inventories. It might be argued that double-entry bookkeeping and accrual accounting are merely a means of operationalizing this on a daily basis, and need to be checked annually to see if this approximation is in line with perceived inventory values.

Financial instruments French accounting regulation does not have any general concept of financial instruments in the way in which that appears in the international literature. However the law of 2 July 1996 on modernization of financial activities defines these instruments as 'shares and securities which give direct or indirect access to the capital, debt, or interest in collective investment vehicles and limited term financial instruments'. The accounting rules which are derived from this are consequently partial and specific.

- Titres de participation (non-voting equity instruments) should be valued at balance sheet date at their 'useful value' which corresponds to the price which the entity would be willing to pay to acquire them (PCG 332-1 and 332-3).

- Titres immobilises de l'activité de portefeuille (investment securities) are valued individually taking account of the expected future evolution of the company concerned and their market value (PCG 332-5). Only impairments are taken into account.

- Other securities are valued at the balance sheet date at the average price of the previous month if they are quoted, and at their probable market value if they are not quoted (PCG 332-6). In the event that there is an unusual and temporary drop in the value of such securities, gains on some assets can be used to offset losses on others in calculating the net impairment.

- Futures contracts, fixed or conditional, are not recognized in the balance sheet. The off balance sheet liability has to be disclosed in the notes to the accounts if they are likely to generate a loss. Fluctuations in value are dealt with differently depending upon whether or not the instrument is designated as a hedge. Information must be given in the notes for all material contracts (PCG 372-1 to 372-3).

Deferred taxation is recognized only in the consolidated accounts. Since the adoption of Regulation CRC 99-02, deferred tax provisions have been calculated on the balance sheet method. Deferred tax assets are not recognized unless their realization is not dependent upon future profits, or if profits are being generated in the current period. The tax rate used is the current rate and both assets and liabilities are discounted (unless the transaction giving rise to them has itself been discounted) if their value is material and if a timetable for their reversal can be established. Detailed information should be given in the notes (CRC 99-02 §310-316).

To conclude this section on valuation rules in consolidated accounts, it should be stressed that in France there are certain accounting principles provided in the Commercial Code which are optional but which are designated as 'preferred' in the CRC Regulation 99-02 and are obligatory in IAS. These preferred rules, cited in CRC 99-02 §300 are as follows:

- restatement of fixed assets acquired through a financing lease (art. D248.8e);

- recognition over the period of the loan discounts and premiums on bond issues (PCG art. 361.5/6);

- systematic creation of provisions for pension (Commercial Code L123-13 and PCG art. 335.1);

- recognition in the income statement of gains and losses relating to outstanding monetary items denominated in a foreign currency (D 248.8g);

- systematic application of the percentage of completion method for long-term contracts (PCG art. 380-1).

The choice of the preferred methods cannot subsequently be reversed. In the event that the preferred method is abandoned or not applied, the entity must quantify the effects of that for the balance sheet and income statement.

Consolidation methodology

The French consolidation approach differs in some details from that proposed in IAS 27. The differences relate to the presentation of the accounts, the scope of consolidation and the methods. The French concept of a subsidiary is more narrowly defined than in IAS 27. A company is considered to be a subsidiary of another company when that company holds more than 50% of the capital of the investee. This difference does not make the two sets of rules incompatible. Subsidiaries whose activities are different from those of the rest of the group and whose consolidation would not result in a true and fair view of the group are consolidated by use of the equity method (in France the equity method is seen as a form of consolidation and not as a valuation method). The exclusion of subsidiaries held for resale is optional.

The French rules for the adjustments to be made when a subsidiary has an accounting date different to that of the group are more restrictive than IAS 27. They prohibit the consolidation of figures whose balance sheet date is later than that of the group. Interim accounts must be prepared, while also taking account of the rules for post-balance sheet events.

The notion of an associated company does not have a statutory definition in France. This does not present an obstacle in applying IAS 28. However, it should be remembered that the equity method required by this standard for accounting for investments of this type in the consolidated accounts is considered by French law as a consolidation technique. It is applied only to companies in which the consolidating company is able to exercise a significant influence on the management and financial policies of the associated companies.

Business combinations

New combinations of businesses are achieved through the purchase of a controlling interest or a merger or even through the acquisition of assets in exchange for shares which enjoys a privileged tax treatment. As far as the accounting treatment is concerned, French standards provide for two different methods. The first is the acquisition method (CRC 99-02) which is wholly in conformity with IAS 22, and the second is a derogation from the cost of acquisition (CRC Regulation 2000-07 which modifies §215 of CRC 99-02) which corresponds to the pooling of interests method, formerly recognized in US GAAP, and the uniting of interests recognized by IAS 22. The details of this method have been set out above. A significant difference with IAS 22 is that the IAS specifies that neither of the two merging companies can be identified as the acquirer and that this method is obligatory when there is a genuine sharing of interests. The French method does not make any reference either to the relative size of the two companies. This method, which has been used by a number of large French companies, would not have been possible if the companies were basing their accounts on IAS.

Segment information

The segment information required in France is less extensive than that required by IAS 14. It comes down to a disclosure in the notes to the consolidated accounts of an analysis of turnover, fixed assets or assets employed by geographical or monetary area and by sector of activity. The regulations also provide for the publication of the trading result by geographical zone or by line of business.

Cash flow statement

Publication of a cash flow statement is obligatory in consolidated accounts. (CRC Regulation 99-02). It appears in the notes to the accounts and follows a format which is essentially the same as IAS 7.

Notes

1. The respective influences of the occupying power and the Vichy government in the preparation of the 1942 plan are analysed in Standish, P. 'Origines du Plan Comptable Général: évaluation des pressions allemandes et françaises' *Actes du XIe congrés de l'Association Franáaise de Comptabilité* 1991 pp. 375–401.
2. For a more detailed history see Mikol (1995).
3. *L'information financière 2001, groupes industriels et commerciaux européens*, Editions Communication et Profession Comptable, Grenoble, 2001.

References

Alexander, D. & Burlaud, A. (1993) Existe-t-il une ou plusieurs images fidèles en Europe? *Revue du Droit Comptable*, No. 03–2, pp. 5–34.

Burlaud, A., Friedrich, M. and Langlois, G. (2002) *Comptabilité Approfondie*. Foucher, Paris.

Colasse, B. (1991) Où il est question d'un cadre comptable conceptuel français. *Revue de Droit Comptable*, No. 91–3, pp. 3–20.

Collins, L. (1992) Auditing implication in early warning systems – the French experience. *The European Accounting Review* **1**(2): 447–452.

Conseil National de la Comptabilité (2000) *Plan comptable général 1999*. Imprimerie Nationale, Paris.

Esnault, B. and Hoarau, C. (2001) *Comptabilité financiére*. 3rd edn, PUF, Paris.

Hoarau, C. (1992) La France doit-elle se doter d'un cadre conceptuel comptable? *Revue Française de Comptabilité* February: 58–62.

Hoarau, C. (1995) International accounting harmonization: American hegemony or mutual recognition with benchmarks? *European Accounting Review* **4**(2): 217–233.

Hoarau, C. (2002) *Comptabilité et management*. Foucher, Paris.

Hoarau, C. and Naciri, A. (2001) A comparative analysis of American and French financial reporting philosophies: the case for International Accounting Standards. *Advances in International Accounting*, **14**: 229–247.

Mikol, A. (1993) The evolution of auditing and the independent auditor in France. *The European Accounting Review* **2**(1): 1–16.

Mikol, A. (1995) The history of financial reporting in France. In Walton, P. (ed.) *European Financial Reporting – A History*. Academic Press, London.

Ordre des Experts Comptables *Encyclopédie permanente des recommendations à l'usage des membres de l'ordre*, Vol I & II. Conseil supérieur de l'OEC, Paris.

Scheid, J.-C. and Standish, P. (1989) La normalisation comptable: sa perception dans le monde anglophone et en France. *Revue Française de Comptabilité* May: 90–99.

Accounting in the United Kingdom

Peter Walton

The distinguishing characteristics of the United Kingdom as an accounting jurisdiction are that accounting is dominated by a highly organized accounting profession, but that accounting rules address only limited liability companies and no other commercial entity, and that fiscal accounting has developed separately from commercial accounting. Public sector accounting follows its own, different rules. Commercial accounting rules are oriented primarily round the needs of large companies listed on the stock exchange. Financial statements are supposed to give a 'true and fair view' of the financial position of a company, but what exactly that means is not certain. As in other Anglo-Saxon accounting jurisdictions, rule-makers have at times been innovative, while companies have also been known to push interpretation of the rules to extremes.

Legal and institutional basis of accounting regulation

Company law

The current legal instrument ruling the accounting of limited liability companies is the Companies Act 1985 (CA1985), as amended by the Companies Act 1989 (CA1989). CA1985 is what is known as a 'consolidation act', which introduced no new rules but brought together into a single statute the rules which existed previously in several different statutes. It reflects an evolution of company law since the beginning of the nineteenth century which has been overlaid in the 1980s by legislation to introduce the European Directives, notably the Fourth (1982) and Seventh (1989).

Those interested in a more detailed analysis of the evolution of regulation and institutions should look at Napier (1995). The key points are that prior to the nineteenth century, the creation of share-issuing corporations was possible only by royal charter (e.g. The East India Company) or by individual Act of Parliament. The Industrial Revolution brought about a rapid development of infrastructure and created a need for vehicles which could group together sufficient finance. Many railway companies were formed by individual acts, but this impetus led to legislation, starting with the 1844 Joint Stock Companies Act, to permit the systematic formation of share-issuing companies without an Act of Parliament. Successive Acts (1856, 1862) introduced limited liability and provided model rules which included, but on an optional basis, shareholder audit.

These acts created a pattern that still exists today, even if it has been much modified over time, of the law stating minimum disclosures of accounting information and relying partly on some general qualitative clause, such as the necessity to give a true and fair view, and partly on professional guidance by accountants in formulating detailed accounting rules, to ensure that companies provided statements which were not too misleading. The 1844 Act referred to a 'full and fair' balance sheet, while the 1862 Act called for statements to be 'true and correct'.

In 1900 a new act made audit compulsory; this remained an audit by shareholders for shareholders, although it was often actually carried out in larger companies by professional accountants. There was a landmark court case in 1931, concerning the Royal Mail Shipping Line and dealing with the use of secret reserves to smooth profits and hide trading losses. At this time the annual profit was a one line disclosure and the evidence given in the case made it clear that both auditors and company management regarded it as normal practice that the figures should be manipulated to provide a consistent profit and dividend. The reaction to this trial showed that attitudes were changing and shareholders wanted more unbiased information about company performance and were less willing to put their trust in a paternalistic management. The publication of consolidated accounts had been pioneered earlier in the USA and from this period some companies, notably Dunlop, started to produce experimental statements.

The great reform of company law occurred in 1947 (Companies Act 1947: CA1947), following on the Cohen Report of 1945. This marked a shift in emphasis away from the balance sheet as the sole financial statement and towards the provision of more profit and loss information, even though publication of a complete profit and loss account was to wait until implementation of the Fourth Directive. CA1947 banned secret reserves and introduced definitions as to what constituted a provision (expense which reduces profits before tax) and a reserve (allocation of after-tax profits within equity). It made the preparation of consolidated accounts compulsory where the parent had more than 50% of the votes in another company, and it required that the audit was carried out by professionally qualified accountants. The 'true and correct view' of the financial position which was the overriding objective of the annual statements was changed to become 'a true and fair view'. The Act also required disclosure of the carrying value of fixed assets, showing both original cost and accumulated depreciation – although, curiously, there was no requirement to depreciate assets.

The next series of reforms were largely the result of implementation of European Community Directives. The first of these to be noticeable was the creation (in 1980 following the Second Directive) of two different classes of limited company: the private limited company (Ltd) and the public limited company (PLC). This is a rather artificial distinction which underlines that the UK has never had a corporate vehicle designed primarily for small and medium-sized business. Where Germany adopted the share-issuing limited liability company (Aktiengesellschaft) for major enterprises and then developed a number of other vehicles for smaller companies, including notably the Gesellschaft mit beschränkter Haftung (GmbH), which does not have shares as such, the UK had only the share-issuing company, which was used alike by large and small businesses. The European Directives are predicated on the assumption that jurisdictions have two quite distinct vehicles, generally used for quite different scales of operation and entailing different reporting and auditing environments.

In 1981 a new Companies Act passed regulations implementing the Fourth Directive. This had been met with some alarm by UK companies (see Walton 1990) not least because it entailed a complete analysis of expenses in the profit and loss account. Until then, disclosure of detail had been limited to turnover and net profit before tax, with detailed analysis of appropriations and some disclosure of detail (directors' salaries, depreciation, interest and audit fees) in the notes (the requirement to provide this detail was never repealed, which is why it is still disclosed in the notes to the accounts of British companies even though full expenses by function are given in the profit and loss account). In fact a much thornier problem introduced by the Fourth Directive was the requirement that goodwill should be depreciated, but that did not make itself felt until much later (see below).

In general terms one could say that the Fourth Directive introduced detailed accounting rules into UK law and significantly reduced the flexibility which had previously been a characteristic of UK regulation. Although the Fourth Directive includes a number of specifically British elements (the true and fair view, extraordinary items), the fact that these are embodied in the law is sometimes seen as a constraint by UK regulators who perceive a need for regulation to evolve more quickly to reflect corporate practice.

Nevertheless, British regulators were happy enough in 1989 to take advantage of optional rules from the Seventh Directive to change the criteria for the consolidation of subsidiaries from one of majority voting power to one of control or 'dominant influence', to help combat the use of off balance sheet financing vehicles which depended upon not having majority voting by the 'parent' to keep them out of the consolidated balance sheet. CA1989 is also important for increasing the importance of accounting standards. This was done partly by requiring that companies state that they have complied with standards and explain any departures. The Act also gave the Department of Trade and Industry (the ministry responsible for companies, accounting, auditing, etc.) the right to appoint a body to oversee financial reporting.

Company law allows all the balance sheet and profit and loss account formats provided in the Fourth Directive, and also allows that tangible fixed assets may be valued on a basis other than historical cost. The main body of CA1985 sets out the true and fair reporting requirement, audit requirement, obligation to maintain adequate accounting records, report to shareholders etc., while the detailed accounting and valuation rules are to be found in an appendix, Schedule 4A.

The accounting profession

The profession of accountancy can generally be traced back to the early nineteenth century, albeit with some confusion as to what constitutes the appropriate work of an accounting professional. Some authors suggest that work such as rent-collecting was an early feature, and that some independent accountants were 'general financial agents' of a sort. A detailed study (Jones 1981) looks at the evolution of Whinney Murray, a constituent firm of Ernst & Young (a large part of which was the firm Ernst & Whinney until its merger with Arthur Young in 1989). This traces the evolution of an early partnership which started in London in the 1840s and notes that much of its work in the middle of the nineteenth century was concerned with liquidations of limited companies. Only towards the end of the nineteenth century did audit work, and to a lesser extent accounting, start to figure substantially, albeit growing very rapidly.

Accountants, particularly in Scotland, were quick to form local professional societies (e.g. Edinburgh 1854), membership of which enabled accountants to attract clients by emphasizing standards of conduct, professional competence etc., and distinguished them from those who were not members. This drive to form professional societies carried with it the benefit that the profession was rapidly seen to be organized and apparently coherent, providing, significantly, the government with representative organizations to which it could address its concerns (and vice versa) without necessarily going as far as legislation. Although, say by comparison with the French profession, the British claims to be independent of government, it has always been true that the British have preferred to exercise governmental influence through confidential meetings with representatives of private sector bodies than through overt regulation. The fact that there were effective national bodies (e.g. Institute of Chartered Accountants of England and Wales – ICAEW – since 1880) was probably a contributory factor in determining the lack of formal accounting regulation.

The professional bodies can be divided into three groups.

'Chartered accountants'

These are members of three bodies which have a regional basis:

- Institute of Chartered Accountants in England and Wales (ICAEW) 120 000 members
- Institute of Chartered Accountants of Scotland (ICAS) 15 000 members
- Institute of Chartered Accountants in Ireland (ICAI) 12 500 members

The ICAEW (or 'English Institute' as it is known amongst British accountants) considers itself the senior body, and clearly its size gives it a dominant position. Typically members will have served an internship with an audit firm while they were taking their professional examinations, and the bulk of the partners in audit firms are members of one of these three bodies. However, many members leave audit practice and take jobs in industry and commerce, which does not entail, as it does in other jurisdictions, ceasing to be a member.

Association of Chartered Certified Accountants (ACCA)

This is the second largest body, with 85 000 members. Historically it has prided itself on open access and has a tradition of opposing the 'closed shop' which chartered accountants seemed to operate in the earlier part of the century when access to their body was only through apprenticeship for which the apprentice had to pay the auditor. The bulk of its members do their internship in industry and mostly stay there, although an increasing number of its members are in small audit firms. It is not limited geographically and has for many years operated in other parts of the Commonwealth, conducting examinations in 130 countries. It now sees itself as having an international vocation and has many members for whom its attraction is precisely that its qualification is widely known and may well be more transferable across borders than a domestic qualification.

Members of these four bodies are recognized by the Department of Trade and Industry as qualified to audit companies, subject, of course, to their having had the appropriate internship in auditing as well as having passed the professional examinations. An individual member needs to have spent three years in an audit firm before being admitted to membership (apart from passing the professional examinations) and then a further three years in an audit firm before being given a 'practising certificate', which entitles the accountant to operate as an independent auditor, set up his or her own firm etc.

Specialist bodies

There are two further bodies not competing in the audit market, but concerned rather with other specialist areas.

The Chartered Institute of Management Accountants (CIMA) is a respected body whose 57 000 members are concerned with the financial management of companies. Their areas of special concern are therefore budgetary control, costing, forecasting etc.

The Chartered Institute of Public Finance and Accountancy (CIPFA) is an equally respected body whose 16 000 members are active in the public sector, particularly in municipal bodies. Their interest is the proper administration of public funds, collection of local taxes, etc.

The term 'chartered accountant', which is often seized upon by translators or accountants from other countries as being synonymous with the term 'independent auditor', is widely misunderstood, since a chartered accountant is not necessarily an auditor, and an auditor is not necessarily a chartered accountant. The term is, however, jealously guarded by the three regional institutes and refers simply to the fact that they were granted a Royal Charter early in their life (indeed the acquisition of a charter was one of the main motivating forces behind the formation of the early institutes) and their members were allowed to call themselves, as a consequence, chartered accountants. In more recent times the other three professional bodies have also been granted Royal Charters (as seen in their current names) but not the right to call themselves chartered accountants as such. ACCA members have since January 1997 been able to call themselves 'chartered certified accountants'.

The six bodies do not necessarily work harmoniously with each other, but they have a joint organization, the Consultative Committee of Accountancy Bodies (CCAB), which provides a joint vehicle on the rare occasions when they see a need to cooperate with each other. There is no bar to people being members of more than one body, but this is expensive in terms of annual membership fees and has no advantages.

A particular attribute of these bodies is that they each operate significant examining activities. Each has its own, separate examination system. It is a notable feature of the UK, that, whatever branch of accounting a graduate wants to go into, membership of one of the six professional bodies is seen by employers as essential, carrying with it a guarantee of technical competence. A university diploma in accounting is virtually disregarded in the employment market. This phenomenon can be explained partly by the early professionalization of accountancy in the UK, partly by British preference for pragmatism (implied by 'on the job' training) as opposed to theory (university training), and partly by the very late entry into business education of the universities. It means that the organized accounting profession has more members and plays a much wider role in the UK than in many other countries, where often membership of a professional body is primarily related to the provision of public accountancy and audit services.

In fact fewer than half of the current membership of the UK professional bodies are operating within independent accounting firms, and the firms offer primarily audit, tax advice and management consultancy. While smaller firms may well provide some accounting services to clients, bookkeeping or data processing is an undeveloped market. Owners of small businesses typically maintain accounting records themselves as a weekend activity, or hire part-time bookkeepers. In this area, audit firms mostly restrict themselves to preparing the annual statements, or simply giving technical advice on their preparation.

Accounting standards

The first attempt by the profession to establish technical guidelines for accounting was the establishment by the English Institute in 1942 of its committee on accounting principles, which issued a series of statements over a period of about 25 years. Apart from the analysis by Zeff (1972), this committee has largely disappeared from the literature on UK accounting, which may be a comment on its lack of impact. It did not address any particularly controversial issues, nor did it work very quickly, contenting itself with more or less routine positions on questions such as depreciation. It issued some 12 statements, which were advisory in nature and addressed, of course, purely to its own members.

The first recognizable standard-setter in modern terms was the Accounting Standards Committee (ASC). It is often the case in accounting regulation that there is a cycle where regulatory equilibrium is broken by some event (often a financial scandal) which leads to a regulatory response (perhaps to block a loophole, but certainly to attempt to restore confidence) and a new equilibrium. Each of these breakdowns of equilibrium leaves a regulatory trace, which, particularly where the response was enshrined in law, may never disappear and gives accounting rules an inconsistent, fragmentary feel because of their incremental nature.

In the case of the ASC there were a number of well-publicized controversies in the late 1960s (notably a contested takeover by GEC (now known as Marconi) of a competitor, but also a lawsuit involving Pergamon Press) which made clear that accounting measurements allowed a large element of choice. This led to public criticism of financial reporting and to some loss of confidence in accountants and their product. The ICAEW responded by forming its Accounting Standards Steering Committee in 1969. The other professional bodies felt that they should be involved too, and finally the ASC emerged over a period of months, under the aegis of the CCAB, as the accountancy profession's official setter of technical standards. It produced Statements of Standard Accounting Practice (SSAPs).

The ASC consisted purely of accountants, and those mostly drawn from audit firms. Its members were all voluntary, with the consequences that the only people available were partners in very large accounting firms (which considered the investment worthwhile) and academics. It had a very small secretariat. It suffered therefore from a lack of resources, and in addition its powers were strictly limited. All its pronouncements had to be submitted for approval to the Councils (management committees) of each of the six professional bodies, thereby giving each body a great deal of power to hold up or veto any aspect of an accounting standard with which they disagreed. Potentially, therefore, it was difficult for the ASC to take a very strict line on any issue.

The fragility of the ASC process was highlighted by a failed attempt to introduce inflation accounting (see Walton 2001), and its credibility – and that of the whole UK financial reporting system – was further damaged by the rise of creative accounting in the late 1980s. Creative accounting is generally treated as a special phenomenon which occurred during the economic boom of the late 1980s and was revealed to an extent during the severe depression that followed. However, the financial reporting of companies' financial positions has always been a creative process up to a point: profit is, after all, a subjective notion, not a matter of ascertainable fact (at least until a company has ceased to exist, when a final calculation may be made). The real point was that choices in accounting were being used in combinations and ways which had not previously been seen and the creativity was being taken to an extreme. This had the result in due course of throwing both financial reporting and auditing into disrepute.

The crisis in confidence provoked a response from the accounting profession, which asked a prominent civil servant, Sir Ron Dearing, to study the standard-setting system and recommend changes. He came up with a system that was largely modelled on the Financial Accounting Standards Board (FASB), but included a surveillance arm to check compliance, a function generally performed by the Securities and Exchange Commission (SEC) in the USA (at least for listed companies) but absent from the British system.

The new system was put in place in 1990. One of the important changes was government involvement. The government took powers in CA1989 to appoint an agent to oversee financial reporting, and it duly nominated the Financial Reporting Council (FRC). The FRC has about 40 members, drawn from a wide range of constituencies involved with accounting. Its job is to safeguard the quality of financial reporting – and also to raise the funds necessary to do this.

The FRC in its turn appointed two subsidiary bodies: the Accounting Standards Board (ASB) to issue accounting standards, and the Financial Reporting Review Panel (FRRP) to check compliance with standards (Figure 6.1). The FRRP is run by a lawyer, and while it has no direct powers of sanction, its threat is that it will bring a complaint of failing to

Figure 6.1 Structure of the Financial Reporting Council (FRC)

provide a true and fair view against companies that do not comply, before the civil courts. Anyone can refer a set of accounts to the FRRP, whose team of experts will come to an opinion about the accounts. If the FRRP takes the view that the accounts are defective in some way, it invites the company concerned, and its auditors, to discuss the points at issue, and potentially to change the accounts.

The FRC's surveillance arm can probably be said to have had an impact, but the more noticeable impact has been made by the ASB, the new standard-setter. This body consists of 11 members, drawn from the profession but also from industry and from users. The chairman and the technical director are employed full time and there is a larger technical support group than was available to the ASC. A key political feature is that the ASB does not have to look elsewhere for any endorsement of its standards: it is free to issue what standards it wishes, without consultation, even if in practice it follows procedures that involve publishing position papers and asking for comment well before deciding on the final standard.

The ASB has an associated body, the Urgent Issues Task Force (UITF), which acts as a fire-fighting force to issue temporary guidance on new technical problems as they emerge. The UITF is largely made up of technical partners of accounting firms who normally act as internal consultants within their own firms and are quickly aware of new problems raised by company reporting. A difficulty faced by the ASC was that, by the time a new practice had arrived on its agenda, so many companies were already doing it as to make a ban difficult. The UITF issues 'abstracts' which are intended to avoid undesirable new practices being taken up widely.

Since it started work in 1990, the ASB has set out to address a number of the issues involved in 'creative accounting', particularly the creation and use of reorganization provisions, extraordinary expenses, and fair values on acquisition. It has made the profit and loss account more detailed and introduced a new financial statement, the statement of total recognized gains and losses. It has set out to prepare a conceptual framework, modelled closely on the IASB's framework. The technical aspects of its standards, known as Financial Reporting Standards (FRS), will be examined later in this chapter. (See also Table 6.1.)

Politically, the ASB has succeeded in not being too closely identified with the accounting profession as such, even if many of the individuals associated with the ASB come from the profession. Its standards have been criticized by preparers in particular, but that tends to add to its credibility rather than damage it!

One aspect of its work which should be underlined is that it takes the view that historical cost is not an adequate valuation base for financial reporting. It thinks that the balance sheet should provide a coherent valuation, based on what it calls 'value to the business', which is the ASB term for what accounting theorists refer to as 'deprival value' (which was also used in SSAP16, the failed inflation accounting standard which damaged the ASC).

Deprival value

Deprival value asks the question: what is the cost to the business of being deprived of asset X? If the business would simply buy a replacement asset, then replacement cost is the deprival value. However, it is possible that the business would not replace the asset because it is not profitable, then the deprival value of asset X is the cash flows derived from its continuing use, either from sale of the products or services provided by the asset, or from sale of the asset itself. This can be summed up as

$$\text{deprival value} = \text{lower of} \begin{cases} \text{replacement cost} \\ \text{cash flow from use (or disposal)} \end{cases}$$

Table 6.1 Accounting standards in force

Statements of Standard Accounting Practice	
SSAP2	Disclosure of accounting policies
SSAP4	Accounting treatment of government grants
SSAP5	Accounting for value added tax
SSAP9	Stocks and long term contracts
SSAP13	Accounting for research and development
SSAP17	Post balance sheet events
SSAP19	Accounting for investment properties
SSAP20	Foreign currency translation
SSAP21	Accounting for leases
SSAP24	Accounting for pension costs
SSAP25	Segmental reporting

Financial Reporting Standards	
FRS1	Cash flow statements
FRS2	Accounting for subsidiary undertakings
FRS3	Reporting financial performance
FRS4	Accounting for capital instruments
FRS5	Reporting the substance of transactions
FRS6	Acquisitions and mergers
FRS7	Fair values in acquisition accounting
FRS8	Related party transactions
FRS9	Associates and joint ventures
FRS10	Goodwill and intangible assets
FRSSE	Financial Reporting Standard for Smaller Entities
FRS 11	Impairment of fixed assets and goodwill
FRS 12	Provisions, contingent liabilities and contingent assets
FRS 13	Derivatives and financial instruments – disclosure
FRS 14	Earnings per share
FRS 15	Tangible fixed assets
FRS 16	Current tax
FRS 17	Retirement benefits
FRS 18	Accounting policies
FRS 19	Deferred tax

The ASB seems to have managed to establish this principle without too much reaction from the accounting community. This may be because, in a discussion paper on valuation, it also stated that it did not see a case for immediate change in the existing system, but rather that one should move towards the preferred basis as the opportunity presented itself. Indeed, the ASB has, when introducing its standard (FRS7) on fair values in acquisition accounting, taken the opportunity to specify that 'value to the business' is the appropriate basis of computing fair value. It should be noted that the ASB notion of fair value is an 'entity-specific' value in contrast with the IASB's notion which is a general market value. It seems likely that the ASB's statement of total recognized gains and losses is intended to serve as a linking statement to bring together unrealized valuation changes arising from a deprival value balance sheet and traditional transaction-based historical cost earnings from the profit and loss account.

Taxation

The UK was probably the first country to enjoy taxation of income, having introduced it in 1799 as a temporary measure to finance the fight with the French. It was substantially revised in 1803, creating a system that is largely retained today, even though it was withdrawn at the end of the Napoleonic Wars (1815) and not reinstated until 1843. It is probably significant that taxation of income was introduced when there were no established rules for measurement of income, and that subsequent accounting rules were addressed only to limited liability companies. In any event, UK tax law is quite clear that only the interpretation of statute law and past jurisprudence can determine what is income for tax purposes, and accounting measurements, though interesting, are in no legal sense determining.

Responsibility for taxes lies with the Treasury (i.e. Ministry of Finance), and tax rates and similar matters are fixed every year in an annual Finance Act. Currently the Chancellor of the Exchequer (i.e. the Minister of Finance) announces his intentions to Parliament in November every year. The fiscal year runs from 6 April, and a Finance Act is normally passed by Parliament in order to set rates for the fiscal year ahead. Under the British system the government must command a majority of votes in the Parliament and therefore the Chancellor's measures are generally passed without major change. Minor changes, though, often take place as a result of lobbying or belated perception of difficulties in application.

One significant aspect of the distance between shareholder reporting and fiscal income is that the Finance Acts determine, for tax purposes, (a) what assets are depreciable, and (b) at what rates they may be depreciated, and these are applied irrespective of what happens in the company's published accounts. This means that there is no tax minimization pressure on companies when selecting their asset valuation and depreciation policies for shareholder reporting purposes. Not all assets that would be depreciated under generally accepted accounting principles (e.g. office buildings, retail premises) are depreciable under tax rules, which gives rise to an extensive jurisprudence on whether expenditure is an 'improvement' (added to the carrying value of a potentially non-depreciable asset) or 'maintenance' (deducted from profit).

The computation of taxable income normally starts from the shareholder profit figure and is then adjusted:

	Shareholder profit
add back:	depreciation charges
	general provisions
	disallowed expenditure

deduct: capital allowances
=   taxable profit

Only specific provisions are allowed as a deduction from profit, and the determining factor as far as the tax authorities (the 'Inland Revenue') are concerned is how accurately the
amount of a provision can be calculated. A number of elements of normal expenditure, in
particular for entertaining, are simply disallowed for tax purposes, while others may be
deemed to be capital expenditure by the Inland Revenue (e.g. agent's and legal fees on the
acquisition of an asset). 'Capital allowances' are in effect tax depreciation and are currently 4% straight line on industrial buildings and 25% reducing balance on other industrial assets, motor vehicles, etc. One oddity of the system is that when an asset is disposed
of, it continues to be depreciated for tax purposes and there is no final adjustment of
depreciation based on the disposal value.

Corporate profits are taxed at 30% with a 20% rate for small companies. The relationship with tax on dividends is dealt with under the imputation system: when the shareholder
receives a dividend it is deemed to be net of tax (income tax is 'imputed'), so there is no
double taxation of corporate profits (both within the company and then within the hands
of the shareholder).

Taxation is calculated on an individual company basis, but 'group relief' is available for
groups of companies – losses in one company in one year can be offset against profits in
another company in the same year.

Objectives, assumptions and qualitative characteristics

Probably one of the most famous aspects of British accounting is the concept of the 'true
and fair view', which in company law is the objective of the annual accounts, to achieve
which other rules may in theory be set aside. The true and fair view has been exported to
many countries, initially Commonwealth countries (see Walton 1986, Parker 1989), but
later to the European Union via the Fourth Directive (see, for example, van Hulle 1993,
Nobes 1993). Despite this extensive traffic, the true and fair view has never been defined
and its role in British accounting is highly ambiguous (see Walton 1993).

The true and fair view is represented by different people as being:

(a) a legal residual clause;

(b) a quality external to accounting;

(c) generally accepted accounting principles.

The residual clause concept is one where the law sets out a list of detailed requirements,
but adds a general qualitative requirement to avoid providing a situation where someone
can stick to the letter of the law while not complying with the spirit. A leading company
law judge (Arden 1997) commented that statute law is often framed to give the courts a
little freedom in its application in order to deal with situations that were not foreseen by
the law, or where there are conflicts between different laws.

Many accountants, however, and some of the literature, claim that the true and fair view
is a call to observe higher principles which exist beyond the accounting rules, although
they do not usually define what these principles are.

The third possibility says that true and fair is a 'term of art' (Edey 1971): a technical
term to be understood within a particular context. Edey argued that profit is an abstract
construct which is determined by reference to a framework of accounting rules. It cannot

therefore be assessed without reference to a set of rules and hence any view of profit relates to the rules. In order to operationalize the true and fair view (of a company's financial position) we have to have measurement rules, and so for practical purposes there is no difference between the rules and the concept.

This is not a debate that is likely ever to be resolved, and indeed, the use of true and fair within the Fourth Directive is likely over time to lead to further complication not less (e.g. see Chapter 4 on Germany). What can be seen is that it is a highly indeterminate notion and it has roles to play other than in a technical accounting sense. Hopwood (1990), for example, sees it as having played a political role in the discussion that led to the Fourth Directive. It should certainly not be assumed that British accounting is truer or fairer than any other, nor that it has higher ideals!

In general terms, accounting rules are drawn up with the large, listed company in mind, and transparency for the financial markets as an objective. However, these companies have been quite successful in making their views heard in the standard-setting process, and the UK lacks an independent oversight body, such as the SEC, to push for greater transparency.

The UK has never developed a vehicle for small companies. The share-issuing company is the standard vehicle for ordinary commercial activities and there are important unlimited partnerships (accounting firms, law firms) whose accounting is totally unregulated. There are also some major non-profit distributing charitable organizations such as the National Trust and the Church of England, which hold major assets. Accounting regulation addresses only share-issuing companies, and primarily those listed on the London Stock Exchange, of which there are approximately 2300, which form the vast bulk of commercial sector economic activity.

There are, however, many small companies – unfortunately the government statistical system does not permit of knowing how many. All companies are entered on a single national register when they are created, and they then have to file an annual return, including their accounts. This return (and the accounts) are available for inspection by the general public. There are 1 300 000 companies on the register, but no one knows for sure how many of these are subsidiaries of the 2300 listed companies, how many are dormant (i.e. have no commercial activity but are kept on the register to preserve trade names, etc.) and how many are in process of liquidation. Estimates of how many active, independent, small and medium-sized businesses exist vary between 300 000 and 750 000.

There are no different accounting rules for these companies and all but the smallest are subject to audit, although there are some limitations on disclosures in line with the small company category of the Fourth Directive. From time to time there is a debate as to whether separate accounting rules are necessary, and historically this has always been rejected. Similarly, a Department of Trade and Industry survey in 1995 came to the conclusion that there was little benefit to be obtained in creating a new legal vehicle for small companies. In 1997 the ASB issued a standard which provides a simplified version of existing standards for small companies, although it does not go so far as to propose the creation of entirely separate rules. It seems clear that the primary users of small company accounts are the Inland Revenue, not shareholders or lenders (although the banks look to the accounts for endorsement of financial information such as management accounts), and suppliers tend to refer to credit reference agencies such as Dun and Bradstreet who rely on a wider information set. So far regulators and accountants have resisted the idea that small companies have different reporting requirements from large ones, even though this view is gaining ground in mainland Europe.

There has been little systematic research in this area, although Page (1984) found some evidence that suggested tax computation as an important aspect of the accounts, and Meyer and Alexander (1991) found when comparing matched listed and unlisted companies that unlisted UK companies had a balance sheet profile more akin to their German counterparts than listed UK companies. In general it should not be assumed that practice is uniform in the UK, certainly not as between large, listed companies and small, private ones, even though current accounting regulation hardly distinguishes between them.

Publication and audit

Since 1967 all limited liability companies, of whatever size, have been obliged to have their accounts audited, to distribute them to shareholders and to file them with the Companies' Registry where they are open for inspection. At the time the addition of small companies to the existing requirements for large companies was seen to be the price for limited liability. Since 1982 small companies, within the terms of the Fourth Directive, have had the right to file abbreviated accounts, but they still have to produce full accounts to their shareholders. Technically, CA1989 introduced a facility for large companies to send simplified accounts to shareholders (who retained the right to have full accounts if they wanted them). This was introduced in the wake of privatizations which left some companies with more than a million small shareholders and a large printing bill, but in practice this possibility has not been widely taken up.

During the 1990s the government experimented with granting exemptions from audit for small companies. Currently, companies whose turnover is below £750 000 need not have a statutory audit, although some research suggests that quite a number of companies continue to have their accounts audited.

Beyond these relatively modest relaxations, all companies are required to have an annual audit and to publish their accounts. Most large companies now see their annual accounts or annual report as an important public relations document which they will happily supply free of charge to anyone who telephones to ask for it and which they reproduce on their web site.

Auditing principles are elaborated by the four professional bodies whose members are potentially allowed to audit (the three chartered regional bodies and the ACCA). They do this through the Auditing Practices Board. A system of independent regulation of the audit profession is being put in place.

The audit industry is dominated by the Big Four Anglo-American firms, which inevitably have the large majority of audits of listed companies. There is, however, an important tier of large firms (such as BDO Stoy Hayward and Grant Thornton) which have substantial national practices and belong to international networks. Economies of scale tend to drive medium-sized firms to amalgamate and there is a continuing process of concentration which mostly concerns firms in the middle range of size. At a national level, firms like BDO Stoy Hayward and Grant Thornton are approaching the size of the Big Four but with a different client profile.

Auditing went through a particularly difficult period at the end of the 1980s and beginning of the 1990s when its credibility began to suffer as a result of a number of company failures. In particular the Maxwell scandal where a company pension fund's assets were 'borrowed' was seen to reflect badly on the auditors (although in that case it is not clear that the auditors were in a position to have prevented this in the short term). Major crashes such as the Bank of Credit and Commerce International, as well as more local ones such as Coloroll and Polly Peck, added to the feeling of disenchantment. Auditing in the UK suffered from the 'expectations gap' which was being identified in other countries at the same time.

Up to a point the focus of attention has since switched from the auditor to the company management. The profession sponsored an enquiry, chaired by Sir Adrian Cadbury, into corporate governance in general. The Cadbury Report, published in 1993, set up a code of practice for company management and the subsequent debate successfully highlighted that the company (not the auditor) is responsible to the shareholders for its accounts. The Report recommended that management should make a statement in the annual report about whether they considered the company to be a going concern, and whether they were satisfied with the internal control mechanisms which they had in place (and on which, of course, the statutory auditors rely heavily). They were also recommended to set up an audit committee and a remuneration committee.

Audit liability, although a difficult matter, has had more favourable treatment by the UK courts than in the USA. The negligent auditor in the UK has a joint and several liability for damages (i.e. if negligence is proved, the auditor can be sued for all damages incurred, not just those directly derived from the negligence). For many years the professional indemnity insurers avoided any cases coming to court because they were afraid that legal precedents similar to those established in the USA in the 1970s would be created. However, in 1989 a case (Caparo) did go to court and in fact the judgment was much more favourable to the profession than expected. The court took the view that the auditor could only be liable to someone who had a direct contractual relationship and therefore that the auditor knew when issuing the report would rely upon it.

Subsequent judgments have modified this slightly, but the volume of cases and damages is much lower than in the USA, partly because contingent fee arrangements with lawyers are not permitted and perhaps also because the loser may be required to pay a major part of the winner's legal costs. None the less, there are still negligence cases and it is still true that the amount of partner time taken up in fighting cases (and not recoverable) means that it is frequently cheaper to offer a financial settlement than fight the case through the courts.

UK financial reporting

Components of annual reports

The annual report of large companies, as in other jurisdictions, usually contains a substantial voluntary section which is unregulated, together with statutory items. The unregulated part usually provides many photographs and visual aids giving an overview (almost unfailingly optimistic) of the company. The regulated part includes what company law calls the 'Directors' Report', which consists of a series of statutory disclosures of a widely disparate nature (directors' interests in shares, employment of disabled people, research and development expenditure, etc.). The ASB issued a recommendation that companies should also provide here an 'Operating and Financial Review' which would

> Include a discussion and interpretation of the business, the main factors, features as well as uncertainties that underlie it and the structure of its financing . . . it should draw out those aspects of the year under review that are relevant to an assessment of future prospects.

This has not so far been widely taken up in the ASB form.

The accounting statements that follow (not always in this order) are:

Profit and loss account

Statement of total recognized gains and losses

Statement of movements in shareholders' equity

Balance sheet

Cash flow statement

Notes to the accounts

Auditors' report.

The profit and loss account follows the Fourth Directive formats, all of which are permitted by CA1985, with substantial majority practice being to show expenses by function and display the figures in a vertical list. However, FRS3 *Reporting financial performance* brought in a requirement to include a new statement, that of total recognized gains and losses, which follows on from the profit and loss account. This statement includes the net earnings figure and then shows unrealized changes in value occurring in the year, including revaluation surpluses and foreign currency translation differences. The statement of movements in shareholders' equity again takes up these figures as well as dividend payments. The details of these statements are dealt with in the sections that follow. British companies take a great deal of freedom about the order in which they present the information. For example, information supposed to be in the Directors' Report might appear in the notes to the accounts, segment data which should be in the notes might be displayed separately before the main statements, etc.

Table 6.2   International Accounting Standards checklist

IAS	UK practice
1	Substance over form is not clearly established in UK standards, although FRS5 talks of reporting the economic substance of transactions. Basic principles and disclosures are otherwise provided in SSAP2.
2	Dealt with similarly in SSAP9 except that LIFO is excluded.
7	FRS1 broadly follows this, but interest, dividends and tax are shown separately with the operating data.
8	The UK definition of extraordinary items is now more restrictive than the IAS.
10	SSAP17 (post balance sheet events) is similar.
11	SSAP9 deals with long-term contracts on a similar basis but provides for a more complex balance sheet presentation.
12	FRS 19 requires full provision of deferred tax, as does IAS 12. However the UK standard allows discounting where liabilities are not expected to be settled for some time, and does not require provisions to be made when non-monetary assets are revalued.
14	SSAP25 provides for the same analysis but also specifies that any segment which has significantly different risks, returns or expectations should be separately identified.
16	FRS15 is similar but tangible fixed assets may be carried at valuation.
17	Very similar to SSAP21.
18	No UK standard, but UK practice in line with IAS.
19	SSAP24 is similar. The successor standard, FRS17 has been deferred until 2005.
20	SSAP4 was originally the same as IAS20 but was revised to permit only recognition of grants as deferred credit.

Table 6.2 International Accounting Standards checklist (*continued*)

IAS	UK practice
21	Developed alongside SSAP20, which has same approach as benchmark.
22	FRS6 provides for acquisition accounting and also deals with mergers (uniting of interests). Goodwill must be capitalized and amortized (FRS10). Fair value should be attributed to acquired assets and liabilities on the basis of 'value to the business' (FRS7).
23	No UK standard; CA1985 provides that borrowing costs directly related to financing the construction of an asset (current or fixed) may be capitalized.
24	FRS8 looks for ability to control or influence business.
26	No UK standard.
27	FRS2 deals with this area in very similar terms.
28	SSAP1 provides for use of equity method where significant influence exists.
29	No UK standard. SSAP20 provides that the accounts of subsidiaries in hyperinflationary economies may be restated before consolidation.
31	Proportional consolidation has traditionally been unacceptable in the UK, but is available (CA1989) for joint ventures.
32	FRS4 provides for balance sheet presentation of hybrid securities as either debt or 'non-equity'. Securities are not split into debt and equity components; they are classified as either equity or not depending upon whether there is any guaranteed payment (reimbursement or income) to the holder of the security. There are no disclosure requirements beyond standard contingent liability disclosures.
33	FRS 14 is largely based on IAS 33.
34	No equivalent standard.
35	Covered in FRS 3.
36	FRS 11 requires assets to be held at lower of cost or recoverable amount (cash flows from sale or use of the asset).
37	FRS 12 was developed alongside IAS 37 and is very similar.
38	FRS 10 mandates capitalization of cost and amortization, with a rebuttable presumption of a maximum life of 20 years.
39	No equivalent standard.
40	SSAP 19 allows measurement at current valuation.
41	No equivalent standard.

Measurement and recognition practices

These are approached first by comparing with International Accounting Standards (Table 6.2), and then by an examination of those areas that are different from IAS.

The presentation of the *profit and loss account* has been much affected by FRS3, whose objectives included an attempt to provide more detailed information and to discourage analysts from looking for a single profit figure. The standard calls for a breakdown of the operating figures between those for continuing and discontinued operations, and then a further breakdown of continuing operations between those which were acquired during the year and the rest.

The Fourth Directive format provides for an extraordinary result, a facility that was much abused in the creative accounting days. FRS3 redefines extraordinary items as those thought unlikely ever to recur, while specifically identifying reorganization provisions and profits and losses on the disposal of assets as 'exceptional' items. These have to be shown separately in the profit and loss account or be disclosed in the notes, but form part of the ordinary result.

Typically UK companies are expected to show turnover from their core activities (net of turnover taxes) as the main revenue in the profit and loss account, while ancillary income, such as rentals from unused premises or similar activities (other than financial income from investments), is shown separately within the operating result and not included in turnover. The only other analysis of income is provided in the segment analysis, which is usually in the notes.

Companies must show *earnings per share* (eps) on the face of the profit and loss account, and this is defined in FRS14. The definition of eps takes earnings after minority interests and after extraordinary items, while shares are calculated (a) on the average in issue and (b) 'fully diluted' on the assumption that all outstanding options, warrants, etc., are exercised. When the ASB introduced this definition as part of its fight against the abuse of extraordinary items, financial analysts (the Institute of Investment Management and Research – IIMR) responded by offering an alternative definition which welcomed the standard as 'realistic and constructive' but said that analysts need a benchmark figure. This is calculated by excluding all capital items from earnings (gains and losses on the disposal of assets or businesses). It is known as IIMR headline earnings, and many companies now produce eps figures calculated according to both the standard and the IIMR method.

As far as *intangible fixed assets* are concerned, there are standards on research and development expenditure (development costs may be capitalized as long as the project is judged to be commercially exploitable and the company has the resources necessary) and goodwill (see below). Beyond that CA1985 calls for amortization over the useful life of the asset. There are no special rules for computer software.

The application of the rules is, however, more nuanced. In recent times there has been a tendency by acquisitive companies to capitalize brand assets and not amortize them. Cadbury Schweppes, for example, expenses all research and development expenditure, but has capitalized all brands acquired since 1985. Its accounting policy note says: 'No amortisation is charged as the annual results reflect significant expenditure in support of these brands and the values are reviewed annually with a view to write down if a permanent diminution occurs.'

Tangible fixed assets are normally accounted for at cost (including all expenditure necessary to bring the asset into service) and depreciated over their useful life, except for 'freehold' (owned outright) land (CA1985). However, tangible fixed assets may also be held at valuation, but in that event must be depreciated on the basis of the revalued amount – so many companies that revalue assets only revalue non-depreciable ones, typically land. The increase in value is treated on the equity side by recognizing a revaluation reserve. Write-downs of asset values are not necessary on a year-to-year basis. The entry value can be maintained as long as the asset value is 'recoverable in use' and there is no 'permanent' loss of value.

Systematic depreciation (which has no tax consequence) is calculated (FRS15) after taking account of any estimated residual value. Straight-line depreciation is virtually universal, with companies typically applying a 2% rate to buildings, 10–15% to industrial plant and equipment, and 20% to motor vehicles. Depreciation disclosures in company accounts tend to be very vague in the area of plant and equipment and to aggregate many different kinds of asset, so it is difficult for the user to determine what rate is applied to (say) computers or even motor vehicles.

The lack of tax linkage means that companies have some freedom to juggle with depreciation. One manifestation of this is a tactic often used by British retailers and hotel companies which charge no depreciation on their buildings. The argument advanced is that buildings and furniture are necessarily maintained to a very high standard, with the consequence that the estimated residual value is greater than the historical cost, so there is no sum to be depreciated.

An English Institute working party published a report in 1992 claiming that many companies did not charge sufficient depreciation. It cited, amongst other problems, a failure to distinguish between different parts of investments which had different useful lives (e.g. airframe and engines of aircraft). A consequence of under-depreciation is that asset disposals show accounting losses, but these are now shown (FRS3) as exceptional items, and analysts on the whole tend to disregard exceptional items in their forecasting, so there is little incentive for companies to make large depreciation charges.

Investments, whether short term or long term, are held at the lower of cost or market value. This rule applies to all *current assets*. Stock (SSAP9) is valued on a FIFO basis almost universally with LIFO specifically prohibited by the standard. Production overheads should be included in the computation of stock values. The standard says the company should classify all overheads according to function (production, distribution, administration) and allocate them accordingly.

The same standard deals with profit on long-term contracts, requiring that annual profit should fairly reflect 'the profit attributable to that part of the work performed at the accounting date'. There are several ways to calculate this, including a valuation by a relevant professional, or taking a proportion of total contract turnover, which is derived by applying the ratio of costs incurred to total contract costs. Any expected losses must be provided for immediately.

Liabilities are split in the balance sheet between current (maturing in less than one year) and long term. Borrowings are therefore split across the two parts of the balance sheet, and current liabilities do not strictly represent purely working capital items. Companies are supposed to analyse debt by repayment period and by currency.

By comparison with the traditionally more prudent accounting countries such as Germany or Switzerland, the volume of *provisions* in UK company balance sheets is likely to be relatively small and possibly different in nature. As regards pensions, the state provides a low basic pension which is funded through social security contributions. The more important pension comes from the employer, who pays premiums to an independent fund on a year-to-year basis. The accounting standard (SSAP24) requires that pension liabilities are calculated at balance sheet date and compared with the assets in the pension fund, and any excess of liabilities should appear in the balance sheet. The new pension standard, FRS17, requires pension assets and liabilities to be brought onto the balance sheet. However, implementation has been delayed until 2005. Recent estimates suggest that the decline in stock values has created a significant shortfall in funds.

A more common provision for expenses is that for reorganization. In a management culture that views each large company as a portfolio of projects where old, failing projects should be sold and new, growth projects should be bought, reorganization is a permanent state, but provisions must be made as soon as the reorganization is formally agreed upon. Other routine provisions concern goods on sale or return, obligations under guarantees etc.

The old standard on *deferred taxation* (SSAP15) was felt to be largely out of line with international practice. The standard calls for partial provision only and this is calculated on a deferral basis. At the time the standard was formulated, the UK government gave 100% depreciation allowances in the first year for some industrial assets, giving rise potentially to very large deferred taxation provisions. However, preparers argued, success-fully, that these provisions would never reverse since large companies are constantly renewing their asset portfolio. Consequently the standard calls for deferred tax provisions only in so far as the liability will crystallize within the foreseeable future (two to three years). The new standard, FRS19, comes into force in 2003 and requires full provision of deferred tax liablities.

Provisions for other risks and expenses tend to be minimal. This is probably a function of both the orientation of reporting towards profit maximization for the capital markets, and a lack of tax incentives. The Inland Revenue allow provisions as a deduction from profit only when they are (a) specific to a particular anticipated expense relating to a past event, and (b) can be calculated with reasonable accuracy. General provisions are not allowed.

FRS 12 *Provisions, contingent liabilities and contingent assets* was developed along-side IAS37. A provision should be made when an entity has a legal or constructive oblig-ation arising from a past event, it is probable that a transfer of economic benefits will be required to settle the obligation, and a reliable estimate can be made of the amount. Con-tingent liabilities should be disclosed if there is more than a remote possibility of a cash outflow.

The main accounts of UK companies are the *consolidated accounts*, and the individual accounts of the parent are seen as largely irrelevant, even though the parent balance sheet still has to be provided alongside the group balance sheet. The biggest problem in group accounts is that of accounting for goodwill. Until adoption of the Fourth Directive, this was treated as a non-depreciable asset, and subsequently the accounting standard (SSAP22) allowed for immediate write-off at acquisition against reserves. This avoids a goodwill amortization charge against profits but acquisitive companies deplete their reserves substantially, leading to problems with debt/equity ratios. One way out of this is to recognize a brand value or similar intangible. Aggressive accounting companies also used this route to enhance future profits: they wrote down acquired assets substantially, and created reorganization provisions, which increased the goodwill but substantially reduced the future depreciation and running costs of the acquired company.

The debate about goodwill and the feasibility of recognition of brands and similar intangibles still continues. However, a 1997 standard FRS10 banned the write off of good-will against reserves. It required capitalization and amortization, while allowing recogni-tion of brands and similar intangibles, and conceding that their carrying value should be based on annual valuation rather than being amortized systematically. The change in policy in the USA will put pressure on the UK ASB to return to non-depreciation of goodwill.

The creation of reorganization provisions on acquisition has been banned under FRS6 (acquisitions and mergers). The standard also addresses the question of accounting for a business combination as a uniting of interests or merger, which had also been abused in the creative accounting period. It provides not only that the combination must take place by share exchange but that the companies must show that the management of both companies continue to participate in and share the management of the combination.

In general, the assumption is that acquisition accounting is the norm, with the assets and liabilities of the acquired company valued at fair value at the time of acquisition and good-will recognized. The calculation of fair value is also the subject of a standard, FRS7, which requires the application of 'value to the business' or deprival value (see above), which in most cases will be replacement cost. Analysis of the difference between fair value and the historical cost amounts of the subsidiary has to be disclosed in the notes at the time of the first consolidation.

Translation of the accounts of foreign subsidiaries is dealt with in SSAP20, which was evolved jointly with IAS 21 and SFAS 52 and is therefore broadly similar to them. The UK standard says the preparer must distinguish between quasi-autonomous subsidiaries (closing rate method) and those that are extensions of the parent (temporal method). There is no direct equivalent of the US functional currency approach. The UK standard calls for recognition of unrealized exchange losses *and gains* on outstanding foreign currency balances, restated at balance sheet date.

Associated companies are accounted for by the equity method. This usually includes joint ventures as well, although CA1989 introduced the possibility of accounting for these by proportional consolidation, a technique that had previously been regarded as unacceptable.

FRS1 introduced a US-style *cash flow statement* which replaced the previous funds flow statement; the statement has no statutory backing as such. The UK version shows payments of interest, dividend and taxation on the face of the statement, following the computation of operating cash flows.

The notes to the accounts have the same legal status as the main statements. They must detail the main accounting policies (though these are often presented separately from the other notes). The analysis of fixed assets (cost, accumulated depreciation, etc.) is usually provided in the notes as well, and is part of a general trend towards keeping the profit and loss account and balance sheet as simple as possible while providing detailed analysis in the notes.

A survival of the days when little profit and loss account detail was given is disclosure of the total depreciation figure, interest, directors' remuneration and the audit fee. Recently companies have also been required to disclose fees for non-audit services paid to their audit firm, which has provided some interesting material. It seems that, while there are significant variances, on average the audit fee represents only half of what is paid to the auditor.

The notes should also contain segmental disclosures, called for by SSAP25. These should provide turnover, operating profit and net assets for each industry segment and geographical segment. The choice of segments is left to the preparer, but the standard calls for identification of segments with a significantly different risk or rate of return. The quality of segment reporting varies quite substantially and probably depends to an extent on whether the group's structure lends itself to that kind of analysis (i.e. is it organized strictly on product lines or are there many mixed facilities, etc.).

There are no special disclosures required for financial instruments at present. The notes should contain details of all borrowings (including currencies and maturities) and all equity instruments.

Conclusion

It is clear that the whole infrastructure of UK accounting is oriented around the needs of large, listed companies, and is dominated by the accounting profession. Accounting standards have been more demanding since 1990 and the creation of the ASB. However, the culture of the profession is still one that sees itself as serving the large companies, and the profession generally does not see any need for independent regulation of accounting. Consequently, the reporting regime remains largely one that large companies are comfortable with.

Curiously, despite the existence of a large number of small businesses and small accounting firms which service their needs, this area of the economy is largely neglected, and the voice of the small practitioner is generally not heard in the professional bodies. It may be an accident of history that no separate vehicle for small companies has been developed, but the trend towards polarization and the switch to IFRS for listed companies in 2005 may mean that a divergent accounting culture will finally emerge.

References

Arden, J. (1997) True and fair view: European prospective. *European Accounting Review* **6**(4).

Edey, H. (1971) The true and fair view. *Accountancy* August: 440–441.

Hopwood, A.G. (1990) Ambiguity, knowledge and territorial claims: some observations on the doctrine of substance over form. *British Accounting Review* March: 79–87.

van Hulle, K. (1993) Truth and untruth about true and fair. *European Accounting Review* **2**(1): 99–104.

Jones, E. (1981) *Accountancy and the British Economy 1840–1980*. Batsford, London.

Meyer, C. and Alexander, I. (1991) Stock markets and corporate performance: a comparison of quoted and unquoted companies. Mimeo, Centre for Economic Policy Research, London.

Napier, C. (1995). The history of financial reporting in the UK. In P. Walton (ed.) *European Financial Reporting: a History*. Academic Press, London.

Nobes, C. (1993) The true and fair view requirement: impact on and of the Fourth Directive. *Accounting and Business Research* Winter: 35–48.

Page, M. (1984) Corporate financial reporting and the small independent company. *Accounting and Business Research* Summer: 271–282.

Parker, R.H. (1989) Importing and exporting accounting: the British experience. In A.G. Hopwood, (ed.) *International Pressures for Accounting Change*. Prentice Hall, Hemel Hempstead.

Walton, P. (1986) The export of British legislation to Commonwealth countries. *Accounting and Business Research* Summer: 353–357.

Walton, P. (1990) Les directives européennes et leurs incidences en grande Bretagne. In D. Boussard and P. Delvaille (eds) *Etudes en comptabilité internationale*. ESCP/OECCA, Paris.

Walton, P. (1993) The true and fair view in British accounting. *European Accounting Review* **2**(1): 49–58.

Walton, P. (2001) L'éphémère introduction du coût de remplacement en Grande Bretagne: bilan d'une tentative pour remettre en cause le modèle en coûts historique. In Casta, J.-F. and Colasse, B. (eds.) *La juste valeur*. Economica: Paris.

Zeff, S. (1972) *Forging Accounting Principles in Five Countries*. Stipes Publishing, IL.

Further Reading

Freedman, J. (1987) Profit and prophets – law and accountancy practice on the timing of receipts – recognition under the earnings basis (Schedule D cases I and II). *British Tax Review* No 2 & 3: 61–79, 104–133.

Gordon, P.D. and Gray, S.J. (1994) *European Financial Reporting: United Kingdom*. Routledge, London.

Mumford, M.J. (2000) United Kingdom. In D. Alexander & S. Archer (eds.) *European Accounting Guide*, 4th edn. Aspen Publishing.

Turley, S. (1992) Developments in the structure of financial reporting in the United Kingdom. *European Accounting Review* **1**(1): 105–122.

Whittington, G. (1993) Corporate governance and the regulation of financial reporting. *Accounting and Business Research* **23**(91a): 311–319.

Willmott, H. (1986) Organising the profession: a theoretical and historical examination of the development of the major accountancy bodies in the UK. *Accounting, Organizations and Society*, pp. 555–582.

Accounting in Japan

Etsuo Sawa

Japan as an accounting jurisdiction is characterized by the dominance of the state. The accounting rules have been set out in the past 50 years as statute law with an implicit objective that accounting should contribute to the growth of the national economy. Until very recently, the accounting profession had played a minor role in shaping accounting practices. The accounting profession, or more accurately auditing practice, was also created by law soon after World War II as a discipline needed to reactivate the securities market in Japan. Even auditing standards, again until very recently, have been promulgated by the government. Changes, however, have been taking place in the past several years with a shift toward making financial reporting more investor and creditor oriented by conforming rapidly to internationally recognized standards and giving the accounting profession a more prominent role in developing accounting and auditing standards.

Legal and institutional basis of accounting

Mueller, Gernon and Meek (1994) classified nations into four major groups according to their accounting characteristics and put Japan, together with most countries in continental Europe, in the Continental accounting model, where

> Financial accounting is legalistic in its orientation, and practices tend to be highly conservative. Accounting is not primarily oriented toward the decision-making needs of the capital providers. Instead, it is usually designed to satisfy such government-imposed requirements as computing income taxes or demonstrating compliance with the national government's macroeconomic plan.

Arai and Shiratori (1991) agree with these observations as far as the legal framework of accounting in Japan is concerned, but point out that in the area of financial disclosure, Japanese accounting may be classified as conforming to the British–American model, which is oriented towards the decision needs of investors and creditors. The view expressed by Arai and Shiratori is shared by many Japanese writers in attempting to explain the accounting system in Japan.

Accounting as it is practised in Japan today is indeed legalistic in its orientation as the more important accounting rules are contained in laws, regulations (usually in the form of ministerial ordinances) and ministerial pronouncements. These are the Commercial Code, Securities and Exchange Law (SEL) and Corporate Tax Law and supplementary regulations and ministerial pronouncements that stem from these respective laws. In general, the

Commercial Code can be said to set the basic recognition and measurement principles, the SEL lays out presentation and disclosure standards and the Corporate Tax Law prescribes specifc and detailed recognition and measurement rules. All these, together with the Business Accounting Principles (BAP), are combined, as will be seen later, in drawing up published financial statements of large Japanese companies.

Some writers call this working of the three areas of law the 'triangular legal system' of accounting (Arai and Shiratori 1991). The interrelationships can be shown, for example, by accounting for provisions. Article 287-2 of the Commercial Code states that a provision for specific expenditure or loss may be recognized in the balance sheet, to the extent of the amount that should properly be accounted for as an expense of the business year. The interpretation of this article, however, is not found in the Code itself or its related regulations. One would need to look to the BAP and tax law. The BAP says in its Explanatory Note No. 18 that future losses or expenses that arise from past events, have a high probability of occurrence and can be estimated in a reasonable manner shall be provided for to the extent of the amount attributable to the current period. This definition of provisions is very similar to the definition of a liability and the recognition criteria for an element of financial statements in the IASC Framework, as well as the recognition standard for provisions in IAS37.

Explanatory Note No. 18 of the BAP cites the following examples – provisions for product warranties, sales rebates, sales returns, bonuses, construction guarantees, retirement benefits, repairs and maintenance, special maintenance, loss from debt guarantees, casualty loss and bad debts. It specifies that provisions should not be set up for expenses or losses relating to contingencies that have a low probability of occurrence. One would then go to the tax law for guidance on measurement.

The tax law currently allows six of the above provisions to be deducted for tax to the extent that they are within the limit prescribed by the tax authorities. Since any amount in excess of the ceiling would not be tax deductible and because, as discussed below, deferred tax accounting was not permitted until 1999, the tendency of preparers would be to provide for amounts up to the tax limit in their financial statements issued under the Commercial Code, as well as those issued under the SEL (see below) – even in situations where a larger provision might be more appropriate (see *FT World Accounting Report*, April 1996). Conversely, enterprises may avail themselves of a tax reduction by providing for the maximum, even though a lesser amount is more appropriate for financial reporting purposes.

Commercial Code

The Commercial Code, enacted in 1899 in the present form, has a part (Book II) that deals with companies. Chapter 4 of Book II sets out rules for limited liability companies (Kabushiki Kaisha), such as, for example, incorporation procedures, issuance of shares and duties and responsibilities of directors and statutory auditors. The accounting rules are dealt with primarily in Section 4 of this chapter and these rules are often referred to as the 'computational provisions' (Keisan Kitei) of the Commercial Code. It is true that the number and nature of items dealt with in such provisions are surprisingly few and often one has to go outside the Code for guidance and interpretation. Yet the Code sets the legal framework of accounting in Japan and is in the centre of the triangular legal system, having the status of the fundamental law (Arai and Shiratori 1991). Given its generality, coupled with an implicit and persistent belief in Japan that accounting should eventually contribute to the development of the national economy as a whole (i.e. 'demonstrating compliance with the national government's macroeconomic plan') (Arai and Shiratori 1991), the Code, together with the BAP, has helped large banks and major businesses to accumulate capital through 'flexible' accounting, especially in the years of high economic growth (Kawai and Terashima 1983).

Securities and exchange law

Whereas the accounting rules of the Commercial Code apply to all limited liability companies regardless of their size and whether they are publicly or privately held (there were approximately 1 200 000 such companies in 1991, but this number might have been reduced due to the new minimum capital requirement of ¥10 million effective from 1 June 1996), the SEL and related regulations and circulars apply only to publicly held companies and those about to go public. The SEL, which was enacted in 1948 and modelled after the 1933 Securities Act and 1934 Securities Exchange Act of the United States, is administered by the Ministry of Finance[1] (MOF), whereas the Commercial Code is in the domain of the Ministry of Justice.

The SEL's accounting regulations and circulars set out requirements for the presentation and disclosure of financial information, which are prescribed in a very detailed and exact manner. Companies (and their independent accountants) take pains to ensure that they are complied with to the last detail; for example, the wording used in a note to the financial statements on, say, retirement benefits is the same for practically all companies. Compliance, and therefore uniformity, is the rule (Cooke and Kikuya 1992). In fact, one of the items on which the independent accountant is required to express an opinion in the audit report is whether the presentation and disclosure in the financial statements complies with the Regulation Concerning Financial Statements. Accordingly, the financial statements would, on the surface, seem highly comparable among Japanese companies, but because of the flexibility in the underlying measurements, as explained in the preceding section, they are not really so.

The Regulation Concerning Financial Statements, more precisely Regulation Concerning the Terminology, Form and Preparation Method of Financial Statements, issued in 1963 as MOF Ordinance No. 59, and its Interpretative Guidance stipulate the terms, form and content of unconsolidated financial statements that are required to be prepared by listed companies for filing with the MOF. The content is similar to part of article 4, Rules of General Application, article 5, Commercial and Industrial Companies and article 12, Form and Content of Schedules of the US Securities and Exchange Commission's (SEC's) Regulation S-X.

In addition to these, there are similar regulations and guidance for consolidated financial statements (issued in 1976) and interim, i.e. mid-year, unconsolidated financial statements (issued in 1977). Further, there are other separate MOF ordinances and circulars which set out financial statement disclosure requirements, for example the Ordinance Concerning Company Disclosure (issued in 1973) prescribes, among other things, the forms and regulations for the preparation of company registration statements and securities reports.

Generally, the SEL is a financial disclosure law for listed companies and had not set out accounting recognition and measurement rules, with the notable exceptions of lease accounting and foreign currency transactions, until very recently. The lease accounting rules, however, are in substance a disclosure rule in that although finance leases are accounted for as such, the resulting amounts, i.e. assets, depreciation, liabilities and interest expense of lessees, are not reflected in the basic financial statements as such. Rather, a disclosure of information on a capitalization basis is made in a note to the financial statements. The reason for dealing with lease accounting in this manner is not necessarily because it was in conflict with the Commercial Code framework, but rather for political reasons.

Business accounting principles and the BADC

Some would say that the BAP should be considered as being under the SEL umbrella, while others would raise them to a higher status – the Japanese framework for applied accounting. The BAP (Kigyo Kaikei Gensoku – it is also translated as Financial Accounting Standards for Business Enterprises) were issued in 1949 by the predecessor of the MOF's Business Accounting Deliberation Council[2] (BADC) with the primary purpose of fostering nationwide uniformity in financial accounting practices (Mueller and Yoshida 1968). The 1949 Preface to the BAP says in part that they are a condensed version of the accounting conventions, selected from among those developed over the years in practice, which are generally acknowledged to be fair and sound (i.e. generally accepted accounting principles – GAAP) and that although not necessarily enforceable as law, they are the standards that must be observed by every business enterprise. The preface also states that the BAP should be reflected when, in the future, the Commercial Code, tax laws, etc. are enacted, amended or repealed. The BAP had high ideals and have permeated through the Japanese accounting system. They have influenced the tax law, one evidence of which is the introduction in 1967 of a provision, in article 22-4 of the Corporate Tax Law, stating that taxable income should be computed in accordance with generally accepted accounting principles (unless, needless to say, the tax law provides otherwise). The BAP were translated into the SEL's Regulation Concerning Financial Statements in 1963 and provided the basis for financial statement audits of independent accountants in 1951. The reference in the independent accountant's audit report to generally accepted accounting principles is meant to be the BAP. They have also influenced the Commercial Code to a great extent.

The BAP consist of three parts – general principles, income statement principles and balance sheet principles – and are accompanied in the present version (last amended in 1982) by a total of 24 explanatory notes. Both conceptual and measurement matters are dealt with in the BAP. A large part is devoted to outlining the structure of the classified statement of income and unappropriated surplus (retained earnings) and the balance sheet, with a list of items to be included in each category, but the measurement rules cover little that goes beyond the items mentioned in the Commercial Code. The explanatory notes address a wider range of issues.

The BAP reflect the income statement approach to accounting, rather than the balance sheet approach, then prevailing in the USA. This approach was embodied in the BAP in terms of the accruals and realization basis of accounting and the matching principle. The Commercial Code, however, had traditionally taken the balance sheet centred approach, as in Germany, and assets were required to be valued at not more than market value.

This market or lower principle (Jikaikashugi) of asset valuation was changed in 1962 to conform with the historical (acquisition) cost principle, with an option for the lower of cost or market method to be applied, as given in the BAP. This was expanded to include as assets, among others, goodwill and in an effort to become more income statement oriented, the Code additionally allowed set-up costs and research and development costs to be capitalized as assets and introduced a stipulation for provisions. However, the relationship between the BAP and statutory accounting rules has not always been the former influencing the latter. Sometimes the Code took the upper hand.

The 1963 amendment to the BAP (there were amendments in 1954, 1963, 1974 and 1982) was made with the objective of bringing the BAP into conformity with the Code. The Preface to this amendment states:

> The Commercial Code's (accounting) computational provisions are still left with some which are at variance with the BAP, therefore, in view of the fact that the

Commercial Code is an enforceable law, it has become necessary to amend the Business Accounting Principles in respect of these.

Some observers have remarked (e.g. Kawai and Terashima 1983) that although the 1963 revision to the BAP was partial, the BAP, which at the time had come to be looked upon lightly, started to show signs of changing their relationship with practice and the Code. This started with the 1962 revision to the Code (see above), made for the purpose of protecting entities in the age of open economic policy, and which had the effect of promoting the view that statutory requirements have priority over GAAP in accounting practices.

A further attempt at unifying accounting standards and bringing the BAP closer to the Code was made by the BADC in 1974. In the 1974 revision, among other changes, the consistency principle was relaxed and special provisions, deductions from earnings for specific purposes, were allowed to be recognized in the liabilities section of the balance sheet. These were made not so much to make compromises with the Code, but more as compromises to practice. Kawai and Terashima (1983) claim that a relaxation of this sort is a reflection of the desire embedded in businesses for creative and free accounting practices, sometimes, in the name of conservatism. Some would regret this as a downgrading of the BAP, which had once high ideals and had influenced the shaping of the Japanese accounting system (Someya 1996), and consider the BAP now as only a part of the SEL.

The Business Accounting Deliberation Council (BADC) of the Ministry of Finance[3] sets out financial accounting and reporting standards for publicly held companies that are required to file registration statements or periodic securities reports under the SEL. As previously mentioned, the BADC's standards-setting activities in the sense of, say the FASB or IASC, had been limited to establishing primarily the Business Accounting Principles (1949) and the Principles of Consolidated Financial Statements (1975) and issuing the standards on foreign currency transactions and translation (1979), segment information (1988), disclosure of market value information of certain financial instruments (1990) and leases (1993). However, within the 20-month period from June 1997 to January 1999, the BADC issued new accounting standards or made major revisions to existing standards with a view to bringing the Japancese accounting requirements for listed companies closer to internationally recognized standards.

The items covered in the new and revised standards are consolidation policy and procedures, cash flow statement, retirement benefits, research and development costs, deferred tax accounting and financial instruments. These standards became effective over the three-year period beginning on 1 April 1999. In this chapter, they are incorporated in the 'Recognition and Measurement' section that follows.

Corporate tax law

Because of the flexibility that exists in the recognition and measurement aspects of accounting under the Commercial Code, the SEL and the BAP (some would see it as a relatively large vacuum), and further, because of the tax law requirement to use financial statements that have been submitted and approved at the annual shareholders' meeting, the adoption of tax accounting for general purpose financial reporting is relatively common in Japan. This tie between the tax accounts and Code accounts is commonly referred to as the 'principle of final accounts (Kakutei Kessan Shugi)' and makes it difficult for financial reporting under the Code (for the protection of creditors) and SEL (for the interest of investors) to be different from the measurement bases used in the computation of taxable income.

For example, article 285-2 of the Commercial Code states that current assets (principally inventories) should be valued at the acquisition cost (purchased or manufactured), except when the market value is substantially lower than the acquisition cost, in which case the carrying amount should be the market value. However, such a write-down is not required when a decline in value is expected to be temporary. The Commercial Code is, however, silent on what would constitute a substantial decline in market value, and the practice has developed over the years of interpreting it to mean the same thing as the tax rule (tax circular) allows, i.e. when the market value is lower than the carrying amount by 50% or more.

Accordingly, a company, especially when its financial statements are subject to audit by independent accountants, has no alternative but to recognize a loss in such circumstance and would claim a tax deduction. More conservative companies, however, would apply the rule to a decline of less than 50%, say 20%, and recognize the loss for financial reporting purposes even though the loss is not tax deductible unless the decline is 50% or greater. Thus, there is flexibility in adopting the accounting policy for recognizing valuation losses – in this case a decline in the range between 20% and 50%. However, the tendency of Japanese companies is not to recognize income, expenses, gains and losses for financial reporting purposes if they are treated differently under the tax law. Deferred taxation, which might have mitigated this, had not been allowed in unconsolidated accounts until 1999.

Not all items of income, expense, gain and loss for financial reporting purposes need be the same as those for tax purposes. For example, dividend income and entertainment expenses, as recorded in the books of account, are adjusted in the tax return (Schedule 4 to tax return) so as to exclude the former from taxable income and exclude the latter from deductible expenses. However, there are certain expenses and losses that must be recorded in the books of account in order to claim them as tax deductions and cannot be introduced through Schedule 4 as above. These include, among others, depreciation (including special bonus depreciation), retirement benefits to directors and provisions (Hikiatekin) and reserves (Junbikin) prescribed in the Special Taxation Measures Law.

There is a tendency, which is difficult to challenge, for companies, large and small, to align themselves conveniently on tax rules in the selection of accounting policies for general purpose financial reporting. This tendency is criticized by some as being 'a reverse influence of tax law on generally accepted accounting principles'. The relative superiority of tax law over other accounting regulations in the mind of corporate accountants is illustrated in a survey (Hiramatsu 1994). This showed that, for them, corporate tax rules are the most important of all accounting rules, followed by the SEL's Regulation Concerning Financial Statements (presentation and disclosure).

Accounting profession

There are two groups of accounting professionals that provide services to third parties. One is the licensed tax practitioner (Zeirishi) and the other is the certified public accountant (Konin Kaikeishi).

Tax practitioners are individuals who have passed the required examinations or obtained the required qualifications in some other way (for example, by working as a tax agent of the Japanese Tax Administration Agency for a certain number of years or by holding a certified public accountant's qualification) and who are registered with the appropriate regional Certified Public Tax Accountants Associations. They practice as sole practitioners and principally provide tax compliance and consulting services to corporate and individual clients. Their services also include bookkeeping, preparation of financial statements, business consulting, computerization and consultation in specialized areas of taxation such as inheritance tax.

Due to the nature of their services and the size of their firms, the clients they serve are normally individual operators and small to medium-sized companies, but they may be retained by large corporations as tax consultants. Accordingly, except in the area of financial statement attest services, which can only be provided by certified public accountants, the two groups are in competition and can be said to share the public accounting, tax and consulting markets in Japan. Approximately half of the certified public accountants are also registered as tax practitioners. As of the end of 2000, the total membership of the Japan Federation of Certified Public Tax Accountants Associations was approximately 65 000.

Certified public accountants and audit corporations are authorized under the Certified Public Accountants Law to engage in the practice of public accountancy, the most significant and exclusive of which is the financial statement attest service. The related services provided by certified public accountants are tax compliance and planning and, to a lesser extent, business consulting, mergers and acquisitions, assistance in stock exchange listing, electronic data processing consulting and systems review, and international consulting. Except for financial statement attest and tax work – in which only certified public accountants and licensed tax practitioners, respectively, are permitted to engage – there are no qualification requirements for other work.

The practice of public accountancy is open to those who have passed the Japanese certified public accountants' (CPA) examination and registered with the Japanese Institute of Certified Public Accountants (JICPA). The CPA examination is administered by the Ministry of Finance and conducted by the CPA examination board, the members of which are appointed by the Ministry. The examination consists of three phases.

The first examination comprises Japanese language, mathematics, a foreign language and a thesis. Candidates who have completed two years of study at a university or college are exempt from this requirement. The second examination is given once a year and allows candidates two and a half days to complete the papers. It comprises bookkeeping, financial statement theory, cost accounting, auditing theory and commercial law and two out of the following subjects: business management, economics and civil law. The pass rates over the period 1985 to 1995 were between 6.9% and 10.6%, with the numbers of candidates increasing from 4000 to over 10 000 over the period.

Candidates who complete the second examination successfully are given the title of Junior CPA upon registration with the JICPA. Then they are required to complete a further training course for one year, conducted usually in the evening, and to gain experience in public accounting or accounting-related work for two years before becoming eligible to sit for the third examination. The third examination comprises accounting practice (including tax), auditing practice, financial analysis and a thesis. It consists of written and oral parts. Candidates who complete the third examination successfully must become members of the JICPA in order to qualify as CPAs. As of the end of 2000, the JICPA had the following members:

CPAs	13 220
Foreign CPAs	6
Audit corporations	149
Subtotal	13 375
Junior CPAs	4 038
Total	17 413

The practice of public accountancy by CPAs may be conducted by sole practitioners or, since 1966, by audit corporations (Kansa Hojin) that have a minimum of five partners, all of whom must be CPAs. Each partner has unlimited, joint liability. Historically, there have not been many CPAs who work in areas other than public accounting. Out of approximately 17 000 CPAs and junior CPAs who are members of the JICPA, only around 2 to 3% work in the teaching profession, industry and government.

The statutory audit market in Japan, especially with regard to SEL audits, is dominated by four large audit corporations. These firms, most of which have partners and professional/administrative staff exceeding 2000 each, started as medium-sized firms and have grown to their present size primarily through mergers with similar and smaller firms. Since audit corporations under the law can only provide attest and other restricted services related to financial statements, tax and consulting work for their audit clients and others is normally undertaken through their affiliates. The largest audit corporations and their affiliates are members of the world's Big Four accounting and financial services firms.

The Japanese Institute of Certified Public Accountants

The JICPA is the only professional body of certified public accountants with its legal base in the CPA Law. In addition to being the registrar of CPAs, the Institute has overall responsibility under the law to supervise, guide and develop its members and the profession. The business of the JICPA is directed by its officers, who are elected every three years, and carried out through various standing and special committees of members.

The technical committees, such as the Accounting Standards Committee and Auditing Standards Committee, issue guidelines and interpretations for the members to follow. In the 1990s, the JICPA became more involved in preparing research papers on specific accounting issues for consideration by the BADC and supplementing the accounting standards and opinions issued by the BADC by issuing implementation guidance. There are various other committees, such as those that deal with professional ethics, member disciplinary matters and training and publications (JICPA publishes a monthly journal). The committees usually meet once a month or as often as necessary. The committee activities and other businesses of the JICPA are supported by some 150 full-time administrative and technical staff, including those specializing in technical information and research activities and those working for regional chapters.

Internationally, the JICPA is a council member of the International Federation of Accountants (IFAC) and an executive committee member of the Confederation of Asian and Pacific Accountants (CAPA).

Financial reporting, disclosure and audit

Assumptions and qualitative characteristics

The BAP mention seven qualitative characteristics of business accounting, such as truthfulness of reporting, understandability, consistency of application and conservatism in general terms. By way of example, with respect to conservatism, it says, 'Financial accounting for business enterprises should include prudent accounting practices in providing for possible unfavourable effects upon the financial condition of a business enterprise' (JICPA translation). The underlying measurement concepts of the accrual basis of accounting, the realization principle and the principle of matching revenue with expenses, are found in the part of the BAP dealing with the income statement.

Financial reporting under the Securities and Exchange Law

The annual securities report (Yukashoken Hokokusyo) of a publicly held Japanese company is a detailed document and for large companies with diversified operations, it runs to about 100 pages on average. The report is filed with the MOF, submitted to each of the stock exchanges on which the securities are listed and available to the public. Included in the securities report are details about the company, its operations (including research and development activities), its production and sales data (including production facilities) and capital expenditure. Two sections are financial – one is prepared on a company-alone (unconsolidated) basis and the other on a group (consolidated) basis for each of the two years presented.

The information contained in the securities report is all statutory in compliance with the rules and regulations issued by the MOF and its Securities Bureau. Company reports lack any voluntary information and are highly standardized, using uniform terminology, form and content. In many respects, the securities report is similar to Form 10-K prepared by publicly held companies in the USA.

Reporting under the Commercial Code

A business report (Eigyo Hokokusyo) is required under the Commercial Code for all limited liability companies, irrespective of whether they are publicly held or private companies, and is sent to shareholders. The business report is less voluminous than the securities report, and averages about 20 pages. Presently, 11 supporting schedules are required, showing items such as liens on assets, guarantees of indebtedness of others and compensation to directors and statutory auditors, but these schedules are not usually included in the business report sent to the shareholders. The financial statement section of the report comprises the balance sheet, income statement and proposal for appropriations of retained earnings and limited, simple accompanying notes. The financial statements are for the current year only and are prepared on an unconsolidated basis. The last of these statements, i.e. proposal for appropriations of retained earnings, which state, among others, the directors' proposal for the amounts of dividend and directors' bonus for the year, requires approval at the annual shareholders' meeting.

The Commercial Code requires that the business report and the supporting schedules be audited by statutory auditors (Kansayaku – see below). Further, when the company's share capital is ¥500 million or more or when total liabilities are ¥20 000 million or more, the business report, including those items in the descriptive sections which relate to the accounting records, is audited by independent accountants.

The business report, together with the statutory auditors' report and where applicable, the independent accountants' report, is kept at the company offices for inspection by shareholders and creditors, but is not available to the public nor is it filed with any governmental agency. However, large corporations (those that fulfil the size requirement for an independent accountant's report) need to publish a condensed balance sheet and income statement in the newspaper or official gazette as set out in the Commercial Code. Smaller corporations need to publish only a condensed balance sheet.

Other financial reporting

In addition to the two statutory reports, some large publicly held Japanese companies voluntarily prepare and publish annual reports of the type seen in the USA and elsewhere. These are primarily for foreign users and usually in the English language with the monetary amounts expressed in US dollars. The financial statements and other financial information included in them are, however, commonly still those of the Japanese statutory report, except that the presentation structure has been modified to reflect the terminology and form of, for example, a US report. Some of the note disclosures required in the Japanese securities report, such as the explanation about the presentation of consumption tax, are usually deleted from these annual reports while others, such as the description of principles used for accounting for retirement benefits, are expanded.

Among those Japanese companies that prepare these secondary annual reports for the convenience of foreign users are some 30 or 40 that have adopted US GAAP in the preparation of these financial statements. While most of them prepare these US GAAP financial statements because they are registered with the Securities and Exchange Commission (SEC) (see Chapter 17), others prepare them on a voluntary basis. As of the time of writing (January 2003), there is no known case of a Japanese multinational preparing its financial statements, either for local statutory purposes or for the convenience of the foreign reader, in accordance with International Accounting Standards.

Auditing

Financial auditing as practised, for example, in the USA, formally came into being in Japan with the enactment of the SEL and the Certified Public Accountants Law in 1948. In order that the aspects of these laws as they relate to the preparation of financial statements and their audits would be administered in a smooth manner, the predecessor of the BADC was established in the same year to develop financial accounting and auditing standards.

The *Auditing Standards*, which contain in the current version four general standards, three standards of field work and four standards of reporting, were first issued in 1950. To supplement these auditing standards, which are by their nature general statements of auditing, and to provide a degree of uniformity in their implementation, *Working Rules of Field Work* was also issued in 1950 and *Working Rules of Reporting* in 1956. Because the audit of financial statements was virtually non-existent before the 1950s, the newly created body of certified public accountants needed time to learn how to apply them, and publicly held companies, whose financial statements became subject to audit under the SEL, also needed time to improve their accounting systems so that they would be auditable. Accordingly, the first auditing under the statute, which was in 1951, was limited to a review of the company's accounting procedures and internal controls. This was followed over the next few years by the audit of limited numbers of financial statement items, with increasing coverage resulting in the full audit of financial statements in 1957.

With the expansion of the Japanese economy and the capital market, the number of publicly held companies needing to be audited increased proportionally. In 1974, a new law was added to the Commercial Code to require companies of a certain size (share capital of ¥500 million or more or total liabilities of ¥20 000 million or more) to be audited, regardless of whether they were held publicly or privately. Consequently there are two major statutes – the SEL administered by the MOF and the Commercial Code administered by the Ministry of Justice – which require the audit of financial statements of certain companies by independent auditors qualified by law to practise in Japan. Such audits are often referred to as statutory audits (Hootei Kansa). Separately from the audit of financial statements by independent auditors introduced in 1974, the Commercial Code requires the designated company personnel, called Statutory Auditors (Kansayaku) and whose function it is to 'audit' the directors' discharge of their duties (not unlike the sindaci in Italy), to audit the financial statements as well.

There are other statutory audits, such as those required for private schools that receive government subsidies and labour unions, but the number is not significant and the audits are normally performed by sole practitioners and small to medium-sized firms. The number of non-statutory, or voluntary, audits is also insignificant (if one disregards the Japanese subsidiaries and affiliates of foreign entities whose financial statements are audited or reviewed for inclusion in the group accounts).

As of 31 March 1996, the numbers of companies subject to statutory audits under the two laws were approximately as follows:

SEL	3700
Commercial Code (excluding those that are also subject to audit under SEL)	5000
Total	8700

Japanese auditing standards and related working rules, which previously included audit procedures in the form of an audit programme, have been amended several times by the BADC in order to respond to the changes that have occurred since the 1950s. The most recent of these revisions, made in 1991, marked a distinct change in standard-setting in that the role of specifying auditing procedures was shifted from the public sector (BADC) to the private sector (JICPA). Although the public sector still retains responsibility for setting general auditing standards and related working rules of field work and reporting, the profession as a whole has become responsible for developing auditing procedures within the overall frame of reference established by the BADC.

The auditing procedures, called the Auditing Standards Committee Reports, are issued by the JICPA and are similar in style and content to the AICPA's Statements on Auditing Standards (SASs) and the International Standards on Auditing (ISAs) and International Auditing Practice Statements (IAPSs) issued by the IFAC's International Auditing Practices Committee. Since its inception in 1992 at the recommendation of the BADC, a total of 17 such reports had been issued by the JICPA by early 1999. Examples of the subject matters dealt with in these reports are analytical procedures, internal control, audit risk and materiality, irregularities and errors, illegal acts (by clients), quality control and audit of accounting estimates. The going-concern issue is currently being addressed.

Recognition and measurement

In general, the basic accounting principles and procedures in Japan as they relate to the recognition, measurement and disclosure of transactions and events are in many ways similar to those of International Accounting Standards (IAS) or of countries such as the USA. These principles reflect such concepts as matching revenue with expenses, the accrual basis accounting, the going-concern assumption, the realization principle, etc. However, as discussed above, measurement principles are frequently influenced by tax considerations, and there are more extensive disclosures for listed companies. Table 7.1 compares Japanese practices with IAS.

The following is a summary of Japanese methods of accounting for certain elements of financial statements.

Table 7.1 International accounting standards checklist: comparison of Japanese practices with IAS

IAS	Japanese rules
1	Commercial Code (CC) and Business Accounting Principles (BAP) similar to IAS.
2	Valuation at cost (LIFO, FIFO or weighted average) or optionally at lower of cost or market.
4	Similar, but tax rules generally followed.
7	Only listed companies have obligation to publish, form and content similar to IAS.
8	Extraordinary category used for wider range of transactions, including asset disposals and adjustment to prior period provisions. Major extraordinary losses can be deferred and amortized. No retrospective change in opening balances is permitted. Fundamental errors are taken to current result in special section of income statement relating to prior period adjustments.
10	Companies must disclose these.
11	Both completed contract and percentage of completion allowed.
12	Similar to IAS.
14	Listed companies required to disclose analysis of sales, results, assets, depreciation and capital expenditure by major business segments; sales, result and assets by geographical segments; foreign sales by geographical locations.
15	No rules.
16	Historical cost, however, temporary measure available for revaluation. Write-down required for any permanent diminution of value.
17	Finance lease defined as one where the rental cannot be cancelled during an agreed period of time and for which lessee accepts substantially all risks and rewards. Treatment as IAS but disclosed in notes, not incorporated into balance sheet, except for those in which ownership transfers during lease period.
18	BAP in line with IAS.
19	Substantially similar to IAS with respect to retirement benefits.
20	Government grants related to assets are normally deducted in arriving at the carrying amount of the asset.
21	Transactions are reported similarly to IAS, except that long-term monetary items are reported using the historical rate, unless there is material unrealized loss, which is recognized through application of the current rate. Translation of subsidiaries: current rate for assets and liabilities, historical for income statement. Translation differences are capitalized as assets or liabilities.
22	Method resembles pooling of interests. Assets and liabilities are revalued for consolidation purposes. Goodwill normally capitalized and amortized over twenty years or less.
23	May be capitalized.
24	Listed companies must disclose ten largest shareholders, and other requirements are more extensive and detailed than IAS.
25	Long term carried at cost with obligatory write-down for permanent impairment. Short term carried at cost or optionally at lower of cost or market value.
26	No rules.
27	Listed companies only. Scope of consolidation and equity method is determined by control and significant influence criteria, respectively.
28	In group accounts only, equity accounting used.
29	No rules.
30	Separate statutes.
31	No rules, but normally accounted for by the equity method in group accounts.
32	Market values of securities, futures and options are required to be disclosed by listed companies.
33	Similar to IAS.

Table 7.1 International accounting standards checklist: comparison of Japanese practices with IAS (*continued*)

IAS	Japanese rules
34	Semi-annual financial statements, comprising balance sheet, income statement, cash flow statement and notes, are required only of publicly held companies.
35	No rules.
36	No separate standard.
37	General rule in BAP with list of provisions that may be recognized.
38	Examples of intangible assets mentioned in CC. Research and development costs are charged to expense when incurred, certain computer software should be capitalized and amortized over useful life.
39	Substantially similar to IAS.
40	No separate standard. Measured normally at cost less depreciation.
41	No rules. Income not normally recognized until items are sold.

Assets

Property, plant and equipment

Fixed assets are valued at acquisition or production cost, and must be written down to market value where a severe and permanent diminution of market value takes place. Capitalization of interest cost, although permitted, is not a general practice for commercial and industrial companies. Property, plant and equipment is shown in the financial statements at acquisition cost less related accumulated depreciation. Depreciation is generally computed by the declining balance method or straight-line method in accordance with the tax law.

Leases

Assets held under finance leases in which ownership is deemed to pass to lessees are required to be accounted for as assets and liabilities by the lessees. The government began to phase in this ruling on 1 April 1994, intending that full implementation would be achieved for individual company financial statements by 1 April 1996 and for consolidated financial statements two years thereafter. Other finance leases which individually have total minimum lease payments of ¥3 million or more need not be capitalized, provided that a disclosure based on the assumption that the leases have been capitalized is made in a note to financial statements. All other leases are accounted for as operating leases. This standard for certain finance leases is applicable only to publicly held companies in their reporting under the SEL.

Research and development costs

Previously, research and development costs could be either charged to expense when incurred, or capitalized and amortized over a period of five years or less. However, under the new standard on accounting for research and development costs and related items effective for fiscal years beginning on or after 1 April 1999, all costs and expenses associated with research and development activities, which are defined similarly as in IAS 38, should be charged to expense when incurred. Costs of producing product masters of computer software for the purpose of marketing their copies, exclusive of costs that are of a research and development nature, should be capitalized as an asset. Also, the costs of computer software created internally or purchased for internal use should be capitalized when it is deemed that provision of administrative services from its use would generate future revenues or result in cost reduction.

Computer software costs capitalized as intangible assets should be amortized using a method based on the estimated number of units expected to be sold or other reasonable method in accordance with the nature of such software. The amount of amortization for each period, however, should not be less than the amount computed using the straight-line method over the remaining life. The standard requires a footnote disclosure of the total amount of research and development costs charged to expense in the period.

Financial instruments

Financial instruments, until the issuance of a new standard in early 1999, were accounted for principally at cost with an option to value them at the lower of cost or market method determined on the individual security (issuer) basis. Market value information was required to be disclosed for quoted debt and equity securities as well as financial derivatives, such as futures, options and forward exchange contracts.

The new standard on financial instruments, which would become effective over the two-year period beginning on 1 April 2000, is similar in most of the material respects to IAS 39. As a matter of fact, the preamble to the standard says, among other things, that there is a need for an increased transparency in financial reporting and specifically makes reference to the IASC standards and FASB statements that had already been developed on financial instruments at the time. The standard covers the scope of financial instruments (instead of providing a definition, it states that cash and cash deposits, monetary receivables and payables, securities and net monetary receivable or payable arising from derivative transactions are financial instruments), recognition and derecognition of financial assets and financial liabilities (adopted the 'financial components' approach rather than the 'risks and rewards' approach in accounting for the transfer of a financial asset), valuation (measurement) of financial instruments, computation of estimated amount of bad debt, hedge accounting and compound financial instruments.

For the purpose of measuring debt and equity securities subsequent to intial recognition, the standard classifies them into four categories as follows: (1) held for trading, which are measured at market (fair) value with changes in market values included in net profit or loss; (2) debt securities held to maturity, which are measured at amortized cost; (3) equity securities of subsidiaries and affiliates, which are measured at cost in the parent's separate financial statements; and (4) other securities (other than (1), (2) and (3) above), which are measured at market value with changes in market values recognized principally as a separate component of equity or, alternatively, gains recognized in equity and losses in net profit or loss. When other securities whose valuation gains or losses were previously recognized directly in equity are sold, the difference between the selling price and cost should be included in net profit or loss, i.e. the cumulative valuation gain or loss is recycled through the income statement. For debt and equity securities held other than for trading purposes, when there is a significant decline in market value which is not expected to recover, the carrying amount should be adjusted to market value with loss included in profit and loss. Because of significant implications of fair valuing the equity shares held under mutual-shareholding arrangements among Japanese companies and banks that would be classified as other securities, the effective date of implementing this particular requirement was delayed for one year to 1 April 2001.

As can be seen and has been mentioned previously, the new standard on financial instruments is similar in most material respects to IASs 39 and 32. However, there are some options provided in the Japanese standard that are not available under these IASs and some differences. For example, provided that it is used consistently, average market value of the one-month period preceding the reporting date may be used in lieu of the reporting date market value in measuring other securities. Another example of options is with respect to accounting for convertible debt by an issuer. Although debt issued with stock purchase warrants is required to be classified separately into the debt and equity portions by both the issuer and the acquirer, the issuer of a convertible debt may either treat the whole instrument as a liability or separate it into two components. When separated, the amount assigned to warrants or conversion right is recognized as a liability instead of, as in IAS 32, an equity until, in the case of warrants, they are exercised at which time the liability is reclassified into equity. When the warrants expire, the liability is transferred to net profit and loss.

One of the differences that exist between the Japanese standard on financial instruments and IAS 39 is in the area of hedge accounting. Instead of the complex rules stipulated in the latter, the Japanese standard follows the traditional 'deferral hedge accounting', under which a gain or loss arising from remeasuring the derivative hedging instrument is deferred as an asset or a liability until the hedged item is recognized in profit and loss. The standard also allows a method whereby the recognition of gains and losses of the hedged item is accelerated to offset those recognized on the hedging instrument.

Current assets

For current assets, inventories are valued at cost (for example, specific identification, FIFO, LIFO, weighted average, etc.) or, optionally, at the lower of cost or market. However, if there is a significant or permanent decline in market value, the market becomes the carrying amount even under the cost method. Allowance for doubtful accounts receivable is normally provided on the basis of certain percentages of receivables which are determined on the basis of several industry classifications, as stipulated in the tax law. In 1996, for example, the percentages of receivables that could be provided as tax deductible bad debt allowance were 0.3% for financial institutions and insurance companies, 0.8% for manufacturers and 1.0% for wholesalers and retailers. However, the new financial accounting standard on financial instruments (see above) stipulates the method of computing the amount of estimated bad debt losses relating to receivables and loans (receivables).

The standard requires the receivables to be classified into three categories based on financial condition and performance of debtors as follows: (1) receivables from debtors who are not in financial difficulty, for which an estimated bad debt amount is computed on a reasonable basis, such as past bad debt ratios for similar receivables; (2) receivables from debtors who are not yet in the state of bankruptcy but have a high possibility of delinquency in principal and interest payments, for which the amount of bad debt loss or impairment is computed on the balance of receivables remaining after deduction for amounts collectible from collaterized assets and guarantees, or obtaining the present value of expected future cash flows discounted at the original interest rate of the receivables; and (3) receivables from debtors who are in bankrupcy or substantially in such condition, for which the loss is provided to equal the amount of receivables reduced by collaterized assets and guarantees.

Liabilities

Retirement benefit costs

Many Japanese companies have an unfunded lump-sum severance indemnity plan, under which benefits are usually determined on the basis of the reason for termination (either voluntary or including termination at normal retirement age, involuntary), length of service and current rate of pay. These companies used to provide for this liability at amounts ranging from 40% (the limit deductible for tax) to 100% of the amount that would be required if all employees terminated their services voluntarily as of the balance sheet date. With respect to pension plans, which are funded, the past practice was to charge pension premiums to income. However, effective for fiscal years beginning on or after 1 April 2001, a new standard on accounting for retirement benefits becomes applicable. For the one-year period preceding the mandatory implementation, disclosure of the amount of retirement benefit obligation and other pertinent matters is permitted in lieu of fully incorporating the standard in the financial statements.

In the new standard, no distinction is made between lump-sum payment plans (usually unfunded) and pension plans (funded) for accounting purposes, and the approaches adopted for the standard and accounting and disclosure requirements are substantially the same as those under IAS 19. There are, however, some differences. For example, in recognizing the past service cost as an expense, the Japanese standard states that such cost, in principle, should be charged to expenses over a fixed period within the average remaining lives of the employees participating in the plan rather than, as in IAS 19, over the average period on a straight-line basis until the benefits become vested. However, the entire amount of the portion applicable to retired employees may be charged to expenses in the period it arises. Another example is the transitional treatment for defined benefit plans on adopting the standard for the first time. On first adoption of the Japanese standard, an enterprise many recognize the transitional liability by a charge to expense over a fixed period not exceeding 15 years on a straight-line basis. Some companies have chosen to recognize the entire amount immediately while others opted for a five-year or longer period. When the transitional liability is recognized over a period of five years or less, the expense is shown under the category of special losses/gains in the classified income statement prescribed in Japan.

Capital

Legal reserve

The Commercial Code requires that an amount equal to at least 10% of cash distributions paid out of earnings be appropriated as a legal reserve until this reserve equals 25% of the capital stock account. This reserve may either be used to reduce a capital deficit or be transferred to a capital account.

Free share distribution

A company, by resolution of the board of directors, may issue new equity shares to existing shareholders on a pro rata basis by transferring an amount (normally at par value) from the capital surplus or legal reserve account to the capital stock account. This type of distribution, called free share distribution, is distinguished from stock dividend paid out of profits.

Treasury stock

Transactions in a company's own equity shares are generally prohibited. However, acquisitions for certain specified purposes, such as for transfer to an employees' stock ownership plan and for cancellation, became possible from April 1995.

Income statement

Long-term contracts

Both the percentage of completion method and completed contract method are allowed in accounting for revenue on long-term contracts.

Instalment sales

The instalment method of recognizing revenue is acceptable when sales transactions are structured as such. The cost recovery method is not generally practiced.

Discounting of notes receivable

It is a common business practice in Japan that promissory notes (commonly 90 to 120 days) are received for sales made on credit. The notes are then often discounted, usually with recourse, for cash at banks and other lending institutions. The excess of the face amount of the note discounted over the amount of cash received is amortized over the remaining term of the note, rather than recognizing this transfer as a sale and the difference as a loss. The total amount of notes receivable discounted and still outstanding at year end is reported off balance sheet as a contingent liability.

Bonuses to directors and statutory auditors

These are paid upon approval at the annual shareholders' meeting and recorded as an appropriation of retained earnings rather than as a charge to income, as is customary in Japan. The fixed remuneration, however, is charged to income.

Income taxes

Currently payable taxes based on taxable income are recognized in the financial statements. Deferred tax accounting was not permitted in individual company financial statements, although a partial recognition that relates to inter-company profits eliminated in consolidation was acceptable in consolidated financial statements. However, effective for fiscal years beginning on or after 1 April 1999, deferred tax accounting has become a requirement in the preparation of both the individual and consolidated financial statements. The substance of the new standard is the same as that contained in IAS 12, including the definition of temporary differences for which a deferred tax liability or an asset, subject to recoverability, should be provided. Although not a significant difference, the Japanese standard has taken the position to require, in principle, to present deferred tax assets (liabilities) as current and non-current as appropriate.

Dividends

Under the Commercial Code, distributable profits are limited to the excess of net assets over the aggregate of: stated capital, capital surplus, legal reserve, including the amount currently required to be set aside; and the excess, if any, of unamortized pre-operating expenses and deferred research and development expenses over the sum of capital surplus and legal reserve.

Foreign currency transactions and translation

Foreign currency transactions are translated into the reporting currency at the exchange rate prevailing on the transaction date (historical rate), except when the amount in reporting currency is fixed by a forward exchange contract or other means. At the year end, short-term foreign currency monetary items are translated at the closing exchange rate and the resulting exchange gains and losses are recognized in income. Long-term foreign currency monetary items are translated at the historical rate, except when there is a material loss, in which case such loss should be recognized currently by applying the current rate. Non-monetary items remain translated at the historical rate at year end.

The financial statements of a foreign branch are translated in the same manner as above as if the transactions of the foreign branch had been those of the reporting enterprise itself. On the other hand, the financial statements of foreign subsidiaries and affiliated companies, as distinguished from foreign branches, are required to be translated as follows for the purposes of incorporating them in the consolidated financial statements: assets and liabilities, both monetary and non-monetary, are translated at the closing rate, and income and expense items at historical rates, and the resulting translation differences are classified as an asset or a liability.

Changes in accounting policies are applied prospectively in Japan, that is, the new accounting treatment is applied to the existing balance from the beginning of the period in which the change is made. An adjustment to the opening balance of retained earnings, based on a retroactive computation, is not permitted except when specifically prescribed for first adoption of a new standard as in the case of deferred tax. Fundamental errors, if any, would be reported as prior period adjustments under the special income or loss category of the classified statement of income and included in the determination of net profit or loss for the current period. In this connection, the Japanese definition of special income or loss items is broader than the IAS 8 definition of extraordinary items and includes, for example, in addition to losses from natural disaster, gains and losses from sale of property, plant and equipment, gains and losses from sale of securities purchased originally for purposes other than resale, adjustment to provisions set up in a prior period and correction of inventory valuation of a prior period.

Group accounts

Mergers and consolidation

Mergers in Japan are accounted for primarily by what the tax law dictates, and this resembles the pooling of interests method. The net assets as recorded in the books of the merged company may or may not be adjusted to reflect their fair value. However, such adjustment is not normally made in practice as an upward adjustment would give rise to taxable income. Goodwill purchased for consideration (called Noren or Eigyoken), but not consolidation goodwill, is deductible for tax purposes over a period of five years or less.

A proposal to amend the consolidation policy and procedures was made in 1997 to become effective from fiscal years beginning on or after 1 April 1999. Major changes for business combinations that are acquisitions are summarized as follows. As to the scope of consolidation and accounting for investments in associates by the equity method, the concept of control and significant influence was introduced to supplement the ownership criteria of 50% and 20% of voting shares for consolidation and equity accounting, respectively. With respect to the use of uniform accounting policies for like transactions and other events in similar circumstances in the preparation of consolidated financial statements, the prior requirement of 'to the extent possible' to those of the parent company was changed to read that, in principle, they should be the same. Another requirement made, which was previously optional, is to fair value the assets and liabilities of the subsidiary at the time of its acquisition for consolidation purposes. In this connection, a new option has been provided to allow for fair valuing all assets and liabilities, including the minority's interest in net assets, in order to embrace the allowed alternative treatment under IAS 22. Lastly, the amortization period of consolidation goodwill (called Renketsu Chosei Kanjyo, meaning consolidation adjustment account), arising on business combinations has been extended from five years to the maximum of 20 years.

Cash flow statement

One other new reporting standard put in place as of 1 April 1999 is the preparation of a consolidated cash flow statement as one of the basic financial statements of publicly held companies. Previously, these companies were required to include in the registration statement/securities report a funds-flow statement outside the financial statements on an unconsolidated basis, but the form and content were different from those required under the new standard. The standard in all material respects is the same as IAS 7, including, for example, what would constitute cash equivalents, presentation of cash flows under three categories (operating, investing and financing) and disclosure of pertinent non-cash transactions. As in IAS 7, interest paid and interest and dividends received may be presented under the operating activities classification because they enter into the determination of net profit or loss or, alternatively, interest and dividends received may be classified as investing cash flows and interest and dividend paid as financing cash flows.

Conclusion and prospects

As has been seen, accounting in Japan is largely statutory with rules contained in a multitude of laws and regulations. This makes it rather difficult for non-Japanese researchers to gain an in-depth understanding of the accounting system in Japan. Even for Japanese accountants working in industry and in public practice, the task is not an easy one in that they need to know, for example, which rules are found where (often the term used in one group of rules is different from another for the same thing) and the intertwining relationship between different laws and regulations. The task would be easier if, for one thing, these accounting rules and standards were promulgated in serialized pronouncements, such as the US Financial Accounting Standards Board's statements and IASC's standards, with recognition and measurement issues addressed together with related disclosure issues.

An attempt has been made in this chapter to give a realistic idea of Japanese accounting as practised by large companies. Emphasis has been put on the interrelationship of the three major groups of law – the Commercial Code, the SEL and the Corporate Tax Law. For listed companies whose financial statements are made public, the accounting treatments followed are generally those prescribed in the Code (broad yet fundamental) and tax law (specific) and disclosure is made in accordance with SEL (precise and detailed). Because of the constraints of the Code, which has adopted the historical cost accounting model, and the pressure of businesses, sometimes a note disclosure is used as an alternative to recognizing items in the financial statements, for example, a disclosure of finance leases. If it may be construed that such a substitution rectifies the failure to recognize the items in the financial statements, as some would believe in Japan, then financial reporting in Japan may reflect the British–American model. However, some accountants believe that recognition of items in the balance sheet or income statement cannot be replaced by disclosure made outside the financial statements.

In 1996 the Japanese govenment announced that it would take the necessary steps to put in effect by year 2001 a series of financial deregulation measures so as to reach a position where the Japanese financial market will be more transparent, international in approach and operating under market principles ('free, fair and internationalized'). As an integral part of this plan, the MOF's BADC had launched a major project to review the then existing Japanese accounting rules with the objective of bringing them closer to internationally recognized standards and practices. This resulted in the issuance of several revised and new standards between a relatively short period from June 1997 to January 1999 with implementation over a three-year period beginning on 1 April 1999. This effort has often been called the 'Accounting Big Bang' in Japan and includes, among others, revised or new standards on consolidation, cash flow statement, retirement benefits, deferred tax accounting and financial instruments.

When these standards are fully implemented by 2002, few differences from IAS will remain. This would include inventory pricing (commonly measured at cost), recognition of construction contract revenue (completed contract method may be used), accounting for finance leases (commonly accounted for as operating leases with disclosure of information on the basis of 'as if capitalized'), accounting for business combinations (especially legal mergers and classification between an acquisition and a uniting of interests), reporting of discontinuing operations and accounting for impairment of assets. Of these, business combinations and impairment of assets and together with auditing implications, the going-concern issue are currently addressed by the BADC.

Another important development is the work currently in progress to transfer the standards-setting responsibility from the government to the private sector in the hope that the new body, scheduled to come into existence in 2001 and functioning independently under a foundation which is financed primarily by contributions from listed and over-the-counter companies, will be more transparent in the standard-setting process, independent and responsive to the changing environment in financial reporting.

Notes

1. As a result of reorganization of the executive branch of the Japanese government effective 1 July 2000, the SEL, as well as the Business Accounting Deliberation Council, is administered by the newly created Financial Services Agency.

2. This was called the Investigation Committee of Enterprise Financial Accounting System of the Economic Stabilization Board.

3. See note 1.

References

Arai, K. and Shiratori, S. (1991) *Legal and Conceptual Framework of Accounting in Japan*. Japanese Institute of Certified Public Accountants, Tokyo.

Cooke, T.E. and Kikuya, M. (1992) *Financial Reporting in Japan*. Blackwell, Oxford.

Coopers & Lybrand (International) (1991) *1991 International Accounting Summaries*. John Wiley, New York.

FT World Accounting Report (1996) Disclosing loan losses, pp. 7-8. Financial Times Financial Publishing, April.

Hiramatsu, K. (1994) *Kokusai Kaikei no Shindoukou (New Trends in International Accounting)*. Chuo Keizai Sha, Tokyo.

Japanese Institute of Certified Public Accountants (1994) *Corporate Disclosure in Japan – Accounting*. JICPA, Tokyo.

Kawai, N. and Terashima, H. (eds) (1983) *Sengo Kigyo Kaikei Seidono Tenkai ('Postwar Developments in Business Accounting Systems')*. Houritsu Bunka Sha, Kyoto.

Mueller, G.G. and Yoshida, H. (1968) *Accounting Practices in Japan*. Graduate School of Business Administration, University of Washington, Seattle.

Mueller, G.G., Gernon, H. and Meek, G.K. (1994) *Accounting – An International Perspective*. Irwin, Burr Ridge, Illinois.

Someya, K. (1996) *Japanese Accounting*. Clarendon Press, Oxford.

Accounting in Italy

Stefano Zambon

Italian accounting is frequently regarded as law-based, tax-driven and primarily oriented towards creditor protection and, as such, conservatively biased. Moreover, professional accounting standards have had only a residual role so far, and it is only recently that the accounting profession has started to assume a significant profile in socio-economic terms. Listed companies stand apart since they have to satisfy supplementary accounting rules and requirements. The 'Economia Aziendale' (business economics) tradition has also exerted some influence on accounting practice (see Zambon 1996 for further analysis), but today the European directives have, of course, played a most significant role.

The main features of the Italian economic context can be summarized as follows: the primary role of the banking system in company financing; a parallel weakness of the stock exchange as a mechanism for resource allocation (only 297 companies listed on the Milan Stock Exchange as of 31 December 2001); the prevalence of small and medium-sized enterprises; the presence, even in large companies, of families as a predominant factor in business life (which means that ownership goes together with control); the reliance of the state for its revenues on the results of the individual companies, which produces a substantial overlapping of the tax numbers with the accounts drawn up for legal and commercial purposes.

This ownership structure and financing situation has implications for accounting. If firm size tends to be limited, entrepreneurs frequently run their own firms, and so the external demand for detailed and reliable accounting information is relatively low. It derives mainly from tax authorities and banks, and often exclusively from the former, since for bank lending decisions either financial statements are not considered or, frequently, ad hoc accounts are prepared. Multiple accounting statements are hence likely to be quite normal in practice. The demand for independent auditing is also reduced. None or very few shareholders are really outside the company, and they generally have direct access to the data they need. Accordingly, the general level of disclosure is relatively satisfactory in comparative terms, and essentially complies only with legal requirements (which have been increased dramatically).

Conservatism and secrecy are still recognized as important values in business activity. Italian accounting regulation has largely been influenced by fiscal rules, and therefore the objective of minimizing taxable income is, by and large, the main one for accounting professionals and for the financial directors of companies, especially in the case of small and medium-sized enterprises.

Legal and institutional basis of accounting regulation

Civil Code and Commercial Regulation

Italy has a legal system of Roman-Justinean derivation and statutes are expected to play a dominant role in ruling commercial issues, including accounting and related matters. The most important instrument regulating accounting is the 1942 Civil Code, as amended in 1991 by the adoption of the Fourth and Seventh European Directives. Those interested in a more detailed analysis of the evolution of regulation and institutions should look at Zambon (2001 and 2002) and Took (1995). The key points are the following: Italian commercial regulation has its roots in the French Commercial Code of 1807, which was introduced into the Italian Kingdom during the period of Napoleon's domination (the King of Italy was Napoleon himself). These rules were basically maintained in the 1865 and 1882 Italian Codes (Italy as a unitary state came into existence in 1861).

The obligation to draw up financial statements emerged implicitly through the 1865 Civil Code requirement to distribute dividends only from 'actually realized profits'. In a laissez-faire political climate, no detailed rules were given concerning accounting principles or statements. However, the 1882 Commercial Code introduced the general principle that the accounts should give the financial situation and results of a company with *evidenza e verità* (straightforwardness and truth). The mandatory filing of financial statements with commercial courts, as well as the publication of extracts from these statements, has been required from all *società anonime* (public limited companies) since 1865.

The 1942 Civil Code replaced the previous Codes and regulated company accounts in a more comprehensive way. It introduced a new general principle (without substituting the previous one) that the balance sheet and the profit and loss account should present with *chiarezza e precisione* (clarity and precision) a company's financial position and results. The formula was intended as a guideline in relation to which specific rules had to be interpreted. It was generally accepted that both 'clarity' and 'straightforwardness' referred to form and content, while both 'precision' and 'truth' referred to valuations. The 1942 Code set a minimum content for the balance sheet but did not specify the contents of the income statement. Departures from legal rules were permitted for 'special reasons' relating to the company or to a specific asset. This overriding principle was much debated: the simplicity of its form contrasted with its problematic application.

Several revaluation laws have been issued in a non-systematic way since the 1942 promulgation of the Civil Code. These laws have been different in aims, scope and revaluation mechanisms. The more recent of them are law no. 576/1975 (so-called 'Visentini law'), law no. 72/1983 (so-called 'Visentini-*bis* law'), law no. 408/1990, law no. 413/1991 and law no. 342/2000. These laws have generally permitted a tax-free revaluation of the assets, apart from the latter three, which taxed the revalued amounts.

A further step in the evolution of financial statement regulation in Italy came with law no. 216 of 1974. This set the format and minimum content of the income statement, and established the presentation of the directors' report and a requirement for interim results to be produced by listed companies. The *Commissione Nazionale per le Società e la Borsa* (CONSOB – National Commission for Companies and the Stock Exchange) was set up to monitor quoted companies, and during the ensuing years its power and scope have been increased.

Progress in regulating consolidated accounts has been much slower. Consolidated financial statements were not traditionally prepared in Italy, apart from a few categories of firms – notably listed companies – for which consolidated reporting was compulsory. Until 1991, in fact, no general legal requirement for group accounts was established in law, even though some large groups did present consolidated accounts on a voluntary basis, especially to support bank lending applications.

At the beginning of the 1990s accounting regulation in Italy underwent a period of major change. The rapidity and magnitude of this revolution are quite impressive, especially when compared with the relatively stable situation that characterized accounting previously. In a few years virtually all the previous regulation dealing with the technical and professional side of accounting was swept away and replaced. The main thrust of this change concerned the formats and principles for the annual accounts of companies and financial institutions (including banks), consolidated financial statements, three revaluation laws and the relationship between commercial and fiscal rules as well as the accounting profession itself and the role of the collegio sindacale in listed companies. Most of these innovations derived from the implementation of European directives, but other innovations have their origin in the autonomous trajectory of Italian accounting.

Taxation

Tax legislation undoubtedly has a significant effect on individual company financial reporting in Italy. Since the 1970s, tax distortions of the commercial accounts have been common in order to obtain fiscal benefits. Tax rules, which were comparatively more exhaustive than the accounting legislation, were regarded de facto as providing the operational detail to amplify the very general 1942 commercial legislation. This view, which is traditionally referred to as the 'single track approach' ('teoria del binario unico'), argues in favour of the tax influence on the annual accounts, so that there is a sort of reverse dependence of the commercial rules on the fiscal ones ('reverse congruence' – see Chapter 4). Taxation in Italy, therefore, affects income measurement, albeit with companies sometimes providing explanations in the notes (which became mandatory in 1993).

This reverse congruence found a legislative basis from 1973 with the reform of income tax (called the Visentini reform), which linked tax measurement to accounting numbers in a way similar to that in Germany (*Massgeblichkeitsprinzip*). This link was confirmed in 1986 by the Testo Unico delle Imposte sui Redditi (TUIR – Consolidated Act on income tax). The prevalence of the single track approach has been caused mainly by the combined effect of two fiscal rules. The first requires that company taxable income is in principle that resulting from the accounting records kept for commercial purposes (art. 52, TUIR), while the second makes it compulsory for Italian companies to include certain expenses in the profit and loss account in order to deduct them for tax (art. 75, section 4, TUIR).

An attempt to overcome the problematic relationship between commercial law and fiscal rules was made by the decree no. 127/1991, which required that the final section of the income statement included adjustments resulting purely from the application of tax legislation. As an example, accelerated depreciation exceeding the 'correct' amount under the Civil Code had to be shown in the section for fiscal adjustments – a treatment similar to that in France (see Chapter 5).

This fiscal section of the income statement format became a source of interpretation and technical problems and cultural resistance arose. In particular, many firms complained that the new treatment for excess depreciation was too complicated in that the credit entry went to equity instead of being deducted from the asset carrying value, and this triggered a deferred tax provision, which is fairly uncommon for individual company accounts in Italy.

As a consequence, a new rule was issued in 1994 (art. 2-*bis*, law no. 503/1994), which cancelled the fiscal section in the income statement format. It established that fiscal considerations could be used in company accounts, and that the reasons for the fiscal adjustments and the related amounts should be disclosed in the notes. The effect of this regulatory change is that virtually no value in company income statements is now free from fiscal influences. The principle of dependence of commercial accounting rules on tax rules was confirmed, and in addition, art. 2-*bis* of law no. 503/1994 cancelled a requirement that consolidated accounts should be drawn up free from the fiscal interference existing in company accounts. It simply required a disclosure in the notes as for individual accounts.

It would seem that the Italian tax authorities relied to a large extent on accounting numbers and yet in recent times a contradictory trend has emerged. The large amount of tax evasion and the urgent need to cope with a large public deficit induced the Italian government to introduce both a minimum income to be declared by a large number of categories of taxpayers in several fiscal years, and a series of indices aimed at an artificially determined minimum income (*coefficient presuntivi di reddito*). So, the fiscal system in Italy has shown in the recent past a sort of schizophrenic approach to accounting. On the one hand, taxation is formally based on the accounting results, and on the other, it is also moving away from them.

At the beginning of 2002 Parliament approved a law requiring the government to issue, within one year, a regulation aimed at disconnecting accounting numbers from fiscal rules, thus paving the way to a new phase of the relationship between tax and financial reporting. This law was eventually promulgated (legislative decree no. 6/2003) and it will come into force as of 1st January 2004.

The accounting profession

The accounting profession has a long history in Italy. In fact, the first accounting professionals were to be found in Venice at the beginning of the sixteenth century (the *rasonati* – literally the accountants), with the function of auditing the Doge's expenses. Later in that century the *Collegio dei Rasonati* was created. This imposed, amongst other things, an apprenticeship period of six years and a professional examination. The first law concerning the accounting profession issued after the unification of Italy was passed in 1865 and during the latter part of the nineteenth century Italian accountants and scholars continued to institutionalize their competences and knowledge, building on an autonomous and distinct professional base.

Up to 1929, the accounting profession in Italy consisted exclusively of *ragionieri* (the modern term for *rasonati*). In that year, the law no. 588 set up a second professional category, the *dottori commercialisti*, with duties similar to those of ragionieri. This development was a result of the creation of educational establishments to study commercial subjects, which subsequently became faculties of economics and commerce, where subjects such as accountancy, business management, banking, commercial and industrial activity acquired the status of university subjects. In 1953 two different laws, still in force, reorganized the accounting profession, confirming the two professional bodies.

Currently, accounting professionals are an increasingly important phenomenon in Italian society. Their total number is rapidly expanding, and is now around 90 000, 85% of whom are in practice (those not in practice do not lose their professional qualification). The average age is below 45 years. This growth is linked to the complexity of the tax legislation, and to the accountants' fundamental role in helping the huge number of small and medium-sized companies. It is customary in Italy for such companies to have an external professional deal with their financial accounting and tax management.

The Italian accounting profession has a certain number of distinctive features as compared to its European neighbours. It is organized into two bodies (the dottori commercialisti and the ragionieri) which are approximately the same size. In 2004 the two bodies will merge to form one professional body, as a consequence of a new government regulation and university reform. Two sections will be created in the new roll: section A will be staffed by the dottori commercialisti, and the section B by the esperti contabili (accounting experts). The members of the two sections will be differentiated on the basis of the diverse tasks that they will be allowed to perform. The path to these two distinct qualifications will also change (see Figure 8.1).

Another distinguishing element of the Italian accounting profession is the existence of a quite sharp division between external auditing, which is provided by audit firms, and commercial accounting and related legal services such as tax requirements and declarations, which are provided by dottori commercialisti and ragionieri.

Auditing

Auditing in Italy is a quite complex and idiosyncratic issue because of the legislative maze produced by the different laws that have been introduced over about 60 years. Above all, the Italian audit is characterized by an evident anomaly. Since 1975 there have been two competing approaches to audit: an institutional-administrative one, performed by the *sindaci*, and an external one, run by the audit firms.

Audit by the 'Collegio Sindacale'

The Civil Code requires that limited liability companies with a share capital exceeding €120,000 must appoint, at the annual general meeting, a *collegio sindacale* consisting of three to five members, who remain in charge for three years, but can be reappointed indefinitely. Their main duties are: (a) to control the administration of the company; (b) to verify general compliance with the law and the articles of association and the legality of the accounting records; (c) to check that the balance sheet and income statement conform with the underlying accounting records; and (d) to ensure the conformity to legal rules of the financial statement valuations.

It is clear that this type of audit is different in scope from the accounting-centred one characterizing the Anglo-Saxon tradition.

The collegio sindacale prepares an annual report, which is included in the financial statements, and for which there is no legally prescribed format, but which generally limits itself to confirming the stated figures and to proposing their approval by the general meeting. Since 1994 the sindaci have also had to verify and control group accounts, if the company is a parent undertaking (art. 41, decree no. 127/1991). However, since July 1998,

Figure 8.1 Access to the accounting profession in Italy

Section A
Dottore Commercialista
(Chartered accountant)

Long university degree in economics or business administration
with some compulsory subjects passed (5 years)
+
apprenticeship (3 years)
+
state exam

Section B
Esperto Contabile
(accounting expert)

University degree in economics or business administration
with some compulsory subjects passed (3 years)
+
appenticeship (3 years)
+
state exam

as part of a wider reform of financial markets, the audit competences of the collegio sindacale of listed companies have been entirely transferred to external accountancy firms, while its supervisory powers on the company compliance with the law and the adequacy of its administrative and organizational structure have been strengthened (this change making the collegio sindacale of listed companies look more like a German-type supervisory board). Until 1995 (the effective date of legislative decree no. 88/1992) virtually anybody could be a sindaco, and consequently not all the persons carrying out such a function had an appropriate qualification. Nevertheless, in most cases the sindaci are independent accounting professionals (dottori commercialisti and ragionieri).

Since 1995 all sindaci must be on a special register under the supervision of the Ministry of Justice. Following the implementation of the Eighth Directive in Italy through decree no. 88/1992, from 1995 *only* those who have the qualification of *revisore contabile* (auditor) can carry out auditing activity, and be appointed as sindaci of a company. As mentioned earlier, in order to be admitted to the register of the revisori contabili, it is necessary to have a three-year university degree in economics, business administration or law, to serve an apprenticeship period of three years under the guidance of a revisore contabile and to pass a state examination. It should be pointed out that the pattern of access to the accounting profession (as dottore commercialista or ragioniere) and that to the auditing profession (as revisore section B of the new roll) is now the same.

With regard to Italian listed companies, decree no. 162/2000 by the Ministry of Justice sets different eligibility criteria for the members of the collegio sindacale: at least one of them must be a 'Revisore contabile' with audit experience of three years or more, but the other two effective members could be persons who

- have carried out, for at least three years, managerial or administrative tasks in companies with a share capital of not less than 2 billion euro; or
- are professionals or university teachers with at least three years experience in subject areas which are strictly close to those of the company (e.g. a professional biologist or a chemist could be appointed as a member of the collegio sindacale, respectively, of a biotechnology or a chemical listed company); or
- are executives of public administrations operating in law, economics, the financial sector or in subject areas strictly close to those of the company.

As at February 2001 there were nearly 120 000 revisori on the new register. The Italian accountancy bodies in 1995 issued some ethical guidelines for the collegio sindacale in an attempt to cope with the lack of incisiveness of this function.

From 2004 the collegio sindacale of all limited liability companies will be made up of at least one revisore contabile while the remaining members should come from professional roles or be academics in law or economics

Audit by External Independent Firms

The external audit, carried out by an independent professional, which conforms most closely with that of the Anglo-Saxon countries, can be carried out in Italy under two different forms which only partially overlap. These forms are:

(a) *società di revisione* (audit company) (legislative decree no. 58/1998);

(b) *revisore contabile* (legislative decree no. 88/1992).

Another important interpretative dimension of external auditing in Italy is the distinction between *voluntary* and *statutory* audit. A voluntary audit can be performed by both kinds of entities mentioned above, but a statutory audit can be carried out only by the società di revisione.

Società di revisione

As an important part of the reform of share-issuing companies in 1974 (enacted by law no. 216 of 7 June 1974, which also established the CONSOB), Presidential decree no. 136 of 31 March 1975 introduced into Italian company law the requirement for listed companies to submit their annual accounts to independent external audit. The same requirement was later introduced for newspaper companies (now excluded), insurances, state-owned commercial entities, financial companies, public utilities, investment funds and a few others. This change was a response to the perceived general unreliability of the audit performed by sindaci. In order to accomplish this, a 'Special Roll' of auditors was set up, under the supervision of CONSOB, where only audit firms with particular characteristics of professional competence and financial soundness could enter.

Admission to this Special Roll is granted when (art. 161, section 2, decree no. 58/1998, which refers to the conditions for admission to the Register of revisori Contabili stated by art. 6 of decree no. 88/1992): (1) the firm's objects – according to the Memorandum – are limited to the auditing and accounting organization of a company, and specifically exclude any other professional activity (e.g. consultancy); (2) the partners underwriting audit reports, as well as the majority of partners, belong to the register of revisori contabili; (3) the majority of its capital is owned by physical persons included in the register of revisori contabili; the same qualification is possessed by the majority of the partnership or company members; (4) the company or partnership must be 'technically suitable (i.e. capable)' (this is to be assessed by the CONSOB); and (5) an insurance guarantee which is judged adequate by CONSOB is available to the audit firm (at the moment 'adequacy' is set around 500 000– 1 million euros). Italian subsidiaries of foreign auditing firms may also be registered on the 'Special Roll', provided that they respect the rules set for the other firms. As of 31 December 2001, there were 24 auditing firms on the CONSOB Special Roll.

The audit appointment is made by the annual general meeting of the company which should – according to CONSOB requirements – choose between three competing proposals from different Società di revisione. The appointment lasts for three years and can be renewed not more than twice (i.e. in total nine years). After that it can be assigned again to the same audit firm only after a gap of at least three years. In 1994 most of the major Italian groups changed auditors. The nine-year limit does not apply to an audit undertaken on a voluntary basis.

At the end of the auditing process, the auditor issues a professional judgement on the quality of the accounts audited. In 1983 the CONSOB specified a model for the audit report which was slightly modified in 1987, 1994 and most recently in 1999. It should be noted that it is possible in Italy to deliver an auditors' report with a qualified opinion. The audit report should state compliance with legal rules only (decree no. 127/1991).

The relationship between collegio sindacale and the external audit firm, when they are both present in a company, is traditionally not very clear either in law or in practice. The two forms of audits involve carrying out tasks which overlap and are not thoroughly specified by the law. Even though the law requires that the external audit firm must inform sindaci about the existence of irregularities that have a material impact on financial statements, one may assume that the linkage between the two processes is in the vast majority of cases ambiguous or, more likely, non-existent. Following the 1988 reform of the law on financial markets, the relationship between the collegio sindacale and the external audit firm has been made clearer at least for listed companies, in that all audit activity has been removed from the former and fully attributed to the latter.

Revisore contabile

Beyond being appointed as a sindaco in limited liability companies, the revisore contabile can also perform the voluntary audit, that is an audit which is freely undertaken by companies (which are not bound to do so). This professional service may be attributed to a physical person, a partnership (società in nome collettivo or società in accomandita semplice) or a limited liability company which are included in the register of revisori contabili. Of course, the appointment as a sindaco of a company is instead reserved only to physical persons (even though each of them may have his/her own audit firm).

The total turnover of the external audit business in Italy is estimated at around €450m a year. However, it is remarkable that the number of companies that undergo a voluntary audit (generally either for purposes of external profile or for bank purposes) is much larger than that of companies for which audit is legally required. The market for voluntary auditing represents about 75–80% of the total audit market.

In independent external auditing, the international crisis of confidence in auditors and their work has progressively emerged also in Italy. A number of the Big Four audit firms have been the subject of lawsuits. Furthermore, as a by-product of the big bribery scandals and the related judicial inquiries (so-called *mani pulite*), some firms are being investigated in relation to their failure to find any traces of bribes paid by large companies. In 1993 CONSOB tried to address the situation by inviting audit firms and sindaci to carry out extra enquiries in order to identify and report any possible problems linked to bribe payments. In 1999 the two professional bodies issued a code of ethics for sindaci of listed companies. Despite this, many are questioning the true meaning and role of the collegio sindacale as well as that of external independent auditing.

Accounting Standards (Principi Contabili) *and Auditing Standards* (Principi di Revisione)

For many decades no need for accounting standards was felt in Italy. This was probably due to the code law system, which obliges companies to follow detailed legal prescriptions, to the penetration of tax measurement and to the strong and lasting resistance of Italian academics to any standardization process for company financial reporting. However, as discussed above, compulsory external auditing was imposed on listed companies in 1974, and decree no. 136/1975 (art. 4, section 2) required that the auditors had to verify whether the company financial statements complied with *both* legal rules *and* 'corretti principi contabili' ('correct accounting principles'). At the time no such body of standards existed nor was there any standard-setting body.

Some institutions such as the Ministry for State-owned groups (Ministero per le Partecipazioni Statali) and the Association of Italian Public Limited Companies (Assonime), started issuing their own accounting standards, trying to legitimize them in their 'territory of competence'. The most authoritative professional body (Consiglio Nazionale dei Dottori Commercialisti – CNDC) set up a committee in 1975 to cope with the issues arising from the introduction of compulsory external audit. This started issuing 'principi contabili' (accounting principles) on valuation and presentation. For some years different sets of standards were competing in Italy, until CONSOB made a choice in 1982 in favour of the standards prepared by the accounting professional bodies, with the backing of the audit firms. In 1982 the CONSOB also added that, when the Italian Standards were absent on a given topic, reference should be made to the International Accounting Standards (IAS). At this time the other Italian professional body (Consiglio Nazionale dei Rugianieri) joined the standard setting venture. In December 1999, the CONSOB modified its 1982 advice, and put Italian accounting standards and the IAS at the same level, both being 'a useful reference point' for listed companies.

The standard-setting committee is composed of 21 members, of whom 11 are dottori commercialisti and 10 ragionieri. The Chairman is a dottore commercialista. The majority of members work in their own 'studio', but some of them come from audit firms. Some academics are also involved.

To date, 30 statements have been published (see Table 8.1). As a consequence of criticisms about the slowness with which standards are prepared or updated, a wide revision was made in the 1990s in order to take into consideration the new legal framework for accounting arising from the adoption of European directives. The main aim of the revision process was to make standards as close as possible to legal rules in order to play an interpretative role.

In November 2001 a new standard-setting body was set up in Italy, the Italian Accounting Body (*Organismo Italiano di Contabilità* – OIC). It differs from the predecessor body, in that this new body is representative of various interested parties (preparers, users, professionals, financial institutions, stock exchange, relevant state agencies, public administration and so on). A technical committee will draft national accounting standards, and these will have to be approved by the new body's executive committee.

Accounting standards are not compulsory either in legal or professional terms. The 1975 reference in the law to accounting principles was cancelled in decree 127/1991. The audit should now verify the conformity of the accounts *exclusively* to commercial regulation, even though the ministerial commentary to the decree confirmed the role of standards in the interpretation of the law. In general terms, though, the significance and effectiveness of these standards within a code law system remains problematic. The contradictory and ambiguous nature of accounting standards in Italy did, and does, influence their limited application and recognition by professionals and companies.

However, it should be noted that in December 1997 a newly introduced tax called IRAP (Regional Tax on Production Activities) which hits a value added-like figure, again gives a legal recognition to Italian accounting standards, assigning them a role in correctly classifying revenues and costs within the income statement. This provision was cancelled in December 1999.

As a final remark it has to be pointed out that from July 1998 Italian companies listed on both an EU market and a non-EU market can depart from national rules and refer to 'accounting standards of international recognition' which are compatible with EU Directives in order to prepare consolidated financial statements, provided that these standards are acceptable to the non-EU market. These 'alternative' standards are to be identified by an ad hoc decree of the Ministry of Justice, and are likely to correspond to those issued by the International Accounting Standards Board (IASB). However, to date the decree has not been issued, and the system is thus not operational. The 2002 EU Regulation on IAS will supersede this rule.

The issuance of auditing standards (principi di revisione) was also started in 1975. To date many statements have been published dealing with all aspects of audit activity and which reflect international practice.

Objectives, assumptions and qualitative characteristics

An Italian view of the 'true and fair view'

The fundamental principle of the new legislation, which drives the whole process of accounts preparation in Italy, is a derivation – according to the ministerial commentary (which accompanied decree no. 127/1991) – of the British 'true and fair view' formula. It has now become established in Italian law that accounts shall *rappresentare in modo veritiero e corretto* (represent in a true and correct manner) a company's economic and financial situation and year's results (art. 2423, Civil Code, section 2). No definition of this is given either by the official commentary or by the law itself.

Table 8.1 Italian accounting standards jointly issued by the 'Consiglio Nazionale dei Dottori Commercialisti' and 'Consiglio Nazionale dei Ragionieri'

1.	Financial statements: objectives and postulates (1977, but approved in 1975; superseded by standard no. 11)
2.	Formats (1977; superseded by standard no. 12)
2.*bis*	Interpretations of and clarifications to accounting standard no. 2 (1982)
3.	Stocks (1978; superseded in standard no. 13)
4.	Tangible fixed assets (1979; superseded by standard no. 16)
5.	Liquid funds and bank overdrafts (1980; superseded by standard no. 14)
6.	Debtors (1980; superseded by standard no. 15)
7.	Creditors and other liabilities (1981; superseded by standard no. 19)
8.	Investments, participating interests and consolidated accounts (1983; superseded by standards nos 17, 20 and 21)
9.	Translation of items in foreign currency (1988; superseded by standard no. 26)
10.	Long-term contracts (1991; superseded by standard no. 23)
11.	Financial statements: objectives and postulates (1994)
12.	Formats (1994)
13.	Stocks (1994)
14.	Liquid funds (1994)
15.	Debtors (1996)
16.	Tangible fixed assets (1996)
17.	Consolidated financial statements (1996)
18.	Prepayments, accrued income, accruals and deferred income (1996)
19.	Creditors and other liabilities (statutory provision for severance indemnities, provisions for risks and future costs) (1996)
20.	Securities and participating interests (1996)
21.	Equity method (1996)
22.	Memorandum accounts (1997)
23.	Long-term contracts (1997)
24.	Intangible fixed assets (1999)
25.	Income taxes (1999)
26.	Operations and items in foreign currency (1999)
27.	The introduction of euro as monetary unit (1999)
28.	Shareholders' equity (2000)
29.	Changes in accounting policies, changes in estimates, fundamental errors, extraordinary items, events after the balance sheet date (2001)
30.	Interim financial reporting (2002)

Accounting Standard Interpretation Series

1.	Classification of revenues and expenses in the income statement according to correct accounting standards – Interpretative statement of accounting standard no. 12 (1998)

In addition, accounts also have to be drawn up with 'chiarezza' (clarity). These requirements apply also to the accounts of groups and financial institutions (art. 29, decree no. 127/1991; and art. 2, decree no. 87/1992).

There was concern in Italy about how to interpret the formula, given that the transfer of such a context-specific concept from one jurisdiction to another is problematic, especially one from a common law system to a code law system. However, despite some optimistic expectations linked to its introduction in Italian accounting, it appears that the role of any general legal principle will probably remain limited in practice, because, where specific rules are given, these must be followed. Their application then leads quite automatically – by a sort of legal presumption – to the respect of the general principle (i.e. strict adherence to specific accounting rules leads automatically to compliance with the principle of reppresentazione veritiera e corretta).

The general, well-known accounting postulates such as prudence, accruals basis, consistency and going concern are also specified in the new provisions (art. 2423-*bis*, Civil Code). However, these were already applied as common practice and in the main already implicit in the previous law. No particular differences exist with the Anglo-American interpretation of the same postulates.

General characteristics of accounts

Individual company accounts

The individual company (as well as group) annual report could be composed of the following documents:

1. balance sheet (stato patrimoniale);
2. income statement (conto economico);
3. notes to the accounts (nota integrativa);
4. report on operations (relazione sulla gestione);
5. changes in shareholders' funds statement (prospetto delle variazioni di capitale netto);
6. flow of funds statement (rendiconto finanziario);
7. chairman's statement (relazione del Presidente);
8. directors' report (relazione del Consiglio di amminstrazione);
9. auditor's report (della societè di revisione);
10. collegio sindacale's report (relazione del collegio sindacale).

Only the first four statements must be produced by all limited liability companies in Italy (mainly Società per azioni or S.p.A. – public share-issuing company; Società a responsabilità limitata or S.r.l. – private limited company; Società in accomandita per azioni or S.a.p.a. – quasi-partnership with shares, little used now). Of course, the collegio sindacale's report is also mandatory, as detailed above. The first three statements are considered as a single whole from a legal point of view, comprising the 'bilancio d'esercizio' (annual financial statements) (art. 2423, section 1, Civil Code).

Items 5 to 8 are presented on a voluntary basis, and generally prepared only by medium-large companies (quoted or not). Italian law does not require a flow of funds statement in any form. The professional accounting standard no. 12 (see Table 8.1), does, though, ask for such a statement.

Listed companies also have to produce quarterly reports, of which the six-monthly report (the relazione semestrale) has a particular relevance. This report is drawn up by company directors according to the criteria established by CONSOB, and from 1999 is partially audited. All these reports have to be made public (art. 2427 Civil Code, section 3).

There also exists an abridged form of company financial statements (bilancio in forma abbreviata), which is allowed for small companies not exceeding – for two consecutive financial years or in the first year of their existence – two of the three size thresholds indicated in Table 8.2 (art. 2435-*bis* Civil Code).

Corporate firms without limited liability (impresa individuale – sole proprietorship; società in nome collettivo or S.n.c. – comparable to a partnership; società in accomandita semplice or S.a.s. – a quasi-partnership) have to prepare only a balance sheet (as a by-product of the annual stock-taking) and an income statement, but they do not have to comply with the formats and rules set for limited companies, except for the valuation criteria, which are the same. The general principle to be followed by these firms is that their accounts shall give 'with straightforwardness and truth' the firm's financial situation and year performance (art. 2217, section 2, Civil Code). The accounts are not published.

A quite recent – although still limited – accounting phenomenon in Italy is the publication by a growing number of companies of an environmental report (bilancio ambientale) and/or a social report. In 2001 the Italian Banking Association officially recommended the preparation of social reports by its member banks.

Group accounts

Prior to the 1991 decree, group accounts were only a requirement – since the early 1980s – for groups that included listed companies and a few other special categories, such as newspaper publishers, insurance companies, public utilities and in general entities receiving public support on a regular basis. However, virtually all large, non-listed groups have presented consolidated accounts on a voluntary basis since the second half of the 1980s. Quite often these consolidated reports are also published in English. This is especially the case when Italian companies are listed only on foreign stock exchanges, in particular the NYSE and NASDAQ (e.g. Fiat, Montedison, Benetton, Luxottica, Natuzzi, Fila, De Rigo, Saes Getters).

The implementation of the Seventh Directive introduced for the first time a generalized obligation for any group of companies to prepare consolidated accounts, starting with the 1994 financial year. Exemptions from consolidated accounts are automatic only for groups that exceed – for two consecutive financial years or in the first year of their existence – two of the following three size thresholds (art. 27, decree no. 127/1991):

(a) total assets €12.5m (gross of consolidation adjustments);

(b) turnover €25m (gross of consolidation adjustments); and

(c) 250 employees.

The 1991 limits were transitionally doubled until 1999 (art. 46, section 2), with the obvious consequence that until that year only large groups had to comply with this requirement.

Table 8.2 Size thresholds for abridged financial statements (art. 2435-*bis* Civil Code)

Assets (net of depreciation)	€3.125m
Sales (net of discounts)	€6.250m
Employees (financial year average)	50

In order to benefit from the special (balance sheet) format and abridged notes and report on operations, the above limits have not to be exceeded for two consecutive financial years (or for the first year of life of an undertaking).

As to the scope of consolidation, the general principle states that a company must be consolidated when it is a subsidiary, which is determined by the parent's capability to control or exert a dominant influence over it, through either (a) direct or indirect voting rights in the ordinary general meeting, or (b) a control contract or an Article of Association producing a similar effect, or (c) agreements with other shareholders (art. 26). Domestic and foreign subsidiaries must be included, and this is irrespective of the legal form and geographical location of the subsidiary. The decree did not take up the option to extend consolidation to companies where the parent exercises a de facto dominant influence. Subsidiaries have to be fully consolidated using the acquisition method. No mention is made by law of the merger accounting method (or pooling-of-interests method).

Subsidiaries have to be excluded from consolidation if their activities are so divergent that their inclusion would compromise the 'true and correct representation' (art. 28, section 1). Subsidiaries may also be excluded if they are immaterial, if the parent's actual control is restricted, if they are only temporarily under the control of the parent, or if there is difficulty in obtaining in time, or without a disproportionate expense, the necessary accounting information (art. 28, section 2).

Joint ventures may be included in the scope of consolidation when (a) one of the group companies has a joint control of it, and (b) the participating investment reaches at least 20% (or 10%, if the joint venture is listed) of the share capital of this enterprise. If these requirements are met, joint ventures should be accounted for by proportional consolidation (art. 37), or by the equity method. If they do not exceed the threshold under (b), they have to be stated at cost in consolidated financial statements.

Additional statements (e.g. consolidated funds flow, chairman's report, changes in shareholders' funds, and so on) are voluntary, even though it is fair to say that most of the groups producing consolidated accounts (for legal reasons or on a voluntary basis) provide these supplementary statements.

An additional issue in the preparation and interpretation of group accounts is their relationship with fiscal values. As in other European countries, consolidated financial statements are tax-neutral in Italy, since income taxes are levied upon individual company account figures. As pointed out earlier, the art. 2-*bis* of the law no. 503/1994 allows groups to disclose fiscal distortions in the notes to consolidated accounts. Similar to Germany, but unlike France, there is no requirement then to purify these accounts and remove tax-driven values.

Formats of published accounts

Decree no. 127/1991 introduced compulsory formats into Italy for the first time. Highly rigid formats and contents have been introduced not only for the profit and loss account and balance sheet, but also for the notes and the report on operations.

Balance sheet

From the options available in the Fourth Directive, Italy has chosen the traditional, horizontal balance sheet format (art. 9 of the Directive), with assets on the left and set out apparently in the reverse order of liquidity.

Income statement

Italy chose the vertical income statement format, with the cost classification by *nature* rather than by destination.

Notes

They have a compulsory minimum content, which should follow a given sequence in order to facilitate comparison.

Management report on operations

According to art. 2428 of the Civil Code, this Report should (a) be prepared by the directors; (b) discuss the general situation of the company and the trends of its operations, considered both globally and in the various sectors in which it has operated, and its main subsidiaries; and (c) refer especially to company costs, revenues and investments. The report must provide at least the following information: (1) research and development activities; (2) relationships with subsidiary, associate, parent and group undertakings; (3) events occurring after the balance sheet date; (4) predicted evolution of operations.

Publication and audit

For limited liability entities, the company annual meeting (*Assemblea dei soci*) has to be summoned within four months (or within six months, if the company statutes so specify) after the end of the financial year. Group accounts follow the same pattern and timing in preparation and presentation to the shareholders as the parent company individual accounts. However, a fundamental difference is that consolidated financial statements are not submitted to the approval of the shareholders, who can only examine them, without having the possibility of asking for any change. In fact, only the parent's individual accounts need shareholders' endorsement, since the dividend distribution is decided on the basis of these.

In addition to the approved parent company accounts, a copy of the consolidated financial statements, together with the report on operations and the collegio sindacale's report, has to be filed in the 'Register of undertakings' at the local Chamber of Commerce. The filing has to be reported in the BUSARL (official bulletin). Unlimited liability firms do not have to file their accounts publicly.

As to audit, it has already been pointed out that limited companies with a capital exceeding €120,000 must have a collegio sindacale, while only listed companies, insurances and a few other categories of firms are subject to compulsory external audit. However, many medium–large-sized companies have their accounts audited voluntarily. Consolidated accounts have to be audited by the same body responsible for the audit of the parent's accounts.

Rules, policies and practices in measurement criteria

Table 8.3 summarizes the main differences between Italian regulations and International Accounting Standards (IAS).

Measurement criteria in individual company accounts

In addition to those changes discussed earlier, the decree no. 127/1991 introduced more detailed measurement criteria (new art. 2426, Civil Code). As has already been pointed out, the valuation rules set by fiscal law (particularly the TUIR, see above) are also extremely relevant in the Italian environment, and are often the actual source when drawing up individual company accounts. A further source on measurement issues is the accounting standards issued by the Italian profession, but these statements are not generally considered as very authoritative. Some of the main measurement issues are analysed below, giving a comprehensive idea of the sources of regulations.

Table 8.3 International Accounting Standards checklist

IAS	Italian rules (if not otherwise specified, the primary reference is to the Civil Code)
1	Materiality and substance over form are not concepts established in the law. They are included in the accounting standard no. 11. However, the Italian law implementing the Fourth Directive on bank accounts expressly requires the application of these two concepts. Offsetting between values is expressly forbidden. A horizontal balance sheet format is compulsory. There is no specific section for current liabilities. Short-term receivables of a financial nature are to be included in the investments, while long-term receivables of a commercial nature are reported within the current assets.
2	The general rule is the lower of cost and net realizable value. As to cost formulas, LIFO, FIFO and weighted average are all allowed, but LIFO is the most widely adopted in practice. Overheads have to be allocated to inventory cost for a 'reasonable amount'.
4	Residual value is not mentioned in the law. Any modifications in depreciation criteria or coefficients must be explained in the notes. All changes relating to fixed assets (e.g. revaluations, acquisitions and disposals, depreciation and losses, and so on) should also be disclosed in the notes. In practice tax rates are applied. Tax accelerated depreciation, when adopted, is to be calculated in the first three fiscal years of an asset's use and it could be treated either as an equity reserve (preferred treatment by accounting standard no. 16), or as part of the accumulated depreciation.
7	Cash flow statements are not compulsory, but are recommended by accounting standard no. 12. Quoted companies generally provide one in practice.
8	The compulsory income statement format (of a vertical type with cost by nature) does not identify a sub-total which clearly corresponds to profit/loss from ordinary operations. Extraordinary items are shown separately and divided in gains and losses. No clear legal definition of them is given (items are extraordinary if they do not relate to the company's ordinary activities). Accounting standard no. 12 gives some guidance on that. Valuation criteria cannot be changed from one accounting period to another, apart from when exceptional circumstances occur. According to CONSOB and accounting standard no. 29, the effects of changes in accounting policies and of the correction of fundamental errors have to be taken to the income statement as an extraordinary item (allowed treatment by the International Accounting Standard). For listed companies it is compulsory to produce a pro-forma statement when facing a change in accounting policies.
10	No explicit statutory guideline for the recognition of post balance sheet events and contingencies. Significant post balance sheet events are to be disclosed in the report on operations. Accounting standard no. 29 is in line with the International Accounting Standard.
11	Percentage-of-completion method is allowed by the Civil Code and preferred by the tax law and accounting standard no. 23. Complete contract method is also permitted legally but less adopted in practice.
12	No legal requirement for recognizing deferred taxes either in individual company or group accounts. There is only a requirement for disclosing the deferred tax effects in the notes. From 1999 accounting standard no. 25 requires the recognition of deferred taxes in both individual company and group accounts. However, deferred tax assets are to be recognized only where there are no reasonable doubts (not only when it is probable) that a taxable profit will be available; while deferred tax liabilities are to be recognized only when it is likely that a future liability will arise (and then not on all

Table 8.3   International Accounting Standards checklist (*continued*)

IAS	*Italian rules (if not otherwise specified, the primary reference is to the Civil Code)*

taxable temporary differences). The flow-through method is customary in practice, but listed companies traditionally provide for deferred taxation in consolidated accounts.

14   If the information is significant, segmental reports of the sale revenues by industry and geographical area are to be provided in the notes. No reconciliation between segments and aggregated information is explicitly required. This applies to all limited liability companies.

15   Limited and unlimited liability entities exploiting the revaluation possibilities allowed by ad hoc laws, which are issued from time to time, have to disclose the amount of the revaluations carried out.

16   Property, plant and equipment are valued at historical cost less any accumulated depreciation. Subsequent expenditure can be capitalized. Devaluations are allowed only if the item has suffered a lasting reduction in value. When this reduction ceases, the item should be revalued to its previous cost. Revaluations above the historical cost, which are sometimes tax-free, are granted from time to time by ad hoc laws (see above). Revaluation to current value is not necessarily required – sometimes special parameters have to be applied.

17   No capitalization of finance leases by the lessee is required. The amount of lease debt is generally disclosed in the memorandum accounts at the bottom of the balance sheet. Lease capitalization is frequent in the consolidated accounts of large groups and requested by accounting standard no 17.

18   There is no Civil Code guideline or requirement on revenue recognition. The tax law gives a list of the items to be recognized as revenues. Dividends are recognized on a cash basis. When they are paid by subsidiaries, CONSOB allows listed parent companies (only) to account for dividends on an accrual basis.

19   An employee severance indemnity is accrued in a special non-funded provision. (This is likely to change soon, though, and part of the severance indemnity could actually be paid to ad hoc external pension funds.) Employee pension costs are generally paid to a state-run agency on a monthly basis and thus recognized as a period expense. See also IAS 26 and IAS 37.

20   No general legal criteria for recognizing public grants. Tax rules suggest that grants related to the purchase of assets should be deducted from the assets' historical cost. Accounting standard no. 16 expresses a preference for treating this type of grant as deferred income. Grants related to income are to be taken to the income statement when they are cashed or gradually within a period not exceeding five years.

21   No Civil Code indication as to the method to be used for translating either transactions or financial statements in foreign currency. Whichever method is adopted should be disclosed in the notès. As to foreign currency transactions, Italian accounting standard no. 26 follows the IAS with some exceptions, the most relevant of which is that exchange gains on long-term debtors and creditors are to be deferred and taken to an ad hoc provision in the balance sheet. Italian fiscal law allows the use of both the closing rate method and the temporal method, but the former is the most widely adopted in practice. As to the translation of the accounts of foreign subsidiaries, Italian accounting standard no. 17 is in line with the IAS. According to Italian accounting standard no. 27, the exchange differences arising from the changeover to the euro can also be capitalized and amortized through time (e.g. four

Table 8.3   International Accounting Standards checklist (*continued*)

IAS	Italian rules (if not otherwise specified, the primary reference is to the Civil Code)

years) instead of being taken immediately to the income statement (as required by the International Accounting Standard).

22   The pooling-of-interests method of accounting for business combinations is not mentioned but is adopted in practice in dealing with legal mergers. Goodwill arising on consolidation can be either capitalized and amortized over up to five years or a slightly longer period, provided that this does not exceed the period of asset's use (the same rules apply also to purchased goodwill), or written off against reserves. Negative goodwill should be taken – depending on its nature – either to reserves or to a special provision ('consolidation provision for risks and future expenses'). Before recognizing consolidation goodwill, the difference resulting from offsetting the parent's interest against subsidiary's net equity is to be attributed to acquired assets and liabilities. No explicit legal guideline exists for such a revaluation process.

23   According to the law, borrowing costs, when relating to an acquisition, construction or production of an asset, could be capitalized 'for a reasonable amount' and until the moment from which the asset can be used. Tax law, which conforms in the main to the international standards, is followed in practice.

24   Disclosure is to be made in the notes of the identity of related parties, the amounts of the participating interests in them, and the corresponding share in the related party's equity. In the management report, disclosure should be made of the transactions carried out and any other type of involvement with related parties.

25   Current investments should be carried in the balance sheet at the lower of cost and net realizable value. Long-term investments should be valued in the balance sheet at cost, which is to be reduced to recognize a decline other than temporary in their value. Revaluations above cost are possible only when they are allowed by special laws.

26   It is not customary for Italian companies to set up their own retirement pension schemes for employees, even though a few companies do it on top of the statutory government-run one. Pensions are paid by the state or state-controlled agencies only, partly from payments made by the company on the basis of a statute law. Thus, no provisions for this are necessary. However, a severance indemnity is paid when the employee leaves the company for whatever reason. This indemnity is built up year by year in relation to an employee's salary. The yearly amount of the severance indemnity is determined by a legal mechanism, and is accrued in an ad hoc non-funded provision (fondo di trattamento di fine rapporto). See also IAS 19 and IAS 37.

27   Control for consolidation purposes is linked to a legally based dominant influence of the parent on a subsidiary. Subsidiaries whose activities are dissimilar from those of the other group undertakings have to be excluded from consolidation, even though CONSOB has reduced the scope of this legal rule to the minimum extent. An exemption from preparing consolidated accounts is permitted for small groups. Minority interests should be included as a separate item in the consolidated shareholders' equity and as a share of the group's profit/loss for the year in the consolidated income statement. In the group accounts subsidiaries that have been excluded from full consolidation are to be valued by the equity method following the International Accounting Standard.

28   Significant influence is presumed to exist when an investor holds, directly or indirectly, 20% or more (10% for listed companies) of the voting power of the investee. In the parent's individual accounts investments in associates should be

Table 8.3 International Accounting Standards checklist (*continued*)

IAS	Italian rules (if not otherwise specified, the primary reference is to the Civil Code)

carried either at cost or by the equity method (the resulting profit should be credited to an ad hoc equity reserve). Practice follows in the main the former method. In the consolidated accounts investments in associates should be accounted for using the equity method according to the International Accounting Standard.

29 No ad hoc legal or professional regulation dealing with financial reporting in hyperinflationary economies exists.

30 The law no. 87/1992 implementing in Italy the Fourth EC Directive for bank and financial institution accounts sets the legal disclosures to be provided by this type of company. Contingencies are to be disclosed in the notes and in the memorandum accounts at the bottom of the balance sheet. Offsetting between assets and liabilities and revenues and costs is explicitly forbidden. The Bank of Italy has issued special regulations on this subject. The resulting level of disclosure by banks and similar institutions is likely to be slightly lower than that required by the International Accounting Standard.

31 If a participating undertaking holds a share superior to 20% of a joint venture (10% if the joint venture is listed), the participating undertaking is allowed to include the joint venture in the group accounts. In this case proportional consolidation could be used to account for this joint venture.

32 No specific legal rules exist for the presentation and disclosure of financial instruments in the accounts of non-financial companies. Instruments permitting off balance sheet financing should be disclosed in the notes to both individual company and consolidated accounts.

33 No legal regulation deals with earnings per share. Accounting standard no. 28 offers some indications in line with the International Accounting Standard.

34 Since the 1990s listed companies have to produce a half-year interim report, which is subject from 1998 to the so-called 'limited external audit procedure'. Since 2000 listed companies also have to produce quarterly reports according to the requirements of CONSOB, which are in line with the IAS. The Italian accounting standard no. 30 is also in line with the IAS.

35 No ad hoc legal or professional regulation dealing with discontinuing operations exists. For listed companies CONSOB has recommended reference to the IAS.

36 The writing down of fixed assets is compulsory when an enduring loss in their value has occurred. The devaluation of current assets is compulsory whenever the market value of the asset is lower than its historical cost. No indication is given as to how the impairment test should be carried out.

37 Provisions for risks and future costs are to be related to losses or debts with a specific nature and whose existence is certain or probable, but of which either the amount or the date of occurrence is indeterminate. The provision for severance indemnity is an Italian specificity. Also contingent losses which have a specifically identified nature and which are likely to occur in the foreseeable future, are to be provided for. Contingencies are to be disclosed in the notes or in the memorandum accounts at the bottom of the balance sheet. Accounting standard no. 19 is in line with the IAS. For fiscal purposes it is possible to account for tax-deductible provisions only in relation to causes expressly identified. See also IAS 19 and IAS 26.

38 It is possible to capitalize start-up, research and development and advertisement costs

Table 8.3   International Accounting Standards checklist (*continued*)

IAS	Italian rules (if not otherwise specified, the primary reference is to the Civil Code)
	with the consent of the collegio sindacale. However, no legal definition of these expenses is given, and no legal conditions are set for capitalizing them. They have to be amortized within five years. Their capitalization, however, constrains distributable profit, unless the net amount is less than or at most equal to the free reserves available. It is not possible to revalue intangible assets, except when an ad hoc revaluation law is issued. Accounting standard no. 24 limits itself to detailing the Civil Code rules.
39	No ad hoc legal or professional regulation dealing with financial instruments exists. Fair value cannot be adopted by non-financial institutions due to the adherence to the historical cost principle. Therefore, the IAS can be applied asymmetrically: financial instruments can be devalued if their year-end market price is below the historical cost, but they cannot be revalued above this threshold. The use of fair value for financial instruments is allowed for banks and financial institutions.
40	No ad hoc legal or professional regulation dealing with investment property exists. These assets have to be valued in the same way as all other fixed assets, i.e. at depreciated historical cost. Fair value is not allowed in such cases.
41	No ad hoc legal or professional regulation dealing with agriculture accounting issues exists.

The general principle for asset valuation given by art. 2426, Civil Code is historical cost, which may be either purchase cost (costo di acquisto) or production cost (costo di produzione).

Tangible fixed assets have in principle to be valued at historical cost; they must be written down only if an enduring loss in value occurs, but their historical cost has to be restored if the situation reverses. Tangible assets whose life is finite have to be depreciated systematically over their useful (economic) life 'in relation to their residual possibility of use'. However, the historical cost principle is compromised by legal revaluations. An ad hoc revaluation law is occasionally issued in Italy in order to allow companies legitimately to overcome the limit of the historical cost. The most recent revaluation laws were passed in 1990, 1991 and 2000 (law no. 408/1990, law no. 413/1991 and law 342/2000). In the last 50 years only three similar laws were passed (1952, 1975, 1983). The old revaluation laws granted free-tax revaluations, but the three most recent acts taxed the revaluation gains (although at a reduced rate). It is possible that the 1990 and 1991 laws were mostly motivated by government financing problems rather than by inflation, which nevertheless affected the Italian economy in the second half of the 1980s. This interpretation is supported by the unusually short time lag between the two acts: the failure of the first law which permitted optional revaluation to achieve tax inflows may explain the need – after only one year – for a second revaluation law, this time compulsory in application. The 2000 law should be interpreted in the context of the introduction of the euro. As a result of these laws, the annual accounts of Italian companies clearly cannot be said to be drawn up in accordance either with the current value principle or with the historical cost one. On the contrary, instead of leading to some amelioration in the consistency and quality of the published accounting data, the recent revaluation laws are likely to have produced further distortions as a result once again of using the accounts as a fiscal tool for collecting money.

The tax rules dealing with tangible fixed assets are very influential and de facto substitute for commercial law rules. The amount by which tax depreciation exceeds commercial depreciation can be accounted for as normal depreciation in the income statement, or alternatively is credited to a special reserve in the shareholder's funds (solution preferred by Italian accounting standards). If the accelerated depreciation is treated as commercial depreciation (which is the most customary treatment so far), the formation of hidden reserves is in effect taking place. Traditionally tax depreciation charges have to be taken to the income statement in order to be deductible. At the end of the 1990s the Ministry of Finance granted the possibility of deducting accelerated depreciation charges directly in the tax declaration, thus opening the way to companies to free their income statement from this particular fiscal interference. Most recently, the Ministry of Finance has also allowed companies to classify the accumulated accelerated depreciation as part of the shareholder's funds: this solution offers companies some fiscal advantages, and therefore has begun to be commonly followed in pratice. In this case, the tax-recognized 'provision' for accelerated depreciation is set up using part of the profit for the year and establishing a correspondent equity reserve.

Intangible asset valuation rules follow in principle those for tangible assets. However, some legal provisions deal specifically with intangibles. In particular, unlike other countries, the capitalization of research and development, advertising and business start-up costs is allowed. They have to be amortized over a maximum of five years. However, the capitalization of research and development costs, as well as advertising expenses, prevents dividends from being distributed, unless the unamortized amount of these assets is counterbalanced by at least an equivalent amount of free reserves.

Goodwill can be recognized – with the consent of the collegio sindacale – only if a cost has been incurred by the company for its acquisition. It has in theory to be amortized over five years, but this period can be extended for a limited number of years if the useful life of the goodwill is estimated to be longer. The capitalization of internally-generated brands is not permitted.

The tax rules provide that, to be deductible for tax purposes, (a) the amortization charges for the cost of royalties and patents cannot exceed one third of their book value, (b) the yearly amortization provision for brands cannot be superior to one tenth of their cost, (c) the amortization period for licences is the same as their contractual or legal life, (d) amortization allowances for goodwill cannot exceed one tenth of its book value (quite similar to the Civil Code rule) (art. 68, TUIR), (e) research and development costs can be either expensed immediately or amortized by the straight-line method within four years, (f) advertising can be either expensed immediately or amortized straight line over five years (art. 74, TUIR). No detailed rule is provided for amortization of start-up costs and it is considered acceptable for fiscal purposes to use the period fixed by Civil Code (five years).

Equity investments can be valued either at cost or by the equity method. A major innovation imported by the decree no. 127/1991 is the option to use the equity method for valuation of investments in individual company accounts where the investor has a dominant or significant influence. Nevertheless, in this case the application of the equity method takes place in a particular way: income from associates has to be credited to an undistributable equity reserve in the balance sheet, and not to the profit and loss statement, insofar as that income corresponds to unrealized gains (dividends are recorded in the income statement).

For tax purposes, investments (apart from those valued by the equity method) have to be valued at LIFO (on an annual basis), or FIFO or weighted average, as for stocks (see below). Any increase above historical cost (not allowed, though, by commercial rules) is taxable. In 1994 the law decree no. 416/1994 changed the fiscal approach to the equity method, considering income from subsidiaries and associates – exceeding any previously deducted loss in value – as non-taxable (new art. 54, section 2-*bis*, TUIR). This innovation should favour the adoption of the equity method, but this is not expected to be very extensive in any event.

Short-term financial assets (C.III. of Assets) are to be held at cost, subject to write-down for any loss in value. They have to be restored to their historical cost if their value goes up again. Also financial instruments (swaps, futures, and so on) are to be valued at cost.

The rule of lower of cost and net realizable value applies to the valuation of *stocks*. The LIFO method is permitted, as well as FIFO and weighted average. The current cost of individual categories of stocks should be disclosed in the notes, if this is materially different from that stated in the accounts. Tax rules follow in the main the commercial legislation, allowing all the three valuation bases.

Accounting for assets held under finance leases is a point deliberately not addressed in the valuation rules, even though the prevailing legal opinion is that capitalization is not permitted. No change is expected in the current practice of taking rents to the income statement and of disclosing the amount of the residual debt only in the memorandum section of the balance sheet.

According to the Civil Code rule, *trade debtors* have to be valued at their net realizable value. Practice concerning the creation of provisions is heavily influenced by the tax rules. These accept as deductible a figure not exceeding 0.5% of the nominal value of debtors at the end of the financial year. This is allowed until the related provision reaches 5% of the amount of trade debtors. The annual deductable figure applicable to banks and financial institutions is raised to 0.6% of the nominal value of their debtors.

In Italy, as in France, *pensions* are generally paid by the state or by public entities, from contributions made both by companies (mostly) and by employees, throughout their working life. Thus no balance sheet provisions for this are necessary, and the Civil Code requires only that the amounts paid by the company are recorded in accordance with the accrual principle in the income statement. Sometimes additional company or group pension schemes exist.

When an Italian employee leaves a company, a *severance* (or *termination*) *indemnity* must be paid. A non-funded allowance is to be annually calculated for each company employee according to legally set parameters, and taken to the income statement and to an ad hoc provision of the balance sheet.

As to *long-term contracts*, the percentage of completion method may be used according to the Civil Code, but the completed contract method is not excluded. Technical guidelines for the implementation of the two valuation methods can be found in Italian accounting standard no. 23. Tax rules set as a preferred principle the percentage of completion method, with some minor adjustments in favour of the taxpayer.

There is no rule in the Civil Code on *foreign currency transactions* within an individual company's own accounts. There is only the requirement to disclose the accounting policy adopted. The Italian accounting standard no. 26 follows IAS 21 with some exceptions, the most relevant of which is that exchange gains on long-term debtors and creditors are to be deferred and taken to an ad hoc provision in the balance sheet. Italian fiscal law allows two accounting methods: (a) year-end exchange rate method, with the recognition of gains or losses from the translation process as tax relevant (art. 76, section 2, TUIR); (b) historical exchange rate method, with negative translation differences provided for through a yearly tax-deductible allowance in the income statement, which is accrued to an ad hoc fund (*fondo rischi su cambi* – provision for foreign exchange risks) to be decreased when a loss is realized or an unexpected gain occurs (art. 72, TUIR).

The method generally applied to accounting for *taxes* is the 'flow-through' one. Accounting for deferred tax in individual company accounts is quite rare even though the publication of accounting standard no. 25 should favour the spread of a more sophisticated treatment of income taxes. The income tax burden on limited companies is today (February 2002) around 40.25% of taxable income (36% being state income tax – 35% from 2003). A tax credit is recognized on company dividends paid to shareholders, which is up to 56.25% of the amount distributed. A five-year carry forward of accounting losses is allowed for all limited and unlimited entities.

Measurement criteria in group accounts

Group accounting policies must be uniformly applied to the accounts of all subsidiaries included in the consolidation. Unconsolidated subsidiaries and associates are to be accounted for by the equity method (however, contrary to the practice in individual company accounts, income from associates has to be taken into the income statement). Joint ventures are to be treated by the same method or by proportional consolidation, if the participating interest in them exceeds 20% (10% if the joint venture is listed). If this interest amounts to less than this, they have to be valued at cost. In principle, valuation criteria used in the parent's individual accounts are transferred to group accounts via the consolidation process: thus the single company rules relate also to group accounts. However, there are some valuation issues which could be considered specific to consolidated reporting.

The *acquisition or purchase method* has to be applied in consolidating subsidiaries. Merger accounting (or pooling-of-interests) is not allowed and not even mentioned by decree no. 127/1991 but it is sometimes applied in practice to legal mergers. The difference between the cost of acquisition of a subsidiary and the correspondent book value of the subsidiary should first be allocated over the latter's individual assets and liabilities, probably up to their current value (no definition is specified, though, by the law).

Any residual difference is to be treated according to its sign. A positive difference (acquisition cost exceeding the updated book value of the subsidiary) has to be treated as an intangible asset (called *differenza di consolidamento* – difference on consolidation) or, alternatively, written off immediately against group reserves. Consolidation goodwill, a purchased goodwill, should be amortized over five years, but the period may be extended for a limited number of years if its useful life is reckoned to be longer. The consent of the parent company's collegio sindacale is required for the recognition of goodwill as an intangible asset. If goodwill is negative, its treatment varies according to the cause. A negative difference (subsidiary updated book value exceeding the cost of acquisition) has to be allocated to an ad hoc reserve when deriving from a perceived bargain purchase, but is classified as a liability when it represents future losses (*fondo di consolidamento per rischi ed oneri futuri* – consolidation provision for future risks and expenses).

No specific rule exists for *translation of the accounts of foreign subsidiaries*, but only a requirement to indicate in the notes the criteria adopted. Italian accounting standard no. 17 is in line with what is recommended by IAS 21 (use of the current rate method for subsidiaries which are operationally and financially autonomous from the parent company; use of the temporal method for subsidiaries which are operationally and financially integrated with the parent company).

There is no rule allowing for capitalization of finance leases. However, even before the implementation of decree no. 127/1991, Italian groups capitalized leasing in their consolidated accounts.

All major Italian groups used to account for *deferred* tax in their consolidated statements. The cancellation of section 5 of art. 31 by law no. 503/1994 (discussed above) seems to have had the effect of only permitting the elimination of fiscal interferences in group accounts. In this respect, contradictory treatments of deferred tax have arisen on the occasion of the application of the new legal rules on consolidated statements (see below). After the publication of Italian accounting standard no. 25, the general practice is now to fully account for deferred taxes.

The valuation policies of all major Italian groups, as well as their account formats and notes, faced a major discontinuity in legal rules with reference to the 1994 financial year. An empirical survey conducted by the author on 30 Italian medium-large groups (most of them listed on the Milan Stock Exchange) reveals a substantial inertia in changing the key accounting policies (e.g. elimination of intra-group items and margins, treatment of consolidation goodwill, foreign currency translation, fiscal interferences) between the consolidated accounts of 1992 and 1994.[1]

As a significant example, all but one of the 20 groups that accounted for deferred taxes in 1992 did the same in 1994, while the groups that did not provide for deferred taxes in 1992 maintained this policy also in 1994. Only marginal adjustments can be detected as a consequence of the coming into force of the new commercial rules on accounting. For instance, a remarkable shift in the positioning of minority interests in the balance sheet has occurred: in 1992 17 groups showed this item between liabilities and equity and 7 within liabilities; in 1994 28 groups included minority interests in equity according to the then new legislation. Further, deferred taxes were treated by the majority of groups as a long-term liability in 1992, whilst most of the groups put them in the balance sheet as a provision in 1994.

As aforementioned, from July 1998 Italian companies which are listed on both EU and non-EU markets are allowed to prepare their consolidated accounts in accordance with 'accounting standards of international recognition' which are compatiable with EU Directives. However, this statutory rule has not come into force as yet.

Conclusion

The innovations which took place in the 1990s in the Italian regulatory framework for accounting, arising from the adoption of the European directives, have opened a new era in this country's financial reporting regulatory system. One could say that Italian accounting has surely been changed in form and probably improved in certain areas such as disclosure and group accounts. However, the actual depth of the innovations may be questioned. The reforms do not seem in fact likely to have led to a radical change in the socio-economic foundations of Italian accounting, which will probably continue to be inspired for a certain period by the same issues of fiscal consequences, conservatism and secrecy. However, the merger of the two professional bodies and the reform of company law might produce a quite substantial discontinuity. Indeed, as mentioned earlier, a major reform was introduced at the beginning of 2003 (coming into force as of 1st January 2004) which is aimed to disconnect tax and accounting and to consider the deferred tax effects; to entitle 'internationally-oriented companies as well as financial institutions' to use 'accounting standards of international recognition' for the preparation of consolidated accounts; to adopt fair value as a generalized valuation criterion for financial instruments; to allow the capitalization of leasing operations; and to allow companies to have a 'supervisory committee' (similar to the German approach) instead of the traditional collegio sindacale. It is quite evident that the range and depth of the expected changes are potentially able not only to have an impact on accounting regulations and practices, but also to foster the latter's socio-economic role and perception in the Italian context of the new decade.

Notes

1. The 30 groups whose financial statements have been considered by the author for this survey are: Ansaldo Trasporti, Benetton Group, Cartiere Burgo, Cartiere Sottrici Binda, Cementir, Cofide, Cucirini Cantoni Coats, Dalmine, Eni, Falck, Fiat, FMC, Italfarmco, Italgas, Jolly Hotels, Linificio Canapificio Nazionale, La Magona, Navigazione Alta Italia, Nuovo Pignone, Rai, Recordati, Rinascente, Saffa, Schiapparelli, Sirti, Stet, Unicem, Zignago and Zucchi.

References

Took, L. (1995) The history of financial reporting in Italy. In P. Walton (ed.) *European Financial Reporting. A History*. Academic Press, London, pp. 157–168.

Zambon, S. (2001) Italy. In D. Alexander and S. Archer (eds) *The European Accounting Guide*, 4th edn, Aspen Publishing. New York, pp. 520–667.

Zambon, S. (1996) Accounting and business economics traditions: a missing European connection? *European Accounting Review* **5**: 401–411.

Further Reading

Canziani, A. (1994) Gino Zappa: accounting revolutionary. In J.R. Edwards (ed.) *Twentieth-Century Accounting Thinkers*. Routledge in association with ICAEW, London and New York, pp. 142–165.

De Ste. Croix, G.E.M. (1956) Greek and Roman Accounting. In A.C. Littleton and B.S. Yamey (eds) *Studies in the History of Accounting*. Irwin, Homewood, Ill., pp. 14–74.

Riccaboni, A. and Ghirri, R. (1994) *Italy*. Routledge in association with the ICAEW, London.

Zambon, S. and Saccon, C. (1993) Accounting change in Italy: Fresh Start or *Gattopardo's* Revolution? *European Accounting Review* **2**(2 September): 245–283.

Zambon, S. (2002) *Locating Accounting in its National Context: The Case of Italy*. Franco Angeli, Milan.

Zan, L. (1994) Toward a history of accounting histories: perspectives from the Italian tradition. *European Accounting Review* **3**(2): 255–307.

Accounting in Belgium

Ann Jorissen

Belgian financial reporting and financial accounting practices provide another example of the continental European model. Influences from French accounting (e.g. the obligation to use a standard chart of accounts, defined in the law) and German accounting (e.g. the dominance of conservatism, a very detailed accounting law and a close relationship between financial reporting and taxation) are to be found in Belgium.

The business community in which financial reporting slowly developed in Belgium consisted of a large number of small and medium-sized family enterprises. These companies were predominantly financed through family capital and loans from creditors, particularly banks. The owners of these businesses usually succeeded in obtaining their financial information directly through the management of the company. Very often the management team consisted of family members. Only a few large companies existed in the nineteenth and at the beginning of the twentieth century. As there were only a limited number of large companies the Belgium stock exchange remained rather small with only a few companies listed and a small trading volume. There was no investor community which asked for financial statements containing useful information for investors.

At the start of the twenty-first century these characteristics are changing. More and more companies are finding their way on to the stock exchange and the investor community is also steadily growing. Until the implementation of the EC directives, financial reporting was oriented towards providing information to creditors instead of investors. Therefore Belgian accounting was and still is dominated by the prudence principle. In the 1970s, following the adoption of the EC directives, new and extensive accounting legislation was introduced in Belgium. The accounting law and its accompanying royal decrees were very detailed because Belgium has a tradition of a codified law system as in Germany. In addition, preparers of financial information and the auditing profession share the view that compliance with these detailed legal rules results in statements that give a true and fair view. The new millennium will divide Belgian companies into two groups with respect to financial reporting. Listed companies will prepare their consolidated accounts to IAS or IFRS. Other non-listed large groups will probably adopt IAS or IFRS in the near future. The medium-sized and small companies will retain the traditional Belgian accounting legislation.

Legal and institutional basis of accounting regulation

Company law

Prior to the accounting law of 1975, legislation on company accounting was almost non-existent in Belgium. Only a few articles in the Code of Commerce dealt with the financial reporting requirements of companies. These articles had been taken from the Colbert/Savary ordonnance of 1673 (see Chapter 5 on France) and since their introduction to Belgian law relatively few changes occurred until 1975. The first Belgian Code of Commerce (18 May 1873) only included the requirement to prepare a balance sheet and a profit and loss account. The Act did not require any specific content or layout for these annual statements, nor were any valuation rules specified. As a consequence the annual accounts published in the official journal were not comparable with each other and were for the most part incomprehensible to third parties. The law only stipulated that all necessary depreciation had to be registered in the profit and loss account.

With the amendment of the law in 1913 a minimum layout for the balance sheet was introduced. This consisted of the following headings: on the asset side permanent assets and realizable assets had to be shown separately; on the liability side internal debts, debts on pledged assets and unsecured debts had to be presented (art. 75). This law, which ruled financial reporting up to 1975, remained silent with regard to valuation methods.

In the late 1960s the protest movement of workers and students against the establishment and the capitalist system, which was experienced in many European countries, had the effect in Belgium of leading the unions to question the rules governing financial disclosure by companies (Michielsen 1975, p. 179). The requirements of company law were not seen as stringent enough in the eyes of the labour movement, and the government was forced to change the existing financial reporting rules. On the basis of reports from interested parties and partly also of the first draft of the Fourth Directive on individual accounts (see Chapter 1), the legislator issued on 17 July 1975 the Wet op de Boekhouding en Jaarekening van Onderneming/Loi relative à la comptabilité et aux comptes annuels des entreprises (Accounting Law on bookkeeping and financial reporting for industrial and commercial companies). The provisions of the law were implemented by royal decree (RD) on 8 October 1976. The 1975 Law, together with the royal decree of 1976, covers aspects of bookkeeping, the form and content of the annual accounts, valuation rules, disclosure requirements and a basic standard chart of accounts. The law and the royal decree were amended by subsequent royal decrees. In 2001 the articles of the royal decree of 1976 were incorporated into company law. The articles are now part of the royal decree of 30 January 2001, enacting company law. These royal decrees are also issued by the parliament and they have the same status as a law.

The introduction of this legislation, although it dealt only with individual accounts, was a milestone in the history of financial reporting in Belgium.

Along with the royal decrees, the Law is the sole source of obligatory regulations on bookkeeping and accounting for industrial and commercial companies. Being part of a codified law system, the Accounting Law and the accompanying royal decrees are very detailed. They contain numerous requirements on bookkeeping and prescribe formats not only for the balance sheet and the profit and loss account, but also for the notes.

A second source of accounting regulation in Belgium, but not a binding one, are the opinions issued by the Commission des Normes Comptables, CNC/Commissie voor Boekhoudkundige Normen, CBN (Commission on accounting standards). The Accounting Law contains the articles governing the creation of the CNC/CBN. Its responsibilities are laid down in art. 14 as follows:

1. To put forward opinions to the government and parliament as required or on its own initiative.

2. To develop a body of accounting thought and to formulate the principles of proper accounting by way of opinions or recommendations.

Representatives of the accounting and audit professions and of the preparers of financial statements together with representatives from the Ministry of Finance and the Ministry of Small and Medium-size Enterprises sit on the board of the CNC/CBN. The opinions of the commission are considered to be 'authoritative' pronouncements, but they do not have the force of the law. Since its establishment, the CNC/CBN has issued 47 bulletins, which set out opinions on the application of particular articles of the law or the royal decrees. Some opinions have since been revised, and others have been subsequently enacted by law or royal decree. The CNC/CBN does not circulate drafts of opinions before they are issued, although in fact an exception was made in the case of foreign currency transactions.

Until 1990, companies were only obliged to prepare individual accounts. Consolidated accounts were regarded as an exotic item and companies did not prepare them voluntarily, mainly because they were unfamiliar with the concept. With the royal decree of 6 March 1990, the Seventh EC Directive was implemented in Belgium. Given the novelty of the requirement, the legislator chose to impose the obligation to prepare consolidated accounts only on very large groups until 1999. In many countries the option to prepare annual accounts according to rules other than national ones was introduced by law. The Belgian legislator did not choose to take that approach at the end of the twentieth century. A much more restrictive approach was taken. If a Belgian company wants to prepare its accounts according to international or foreign GAAP, it must seek permission to do so. The government decided to work with individual exemptions, which will be granted by the Minister of Economic Affairs. In Bulletin no. 44 (June 1998) issued by the Commission on Accounting Standards the criteria the Minister will use to grant an exemption were described. Companies which are eligible to apply foreign or international accounting standards are the so-called 'global players'. A global player is a company which fulfils one or more of the following criteria:

1. the enterprise is listed (or is planning to be listed) on international or foreign capital markets, or

2. the enterprise has significant international activities, or

3. the parent company of the enterprise uses non-Belgian accounting rules in its consolidated financial statements, or

4. the operations of the enterprise are situated in certain sectors (such as oil) where the use of foreign accounting rules is widespread.

Furthermore these exemptions will only be granted in relation to the consolidated accounts. Departure from EC Directives is prohibited. Individual accounts must always be prepared according to Belgian GAAP. After issuing Bulletin no. 44 the Commission on Accounting Standards also stressed that in the case of optional consolidation an exemption should be sought. The Commission made this point because small groups (which according to the legal criteria did not have to prepare consolidated accounts) presented their accounts in GAAP other than the national ones, without asking for permission first.

In the wake of the EU regulation requiring EU-listed companies to apply IAS, the Belgian Commission on Accounting Standards published a paper in which they stated that non-listed companies could also opt to apply IAS standards for their consolidated accounts.

This implies that companies no longer have to apply for an exemption if they want to use IAS as their sole reporting basis.

Taxation

The principle of fiscal neutrality

The first tax laws were passed in 1830 when Belgium became independent, but the concept of corporate income tax was introduced only in 1913. As the tax statutes remained rather vague on the definition of taxable income, a rich body of tax regulations (issued by the tax authorities and arising from court decisions) was developed. For the first seventy years of the twentieth century companies valued their assets, liabilities, expenses and revenues according to the fiscal rules in order to determine their taxable income. De facto these fiscal rules became the implicit accounting rules (Gelders 1984, p. 1301), because company law did not provide any valuation rules. In this way a strong link was created between accounting and taxation, a link that still exists today.

From the mid-1970s a new situation emerged. Companies were faced with a completely new set of accounting rules with the introduction of the 1975 Accounting Law as well as the existing set of fiscal rules. In many other industrial countries companies are in a similar situation, and differences between financial reporting and taxation were overcome by the introduction of deferred taxes into the annual accounts. However, in the mid-1970s the concept of deferred taxes was totally unfamiliar to members of the Belgian business community. Furthermore, they were used to preparing only one set of annual accounts for both publication and fiscal purposes. They opposed the idea of preparing two sets of accounts, which they considered to be too big an administrative burden. As a solution to this problem, the government introduced the principle of fiscal neutrality (Jorissen and Maes 1996, p. 918).

The introduction of this principle was also a political choice because the government did not want the tax system and the computation of taxable income to be changed through the introduction of this new accounting legislation. It noted in the explanatory memorandum to the Law of 1975: 'The government will make sure that fiscal neutrality is guaranteed and when necessary it shall take the necessary legal and administrative initiatives and measures.' Fiscal neutrality was to be achieved in the following way. The fiscal administration would accept for tax purposes all the rules of the Accounting Law and its decrees with regard to depreciation, write-offs, write-backs, provisions and other valuation rules in order to determine the taxable amount unless tax law expressly provided otherwise. In the preamble to the royal decree of 18 October 1976, the parliament expressed its will to permit fiscal rules to differ from accounting rules only in exceptional circumstances. On this basis, accounting law overrides fiscal law except as far as concerns some special issues.

At first there existed many distortions between fiscal law and accounting law. In order to eliminate these, the government proceeded in several ways: first, it changed certain aspects of the fiscal statutes to bring these into line with the Accounting Law; secondly, items in the Accounting Law were changed to harmonize with their fiscal treatment. Almost 20 years after the introduction of the Accounting Law and the principle of fiscal neutrality, one might say that the latter has been achieved only in part. In many cases fiscal law and the tax administration accept the accounting rules. However, neutrality is constantly threatened by the fact that parliament often uses fiscal measures to stimulate the economic activity of enterprises. Moreover, where tax relief is proposed to stimulate the economy, company accounts are obliged to reflect this, which results in tax-biased annual accounts. Examples of tax-driven accounting are given later in the chapter.

The system of corporate income tax

The Belgian tax system includes the following four main types of taxes:

1. taxes on income, including corporate income tax, the legal entity income tax, individual income tax and non-resident income tax;

2. taxes on the transfer of property, goods and services, consisting of value added tax (VAT), registration and stamp duties, customs and excise duties, and succession (inheritance tax) and gift taxes;

3. taxes on property, including real estate tax and 'movable property' tax on dividends, interest and royalties;

4. communal (i.e. local) taxes.

For companies corporate income tax is the most important. Although the official flat corporate income tax rate is 39% (companies with profits below €322 300 ($350 000) may benefit from a lower rate), the effective tax rate calculated from the published profit and loss accounts of many large companies varies between 10% and 30%, and for small and medium-sized companies between 20% and 30%. These figures prove that many Belgian companies make use of special tax-deductible items or other tax avoidance structures. It is not unusual to find annual accounts in which one sees a profit figure with virtually no tax deduction. The opposite situation is more rare.

Consolidated accounts are not used for tax purposes. The starting point for the calculation of corporate income tax is the accounting profit in the individual company accounts. To this are added depreciation, write-offs and provisions that are not accepted for tax purposes and other disallowed business expenses (e.g. 50% of hotel and restaurant expenses). Write-backs that are not taxable are deducted from profit. Taxable income can also be reduced by the following items: profits attributable to foreign permanent establishments located in a tax treaty country, tax-free charitable donations and tax exemptions granted for extra personnel that have been hired. Inter-company dividends are not taxed and if a company has invested in new assets during the financial year a certain amount called 'investment deduction' can be deducted from the taxable income. Prior year losses can be carried forward for offset against taxable income.

The accounting profession

The accounting profession developed very slowly in Belgium. Because most companies in Belgium were financed through family capital and external loans and the parties involved were satisfied with the information they had directly, there was no need for a highly developed accounting profession which could take the lead in developing accounting standards. The Institut des Reviseurs d' Entreprises/Instituut van Bedrijfsrevisoren (Institute of Auditors) was only created in 1953 (by the Law of 22 July). The influence of the profession on accounting practice is very limited. Even in the 'turbulent' years of the mid-1970s, the accounting and audit profession played a very passive role (Pauwels 1979, p. 41). The Institut des Réviseurs addresses particular accounting problems but never issues pronouncements on them. The results of its analyses are communicated only to its members. Furthermore, as the profession is accustomed to working within a codified law system, the Institut feels quite comfortable with this situation where the law supplies all regulatory needs.

The implementation of the Eighth Directive required amendment of the 1953 statute and the profession was in effect reorganized through the law of 21 February 1985. This created a second professional body, the Institut des Experts Comptables/Instituut der Accountants (Institute of Accountants). The Insitute of Accountants was reorganized in 1999 (law of 22 April 1999) into the Institute of Accountants and Tax Advisers (Instituut voor Accountants en Belastungconsulenten (IAB)/Institut des Experts-comptables et des Conseils fiscaux (IEC)). The Hoge Raad voor het economisch beroep/Conseil Supérieur des Professions économiques (Higher Council for the Economic Professions) set up under the statute, has defined the separate functions of an auditor and an accountant and governs the relationship between the two institutes. Only members of the Institut des Réviseurs (about 800 members) may perform all functions with which public auditors are exclusively entrusted by law, in particular the statutory audit of the financial statements of large enterprises. The main task of members of the Institute of Accountants and Tax Consultants (Instituut van de Accountants en Belastingconsulenten/Institut des Experts-comptables et des Conseils fiscaux) (approximately 8000 members) is to provide help to small and medium-sized firms with the preparation of their annual accounts and by giving them legal and tax advice.

Objectives, assumptions and qualitative characteristics

The concept of 'true and fair' was introduced into Belgian accounting legislation as part of the harmonization process. This concept was new to the Belgian accounting world but is interpreted as meaning that the annual accounts as a whole have to present a true and fair view and that when the balance sheet and the profit and loss account fail to present a true and fair view due to extreme conservatism or tax-driven accounting, a corrective statement has to be made in the notes. In fact the concept of true and fair was never really absorbed into Belgian accounting measurement practices, as it clashed constantly with conservatism or tax-driven requirements. Even the legislation states that when for tax reasons the balance sheet and profit and loss account do not present a true and fair view, a disclosure in the notes is sufficient to correct the situation.

For example in art. 61 of the royal decree of 2001 the legislator states that in accordance with the relevant tax regulations, an accelerated depreciation plan may be applied. Should the application of such an accelerated plan lead to more rapid depreciation than can be justified on economic grounds, the difference between the accumulated depreciation charged and the amount of the depreciation that is economically justifiable shall be disclosed in the notes. The notes shall also disclose the impact of the accelerated depreciation charged during the period or during previous periods on the amount of depreciation shown in the profit and loss account of the period.

With regard to the question of the relationship of substance over form, the legal form is usually adhered to, although in recent years there have been some signs of change, such as a requirement to capitalize financial leases, where economic substance has overruled form.

Overall, Belgian annual accounts present a prudent view of the financial situation of a company and one that is heavily influenced by tax rules. This applies not only to individual company accounts, but also to consolidated statements (see below). Preparing financial statements is considered by the business community and by the profession as a fulfilment of the detailed requirements laid down in the accounting statutes. Special laws and royal decrees exist dealing with the annual reports of holding companies, banks, insurance companies, pension funds and hospitals.

The accounting law on the individual accounts of a company contains detailed regulations with regard to bookkeeping procedures, includes a detailed standard chart of accounts and a detailed format not only for the balance sheet and the profit and loss account but also for the notes. The royal decrees on consolidated accounts contain a detailed format for the consolidated balance sheet and profit and loss account but no detailed format for the notes.

The accounting statutes contain several, rather vague, general valuation principles as well as a set of detailed valuation rules for specific balance sheet and profit and loss items. The legislator states that

> Each enterprise, taking into account the particular nature of its business, must define the rules to be used in the valuation of the inventory of its business and in particular for establishing and adjusting depreciation, amounts written off, provisions for liabilities and charges and revaluations. Valuations, depreciation, amounts written down and provisions for liabilities and charges shall satisfy the criteria of prudence, sincerity and good faith.

The criterion of prudence is discussed further in the law, but the criteria of sincerity and good faith are not explicitly defined. Furthermore, the legislator prescribes that the going concern principle, consistency, realization and matching and the principle of individual valuation have to be adhered to but does not define them.

Although the general valuation rules remain vague, this does not mean that preparers of financial statements have much room for judgement when they consider the valuation of assets, liabilities, costs and revenues. For many items in the balance sheet and the profit and loss account a detailed valuation and recognition procedure is prescribed in the legislation. Preparers normally apply those detailed procedures without difficulty. The most important of them will be analysed in the section on measurement and recognition practices. The valuation and recognition procedures are typically very pragmatic and take account of the interests of the business community and the fiscal environment. Before a royal decree or a law is passed, the preparers of annual accounts, the profession but also the government and the fiscal authorities have the opportunity to lobby on behalf of their interests and to influence the process within the Commission des Normes Comptables on which they are represented. So the accounting statutes are usually not controversial in Belgium and are generally based on a broad consensus.

Publication and audit

Individual accounts

Over 200 000 companies prepare and publish individual accounts each year. All enterprises subject to the Accounting Law of 1975[1] are required to set up a bookkeeping system and to prepare annual accounts. The format of the accounts and the audit requirements will differ according to the size of the company.

First of all there are unincorporated individuals and general or limited partnerships which are permitted to adopt a simplified system of accounting, if their turnover does not exceed €495 787.05. This means that they do not have to set up a system of double entry bookkeeping, they can choose their own format for their financial statements and choose their own valuation rules. They do not have to publish their annual accounts.

Second is the type of company that has to conform to the accounting chart but is allowed to prepare its annual accounts in abbreviated format. The enterprise must not have exceeded more than one of the following criteria in the financial period to which the annual accounts relate:

Number of employees: 50

Turnover: 6.25m euro

Balance sheet total: 3.125m euro

If the company has more than 100 employees, it is required to present its annual accounts in full format irrespective of the other criteria. The expression 'small and medium-sized companies' is generally considered in Belgium to refer to those entitled to prepare only abbreviated accounts.

The third group of companies, those that do not meet the criteria mentioned above, have to respect the chart of accounts and prepare their annual accounts in the full format. It is worth noting that Belgium has not introduced any exemptions for an intermediate category of companies, as the Fourth Directive allows.

Public limited liability companies, partnerships limited by shares, private limited liability companies and cooperatives with limited liability have to publish their annual accounts in abridged or full form together with the directors' report. Enterprises otherwise incorporated (cooperatives with unlimited liability, limited partnerships, general partnerships) have to publish their annual accounts only if they have to prepare their annual accounts in full format because they exceed the size limits. An exception is made for general partnerships, limited partnerships and cooperatives with unlimited liability in which the liability of all the partners is unlimited. Even if such businesses have to prepare their annual accounts in full format they do not need to publish them.

The publication of the annual accounts is organized through the Banque Nationale de Belgique. A company files its annual accounts with the branch of the central bank which is in the same commercial court jurisdiction as the headquarters of the company (until relatively recently annual accounts were filed with the commercial courts, as in the French commercial code model). Companies have to use standard forms but may also submit their annual accounts on diskette, if they use a software package approved by the bank. All individual annual accounts filed with the Banque Nationale are available to the public on microfilm, magnetic tape or CD-ROM. It is also possible to obtain a copy of the financial statements of a particular enterprise at any of the offices of the bank.

The audit of the financial statements is required for all public limited liability companies, private limited liability companies, cooperatives and partnerships limited by shares, which correspond to the criteria of large enterprises, as set out above.

Consolidated accounts

Only a few hundred companies (about 400) prepared their consolidated accounts since the requirement came into force in 1991. From 2000 onwards, this number increased significantly because of a decrease in the limits for small group exemptions. Commercial and civil companies of a legal form governed by Belgian law, and public organizations governed by Belgian law whose activities are of a commercial, financial or industrial nature are required to prepare consolidated accounts. However, there are two grounds for exemption: sub-consolidation (where the group is a member of a larger group reporting within the EU) and small groups. A group qualifies for the small group exemption if the controlling company and its subsidiaries, on a consolidated basis, do not exceed more than one of the following limits:

Annual turnover: 25 000 000 euro

Balance sheet total: 12 500 000 euro

Average number of employees: 250

For financial periods beginning before 1 January 1999, the limits were much higher. If companies exceed the new limits for two consecutive years they have to prepare consolidated accounts.

All consolidated accounts must be audited and published. In principle all consolidated accounts have to be audited by the statutory auditor of the parent company.

The procedure for publication of the consolidated accounts is the same as that for the individual accounts.

Belgian financial reporting

Components of annual reports

The regulated part of the annual report consists of the balance sheet, profit and loss account and the notes to the accounts. The balance sheet has to be presented after appropriation of the result, which is shown in an appropriation account as part of the profit and loss account.

From the Fourth Directive presentation options, Belgian legislation has settled on the horizontal balance sheet format. The profit and loss account for individual company accounts uses the layout in which the charges are presented by nature but companies may choose between the horizontal or vertical form of presentation. In the consolidated accounts companies may present charges either by nature or by function.

Limited liability companies, private or public, cooperatives or partnerships limited by shares have to include a directors' report, and of course an audit report if they are subject to audit. The publication of other statements, such as cash flow or environmental reports, is optional. However, in order to be able to evaluate the results of government initiatives to create jobs, companies are now obliged by law to give specific data about their employment policy. From 1995 the social balance sheet became an integral part of the financial statements of a company. All companies that have to prepare and publish financial accounts have to add a social balance sheet.

This social balance sheet consists of four chapters. Chapter one includes an overview of the number of personnel employed at balance sheet date, analysed between full and part time and by category (e.g. manual, skilled production, office staff, management). Chapter two gives explanations for changes in the number of people employed over the past year. Chapter three includes information about the use the company has made of government incentives. Chapter four includes information about the amount spent on education and training and the number of employees that participated in these. Companies that are allowed to present their annual accounts in an abbreviated version are also allowed to publish an abbreviated version of the social balance sheet.

Listed companies have to disclose (royal decree of 17 December 1998) periodic information reports and occasional information reports.

Periodic information consists of a half-year report and an annual report. In the half-yearly report the following elements, at least, must be disclosed: the net turnover for the six-month period, the operating result, the financial result, the extraordinary results and the results before and after tax. The report must contain quantitative information together with an explanation of the results and a statement on the situation of the company. Comparative figures for the year should be included. This interim report should be available, at the latest, by three months after the end of the half-year period. The quantitative items in the interim report should be calculated and valued according to the provisions of the accounting law. The interim report should mention whether these figures are audited.

The annual report consists of the individual accounts, the consolidated accounts, the directors' report, the auditor's report and an annual information bulletin (jaarlijks communiqué/communiqué annuelle). This annual information bulletin is a new requirement which was introduced with recent amendments to the law. This bulletin contains the same information items as the half-year report, however, the figures are now based on a 12-month period. These quantitative data should be accompanied by an explanation of the results and information on the activity of the firm. Furthermore, it should be mentioned whether the data have been audited and whether the auditor has issued a qualified report. In such a case, the contents of the qualification should be disclosed as well. This annual information bulletin must be made available, at the latest, by three months after the year end.

In addition, listed companies have to communicate immediately, via an occasional report, any information which might influence the price of shares or other financial instruments issued by the company, if that information were to become public.

Companies listed on the new market must publish quarterly information on their turnover and results, together with estimates for the future.

Companies that have an employee council (as in France, this is those with more than 50 employees) must prepare a special report on the financial situation of the company for this. In the early 1970s workers' representatives and the unions attached great importance to the disclosure of financial information. They played an influential role in working out the details of the Accounting Law of 1975. As a result of their lobbying, they secured the right for employee councils to be provided with a good deal of financial information at regular intervals. The information presented to the workers' council can be approved by the auditors. The auditors will then analyse it and declare that the information represents the situation of the company fairly and attend the employee council meeting to answer questions.

Measurement and recognition practices

A comparison of Belgian regulations with International Accounting Standards (IAS) is given in Table 9.1. In Belgium measurement and recognition practices are almost identical to the procedures laid down in the law.

Valuation rules for the balance sheet and profit and loss account items are usually the same for both individual accounts and consolidated accounts. Most valuation rules are conservative and very often the legal form dominates over substance. There is no general definition of assets, liabilities, expenses and revenues in the Accounting Law or in the accompanying royal decrees. The creation of a conceptual framework was never regarded as necessary in Belgium for the development of financial reporting. The legislator and the CNC/CBN have developed detailed individual rules, which is typical of a codified law system, rather than general definitions and principles. Consequently, on the one hand, several types of assets and some liability items are defined explicitly in the statutes, while on the other hand, certain other balance sheet items are not defined at all.

The valuation rules for the most important balance sheet items are described below, together with differences between rules for individual accounts and consolidated accounts. Valuation issues related especially to consolidated accounts will be dealt with separately thereafter. Valuation concepts like impairment and fair value accounting have not been introduced into the Belgian Accounting Law.

Intangible assets

The asset side of a Belgian balance sheet starts off with a separate item for formation expenses, under which formation, reorganization and loan issue costs may be capitalized. As they are in nature deferred charges rather than saleable assets, they have (except for loan issue expenses) to be amortized over a period not exceeding five years.

Table 9.1 International Accounting Standards checklist

IAS	*Belgian accounting law and standards*

1 The same accounting principles are included in the accounting statutes. As regards substance over form, the legal form usually dominates. With regard to the content of the financial statements, a cash flow statement is not required in Belgium and a statement of changes in equity is only required for consolidated accounts.

2 Dealt with similarly in arts 32 and 35–39 (RD 2001); FIFO, LIFO and weighted average are accepted. Variable costing is allowed for the calculation of the cost of conversion.

7 No regulation on cash flow statements.

8 Ordinary and extraordinary results are approached in a similar way in part IV of RD 2001, there is no regulation concerning correction and fundamental errors; a restatement of the opening balance of retained earnings is not allowed; accounting changes dealt with in arts 30 and 127, only changes in valuation rules and presentation are mentioned and the only requirement is disclosure in the notes.

10 The basic approach is similar under both sets of rules: post balance sheet events can only lead to adjustments if they relate to conditions existing at the balance sheet date.

11 Dealt with in RD 2001, both valuation methods are allowed: completed contract method or percentage of completion method.

12 Only deferred tax liabilites are recognized. The preferred valuation method is the liability method combined with the partial method for the recognition of temporary differences.

14 In the notes to the accounts the turnover of different industry and geographical segments should be reported.

15 The effect of changing prices is not addressed in Belgian legislation.

16 Dealt with similarly in arts 35–39, 42–49 (RD 2001).

17 Dealt with in art. 95 (RD 2001). The basic principles for qualifying as a financial lease or operating lease are defined further in the text (see tangible assets on p.231).

18 The concept of revenue is not explained in Belgian accounting law.

19 Only art. 54 (RD 2001) deals with pensions and is limited to the description of those situations in which no pension provision should be presented on the balance sheet (more information below).

20 Government grants related to assets have to be presented on the balance sheet split between equity and deferred taxes. The presentation of grants related to assets is in conflict with IAS 20. All other grants have to be presented as income (art. 95, RD 2001).

21 Foreign currency transactions are only dealt with in Bulletin 20 of the CNC/CBN. The treament is in line with IAS 21, except that unrealized gains should be reported as deferred income. For translation of the financial statements of foreign subsidiaries, the consolidation decree allows the aplication of two methods: the monetary/non-monetary method and the closing rate method, but does not prescribe when each of them should be applied.

22 Tax-free reorganizations are prescribed using a method comparable to the pooling of interests method with some exceptions:
– taxable reorganizations: purchase method of accounting with some exceptions;
– consolidaton: purchase method of accounting.

23 Both treatments are allowed: capitalizing and expensing.

Table 9.1 International Accounting Standards checklist (*continued*)

IAS	Belgian accounting law and standards
24	Disclosure should be made in the notes of financial assets, receivables and investments held in related entities, debts owed to related parties and financial results obtained from them. Also the amount of debts of the related party secured by the company should be disclosed in the notes.
26	A special royal decree (19 April 1991) deals with the financial statements of pension funds. These financial statements have many similarities with the financial staements of insurance companies in Belgium and are not in line with the net assets statements required by IAS 26.
27	The consolidation decree of March 1991 is in line with the Seventh Directive, and therefore to a large extent is the same as IAS 27. Only investments in subsidiaries in the parent's separate financial statements should be carried at cost or a revalued amount. Horizontal consolidation is required according to the Belgian legislation and small groups are exempted from consolidation. The concept of dissimilar activities is interpreted much more broadly in Belgium.
28	Investments in associates should be accounted for in the consolidated statements using the equity method, but in the individual accounts the cost method or a revalued amount should be used.
29	No regulation on hyperinflation.
30	There are no conflicts between IAS 30 and the royal decree of 4 August 1996 which governs financial reporting by banks and other financial institutions.
31	Proportional consolidation should be used for reporting interests in joint ventures.
32	No specific rules with regard to new financial instruments. The CNC/CBN has issued an opinion (28) on stock options and a recommendation on forward contracts.
33	This topic is not addressed by the Belgian legislator.
34	The interim report consists only of a condensed income statement and selected explanatory notes in Belgium (see components of annual reports on p.227).
35	The Belgian accounting legislation does not provide any definition of discontinuing operations.
36	The RD of 30 January 2001 only indicates in broad terms when exceptional depreciation should be recorded or reversed. The concept of the cash generating unit is not defined under Belgian legislation.
37	The probability that the enterprise will incur changes as a result of a past event is sufficient (art. 51, RD 2001). No obligation should exist at the balance sheet date. A provision for major repair and mainteance costs may be set up. A decision to restructure taken by the board of directors before the balance sheet date is sufficient to set up a provision. Contingencies are similarly dealt with in arts 50 and 51 (RD 2001).
38	Under Belgian legislation no distinction is made between research costs and development costs, both may be capitalized. With regard to internally generated intangible assets indirect costs may be included.
39	No specific rules with regard to financial instruments. The CNC/CBN has issued an opinion (28) on stock options and a recommendation on forward contracts.
40	Under Belgian legislation only the valuation under the historical cost model with revaluation is allowed.
41	These items are not addressed in Belgian legislation.

Intangible assets as such is the next item on the balance sheet. They must be valued at cost, subject to a ceiling that the sum capitalized may never exceed the amount of future income that is expected to be created by the intangible asset. Revaluation of intangible assets is not permitted.

Goodwill in individual accounts arises only in two very specific situations. First of all it can arise when a company buys another company or part of it. Goodwill is then defined as that portion of the cost of acquiring an enterprise or business segment which exceeds the net value of the enterprise or segment acquired. Secondly, goodwill will arise in the event of a merger or acquisition by an exchange of shares in the following well defined situation: when (1) the acquirer has a percentage of the shares of the acquired company among its assets and (2) the carrying value of those shares in the balance sheet of the acquirer is greater than the equity value of the shares in the books of the acquiree. If such difference occurs, an attempt should first be made to eliminate it by adjusting the values of certain assets or liabilities. If after that a difference remains it should be shown in the books after the merger or the acquisition as goodwill. Goodwill in the consolidated accounts will be discussed together with the other consolidation issues.

Tangible assets

Tangible fixed assets are normally accounted for at cost (including all expenditure necessary to bring the asset into service) and depreciated over their useful life. The Accounting Law does not specify which depreciation methods should be used. Fiscal law, however, only allows the straight-line depreciation method and the fiscal reducing balance method for tax purposes. In addition, the depreciation charges are only accepted as tax-deductible costs if they are recorded in the books and in the annual accounts of the company. So in practice only the fiscally accepted methods are used in the individual accounts. Very often the book value shown under tangible assets does not really present an economic view, as assets depreciated using the fiscal reducing balance method are often undervalued.

This situation occurs very often with the result that many published annual accounts are biased. This is true not only for individual accounts, but possibly also for consolidated accounts, even if they are not used for determining corporate income tax. In the consolidation decree the legislator introduced an escape clause from the obligation to present assets according to their economic value: enterprises are permitted not to restate the value of their assets on consolidation, if the impact of tax regulation is disclosed in the notes.

Tangible assets may be revalued when the increase in value is of a permanent character. The revaluation amount recorded on a tangible asset with a finite useful life should be depreciated. These additional depreciation charges are not accepted for tax purposes, and the revaluation surplus is not taxable.

In Belgium, legal form usually dominates substance. A well-known exception, however, is leased assets. Over the last 20 years the Belgian legislator has changed the definition of financial leasing several times in order to keep leasing contracts on the balance sheet, as the business community was and still is extremely inventive in trying to circumvent the law. According to the current legislation, a contract is considered to be a financial lease when the instalments projected in the contract cover the investment together with interest and ancillary costs. In the case of a movable property, the instalments may be increased by the price of the purchase option, if the option does not exceed 15% of the capital invested by the lessor.

Financial assets

Financial assets are recorded at cost or at a revalued amount in the individual accounts. A distinction is made between amounts invested in subsidiaries, in associates and in other companies, which must be shown separately. The use of the equity method is not permitted in individual company accounts.

All debtors receivable in more than one year and all liabilities payable after more than one year are valued at nominal value.

Current assets

Stocks are valued at the lower of cost or market value. Companies may choose whether or not to include overhead costs in their production cost. If the production period exceeds one year companies may also include interest charges in the production cost. On long-term contracts, companies may choose between the completed contract method and the percentage of completion method. In practice the completed contract method is mostly used because of the tax consequences.

Short-term receivables, investments, liquid assets, deferred charges and accrued income must be carried at the lower of cost or market value. So unrealized losses on investments will be charged to the profit and loss account, whereas unrealized gains are not recognized. Fixed income securities should be valued at acquisition cost. But discounts and premiums against redemption value should be released to the income statement on an actuarial basis, taking into account the actuarial yield at acquisition.

Liabilities and provisions

Liabilities are split in the balance sheet between current and long term and also as to their type (e.g. financial debts, trade debts, etc.). Information on whether these borrowings are secured or guaranteed is disclosed in the notes. Provisions, including deferred taxes, are presented between the liability and equity sections. Provisions are subdivided into four categories (pensions, taxes, maintenance and major repairs and other provisions). According to the Belgian legislator a provision is intended to cover losses or charges, the nature of which is clearly defined, and which at the balance sheet date are either likely or certain to be incurred, but the exact amount of which is uncertain (art. 33). Although Belgian financial reporting practices are conservative, large amounts are not normally found under provisions in the annual accounts, because the tax authorities are reluctant to accept provisions as tax-deductible items. Preparers of accounts will generally only record on the balance sheet those provisions that have also been accepted by the tax authorities.

In the Accounting Law the different types of pension plans are not defined, nor is the concept of pension cost. Neither a valuation method for the calculation of pension costs nor the way in which they have to be reported on the profit and loss account is prescribed. A royal decree deals only with the question of when a pension provision should be disclosed in the balance sheet of the employer: companies have to show a provision for pensions when the accrued pension rights of employees are not covered by assets in the pension fund (art. 45, royal decree of 1987). However, when companies do not have to finance their pension commitments, or a part of them, in a separate fund because they comply with the exemption criteria of a decree of May 1985, they are also exempted from the requirement to show a provision for pensions on the balance sheet. These exemptions are transitional in nature, but for the moment their effect is that many pension commitments remain off balance sheet in Belgium.

The balance sheet item 'provision for taxation' is meant to be used for provisions made to cover tax charges resulting from adjustments of taxable income or from changes in the method of computing tax. This type of provision is hardly used in practice.

In 1991 the provisions section of the official balance sheet format for individual accounts was extended to include deferred taxes. With the royal decree of 31 December 1991 (now the royal decree of 30 January 2001) the concept of deferred taxes was in effect introduced, albeit only to a very limited extent. Deferred taxes have to be reported in the balance sheet of individual accounts in the following two situations: (1) tax deferred to later financial periods on investment grants obtained from public authorities for investment in fixed assets, and (2) tax deferred to later financial periods on gains on the disposal of tangible and intangible fixed assets and of securities issued by Belgian public authorities, when the tax on these gains is deferred.

Consolidated accounts

When the Seventh Directive was adopted in Belgium with the issuing of the consolidation decree (royal decree March 1990), in effect a new method of financial reporting was being introduced. Up to that time, only a small number of holding companies (about 90) had had to prepare consolidated accounts. Because the Belgian business community was unfamiliar with the concept of consolidated accounts and all the related problems, the legislator opted for a very gentle introduction of these. This was achieved by putting forward high limits for the exemption criteria for small groups (see above) until 1999. In 1992 a total of 398 sets of consolidated accounts relating to the financial year 1991 were filed. However, it is not known how many companies should have filed their consolidated accounts (Servais 1993). This number included about 100 financial holding companies.

Scope of the consolidated accounts

For the definition of the group concept, the Belgian legislator followed the criteria of the Seventh Directive, which means that not only vertical groups but also consortia or horizontal groups (e.g. 15 in 1993 according to the Servais (1993) survey) are consolidated. The determining factor for the requirement to consolidate is the existence of a control relationship. According to the legislation, control can be de jure or de facto. De jure control exists (company law 2000, art. 5) where a company holds a majority of the voting rights, where a shareholder has the right to appoint or remove the majority of the board, where a company has power of control by virtue of the company statutes or any other agreement with other shareholders.

Control is de facto where it derives from factors other than these. In the absence of evidence to the contrary, a shareholder or member of an enterprise is presumed to have de facto control over the enterprise if, at the two previous general meetings of the enterprise, the shareholder or member exercised voting rights representing the majority of the votes attached to the shares represented at those general meetings.

In addition to the two basic exemptions from consolidation included in the Seventh Directive, the Belgian legislator introduced the following optional exclusions from the consolidation: non-materiality, the existence of a restriction on long-term control, disproportionate expense or undue delay, having the intention to re-sell; and the following compulsory exclusions: divergent activities, incompatibility with the true and fair view principle, company in liquidation. Where a subsidiary is excluded for one of the optional reasons, it is stated in the consolidated balance sheet at cost or a revalued amount, while in the case of a compulsory exclusion the subsidiary has to be included in the consolidated balance sheet using the equity method. Although the legislator stated explicitly that these criteria for exclusion should be applied in a restrictive manner, practice shows that companies often make use of the true and fair view and the divergent activities clauses to exclude subsidiaries from consolidation (Servais 1993).

In preparing consolidated accounts, the following methods have to be used: full consolidation for subsidiaries, proportional consolidation for joint ventures, equity method for associated companies and the cost method for other companies in which shares are held.

Valuation methods and consolidated accounts

The valuation rules for the consolidated accounts are generally the same as those for individual accounts, but differences exist in respect of goodwill, deferred taxation and translation methods. Positive differences between the cost of the investment and the underlying net assets are recognized as a goodwill asset while negative consolidation differences are recorded in equity. Goodwill assets should be amortized over a period of five years, while a negative consolidation difference will remain in equity.

For the translation of the accounts of subsidiaries denominated in foreign currencies, the consolidation decree allows for one of two methods to be used, the monetary/non-monetary method and the closing rate method. Translation differences arising under the closing rate method are treated as part of the equity of the group. Under the monetary/non-monetary method, translation differences are taken to the profit and loss account.

The consolidation legislation states (art. 129) that

> Account shall be taken in the consolidated balance sheet and income statement of any difference arising on consolidation between the tax chargeable for the current financial period and for preceding financial periods and the amount of tax paid or payable in respect of those periods, provided it is probable that an actual charge to tax will arise within the foreseeable future for one of the consolidated enterprises. This future taxation must be recorded as a liability in the consolidated balance sheet.

The legislator did not state explicitly which valuation methods for deferred taxes to use but the wording seems to suggest that the legislator is in favour of the liability approach and the partial method for recognizing timing differences. The presentation of deferred tax assets is prohibited under the consolidation legislation.

As concerns these more complex issues, the Belgian accounting law remains rather vague and preparers of financial statements and the profession rely in these circumstances on the general valuation rules specified in the law and thereafter refer to IAS in order to elaborate valuation methods for specific problems. For a few technical issues the CNC has issued opinions. This is the case for forward contracts and stock options. The government in cooperation with the CNC no longer tries to elaborate a set of national accounting rules on these technical topics. Instead they will assimilate the international standards into Belgian practice once the debate at the international level has been translated into a standard.

In general there is no guidance on new financial instruments, but in the case of stock options an opinion (Bulletin 28) was issued by the CNC/CBN in 1992. The essence of the opinion comes down to a requirement that an option should be registered in the books of the buyer as an investment at the lower of cost or market value as long as the option is not exercised. When the option is exercised the option value becomes part of the acquisition value in case of a call option or reduces the sales price of the share in case of a put option. The writer of the option has two possibilities for registration. The writer may show the collected premium under deferred income or record the premium as revenue and create a provision for the risk associated with the option. When a call option is exercised, the difference between the acquisition costs of the shares and their sales value will be recorded as a financial cost. In the case of a put option a write-down has to be recorded equal to the difference between the acquisition cost of the shares and their market value.

In the case of forward contracts, in 1987 the CNC/CBN issued a recommendation, which is not as strong as an opinion. The valuation of the forward contracts should be based on the economic rationale for the company entering into the contract. In the case of hedging, the transaction concerned is recorded at the rate specified in the forward contract. If a contract is taken out for trading purposes the contract is off balance sheet but the premium or discount should be recorded and released to the profit and loss account over the related period. At the balance sheet date the forward rate contracts are valued at the current rate. When the rate at the balance sheet date differs from the spot rate in force at the start of the contract the difference must be disclosed. According to the CNC/CBN these differences must be treated in a conservative way.

Environmental accounting

The issue of environmental accounting is slowly gaining importance in Belgium although the legislation is silent on environmental issues. Preparers of financial statements have to turn to the general valuation rules to find any guidance when faced with reporting environmental costs or provisions. The CNC/CBN issued only one opinion (CNC/CBN 34/1995) that dealt with environmental issues. The following accounting principles are recommended:

1. for waste products that have not been collected at the end of the accounting period, a provision for collection costs must be set up;
2. for waste products that have not been processed at the end of the accounting period, a provision for processing costs must be set up.

For enterprises active in processing waste the commission for accounting standards has issued specific accounting treatments.

Enterprises which exploit land or premises have to provide for the future costs of cleaning up and eventually must consider if a loss of value of the land or premises has to be recorded in the accounts.

Conclusion

Preparing financial statements in Belgium consisted in the past, to a large extent, in applying the detailed accounting regulations issued by the government. Belgian accounting regulation and the valuation rules included in it are conservative in nature, and legal form usually dominates substance. During the twentieth century individual company accounts were the most important source of company financial information in Belgium. Individual accounts were, and generally still are, tax driven. At the end of the twentieth century two developments occurred. First, from the beginning of the 1990s, the consolidated accounts of large companies took on greater importance as a source of financial information. (In many other European countries this had been the case for many years.) Secondly, the influence of IAS, US GAAP and other foreign GAAP on Belgian accounting practice became much stronger due to international harmonization effects.

In the twenty-first century it is expected that a group of large Belgian companies will be seen applying International Accounting Standards, while a larger group of small and medium-sized enterprises will continue to apply traditional Belgian accounting practices governed by the national law and local decrees.

Notes

1 • Individuals carrying on a commercial activity

  • Commercial companies and companies having a legal commercial form

    – Naamloze Vennootschap NV, Société Anonyme SA (public limited company)

    – Besloten Vennootschap met Beperkte Aansprakelijkheid BVBA, Société Privée à Responsabilité Limitée SPRL (private limited company)

    – GEWONE Commanditaire Vennootschap (Comm V.), Société en Commandite Simple SC (limited partnership)

    – Commanditaire Vennootschap op aandelen Covam VA, Société en Commandite par Actions SCA (partnership limited by shares)

    – Vennootschap onder firma VOF, Société en nom collectif SNC (general partnership)

    – Cooperatieve Vennootschap CV, Société Coopérative SC (cooperative society)

  • European economic interest groupings and other economic interest groupings

  • Public organizations having statutory responsibilities of a commercial, financial or industrial nature

  • Any other organization not referred to in the second or third category above, whether having a legal personality or not, that carries on any activity of a commercial, financial or industrial nature, for profit or otherwise, to which the preparation of annual accounts is made applicable under royal decree by category of organization.

References

Gelders, G. (1984) Boekhoudrecht en Fiscaliteit. *Bulletin der Belastingen* **60**(628): 1298–1321.

Jorissen, A. and Maes, L. (1996) The principle of fiscal neutrality: the cornerstone of the relationship between financial reporting and taxation in Belgium. *European Accounting Review* **5**(suppl.): 915–931.

Michielsen, F. (1975) De financiële verslaggeving van de ondernemingen en de in het vooruitzicht gestelde wettelijke hervormingen inzake jaarrekeningen en revisoraat. *Economisch en Sociaal Tijdschrift* **2**: 179–196.

Pauwels, P. (1979) Accounting and Reporting in Belgium. *Accountancy en Bedrijfskunde* **1**: 36–54.

Servais, J.P. (1993). Qualité de l'information financiäre donnée par les comptes consolidés publies depuis l'entrée en vigueur de l' A.R. du 6 Mars 1990 (mimeo). Paper presented at Leuven University, 14 January 1994.

Further Reading

De Ronge, Y., Henrion, E. and Vael, C. (1993) Company law and accounting in nineteenth-century Europe: Belgium. *European Accounting Review* **2**(2): 298–311.

De Ronge, Y., Henrion, E. and Vael, C. (1995) The history of financial reporting in Belgium. In P. Walton (ed.) *European Financial Reporting: a History*. Academic Press, London.

Ettinger, J.C. and Gillet, J.P. (1981) Principes generalement admis et legislation comptable Belge. *Accountancy en Bedrijfskunde* **4**: 48–62.

Ettinger, J.C. and Gillet, J.P. (1982) Principes generalement admis et legislation comptable Belge. *Accountancy en Bedrijfskunde* **1**: 23–27.

Jorissen, A. (1998) Financial reporting in Belgium. In S. Archer and D. Alexander (eds) *Miller's European Accounting Guide*, 2nd edn. Harcourt Brace, San Diego.

Jorissen, A. and van Oostveldt, K. (2001) Belgium – individual accounts. In D. Ordelheide and KPMG (eds) *Transnational Accounting*. Palgrave, London, pp. 375–468.

Jorissen, A. and Maes, L. (1996) The principle of fiscal neutrality: the cornerstone of the relationship between financial reporting and taxation in Belgium. *The European Accounting Review* **5**(suppl.): 915–931.

Kirkpatrick, J. (1982) L'influence du nouveau droit comptable sur le droit fiscal des sociétés en Belgique. *Journal des Tribunaux* **5200**: 193–197.

Lefebvre, C. and Flower, J. (1994) *European Financial Reporting: Belgium*. Routledge, London.

Maes, J.P. and Stempnierwsky, Y. (1990) La transposition en droit belge de la septieme directive du Conseil des Communautes Européennes relative aux comptes consolides. *Tijdschrift voor het Belgisch Handelbrecht* **6**: 460–520.

Theunisse, H. and Aerts, W. (2001) Belgium – consolidated accounts. In D. Ordelheide and KPMG (eds) *Transnational Accounting*. Palgrave, London, pp. 469–530.

Timmerman, G. (1980) Problems in the implementation of the Fourth Directive in Belgium. *Accountancy en Bedrijfskunde* **2**: 53–58.

Van Hulle, K. (1990) De aanpassing van de Belgische wetgeving aan de Zevende Richtlijn inzake de geconsolideerde jaarrekening. *Economisch en Sociaal Tijdschrift* **44**(2): 205–229.

Accounting in the Netherlands

Leo van der Tas

The history of accounting in the Netherlands goes back several centuries when, for example, the Vereenigde Oostindische Compagnie (VOC) was the first public company in the world to publish its financial statements, in the early seventeenth century. The development of accounting in the Netherlands started somewhat independently from other countries, with ideas from Limperg on using replacement value accounting (for further analysis see Camfferman 1995). Researchers have found it hard to classify the Netherlands in relation to other countries and have tended to put it in a special category. More recently, accounting has been increasingly influenced by the development of financial reporting in the Anglo-Saxon countries, as well as by harmonization of accounting with the rest of Europe through implementation of the EC accounting directives. A further characteristic of accounting in the Netherlands is that standard-setting started only recently, through pressure from European rules. Only basic rules are laid down in the law and accounting standards allow considerable flexibility.

Legal and institutional basis of accounting regulation

Legal requirements

It was only in 1970 that accounting requirements of some significance were introduced in law. Before then there were only a few general provisions relating to the requirement to draw up accounts and prescribing some general accounting principles. The development of financial reporting regulation is described in detail in Zeff, Van der Wel and Camfferman (1992). In 1837 the first requirements to keep books and prepare a balance sheet and 'staat' (state of assets and liabilities) were laid down in the Commercial Code. There was no requirement to have the accounts audited or to publish them. A publication requirement was introduced in 1928.

Unlike many other continental European countries, the Netherlands had only one legal form of limited liability company, the public limited liability company (naamloze vennootschap, NV). EC directives, however, distinguish between private and public limited liability companies and the financial reporting requirements of private limited liability companies are less onerous than those for public limited liability companies. This was a major reason for the introduction of the private limited liability company (besloten vennootschap met beperkte aansprakelijkheid, BV) in the Netherlands in 1971.

In 1970 the Act on Annual Accounts (Wet op de Jaarrekening van Ondernemingen, WJO) was adopted and for the first time laid down more detailed rules on the form and content of the annual accounts of public and private limited liability companies. The publication requirement was extended to large private limited liability companies and at the same time an audit requirement for public and large private limited liability companies was introduced. The WJO was the Dutch reaction to the discussions then taking place in Brussels on the draft of the Fourth Directive concerning the annual accounts of companies and its requirements were heavily influenced by these.

One innovation of particular note is that for the first time a formal separation between the financial accounts and the tax return was made by the WJO. Before 1970 accounts had to be drawn up according to 'sound business practice' (goed koopmansgebruik) for both financial reporting purposes and tax purposes. The 1970 Act, which only applied to the financial accounts, however, introduced another general principle. The accounts should provide such an insight that a well-founded opinion (verantwoord oordeel) can be formed of the assets and liabilities and profit or loss of the company. In addition, the balance sheet and the notes thereto should 'faithfully and consistently' (getrouw and stelselmatig) present the size and composition of the net assets at the balance sheet date. The profit and loss account and the notes thereto should 'faithfully and consistently' (getrouw and stelselmatig) present the size and composition of the net result of the financial year.

Later, the general principles were changed slightly (art. 362(1–3), Book 2 Civil Code). The insight given should be according to norms considered acceptable in the economic and social climate (maatschappelijk verkeer). The balance sheet, profit and loss account and notes thereto should present not only faithfully and consistently but also clearly (duidelijk) the assets and liabilities, financial position and profit or loss of a company. This is the Dutch equivalent of 'a true and fair view'. The general principles applying to tax returns were, however, never amended. A detailed description of the historical development of the general principles underlying both financial reporting and taxation can be found in Bos *et al.* (comment on art. 362, Book 2 Civil Code) and Hoogendoorn (1996).

The requirements of the 1970 law were moved to Title 6 of Book 2 of the Civil Code without any substantial changes. The Civil Code was subsequently amended several times to implement EC accounting directives and was renumbered to Title 9.

- Fourth Directive on annual accounts: Law of 7 December 1983 (Official Journal 663, applicable from 1 January 1984). Given that the draft directive had been an influence on the 1970 Law, one would expect its final implementation not to have a large impact. However, the directive had in the meantime been changed considerably, so its implementation had a new influence on financial reporting in the Netherlands.

- Seventh Directive on consolidated accounts: Law of 10 November 1988 (Official Journal 517, applicable from 1 January 1990). This directive did not have a great impact because the law already contained a consolidation requirement for all parent companies.

- Eleventh Directive on branches: Law of 19 December 1991 (Official Journal 710).

- SME Directive on the exemptions for small and medium-sized enterprises and the publication of accounts in ecus: decreee of 6 September 1991 (Official Journal 456).

- Scope Directive on the extension of the scope of the Fourth and Seventh Directives: Law of 17 March 1993 (Official Journal 261).

- Bank Accounts Directive: Law of 17 March 1993 (Official Journal 258).

- Insurance Accounts Directive: Law of 16 September 1993 (Official Journal 517).

In 2002 a bill has been taken to Parliament proposing to allow Dutch companies to apply IFRS in their consolidated accounts and single-entity accounts from financial years 2002 onwards.

Enterprise chamber

A unique characteristic of financial reporting regulation in the Netherlands is the existence of a court called the Enterprise Chamber (Ondernemingskamer). This Chamber was introduced in 1970, together with the WJO. It is one of the Chambers of the Court of Justice in Amsterdam. The Enterprise Chamber has exclusive authority over company financial reporting. Cases can be put before this Chamber by all parties who can prove that they have an interest in a particular annual report. The Attorney-General (procureur generaal) has the right to challenge a set of financial statements and bring the company before the Enterprise Chamber when this would be in the public interest.

So far, however, the Enterprise Chamber has defined 'interested party' and 'public interest' rather narrowly, which means that only a limited body of case law has come out of the Chamber. So far the Chamber has given judgment in only 54 cases. In a considerable number of other cases the Chamber decided the claimant could not bring a claim. The sanctions the Chamber may impose upon the company are twofold. It may require the company to prepare revised financial statements or it may require the company to prepare subsequent financial statements according to the instructions of the Chamber.

Council for annual reporting

When the 1970 law on annual accounts was adopted the government asked the parties it considered to be involved in financial reporting to form a tripartite committee (Tripartiete Overleg) to develop more detailed accounting rules and interpretations of the basic principles laid down in the law. The three parties concerned were the employers, the employees and the accounting profession. The employers were represented by the employers' federations – Vereniging van Nederlandse ondernemingen (VNO) and Nederlands Christelijk Werkgeversverbond (NCW). The employees were represented by the trade unions – Federatie Nederlandse Vakverenigingen (FNV) and Christelijke Nederlandse Vakverenigingen (CNV). The accounting profession was represented by the Nederlands Instituut van Registeraccountants (NIVRA). The Tripartite Committee started issuing 'Beschouwingen' (discussion memoranda). They had no binding status.

In 1981 the Tripartite Committee was replaced by the Council for Annual Reporting (CAR – Raad voor de Jaarverslaggeving). Like the Tripartite Committee the CAR consists of three delegations, but now they represent the preparers, the users and the auditors. The same organizations are represented, but the users' delegation was expanded to include a person representing the financial analysts. Recently, the VNO and the NCW merged into one organization. The CAR issues Guidelines. It has also published a Framework (comparable to IASC's Conceptual Framework). The CAR publishes an English translation of the Guidelines. The status of the CAR Guidelines has been debated frequently. They are not legally binding, but they may be used to interpret legal provisions when considering what constitutes generally accepted accounting principles in the Netherlands. Although large listed companies tend to comply with the Guidelines on major items, there are also frequent deviations from them. In 2000 NIVRA introduced an auditing standard prohibiting the auditor to issue an unqualified opinion if a firm pronouncement of the CAR is not applied.

In the Preface to the Guidelines CAR states: 'included in the various topics are the international standards (IAS) adopted by the International Accounting Standards Committee, except where these are not appropriate to the Dutch situation'. The influence of IAS on the Guidelines is therefore significant.

Accounting profession

Although accountancy as a profession had existed for several centuries it was in the late nineteenth century that it became organized. In 1895 the Netherlands Institute of Accountants (Nederlands Instituut van Accountants, NIVA) was established. Since then several other bodies have been established and merged with each other. It was only in 1962 that the first law on the audit profession was adopted. Some years later in 1967 NIVRA (Nederlands Instituut van Registeraccountants) was established as a public body. Currently there are two institutes of accountants: the Royal NIVRA and the Nederlandse Organisatie van Accountants-Administratieconsulenten (NOVAA). NOVAA members (accountant-administratieconsulenten, AAs) were originally accountants providing bookkeeping services, tax advice and related services to small and medium-sized enterprises.

When the Fourth Directive was implemented in 1983, introducing a general audit requirement for all medium-sized companies, NOVAA requested for its members the legal right to perform this statutory audit because they thought they might risk losing clients. At the same time discussions started on the implementation of the Eighth Directive on the audit profession. It took ten years before the institutes, the government and parliament agreed on a compromise solution. Existing AAs would remain AAs, but they would only be allowed to perform statutory audits after passing a test of competence. New AAs would be licensed to perform the statutory audit after they had passed the normal AA examinations and completed three years' practical training. NOVAA became a public body, like the Royal NIVRA. Both institutes issue partly the same professional standards.

At the end of 2001 Royal NIVRA had around 13 300 members. There is no requirement to be an audit practitioner after registration as a member, and in the past one did not have to have any practical experience in auditing to become a registered accountant. Therefore, a significant proportion of registered accountants are not practicing as auditors. The composition of NIVRA's membership is listed below:

Public accountant	5 000
Government auditor	1 000
Internal auditor	600
Financial/Economic management and others	4 800
	11 400
Not active	1 900
Total	13 300

NOVAA has around 6500 members. The vast majority of the members render bookkeeping, tax advice and related services, although some of them are allowed to perform statutory audits.

Taxation

As explained above, there is no formal requirement for congruence between the financial statements and the tax return. The two have to meet different general norms. The tax return must be drawn up in accordance with 'sound business practice' whereas the financial report must provide a 'true and fair view'. Differences may exist between the valuation methods applied in the tax return and in the financial report. In practice, however, the financial report and the tax return are to a certain degree linked to one another. Small and medium-sized companies tend to draw up only one set of accounts for both purposes. In addition, estimations in the tax return (such as useful lives, provisions for bad debts, etc.) will seldom deviate from the same estimations in the financial report. Moreover, the financial report must always be attached to the tax return.

Many groups operating internationally establish a financing or holding company in the Netherlands, even if they are not very active on the Dutch domestic market. The reasons for this are twofold. Dutch tax law allows for some interesting tax exemptions and to avoid double taxation the Netherlands have negotiated an extensive network of tax treaties with other countries. One of those tax exemptions relates to profits distributed from investments, so dividends received by a Dutch holding company from a foreign subsidiary do not attract further tax. A number of requirements should be met, including the requirement that at least 5% of the shares of the investee company should be held.

Income taxes are based on the historical cost principle. There are no detailed requirements on the way income should be calculated and there are no detailed requirements on, for example, the useful lives of particular assets or the way bad debts must be provided for. Such matters are, subject to reasonable limits, left to the discretion of management.

Objectives, assumptions and qualitative characteristics

The Netherlands Civil Code contains the general principles laid down in the Fourth Directive, such as the principle of realization, prudence, accruals, going concern, separate valuation, etc. These principles apply to both the individual company and consolidated accounts. The principle of substance over form is not dealt with explicitly in the law, but is presumed to be part of the Framework (see below) underlying the guidelines of the CAR (Guideline 110.116 and 130.106–112.114).

The CAR issued a 'Framework for the preparation and presentation of financial statements'. This is a translation of the IASB's 'Framework for the preparation and presentation of financial statements'.

Requirements to publish accounts and have them audited

The general accounting and reporting requirements apply to:

- the public limited liability company (naamloze vennootschap, NV);
- the private limited liability company (besloten vennootschap met beperkte aansprakelijkheid, BV);
- the cooperative (coöperatie);
- the mutual insurance company (onderlinge waarborgmaatschappij);
- the limited partnership (commanditaire vennootschap, CV) and the unlimited partnership (Vennootschap onder Firma, VOF) if all unlimited partners are established as a limited liability company according to the law of another country;

- large associations (verenigingen) and foundations (stichtingen) having a business activity;
- foreign companies having no effective link with the country under which law they were established and whose main activities are carried out in the Netherlands.

All categories of companies listed above are required to prepare and publish accounts, although some exemptions exist. The legal requirements differ as between large, medium-sized and small companies. A company is considered to be small if it meets two of the following three criteria in two consecutive financial years:

- net turnover is less than €7 million (US$7 million);
- the balance sheet total is less than €3.5 million (US$3.5 million);
- the average number of employees is less than 50.

A company is considered to be medium-sized if it meets two of the following criteria in two consecutive financial years:

- net turnover is less than €28 million (US$28 million);
- the balance sheet total is less than €14 million (US$14 million);
- the average number of employees is less than 250.

Small companies are allowed to prepare only a short-form balance sheet, an abbreviated profit and loss account and notes. They need not prepare an annual management report (directors' report) and only need to publish an abbreviated balance sheet and notes. Medium-sized companies are allowed to prepare an abbreviated profit and loss account and notes. They are required to prepare a full balance sheet and an annual management report. They are allowed to publish an abbreviated balance sheet, the abbreviated profit and loss account and the abbreviated notes, together with the management report.

The Netherlands is one of the few EU member states that implemented art. 57 of the Fourth Directive, which gives companies an exemption from preparing and publishing accounts, provided certain conditions have been met. Art. 403 of the Dutch Civil Code provides that companies are exempted from the legal requirements to prepare and publish accounts under the following conditions:

- a short-form balance sheet and profit and loss account is prepared;
- the members or shareholders of the company approve of the application of the exemption;
- the financial information of the company has been included in the consolidated accounts of a company to which the provisions of the EC accounting directives apply;
- those consolidated accounts are published in the Netherlands, together with the annual report and the auditor's report;
- the company preparing those consolidated accounts has assumed joint and several liability for any liabilities arising from the legal acts of the exempted company;
- the approval of shareholders and the declaration of liability are published in the Netherlands.

Small legal entities whose aim is not the making of profits are exempted from the publication requirement, provided their accounts are presented to shareholders and creditors upon request and a certificate from a public accountant certifying that the legal entity is entitled to make use of the exemption is deposited at the commercial register.

The stock exchange supervisory authority requires listed companies to include a statement of sources and uses of funds in their prospectuses. Although there is no legal requirement to include such a statement or a cash flow statement in their financial reports, most of those companies choose to present a cash flow statement.

Publication of financial statements is effected by depositing them at the commercial register kept by local Chambers of Commerce and Industry (Kamer van Koophandel en Fabrieken). There is a central, automated, database kept by the Chambers of Commerce and Industry.

All companies in the legal forms mentioned above need to have their accounts audited, except for small companies and the companies applying the group company exemption under art. 403 of the Civil Code (see above). NIVRA issues auditing standards, which are in most respects identical to the International Standards on Auditing of the International Federation of Accountants (IFAC) (see Chapter 20). In 2000 a book (NIVRA 2000) was published containing all auditing standards, including an English translation of all the standards. NIVRA is a member of IFAC, NOVAA is not.

Auditors do not have a joint and several liability for damages, but a liability proportional to the extent of damage caused by their negligence. The number of cases against public accountants has increased but is in no way comparable to the situation in the USA. The public accountant has not come in for the same criticism as in the USA or the UK although the debate in those countries had an impact on the perceived role of the auditor in the Netherlands. In 1996 a national committee was set up to look at corporate governance, including the role of the statutory auditor. The auditor is already required to report cases of alleged fraud that are found during the course of the audit but not corrected appropriately. He is also required to report to the supervisory board (raad van commissarissen, non-executive directors) and the management on his findings in respect of the reliability and continuity of the company's automated data processing systems.

Components of annual reports

The annual report consists of the annual accounts, the directors' report and 'additional information' (overige gegevens). The annual accounts consist of a balance sheet, a profit and loss account and the notes to those accounts. The consolidated accounts are considered as a part of the notes on the individual accounts. Therefore they are not considered to be a separate legal document.

Companies may choose between two formats for the balance sheet and four formats for the profit and loss account, as in the Fourth Directive. The CAR issued a format for the cash flow statement which is comparable to the format issued by IASC.

Although the CAR recommends the disclosure of a *value added statement*, only a small minority of companies actually include such a statement in the annual report.

Article 391 of Book 2 Civil Code requires companies to disclose in the *directors' report* the expected development of the business, and, to the extent that disclosure is not harmful to its interests, particular attention should be paid to investments, financing, the number of personnel and to the circumstances upon which the development of turnover and profitability depends. Information should be disclosed in respect of activities in the field of research and development. The effect on expected future performance of particular events, which need not be reflected in the annual accounts, must be stated. The CAR issued a Guideline on the contents of the directors' report which goes significantly further than the legal requirements. The directors' report should contain general information on the legal entity and related companies, covering among others the purpose of the company (mission statement), its core business, including a description of the main products, services, geographical areas and categories of suppliers and clients. Management must follow up on any expectations expressed and risks mentioned in the previous directors' report.

The *additional information* comprises the audit report, the appropriation of profit for the year and the provisions in the articles of association concerning the appropriation of profit. In addition, any events occurring after the balance sheet date with a significant impact should be explained. Where applicable, a statement of the existence of branches and of countries where there are branches, and of the trade names used by these if they are different from that of the legal entity, must be disclosed.

Measurement and recognition concepts and practices

Table 10.1 compares the Dutch legal requirements and accounting standards applicable to fiscal year 2002 with International Financial Reporting Standards (IFRS). The CAR publishes Guideline 920 which provides an overview of the extent to which IFRS have been incorporated in the Guidelines. Table 10.1 is based upon this appendix.

Intangible fixed assets comprise capitalized research and development costs, concessions, licences and intellectual property rights and costs of goodwill acquired from third parties. Intangible assets must be valued at historical cost. Capitalized research and development costs must be amortized within a maximum period of five years. In recent years, publishing companies and other companies with considerable intangible assets have started to capitalize these assets without depreciating them on a systematic basis. In 1990 three large publishing companies (Elsevier, VNU and Wolters Kluwer) decided to distinguish between purchased publishing rights and goodwill on the acquisition of subsidiaries. Before that, the whole difference between purchase price and net tangible assets was treated as goodwill. One of the reasons may have been the lack of net equity against which to write off goodwill. The publishing companies also decided not to amortize the publishing rights, but to perform impairment tests, based on the profitability of the titles. A similar accounting treatment could be found with PolyGram and Philips in their valuation of music rights. The CAR has now issued Guideline 210 on Intangible Assets which is identical to IAS 38 on this issue.

Internally generated goodwill may not be capitalized. Goodwill arising from consolidation of an acquired subsidiary must be capitalized and amortized. Capitalized goodwill must be written off according to the expected useful life. If goodwill is amortized over a period of more than 20 years, the enterprise must do an annual impairment test during the entire life of the goodwill.

Tangible fixed assets must be capitalized and amortized over their economic life, taking into account any expected residual values. Valuation must be at either historical cost or current value. Historical cost may be either purchase price (plus expenses related to the purchase) or production cost (direct costs plus attributable indirect costs, excluding sales costs). Interest may only be capitalized to the extent that interest payable to third parties is attributable to the manufacture of the asset.

Where current value is applied, tangible fixed assets should be shown at replacement cost if it is reasonable to suppose that they will be replaced by an asset of equivalent economic value in the context of the activities of the company. Tangible fixed assets should be shown at the recoverable amount if they are not to be replaced, but they continue to be used in connection with activities or are intended so to be used, and at net realizable value if they are not to be replaced, are not used in connection with activities or it is not the intention to use them for this purpose. Where current values are applied, the difference between

Table 10.1 International Accounting Standards checklist

IAS	Netherlands practice

1 Presentation of Financial Statements. Dutch law and CAR Guidelines contain similar requirements.

2 Inventories. Dutch law and the CAR Guidelines are in conformity with IAS 2.

7 Cash flow statements. The CAR Guidelines contain similar requirements (Guideline 360).

8 Net profit or loss for the period, fundamental errors and changes in accounting policies. The law and CAR Guidelines contain similar requirements, except for the following:
   - Compared to IAS 8 the CAR Guidelines and legal provisions permit more instances in which amounts may be taken direct to equity; these are mentioned in Guideline 240.211.

   - The interpretation of extraordinary income and expense in the CAR Guidelines is slightly broader (Guideline 270.211) than the definition in IAS 8.

10 Events occurring after the balance sheet date. The law and CAR Guidelines contain similar requirements.

11 Construction contracts. The law and CAR Guidelines contain similar requirements.

12 Accounting for taxes on income. Taxes on income must be accounted for by way of the liability method. There is no guidance on the choice between the partial and the comprehensive method and the CAR guidelines allow discounting of deferred taxes. A tax loss carry forward must be treated the same way as any other deferred tax assets.

14 Reporting financial information by segment. Apart from the segmental net turnover information required by law, there are only recommendations for large and listed companies to disclose further segmental information.

16 Property, plant and equipment. The law and CAR Guidelines contain similar requirements.

17 Accounting for leases. The law and CAR Guidelines contain similar requirements.

18 Revenue. No specific legal requirement or CAR Guideline, but Dutch practice basically in line with IAS 18.

19 Retirement benefit costs. IAS 19 has not been reflected in the CAR Guidelines yet. See below for a further description of accounting for pensions in the Netherlands.

20 Accounting for government grants and disclosure of government assistance. The CAR Guidelines contain similar requirements.

21 The effects of changes in foreign exchange rates. The law and CAR Guidelines contain similar requirements, except for the following. IAS 21 prescribes that in the event of a foreign entity being disposed of, translation differences directly accounted for in equity (and separately recorded), together with the capital gain realized on disposal, should be included in the profit and loss account. The Guidelines are silent on the subject.

22 Business combinations. Dutch law and CAR Guidelines contain similar requirements. However, the CAR does not allow the IAS 22 benchmark treatment for the allocation of cost of acquisition to minority interests on acquisition and the CAR is a little more flexible on the recognition of a restructuring provision on acquisition.

23 Borrowing costs. The law and CAR Guidelines contain similar requirements (Guideline 120.407).

Table 10.1 International Accounting Standards checklist (*continued*)

IAS	*Belgian accounting law and standards*

24 Related party disclosures. The law and CAR Guidelines contain similar requirements (Guideline 330).

26 Accounting and reporting by retirement benefit plans. The CAR issued Guideline 610 on accounting for pension funds. This Guideline is very different from IAS 26 and specifically focuses on the Dutch pension system.

27 Consolidated financial statements and accounting for investments in subsidiaries. The law and CAR Guidelines contain similar requirements, except for the following.

- The Guidelines do not prohibit consolidation of a subsidiary that operates under severe long-term restrictions which significantly impair its ability to transfer funds to the parent, but require a provision to be formed for the special risks involved (Guideline 214.230).

- The law and the Guidelines prohibit consolidation in the case of activities that are so dissimilar to the other activities that consolidation would be incompatible with the statutory true and fair view. In that event, the annual accounts of the entity not consolidated should be added as a separate part of, and information on invisible consequences should be given in the notes (art. 406(3), Book 2 of the Netherlands Civil Code, Guideline 510.104).

28 Accounting for investments in associates. The law and CAR Guidelines contain similar requirements.

29 Financial reporting in hyperinflationary economies. The law and CAR Guidelines contain similar requirements.

31 Financial reporting of interests in joint ventures. The law and CAR Guidelines contain similar requirements.

32 Financial instruments: disclosure and presentation. The CAR Guidelines contain similar requirements, except that the Guidelines recommend but do not require the splitting up of issued hybrid securities into a debt component and an equity component (Guideline 290.215).

33 Earnings per Share. CAR Guideline 340 contains similar requirements.

34 Interim Reporting. CAR Guideline 550 contains similar requirements.

35 Discontinued Operations. CAR Guideline 345 contains similar requirements.

36 Impairment. CAR Guideline 121 contains similar requirements.

37 Provisions. CAR Guideline 252 contains similar requirements with the following exceptions:

- provisions are not required to be discounted.

- the criteria for recognizing a restructuring provision are more flexible.

38 Intangibles. CAR Guideline 210 contains similar requirements. However, intangibles may never be revalued.

39 Financial Instruments: Recognition and Measurement. This standard has not been implemented in the CAR Guidelines yet, although there is a draft Guideline 290a which is identical to IAS 39.

40 Investment Properties. This standard has not been implemented in the CAR Guidelines yet, although there is a draft Guideline 213 which is identical to IAS 40.

41 Agriculture. There are no comparable standards in the Netherlands.

current value and historical cost must be taken to a revaluation reserve, which is non-distributable until the realization of the asset (by way of sale or depreciation).

Although the application of current value accounting was quite popular in the Netherlands after World War II, the number of companies valuing all tangible fixed assets at current value has diminished significantly. In 1979 7% of listed companies applied current values on an integral basis while 41% applied current values to part of their assets. In 1994 these figures had dropped to 3% and 31% respectively (Brink and Langendijk 1995, p. 25). This may have been caused by the substantial decrease in the rate of inflation (almost 10% in the mid 1970s to less than 3% in the early 1990s). The international trend towards application of historical cost will probably have had an impact as well.

Participating investments are presented as *financial fixed assets*. They must be valued at either historical cost, current value or net asset value, depending on the type of investment. Participating investments are defined as investments by way of contribution of capital with the object of establishing a long-term relationship with the investee for the furtherance of the activities of the investor. The investor must value the investment at net asset value if it exercises a significant influence on the business and financial policy of the investment. This is presumed to be the case if the holder can exercise one fifth or more of the voting rights. In other cases the participating interest must be valued at either historical cost or current value.

The requirement to use net asset value for participating investments on which a significant influence on the business and financial policy is exercised applies not only to the consolidated accounts but also to the individual accounts. This rather unique phenomenon leads to the fact that net equity in the individual and consolidated accounts is exactly the same, except for certain rare exceptions. For some reasons Dutch accountants think it important that this equality should be preserved. No theoretical or conceptual arguments exist to support this view, but it is practical and easy to understand when both equity values are identical. This is probably unique in the world.

Stocks may be valued at historical cost or current value. If historical cost is used, various variants are allowed including FIFO, LIFO, the base-stock method and weighted average cost. However, according to the CAR Guidelines additional information should be disclosed if LIFO or the base-stock method is applied.

If current values are applied, the value is equal to the lower of replacement cost and net realizable value if it can be assumed that the stocks will be replaced. Where the assumption of replacement cannot be made, stocks should be stated at net realizable value. The difference of value with historical cost must be taken to a revaluation reserve which is non-distributable until realization by way of sale or usage. Article 387(3) of Book 2 Civil Code and the CAR Guidelines permit, as in Germany, extraordinary diminutions in the value of current assets which are reasonably foreseeable in the short term to be taken into account when determining the carrying value of such assets, even if these are not related to the situation at the balance sheet date (Guideline 226.206).

Provisions must be made (art. 374, Book 2 Civil Code) for:

- all liabilities and losses the extent of which is uncertain on the balance sheet date but which can reasonably be estimated;
- risks existing on the balance sheet date in respect of certain expected liabilities or losses the extent of which can reasonably be estimated;
- expenses to be incurred in a subsequent year, provided such expenses originate at least partly in the year under review or in a prior year and the purpose of the provision is to spread the charges evenly over a number of years.

Companies are in general required to insure any pension liabilities with an insurance company or a pension fund. Some large companies have their own company pension fund (ondernemingspensioenfonds), which must be independent of the company. But most companies have insured their pension liabilities with a pension fund connected to the industry they are operating in (bedrijfspensioenfondsen). Both insurance companies and pension funds are under the supervision of the Insurance Chamber (Verzekeringskamer). Premiums paid to the pension funds and insurance companies are expensed. If pension rights are introduced or improved, past-service charges may arise. Unconditional rights must be provided for in as far they have not yet been funded (CAR Guideline 271). The CAR recommends that companies provide for most conditional pension rights as well. Provision must also be made for any deficits in company pension funds for which the company is legally liable. If a company is affiliated with an industry pension fund which is not fully funded, the participating companies have a joint liability to make further contributions. The CAR recommends companies to provide for their share in the deficit. Pension provisions are normally calculated by using actuarial methods, applying a conservative low discount rate, but not taking into account expected salary increases. Recently, pension funds have performed quite well, allowing some companies with their own pension funds to take a pension holiday. In one case part of the surplus of the pension fund was paid back to the company.

Provision must be made for early retirement and other non-active personnel schemes if (CAR Guideline 271.405):

- employees have already opted to avail themselves of the scheme;
- there are employees who have the right to opt for early retirement under the existing scheme but who have not yet done so;
- there are employees who are not yet able to opt for early retirement but who may do so in the future before the existing scheme comes to an end.

Provision must be made for all *deferred tax* liabilities. The liability method must be applied. A deferred tax claim should be included in the balance sheet if it is reasonable to suppose that it will be possible to realize the claim in due course. Failing this, a deferred tax claim should be carried in the balance sheet in an amount not exceeding an existing deferred tax liability, provided that (CAR Guidelines 272.309–311):

- it is reasonably certain that the deferred tax claim can be set off against the deferred tax claim;
- the deferred tax liability is not the result of revaluation;
- the deferred tax liability is not the result of disputes with the tax authorities.

Tax losses may be carried forward indefinitely. Deferred tax liabilities resulting from tax loss carry forwards are treated as any other deferred tax liabilities. The amount of any loss carry-forward not taken into account must be disclosed in the notes.

Shareholders' equity must be analysed into issued capital, share premium, revaluation reserves, statutory reserves, reserves required by the articles of association and undistributed profit. A company may purchase its own shares. If shares of a company are purchased by that company or its subsidiary, the purchase price of those shares must be deducted from free reserves. They may not be accounted for as an asset or written off against share capital (unless of course those shares are cancelled). Insofar as such information is available, a legal entity should disclose in the notes the number, class and nominal value of own shares held. If a company has committed itself to repurchasing outstanding shares or depositary receipts for shares in the legal entity's capital, this should be disclosed in the notes, stating the nominal value of the shares or depositary receipts, the agreed price and any other relevant conditions. Disclosure must also be made in the notes of rights to subscribe for shares (such as options and warrants) granted conditionally or unconditionally to shareholders, employees or others. This also applies to conversion rights attaching to convertible bonds.

Segmental disclosures: net turnover must be analysed by type of activity and by geographical area (art. 380, Book 2 Civil Code). In addition, the CAR recommends that large legal entities should provide an analysis of their operating results and tangible and intangible fixed assets, both by type of activity and by geographical area (CAR Guideline 350). It is interesting to note that the law at one time contained a requirement to disclose the extent to which each category of activities contributed to the net result of the year. This requirement was deleted by the law implementing the Fourth Directive. The government considered this information to be commercially sensitive and reasoned that Dutch companies should not be put at a competitive disadvantage compared to other companies within the European Union. Not all companies provide segmental earnings information. Dijksma and Schoonderbeek (2001, pp. 59–62) found 29 out of 42 listed Dutch companies provided segmented operating results by category of activities and 14 by geographical area. It is also interesting to note that many Dutch companies provide segmental information in the directors' report instead of the notes.

In the profit and loss account a distinction is made between results from ordinary activities and *extraordinary income and expenses*. No definition of extraordinary items exists, but the CAR considers the frequency of occurrence in relation to the duration of the typical production cycle for the business as an important criterion. Examples of instances in which classification as extraordinary depends on the nature and size of the company's business would include the settlement of insurance claims resulting in book gains and losses, reorganization expenses and special provisions, such as those for litigation. Items which are not classified as extraordinary but nevertheless are of an unusual nature should be shown separately in the profit and loss account or quantified in the notes (CAR Guideline 270.212).

Government investment grants should either be deducted from the book value of the assets concerned (thereby decreasing the amount of subsequent depreciation over the useful economic life of the asset) or be capitalized in an equalization account. This amount may not be presented as equity and must be amortized on a systematic basis, reflecting the way in which the expenditure for which the grant was made is itself treated in the annual accounts (CAR Guideline 274). In practice companies apply the latter method and show the equalization account as an item directly following equity and as part of 'guarantee capital' or 'group capital'.

Although there is no legal requirement to provide *earnings per share* information, CAR 'requires' listed companies to disclose this information in the notes to the accounts. CAR Guideline 340 is identical to IAS 33.

There is no legal requirement to include a *cash flow statement* in the financial statements. The CAR 'requires' large and listed companies to include a cash flow statement and recommend other companies to do the same. The content of the cash flow statement is almost identical to that described in IAS 7.

Group accounting: Dutch enterprises have a long tradition of preparing consolidated accounts, which is why the Dutch government did not find it necessary to include detailed rules in the law concerning the technicalities of consolidation. In general, consolidation is required of all controlled companies, irrespective of whether this is based upon a legal right to control or on any other basis (i.e. economic approach instead of legal approach).

These subsidiaries must be consolidated in full. Proportional consolidation is allowed, but not required, in the case of joint control of another enterprise.

Conclusion

It can be seen from the above description of accounting in the Netherlands that the legal requirements lay down only broad principles and that the status of the more detailed Guidelines of the CAR is somewhat vague. It is therefore fair to say that the Netherlands ranks among the countries having a very flexible accounting regulatory system. This is evident from empirical research. The tendency for Dutch accounting will be increasingly to follow IFRS. The CAR has made this its formal policy and will only deviate from IFRS when the Dutch business environment or legal requirements make this necessary.

In the light of the EU Regulation requiring Dutch listed companies to apply endorsed IFRS from 2005 onwards and the fact that the Dutch Minister of Finance has expressed his intention to require all banks and insurance companies also to apply IFRS from 2005, the expectation is that many non-listed companies will follow suit.

References

Bos, E. *et al.* (eds), *Fiscale Encyclopedie De Vakstudie*. Jaarverslaglegging, Kluwer, Deventer (looseleaf).

Brink, H.L. and Langendijk, H.P.A.J. (1995) Actuele waarde in de jaarrekening. In H.L. Brink and L.G. van der Tas (eds) *Jaar in jaar uit 9*. Kluwer Bedrijfswetenschappen, Deventer, pp. 1–30.

Camfferman, K. (1995) The history of financial reporting in the Netherlands. In Walton, P. (ed.) *European Financial Reporting – A History*. Academic Press, London.

Council for Annual Reporting (1995) *Guidelines for Annual Reporting in the Netherlands*. Kluwer Bedrijfswetenschappen, Deventer.

Dijksma, J. and Schoonderbeek, W.J. (2001) Segmentatie. In J.A.G.M. Koevoets, G.M.H. Mertens and R.G.A. Vergoossen (eds) *Het Jaar 2000 Verslagen*. Kluwer, Deventer, pp. 49–68.

Hoogendoorn, M. (1996) Accounting and taxation in the Netherlands. *European Accounting Review* **5** (Supplement).

Kapteijn, J.H.N., van Offeren, D.H. and Vijge, G.W.A. (1992) Goodwill. In M.N. Hoogendoorn C.D. Knoops (eds) *Jaar in jaar uit 6*. Wolters-Noordhoff, Groningen, pp. 55–75.

Knoops, C.D. and van Offeren, D.H. (1995) Gesegmenteerde informatie. In H.L. Brink and L.G. van der Tas (eds) *Jaar in jaar uit 9*. Kluwer Bedrijfswetenshcappen, Deventer, pp. 131–163.

Nederlands Instituut van Registeraccountants (2000) *Richtlijnen voor de Accountantscontrole*. Amsterdam.

Zeff, S.A., van de Wel, F. and Camfferman, K. (1992) *Company Financial Reporting: a Historical and Comparative Study of the Dutch Regulatory Process*. North-Holland, Amsterdam.

Further Reading

Dijksma, J. and Hoogendoorn, M.N. (1993) *European Financial Reporting: the Netherlands*. Routledge, London.

Ernst & Young (2002) *International Accounting Standards – Comparison with Dutch law and regulations*. Rotterdam.

Hoogendoorn, M.N. (1995) The Netherlands. In D. Alexander and S. Archer (eds) *The European Accounting Guide*. Harcourt Brace, San Diego, pp. 555–659.

Klaassen, J. (2001) Netherlands: individual accounts. In D. Ordelheide and KPMG (eds) *Transnational Accounting*. Palgrave, Basingstoke/New York, pp. 1909–2014.

Klaassen, J. (2001) Netherlands: group accounts. In D. Ordelheide and KPMG (eds) *Transnational Accounting*. Palgrave, Basingstoke/New York, pp. 2015–2046.

Maijoor, S.J. (1991) *The Economics of Accounting Regulation: Effects of Dutch Accounting Regulation for Public Accountants and Firms*. Datawyse, Maastricht.

Parker, R.H. (1998) Financial reporting in the Netherlands. In C.W. Nobes and R.H. Parker (eds) *Comparative International Accounting*. Prentice-Hall, Hemel Hempstead, pp. 153–171.

Accounting in Spain

Begoña Giner Inchausti

A ny study of the Spanish accounting system needs to distinguish clearly between two periods, before and after the adoption of the European accounting directives. The traditional lack of detailed professional accounting standards has been filled in part by commercial regulation, but even more importantly by fiscal legislation. The influence of these types of rules may be clearly discerned in the two distinguishing characteristics of the old accounting system: conservatism, which results from the concern for the protection of creditors, and the interaction of taxation rules with accounting rules. These refer mainly to formal aspects of bookkeeping and are addressed to all types of business corporations and individual traders.

Although the adoption of the EC directives in 1989 brought substantial change to the Spanish accounting system, this was able to build upon reforms of the 1970s. The adoption in 1973 of the accounting plan and the creation in 1979 of a professional body, Asociación Española de Contabilidad y Administración de Empresas (AECA), marked a major shift in attitudes to accounting. During the 1980s tax authorities allowed some degree of independence between fiscal and financial accounting. A full-scale revamping of the financial reporting system followed membership of the European Union (EU), with new statutes, a new accounting plan, and an extensive reform of audit. However, as far as the accounting system is concerned, prudence is still the overriding principle.

Legal and institutional basis of accounting regulation

The influence of the legal system

The Spanish legal system relies on detailed codes, such as the Commercial Code and the Civil Code, and the rules contained in these are meant to cover all eventualities. Spanish commercial legislation has traditionally been much more concerned with formal record-keeping requirements than with principles and valuation criteria. It was not until the twentieth century that these matters were addressed. A more detailed analysis of the evolution of commercial legislation and institutions is provided in Giner (1995b), but the key points are set out below.

Spain was the first country to prescribe the double-entry bookkeeping system in law. In 1549 and 1552 laws were passed which applied to any person engaged in business in the kingdom of Castile. They defined the accounting requirements for trading establishments, including keeping accounting books according to the double-entry method. The duty to prepare a periodical balance sheet was stated in the 1737 Ordinances of Bilbao. It can be inferred from the general content of the Ordinances that the principle of unlimited liability applied to the first trading companies, although in practice it was possible to limit the liability of some partners. As in other European countries, there were also specially privileged share-issuing companies whose example facilitated the transition from the unlimited to the limited company. These companies in Spain were really owned by the state.

The existence of limited companies was recognized by the 1829 Commercial Code, but in 1848, a Law on Share-issuing Companies virtually prohibited them, except for some specific purposes, thereby causing an uneven development between sectors of the economy. In 1868, the Government adopted a more liberal economic policy and issued a decree abolishing the 1848 law. It was followed the next year by a new Law on Share-issuing Companies that tried to promote this type of company in order to stimulate industrial development and the modernization of Spain.

In 1885 a new Commercial Code was promulgated, which still remains in force, although the section referring to accounting requirements has been modified three times. According to the Code, companies may choose between three different types of legal organization:

- general partnership
- limited partnership
- share-issuing limited company.

There are no references in Spanish legislation to private companies with limited liability until the twentieth century.

The annual profit and loss account and the notes to the accounts were first introduced by the 1951 Law on Share-issuing Limited Companies, and were extended to all types of business in 1973, through a reform of the 1885 Commercial Code. This law is still in force, although it was substantially amended in 1989. It indicates the accounting duties of management, it recognizes the shareholders' right to have access to accounting information before their annual meeting, and introduces the concept of the shareholder auditor (see below).

The 1973 change did not compensate for the shortage of accounting details in the Code, but it did list a series of items to be included in the financial statements. It also stated some valuation rules based on historical cost and established the duty to depreciate fixed assets. In order to protect creditors' interests, some rules about distribution of dividends and the creation of a legal reserve were established. The criteria governing financial reporting were: *clarity and accuracy*.

A Law on Private Limited Companies was passed in 1953, and this too was amended in 1989. This new type of company can be considered as a flexible limited company, which does not issue shares. Its accounting obligations are very similar to those of public limited companies, although private companies were not obliged to have their accounts audited.

Accounting plans and regulation

In 1965 the Ministry of Finance[1] took the first steps towards an accounting plan. Its main purpose was to cover the lack of accounting rules in the legal system and to improve the quality of accounting information. The Comisión Central de Planificación Contable (CCPC – Central Accounting Planning Commission) was established that year, and was later reorganized in 1971. It followed the French system of accounting, and it developed the Plan General de Contabilidad (PGC – General Accounting Plan) with the help of experts from the private sector. It became effective with Decree 530 of 22 February 1973, which approved the PGC. The PGC was a consequence of a 1964 Law, which offered a tax amnesty. To control its application, it gave the Ministro de Hacienda (Minister of Finance) the possibility of requiring companies to prepare balance sheets according to a special format, but specification of this was left to wait until the PGC was published.

Although the PGC was not in itself compulsory, due to the 1964 law it was adopted by the companies that benefited from the amnesty. Later on there were other similar measures that imposed the obligation to follow this plan. Therefore the 1973 PGC was adopted by many companies.

In 1974 a plan for small and medium-sized companies was enacted which was a simplified version of the PGC. From 1976 to 1988, 19 sector plans were issued, and in 1978, Group 9 of the PGC referring to cost accounting was published. In 1982 non-compulsory rules for consolidated accounts were established, although they were not generally followed by groups. These subsequent developments of the accounting plan were produced by the Ministry of Economy and Finance's Instituto de Planificación Contable (IPC – Accounting Plans Institute), which was created in 1976. The Law 19/1988 On Audit replaced it in 1988 by the Instituto de Contabilidad y Auditoría de Cuentas (ICAC – Accounting and Auditing Institute), which remains the official regulatory body.

ICAC is an autonomous body, forming part of the Ministry of Economy. It is under the executive control of its chairman, who approves standards before they are legally enforced. He or she chairs the ICAC Comité Consultivo (Advisory Committee), which has 11 other members who are appointed by the Minister of Economy. Five of these are civil servants from the Ministry, and the rest are proposed by the three professional auditing bodies and the Asociacion Española de Contabilidad y Administracion de Empresas (AECA – Spanish Accounting and Business Administration Committee). This Committee has two subordinate committees, for auditing and for accounting. Each is composed of 24 members appointed by the Chairman of ICAC.

As far as accounting is concerned, discussion and drafting of accounting standards takes place in specific working groups. Each working group has about 10 members, some are ICAC technical officers, and others are outside experts from government, auditing firms, universities, etc. Each group is set up with the purpose of preparing a draft on a specific subject, which is then submitted to the accounting committee and ultimately to the Comité Consultivo. The next stage is exposure through the ICAC Gazette in order to receive comments, and finally it is approved by the chairman. In spite of the very important role of the working group in the development of any accounting standard, its final form is determined by the chairman, who may decide to add, eliminate, or change some of the working party's recommendations (for more details see Cañibano and Cea 1995).

The 1973 accounting plan was divided into four sections:

1. Chart of accounts
2. Accounting definitions
3. Model annual accounts
4. Valuation rules.

It specified acquisition cost, consistency, accruals, and going concern principles. However, probably due to its source, this plan was more concerned with the fiscal content of accounting than with obtaining a meaningful reflection of the economic situation of companies.

Law 19/1989 implemented the EC company directives (see Giner 1993). This introduced the Fourth Directive references to: (i) *generally accepted accounting principles* (GAAP), and (ii) the *imagen fiel* (true and fair view). The legislation establishes that in the case of conflict between those principles, the one that better leads to the true and fair view of the net worth, financial position and results of the company during the period should be the one to prevail. However, in line with the Spanish tradition, the principle of prudence is still considered as the overriding one. The mandatory principles imposed by the 1989 law are: going concern, consistency, prudence, accruals, no offsetting, and acquisition cost.

ICAC in 1990 issued a new PGC adjusted to take account of the revisions in company rules. This plan was issued by means of Royal Decree 1643, of 20 December 1990. It keeps the same structure as the 1973 PGC, but includes another section entitled Accounting Principles. It adds three more principles to those contained in the 1989 law: matching, materiality and recording. The last section is Valuation Rules, and it contains a detailed description of the valuation methods to be used for different items. These two sections and the one referring to Annual Accounts are compulsory, not only for all types of companies, but also for partnerships and individual traders.[2]

Consolidated financial statements have been compulsory since the reform of commercial legislation. The revised Commercial Code establishes this obligation for corporate groups when there is *de jure* control between two companies. Several situations lead to this obligation:

- having the majority of voting rights,
- having the right to appoint the majority of directors, or
- by virtue of agreements with other shareholders having the majority of voting rights.

The only situation of de facto control that implies preparing consolidated accounts is when the company has appointed the majority of directors exclusively with its votes.

The Code has been very restrictive in its interpretation of the Seventh Directive. There are only two reasons to justify the exemption to consolidate, provided that none of the affected companies are listed on the stock exchange:

- small group size (the same limits as for abridged profit and loss account)
- subgroup within EC parent company.

The preparation of consolidated annual accounts was regulated in 1991 by Royal Decree 1815.

After completing the accounting reform, the ICAC has focused on the development of further rules, which are compulsory for sole traders and companies, apart from those in regulated sectors such as credit and insurance entities. It has issued several *Resoluciones* concerning valuation of tangible and intangible assets, income tax recording, etc. The ICAC is also developing adaptations of the PGC to particular industries; these rules are ultimately enacted by Ministerial Orders. Currently ten specific plans have been implemented (construction companies, sporting federations, real-estate agencies, sporting public companies, health service companies, electric utility companies, private non-profit entities, toll highway companies, water utility companies and vine-growing companies), and there are more under preparation.

Official rule-making bodies

As has been noted, ICAC is the body that is responsible for the general accounting system as well as the practice of auditing. There are other bodies with powers related to accounting regulation: the Bank of Spain, the Dirección General de Seguros (DGS – Directorate General of Insurance), and the Comisión Nacional del Mercado de Valores (CNMV – National Securities Market Commission). However, as far as accounting regulation is concerned, the role of the CNMV is limited to entities using the stock market and collective investment institutions. These entities generally follow the guidelines established by the ICAC *Resoluciones* when they provide specific accounting rules.

Accounting standards issued by professional bodies

AECA is a private, non-profit professional association created in 1979 by a group of well-known accountants, auditors and scholars. In the words of its vice-chairman, it was established

> In order to contribute to the scientific development of accounting and business administration, to foster studies on these matters, to establish contacts and exchanges of know-how with other institutions and associations both in Spain and abroad, etc. . . . one of its basic goals being that of contributing to the formation of a regulatory framework in the field of accounting in order to permit the attainment of sufficient reliability in the financial and accounting information which Spanish companies must periodically prepare.
>
> (Cañibano 1992, pp. 85–86)

In short, its main purpose was defining the core of accounting principles that could help the accounting profession, and at the same time could be useful for rationalizing business activity.

Its pronouncements on accounting rules and principles have made a major contribution to changing the mentality of businessmen, consultants, and even government officials, which is particularly surprising given the non-compulsory character of its pronouncements. It is perhaps the wide spectrum of its membership which has allowed its influence to grow throughout Spain. Currently it has about 5000 members (4000 individuals and 1000 corporations).

Possibly its most important contribution was made before the 1989 reform when there was a lack of accounting rules, and the AECA recommendations (opinions and statements) were able to fill this vacuum. Moreover these recommendations were taken into account to a large extent when the legislation was reformed, and they also particularly influenced the 1990 PGC. Some of the AECA's opinions were published in order to make public its views on key aspects of the drafts of statutes which were under discussion (e.g. the Law on Limited Companies, tax regulations, the Audit Law, the new PGC, the consolidated accounts rules, etc.).

The first 15 AECA Statements were issued before the 1990 PGC, and their influence may easily be seen in rules for the recording of financial leasing operations as assets and debts, the adoption of the deferred tax system, the recording of the pension commitments on an accrual basis, etc. Before the notion of *generally accepted accounting principles* existed, and a reference to them was introduced in the Commercial Code after the reform made in 1973, the first AECA Statement specified those accounting principles necessary to provide a *true and fair view* of the economic activity of the company.

AECA Statement 1 (1980) thereby introduced two new and important concepts into Spanish business thinking: the true and fair view concept, typical of the Anglo-Saxon accounting system, but also assumed by the Fourth Directive as the ultimate object of financial statements, and the list of the principles that should be followed in order to attain that objective. These principles were basically the ones included in the 1989 law and in the 1990 PGC. This statement also established a new purpose for accounting information, that of being *useful* for the decision-making process of those interested in the activity of companies, and it stated the *nature* of accounting information needed for this purpose. They are in line with the qualitative characteristics indicated in the US conceptual framework (see Chapter 3) SFAC 2 (Financial Accounting Standards Board 1980), although no hierarchical order is offered.

Since the enactment of the new PGC, AECA has continued with its activity, focusing on areas where there are no accounting rules in Spain, such as commodity futures and options, cash flow statements and the conceptual framework, which is in line with those of FASB and IASB. Other projected statements refer to the earnings per share (EPS) ratio, changes in accounting principles, the use of the equity method in the parent accounts, accounting for non-profit organizations, etc.

Therefore there is now a framework of accounting principles and standards in Spain. In addition to the legal accounting rules, under the control of ICAC, there are the professional statements issued by AECA. Although these standards do not have the status of law and are compulsory neither for auditors nor for companies, they do command wide support. These are normally in advance of legislation but are often taken up later by the government regulators.

AECA statements

Conceptual framework

1. Accounting principles and standards in Spain
2. Tangible fixed assets
3. Intangibles and deferred charges
5. Suppliers, creditors and other payable accounts
6. Trade receivables, debtors and other receivable accounts
7. Accrual accounts and deferred collections and payments
8. Inventories
9. Income tax
10. Accounting principles for equity
11. Provisions, contingencies and events subsequent to the date of the financial statements
12. Deferred revenues
13. Revenues
14. Reversion reserve
15. Financial investments
16. Pension plans
17. Expenses
18. Long-term financial liabilities
19. Commodity futures and options
20. Cash flow statement
21. Income tax in consolidated accounts.
22. Foreign currency exchange differences and translation of financial statements in foreign currency.

(as at January 2002. All the statements were revised in 1991.)

AECA has several committees engaged in different areas related to accounting and business administration. The Accounting Principles and Standards Committee has 25 members drawn from the profession, academic institutions and government agencies. The Committee operates through plenary sessions, and in working parties (about 8–10 persons). Its pronouncements are first published as exposure drafts, which are open to suggestions and comments, and then issued as AECA Statements in six months' time. For more details see Cañibano and Cea (1995).

Users, qualitative characteristics and objectives

The 1990 PGC does not mention any particular user of the annual accounts, but in its introduction it says 'Annual accounts ought to be available to the economic agents interested in the current and future situation of companies, such as shareholders, creditors, employees, the Public Administration, and even competitors'. It also mentions the following qualitative characteristics of the accounting information:

- Understandability
- Relevance
- Reliability
- Comparability (including consistency)
- Timeliness.

Understandability is defined as the quality of being easy to understand for users, but provided that the users fall within the PGC definition, it may be inferred that they will have a reasonable knowledge of business and accounting. Relevance is defined as containing significant information for users. Information is reliable if it does not contain significant errors. Comparability implies consistency over time and uniformity between companies. Lastly, information must be timely in order to be useful for users. However, according to the calendar established in the commercial legislation, annual accounts are normally disclosed one semester after the year end.

These characteristics may be considered as an approximation of those established in the IASC's conceptual framework. The PGC also mentions the need to arrive at a balance between these characteristics in order to achieve the overall objective of providing the *imagen fiel* (true and fair view). It is now required that financial statements provide the *imagen fiel* of the net equity, the financial position and results of the company. However, given that this concept has not been defined in the British literature (see Walton 1993), it is even more difficult to understand it in a different context. Several interpretations have been offered by Spanish authors. Tua (1982) maintains that some of the aspects previously addressed in the Commercial Code are not very far from it. He refers to the terms *clarity and accuracy*. However, this interpretation of the concept may be accepted only in the particular cases where the economic context and the company characteristics are extraordinarily simple.

Another approach to consider is the legalistic one and assumes that the true and fair view is a *consequence of the adoption of GAAP* (Montesinos 1980). This approach opens a new dilemma because GAAP are not unique. They may differ from one country to another and change with the economic and legal circumstances. To avoid misunderstandings, it is necessary to provide information to the users of accounts about the accounting rules that have been used.

Since there are no rules that cover every economic transaction, it is advisable to provide general guidance for registering. For this purpose IAS 1 states the preference of *substance over form*, which according to Gabás et al. (1986) may be considered as another interpretation of the true and fair view. Finally these authors consider that the concept could also be taken to mean *usefulness for users*. This implies that it is necessary to keep in mind the final purpose of the accounts when recording economic events.

Consistent with the Commercial Code, the legalistic approach is accepted and the general opinion is that the *imagen fiel* is achieved when the accounting principles and rules established in the PGC are applied in the preparation of the annual accounts. Although, in line with the Fourth Directive, the Commercial Code considers the possibility of deviating from the legal rules in order to obtain the true and fair view, this is left to the auditor's judgement, and will normally be applied only in an extreme situation. Therefore it could be said that there is a general consensus that Spanish GAAP are adequate to provide an *imagen fiel*, which may be considered to be a literal interpretation of the standard opinion in the auditor's report.

The influence of the tax system

In Spain, just as in France and Italy, the influence of tax on accounting has traditionally been strong, and there has been a total congruence between financial statements intended for external purposes (Besteiro 1985, Cea 1988). However, this situation has changed and nowadays there is independence between tax and accounting rules.

Although tax on profits has existed since the middle of the nineteenth century, it only applied to certain types of activities, and it was only in 1922 that it was extended to all types of businesses. The 1922 law based the tax amount on the accounting profit, which was calculated according to commercial rules, but at the same time fiscal regulations made special references about which items could be considered as revenues and expenses. The interferences of tax rules with the accounting system increased as a consequence of a new tax on companies introduced in 1957.

During the 1970s there was another general fiscal reform, and Law 6/1978 On Corporate Income Tax laid out a new framework for enforcing this tax system. This law and its later regulation by Royal Decree 2631/1982, both of which were abolished in 1995, seemed to have a different view of the relationship between accounting and taxation, and the tax authority recognized that accounting and tax rules could be different. However, Royal Decree 2631 was contradictory, for although it stated that fiscal valuation criteria would only be considered for determining the tax amount, it did not allow the use of accounting valuation rules when they were different from those included in its articles. These valuation rules did not always agree with the 1973 PCG in force at that time, nor do they with the 1990 PCG.

Subsequent fiscal rules, such as Law 18/1982 which referred to the tax system for temporary groups of companies, have not always accepted this attitude towards the separation of tax and accounting rules, and they have imposed the obligation to adopt the same rules for tax and economic purposes.

However, after the 1989 and 1990 reforms of the accounting regulation, it is not possible to use tax rules to account for economic events. Commercial accounting rules must be used in the preparation of general-purpose individual company and consolidated financial statements that are directed to the general public, and accounting rules issued by the tax authorities are only applicable for income tax reporting purposes. The tax effects of the differences between tax and accounting criteria concerning expenses and revenues have to be recognized in the financial statements.

There is a general view amongst accountants that in practice tax-oriented measurement rules have been favoured by Spanish companies (with the exception of large and listed ones) even after the new PGC. This is due perhaps to a lack of understanding of the utility of the 'economic' profit (as opposed to a tax-oriented profit) and the small significance attached to possible comments or even qualifications in the auditor's report, where one is required. A 1995 study by Ernst & Young states that the proportion of large companies (usually listed companies) that account for prepaid and deferred taxes has increased from about 38% in 1992 to 46% in 1993. Although another study by Gandía et al. (1994) concludes that the returns of the 71 largest Spanish companies were not significantly changed by accounting for deferred taxation (as opposed to those that they would have shown under the flow-through method).

In December 1995 a new Corporate Tax Law was passed which attempts to adapt the fiscal accounting rules to those of commercial accounting, in order to avoid the conflicts that existed between accounting and fiscal rules. Law 43/1995 and its regulation by Royal Decree 537/1997 takes the accounting profit as the basis of taxable profit, but introduces some specific rules to that end. The main areas of difference are: the depreciation of intangible assets such as goodwill, transfer rights and transferable administrative concessions, where the useful life for tax purposes is 10 years; provisions for bad debts, which can only be expensed for tax purposes if they are more than 12 months old; profit on disposal of fixed assets may be reduced by indexing the historical cost, and the revised profit may be spread over seven years if it is reinvested in fixed assets; there are special rules for related party transactions and those concerning companies in tax havens. The standard rate of tax on corporate profits is 35%, but there are reduced rates for some specific types of companies (cooperatives, investment institutions, reciprocal guarantee companies, and rural savings banks). Although taxes are usually calculated for individual companies, groups may choose to be taxed on consolidated income.

The Ministerio de Hacienda (Ministry of Finance) is responsible for taxes, and tax incentives – mainly relating to investment and job creation – are determined each year by the Ley de Presupuestos (Budget Law). The fiscal year runs from 1 January.

Auditing of accounts

The first reference to auditing appeared in 1848. According to the Regulation of the 1848 Law of Share-Issuing Companies (limited partnerships and companies), the annual balance had to be audited by the civil governor and published in the Official Bulletin of the Province. However, this external control disappeared with the abolition of the Law twenty years later. There were no further references to auditing until the 1951 Law.

Not surprisingly, the development of the auditing profession also had to wait until the twentieth century. In 1912 the Institute of Public Accountants of Spain was created, but it disappeared after a short period. Some years later, local associations of public accountants were established in different cities: Bilbao in 1927, and Madrid, Barcelona and Vigo in 1936. Finally they were grouped into the Instituto de Censores Jurados de Cuentas de España (ICJCE – Spanish Institute of Certified Public Accountants) in 1945.

The 1951 Law (see above) introduced the concept of the shareholder auditor, whose object was to control the clarity and accuracy of the annual accounts of limited companies, and which was available exceptionally, when one third of the shareholders requested it. The shareholders could check any accounting document on their own, or with the help of an expert. Neither the shareholder auditors nor the expert needed to belong to any special body or to have any special knowledge. In practice, nobody examined the accounts. In the event that there were disagreements over the election of the shareholder auditors (two were elected, together with deputies), the law recognized the right of a minority (owning at least 10% of the company's shares) to name another auditor and deputy, who had to belong to the ICJCE.

Some years later two statutes were enacted that might have brought about changes in this area. The Decree Law 7/1964 established that companies and investment funds listed on the stock exchange should have their financial statements certified (not audited) by a member of the ICJCE. To certify was generally understood (by the stock exchange authorities and most members of the ICJCE[3]) as simply checking that what was sent to the stock exchange was consistent with the company's books. Although this rule was not followed by companies, there were no penalties. After the 1973 amendments, the Commercial Code included a requirement to have the accounts verified by an expert (not necessarily a member of ICJCE) in several situations: when a law established the duty to do so, when a judged asked for it, or when the stock exchange requested it. This, apart from anything else, allowed access to auditing by other professionals.

During the 1980s, auditing became more common, because the Government enforced the audit of state-owned businesses and companies in regulated industries. The establishment of foreign manufacturing companies also made the practice of auditing more widespread, so the multinational auditing firms came to Spain and brought in experts from outside. These firms were essential in the development of another important body of public accountants, the Registro de Economistas Auditores (REA – Register of Economist Auditors), which belong to the Consejo General de Colegios de Economistas de España (General Council of Spanish Economists' Associations). This new Register formally opened the auditing activity to economists, and weakened the position of the traditional ICJCE. Following this tendency, the Consejo Superior de Colegios Oficiales de Titulados Mercantiles y Empresariales de España (Supreme Council of Spanish Commercial Graduates' Associations) also created the Registro General de Auditores (REGA – Register of Commercial Graduate Auditors), in order to give their members the possibility of acting as auditors.

These three auditors' bodies have focused on the technical standards for the practice of auditing, and only in some cases have these rules had an effect on accounting, such as the interpretation of certain principles, mainly going concern and materiality, that are relevant to the auditors' task.

The auditing of accounts, as it is now understood, was made a general requirement by the 1989 law, but it was the Audit Law of 1988 that established the necessary framework for the development of statutory audit.[4] This law created ICAC, defined the educational requirements, and obliged auditors and auditing firms to be registered in the Registro Oficial de Auditores (ROAC – Official Register of Auditors). Since that date, the ICAC has been issuing technical rules about auditing, and only members of the Register are allowed to perform the auditing of accounts. Members of the three professional bodies (ICJCE, REA and REGA) were given the opportunity to be included in ROAC. Since then, practitioners must comply with the requirements of the 1988 law, including successfully taking the official professional examinations, which are organized by the three auditors' organizations, and recognized by ICAC.

In 1999 there were around 16 000 registered auditors, of whom approximately 4900 belonged to ICJCE, 3000 were members of REA and 1600 of REGA. The remainder did not belong to any professional association, so they were dependent only on ICAC. From 1990 to 1999 the number of auditors registered in ROAC increased slightly from 12 500 to 16 000, but the percentage of active auditors has decreased from 44% to 29%. Total revenues from auditing activities are distributed as follows: 12% is earned by individuals and 88% by auditing firms, of which the Big Four represent 65%.

The following companies must be audited: listed companies, companies that issue debentures to the general public, financial intermediaries, companies regulated by the Private Insurance Law, and companies that receive subsidies or other aids or perform work or services for the state and state agencies. The 1989 Law extended the requirement to all kinds of limited companies or partnerships, as well as to employee-owned companies, unless they were allowed to present abridged annual accounts (see above), and to consolidated annual accounts.

There has been an increase in audits performed from 25 000 in 1991, to 39 500 in 1999. It is interesting to note that compulsory audits make up approximately 61% of this. As in other developed countries, the profession is suffering from the so-called expectations gap, which is also probably influenced by financial scandals, such as the failure of the Banesto bank. Apparently auditors are not satisfying users' needs.

Publication of accounting information

Although 1989 Law is normally cited as the first to have introduced the obligation to provide accounting information to the general public, this is not totally true. There have been a number of intiatives at different times to make accounting information public (see Giner 1995a). Nevertheless, publication was extended in 1989 to private limited companies, partnerships limited by shares and reciprocal guarantee companies. However, 25% of the companies that are under this obligation do not meet it, and since 1995 penalties may be imposed on them.[5]

Companies listed on the stock market have been required to publish annual information since the 1960s. Law 24/1988 referring to the Mercado de Valores (Stock Exchange) created the Comisión Nacional del Mercado de Valores (CNMV – National Stock Exchange Commission), which is now the overall authority. The CNMV supervises and controls all operations in the capital markets. To this end it issues mandatory accounting rules for companies listed on the stock exchange and collective investment entities. The accounting rules concern financial and non-financial information in the annual and interim accounts to be provided by listed companies. The accounting elements as such are broadly in line with the PGC (for further details see Sánchez de la Peña 1992).

There are four local markets (Madrid, Barcelona, Valencia and Bilbao). In 1989 a trading system interconnected by computer, called the continuous market, was created and has become the largest one. The Spanish market is similar in size (total equity and volume of trading) to those of Italy and Holland. The number of companies quoted in the continuous market is only around 150. Spanish companies still rely on bank loans as their main source of financing. Therefore accounting information is mainly addressed to proprietors and banking institutions, which explains the fundamental role of the prudence principle.

Financial reporting in Spain

Components of annual accounts

According to the 1989 Law and the 1990 PGC, annual accounts are composed of the balance sheet, the profit and loss account and the notes. These documents form a unit, and must be prepared according to the very precise rules established by the PGC. Generally the accounts of large companies are included in a wider report to shareholders, which also contains the management report, the auditor's report and some additional information. As is common, this voluntary information normally tries to give a positive view of the company, and adopts a more visual approach, by using photographs, tables, and so on.

The management report is regulated by the 1989 Law and is compulsory for limited companies, whether public or private. This document must provide an *exposición fiel* (true and fair description) of the evolution of the business and the position of the company. It should also contain information about significant events that have occurred since the year end, as well as research and development projects, and any purchases it has made of its own shares.

The structures of the balance sheet, the profit and loss account and the notes to the accounts were established in the 1989 law, and were developed in the new PGC. All individual traders and those companies that meet two of the following conditions for two consecutive years (about 575 000 companies are within these limits) are allowed to present abridged annual accounts at the end of the year:[6]

(a) Net assets: 2.37 million euro

(b) Net turnover: 4.75 million euro

(c) Average number of employees: 50.

The limits for presenting a normal balance sheet and notes, but an abridged profit and loss account are the following:

(a) Net assets: 9.49 million euro

(b) Net turnover: 18.99 million euro

(c) Average number of employees: 250.

The balance sheet adopts the basic structure outlined in the Fourth Directive, but only the horizontal one is allowed. The profit and loss account follows the account format, classifying revenues and expenses by nature. It is possible to include another income statement organized by function in the notes, which offers significant intermediate data (e.g. value of production, added value, gross and net operating income). The format of these documents cannot be changed from one year to the next, and they have to include the figures for the current and the preceding year.

The notes to the accounts are a new element in financial statements. Although the 1973 PGC already included notes, they were not so developed and they were disregarded by companies. The notes include: a funds statement that expresses changes in working capital, another statement containing the proposed dividend, the valuation criteria, segment information by sales, directors' remuneration and loans, movements of fixed assets and other elements, and information about the company, such as its line of business, main shareholders. The abridged notes do not include either a funds statement or segmental data. A description of the structure of annual accounts may be seen in Gonzalo and Gallizo (1992).

Measurement and recognition practices

Rather than providing a complete description of Spanish practices on measurement and recognition, this issue will be dealt with by examining the main differences between Spanish principles (as embodied in the PGC, the ICAC Resolutions and some AECA Statements) and International Accounting Standards (Table 11.1) and examining those aspects that in the author's opinion help to give a clear idea of the Spanish accounting system.

Several specific areas of accounting are discussed in more detail below. Ten items are devoted to different elements of the financial statements, one deals with presentation in the balance sheet, another looks at the content of the notes and the last refers to consolidated accounts. This structure does not follow the IAS checklist, but rather an accounting rationale which may be more useful to the reader.

Inventories have to be valued at acquisition price or production cost. The first criterion includes the invoice price plus all additional expenses up until the stocks are in the warehouse. Production cost includes the acquisition price of raw materials plus all costs directly allocatable for production and, in line with IAS 2, a reasonable part of the indirect cost

Table 11.1 International Accounting Standards checklist

IAS	Spanish practice
1	Substance over form is not mentioned in the Spanish rules. Basic principles are provided by PGC and AECA Statement 1, although they do not appear in the AECA conceptual framework (1999).
2	Spanish rules allow that certain stocks are valued at a fixed quantity and value, and IAS 2 do not.
4	The subject is similarly dealt with in PGC.
7	The notes to the accounts include a source and application of funds statement. PGC gives details to deal with it. AECA Statement 20 refers to the cash flow statement.
8	The definition of extraordinary items is very wide in the PGC. Retained earnings cannot be re-stated.
10	AECA Statement 11 and PGC treat this item consistently with IAS 10.
11	Valuation rule 18 of the sectorial plan for construction companies establishes the percentage of completion method, but provides also for the use of the completed contract method in certain exceptional cases.
12	AECA Statement 9 and Valuation rule 16 are in line with old IAS 12. However after the change in the IAS 12 (1996) to adopt the balance sheet approach, there are differences.
14	Notes to the accounts include a breakdown of sales by activities and markets.
15	Not applicable.
16	Under AECA Statement 2 and Valuation rule 3 historical cost is the only accepted criterion.
17	AECA Statement 2 and PGC Valuation rule 5 allow capitalization. PGC treats them as intangible assets and includes finance costs as deferred expenses.
18	AECA statement 13 and PGC Valuation rule 18 are in line with IAS, but no revenue is generated after any exchange or swap of any type of goods.
19	AECA Statement 16 and PGC Valuation rule 19 follow the accrual system.
20	PGC Valuation rule 20 does not allow deduction from the asset.
21	PGC Valuation rule 14 provides more conservative rules than IAS. However new AECA statement 22 is in line with IAS 21. At the time of writing, PGC is under discussion.
22	These accounting rules are under discussion at the time of writing.
23	No specific rules, but it is possible to capitalize interest costs in certain circumstances.
24	PGC asks for related party disclosures in the notes.
25	AECA Statement 15 and PGC Valuation rule 8 do not allow the portfolio approach indicated in IAS. The prudence principle does not allow investments to be valued higher than historical cost.
26	AECA Statement 16 does not allow compensation of assets and liabilities. The 'corridor approach' is not in line with the Spanish valuation rules for provisions.
27	The treatment of investments in subsidiaries in the parent's financial statements does not depend on whether or not they have been included in consolidated accounts.
28	Same comment as above. No exemption from consolidation is allowed by Spanish rules.
29	This subject is not dealt with in the PGC as annual accounts must be expressed in euro, and the PGC is established using an assumption of relative stability of prices. As regards consolidation rules for foreign companies which are based in countries with high inflation, either the closing rate or the monetary/non-monetary method should be followed, depending upon which gives a true and fair view.

Table 11.1 International Accounting Standards checklist (*continued*)

IAS	Spanish practice

31 Same comment as for IAS 27. The two exemptions from consolidation are not allowed by Spanish rules.

32 No accounting standard in Spain.

33 At the moment there are no rules. AECA has a project to deal with EPS.

34 No accounting standard in Spain. Listed companies have to provide biannual information to the SE.

35 No accounting standard in Spain.

36 Impairment of assets is dealt with through provisions if the loss is temporary, or reductions in value if the loss is permanent. The notion of the cash generating unit is not reflected in the PGC.

37 Spanish rules allow the creation of provisions for liabilities and charges, even if there are no third parties affected. Contingent assets are never recognized.

38 PGC valuation rule 5 allows the capitalization of research expenses (as well as development), but the later ICAC Resolution introduced limitations, and AECA Statement 3 does not allow it. Financial expenses cannot be included in the cost of intangibles under the Spanish rules.

39 No accounting standard in Spain.

40 Fair value is not allowed for investment property. This asset is valued under the same rules that any other fixed asset.

41 No Spanish standards on this topic.

originated during the manufacturing period. As an exceptional case that is not considered by IAS 2, Spanish rules allow for certain stocks to be valued at a fixed quantity and value if their quantity, value and composition do not vary materially and their amount is not significant. With reference to valuation criteria, the PGC allows the consistent use of FIFO, LIFO or weighted average cost methods.

Periodical revaluations are not allowed either for *fixed assets* or for *investments*. According to the prudence principle, valuation at market price is not permitted when it is higher than cost. Nevertheless, there have been some exceptions due to the influence of the tax system. The first exception took place when Law 76/1961 permitted fixed and certain other assets to be revalued, but for both tax and accounting purposes. Later on, during the 1970s and 1980s, other similar laws allowed revaluations; the last one was in 1983. The revalued figures have been accepted by the 1990 PGC as historical values. Revaluation was also allowed by Royal Decree 7/1996, which gave companies the opportunity to revalue fixed assets and some specific intangible assets (capitalized finance leases) in the 1996 accounts. According to the preamble to this decree, this measure aimed to adjust for the depreciation of the currency since 1983.

The restatement of asset values is also possible following a merger, because of a law issued in 1980 on their taxation. Increases in assets disclosed as a result of the merger were not considered as fiscal income, but these tax benefits were eliminated in 1991. Another more recent regulation – the Ministerial Order of 23 March 1994 – has also altered the historical cost of certain assets. It allowed airline companies Iberia, Viva and Aviaco to add negative differences in foreign currency translation relative to debt not yet matured to the aircraft values already in use. As a consequence of all these measures, for some companies asset values differ from historical cost, and the annual depreciation is not based exactly on this value.

Straight-line *depreciation* is commonly used by Spanish companies, and the rates applied are usually linked to the rates allowed for tax. Reducing balance is also accepted for tax purposes, but special depreciation plans need the approval of the tax authorities on a case-by-case basis. In spite of these comments, it should be said that depreciation for accounting purposes is not constrained by tax rules. In line with IAS 4, the ICAC Resolución of 30 July 1991 states that when calculating the annual depreciation, residual value should be deducted from historical cost if that amount is material.

As far as *leased assets* are concerned, there are some interesting aspects that are worth highlighting. First, for a leasing contract to be considered as a finance lease, the PGC requires that a purchase option be included in the contract and that its exercise is likely. There is no mention of transfer of the risks and rewards of ownership as provided by IAS 17. The ICAC Resolución of 21 January 1992 modifies the PGC slightly by specifying that exercise can be assumed if the cost of exercising the option is less than the residual value of the asset at the exercise date, or if the cost is very small by comparison with the total value of the lease payments. The Resolución does not exclude other possible cases.

Where the asset is considered to be held under a finance lease, it is accounted for as an intangible fixed asset which is to be depreciated over its useful life. The corresponding liability is measured as the total amount of payments under the lease (including exercise of the purchase option), while the interest element is capitalized as a deferred expense. As Chauveau (1995, p. 136) points out: 'A compromise is made between the legal commitment and the adequate disclosure of the economic nature of the finance agreement'. The Resolución also clarifies that when the option is exercised the asset should be reclassified as tangible.

Goodwill arising from consolidation has to be written off in 20 years maximum,[7] provided that the investment can be shown to produce income over this period; otherwise, the maximum period will be five years. As in IAS 22, it cannot be immediately deducted against reserves. When consolidated accounts are prepared for the first time, the acquired assets and liabilities have to be revalued to their market value. If a positive difference between the total price of the investment and the revalued net worth still exists, it is considered as a goodwill asset, and depreciated accordingly. If the difference is negative, it will appear on the liability side of the balance sheet and is treated as deferred income or as a provision for liabilities and charges. It will be released to the profit and loss account when the capital gain is realized through a sale of the investment, or when expenses are later incurred to make the company viable or the expected losses are realized. IAS 22 also adopts a contextual approach for the negative goodwill, being consistent with the Spanish rules when it is considered as a provision, but differs when it does not relate to future losses or expenses.

Although the PGC allows capitalization of *research and development* expenses, ICAC Resolución of 16 January 1992, states certain conditions that make it very difficult to capitalize research. The amortization period is five years maximum from the completion of development activities. In the unlikely case of capitalizing research expenses, they should be amortized in five years maximum, from the capitalization date.

In application of the accruals and matching principles, *internally funded pensions and related commitments* must be registered as an expense from the inception of the relevant pension plan, and during the active life of the employee the provision for pensions is treated as a liability in the balance sheet. Disclosure in the notes is compulsory for details of the method used to calculate the annual expense and the interest rate used as well as the risks covered by the pension plan. There has so far been no official advice as to the method to be used in calculating the pension cost.

The PGC established a transitional rule to help companies adjust to the rules for pension accounting and make provision for the accumulated liability not previously recognized in the balance sheet. Companies were given a seven-year period to create provisions for pensions or other benefits where the employee was already entitled to receive benefit and a 15-year period for active employees. The reference date is the first accounting period ended after 30 June 1990. A later Order of 1 July 1991 extended these terms for the electric industry to 10 and 20 years and specified that the transitional provisions could be charged against retained earnings if the company had any.

Traditionally corporate income tax has been considered as a distribution of income, but since the 1989 Law it is treated as an expense. The PGC clearly differentiates between accounting and taxation rules, and insists on the necessity of not having interference between the two. Consequently, the *deferred tax system* has been adopted. Although the PGC states that all temporary differences will produce either a deferred tax liability or a pre-paid tax asset, the later ICAC Resolutión of 25 September 1991, limits the recognition of deferred tax assets to those reversing in 10 years. This period may be extended if there are deferred taxes of similar amount that will reverse in a longer period. The notes to the accounts must reconcile the accounting result with the taxable amount, and provide details about tax incentives, loss carry-forwards, and other information that is important for the full appreciation of the company's fiscal position.

Foreign currency receivables and payables must be adjusted to the closing exchange rate. Negative differences are considered expenses for the period, but positive differences are treated as deferred income until the related transaction is settled. As an exception, positive differences may be included as income for the period if there are negative differences produced in similar currencies arising from balances due for settlement in the same year.

The application of the translation rules forced companies to reflect substantial losses when the peseta was devalued in 1992 and 1993. Regulated companies that could not increase their prices were particularly affected by the measures, and later on the Ministerial Order of 12 March 1993, and the subsequent one of 18 March 1994, allowed certain regulated companies to consider the negative differences in foreign currency translation related to debt not yet matured as a deferred charge. A third exception to the general rule was made for certain companies in the air transport industry (see above).

The PGC establishes the inclusion under the heading of *extraordinary items* of transactions that are not treated as extraordinary by IAS 8, such as disposals and other transactions related to fixed assets and long-term financial investments, and those arising from transactions with the company's own shares and debentures. Non-recurrent items that are not typical of the company's normal activity are also considered as extraordinary (e.g. accrued government grants, fines, penalties, etc.). Revenues and expenses relating to previous accounting periods are also included under extraordinary items, but if not material may be treated as ordinary and appear under the analysis of expenses by nature.

As a consequence of the many items that are considered as extraordinary by the PGC it is normal for most companies to have some items under this heading in their profit and loss account. The 1995 Ernst & Young study shows that two-thirds of the 150 large companies surveyed (mostly listed companies) included extraordinary items, either positive or negative, in their profit and loss account. However, the study did not carry out any analysis to attempt to show whether companies use this category to try to manage their results. There is some evidence of listed companies selling fixed assets to boost their earnings and maintain the dividend.

The effect of any change in accounting principles and estimates must be included in the profit and loss account, with the part that relates to prior years being treated as an extraordinary item. As an exception companies in the electric industry are required to charge provisions for pension commitments to reserves (see above), which contradicts the general rule established in the PGC.

Assets and debts are classified as *current or fixed*, on the basis of whether they mature in more or less than one year, but provisions for liabilities and charges (including pension commitments, deferred taxes, etc.) are not split in these two categories. Deferred charges, on the asset side, and deferred income, on the liabilities side, are not split either.

As far as the *notes to the accounts* are concerned, they have to provide details to help users to better understand the other statements (activity of the company, its accounting policies, information about fixed assets, etc.). There are no criteria regarding the identification of a segment, and analysis of sales information only is required by the PGC. Many Spanish companies would consider information about segment assets and profit too dangerous. Spanish legislation allows non-disclosure of segmental information when it could be harmful for the company. A study by Cervera *et al.* (1996) shows that only half of the companies analysed identify relevant segments based on IAS 4, and it is difficult to appreciate the relevance of the segments disclosed.

At this moment there are no requirements to provide environmental information, and voluntary information is almost non-existent in the annual report. Giner (1995a) states that since the enactment of the reform in 1989 there has been a reduction in the amount of voluntary information. The only element in the notes considered optional by the PGC – the income statement by function – has been disclosed by less than 10% of companies (Aibar *et al.* 1995).

Regarding *consolidated accounts*, the normal method to be followed for dependent companies is *full consolidation*, although a company that meets the definition of subsidiary can be excluded from consolidation, if certain conditions are satisfied. When any company of the group has a considerable influence over another one, meaning that it holds 20% or more of the voting rights (3% if it is listed), the consolidated accounts have to include the investee company using the *equity method*. Consolidated accounts also include companies over which any company of the group exercises a significant influence, and which are jointly owned and managed with other companies outside the group. The method applied may be *proportional consolidation* or the equity method (for more details see Condor 1991).

Before concluding this section on Spanish accounting rules it would perhaps be useful to mention that although IASB standards have had a clear influence on AECA pronouncements and on the PGC valuation rules, they are not directly applied by any Spanish companies. This is a direct consequence of the legalistic approach (see Puxty *et al.* 1987) of the Spanish accounting system. According to the last valuation rule of the PGC (no. 22) the only accounting rules that may be applied in Spain are those included in:

(a) the Commercial Code and other company statutes

(b) the PGC and industry adaptations of it

(c) the supplementary accounting rules issued by ICAC

(d) other legislation that may apply in specific circumstances.

Consequently auditors would not approve the use of any other rules that could be in conflict with these. Only if there is a legal vacuum on a particular point would they accept other rules and then only provided that they were in line with the legal context at a national level or eventually at an international level such as the IASB.

Conclusion

During the 1970s the orientation of accounting information started changing in Spain, but it was not until the end of the 1980s that the situation developed in accordance with international accounting rules. Several forces have had a clear influence on the new situation: on the one hand the professional body, AECA, introduced a new view of accounting and accountants; on the other hand, the adoption of the European directives produced some legal changes.

Nowadays it is assumed that the purpose of accounting information is usefulness for the decision-making process of those interested in the economic activity of business. Therefore accounting is no longer attached to tax rules, although accounting information may be useful to the tax administration. Conservatism, the other traditional quality of the Spanish accounting system, has a fundamental role, as long as the prudence principle is the overriding one according to the new commercial legislation. Auditing and submitting annual accounts are two new requirements of the legal system that help increase the quality of accounts and the possibility of their being useful for a wide audience. As far as measurement and recognition practices are concerned, it may be said that Spanish practices are in line with international accounting practice, although they tend to be more conservative.

Notes

1. The structure of the government has changed over time. This ministry is now that of Economy.

2. However, business activity is nowadays carried out mainly by companies having adopted limited status. There are some 900 000 companies registered in the Mercantile Register.

3. The 1973 conference of the ICJCE formally approved this view, allowing members to certify without auditing, and although the ICJCE changed its view three years later, it was nearly impossible to change the view of their members.

4. Law 44/2002 has updated the Audit Law.

5. Penalties may be by way of fines (max: 60 000 euro) or by way of impeding them in carrying out certain economic transactions, such as US increases of capital, mergers and so on, that need to be registered.

6. The limits were increased by Royal Decree 572/1997.

7. Law 37/1998 extended the maximum life from 10 years up to 20 years in line with IAS 22.

References

Aibar, B., Canay, J.R., Maside, J.M. and Vidal, R. (1995) La información económica en el análisis de estados financieros: ¿una referencia obligada a la cuenta de pérdidas y ganancias analítica? *Economía de los servicios profesionales (I): Contabilidad y Auditoría*, (Consejo General de Colegios de Economistas de España ed.), Imprenta Pérez Galdós, Gran Canaria, pp. 193–202.

Besteiro, A. (1985) *Análisis de la Relación Actual Contabilidad–Derecho Tributario. Propuesta modificadora para España.* IPC, Madrid.

Cañibano, L. (1992) Professional standards: AECA Accounting Principles. In J. Gonzalo (ed.) *Accounting in Spain 1992.* AECA, Madrid, pp. 85–99.

Cañibano, L. and Cea, J.L. (1995) *Regulation of Financial Reporting. Accounting Requirements in Spain.* Documento IADE 42, April.

Cea, J.L. (1988) *Principios Contables y Fiscalidad*. Monografía 10, AECA, Madrid.

Cervera, N., Giner, B. and Ruiz, A. (1996) Segmental reporting and the identification problem: A survey of the disclosure by Spains Companies. Paper presented at the 19th Annual Congress of the EAA.

Chauveau, B. (1995) The Spanish *Plan General de Contabilidad*: agent of development and innovation? *European Accounting Reveiw* **4**(1): 15–29.

Condor, V. (1991) The impact of EC Directives on Spanish accounting law, with special reference to group accounts. *European Accounting*, pp. 33–39.

Ernst & Young (1995) *Soluciones Prácticas para la Elaboración de las Cuentas Anuales*. Cinco Días, Madrid, Tomos I à X.

Gabas, F., Castro, E. and Gonzalo, J.A. (1986) Los Principios Contables Fundamentales en la Actualidad. Ponencia presentada al VII Congreso Nacional de Censores Jurados de Cuentas de España. *Auditoría y principios de Contabilidad*. ICJCE, Madrid, pp. 133–240.

Gandía, J.L., Labatut, G. and Rodriguez, V. (1994) The Relevance in Financial Statements of the Income Tax Treatment in Spain: an empirical research in 1991 and 1992. Paper presented at the 17th annual congress of the EAA, Venice.

Gay de Montella (1936) *Código de comercio español comentado*. Bosch casa editorial, Barcelona.

Giner, B. (1993) The Spanish Accounting Framework: Some Comments. *European Accounting Review*, September, pp. 379–385.

Giner, B. (1995a) *La divulgación de información financiera: Una investigación empírica*. ICAC, Madrid.

Giner, B. (1995b) The history of financial reporting in Spain. In: *European Financial Reporting. A History* (P. Walton, ed.), Academic Press, London, pp. 203–220.

Gonzalo, J.A. and Gallizo, J.L. (1992) *European Financial Reporting. Spain*. Routledge–ICAEW, London.

Montesinos, V. (1980) *Las normas de contabilidad en la Comunidad Económica Europea*. IPC, Madrid.

Puxty, A.G., Willmott, H.C., Cooper, D. and Lowe, T. (1987) Modes of regulation in advanced capitalism: locating accountancy in four countries. *Accounting, Organizations and Society* **12**(3): 273–292.

Sanchez de la Peña, R. (1992) Financial reporting by regulated Enterprises. In J.A. Gonzalo (ed.) *Accounting in Spain 1992*. AECA, Madrid, pp. 131–148.

Tua, J. (1982) El Principio de Imagen Fiel: Aspectos jurídicos y Contables. *Revista Técnica del Instituto de Censores Jurados de Cuentas de España* **5** (June): 15–29.

Walton, P. (1993) The true and fair view in British accounting. *The European Accounting Review* **2**(1): 49–58.

Further reading

Gonazalo, J.A. (1992) *Accounting in Spain 1992*. AECA, Madrid.

Lainez, J.A. (1993) *Comparabilidad internacional de la información financiera. Análisis y posición de la normativa española*. ICAC, Madrid.

Larriba Diaz–Zorita, A. (1991) *Formulación de las cuentas anuales*. Ediciones Ciencias Sociales, Madrid.

Several authors (1993) *Comentarios Sobre el Nuevo Plan General de Contabilidad*. ICAC, Madrid.

Tua Pereda, J. (1990) El Plan General de Contabilidad y el Derecho Contable. *Revista Española de Financiación y Contabilidad* Octubre–Diciembre, pp. 823–837.

Accounting in Australia

Terry Heazlewood

Introduction

Australia, an island continent, was inhabited by nomadic tribes of aborigines prior to the establishment of a British penal colony in New South Wales in 1788. Further colonies established around Australia formed the basis of today's six States and two Territories, the leaders of whom agreed to the formation of a federal system of government in 1900, a written constitution and the creation of an Australian nation in 1901. The constitution divided power between the State and Australian governments with any residual power for unspecified matters becoming a federal responsibility, unlike the situation in Canada and Switzerland.

As a former British colony and continuing member of the Commonwealth, ties with the United Kingdom are still significant and have resulted in the adoption of UK company law and accounting practices to serve the growing nation's needs in commerce, industry and government. As a result of the constitution, both State and federal governments are involved in regulating business activity. Since World War II increasing trade contacts with the USA have seen the introduction of American accounting principles as well as a number of locally developed standards.

While the accounting profession exercised significant influence over the development of accounting standards the need for enforceability has seen an increasing government involvement in the regulatory structure.

As a founder member of the IASB, Australia has always played an active part in accounting standard-setting at the international level.

Distinguishing features of the Australian system are:

(a) its federal nature with the States only recently ceding their powers over companies to the federal government;

(b) the development of accounting standards not only for companies but for other (reporting) entities as well resulting in,

(c) there being two sets of accounting standards – one enforced under Corporations Law (AASB) and one by the profession (AAS). The AAS series is now being phased out,

(d) two standard-setting boards, the Australian Accounting Standards Board (AASB) and the Public Sector Accounting Standards Board (PSASB), both being provided with technical support by the Australian Accounting Research Foundation (AARF) until May 2000 when the 'new' AASB (now also encompassing the PSASB) commenced operations with its own secretariat/technical staff, and

(e) the involvement of the Australian Stock Exchange (ASX) and the Australian Securities and Investments Commission (ASIC) in the process.

Legal and institutional basis of accounting regulation

Introduction

In Australia the rules governing accounting and corporate reporting have come from three sources.

1. Government legislation – companies acts and codes administered by State Corporate Affairs Commissions (CACs), the National Companies and Securities Commission (NCSC) and now their replacement organization the Australian Securities and Investments Commission (ASIC).
2. The accounting profession – CPA Australia (CPA)[1] and Institute of Chartered Accountants in Australia (ICAA) through accounting principles and standards, codes of practice and disciplinary procedures.
3. The Australian Stock Exchange (ASX) through listing requirements.

Prior to the 'nationalizing' of legislation, each (State) Companies Act required of public companies:

- proper books (records) and accounts to be kept;
- a profit and loss account and balance sheet be presented to shareholders at the annual general meeting and a copy lodged with the CAC;
- the accounts presented show a true and fair view of the company's profit or loss and state of affairs;
- the disclosure of matters (usually by the way of note) prescribed by regulations; and
- an auditor's report on compliance with the above.

The Act(s) never specified accounting measurement rules and thus relied on the accounting profession for accounting standards on measurement and disclosure that would provide a true and fair view. Members of the profession were required to observe the standards under K1 – 'Conformity with Institute Technical Statements', May 1971, ICAA, now APS 1, 'Conformity with Accounting Standards and Urgent Issues Group Consensus Views', June 1995. However, without legislative support enforcement was a major problem.

The ASX listing regulations on disclosure requirements included provision of annual and half-yearly reports (quarterly for mining companies) and additional information not normally required by accounting standards or corporate legislation.

Company (Corporations) Law

The current legal instrument determining the accounting (and financial reporting) of limited liability companies is the Corporations Law (CL) which came into operation on 1 January 1991 under four main sets of legislation.

1. The Corporations Act 1989
2. The Corporations Law (sec. 82 of the Corporations Act)

3. The Australian Securities Commission Act 1989 (now the ASIC Act)

4. The Applications Acts (of each State and Territory)

Since this legislation successive federal governments included corporate law simplification proposals as part of an economic reform agenda. The First Corporate Law Simplification Act reclassifed companies for reporting purposes while later legislation including the Company Law Review Act 1998 and the Corporate Law Economic Reform Program (CLERP) Act 1999 have introduced amendments changing terminology and embodying in legislation a number of objectives relating to the role of accounting standards.

A major problem has been the number of legal challenges being mounted against the CL (by individuals and companies) on constitutional grounds which, unless carefully addressed could undermine the CL framework (see p. 294).

Australian company legislation developed slowly on an individual State (and Territory) basis generally following that of the UK. Changes usually came about as a result of major company failures leading to the claim that

> By the early 1960s there was a tradition of legislative regulation of financial reporting based upon the view that compulsory disclosure of historical accounting information was the key to the prevention of fraud, deception and investor losses.
>
> Peirson and Ramsay (1983, p. 288)

Despite substantial changes to company law over the period including the passing of uniform legislation in each jurisdiction in 1961, there was little action on the profession's part until the 1960s when the diversity of acceptable accounting practices came under attack following a string of major company crashes. This culminated in a threat from the New South Wales Commissioner for Corporate Affairs in 1967 that the State government might have to legislate to provide for accounting principles that would provide a true and fair view.

In addition, abuses evident during the mining boom of the late 1960s highlighted first, the inability of individual State jurisdictions to deal adequately with interstate fraud and market manipulation, and second, the need for greater interstate cooperation.

This resulted in the establishment of what was known as 'The Co-operative Scheme for Uniform Companies and Securities Law' in November 1978 whereby the Commonwealth and State governments agreed to operate under identical law (the Companies Code) administered by the NCSC and the various CACs. The oversight body was the Ministerial Council for Companies and Securities comprising the federal and State attorneys-general. The NCSC was responsible for policy advice, administration and regulation of the scheme. In fact, day-to-day matters were delegated to the CACs, as were major prosecutions.

The dearth of funding, resentment by the CACs, and lack of accountability (not to Parliament, only the Ministerial Council) by the NCSC, plus its high profile, added to the dissatisfaction felt with the cooperative scheme and led to the proposal of a National Scheme (responsible only to the federal government). The Corporations Bill of 1988 was passed into law in 1989 but was challenged by three States as unconstitutional. The High Court held in favour of the States finding that the federal government did not have the power to legislate for the incorporation of trading and financial corporations. Following intensive negotiations with the States the impasse was finally overcome in the later half of 1990 through substantial payments to the States for the loss of revenues from their CACs.

The effect of the introduction of the Corporations Law in 1991 was to place control of corporate regulation in the hands of the federal government and the ASIC, which not only superseded the NCSC but also took over all the CAC's functions through the establishment of State and regional business centres.

In terms of accounting and financial reporting there has not been a substantial change in the major requirements of the Code or Corporations Law nor, apart from accounting standard enforcement, with the Uniform Companies Acts.

However, the true and fair view override of accounting standards has now been reversed with the 1991 Amendment Act deleting s 298(2) of the Corporations Law (which gave the true and fair view priority over compliance with accounting standards) and major changes since enacted to the standard setting process through CLERP.

Stock exchange listing requirements

Individual (State) exchanges issued their own listing requirements until 1954 when the ASX took over on a national basis. Prior to 1987 (when the six State exchanges united under a new name, ASX, and structure) they were collectively known as the Australian Associated Stock Exchanges.

The listing rules required the publication of funds statements, turnover data and provision of half yearly reports none of which were compulsory under earlier legislation or accounting standards. Following the 1987 share market collapse, the ASX reviewed its listing rules and in October 1990 issued a discussion paper, which had as its objective the strengthening of financial reporting disclosures to bring them into line with best practice overseas. Following comment on the document, revised proposals were released in June 1991 and the Official Listing Rules were amended, effective from 1 January 1992.

These amendments and continuous updating to ensure, for example, that companies prepare financial statements (including a cash flow statment) in accordance with accounting standards represent the current push by the ASX to a continuous disclosure regime based in part on US practice but falling short of requiring the automatic provision of quarterly financial reports.

The accounting profession

In comparison with activities by the legislatures and stock exchanges, the development of accounting standards is a much more recent process despite the existence of professional bodies as far back as 1885 (Adelaide Society of Accountants). In keeping with other developments, the societies were mainly formed at the State level and it was only after a number of amalgamations that the two national professional bodies emerged. The ICAA was incorporated by Royal Charter in 1928 and the CPAs in 1952.

Table 12.1 provides a statistical breakdown of the respective memberships.

CPA Australia because of its size has offices in all States and Territories in Australia as well as in Hong Kong, Malaysia, New Zealand, Papua New Guinea, Singapore and the United Kingdom. While the major focus of the Institute is in public practice (including substantial representation from the Big Four accounting firms) the CPAs in absolute terms has more members employed in this area.

There have been four proposals to amalgamate the two professional bodies on the grounds of presenting a united voice on matters concerning the profession and rationalization of activities and costs. However, while the required majority in favour has been achieved by the CPAs, this has not been the case with the Institute. Despite these setbacks, both bodies work together in a number of areas including support for the standard-setting body, research and education.

The basic membership requirement for both bodies is the possession of a recognized University degree and a major in accounting. For those wishing to enter public practice their studies should also include company law, taxation and auditing. To become a CPA or CA both practical experience, further study and examination is required.

Table 12.1   Membership of CPA Australia and ICAA (31 December 2002)

	CPA[2] *(approx. 98 500 members)* %	ICAA *(approx. 38 000 members)* %
Male	66	74
Female	34	26
Overseas	21	10
Employment area		
Business, commerce, industry	49	39
Government	11	39
In public practice	19	42
Retired	8	19
Other	10	19
Academic	3	19
Total	100	100

CPA members undertake the CPA programme and must have three years' supervised or mentored relevant work experience. Institute members must pass the CA Program and have three years' mentored practical experience. Until recently this experience was in public practice. However, nominated employers in commerce and industry can now also provide the required supervision.

A company auditor must hold appropriate accounting qualifications, have practical experience, be of good character, a member of a recognized professional body and registered with the ASIC.

A number of organizations have emerged over the last decade offering 'professional' memberships for accounting and related functions. The National Institute of Accountants (NIA), originally established by the CPAs to provide a para-professional qualification for accounting technicians, has a membership well over 10 000 and continues to press for full professional status. The basic education requirement for admission is an associate diploma in accounting from the technical and further education system. Other professional bodies have been established to support the ever growing band of taxation practitioners.

Accounting standards

The ICAA in 1946 issued a series of five 'Recommendations on Accounting Principles' based on those issued by the ICAEW (in 1942) but also incorporating relevant provisions of the Victorian Companies Act (1938) concerning the form of the income statement and balance sheet. 'As early as 1948 concern was expressed at the high level of non-compliance with the ICAA's recommendations but no action was taken. Nor were further recommendations made until the 1960s' (Godfrey *et al.* 2000, p. 362).

The incentive for further action followed the outcry resulting from the company crashes of the early 1960s and the threat of political action which saw the ICAA and CPA join forces in 1966 to form the Australian Accounting Research Foundation (AARF), whose aim was to provide a research base and prepare accounting standards for the profession's endorsement.

In August 1979 the profession's standards were designated AAS (Australian Accounting Standards) and prior to the formation of the Accounting Standards Review Board (ASRB) some 14 standards had been issued. The creation of the ASRB resulted from the interplay of many factors including suitability of existing accounting standards and problems of enforcing compliance, especially from non-members of the profession. These concerns and that of the meaning of a true and fair view were continually raised during the 1970s, leading to a review of the accounts provisions of the Companies Act and accounting standards. The resulting report (Chambers 1978) recommended that suitable accounting standards be given statutory recognition. However, in Chambers' view the existing (historical cost based) standards were not suitable.

The Committee of Inquiry into the Australian Financial System, (Campbell Committee, November 1981) recommended that:

(a) the professional accounting bodies should continue to be responsible for the design and development of accounting standards;

(b) an ASRB should be established with responsiblity for deciding on the adoption of accounting standards having regard to the needs of different users; the NCSC, professional accounting bodies and other interested parties should be represented on the board; and

(c) accounting standards approved by such a board should be given legislative support (Parker *et al.* 1987, p. 235).

The Campbell Report provided further impetus for establishment of an ASRB, the main debating point being its functions and control. The profession's preferred view was to follow Canadian precedent whereby their standards would be given legislative backing, or, if a separate ASRB was established, it should be profession sponsored (like the US FASB) with the majority of members being accountants, nominated by the profession. The Board's major function would be to accept or reject proposed standards (from the profession).

These views were not accepted and the NCSC recommendation to Ministerial Council (release 405) canvassed the possible recognition of standards developed by 'non-accounting' organizations. In addition, the NCSC and NSW CAC jointly recommended that the ASRB sponsor the development of standards and determine its own priorities.

The ASRB was formally established in January 1984 not by legislation but by resolution of the Ministerial Council (a joint government initiative), which gave the Board a much broader role than that originally envisaged and one not restricted by legislative fiat.

This followed the 1983 Companies and Securities Legislation (Miscellaneous Amendments) Act which, for the first time, gave legislative backing to accounting standards by requiring companies to prepare their accounts in accordance with applicable approved accounting standards, i.e. those issued by the ASRB.

In 1983 the profession had expanded its own standard-setting role with the formation of the Public Sector Accounting Standards Board (PSASB) to improve public sector financial reporting. This was in addition to the AcSB (Accounting Standards Board) which prepared the standards jointly issued by the CPA and ICAA. The PSASB and AcSB agreed to work in unison in order to produce a common set of accounting standards for both private and public sectors.

With two competing private sector standard-setting bodies (ASRB and AcSB) friction developed at a very early stage when it became apparent that the ASRB was not going to rubber-stamp the profession's standards but take an independent approach in line with its charter.

The Australian Accounting Standards Board

ASRB Release 200 (1985) provided information on the approval of standards and the functions, establishment, constitution, powers and duties of the Board.[3]

One of the Board's first tasks was to encourage development of a conceptual framework to ensure that approved accounting standards were logically well developed and consistent. The expectation was that standards would normally come from AARF while those from other sources would go to AARF for comment prior to approval.

A due process procedure was put in place providing for comment on proposed standards and public hearings.

ASRB Release 100 (1985) specified the criteria for approval of a standard and the accounting process assumptions needed while the conceptual framework was being developed. ASRB Release 101 (1985) added a measurement assumption.

The Board's role cut across many of the activities carried out by AARF, which was of concern to all parties, and the NCSC Chairman expressed disappointment over the time taken to issue approved standards, resulting in the Board bypassing its own due process procedures in order to fast-track standards.

Despite scope to allow other organizations to submit accounting standards for approval, only one was successful, ASRB 1003, 'Foreign Currency Translation – Disclosure', submitted by the NCSC. Reliance on AARF for technical advice and support allowed AARF to influence which of the profession's standards would be made available for fast-tracking although the ASRB determined the order of implementation.

The problem of having two standard-setting bodies for the private sector placed strains on the system and saw no new AASs issued for 18 months in the mid-1980s. AARF time was being spent assisting the ASRB to finalize approved standards, develop the PSASB and work on the conceptual framework. As a consequence pressure arose from the profession (and business) to rationalize procedures through a merger of the ASRB and AcSB, which was formalized in September 1988.

Conditions of the merger included:

- dissolution of the AcSB,
- an increase in board membership from seven to nine (one extra from both the CPA and ICAA),
- continuing Ministerial Council control over the appointment of members (on advice from the NCSC),
- the Ministerial Council veto of standards remaining, and
- funding arrangements to continue as before (with the public sector financing the ASRB and private sector, the AARF).

These new arrangements were seen as

> The first step in the rationalisation of the accounting standard setting process with the objective of establishing the most efficient structure for the allocation of scarce standard setting resources. The second phase is intended to see the merging of the reconstituted ASRB with the Public Sector Accounting Standards Board of the AARF, resulting in a single body setting accounting standards for both the public and private sectors.
>
> (McGregor 1989, p. 48)

The merger removed the duplicity of standards applicable to listed companies, modified the due process procedures and allowed work on the conceptual framework to proceed in the manner desired by AARF.

In December 1987 AARF issued four exposure drafts on the conceptual framework followed by two more in April 1988. In October 1989 five AASs were given immediate approval as AASBs subject to a more detailed review, due process being bypassed on the grounds of expediency. In August 1990 AARF issued exposure drafts on the definition of equity and definition and recognition of revenues together with the first three statements of accounting concepts (SAC):

- SAC 1, 'Definition of the Reporting Entity'
- SAC 2, 'Objective of General Purpose Financial Reporting'
- SAC 3, 'Qualitative Characteristics of Financial Information'

Accompanying the issue of the first SACs was a revision of Release 100 requiring accounting standards to meet the SAC 3 criteria.

September 1990 saw the release by the AARF Board of Management of an invitation to comment on the recommendations of the Peirson Report. Following the merger of the ASRB and AcSB in 1988, Professor Peirson had been commissioned to prepare a Report on the institutional arrangements needed for setting accounting standards in order to facilitate the formation of one single national accounting standard-setting body. The terms of reference included:

(a) to review the existing institutional arrangements for the setting of accounting standards in Australia in respect of both the public and private sectors; and

(b) to review institutional arrangements for the setting of accounting standards in the public sectors in other relevant countries. In particular, to review the arrangements in the United States, Canada, United Kingdom, New Zealand and the Netherlands.

The major reforms proposed by Peirson (1990) were:

- The formation by 1992 of two broadly constituted consultative groups, one for the private sector and one for the public sector.
- The establishment by 1995 of a foundation to be called the Australian Accounting Standards Foundation which would be independent of the accounting profession, business and government, and whose funding would be broadly based.
- The establishment by 1995 of one national accounting standard-setting board within the Foundation to be called the Accounting Standards Board. This Board would result from a merger of the ASRB and the PSASB.

In general terms the recommendations are in line with those that have been operating in the USA for some time and are now in place in the UK following the Dearing Committee proposals.

The federal government declined to implement the Report at that time but increased membership of the AASB by two and set up a working party to consider amalgamation of the ASRB and PSASB. The working party reported in the affirmative (September 1993) although no action was taken until the implementation of the CLERP Act in 2000. The ASRB was replaced by the Australian Accounting Standards Board (AASB) in January 1991 (ASC Act, Section 224).

The issue of SAC 4, 'Definition and Recognition of the Elements of Financial Statements' (March 1992), sparked the most controversial debate in Australia's standard-setting history and provoked further review of due process, a situation foreshadowed by the responses to the fast-tracking of AASB1026, and the manner in which the cash flow statement debate had been stalled by AARF (Walker and Robinson 1994).

Opponents of SAC 4 claimed it was 'academic (the ultimate criticism), radical, leading the world (a heinous crime) and evidence of a plot by the standard setters to supplement historical cost with some new unspecified system. This reaction . . . was not expected', and came in the main because of the mandatory status of the SACs (Henderson 1993, p. 12). This was unfortunate given the lengthy exposure time and the change in economic climate over the period. It has been noticeable that as the economy moves into a growth situation the penchant for corporate reform diminishes.

Rahman (1991) has also concluded that the Australian standard-setting process did not provide 'outsiders' with an opportunity to become involved in all aspects of the process, a situation finally addressed by Policy Statement One (1993).

The formation of an Urgent Issues Task Force similar to those in the UK and USA was initially not adopted as the AASB felt the need to clarify the role and resource requirements to operate such a task force (AARF and AASB Report, September 1993). However, the formal retraction of the mandatory status of SAC 4 (and as a corollary SACs 1, 2 and 3) in December 1993 can be viewed as the point where business interests succeeded in wresting the standard-setting initiative from the accounting profession and AARF. One immediate result was the issue of a discussion paper on the formation of an Emerging Issues Group (EIG) also in December 1993. Following a review of responses to the EIG discussion paper, an Urgent Issues Group (UIG) was formed and commenced operation in March 1995.

The 15-member UIG is dominated by the profession, comprising a senior partner from each Big Four firm, and representatives from the AASB (chairman), a second tier accounting firm, user and preparer groups, academia and public sector with an ASIC observer. Technical support was initially provided by AARF but now the AASB. Eleven votes are required to make a ruling; four negative votes ensure the matter is lost. The UIG meetings are open to the public and submissions invited. However, there is no due process as the Group only has 3 + 1 meetings in which to resolve an issue. The AASB has the power of veto over UIG decisions. Appendix 4 provides a list of the 52 Abstracts issued to date.

The most interesting ruling made by the UIG in the course of its first year of operations was Abstract 5, 'Methods of amortization of goodwill', which bans the inverse sum of the years digits method. This matter was referred to the AASB when reviewing the goodwill standard (AASB 1013) and has been incorporated therein. The decision on goodwill amortization 'followed' the June 1995 ASIC ruling on the matter, thus averting a major clash between AARF/AASB/UIG and the ASIC on the issue.

March 1995 also saw the release of the revised SAC 4 without the contentious examples (especially that of agreements equally and proportionally unperformed). Without mandatory status attaching thereto this release has attracted little comment.

The Corporate Law Reform Act of September 1994 ensconced the role of the ASX as a co-regulator with regard to the enforcement of listing and business rules on continuous disclosure. The main disclosure requirement was listing rule 3A(1). The First Corporation Law Simplification Bill was enacted in September 1995. Its major thrust was to change the classification of proprietary companies from the reporting (entity) concept developed by AARF/AASB to one based on a definition of 'small' and 'large' companies. To be a small company *two* of the following three criteria must be met:

- Gross consolidated revenue < A$10 million (about US$6 million)
- Consolidated total assets < A$5 million (about US$3 million)
- Fewer than 50 full-time employees.

This means that company status is now determined on an annual basis following a legalistic approach rather than one of 'substance' over form preferred by the profession.

Companies defined as 'small' have much less stringent accounting and financial reporting requirements to meet than 'large' companies, which must prepare and lodge (with the ASIC) audited accounts in accordance with accounting standards.

Notwithstanding the fluctuating fortunes of the various interest groups over the last decade, the increasing globalization of financial markets and need for capital raising and operations offshore has brought some agreement with regard to the international compatibility and harmonization of accounting standards. The president of G100[4] used this as a platform to promote yet another (unsuccessful) merger attempt of the CPAs and ICAA as well as an overhaul of the standard-setting process. A proposal that Australia replace its standards with International Accounting Standards (IAS) for domestic reporting purposes was greeted with dismay by AARF (possible loss of influence) and concern was expressed by the G4 + 1 (IASB) group who noted it was not IASC policy for IAB to replace national accounting standards.

The AASB and AARF agreed on the adoption of IAS except where there may be conflict with Australian standards. This is in keeping with the policy of cross-Tasman (Australia and New Zealand) involvement and international harmonization, which was actively promoted by the past Australian IASB chairman and the IASB secretary-general.

A further development during 1996 saw the ASX (with strong G100 support) impose a special levy on all listed companies to raise A$1 million over two years to enable the AASB and PSASB to pursue a programme of harmonizing Australian accounting standards (AASBs) with those of the IASB by the close of 1998. This programme is now ongoing.

The complex nature of the Australian accounting and financial reporting regulatory framework prior to the CLERP reforms is depicted in Appendix 1. The more simplified approach following the CLERP reforms is depicted in Appendix 2 together with a listing of the reforms undertaken (see also Table 12.2).

Table 12.2 Accounting standards in force as at 31 December 2002. AASB and AAS-series accounting standards

AASB series	AAS series	Title	Issued (re-issued #)
1001	6	Accounting policies	# 3/99
1002	8	Events Occurring After Reporting Date	# 10/97
1004	15	Revenue	# 6/98
1005	16	Segment Reporting	# 8/00
1006	19	Interests in Joint Ventures	# 12/98
1008	17	Leases	# 10/98
1009	11	Construction Contacts	# 12/97
1010	10	Recoverable Amount of Non-Current Assets	#12/99
1011	13	Accounting for Research and Development Costs	5/87
1012	20	Foreign Currency Translation	# 11/00
1013	18	Accounting for Goodwill	# 6/96
1014	23	Set-off and Extinguishment of Debt	# 12/96
1015	21	Acquisitions of Assets	# 11/99
1016	14	Accounting for Investments in Associates	# 8/98
1016A	—	Amendments to Accounting Standard AASB 1016	10/98
1017	22	Related Party Disclosures	# 2/97

Table 12.2 Accounting standards in force as at 31 December 2002. AASB and AAS-series accounting standards (*continued*)

AASB series	AAS series	Title	Issued (re-issued#)
1018	1	Statement of Financial Performance	# 6/02
1019	2	Inventories	# 3/98
1020	3	Accounting for Income Tax (Tax-effect Accounting)	11/89
1020	3	Income Taxes	12/99
1020A	3	Amendments to Accounting Standard AASB 1020 and Australian Accounting Standards AAS 3	6/02
1020B	3	Amendments to Accounting Standard AASB 1020 and Australian Accounting Standards AAS 3	12/02
1021	4	Depreciation	#8/97
1022	7	Accounting for the Extractive Industries	10/89
1023	26	Financial Reporting of General Insurance Activities	# 11/96
1024	24	Consolidated Accounts	# 5/92
1025	—	Application of the Reporting Entity Concept and Other Amendments	7/91
1026	28	Statement of Cash Flows	# 10/97
1027	—	Earnings per Share	6/01
1028	30	Employee Benefits	# 6/01
1029	—	Interim Financial Reporting	# 10/00
1030	—	Application of Accounting Standards to Financial Year Accounts and Consolidated Accounts of Disclosing Entities other than Companies	12/94
1031	5	Materiality	9/95
1032	32	Specific Disclosures by Financial Institutions	12/96
1033	33	Presentation and Disclosure of Financial Instruments	# 10/99
1034	37	Financial Report Presentation and Disclosures	# 10/99
1036	34	Borrowing Costs	12/97
1037	35	Self-Generating and Regenerating Assets	8/98
1037A	35A	Amendments to Accounting Standard AASB 1037	7/99
1038	—	Life Insurance Business	11/98
1039	—	Concise Financial Reports	# 6/02
1040	36	Statement of Financial Position	10/99
1041	38	Revaluation of Non-Current Assets	# 7/01
1042	—	Discontinuing Operations	8/00
1043	—	Changes to the Application of AASB and AAS Standards and Other Amendments	12/00
1044	—	Provisions, Contingent Liabilities and Contingent Assets	10/01
1045	—	Land Under Roads: Amendments to AAS 27A, AAS 29A and AAS 31	10/02
—	25	Financial Reporting by Superannuation Plans	3/93
—	27	Financial Reporting by Local Governments	# 6/96
—	27A	Amendments to the Transitional Provisions in AAS 27	12/99
—	29	Financial Reporting by Government Departments	# 6/98
—	29A	Amendments to the Transitional Provisions in AAS 29	12/99
—	31	Financial Reporting by Governments	6/98
—	31A	Amendments to the Transitional Provisions in AAS 31	12/99

Taxation

While the Australian Constitution allows State and federal governments to levy a tax on income, in 1942 the States agreed to hand over this power to the federal government (as a wartime measure) in return for a share of the collections (grants). The federal government has retained control of income tax since that date. Income tax is levied on residents of Australia be they individuals or companies and applies to worldwide income (subject to exemptions and double taxation agreements).

The tax rates applying to individuals and companies are usually announced by the Treasurer in the August budget, which must be passed by both Houses of Parliament (the House of Representatives and Senate) and are applicable for the following fiscal year, which runs from 1 July to 30 June. The corporate tax rate as from the 2001/2002 fiscal year is 30%, previously 34%.

While income tax is the major source of federal government revenue, other taxes imposed include sales tax, customs and excise duties, natural resources tax (e.g. on oil and gas), fringe benefits tax and capital gains tax. The States levy stamp duty, payroll tax, land tax and a range of business franchise taxes. In July 2000 a 10% Goods and Services Tax (GST) was introduced replacing the wholesale tax and a range of business franchise taxes.

Taxable income is determined as follows:

Gross income from all sources (excluding exempt income)	A
Add: net capital gains (inflation adjusted or 50% net)	B
= Assessable income	A + B
Less: allowable deductions	C
= Taxable income	A + B − C

For companies in general, taxable income usually correlates with accounting income subject to a number of important exceptions covering valuation of trading stock, depreciation of plant and buildings including prescription of rates, methods (straight line or reducing balance) and special allowances, bad debts (must be written off) and provisions (not usually allowed), carry-forward of losses (indefinitely), treatment of intergroup losses (offset), inter-company dividends (rebateable) and entertainment expenses (not allowed).

While all companies are taxed at the same rate a distinction is made between public and private companies for tax purposes. A public company is either listed or has more than 50 shareholders. A private company is one that is not a public company. Restrictions applied to private companies mainly focus on the treatment of excessive payments, loans or remuneration to the owners, which are treated as dividends (non-deductible) rather than expenses (deductible).

A dividend imputation scheme now operates to avoid the double taxation of dividends. Dividends are franked and provide shareholders with a rebate at the company tax rate. Australia does not operate an advance corporations tax (ACT) as is the case in the UK.

Objectives, assumptions and qualitative characteristics

As a consequence of the legalization of accounting standards coupled with the continuing development of a conceptual framework upon which the standards are based, the notion of a true and fair view has now been given secondary status. Prior to the removal of section 298(2) of the Corporations Law (CL), the position was that directors need not ensure that the financial statements were made out in accordance with accounting standards if compliance would lead to the accounts *not* giving a true and fair view.

Those companies not prepared to comply with selected accounting standards used the override as a means of avoiding compliance. This, plus the difficulties of defining a true and fair view (see Chapter 6 on the UK) resulted in the amendment to the CL which now provides that if compliance with standards will not give a true and fair view then the directors must add such information and explanations as will give a true and fair view rather than depart from the standards in presenting the financial statements (section 297 CL). An unintended consequence of this was the use of multi-column financial statements by a few companies who believed the application of a standard was misleading. This practice is now banned.

While the impetus for developing accounting standards has been to regulate listed companies, there have always been concerns that small companies should not be burdened with unnecessary regulation. The First Corporation Law Simplification Act provided a small business guide to consolidate all statutory provisions affecting small companies in one place. A feature of the Act and subsequent amendments was that any company classified as small has reduced accounting obligations. While sufficient accounting records must be kept to allow annual accounts to be prepared and audited, a small proprietary company (which now only needs one shareholder, previous minimum was two) is not required to prepare formal accounts or have them audited unless the company is requested to do so by 5% of the voting shareholders or the ASIC.

Given that around 98% of Australia's 1.1 million companies are defined as small these new provisions are of major economic benefit to such companies. They must still, however, lodge an annual return (filing) with the ASIC containing details of directors, shareholders, issued shares and registered office.

Publication and audit

Subject to the above provisions for small companies all other companies are required to have their annual financial statements audited and to lodge annual returns with the ASIC. Grandfather provisions (i.e. transitional derogations for existing companies) were introduced to delay this requirement for certain large proprietary (private limited) companies that had previously been exempt.

Auditing principles are determined by the Auditing and Assurance Standards Board (AuASB) of AARF and have been codified as Australian Auditing Standards (AUSs), replacing the existing statement of auditing standards and statements of auditing practice (AUPs). A series of Auditing Guidance Statements has been issued to support the AUSs in place of the existing auditing guidance releases. The AUSs are operative for the first financial reporting period commencing on or after 1 July 1996.

With much of the guidance in the current AUPs based on the superseded International Auditing Guidelines, the AuASB based their review on the International Auditing Practices Committee codification. The aim was to ensure as far as possible the international compatibility of the AUSs.

As with the USA and UK the audit industry is dominated by the Big Four international firms who conduct the majority of listed company audits (87% of the top 150 companies) (Heazlewood and Ryan 1999).

Following the share market collapse of October 1987 and subsequent major company failures, audit credibility was questioned as legal action was taken against audit firms by government, administrators and receivers for providing unqualified audit reports on companies unable to pay their debts. This led to discussions on auditors' responsibilities, the issue of a new scope statement in 1991 and the commissioning by the profession of a report titled 'A research study on financial reporting and auditing – bridging the expectation gap'. The report took a holistic approach and stressed the whole of financial reporting not just audit. The focus then shifted towards corporate governance following the lead of the UK Cadbury Committee. The ASX has now incorporated principles of corporate governance into its listing requirements with all major companies now appointing audit committees comprised in the main of independent (non-executive) directors. These requirements have been further strengthened following the ENRON and WorldCom collapses.

On the matter of audit liability, as in the UK the negligent auditor has a joint and several liability for damages. This had led to a number of high profile law suits being brought against the audit firms. In most cases the claims are settled out of court in order to minimize costs and adverse publicity. Some consolation for auditors was found in a recent case (AWA) where the court was prepared to apportion the damages (blame) between the directors and auditors. As in the UK the level of claims is less than the USA due to the fact that the practice of contingency fee arrangements with lawyers has not been normal Australian practice (although this is changing) and the loser is usually required to pay the winning party's taxed legal costs.

Australian financial reporting

Components of annual reports

The annual report of a publicly listed company contains an unregulated voluntary section usually at the beginning followed by the statutory requirements.

The unregulated section contains the Chairman's and Managing Director's review of the past year and future prospects (usually optimistic in nature). Various company activities are featured in this section as well as environmental and employee matters (62% of companies reporting) and mineral prospects and reserves for mining companies (20% of companies reporting) (Heazlewood and Ryan 1999).

Following amendments by the Company Law Review Act 1998, the key accounting and auditing requirements are found in Chapter 2M, Financial Reports and Audit.

In general terms the legal requirements are as before, however, the terms 'accounting records' and 'accounts' have been replaced by 'financial records' and 'financial report' respectively.

- Part 2M.1 *Overview* spells out in summary form the key annual reporting requirements for disclosing entities [s 285(2)] covering preparation of the financial reports, directors' report, auditor's report, the sending of the reports to members and lodging with the ASIC.

- Part 2M.2 *Financial Records* imposes an obligation on companies to keep adequate financial records.

- Part 2M.3 *Financial Reporting, Division 1*, requires the preparation of a financial report and directors' report each year s 292(1).

- Section 295(1) specifies the basic content of the financial (annual) report as consisting of the financial statements, notes to the financial statements and the directors' declaration about the statement and notes.

- Section 295(2) defines the yearly financial statements as being the profit and loss statement, balance sheet and statement of cash flows and where required by the accounting standards the consolidation version of the above.

- Section 295(3) prescribes the notes to the financial statements as being disclosures required by the regulations, notes required by the accounting standards and any other information needed to give a true and fair view.

- Section 295(4) deals with the directors' declaration stating that the financial statements and notes comply with accounting standards and give a true and fair view, there are reasonable grounds to believe the entity will pay its debts and that the financial statements and notes are in accordance with the Law including s 296 and s 297.

- Section 296 requires the yearly financial report to comply with accounting standards while s 297 requires the financial statements and notes to give a true and fair view of the financial positions and performance of the entity and consolidated entity.

  Where a conflict between complying with accounting standards and presenting a true and fair view arises, this is to be resolved by providing an explanation in the notes [s 295(3)(c)].

- Section 298 requires presentation of an annual directors' report providing both general information as detailed in s 299 and specific information required by s 300.

- Part 2M.3 *Division 2*, deals with half-year reporting while *Division 3* covers audit and the auditor's report requiring that where a financial report has been audited the auditor must form an opinion about whether it is an accordance with the Law including compliance with accounting standards, gives a true and fair view (s 307) and, for the annual financial report, if not why not [s 308(1)]. Where non-compliance with an accounting standard is involved, the auditor must quantify the effect (if possible) s 208(2) or say why it is not practicable. Section 309 provides similar requirements for the audit of half-year financial reports.

- *Division 4* s 314 provides for the sending of concise annual reports to members instead of full annual reports. This reverses the previous requirement of sending a full report to each member unless advised to the contrary.

  Part 2M.5 *Accounting Standards* gives the AASB the authority to make accounting standards (s 334) including equity accounting (s 335) while Part 2M 6 *Exemptions and Modifications* maintains the ASIC's power to make specific exemption orders (s 340) and class orders (s 341) relieving entities from complying with all or certain requirements of Part 2M.2 and Part 2M.3.

The financial reports are usually preceded by the statutory directors' report and are:

- profit and loss statements
- balance sheets
- cash flow statements
- notes to the financial statements (first note specifies accounting policies used)
- directors' declaration
- auditors' report.

The audit report is usually followed by ASX listing rule requirements covering substantial shareholdings and number of shareholders by parcel size. The format of the profit and loss statement and balance sheet is now determined by AASB 1018 and AASB 1040 (see Appendix 3).

Matters covered in the directors' declaration include comment on: review and results of operations, any significant change in state of affairs, principal activities and changes, net profit or loss, dividends recommended and paid, subsequent events, future developments (but prejudicial information may be omitted), directors' interests and benefits, meeting attendance, indemnities and rounding off.

The profit and loss statement requirements also include full details of all transactions affecting the distribution of profits including dividends and transfers to and from reserves.

The directors' declaration requires a statement to the effect that

(a) the accounts give a true and fair view,

(b) the entity will be able to repay its debts as and when they fall due, and

(c) the accounts have been made out in accordance with applicable Australian Accounting Standards.

It should be noted that while the CL refers to the Profit and Loss Statement and Balance Sheet the accounting standards refer to Statement of Financial Performance (AASB 1018) and Statement of Financial Position (AASB 1040).

Measurement and recognition practices

A comparison with International Accounting Standards (Table 12.3) is provided followed by general discussion on major areas of difference. As compliance with accounting standards is mandatory it is important to appreciate that their theoretical underpinning is based on the Statements of Accounting Concepts.

SAC 1 discusses the concept of a reporting entity as the vehicle for which standards are prepared – unfortunately this concept has been clouded by the statutory definition provided for small and large private limited companies. SAC 2 requires reporting entities to prepare general purpose financial reports to those interested parties who are unable to obtain their own specific purpose financial reports, i.e. shareholders, investors and creditors in general. SAC 3 focuses on the key qualitative characteristics required of financial information, of which relevance and reliability feature strongly. SAC 4 provides the definitions of revenue, expense, assets and liabilities with equity as a residual. While no longer mandatory the SACs, and in particular the SAC 4 definitions, are being incorporated into accounting standards as they are issued. The measurement SAC is still being developed now by the AASB. For measurement purposes the accrual basis and going concern convention are implicit and, although the underlying basis is historical cost, there are a number of instances where revaluations are allowed (up and down), the use of present value (discounting) for leases and insurance liabilities, 'mark to market' for insurance assets and fair values for business combinations.

The presentation of the *profit and loss* statement is determined by AASB 1018. An all-inclusive income approach is taken for profit determination with the separate inclusion of extraordinary items. Extraordinary items are narrowly defined to be not only attributable to events or transactions of a type that are outside ordinary operations, but also not of 'a recurring nature'. This has led to a marked decrease in companies reporting extraordinary items from 31% (1991) to 0% (1998) Heazlewood and Ryan (1999, p. 153). Although AASB 1004 requires all companies to disclose gross revenue (turnover), there was no requirement to disclose a cost of goods sold figure and only one top company did so. AASB 1018 (June 2002) now requires the disclosure of cost of sales. Likewise, as the place of revenue disclosure is not specified, only 50% use the profit statement with the remainder utilizing the notes. AASB 1027 defines and requires disclosure of *earnings per share* (basic and diluted) but does not specify location leading to this information also being disclosed in the notes (Heazlewood and Ryan 1999). Extraordinary items but not abnormals are excluded from the calculation.

With regard to the balance sheet there is continuing controversy over the treatment of *intangible non-current assets*. There are standards on research and development (capitalization is allowed if the future benefits arising from these costs are expected beyond any reasonable doubt) and goodwill may be written off (to expense) or amortized over a period

Table 12.3 International Accounting Standards checklist

IAS	Australian practice

1 AASB 1001 conforms with regard to accounting policies.

AASB 1018 conforms to the extent IAS 1 addresses the statement of financial performance and disclosure of changes in equity other than those arising from transactions with owners in their capacity as owners, except that this Standard does not require revenues and expenses from ordinary activities to be separated between operating activities and non-operating activities.

AASB 1034 conforms to the extent of financial report presentation and disclosures (other than those covered in AASB 1018 and AASB 1040) except that IAS 1 requires a departure from an IAS when management concludes that compliance would be misleading and a departure is necessary to obtain a fair presentation.

AASB 1040 conforms to the extent that IAS 1 addresses the statement of financial position.

2 AASB 1019 conforms except for non-disclosure of cost of goods sold which will be addressed in a later Standard. (AASB 1018).

7 AASB 1026 conforms.

8 AASB 1001 conforms to the extent that IAS 8 addresses changes in accounting policies and AASB 1018 to the extent IAS addresses the statement of financial performance.

10 AASB 1002 conforms to the extent that IAS 10 addresses events occurring after reporting date, with one exception relating to an event after reporting date providing evidence the going concern basis is not appropriate. IAS 10 requires the financial effect of the event to be recognized in the financial report; AASB 1002 only requires the financial effect of the event to be disclosed.

11 AASB 1009 conforms.

12 The revised AASB 1020 due for implementation on 1 January 2005 conforms.

14 AASB 1005 conforms.

15 No similar Standard.

16 AASB 1021 conforms to the extent that IAS 16 addresses the recognition and depreciation of physical non-current assets which are expected to be used during more than one financial year.

AASB 1041 conforms with IAS 16 to the extent it addresses revaluations of, and disclosures relating to, non-current assets except that it:

(a) requires revaluation increments and revaluation decrements relating to assets within a class of non-current assets to be offset against one another;

(b) does not require disclosure of the carrying amount of revalued assets that would have been recognized had the cost basis of measuring assets been applied;

(c) does not require the disclosure of restrictions on the distribution to owners of the balance of the asset revaluation reserve (which are specified in the Standard for total non-current assets) to be made for each class of non-current assets.

17 AASB 1008 conforms.

18 AASB 1004 conforms.

19 AASB 1028 conforms except in relation to post employment benefits, some aspects of disclosure, the discount rate and the treatment of interest cost.

20 The AASB 1004 treatment of contributions as revenue is not in conformity with IAS 20.

Table 12.3 International Accounting Standards checklist (*continued*)

IAS	Australian practice

21   AASB 1012 conforms except that IAS 21:
  (a)   applies to foreign currency contracts not classified as hedges, although IAS 39 may be applied to those contracts; and
  (b)   requires that on disposal, or part disposal, of a foreign operation the balance in the foreign currency translation reserve relating to the disposal be recycled as a revenue or an expense in net profit or loss/result in the reporting period in which the disposal is recognized.

22   AASB 1024 conforms to the extent IAS 22 addresses the accounting for and disclosures about the initial recognition of business combinations, except that IAS 22:
  (a)   requires the uniting of interests method to be applied in certain rare circumstances;
  (b)   requires transaction costs arising on the issue of equity instruments to be included as part of the cost of acquisition where the equity instruments are issued as purchase consideration for a business combination; and
  (c)   includes requirements in relation to the recognition of certain liabilities as part of the initial recognition of a business combination.
  AASB 1013 conforms to the extent IAS 22 addresses accounting for goodwill except for the following:
  (a)   where an entity applies a period of amortization exceeding five years, it would be required to disclose a justification of the period adopted in order to comply with IAS 22 and only the straight line method of amortization is permitted;
  (b)   this Standard requires that a discount on acquisition be eliminated proportionately against the fair values of non-monetary assets and where the values of such non-monetary assets are reduced to zero, and remaining discount must be recognized as revenue;
  (c)   under this Standard, assets and liabilities acquired as part of a business acquisition which are identified and recognized subsequent to acquisition are accounted for by adjusting goodwill or discount on acquisition; and
  (d)   IAS 22 requires a reconcilation of movement in balances of goodwill, discount on acquisitions and related amortization during the financial year.

23   AASB 1036 conforms.

24   AASB 1017 conforms with the following exceptions:
  (a)   key management personnel are not directly included as related parties;
  (b)   authorized trustee corporations and fund managers are excluded as related parties where the relationship results solely from normal dealings; and
  (c)   disclosure of pricing policies not as extensive.

26   No AASB; however, AAS 25 is similar, except the IAS allows changes in net market values to be recognized as revenue only in certain specified cases.

27   AASB 1024 is similar.

28   AASB 1016 conforms with the the following exceptions:
  (a)   the cost method is to be applied in the investor's own financial report except where a consolidated financial report is not required to be prepared; and
  (b)   the carrying amount of the investment must not exceed its recoverable amount, however, how recoverable amount is to be determined is not specified.

29   No similar Standard.

Table 12.3 International Accounting Standards checklist (*continued*)

IAS	*Australian practice*

30 AASB 1032 conforms with the following exceptions:
   (a) where there are differences between the requirements of IAS 30 and IAS 32, this and other Standards conform with the requirements of IAS 32, rather than with the requirements of IAS 30; and
   (b) a parent entity need comply with only the basic profit and loss account and balance sheet disclosure requirements of this Standard when the parent entity's financial report is presented with the economic entity's financial report, and the economic entity's financial report applies with Standard.

31 AASB 1006 conforms.

32 AASB 1033 with the following exceptions:
   (a) the requirement to classify the component parts of compound instruments separately does not apply under this Standard to instruments issued prior to 1 January 1998; and
   (b) a parent entity's financial report is presented with the economic entity's financial report, and the economic entity's financial report applies the Standard.
   AASB 1014 conforms with the set-off criteria except that the Standard treats in-substance defeasances as extinguishing the liability when the prescribed conditions are satisfied.

33 AASB 1027 conforms except that it:
   (a) requires the following securities to be considered dilutive:
      (i) potential ordinary shares for which conversion to, calling of, or subscription for, ordinary share capital is mandatory; and
      (ii) potential ordinary shares for which conversion to, calling of, or subscription for, ordinary share capital is at the option of the entity and based on conditions at reporting date it is probable that the entity will successfully exercise its option at some time in the future;
   (b) specifically identifies an additive list of shares for the purpose of calculating diluted EPS; and
   (c) requires an entity that has undergone a major capital restructuring during the reporting period to disclosure of an additional basic EPS and, where applicable, diluted EPS, using an alternative denominator where this is more meaningful than the EPS information calculated in accordance with the other requirements of this Standard.

34 AASB 1029 conforms.

35 AASB 1042 conforms to the extent IAS 35 addresses annual financial reporting, except that:
   (a) IAS 35 prohibits a discontinuing operation from being classified as an extraordinary item; and
   (b) IAS 35 requires the amount of gain or loss before income tax expense (income tax revenue) recognized on the disposal of assets or settlement of liabilities attributable to each discontinuing operation to be disclosed on the face of the statement of financial performance.

36 No similar Standard. However, ED 99 'Impairment of Assets' conforms with the broad principles. Differences from IAS 36 are:
   (a) exploration and evaluation costs carried forward by entities in the extractive industries prior to the development stage are excluded;

Table 12.3 International Accounting Standards checklist (*continued*)

IAS	Australian practice

    (b)   recoverable amount is defined as the maximum amount an entity would rationally be prepared to pay for an asset, measured as fair value for an asset held for continuing use, and fair value less costs of disposal for an asset held for disposal. This differs from the AASB 1010 definition of recoverable amount;

    (c)   the recoverable amount test to be applied to individual assets;

    (d)   reversals of impairment losses for assets other than goodwill where there is evidence that the recoverable amount of the asset has risen above its carrying amount; and

    (e)   prohibition of the reversal of impairment losses for goodwill.

37   AASB 1044 conforms except in selected matters relating to derivatives (that are not financial guarantees), costs of disposal or retirement of long lived assets, criteria for recognition and set-off of expected recoveries of costs relating to provisions, sale of an operation, provision for restructuring and disclosures (timing and uncertainty).

38   No similar Standard. Topic is on the AASB agenda. AASB 1011 is similar for research and development costs.

39   No similar Standard. Draft IASC/JWG Standard on 'Financial Instruments' under discussion by the AASB.

40   No similar Standard.

41   AASB 1037 similar. However, IAS 41 scope narrow as excludes:

–   non-human living animals and plants that are not agricultural activities e.g. forests as carbon sinks, racing animals/birds and performing animals and,

–   non-human living assets other than animals and plats such as viruses and blood cells.

Leases of non-human living assets other than biological assets are covered under IAS 17 and biological asset leases are treated as operating leases in some cases.

There are also different disclosure requirements.

For a comprehensive discussion of differences between IASs and AASBs, see the *Australian Convergence Handbook* (2002).

---

no longer than 20 years. However, the introduction of the goodwill standard led to the development of a range of other intangible assets such as brand names and trademarks, patents, mastheads, television and radio licenses, copyrights, etc., in an effort to bypass the goodwill write-off rules. An exposure draft ED 49 'Accounting for Identifiable Intangible Assets' was issued with a tight asset definition and flexible amortization rules. There was strong opposition to the ED and it was withdrawn 'pending further international developments and the development of the measurement components of the Board's Conceptual Framework' (AARF and AASB Report, September 1994, p. 8).

While this matter is yet to be resolved 18 companies (27 in 1996) reported mastheads in the balance sheet with only 55% amortizing (Heazlewood and Ryan 1999, p. 312).

Concerns over the failure of companies to amortize intangibles led to the issue by the Boards of the first Accounting Interpretation, 'Amortisation of Identifiable Intangible Assets' (June 1999) and a strong pro-amortization stand being taken by the ASIC.

The goodwill debate has focused on the method and time period used to amortize goodwill. Companies appear to be using 20 years rather than reviewing the timeframe for which benefits are derived. Of greater concern was the adoption of the inverse sum of the years digits method of amortization, which minimizes the amount written off in the early years. While this technically complies with the standard, it is a clear abuse of the standard's intent and resulted in the UIG ruling against the method and an amendment made to the standard, which now only allows the straight-line method of amortization.

Tangible non-current assets are normally accounted for at cost (including all expenditure necessary to bring the assets into operation) and depreciated over their useful life. Although land is not depreciable, buildings are, and this has led to qualified audit reports in the past for non-compliance. While depreciation methods are not required to be disclosed around 80% of the top 150 companies did so with straight line being the favoured method (Ryan and Heazlewood 1997, p. 180).

The CL also allows non-current assets to be revalued and AASB 1041 specifies the accounting treatment for such revaluations, requiring the whole class of assets to be revalued, the credit to go direct to an asset revaluation reserve (except if a reversal), a debit to profit and loss account (except if a reversal) and a distinction to be made between assets stated at cost and revalued assets. AASB 1040 requires disclosures of assets and the categories into which they are to be classified. AASB 1010 deals with assets valued at their recoverable amount being 'the net amount that is to be recovered through the cash inflows and outflows arising from its continued use and subsequent disposal'. A statement must also be made as to whether the cash flows have been discounted in arriving at the recoverable amount.

There is no specific accounting standard dealing with *investments*. However, AASB 1040 requires their disclosure and classification into current and non-current categories and they are normally held at lower of cost or market value. Market values may also be disclosed in the notes for investments shown at cost. AASB 1023 para 23 requires that insurance companies measure their investments at net market value at balance date with changes in value being brought to account as revenue or expense in the financial year the changes occur.

For *inventories* the lower of cost and net realizable value is the recommended method and was used in 96% of cases by the top 150 companies while the predominant measures of cost were average cost (32%) and FIFO (42%) (Heazlewood and Ryan 1999, p. 167). Other allowable methods of assigning cost are specific identification and standard cost while the absorption cost method is prescribed for conversion costs.

Liabilities like assets are split in the balance sheet between current (maturing in less than one year) and non-current. While there is no standard on *pension* liabilities, AASB 1028 requires recognition in the accounts of all other employee entitlements at nominal value if due within 12 months, otherwise at the present value of the estimated future cash outflows.

All the top 150 companies applied the liability method of *deferred tax* accounting as prescribed by AASB 1020 with all except three disclosing permanent differences and their nature. Three-quarters of the companies disclosed both deferred tax liabilities and future income tax benefits nearly all of which were classified in the balance sheet as non-current or other (Heazlewood and Ryan 1999, pp. 175).

AASB 1020 was reissued in December 1999 and is not now operative until reporting periods beginning on or after 1 January 2005. The revised Standard takes a balance sheet approach to tax effect accounting compared with the current profit statement approach.

The main accounts of Australian companies are the *consolidated accounts* even though the individual accounts of the parent entity are also required. AASB 1024 specifies that each company required to apply the Standard present consolidated accounts for the economic entity of which it is the parent entity. The key requirement in determining a parent/ subsidiary relationship is control. 'Control means the capacity of an entity to dominate decision-making directly or indirectly, in relation to the financial and operating policies of another entity so as to enable that other entity to operate with it in pursuing the objectives of the controlling entity.' (AASB 1024 para 9)

The major problems with group accounts have concerned goodwill (see above) and the treatment of associate companies. A legal impediment which prevented the use of equity accounting for associates, was finally removed with the issue of AASB 1016 'Accounting for Investments in Associates' (August 1998) which prescribed the circumstances in which the equity accounting method is to be used together with appropriate disclosures. AASB 1015 prohibits the use of the pooling-of-interests method of consolidation. AASB 1006 requires that interests in *joint ventures* be brought to account by including (and disclosing) the venturer's share of assets, liabilities and expenses in the financial statements.

AASB 1012 specifies the accounting treatment for *foreign currency operations*. The standard requires that for foreign currency transactions the exchange gains or losses are recognized in the profit and loss statement (except for qualifying assets) and the financial results of foreign controlled entities are translated according to the level of autonomy exercised.

If the foreign operations are controlled by the reporting entity they are classed as integrated (non-independent) and the temporal rate is used. If they are self-sustaining (independent of the reporting entity) the current rate is used with exchange differences taken directly to a separate 'foreign' currency translation reserve in the shareholders' funds section of the balance sheet. Of the top 150 companies 71% reported foreign exchange operations, the majority being classified as self-sustaining and using the current rate (Heazlewood and Ryan 1999, p. 109).

AASB 1026 requires provision of relevant *cash flow* information about the operating activities and other activities of the entity. The direct method (showing gross cash inflows and outflows) is specified. The standard's appendix encourages the use of investing and financing activity categories.

Classification of interest and dividend cash flows has proved to be a contentious issue, discretion resting with the preparer (similar to IAS 7). The top 150 companies have generally followed the guidelines, with 85% disclosing interest received and paid as operating activities and 69% treating dividends received as operating activities and dividends paid as financing activities (Heazlewood and Ryan 1999, p. 225). The standard also requires a reconciliation of cash flows from operating activities to operating profit or loss (after tax). The definition of cash and cash equivalents is flexible, encompassing highly liquid investments, readily convertible to cash on hand at the investor's option and thus not subject to criticisms levelled at the UK standard.

Disclosures required in the *notes to the accounts* were previously prescribed in Schedule 5 CL and various accounting standards. A major change is removal of the prescribed format for the profit and loss statement (already covered in AASB 1018) and balance sheet AASB 1040. Implementation of AASB 1034, 'Information to be Disclosed in Financial Reports' has seen most disclosure requirements incorporated into the relevant accounting standards.

All the detailed information supporting the profit and loss statement and balance sheet is found in the notes together with prescribed disclosures such as depreciation and amortization amount, dividends, interest, audit (and non-auditing service) fees, executives' and directors' remuneration, amounts charged to provisions, contingent liabilities and capital commitments.

The notes also contain *segmental* disclosures called for by AASB 1005 covering turnover, operating result and net assets for each industry and geographical segment. Two-thirds of the top 150 companies provided segmental information with 74% disclosing industry segments and 77% geographical segments (Heazlewood and Ryan 1999, pp. 60–61).

Given the place of mining companies in the Australian economy, AASB 1022 specifies the method (area-of-interest) and a substantial range of disclosures dealing with exploration, evaluation and development costs when written off or capitalized.

In relation to *financial instruments*, AASB 1033, 'Presentation and Disclosure of Financial Instruments', first issued in December 1996 and reissued in October 1999 is based on the international standard (IAS 32).

Conclusion

The dominant players to emerge from the accounting regulation debate in Australia have been the ASX, ASIC and federal government. While legislative support has been given to accounting standards, the AASB composition has been broadened (with AARF losing its role as research and technical advisor). While the true and fair view has become subservient to accounting standards, the CL relief provisions remain intact. The ASIC has taken a hardline approach to granting relief for non-compliance with accounting standards, arguing that the amendments to the law were aimed at bringing about uniformity, consistency and comparability of accounting information and prevention of creative accounting practices.

With its Financial Statements Surveillance programme the ASIC has assumed in part a similar role to that of the UK Financial Reporting Review Panel to ensure compliance with law and accounting standards. The ASIC (with de facto government support) has pressed ahead with corporate governance requirements along the lines of the UK Cadbury Report and saw early success with the stepping down of the Chairman and Managing Director of Coles-Myer (Australia's tenth largest listed company) due to pressure by institutional investors over related party transactions. However, the regulation of corporate governance is again under review. New institutional arrangements for setting Australian accounting standards came into effect on 1 January 2000, with the replacement of Part 12 of the *Australian Securities and Investments Commission Act 1989* (ASIC Act) by a new Part 12 enacted as part of the legislative reform package contained in the *Corporate Law Economic Reform Program Act 1999*.

Changes still continue at a rapid rate. Following a series of High Court decisions in 1999, doubts were cast on the constitutional validity of the Corporations legislation. Further discussions between the Commonwealth and States resulted in the passing of the 'Corporations Act 2001'. This legislation re-enacted the eight separate Commonwealth, State and Territory corporations' laws as a single federal law. The major outcome of the legislation was to restore the corporations' jurisdiction of the Federal Court.

The Financial Reporting Council (FRC) in determining the AASB's broad strategic direction for 2001–02 placed it more in the context of the longer term objective of international convergence (rather than harmonization) of accounting standards, a direction strongly supported by the business sector on cost and competitiveness grounds. This resulted in the replacement of 'old' Policy statements 4 and 6 in April 2002 by new PS 4, 'International Convergence and Harmonization Policy', and provided the modus operandi for much of the AASB's work programme.

This focus on international convergence also continues with the UIG's review of each interpretation of the IASB's International Financial Reporting Interpretations Committee

(IFRIC). Where the UIG reaches a consensus view that the IFRIC interpretation is applicable to Australian reporting entities, a UIG Abstract will be issued on that matter.

In July 2002 the FRC announced that the AASB is obligated to work towards full implementation of International Accounting Standards in Australia as from 1 January 2005. This strategy was determined by the decision of the EU to require listed companies to prepare their consolidated accounts in accordance with IASB standards as from 1 January 2005.

Given that the AASB has responsibility for setting standards for 'not-for-profit-entities' many domestic standards will vary from those of the IASB. For example, AASB 1044 while based on IAS 37 has additional paragraphs dealing with issues unique to the not-for-profit public sector.

In terms of the accounting regulation framework, it appears that while Australia falls between associationism (as embodied by the UK) and corporatism (Sweden), the increasingly active role of the federal government and its agencies in the regulatory process clearly places Australia into the corporatism sector with its own unique government/professional body/business interaction.

Notes

1. CPA Australia was previously known as the Australian Society of CPAs (ASCPA) and before that the Australian Society of Accountants.
2. CPA Australia is the third largest recognized accounting professional body in the world.
3. The composition of the first board was seven members, a chairman, two nominees of the profession and four members from panels of names proposed by selected organizations with an interest in financial reporting.
4. Senior finance executives from the top 100 listed companies.
5. AASs are intended to apply to all reporting entities in the private or public sectors to which AASB Standards do not apply. AASB Standards are intended to apply to all companies that are reporting entities. Any limitation on the applicability of Accounting Standards would be stated in the text of specific Standards.

References

AASB/IASB (2002) *The Australian Convergence Handbook*, AASB, Melbourne.
ASCPA/ICAA (1993) *A Research Study on Financial Reporting and Auditing – Bridging the Expectation Gap*. Melbourne.
Australian Corporations and Securities Legislation (2002) CCH, Sydney.
Chambers, R.J., Sri Ranathan, T. and Rappaport, H.H. (1978) *Company Accounting Standards*. Report of the Accounting Standards Review Committee. Sydney.
CPA/ICAA (2002) *Accounting Handbook*. Prentice-Hall, Sydney.
Godfrey, J., Hodgson, A., and Holmes, S. (2000) *Accounting Theory* 4th edn. Wiley, Brisbane.
Heazlewood, C.T. and Ryan, J.B. (eds) (1999) *Australian Company Financial Reporting 1999*, Accounting Research Study No 15, AARF, ACAP (Inc), Melbourne.
Henderson, S. (1993) Financial Accounting in Australia – Retrospect and Prospect. *Accounting Forum* September: 4–18.
McGregor, W.J. (1989) The New Standard Bearer. *Charter* September: 48–49.
Parker, R.H., Peirson, C.G. and Ramsay, A.L. (1987) Australian accounting standards and the law. *Companies and Securities Law Journal* **5**(4, November): 231–245.

Peirson, C.G. (1990) *A Report on Institutional Arrangements for Accounting Standard Setting in Australia*. Australian Accounting Research Foundation, Melbourne.

Peirson, C.G. and Ramsay A.L. (1983) A review of the regulation of financial reporting in Australia. *Companies and Securities Law Journal*, vol. 1: 286–300.

Puxty, A.G., Willmott, H.C., Cooper, D.J. and Lowe, T. (1987) Modes of regulation in advanced capitalism: locating accounting in four countries. *Accounting, Organizations and Society* **12**: 273–291.

Rahman, A.R. (1991) Due process and user participation in standard setting. *Australian Accountant* June: 28–34.

Ryan, J. B. and Heazlewood, C.T. (1997) *Australian Company Financial Reporting 1997*. Accounting Research Study No. 14. AARF. ACAP (Inc), Melbourne.

Walker, R.G. and Robinson, S.P. (1994) Competing regulatory agencies with conflicting agendas: setting standards for cash flow /reporting in Australia. *Abacus* **30**(2): 119–137.

Further Reading

Gibson, R.W. (1971) *Disclosure by Australian Companies*. Melbourne University Press, Melbourne.

Miller, M. (1991) Shifts in the regulatory framework for corporate financial reporting. *Australian Accounting Review* **1**(2, November): 30–39.

Miller, M.C. (1994) Australia. In T.E. Cooke and R.H. Parker (eds) *Financial Reporting in the West Pacific Rim*. Routledge, London.

Miller, M.C. (1995) The credibility of Australian financial reporting: are the co-regulation arrangements working? *Australian Accounting Review* **5**(2, November): 3–16.

Nobes, C. and Parker, R.H. (2002) *Comparative International Accounting*, 7th edn. Prentice-Hall, London, Chapter 9.

Parker, R.H. (1989) *Accounting in Australia: Historical Essays*. Garland Publishing, Croydon.

Parker, R.H. (1989) Importing and exporting accounting: the British experience. In A.G. Hopwood (ed.) *International Pressures for Accounting Change*. Prentice-Hall, London.

Rahman, A.R. (1992) *The Australian Accounting Standards Review Board: The Establishment of its Participative Review Process*. Garland Publishing, New York.

Walker, R.G. (1992) Interaction between government and the profession in the regulation of financial reporting: The Australian experience. In M. Bromwich and A. Hopwood (eds) *Accounting and the Law*. Prentice-Hall, London, Chapter 8.

Walker, R.G. (1993) A feeling of deja vu: Controversies in accounting and auditing regulation in Australia. *Critical Perspectives on Accounting* **4**: 97–109.

Whittred, G., Zimmer, I. and Taylor, S. (2000) *Financial Accounting, Incentive Effects and Economic Consequences*, 5th edn. Harcourt, Sydney, Chapter 1.

Appendix 1

Figure 12.1   The Australian Accounting and Financial Reporting Regulatory Framework (prior to the CLERP reforms) *Source*: Adapted from Miller (1995) and PSI.

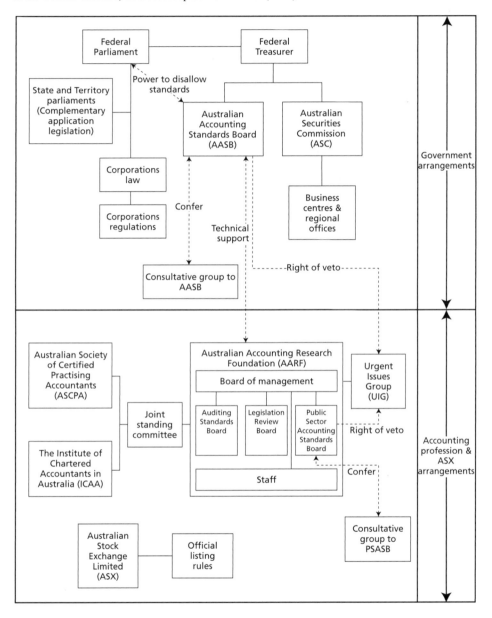

Appendix 2

Figure 12.2   New accounting standard-setting structure

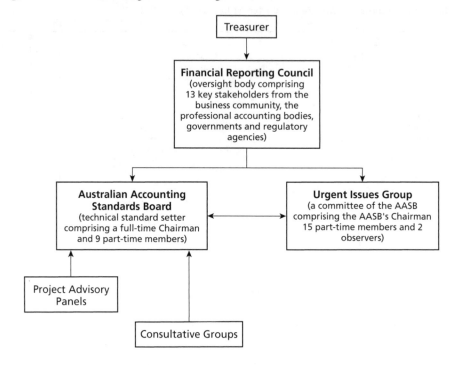

Federal Government's Corporate Law Economic Reform Program (CLERP)

In September 1997 the first CLERP, Proposals for Reform: Paper No. 1 'Accounting Standards – Building international opportunities for Australian business', was issued. This paper reviewed the accounting standard-setting process and made recommendations for change. The key reform proposals (for implementation in 1999) were:

- Setting up a Financial Reporting Council (FRC) (representative of a wide range of interests) to manage funding, appoint the AASC (Australian Accounting Standards Committee) and make recommendations on standard-setting issues to the Treasurer.

- An eight-member AASC to develop and issue standards with meetings open to the public.

- A full-time AASC chairman who will also chair the Urgent Issues Group (appointed by Treasurer).

- The Public Sector Accounting Standards Board to merge with the AASB to form the AASC.

- AASC to influence development of IASs with IASC exposure drafts to be issued as Australian exposure drafts from 1 January 1999.

- Setting up of an independent secretariat (not AARF) for the AASC.

All these reforms have been put in place with the passage of the 1999 CLERP Act, the only variation being the retention of the AASB title rather than AASC.

Appendix 3

Statement of financial performance

This appendix illustrates the format of the statment of financial performance, including the disclosure of non-owner changes in equity.

XYZ Limited

**Statement of Financial Performance
for the financial year ended 30 June 2000**

	Note	Consolidated 2000 $'000	1999 $'000
Revenues from ordinary activities		X	X
Expenses from ordinary activities, excluding borrowing costs expense		(X)	(X)
Borrowing costs expense		(X)	(X)
Share of net profits (losses) of associates and joint ventures accounted for using the equity method		X	(X)
Profit (loss) from ordinary activities before income tax expense (income tax revenue)		X	(X)
Income tax revenue (income tax expense) relating to ordinary activities		(X)	X
Profit (loss) from ordinary activities after related income tax expense (income tax revenue)	9	X	(X)
Profit (loss) from extraordinary items after related income tax expense (income tax revenue)	10	(X)	—
Net profit (loss)		X	(X)
Net profit (loss) attributable to outside equity interests		X	(X)
Net profit (loss) attributable to members of the parent entity	11	X	(X)
Increase (decrease) in asset revaluation reserve	12	X	(X)
Net exchange difference on translation of financial report of self-sustaining foreign operations	13	(X)	X
Increase (decrease) in retained profits on adoption of a new Standard	11	(X)	X
Total revenues, expenses and valuation adjustments attributable to members of the parent entity and recognized directly in equity		X	X
Total changes in equity other than those resulting from transactions with owners as owners	14	X	X
Basic earnings per share		X	(X)
Diluted earnings per share		X	(X)
Dividends per share		X	X

Statements of financial position

This Appendix illustrates the format of the consolidated statements of financial position using the current/non-current and the liquidity presentations.

1. Current/non-current presentations

XYZ Limited
Statement of Financial Position as at 30 June 2000

	Note	Consolidated 2000 $'000	1999 $'000
Current Assets			
Cash assets		X	X
Receivables		X	X
Inventories		X	X
Property, plant and equipment	8	X	X
Other		X	X
Total Current Assets		X	X
Non-Current Assets			
Other financial assets		X	X
Property, plant and equipment	8	X	X
Intangible assets		X	X
Deferred tax assets		X	X
Other		X	X
Total Non-Current Assets		X	X
Total Assets		X	X
Current Liabilities			
Payables		X	X
Interest-bearing liabilities	16	X	X
Current tax liabilities		X	X
Provisions		X	X
Other		X	X
Total Current Liabilities		X	X
Non-Current Liabilities			
Interest-bearing liabilities	16	X	X
Deferred tax liabilities		X	X
Provisions		X	X
Other		X	X
Total Non-Current Liabilities		X	X
Total Liabilities		X	X
Equity			
Contributed equity		X	X
Reserves		X	X
Retained profits		X	X
Parent Entity Interest		X	X
Outside Equity Interest		X	X
Total Equity		X	X

Note: Entities may disclose other assets, liabilities and items of equity in addition to those specified in Section 7 of this Standard. Entities may also choose to provide additional sub-totals.

2. Liquidity presentation

ABC Consolidated Limited
Statement of Financial Position as at 30 June 2000

	Note	Consolidated 2000 $'000	1999 $'000
Assets			
Cash assets		X	X
Receivables		X	X
Inventories		X	X
Investment securities		X	X
Deferred tax assets		X	X
Other assets		X	X
Property, plant and equipment		X	X
Intangible assets		X	X
Total Assets		X	X
Liabilities			
Payables		X	X
Current tax liabilities		X	X
Provisions		X	X
Other liabilities		X	X
Deferred tax liabilities		X	X
Long-term interest-bearing liabilities		X	X
Total Liabilities		X	X
Equity			
Contributed equity		X	X
Reserves		X	X
Retained profits		X	X
Parent Entity Interest		X	X
Outside Equity Interest		X	X
Total Equity		X	X

Appendix 4

Table 12.4   UIG Abstracts – 31 December 2002

Abstract	Title	Issued (re-issued #)
–	Foreword to Urgent Issues Abstracts	9/02
1	Lessee Accounting for Surplus Space Under a Non-Cancellable Operating Lease	6/95
2	Accounting for Non-Vesting Sick Leave	6/95
3	Lessee Accounting for Lease Incentives Under a Non-Cancellable Operating Lease	8/95
4	Disclosure of Accounting Policies for Restoration Obligations in the Extractive Industries	8/95
6	Accounting for Acquisitions – Deferred Settlement of Cash Consideration	12/95
7	Accounting for Non-Current Assets – Derecognition of Intangible Assets and Change in the Basis of Measurement of a Class of Assets	3/96
8	Accounting for Acquisitions – Recognition of Restructuring Costs as Liabilities	6/96
9	Accounting for Acquisitions – Recognition of Acquired Tax Losses	6/96
10	Accounting for Acquisitions – Gold Mining Companies	11/96
11	Accounting for Contributions of, or Contributions for the Acquisition of, Non-Current Assets	12/96
12	Accounting for the Costs of Modifying Computer Software for the Year 2000	4/97
13	The Presentation of the Financial Report of Entities Whose Securities are 'Stapled'	# 5/00
14	Directors' Remuneration	6/97
15	Early Temination of Foreign Currency Hedges	# 12/00
16	Accounting for Share Buy-Backs	1/98
17	Developer and Customer Contributions in Price Regulated Industries	5/98
18	Early Temination of Gold Hedges	# 12/00
19	The Superannuation Contributions Surcharge	7/98
20	Equity Accounting – Elimination of Unrealised Profits and Losses on Transactions with Associates	10/98
21	Consistancy – Different cost Formulas for Inventories	10/98
22	Accounting for the Buy-Back of No Par Value Shares	11/98
23	Transaction Costs Arising on the Issue or Intended Issue of Equity Instruments	# 6/00
24	Equity Accounting – Carrying Amount of an Investment in an Associate	11/98
25	Redesignation of Hedges	# 12/00
26	Accounting for Major Cyclical Maintenance	6/99
27	Designation as Hedges – Sold (Written) Options	7/99
28	Consolidation – Special Purpose Entities	7/99
29	Early Temination of Interest Rate Swaps	# 12/00
30	Depreciation of Long-Lived Physical Assets, including Infrastructure Assets: Condition-Based Depreciation and Other Related Methods	1/00

Table 12.4 UIG Abstracts – 31 December 2002 (*continued*)

Abstract	Title	Issued (re-issued #)
31	Accounting for the Goods and Services Tax (GST)	1/00
32	Designation as Hedges – Rollover Strategies	12/00
33	Hedges of Anticipated Purchases and Sales	5/00
34	Acquisitions and Goodwill – First-Time Application of Accounting Standards	6/00
35	Disclosure of Contingent Liabilities	8/00
36	Non-Monetary Contributions Establishing a Joint Venture Entity	12/00
37	Accounting for Website Costs	1/01
38	Contributions by Owners Made to Wholly-Owned Public Sector Entities	1/01
39	Effect of Proposed Tax Consolidation Legislation on Deferred Tax Balances	# 9/02
40	Non-Reciprocal Transfers Within an Economic Entity for Monetary or No Consideration	9/01
41	Fair Value of Equity Instruments Issued as Purchase Consideration	9/01
42	Subscriber Acquistion Costs in the Telecommunications Industry	10/01
43	Classification of Financial Instruments with Conversion Options	11/01
44	Acquisition of In-Process Research and Development	3/02
45	Subsidiary Becomes a Joint Venture Entity or an Associate	4/02
46	Initial Foreign Currency Translation for Re-domiciled Entities	4/02
47	Professional Indemnity Claims Liabilities in Medical Defence Organisations	6/02
48	Status of Tax Consolidation Legislation	7/02
49	Revenue – Barter Transactions Involving Advertising Services	8/02
50	Evaluating the Substance of Transactions Involving the Legal Form of a Lease	9/02
51	Recovery of Unfunded Superannuation of Universities	12/02
52	Income Tax Accounting under the Tax Consolidation System	12/02

Accounting in Scandinavia

Kristina Artsberg and Hans R. Schwencke

Scandinavia is understood here to include the following countries: Denmark, Finland, Iceland, Norway and Sweden. These countries are more correctly called the Nordic countries – from a strict geographical point of view, the Scandinavian countries are only Norway and Sweden. However, in order not to confuse the Nordic countries with other northern countries they are most often called the Scandinavian countries. The Scandinavian countries are often treated as a group since they share a common history and are culturally close to each other. As far as accounting is concerned, they have many similar attributes. The approach of this chapter is to focus on the general characteristics of Scandinavian accounting, with the specifics of the individual countries mentioned as necessary within this general framework.

Accounting in Scandinavia has changed over time and is still changing significantly. The Scandinavian countries are small ones, heavily dependent on international trade and capital. Since accounting follows trade and capital there is a need to adapt accounting to different international settings, and, as this book demonstrates, there is more than one accounting model in the world. The Scandinavian countries, involved in trade all over the world, have to adapt to this pluralistic environment.

The cultural, political and economic environment

It is important to understand culture and ways of thinking as part of understanding the context which is necessary to interpret different phenomena correctly. This insight has been gained through far too many misunderstandings, and this is true not only for accounting.

The Scandinavian languages are all different, with different grammatical structures. Despite this, it is quite possible for Scandinavians to understand each other since the languages are so close to each other. For example, there are only some 500 words that are completely different between Danish and Swedish. The Finnish language is quite different, but this is most often not any problem in communications between Scandinavians since many Finns speak good Swedish. Most Scandinavians speak English fluently and have also learnt one or two other foreign languages at school, probably German and French. Before World War II, German was the first language learnt in school; therefore many elderly persons still speak German fluently.

Cultural influences often come with language. Before World War II, the German influence on Scandinavia was considerable, but since then the American influence has dominated. One has to go far back in history to trace French influence. The Scandinavian countries have also influenced each other; this influence is often more difficult to trace since it has been reciprocal.

Although there is today a friendly relationship (which is only sometimes disturbed by minor incidents) among the Scandinavian countries, historically it has not always been so. There were frequent wars (particularly between Denmark and Sweden). Finland was part of Sweden for almost 700 years, up until 1812 when Sweden lost Finland to Russia. Finland became independent from Russia in 1917. Although Finland was a part of Russia for 100 years accounting has not been influenced by Russia. Norway belonged to Denmark for almost 300 years between 1537 and 1814, as did Iceland through its union with Norway during that period. Norway was then forced into a union with Sweden between 1814 and 1905. Parts of present Sweden have belonged to Denmark from time to time before the final peace between Denmark and Sweden in 1658.

The Scandinavian countries are comparatively large in area, particularly if compared to their populations which are small, with altogether 25 million inhabitants. This of course influences the way of living and acting. In Scandinavia interaction between people is informal. Since the countries have a long tradition as developed democracies, and relatively few inhabitants, consensus seeking, openness and participation are key words to describe change processes, not least in statutory terms. Consensus rather than conflict is of course important in international contacts for small countries, but it is also a common way of behaving in internal processes within the Scandinavian countries. For example, the right of co-determination for employees is of Scandinavian origin. Another distinctive feature is the right for every person to have access to all public documents (even those concerning individual cases as long as they have not been stamped as secret material, which is not commonly the case).

Finland and Iceland are republics whereas Denmark, Norway and Sweden are monarchies; Denmark is the oldest monarchy in the world. Today the monarchs have no power, only representational duties. Power rests with the parliaments in all countries and governments are based on majority support in parliament. The head of the government is the prime minister. Legislation is proposed by governments, but must be enacted by parliaments. Governments can issue governmental orders which have lesser status than laws.

Denmark, Finland and Sweden are members of the European Union, but Iceland and Norway are not. Denmark has been a member since 1973. Finland and Sweden joined in 1995. As far as accounting is concerned, there is no difference whether or not a particular country is a member of the EU since in 1992 the trade organization EFTA (at that time Norway, Finland, Iceland and Sweden were members) made an agreement with the EU (EAA agreement) that included, among other things, the obligation for EFTA countries to incorporate the European directives on accounting into their legislation.

The judicial systems in Scandinavia are somewhere between the German and the British systems. The laws are not as detailed as in Germany, but more detailed than in the UK. In reaching interpretations of the law, the preparatory work done on a statute has been important and the courts are not as free as in Britain to reach an independent conclusion based purely on the wording of the statute. Generally, there is a strong emphasis on law and regulations, and the involvement of the state, although there are important exceptions. Salary negotiations and other work-related issues are examples of exceptions where the state is generally unwilling to intervene.

Financial policy has been explicitly based on economic theory. This has particularly been the case in Finland and Sweden. The governments wanted to take control of the economy, regulating and guiding it, in order first to plan the war economy and later to plan the welfare state that began to grow after the war. Economic policy was at that time based on Keynesian theory where the state intervened with contra-cyclical policy; this had an impact on accounting, which will be explained later. In the middle of the 1980s there was a shift amongst economists away from the domination of Keynesian theory to Friedman's theories.

Without being much debated, a new agenda was adopted and aimed to deregulate the financial markets, which earlier had been carefully controlled. It turned out to be a too rapid change, with the effect being the bank crises that struck Scandinavia at the end of the 1980s and beginning of the 1990s, costing taxpayers a lot of money. At the same time the Scandinavian countries went into a period of deep recession. The former welfare state was questioned, not in the first place ideologically, but on economic grounds. It was not possible to finance the welfare programmes when fewer people paid taxes and so many more needed the benefits of the state. The Scandinavians had to reconsider and start reducing benefits (Norway was the exception because of oil revenues) and cannot any longer be said to have an outstanding welfare programme, at least not compared to other European countries. By the end of the century, the Scandinavian countries were recovering. In Sweden and Finland the information technology industry has stimulated the economy.

However, the governments in Scandinavia have experienced a decline in power. One reason for this is slower economic growth since the 1970s (again except for Norway). One way to stimulate the economy is to have a more productive private sector and therefore private initiatives have been encouraged. Even if the Scandinavian countries have a tradition of strong, interventionist governments, one should be careful not to overstress the uniqueness of this. It must not be forgotten that they are also strong market economies.

Compared to Britain and even continental Europe, the Scandinavian countries were relatively late to be industrialized. Even in the late nineteenth century Scandinavia was mainly a farming area. Many people emigrated to America because of crop failures at this time. It was not until the turn of the century that industrialization started, but then it evolved quickly. One reason for the rapid industrialization was the good fortune of the Scandinavian countries not to suffer major economic damage during either of the world wars. They were able to benefit from post-war reconstruction demand and industrialization advanced particularly during the 1950s and 1960s, with people migrating to Scandinavia.

Today the Scandinavian countries are dependent upon international trade and co-operation. With a high level of specialization and small home markets, foreign trade is very important. External trade accounts for more than 30% of GNP, with trade between Scandinavian countries forming the largest slice of this while its major trade partners outside Scandinavia are Germany, the UK, the USA and France.

However, there are sectors that have been sealed off from international influences. In Scandinavia, as elsewhere, there was a political will to keep certain sectors under national control, which was achieved through regulation. For example, the financial sector, both banking and the stock market, were for a long time regulated extensively. It was not possible to raise domestic capital for foreign investments, and as a consequence companies that wanted to expand abroad had to find alternative financing. The solution often chosen was to be listed on foreign stock markets. Scandinavian companies also made a significant number of acquisitions in Europe and the United States during the 1980s, to be sure of having access to these markets. Later, when the Scandinavian markets were deregulated, foreign capital found its way there and in several cases built controlling positions in Scandinavian companies.

The structure of business varies somewhat from country to country within Scandinavia. In Denmark, Iceland and Norway, industry is dominated by small and medium-sized companies, while in Finland and Sweden industry is dominated by large multinational companies. One reason for the difference is the type of industrial activity: the larger companies in Finland and Sweden can be explained by a concentration of more capital-intensive heavy industry, whereas in Denmark, Iceland and Norway the industry is lighter, with a concentration in food processing.

Before 1980, the stock markets played a relatively small role in financing industry. Companies were family owned or financed by the banks, and self-financing had also been encouraged by the tax systems. At the end of the 1970s, a period when welfare provision was still growing, the banks were not able to meet all business requirements and the governments also became more concerned about increasing tax revenues, creating a need for equity financing. In all Scandinavian countries the stock markets expanded considerably in the 1980s. Despite this, the banks are still the most important source of finance for Scandinavian companies, either directly through loans or indirectly through equity holdings. Despite strong state management of the economy, there are not many state-owned companies.

Universities, business schools and theories

Accounting has economic consequences. Despite or maybe because of that, normative statements in accounting are often based on theory. There is a need for theory to make it possible to find solutions that are consistent and therefore can persuade and hopefully be accepted. What kind of role has accounting theory played in Scandinavia, and what kind of theory has been influential?

Higher accounting education (i.e. in colleges and universities) started in 1909 in Scandinavia when the Stockholm School of Economics was founded. There was a need for teachers of course, and with no domestic tradition of higher education in accounting, the business schools had to go abroad to find the first professors. At that time it was most natural to go to Germany. Therefore the first professors were Germans or people educated in Germany and the teaching material used was German, even written in German. This German influence lasted at least until World War II, and in some places even longer. In the 1960s there was a shift to American theory. The students could no longer read German, at least not as fluently as English, and American textbooks started to be used all over Scandinavia. This shift took place without any debate. A similar shift from German to American influence can be seen in accounting practice and in accounting standards, but later. So a not too bold guess is that theory does have a role to play in accounting change, but it takes time. The change in practice is lagging behind the change in theory by about 10–20 years; at least this is how it can be seen in Scandinavia.

Although the Scandinavian countries have mostly taken their theoretical influences from other countries, especially Germany and the USA, it is also possible to see influential academic writers who have developed unique national theories, such as Palle Hansen in Denmark, and Martti Saario in Finland.

Professor Palle Hansen introduced marginal costing for inventory valuation and profit measurement in the 1958 edition of a handbook of accounting. The handbook was much used in practice and the marginal costing technique became so widespread that at the end of the 1960s it replaced absorption costing (not only in management accounting but also in financial accounting). The spread from theory to practice was unusually fast in this case, due to the fact that a professor wrote a book that was used by those already in practice. The theory was developed at a time when the Danish economy was dominated by nationally oriented companies.

The theory of Professor Martti Saario was not so much a totally new technique but rather a way to give theoretical rigour to techniques that were seen as economically desirable. Saario started to develop his expenditure–revenue theory after World War II (see Näsi

1995). Saario was influenced by the German academics Schmalenbach, Walb, Rieger and Kosiol and his theory is based strictly on the historical cost concept and the realization principle. The economic consequence of this theory was rapid depreciation of assets, which was supported by the Finnish government since there was a need to build up Finnish industry after the war. Large depreciation charges allowed the companies to retain cash instead of distributing it. The legislation in Finland and also other norms were built on the theory. The theory continues to dominate; even the Finnish incorporation of the EC directives has been discussed in the light of the Saario theory. The dominance of the theory contributed to the long-lasting German influence in Finland. Most Finns believe that it is possible still to use this national theory and at the same time adapt to the present international movements in accounting.

The Danish and Finnish examples illustrate how individual academics can influence accounting practice. There are other influential academics in Scandinavia, not with their own comprehensive theories, but with positions on standard-setting committees and as investigators preparing new legislation. It is difficult to judge the influence of all academics through their participation in the ongoing debate and through their teaching and writing.

Legal and institutional basis of accounting regulation

Accounting in Scandinavia is regulated in a number of ways. Since the beginning of the twentieth century it has been regulated by law and governmental orders. A specific feature of Scandinavian accounting legislation has been the reference to 'good accounting practice'. By using this concept the legislator leaves preparers with a comparatively important role in the development of accounting. Starting in the 1950s, private sector organizations, particularly the auditors, started to formulate standards which were first careful interpretations of the legislation and, later, also guidelines for the development of accounting. In the middle of the 1970s there appeared a new kind of standard-setter with a mixture of private and public sector representatives, known as 'corporatist organizations'. Different state agencies also issue some accounting rules, in particular the tax authorities.

Accounting and company legislation

The legislative process starts when a government commission is appointed to discuss and investigate in depth the topic for which legislation is contemplated. The commission prepares an analysis and proposal for legislation which is then widely exposed for comment from interested organizations. Accounting legislation affects quite a number of interest groups since accounting is used for many purposes in Scandinavia. The main groups consulted are tax authorities, statistical agencies, employees, stock markets, banks and other creditors, business contacts and the public in general. Representatives for all these groups together with technical experts such as academics, auditors, accountants, and civil servants and the representatives of the preparers are invited to give their opinions.

The commission report, together with the comments on it, are then considered by the government and a proposal for legislation put forward. Since the government generally has a majority in parliament, there should normally not be any problem in the proposal being passed. Lobbying parliament against the proposal is not common, because of the opportunity to give input in earlier stages of the process. As indicated above, there is an approach of consensus seeking in Scandinavia and therefore significant interest groups are heard.

It is often said that the accounting legislation in Scandinavia provides only a general framework. It is true that there are general rules for the valuation of current and fixed assets, but there are also specific rules for some items, for example goodwill and research and development. It is in fact sensible to compare the present accounting statutes with the Fourth EC directive since the Scandinavians have mainly been faithful in implementing the European directives, which was not that difficult since the previous legislation was not too different. Some disclosure rules have been added to the existing legislation, and also general principles have been taken into the law where previously they were only to be found in the preparatory work to the legislation, and therefore had a lower level of authority. The Scandinavian statutes do not contain as many options as the directives, since the legislator has, unlike the UK for example, to a great extent chosen between options. The law does not deal with every accounting topic. Where there is no specific rule, the general valuation rules and principles should be applied. In Scandinavia the legislation is seen as providing a framework only, which means that the legislator assumes that certain topics will be determined outside the law, an issue that will be discussed later.

An interesting point concerning the legislative process is that Scandinavians generally interpret the law along the same lines as the Germans, i.e. the will and intent of the legislator have an important bearing, and therefore, the documents issued during the preparatory stages (the commission report and the draft law) of legislation are relevant. For example, researchers and writers, as can be seen in this chapter, rely to a great extent on these to explain and analyse the law. It seems as if the judicial process in the EU is somewhat different, which may well affect the Scandinavians in the future.

Although there are very old public documents with requirements for keeping accounts,[1] specific accounting laws were first passed at the end of the nineteenth century. The obligation to keep accounts became a matter of public interest when the limited liability company became a common business vehicle. However, it was not the information needs of investors that was seen as important for the legislator but rather the need to protect creditors.

Legal rules concerning accounting were first seen in Companies Acts in Sweden and Norway.

In Sweden there was a government order (strongly influenced by French legislation) for companies as early as 1848. The first company law dates from 1895 and this was influenced more by German statutes. Norway enacted legal rules in 1874. Denmark set up a commission in 1901, which produced a proposal for a Companies Act, the content of which reflected influence from Norway and Sweden as well as Germany and the UK. However, because of a scandal involving Alberti, the Minister of Justice, in 1908, it took six proposals before the first Companies Act was passed by the Danish parliament in 1917. This Act included two sections on accounting, but the very first regulation of accounting in Denmark was the Accounting Act of 1912. Finland enacted accounting regulations in 1925.

All these early laws were very general in nature with relatively few clauses. The main objective was to make sure that the companies did keep accounts, and that these accounts were made public. How the accounts should be prepared was hardly regulated at all, except for general expressions such as 'showing a true position at the best estimate of management' (which should not be confused with the British 'true and fair' concept).

Apart from being influenced by France, the UK and especially Germany, the Scandinavians have often looked to each other for inspiration in their legislation. In addition to informal influence, there started in 1934 a formal attempt to harmonize company legislation with the objective of creating a common Nordic market. After eight years of discussions, a common proposal for legislation was published in 1942, but this proposal never reached the statute book because of the war. Sweden, the country least affected by the war, changed its company law in 1944 largely as a result of a financial scandal (Krueger). One important change was to require group accounts, something envisaged in the 1942 proposal.

The harmonization effort was renewed in 1962, and there was a new proposal for companies legislation in 1969. Denmark was the first country to enact this, in 1973. Sweden followed in 1975 and Norway in 1976 with very similar laws. In 1978 Iceland passed a company law that was almost entirely a copy of the Danish statutes. Because of an internal debate about the advantage of Scandinavian cooperation compared to a unique national theory then applied, it was 1981 before Finland enacted a statute based on the common Scandinavian proposal. Ironically enough, in the very year when this harmonization project at last seemed to have reached its goal, Denmark changed Scandinavian harmonization for EU harmonization. It again changed its Companies Act in order to adopt the Fourth Directive. Denmark had joined the EU in 1973 and was at that time the only Scandinavian country that was a member. Today, the Scandinavian countries have again come closer to each other since Finland, Iceland, Norway and Sweden have also adapted their legislation to the European directives. This will be described later.

Current accounting legislation

In the past it has usually been the case that accounting laws were applicable to all business forms. The basic accountability concept has followed the French one that everyone who runs a business should produce accounts. For some sectors such as banks and insurance companies, there is specific legislation that departs somewhat from the norm.

Accounting legislation (see Table 13.1) in all Scandinavian countries is today adjusted to the European directives. When Danish legislation incorporated the Fourth Directive in 1981 it changed the way in which the statutes were organized. Because the number of paragraphs increased significantly the accounting rules for companies that were in a section in the Companies Act were taken out into a specific Financial Statements Act. This Act was amended with adoption of the Seventh Directive in 1990. However, the more detailed technical matters about group accounting were put into a government order that can more easily be changed.

In 2001, Denmark enacted a new Accounting Act. This act is the first 'second generation' implementation of the EC accounting directives. (The first Danish implementation

Table 13.1   The most important contemporary accounting legislation in the Scandinavian countries

Country	Legislation
Denmark	1998 Bookkeeping Act
	2001 Financial Statements Act
Finland	1997 Accounting Act
	1997 Companies Act
Norway	1998 Accounting Act
Sweden	1999 Bookkeeping Act
	1995 Financial Statements Act

was in 1981.) The new Danish act does not seem to follow the directives meticulously, and is more oriented towards IASB rules, which is logical as IASB standards will become obligatory within the EU from 2005. As an example of the IASB orientation, the Danish act explicitly defines assets and liabilities in accordance with the IASB framework.

Finland has maintained the tradition of specifying some of the accounting rules in the Companies Act. The 1978 Companies Act was amended in 1991. The Fourth and Seventh Directives were adopted in 1992 with an amendment to the 1973 Accounting Act. These Acts were amended again in 1997. Sweden, however, while incorporating the EC directives in 1995 followed the Danish model and eliminated the accounting section in the Companies Act and instead created a new specific Financial Statements Act, while retaining the old Bookkeeping Act of 1976. The Accounting Act was amended in 1999. The Bookkeeping Act was amended in 1999. The different laws are applicable in the same way as in Denmark.

As with the Danish 1981 Act, both Finland and Sweden have followed the EC directives quite meticulously. Denmark had the advantage, compared with Finland and Sweden, of having taken part in the process of negotiating the directives and therefore had its unique model of contribution margin accepted by the EU. Sweden discussed whether it was in conformity with the EC directives still to use a balance sheet with untaxed reserves (discussed below) and eventually included such a category, although the EU formats obviously do not have one. Finland was concerned whether or not its unique expenditure–revenue theory could work alongside the EU rules. It finally adopted the EU concepts but also kept the essential concepts of the expenditure–revenue theory. The question to be resolved in the future is how successfully this will work.

Iceland and Norway incorporated the accounting directives in 1994 and 1998 respectively. While Denmark, Finland and Sweden have followed the directives closely, the two non-members, Iceland and Norway, are taking a much more independent attitude. After the government commission in Norway published its proposal for new legislation in 1995, it became clear that in Norway the influence of the IASB is stronger than that of the EU. The commission is largely recommending a market value oriented accounting model, but this was not a unanimous recommendation and since the report was published, there has been a debate, where critics have claimed that the Act is not faithful to the EC directives in all respects.

Influence of taxation

With the introduction of income tax in Scandinavia at the beginning of this century, the computation of taxable income was linked to the commercial accounts, in exactly the same way as was established in Germany. The description of the '*Massgeblichkeitsprinzip*' in Chapter 4 also serves to describe the system as it was introduced and developed in the Scandinavian countries. Since the tax authorities demanded a well organized accounting system, company accounting was improved, especially that of the smaller and medium-sized companies. Tax assessment was built upon the accruals concept and helped ensure a more rapid spread of the practice, replacing a cash basis.

The capital market was insufficient to finance the growing business sector, and therefore the state decided to use the tax system to encourage self-financing by allowing companies to create untaxed reserves. Tax rules were developed that fixed the lowest permitted valuation of net assets. Since the object of the accounting legislation was to protect creditors, the normal accounting rules determined the highest permitted valuation of net assets, thereby leaving companies parameters within which they could choose the most 'suitable' value. Generally companies have opted for the lowest values, set by the tax legislation.

Because of the link between tax and accounting, this choice had to be reflected in the commercial accounts in order to be tax deductible.

Consequently the accounting profit of the year was affected by tax rules. Inventory could, for example, be valued down even to negative values. Depreciation rates on equipment and machinery could be as much as 30% a year on book value. In addition to permitting undervaluation of assets, another technique was to allow an additional charge of 30% of the year's salaries. Companies that were growing and investing could in particular reduce tax payments considerably by taking advantage of all these incentives. Although there were high nominal tax rates of up to 60%, taxable income was so reduced by all these deductions that the effective tax rates (calculated on the income before creation of untaxed reserves) were normally as low as 20–30%.

The tax deductions were conditional upon being reflected in commercial profit, not least so that it should not be possible for the company to distribute untaxed profits. Foreign readers of Scandinavian annual reports were confused by these tax items. When adopting the Fourth Directive in 1981, the Danes discussed how this confusion should be removed, and they decided to split the link between accounting and taxation. The question of the link between accounting and taxation was hotly debated during the 1980s in the other countries, but it was not abolished. Iceland and Norway followed Denmark in the early 1990s in breaking the link. In the Scandinavian countries there were major tax reforms towards the end of the 1980s and beginning of the 1990s, with the object of lowering nominal tax rates (to 25–30%) and broadening the tax base. The number of special tax rules was reduced. However, excess depreciation is still allowed, there are also some kinds of reserves left, but the influence of tax policy has decreased.

Other standard-setters

The legislation in Scandinavia does not give detailed answers to all accounting problems and therefore complementary guidelines exist. Apart from the tax authorities, the auditors' institutes have the longest tradition of issuing these. More recently, standard-setting organizations which involve other interest groups have replaced the work done solely by the auditors. The standard-setting environment in Scandinavia today may, to an outsider, look rather complicated, with several organizations working in parallel. A particular feature of this environment is the existence of corporatist institutions, to which governments appoint representatives (the term corporatist is used here to denote institutions under state control but involving private sector groups). The involvement of the state in the standard-setting is increasing. For an overview of the different standard-setters see Table 13.2.

The term standard is used in this chapter since it is an internationally established term. However, these organizations cannot pronounce standards in, for example, the US way, meaning that they have to be followed by companies using generally accepted accounting principles (GAAP). A more correct word might be guideline or recommendation. The authority of these rules lies primarily in their power to convince or as evidence of agreed best practice; they are not legally binding (not even if they are pronounced by a Ministry or a state agency).

In all Scandinavian countries the auditors were the first to take the initiative to develop standards. They had been giving their opinion informally for a long time. The Swedish auditors' body (Föreningen Auktoriserade Revisorer – FAR) was the first of the Scandinavian institutes formally to set standards for good accounting practice. These standards were developed by their accounting committee, which was set up as a private initiative in 1964 after the model used in the USA. About 10 years later, in the middle of the 1970s, the Finnish, Icelandic and Norwegian professional bodies followed with their own standard-setting organizations. In Denmark, the auditors' body first translated the IASC standards as a substitute for national standards. However, since they did not have as much effect as the auditors had hoped, the Danes also set up an accounting committee in 1986.

For a long time the standard-setting committees of the auditing bodies were quite successful. The committees were small (with no more than eight members) and work was conducted informally without a large research staff (such as the US FASB has, for example). The committee members had both practical experience and an interest in theory. When one considers that the members were part-time volunteers, one must be impressed by the standards they produced. The standard-setting process was similar to the American 'due process'. Different drafts were first published for discussions and comment from outside, but the final standards were the subject of a decision by the boards of the institutes.

FAR, the Swedish body, published 20 standards developed by its accounting committee in the period 1957–1988. The Finnish body (Keskuskauppakamarin hyväksymä tilintarkastaja-yhdistys – KHT) never published any standards of its own but issued guidelines based on IASC standards, especially before its accounting standards board (see below) was established in 1974. The Norwegian institute (Den norske Revisorforening (DnR)) published 17 standards between 1978 and 1988. The Icelandic institute (Félag löggiltra endurskodenda – FLE) published 18 standards between 1976 and 1988. The Danish institute (Foreningen af Statsautoriserede Revisorer – FSR) started to issue standards in 1988.

The authority of these standards was fairly unproblematic until the middle of the 1980s but then preparers started to deviate from them. Therefore, towards the end of the 1980s and the beginning of the 1990s, in Denmark, Iceland, Norway and Sweden, standard-setting was taken over by organizations with different interest groups involved. When Swedish companies started to deviate from the standards issued by FAR, the auditors took the initiative to establish the Redovisningsrådet (RR = the Accounting Council) with representatives from FAR, industry and Bokföringsnämnden (BFN = the Accounting Standards Board, see below). Industry refused, at first, to participate but was finally persuaded to cooperate. The RR replaced FAR but the BFN has continued to work in parallel. Today, the BFN has withdrawn from participation in RR as they have been given a new role by the legislator. The BFN now has overall responsibilty for standard-setting, i.e. the BFN supervises the work of the RR. The RR issues standards for public companies,

Table 13.2 Summary of the different standard-setting organizations in Scandinavia (both historical and contemporary)

| Country | Private | | Corporatist | Public |
	Auditors	Mixed		
Denmark	FSR 1988–	Acc. Panel 1992–		Ehrvervs-og selskabs-styrelsen (Industry Ministry)
Finland			KILA 1974–	
Iceland	FLE 1976–88		Reikningskilarad 1991–	
Norway	DnR 1976–88	NRS 1989–		Regnskapsrådet 1980–91 (Ministry of Finance)
Sweden	FAR 1964–88	RR 1989–	BFN 1976–	

while the BFN issues standards for small and medium-sized companies as well as being the supervisory body for all standard-setting in Sweden.

In 1991 the Danish Parliament expressly demanded that preparer and user groups should be included in the standard-setting, as a reaction to the financial scandal caused by the bankruptcy of Nordic Feather. Therefore the Regnskabspanelet (the Accounting Panel) was set up in Denmark 1992 to include these groups together with the FSR. The new organizations in Iceland and Norway will be described below.

In Scandinavia the bank sector is still a major user of financial reports, but the stock markets have developed substantially since the beginning of the 1980s. Each country has only one stock exchange, in its capital city: Copenhagen, Helsinki, Oslo, Reykjavík and Stockholm. Individually they may not be very large, but taken together they cover 1000 listed companies. The frequency of references to the information needs of the stock markets has increased and become a new argument in debating accounting.

However, with the sole exception of Oslo, the stock exchanges have traditionally played a passive role in accounting. They have not developed any accounting rules of their own, and they do not even involve themselves in other rule-making bodies. Investor-related groups such as financial analysts are relatively small and anonymous and tend also to be passive. In recent years there have been a number of scandals on the stock markets, when companies have manipulated their accounting figures. The stock exchanges have made investigations into these companies and their auditors, but they have opposed any direct involvement in standard-setting. In both Denmark and Sweden the stock exchanges were invited to become members of the standard-setting organizations, but both rejected the invitation. However, in Denmark the stock exchange has since 1986 compelled quoted companies to follow the standards issued by the FRS. The Stockholm stock exchange has been persuaded to recommend the standards developed by the RR, and today the registered companies are obliged to give information about and the reason for any departure from these standards.

The only stock exchange actively involved in standard-setting is Oslo. The Oslo Stock Exchange Accounting Committee issued recommendations from 1977 to 2000. In 1989 the Norsk Regnskapsstiftelse (NRS – the Norwegian Accounting Standards Board), was founded. In 2002 it comprised the following members: the stock exchange, the Norwegian School of Economics and Business Administration (Norges Handelshøyskole, NHH), the DnR, the Norwegian Society of Financial Analysts (Norske Finansanalytikers Forening, NFF) The Norwegian School of Managment, and the organization of 'siviløkonomer'[2] (Norske Siviløkonomers Forening, NSF). Not even these standards are compulsory but the stock exchange expects companies to follow them.

Corporatist and public standard-setters

It is, of course, an issue in accounting, where historically there has been a split between Anglo-Saxon and Code law traditions, as to whether accounting standards should be set in the private or in the public sector. In Scandinavia it is most often neither clearly one nor the other. Both Finland, with its Kirjanpitolautakunta (KILA – Accounting Standards Board), and Sweden (BFN) have had corporatist standard-setting bodies (where the public and private sector work together) since the middle of the 1970s. Iceland established a similar body in 1991 (Reikningsskilarad).

The Finnish KILA, active since 1974, is an organization with members appointed by the government, and in practice the Chief Secretary of the Ministry of Trade and Industry has a great influence in selecting candidates. Candidates are normally selected from the industry, the profession and from the academic world. KILA interprets the accounting legislation, which is a frame law and gives guidelines on bookkeeping issues.

The Swedish BFN was set up by the government in 1976. Members are appointed by government but taken from a wide range of organizations in society, including labour representatives. Auditors, industrialists, academics, tax officials and stock exchange members (as individual experts, not representing the exchange as such) are appointed to the BFN. Despite having a minimal staff, the BFN has published a number of standards of accounting practice and interpretations of the law, as well as giving answers to technical bookkeeping questions and opinions in court cases. Since the BFN, as compared with other standard-setters, has not concentrated so much on profit measurement questions (there are, however, some notable exceptions) it has been seen as a complement to the other standard-setting bodies in Sweden, first to FAR's accounting committee and after 1989 to the RR.

The members of the Icelandic Reikningsskilarad are appointed by the Minister of Finance. The members are nominated by the following organizations: the auditors (FLE), the Department of Economics and Business Administration of the University of Iceland, the Chamber of Commerce, the Minister of Finance and the Auditor General of Iceland.

The level of authority of the organizations set up by governments (KILA, BFN, Reikningsskilarad) is complicated. Since the standards are not voted in the parliaments, their authority is not as strong as law, but the *mandate* to issue standards of these organizations has been granted by the parliaments or governments. The courts (both civil and tax) ask these organizations for comments on matters that concern accounting. If the standard is supported by a court decision then it will of course gain an enhanced legal status. The organizations also respond to questions put forward by private sector organizations, and they have a mandate to interpret the law. The KILA in Finland has dealt with more important questions than the BFN in Sweden, mainly because when BFN was set up there was already a Swedish standard-setting body (the FAR's accounting committee) that dealt with profit measurement questions.

After the scandal of the Nordic Feather in 1991, the standard-setting process in Denmark was reorganized as described above. In addition, there is within the Danish government (connected to the Industry Ministry) the Erhvervs-og selskabsstyrelsen (the Commerce and Companies Agency), which has financial expertise and follows with interest the regulatory process in the private sector and is ready to take over if it does not work smoothly. The government also has the facility to issue ministerial orders in the area of accounting. In Norway the Finance Ministry set up the Regnskapsrådet (the Accounting Council) as an advisory body to the Ministry in 1980. This body was active in issuing statements of preferred accounting practices until it was dissolved in 1991.

The organizations representing the preparers' view are the industry associations. However, accounting is not the only area they are supposed to address, and is not seen as particularly important compared to other topics, such as industry policy, salary negotiations and so on. As has been described, industry has had to be persuaded to participate in formal standard-setting work. One reason may be that the preparers in Scandinavia already have a powerful position. The big companies have considerable power due to their importance for the whole economy, which is especially accentuated in small countries such as the Scandinavian ones. The large companies have several times challenged the standard-setting organizations.

Relationship between legislation, standards and practice

In all Scandinavian countries[3] the concept good accounting practice (hereafter GAP, but not to be confused with GAAP) has been a general concept guiding accounting development and a specific concept related to individual topics that have not been addressed in the legislation but left to practice to resolve. In the preparatory work to the legislation there is usually a discussion and definition of GAP. The literal translation of the Swedish definition of the concept is: 'how a qualitatively representational number of companies do account'. Since companies do account differently there is a need to decide which practice is actually good (or qualitative). The standard-setting bodies are mentioned as those that have to make this interpretation.

The reason for reference to GAP is that the legislation can neither regulate in detail for all matters nor foresee possible future developments. Since the legislative process is a comparatively slow one, there is a need for a dynamic concept to allow practice to solve new accounting transactions. At the same time, it is not possible for practice to change principles for similar transactions; if there is a need to change principles which are regulated in the statutes, then the legislation must first be changed.

Scandinavia mainly has a code law tradition. Despite this, since accounting is seen as a highly technical area, the legislator has left much room for the influence of practice. This can also be seen as an expression of the specific consensus-seeking and cooperative culture of Scandinavia. As long as it works, the legislator prefers this model and the situation puts pressure on practice to be good, since if it is not, there is always a possibility of legislation, which for many in practice is considered a threat.

In discussing the development of accounting practice, one often has the large companies in mind, but influences on these, at least in Scandinavia, are different compared to small and medium-sized companies. The dominating influence on large companies today is international development. But since accounting internationally is not uniform one has to ask which kind of international development? As has been described earlier, the German influence was dominant when accounting was built up and lasted until the 1960s. Thereafter the US influence started to dominate. Besides the American influence, there are also IASB and EU rules. The international influence permeates through several channels: through education, auditors and auditors' institutes and foreign stock markets. One important channel for the spread of new techniques is the companies themselves, through observing each other's practices, through personal contacts and attention in the media and in response to perceived changes in the reporting environment. A few large, internationally listed companies have taken the lead in international development in Scandinavia. Some other companies have followed fairly quickly, then the standard-setters have confirmed the development, and then more companies have changed their accounting. Despite the international influences it is still possible to see national solutions, as was discussed in relation to Denmark and Finland.

For smaller and medium-sized companies that are not dependent on the international capital markets, the tax influence is more important. For these companies the tax authorities are the real main users of financial statements. Accepting a new accounting solution will always mean a risk that the authorities pick up this solution for taxation purposes. Management's concern about taxation is probably as important as the formal tax influence through the tax authorities. Tax influence is also still important for larger companies, besides the international influence. Since these two kinds of influence often go in opposite directions, one may ask how this is possible. The solution, as in other countries such as France, has been that different principles are used for the individual accounts and the group accounts. Since the group is not taxed, principles that give a higher income can be used here without raising the tax burden for companies.

Standards do not automatically constitute GAP unless they are actually followed by preparers; before that they are only guidelines and have no explicit legal support. The argument is sometimes advanced that the different standard-setting organizations have had an important impact on the development of accounting in Scandinavia (as elsewhere). We very much question that thesis in relation to Scandinavia because of the strong will of highly internationalized enterprises. A study (Artsberg 1992) of standard-setting in Sweden during the period 1957–1988, focusing particularly on the standards of FAR, shows that it was the large companies that led development through changes in their own annual reports and through informal discussions between themselves. In some cases FAR tried to resist accounting techniques that in its view breached the law. Despite its resistance and forceful argumentation, FAR had to change its standards several times to come into line with business practice. In the end it gave up and RR was founded and then industry had to be persuaded to take part in the formal standard-setting machinery.

It is also rare for legislation to intitiate rules and force them upon the companies. On the contrary, legislation is changed to be in line with actual practice. There are exceptions though, most often after financial scandals, such as the Krueger crash, which brought about changes in the company legislation in 1944; another later example is the regulation of information about golden parachutes for management. This demand was put into legislation because of intense public indignation about the matter.

Even if the role of the standard-setters is not to take the lead in initiating changes, they should not be dismissed totally. They have a role to play in speeding up the standardization of current developments since there are always those companies that wait for regulation before they change their reporting. The law is often the last element to be changed, but in turn gives legal backing to the practices and standards already in place. Therefore there can be several deviations from the law and still no company has been prosecuted for deviating when it comes to accounting principles. Figure 13.1 illustrates how the relationships probably look some years after a new law.

Can it be GAP then to follow the legislation but not the standard, if there is a difference? Hardly anyone would disagree, but in certain circumstances it is also GAP to follow the standard (in such cases it is argued that the legislation is too old). Standards can also acquire legal backing if they are confirmed by jurisprudence. There are a number of companies that want to be sure and stick to the legislation, waiting for it to be changed before they undertake any change in their annual reports.

The audit profession and auditing

The licence to audit is given by the state, and a two-tier system operates with 'authorized' auditors qualified to service all types of company and 'approved' auditors with a more limited mandate. The professional auditing institutes in Scandinavia have a long tradition of cooperation with each other and they have also created an organization for channelling this cooperation, the 'Nordic Federation of Public Accountants'. Despite the use of the word 'accountant', membership of the institutes is mainly for those in audit practice.

Figure 13.1 Relationship between legislation, guidelines and practice some years after legislation

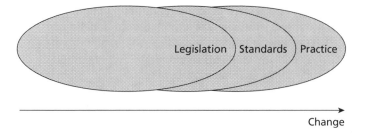

Membership is voluntary, since the licence to practise is given by the state, but most auditors in practice are members.

The auditors' professional institutes and also individual auditors play an important role in accounting regulation. One reason is that they are strong as a result of being highly organized, but the high level of technical education is also a factor. The institutes have an active and powerful lobby; individual members are often members of law committees on accounting, auditing and taxation.

At least one of the auditors in a limited liability company must be an authorized auditor if it is a listed company or if it is above a certain size (defined as more than 200 employees and with net assets above a specified amount). The approved auditors are mainly responsible for auditing small and medium-sized companies.

The Scandinavian auditors' professional institutes are summarized in Table 13.3. The requirements for education and practical training are similar throughout Scandinavia. To become an authorized auditor there is in all countries a need for an academic qualification obtained after four years' study of business and related topics, with accounting as a major and courses in commercial and tax law. In all countries except Norway it is then the auditors themselves who run the subsequent professional education programmes, particularly in auditing techniques, but also taking in more applied accounting and law. The application of knowledge to practical problems is, however, acquired during an internship with an authorized auditing firm, which is as much as five years in Denmark, Finland and Sweden but only three years in Iceland and two years in Norway. In Norway, though, besides the four years of basic academic study, auditors have to undertake an additional 18-month master's course at the Norwegian School of Economics and Business Administration (NHH) or at the Norwegian School of Management (BI).

To become an approved auditor the theoretical demands are somewhat lower. Nevertheless, a Scandinavian approved auditor must meet the minimum requirements of the Eighth European Directive.

After completing the internship period and passing the professional examination a candidate can apply for accreditation, which is administerd by different state or state-authorized agencies in different countries. It is the same authority that subsequently supervises auditors and has the power to withdraw an auditors' accreditation in the event of misconduct.

There are also accountants offering non-audit services and it has not been deemed necessary to regulate these in the same way as auditors. There are dedicated firms of

Table 13.3 The Scandinavian auditors' institutes

Country	Name of institute	Number of members
Denmark	Foreningen af Statsautoriserede Revisorer (FSR) authorized	2000
	Foreningen af Registrerede Revisorer (FRR) approved	4000
Finland	Keskuskauppakamarin hyväksymä tilintarkastaja-yhdistys (KHT) Förening CGR authorized	500
	HTM-tilintarkastajat (HTM) approved	1300
Norway	Den norske Revisorforening	3150
Sweden	FAR authorized mainly	2300
	Svenska Revisorssamfundet (SRS) approved mainly	1800

accountants doing work mainly for small and medium-sized companies. They have campaigned at times for state registration but this has not been given, so today there is only private, voluntary registration of accountants. Auditing and accounting work are mainly carried out by different individuals and may even be seen as different occupations. An auditor can also do accounting work, but not for an audit client. The auditors have taken on more and more consultancy tasks, though, in addition to the auditing work. They provide services concerning tax and legal matters, especially for small and medium-sized companies, and they have also specialized in management accounting and computerization.

Audit requirement

Auditing has been required by law for a long time in Scandinavia; in Sweden and Norway since 1910, in Denmark since 1917 and in Finland since 1925. There are in legislation some specific rules about what the auditor should look for and what kind of opinion should be given. According to legislation auditing should be conducted in accordance with 'good auditing practice'. There is no explicit legal requirement to follow the auditing standards developed by the professional institutes, but implicitly they are of course in a strong position to decide what is 'good auditing practice'. Therefore, it is common in the audit report to note that the audit work has been conducted in accordance with 'good auditing practice'. According to the legislation the audit report should give an opinion as to whether the accounts conform with legislation and 'good accounting practice'. The audit report should guide the annual stockholders meeting whether or not to accept that the board and president of the company have carried out their responsibilities, and it should also comment upon the board's suggestion as to the use of free capital. The auditor is obliged to say in the audit report if there are circumstances or transactions that might lead to liabilities for the board of directors or if they have not followed the law or the company's statutes.

Accounting objectives and principles

As long as there is income tax, there is a need for accounting. In Scandinavia the will to reduce tax cost has been an important determinant of accounting choice since the preparer has an influence on accounting development. The tax cost reducing behaviour of management has more recently had competition from another influence on management, the need to attract capital on the stock markets. In order to do so it is important not to show a too disadvantageous picture.

As discussed, tax has been used actively in connection with government economic policy. Since tax has been linked to accounting, this has also been affected. One purpose of the different policy rules was to help companies with self-financing and make them stronger. Another purpose of the system of untaxed reserves was to smooth out the business cycles in the economy.

The untaxed reserves were used by companies because they lowered the amount paid in tax. One consequence of the system was that at the same time it strengthened the companies, which was to the benefit of the banks and creditors generally which were the main source of finance. The banks were able to ask for information directly and did not need to rely on the published financial accounts. Another consequence of the system and a prerequisite for its acceptance by government was that the profit available for dividends was lowered to the same extent. This was fulfilled by the link between accounting and taxation. One important objective of financial accounting in Scandinavia is to calculate the amount available for distribution to shareholders.

In the 1970s many companies experimented with social reporting, value-added accounting and inflation accounting models. This interest disappeared in the 1980s, but environmental accounting can now be seen. Trade unions have not openly taken part in the accounting debate. One reason may be that the state intervenes (and the trade unions are represented in state committees as well as in the corporatist organizations). Information that has been seen as desirable for the employees or the whole of society has been requested by the state through legislation. The legislator has taken into the law requirements for disclosure of information about employees. The kind of information of interest for employees is information about working conditions but not so much information about profit of the company since wage negotiations are conducted on a centralized level in Scandinavia. Therefore general macroeconomic statistics of the whole industry are used instead.

Information useful for investors is a concern of relatively late date and is a consequence of the growing national stock markets but also the growing number of (mainly on the Anglo-Saxon stock exchanges) internationally listed companies. This kind of information has to a great extent been taken into legislation; for example, disclosure of cash flows for public companies. The demand for information on a number of aspects has increased over the years. The annual reports of Scandinavian public companies today have a high standard of disclosure. Table 13.4 summarizes all the different accounting objectives (with their purposes) that Scandinavian accounts have to fulfil.

Accounting principles

The important principles, mentioned in the Fourth Directive, are: going concern, consistency, prudence, realization, accruals and the inviolability of the closing balance sheet, and to this list should be added matching. In Scandinavia a difference is made between accruals and matching. Accruals has been mentioned in the legislation from the early days in the sense of accounting on a non-cash basis. Matching has established itself as an argument for practical solutions in recent years, which will be pursued below.

The prudence principle has been interpreted differently over the years. Historically it was interpreted in the German way, i.e. building reserves was permitted and even encouraged. Today prudence is more often interpreted in the Anglo-Saxon way as a 'reasonable prudence in accordance with normal business risks'. Figure 13.2 illustrates these two different interpretations of the prudence principle. The reason behind the use of reserves

Table 13.4 Different accounting objectives and purposes in Scandinavia (the economic policy objective hardly used today)

Objective	Purpose
Calculative/administrative	Taxing companies
	Protecting creditors
	Determining dividends
Economic policy	Helping companies with financing
	Encouraging investments
	Smoothing out business cycles (stabilization)
Informative	Informing investors
	Informing employees and society at large

Figure 13.2 Differences in the interpretation of the prudence principle

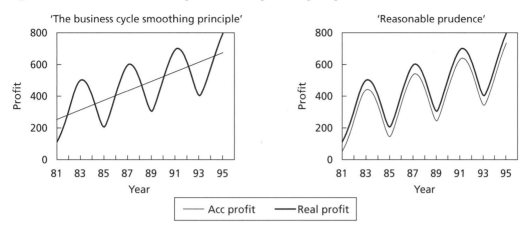

has been explained already. It is worth mentioning again that from the beginning reserves had a more commercial justification, the argument being that they were necessary to compensate for inflation ('excess' depreciation), or for a risk of suddenly falling prices of inventory (inventory reserve). These more commercially justified reserves were later mixed with tax policy rules of a more political nature. Therefore, all kinds of reserves were criticized for being tax incentives with no commercial justification (which can really be questioned). The left-hand graph in Figure 13.2 demonstrates how profit can be adjusted with the help of reserves (the 'real' profit is here expected to follow the variation in the market). The idea with reserves is that they should be created during good years and dissolved during bad years. The effect is that during bad years when reserves are dissolved the company shows a better result than if it has no reserves to dissolve, i.e. the Anglo-Saxon system (demonstrated in the right-hand graph). The system with reserves can be interpreted as a way of manipulating the figures; but it can also be interpreted as a way of calculating profits on a more long-term basis (smoothing the business cycles).

Arguing according to the prudence principle was common until around the middle of the 1980s, when the matching principle started to establish itself in accounting debate (Table 13.5). Norway is the country that has most emphasized the shift from prudence to matching. This shift implies a redefinition of the realization principle, with more emphasis on economic realization and less on legal form and cash settlement.

To summarize, then, the two most important shifts in accounting principles in Scandinavia are the redefinition of the prudence principle and the redefinition of the realization principle. It should be said that it is not generally accepted for all transactions. However, there is a tendency for more and more items to be treated in this new way. More generally this shift is often expressed as a change from the prudence principle (meaning the old prudence principle) to the matching principle.

In Scandinavia the concept of 'good accounting practice' (GAP) is important and has a similarly broad role as the British 'true and fair view', although not formally as an overriding concept. The difference between these two concepts is presented in Table 13.6, and mirrors clearly the more important role of the accounts preparers in the Scandinavian context. Accounting development is more process oriented with the involvement of many interest groups, in the context of a culture of cooperation and consensus seeking. It ought to be easier to decide what is 'good accounting practice' then what is 'true and fair', since the former concept is referring to a set of methods actually used while the second is

Table 13.5   Profit measurement in case of conflict between principles

	Prudence	*Matching*
Revenue recognition	Realization by form	Realization by substance
Cost reporting	Expensing	Capitalizing

Table 13.6   Differences between two general accounting concepts (from Christiansen and Elling 1993)

'Good accounting practice'	*'True and fair view'*
Preparer-oriented	User-oriented
Accounting methods	A holistic concept
Oriented towards the process	Oriented towards the final product

arguably a more philosophical and holistic concept. Although it is not self-evident since the word 'good' is as philosophical as the words 'true' and 'fair'. One consequence of the difference in emphasis is that there are no conceptual frameworks in the Anglo-Saxon sense in the Scandinavian countries.

The EC directives have adopted the British concept of the 'true and fair view'. With the incorporation of the directives in Scandinavian law there has been a debate as to whether or not both concepts are needed and how they relate to each other. The decision reached is to have both concepts in the law. The 'true and fair' concept has been interpreted differently in different Scandinavian countries. In Denmark it is interpreted as an overriding concept for companies in the preparation of accounts. In the other countries it is only overriding for legislators; i.e. the legislator can use 'true and fair' as an overriding concept in the legislative process while interpreting the directives but the standard-setters or the preparers have to follow the legislation and give supplementary information if they think that the regulations do not result in a true and fair view.

Differential reporting

The change in emphasis from the prudence principle to the matching principle, noted above, is most often accepted if it does not influence tax, as in the group accounts. Today, therefore, many companies use different principles for the individual accounts and the group accounts. The individual accounts reflect the legal entity and are used mainly for tax purposes, while the group accounts correspond with the economic entity and are used mainly by investors. Even though both the individual accounts and the group accounts must be registered and thus made public, it is more and more common for just the group accounts to be sent to investors and others with a similar interest of information.

There has been debate as to whether or not it is in accordance with the law to use different principles for individual accounts and group accounts. Generally there are no particular valuation principles or rules specified for groups, the statutes simply state that the group accounts should be drawn up as an aggregation of the individual accounts. Recently legislators in Sweden have explicitly accepted that accounting principles in the group accounts differ from those used in the individual accounts. The present Norwegian legislation seems to differ from the rest of the Scandinavian countries in this area of accounting. Indeed, Norway explicitly requires identical accounting principles to be applied to the group accounts and to the individual accounts of the companies comprising the group. This implies that the choice of accounting principle at the group level may have economic effects (dividends, taxes) on each company in Norway.

When the RR in Sweden decided to publish standards only for the use of public companies there was a discussion about which companies actually are public. The RR means companies whose shares are publicly traded, while some others argued that public should mean companies in which there is a public interest. The legislation in Scandinavian countries does not generally distinguish between whether a company is publicly or privately owned. All limited liability companies have to send in copies of their annual reports to the authorities for registration and a copy can be viewed by anyone, as in the UK.

As a general rule the accounting statutes are applicable to all companies irrespective of sector or ownership. Although there are in Denmark two Companies Acts, one for private and one for public companies, the *accounting* rules do not differ between the two Acts. However, there are some exceptions to this general rule. There is relief for smaller companies from some disclosure rules; for example, there is no need for such companies to publish a cash flow statement and group accounts. It is also possible for smaller companies to publish a short form of the income statement. The exceptions in the legislation are none the less few.

There are distinct differences in how Denmark, Sweden and Norway differentiate accounting rules both in respect of the Accounting Act and in respect of accounting standard requirements. In the new 2001 Accounting Act, *Denmark* has classified companies into four groups, primarily based on size, and enacts different accounting rules for each group. Also, the accounting standards issued by FSR must be applied for listed companies, but are not obligatory (although they are allowed) for other companies. The *Swedish* standard-setter (RR) also issues accounting standards which are obligatory for listed companies. The institution responsible for the development of 'good accounting practice' (BFN), however, explicitly exempts medium-sized and small Swedish companies from certain of the rules of the accounting standards. In *Norway*, the accounting standards set by the NRS are obligatory for all companies except the smallest ones. Instead, a particular accounting standard for all small companies has been issued by the NRS. This standard has a practical orientation, and includes much less detail compared with the general standards. The Norwegian system for small companies is similar to that of the UK.

Format, measurement and disclosure of annual reports

This section deals with regulations concerning specific accounting topics, although it should be stressed that these solutions are not always the same as can be found in company reports. Sometimes preparers deviate from prescribed rules and, while there may be several reasons for that, an important reason is the comparatively major role of company practice in accounting change, as already discussed.

The law requires a company to publish an income statement, balance sheet, notes and director's report. A parent company of a group must also publish a group income statement and balance sheet and give correspondingly relevant information about the group in the notes and the director's report. For larger and/or listed companies it is also compulsory to publish a cash flow statement. All limited liability companies, both private and public, are obliged to file a copy of their annual report with the authorities, and this is available to anyone who wants to see it (or order a copy of it).

The use of notes to give information owes its development to influence from the USA and this practice has increased considerably over the years. There is a trend to move information from the directors' report to the notes, but there is also an increase in disclosure of information. The latest changes in legislation, arising from adoption of the EC directives, continued this trend.

Besides these compulsory components, companies have from time to time experimented with other kinds of reports. During the 1970s several companies went in for social reporting in different ways, ranging from general information to more formal reports such as value-added statements and green accounts. Indeed, the 2001 Danish Accounting Act generally stresses the importance of social reporting and green accounting. Another area of experimentation, especially in Iceland, Finland and Sweden, was inflation reporting. In the 1990s there has been a renewed interest in green accounting.

The format of the obligatory statements follows the EU model, although there are some smaller differences between countries as well as between companies. Before the adoption of the directives, the formats used in the balance sheet followed the American order of reducing liquidity, which is the opposite of the EU model using ascending liquidity. Actually the new format is a return to how statements were before the change to American order. In this respect at least, the international influence is again that of Germany. It has been general practice to disclose information about *contingent liabilities* as a memorandum item at the end of the balance sheet in the German fashion, but owing to international influence this is now sometimes moved to the notes.

The Scandinavian model provides only for an income statement in the form of a list (vertical statement) and a horizontal or account format balance sheet. However, in the income statement expenditure may be shown either by nature or by function, and it is left to the preparer to decide.

In Norway, equity is not only divided into free and restricted capital. The country also divides equity with respect to source: paid in capital and retained earnings. Given the fact that the accumulated distributions to the owners are not disclosed, this division may be regarded as having somewhat reduced interest for users of the accounts. Also, the Norwegian 'double-classification system' of equity may cause practical presentation problems.

A specific feature of the balance sheet in Scandinavia (apart from Denmark which has abandoned the technique) is the inclusion of a category, called *untaxed reserves*, between equity and provisions. Another characteristic on the credit side is that the objective of calculating distributable capital is reflected in the technique of dividing equity into what is *free capital* and *restricted capital*. It is necessary to devote a little space to explaining the use of reserves in Scandinavia, especially the untaxed reserves and the corresponding section *transfers to/from untaxed reserves* in the income statement. Generally reserves in Scandinavia can be one of the three following kinds: appropriations of net income, charges against net income or not related to net income at all. Figure 13.3 summarizes the different forms of reserves and provisions that are used and how they are related to the calculation of income.

There are two kinds of untaxed reserves: those that are charges against net income and those that are not related to net income at all but are only accounted for in the balance sheet. Revaluation reserves are examples of the latter kind. These reserves arise because a reserve is created in the balance sheet in order to recognize, for example, the current market value of investments, but the state, unlike in France, does not tax such an unrealized profit. These transactions normally pass through the income statement when the capital gain is realized. Because of the congruence principle such transactions were initially opposed in Scandinavia, but they are now accepted because of international influence. Revaluation of fixed assets is not conducted systematically in Scandinavia, but is a matter for the individual company.

The other untaxed reserves are used with the intention of reducing taxation and it is this kind of reserve that is the special Scandinavian untaxed reserve. These can technically be created in a number of ways, but there are two broad groups: those that are related to assets and those that are not. The latter group is today supposed to be more neutral because it is supposed to stimulate self-financing without obliging the company to invest in a specific asset. The asset-related reserves can be hidden, which means that it is not possible to work out from the accounts (unless it is disclosed in the notes or in the director's report) how large the reserves are, or they can be accounted for openly. The asset-related reserves can be hidden simply because the reserves can be concealed in the assets' artificially low carrying value. From this it follows that if there are no assets to hide behind, then it is not possible to hide the reserves, and this is the case with the non-asset-related reserves.

Untaxed reserves, openly accounted for, are shown in the balance sheet in this separate category, between long-term liabilities and equity. They are considered to be one part equity and one part deferred tax. This sort of open reserve can also be split into the equity and deferred tax components, and then it is shown in the balance sheet under those headings. This does, however, raise the question of the basis on which deferred tax should be calculated. Figure 13.4 gives a summary of the alternative treatments.

Figure 13.3 Different forms of reserves and provisions used in Scandinavia

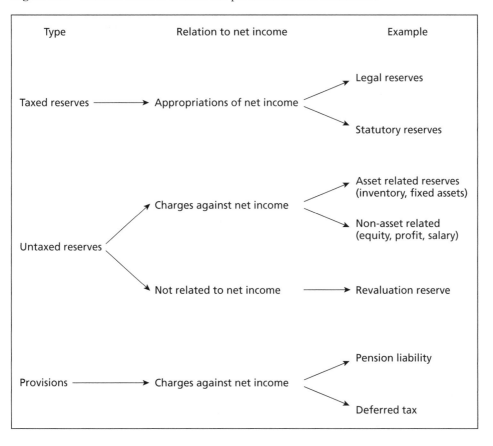

If the reserve is shown openly in the balance sheet, the change in the reserve for the year is also accounted for openly in the income statement as a transfer to or from untaxed reserves. The taxable profit of the year is reduced by the amount transferred to the reserve that year (or increased if the reserve is dissolved), and the company's tax is reduced accordingly. The statement format is the vertical one, and if there is a section of 'transfers to/from untaxed reserves' one must remember that the commercial profit figure cannot be found on the bottom line, but on the line before this special tax section.

In countries where there is a link between taxation and accounting, companies are often allowed to undervalue assets. In Germany the reserves created by undervaluation are generally hidden, in Scandinavia they are most likely open. In order to avoid investors eager for dividends being able to put pressure on management and to enable profit to be calculated on a more long-term basis, these reserves were at first hidden in Scandinavia as well. It can be argued that there actually was a good reason *not* to expose the first kind of reserves that were created, such as excess depreciation and under-valuation of inventories. These reserves were, at least partly, introduced as a way to compensate for inflation. This cannot be said about the specific investment reserves introduced later, which were real tax benefits.

The special category of untaxed reserves in the balance sheet and transfers to/from untaxed reserves in the income statement are rarely seen today (but the most likely countries for it to occur are Finland and Sweden) because, in the interests of international communication, preparers split the untaxed reserves between equity and deferred tax.

Deferred tax remains an issue which is still under discussion in Scandinavian countries, and it is only in the group accounts of some internationally listed companies that deferred tax items are routinely seen today. Denmark is the country with the most intensive theoretical discussion about how the deferred tax problem should be solved, possibly because in Denmark tax and accounting have, compared with the other Scandinavian countries, been separated for a long time. Rules about the definition and measurement of deferred tax are absent from the law in all the Scandinavian countries, including Denmark, so international practice is particularly influential in this area. But since the international solutions are so diverse, practice today is diverse and all kinds of models are used, both full and partial provisions, and both the deferral and liability method.

Measurement rules and practices

Intangible assets if capitalized should be amortized over their useful economic life. Only purchased goodwill can be capitalized. However, most companies expense intangible assets immediately since the expense is tax deductible. The treatment of goodwill is not particularly uniform in practice, with amortization periods varying substantially and going

Figure 13.4 Hidden and open accounting of some untaxed reserves

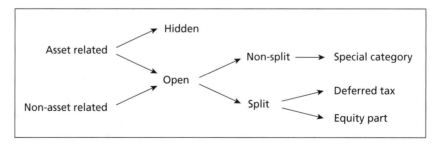

up to the US ceiling of 40 years. Standard-setters tend to follow the IAS 22 and prescribe 20 years as the limit. Research and development costs may be capitalized if they are expected to be of future economic benefit.

The law stipulates that *tangible fixed assets* should be valued at acquisition cost or production cost. Production cost may include overhead and financial costs related to the production period. Tangibles must be depreciated over their useful economic life and the straight-line method is the most commonly used. According to the regulations, an increase in value of the asset is not considered a valid reason for not depreciating it, and instead (except in Norway) there is a rule that permits revaluation if the increase in value is permanent. In Denmark the practice of revaluation is quite common whereas it is forbidden in Norway. In practice though many companies do not depreciate such assets, particularly real estate. If there is a decline in value the asset must be written down. With the introduction of the Fourth Directive there is now a rule that write-offs must be reversed if circumstances change.

For a long time there was no specific legislation for *investments*, and these were valued according to the general rules of valuation for fixed assets and current assets respectively. This meant that fixed investments should be valued at historical cost and current assets at the lower of cost and market value. However, this has been a matter of debate and controversy in recent years because of the international influence. For investments in associates, companies started to use the equity method, even though it broke the regulations. For current investments the mark-to-market rule has become increasingly popular.

For *inventory* until recently it was the tax legislation that determined the value for most companies since it accepted a valuation even lower than cost or market, and for some time periods it accepted an understatement (i.e. the creation of reserves) of up to 60% of stock value. The use of inventory reserves was abandoned in Denmark as early as World War II but for the other countries it lasted until the tax reforms in the late 1980s or early 1990s. The LIFO method is not permitted, only FIFO and weighted average (or similar methods). When deciding the value of inventory in practice, a proportion of fixed costs are sometimes included and also interest incurred during the production process; this issue is, however, not clearly regulated in legislation.

In Denmark there has for some time (from the beginning of the 1950s) been a practice of valuing inventory at variable cost only according to the marginal costing principle. However, in order to bring accounting into conformity with international practice, a new Danish standard was published in 1991 which recommends the use of absorption costing.

Accounting for *long-term contracts* is currently the subject of debate in Scandinavia and is part of the movement in accounting thinking from form to substance. Previously it was seen as self-evident that the completed contract method should be used, because realization was defined according to form and this gave the best tax profile. Subsequently there has been a debate as to whether the percentage of completion method could be used, i.e. whether it was in conformity with the legislation. Today, the percentage of completion method is generally accepted in Scandinavia.

On the liabilities and equity side of the balance sheet, reserves and provisions have been discussed in relation to taxation. *Pension liabilities* are not an issue in Scandinavia because of the state system of pensions because, as in France, the main provision is through social security payments to the state which is then responsible for subsequent pension payments. However, there are also agreements between the unions and the employers for supplementary pension benefits. Despite the prudence principle there has never been any mention in the legislation of recognizing these agreements as liabilities, although standard-setters have tried to address the topic. However, since company benefit plans are often protected through insurance agreements, pensions are commonly dealt with just as contingent liabilities.

Reporting income

The law requires that the values in the closing balance sheet must be the same as those in the opening balance sheet for the next year, which means that all changes in the values of assets and liabilities in the balance sheet must flow through the current year. However, the IAS 8 concerning fundamental errors and changes in accounting policies has been adopted, with the effect that changes in items relating to a prior period are taken directly to equity in the balance sheet. In addition, translation differences in consolidated accounts are taken directly to reserves when using the current rate method. Some companies have also taken goodwill as a deduction from equity, although this is not a common way to treat goodwill, except in Denmark where a majority of companies have followed this practice, although it has since been banned by the 2001 law.

Consolidation practices

The requirement to publish group accounts was enacted for the first time in Sweden in 1944, after the Krueger scandal where transactions between related companies were used to manipulate information and swindle numbers of investors. Group accounts were regulated a bit later in the other Scandinavian countries but had become common practice before that. This is another area where the American influence was important in developing accounting, although it should be noted that the pooling of interests method is almost never used. The law specifies that the acquisition method should be used. Both the law and accounting standards are today in line with both IASB standards and EC directives. A subsidiary is defined as in the Seventh Directive on the basis of both legal control and economic control. Goodwill is computed as the difference between acquisition cost and a valuation of the net assets at fair value to the acquirer. Today an amortization period of up to 20 years and even longer is accepted by the standard-setters.

A company that is not a subsidiary but is managed by a company in the group (and owned jointly together with one or more other companies) can be taken into the group accounts using proportional consolidation. The equity method is compulsory for investments in associated companies in the accounts and is also accepted in the parent company accounts. In the old legislation the equity method was not permitted because fixed assets were required to be valued at historical cost, although it was in practice used in some group accounts. There are some exceptions, in line with the Seventh Directive, to the requirement to publish group accounts.

The translation of the statements of foreign companies for inclusion in the group accounts is not regulated in all countries, but in practice it follows US GAAP and IASB. The current rate method is used for independent subsidiaries (unless they are operating in high inflation countries); otherwise the monetary method is used. As in many other countries, the current rate method has become increasingly popular among the companies.

Other disclosures

As with many topics not related to taxation, the evolution of cash flow statements has followed international developments. Cash flow statements were first prepared voluntarily towards the end of the 1960s, based on the American model, focused on changes in working capital. After a change in approach in the USA with the publication of SFAS 95, practice in Scandinavia changed with both cash flow and funds flow models used. These statements are not regulated in detail in the law, although this requires that large and/or listed companies should publish them for the benefit of investors. The topic was first regulated in the middle of the 1970s as a codification of practice. It was seen as important that companies should have the flexibility to experiment.

A management report is a legal requirement as part of the annual report, and is subject to audit. The auditors in Iceland first resisted the idea of auditing the management report because it contains the board's view on likely future developments of the company. Following a change in 1994 with the new Financial Statements Act, the situation in Iceland is now the same as that of the other Scandinavian countries. The prescriptions in legislation for management reports today follow the EC directives, which mean that the following information should be given:

1. Circumstances that are not shown elsewhere in the annual report but that are important in order to judge the position and income.

2. Events which are important that have taken place during the year or after the balance sheet date.

3. Expected future developments.

4. Research and development activities.

5. Foreign branches.

6. The board's proposal for the disposition of profit and free capital.

As in many other countries, the use of and length of the notes increases every year, although small and medium-sized companies are subject to fewer requirements than large and listed companies. The notes must give an explanation and description of the accounting principles used in the accounts as well as more detailed information and supplementary information concerning the items in the financial statements. The notes form an integral part of the accounts and are audited. Lately, companies have been required to provide information about both risks connected with financial instruments and also, because of recent financial scandals, about golden parachutes for managers and board members.

A particular feature in the annual reports of companies listed on several exchanges is reconciliation statements between different sets of reporting rules. The most common is a reconciliation to US GAAP, but reconciliations to IASB standards can also be seen, and sometimes both. Generally the Scandinavian countries follow the extensive disclosure requirements of the EC directives meticulously and take little advantage of any exemption rules.

Notes

1. For example, Svavarsson (1994, pp. 113–114) mentions that the King of Denmark in 1787 issued a document that included two paragraphs on bookkeeping for merchants operating in Iceland.

2. A 'siviløkonom' is a graduation composed of four years' study in business administration and related topics.

3. The discussion in this section is based on the Swedish experience. There are to our knowledge no similar studies for the other Scandinavian countries, but it is not unreasonable to assume that the relationship between legislation, standards and practice has been and is the same.

References

Artsberg, K. (1992) *Normbildning och redovisningsförändring*. Lund University Press, Lund.

Artsberg, K. (1993) Policy making and accounting change: influences on the choice of measurement principles in Swedish accounting. *European Accounting Review* 141–144.

Christiansen, M. (1993) Accounting regulation in Denmark. *European Accounting Review* 603–616.

Christiansen, M. and Elling, J. (1993) *European Financial Reporting – Denmark*. Routledge, London.

Näsi, S. (1995) The history of financial reporting in Finland. In P. Walton (ed.) *European Financial Reporting – A History*. Academic Press, London.

Svavarsson (1994) Iceland. In J. Flower (ed.) *The Regulation of Financial Reporting in the Nordic Countries*. Fritzes, Stockholm.

Further Reading

Artsberg, K. (1996) The link between commercial accounting and tax accounting in Sweden. *European Accounting Review* (supplement): 795–814.

Christiansen, M. (1993) Company law and accounting in nineteenth-century Europe – Denmark. *European Accounting Review* 312–318.

Christiansen, M. (1996) The relationship between accounting and taxation in Denmark. *European Accounting Review* (supplement): 815–834.

Eilifsen, A. (1996) The relationship between accounting and taxation in Norway. *European Accounting Review* (supplement): 835–844.

Flower, J. (ed.) (1994) *The Regulation of Financial Reporting in the Nordic Countries*. Fritzes, Stockholm.

Hansen, P. (1958) *The Accounting Concept of Profit*. Einar Harcks Forlag, Copenhagen; North-Holland, Amsterdam.

Hofstede, G. (1991) *Cultures and Organizations – on Intercultural Understanding*. McGraw-Hill, London.

Johnsen, A. (1993) Accounting regulation in Norway. *European Accounting Review* 617–626.

Järvenpää, M. (1996) The relationship between taxation and financial accounting in Finland. *European Accounting Review* (supplement): 899–914.

Jönsson, S. (1988) *Accounting Regulation and Elite Structures: Driving Forces in the Development of Accounting Policy*. Wiley, Chichester.

Jönsson, S. (1991) Role-making for accounting while the state is watching. *Accounting, Organization and Society*, no 4/5: 521–546.

Kettunen, P. (1993) Financial accounting and reporting in Finland. *European Accounting Review* 592–602.

Lukka, K. and Pihlanto, P. (1994) Martti Saario – The developer of Finnish accounting theory. In J.R. Edwards (ed.) *Twentieth Century Accounting Thinkers*. Routledge, London.

Monsen, N. and Wallace, W.A. (1995) Evolving financial reporting practices: a comparative study of the Nordic countries' harmonization efforts. *Contemporary Accounting Research* 973–997.

Näsi, S. (1993) Company law and accounting in nineteenth-century Europe – Finland. *European Accounting Review* 319–328.

Nilsson, S-A. and Smiciklas, M. (1993) Company law and accounting in nineteenth-century Europe – Sweden. *European Accounting Review* 362–365.

Puxty, A.G., Willmott, H.C., Cooper, D.J. and Lowe, A.E. (1987) Modes of regulation in advanced capitalism: locating accountancy in four countries. *Accounting, Organizations and Society* **12**(3).

Rundfelt, R. (1993) Standard setting in Sweden. A new regime. *European Accounting Review* 585–591.

Räty, P. (1992) Reforming Finnish accounting legislation. *European Accounting Review* 413–420.

14

Accounting in Eastern Europe: From communism to capitalism

Jacques Richard

S ince accounting first started to ask questions about itself, two particular questions have been posed concerning its nature: is (double-entry) accounting an attribute of capitalism and, in the context of capitalism, is accounting uniform or diverse?

The first question had already been posed by Karl Marx in the latter part of the nineteenth century in a famous sentence:

> Accounting as a means of control and an ideal presentation of the production process is all the more necessary, the more the process takes place on a larger social scale and loses its individual character: ... it is more necessary in capitalist production than in the production of peasants or artisans: it is much more necessary in socialist production than in that of capitalism.

(Karl Marx, *Das Kapital*, Russian edition, Vol II, Complete works of Marx and Engels, p. 153, cited in Makarov 1966).

About half a century later, Werner Sombart had to some extent responded to his compatriot in asserting that 'capitalism and double entry accounting can absolutely not be dissociated. They are to one another as form is to content' (Sombart 1928, p. 118).

The second question appeared in the academic literature much later when the pioneers of international accounting such as Mueller (1967) started to show the extreme diversity of accounting in different capitalist countries and began to propose some sort of classification. The study of Eastern European accounting is especially interesting in respect of these two questions. Thanks to the disappearance of the Communist Bloc, a rich field of evidence has opened up, not only of the impact of transition from a communist type of accounting to a capitalist system, but also, in terms of the choices made in different countries, of the diversity of types of accounting regulation within capitalist accounting, and of the reasons which lead to a particular choice.

This chapter discusses the characteristics of a communist accounting system before the fall of the Iron Curtain. The first type of communist accounting[1] came into the world between 1924 and 1940: 'soviet accounting'. Then at the end of World War II, there was a second wave of communist accounting which appeared in the countries that became satellites of the USSR, and which led to modified forms of the first type.

The soviet accounting model

The birth of soviet accounting did not happen instantaneously: its main characteristics did not begin to emerge until after the New Economic Policy (NEP)[2] and only became completely and finally fixed around 1940–1950. A reading of Makarov's (1966) seminal text (and others[3]) shows evidence of the influence on economic regulation of the state's centralized planning. The influence of this type of regulation manifests itself first by the state centralization of the power of regulation, then by 'formal unity' and by the adoption of specific concepts of assets and income and by standardization and control of costs.

These fundamental ideological elements of soviet accounting were going to influence strongly all the means of accounting control, whether accounting plans, balance sheets, income statements or, in a wider sense, audit techniques.

From the time the soviets took power, it was the state, and in particular the BCHX,[4] which had responsibility for preparing the decrees that governed the new accounting. This state monopoly of accounting regulation lasted until the end of the soviet period. In addition, the role of the state was emphasized by the inclusion in its constitution of the task of bringing in a socialist system of calculation (Makarov 1966).

Unity of reporting

Makarov, in his many criticisms of capitalist accounting, does not fail to emphasize that 'in capitalist businesses there are two accountings' (or two reporting systems): one which serves for management purposes and is the preserve of 'a small number of people collaborating together' in the management of the enterprise and the other, the financial accounting, which is accessible to a larger circle of shareholders, suppliers, customers, etc. Only this second accounting is regulated by the capitalist state. For Makarov this double standard in regulation is an example of a fault inherent in the capitalist system which keeps aside the richest and most exact information, which is contained in the management's accounts (Makarov 1966, p. 305).

According to Makarov the special character (and the superior nature) of the soviet accounting system comes from the fact that the state regulates not only financial accounting but also management accounting, in a way which makes visible all facets of the management of the business: there is a 'regulatory unity'. This unity is the greater in its impact in that it concerns not only accounting but also statistics and operational data. In effect Makarov is setting out the principle of the 'unity of socialist calculation'. This recognizes the three sorts of calculation which permit state control: operational calculations (i.e. physical quantities), accounting calculations and statistical calculations. These are integrated into a conception of the whole architecture of the information system to service the control of the economic plan. One can, however, see (below) that the contradictions inherent in the bureaucratic system often led to this information system splitting back into its components.

Material unity and the full cost principle

In a system of regulation where fiscal policies as used in the West did not exist (tax was conceived as a simple levy), where valuations such as direct costing were considered as an attribute of the crises inherent in capitalism (the need to dump excess production and to adjust prices to variable cost in times of recession), and where the policy of prudence did not have any meaning (see below), there could not, in theory, be any place for a plurality of approaches to valuation.

Makarov emphasizes the primacy of the 'principle of unity' in soviet valuation; that is what we call material unity.[5] In adding to this the 'principle of reality', the soviet accounting theorists came to the conclusion that the only method of valuing assets could be that of full real cost (of acquisition or of production). This principle took its definitive form in 1943 with the prohibition of provisions for doubtful debts. The soviet planners, victorious over economic uncertainties, allowed themselves, it seems, to throw into the dustbin of history the principle of prudence which reigned in the capitalist market economies. Soviet accounting allowed of only one valuation principle throughout the accounting system, and that was full cost, without any modification for a possible market value, since market values did not officially exist.

Unity of form

The organization of accounting on a dual basis (financial accounting and management accounting separated, even if with links) which could be found in some businesses at the time of the Bolshevik revolution was set aside. It was clearly inconceivable that a regime that claimed it wished to have clarity throughout the planning process, particularly as concerns production, should allow a partitioning of the accounting system. Very quickly, at least as far as principles went, the only system to be authorized and put in place was an organization of the accounts that conformed with formal unity (a system with a single circuit, to use current German terminology[6]). In fact, the abandonment of business secrecy, the emergence of material unity and the application of regulatory unity facilitated or even imposed this solution.

A special concept of assets

After the establishment of collective ownership by the state, a certain number of assets disappeared from the balance sheet of soviet businesses, either because they were no longer tradable assets (e.g. land or patents), or because they no longer existed in the context of a centralized management where one business could not own any share of the capital of another business (e.g. investments in subsidiaries). In theory a business could not have in its balance sheet any assets other than the means of production and the trading assets (stocks, debtors) relating strictly to its core activity. This is the reason why from 1933 the term 'fixed assets' was replaced by the term 'fixed means' (Tchenkov 1973, p. 15).

It should be noted, though, that the balance sheets of soviet businesses, having been cleared of capitalist assets, became progressively filled up with all the range of socialist assets (housing, canteens, retirement homes) which were involved in the growing social role of these businesses. Of course, the problematical evaluation of the efficiency of the business implied a distinction between 'productive' assets and 'non-productive' ones.

From 1952 soviet accounting opted for the valuation of assets at their gross value,[7] which was not taken up in other Eastern European countries such as East Germany. However, this does not seem necessarily characteristic of a socialist concept of assets but springs, according to some authors (Tchenkov 1973, p. 36) from an error of logic. We will return to this point later.

It should be emphasized, in conclusion, that although soviet businesses used leased assets, these did not appear in the balance sheet, but rather were recorded off balance sheet. As Makarov remarks, the balance sheet should only reflect what belongs to the business, otherwise it would cause errors at a macroeconomic level. The principle of ownership, albeit socialist ownership, did apply therefore.

A special concept of capital

It is often remarked that accounting in socialist businesses did not have any concept of owners' equity and, in a wider sense, capital (Schroll 1995, p. 828). It is true that in a number of socialist states the structure of the balance sheet (see below) would seem somewhat disturbing to a Western financial analyst in the sense that one could recognize only with the greatest difficulty the owners' equity of Western literature. It is also true that the word capital had been generally replaced by the expression 'statutory fund' (*ustavni fond* in Russian), which referred to state contributions to the company in the form of budgetary allocations.

However, the absence of the Western concept does not mean that there was no concept of owners' equity in the soviet system. It must be understood that from the point of view of a state which controlled all the means of financing, whatever their form (budgetary allocations, loans, self-generated cash flow, etc.), the concept of capital could only refer to the total of resources available. The owners' capital, viewed from the state's perspective, corresponded to the whole of the liabilities and equity of the company. The nature of the concept of earnings, which generally is associated with the notion of capital, substantiates that point.

A special concept of profit

Contrary to the self-management system of Yugoslavia, the soviet system had continued to consider staff remuneration as an expense, and was therefore, on this point, no different from the capitalist system. However, it had been innovative in two areas, treating bank interest and payments of taxes to the state not as expenses but as distributions of profit. If one considers that the state, whether in the form of banker or of tax collector, was the sole 'capitalist' for all these businesses, this concept of profit was very logical.

One should add, by way of further detail, that while in the capitalist system the profit has, since the nineteenth century, generally been considered as being made when the goods are delivered, this was different in the USSR, at least in the period 1970–80. It was only when cash was received that the profit was considered to be made – which implies that debtors should be valued at production cost in the balance sheet.

This odd realization principle was not justified by a concern for prudence, as it would have been in certain capitalist systems in the eighteenth century, but by a practical desire to speed up transactions by requiring businesses to complete their transaction cycle before thinking about any distribution of the profit to the staff.

Standardization and control of costs

Standard-setters in Western types of accounting systems generally require one of two types of classification of expenses: by function or by nature. It is very rare that the profit and loss account provides both kinds of analysis. Countries such as France and Germany prefer classification by nature, while Anglo-Saxon countries prefer classification by function. Soviet accounting also stipulated these two classifications and their communication to the state, but did not, in our opinion, give them more than secondary importance.

The original character of the soviet system came from the fact that it preferred a third system of classification of costs by 'stages' (*stati* in Russian). This classification had a visceral importance because it was used as the basis of pricing (and checking prices), tasks which are obviously essential in a regulatory system where there are no market prices. It consisted of an analysis of the creation of costs by distinguishing direct production costs, indirect production costs and commercial costs, which provided the total cost of production using the following scheme (based on Sumtsov 1975, p. 235).

Costs linked to the technical processes:

1. Raw materials and other supplies
2. *Less* recoverable waste
3. Combustible materials and energy used for production
4. Basic salary for production workers
5. Extra payments for production workers
6. Social security charges
7. Costs of preparing and starting production
8. Costs of maintaining and operating plant

Costs related to administration, organization and general services:

9. Workshop expenses, related to production, and not so related
10. General factory costs, related to production and not so related
11. Loss on rejects
12. Other production costs

Costs related to the sale of products:

13. Charges not connected with production.

Soviet planning required that the business provided planned figures (i.e. budgets), which served the administration as the basis for fixing prices, after adding a margin, and the actual results as a control mechanism. In short, the soviet accountants had regulated cost accounting completely.

Special accounting plans

Lenin had exhorted soviet managers to use the most modern accounting techniques in the service of the new economy. The soviet accountants took a particular interest in German practices and especially the German accounting charts which flourished in the 1920s due to the effect of cartelization under the Weimar economy. It is true that Schmalenbach's famous accounting code (*Kontenrahmen*) was not translated into Russian until 1928 but it is likely that the developments in this area in Germany were followed closely for some years. It is evident that in 1925/26 there appeared for the first time in the USSR some model accounting charts which were, according to Tchenkov (1973, p. 7), 'accounting charts different from those seen before the Revolution'. These charts are, just as are the charts suggested by Schmalenbach and his predecessors, characterized by the principle of unity of form (unity of cost and financial accounting) and by the logic of the production cycle (organization of the accounts in the order of the production cycle – raw material supply, processing, sale). They are very different from the dual type of accounting charts which were put forward in the 1920s and 1930s by opponents of Schmalenbach and which were to establish themselves in countries such as France after 1945.

The choice of these unified accounting charts was absolutely logical because, in giving priority to the production cycle, they gave the soviet state, freed from the constraints of business secrecy and competing valuation approaches, the possibility of concentrating its efforts on controlling the costs of production. The soviets were never to abandon this type of accounting chart. They pursued without remit the task of unifying and standardizing all branches of the country, a task which could be considered as having been accomplished just at the start of World War II, with the appearance of the Unified Chart of 1940 (Tchenkov 1973, p. 26).

Special balance sheets

If one removes the details which are not relevant at this point, the fundamental structure of the soviet balance sheet (after a fairly long evolution) was as follows:

Assets	*Liabilities/Capital*
Standard fixed means	Financing of fixed means
Standard circulating means	Financing of standard circulating means
Non-standard standard circulating means	Financing of non-circulating means

This structure reflected two fundamental characteristics: first, in the Soviet Union financing was allocated to specific purposes and the business had to comply with the financing method provided in the plan for a particular type of asset. Secondly, the assets were, without exception, standardized. The enterprises had to establish standards for assets and for renewals for essential items and comply with these, and give these standards in the balance sheet in relation to the actual figures.[8] The balance sheet, therefore, thanks to its concept of three separate bands of activity, permitted a control of variances in relation to planned investment and planned financing.

In addition, in what some would call a paranoia of control, the Soviet authorities asked the accountants to present the accumulated depreciation on the liabilities side of the balance sheet (which implies that the assets were presented at cost) and to show deductions from the profit on the asset side. This presentation facilitated the control of the use of funds but confused the economic concept of the assets side of the balance sheet. It was not therefore used in other socialist countries.

Special profit and loss accounts

The profit and loss account of soviet businesses uses the concepts described above. Priority is given to a functional classification of expenses which, leaving aside questions of valuation, is very close to that used in Anglo-Saxon countries (sales less cost of goods sold less selling and administrative expenses). Reading the profit and loss account on its own could lead one to believe that cost information was highly aggregated, but it should be remembered that the profit and loss account is only a summary of very detailed information (on costs by nature, by function and by stage as well as on budgeted costs and variances) which the state received to enable it to control adherence to its plan.

Control and audit

The control of the accounts in the USSR was essentially a state control, exercised basically through two groups of people: the chief accountants (*glavni bukhgalter*) and the auditors. The chief accountants were appointed by the manager of the factory and were functionally responsible to him. However, they had to follow the systems imposed by the state and in practice they generally appeared more like spies watching the management and had a repressive image. The auditors answered entirely to the central authorities.

They were considered as the controllers of the controllers and had a responsibility for verifying that the plan had been followed and for protecting the 'socialist property' (against theft, damage, etc.).

An assessment of soviet accounting

Many specialists consider that communist accounting practices were not real accounting. Of course, no one suggests that they did not use double-entry, but rather that it was more to do with keeping the books or counting rather than accounting. The fundamental argument is that of Bailey, who invokes Stiglitz and from earlier times Weber, and suggests that it is not possible to have an accounting system without real prices (Bailey 1995, p. 601). It is incontestable that considerable distortions of prices (and that is a euphemism) could frequently be seen in communist businesses, but does this justify denying the existence of accounting? What was asked of these businesses is that they should reduce their costs with reference to a standard price (even if this was manipulated). Does this type of management which, after all is often that imposed by multinational groups on their subsidiaries, not necessitate accounting, even if only for control purposes?

Should one equally consider that in those capitalist countries where accounting is essentially playing a role in taxation there is no 'real' accounting because the results arrived at do not conform to economic reality? It seems preferable to allow that there are several types of accounting which meet different needs. In this sense communist accounting practice seems a special form, but a form of accounting notwithstanding.

Marxist–Leninist content

Was it a Marxist–Leninist form of accounting? That is certainly the opinion of Seal *et al.* (1995, p. 665). But as regards the author of *Das Kapital*, one can see only with difficulty that this could be Marxist accounting. The two fundamental issues for Marx were (1) the creation of value by work in the sphere of production, and (2) the disappearance of the state in a communist society. In what sense can an accounting system which rejected the creation of a profit to the stage of receipt of money, and which served above all as a means of control by the state, be seen as Marxist?

As far as Lenin is concerned, on the other hand, we know that he particularly insisted on the study of German capitalism. 'Our duty is to put ourselves in the school of capitalism of the German state, and to apply all our energy to assimilating it.'

> We find in this country the last word of the modern techniques of a great capitalism, and of a methodical organization <u>at the service of bourgeois imperialism and the junkers</u>. Delete the underlined words, replace the military state, the state of the junkers, the bourgeois imperialist state, by another state, a state of a different social nature, having a different class, by the soviet state, that is to say, a proletarian state, and you will obtain all the conditions which give socialism.

Is one not justified in thinking, in view of the lessons of history, that the instruments of a German accounting dirigisme fashioned the soviet state socialism?

Objectives of communist accounting

Obviously one could say that this had already been identified as the control of adherence to the state plan, but one can also ask, perhaps naively, what was the point of the plan? The official answer was: the satisfaction of the interests of the workers. But if we examine the accounting system quite objectively (which is, let us agree, easier after the failure of the soviet system than before), we can observe two elements. First, the concept of annual profit was not the value added but a sort of revenue to the state's capital. Secondly, a reading of the financial management books of the communist period[9] shows that this state revenue was compared with the total of capital invested by the state in the enterprise, that is the total value of the balance sheet.

Why not admit that the state tried to withdraw the maximum amount of profit in relation to the capital invested? Of course, at the level of the individual enterprise the calculations made no sense if looked at from the point of view of the private capitalist; but from the viewpoint of the state they had a point. The distortion of prices did not prevent pressure being put on businesses nor the measurement, even if in a (rough) way, of the 'profits'.

Furthermore, we know that in the USSR the total value of the balance sheet was calculated using gross asset values. This could be compared with the practice of measuring the rate of residual income to gross assets which capitalist holding companies require of their subsidiaries: there is a surprising symmetry with the soviet practice.

Obviously such a comparison has its limits since there is no market as such in a communist society. But this explains why accounting, the only possible means of obtaining both microeconomic and macroeconomic figures, had such a crucial importance, at least from the point of view of the state bureaucrats.

The position of accountants

The consequences for accountants (and their techniques) have been considered by several authors, including in particular Bailey, who sums up well the general feeling. This is that the communist accounting system led to an intellectual retreat by accountants, who lacked curiosity, made no innovations, and lived in a closed world which was ignorant of what was going on in the West, and as a result, could only have very rudimentary techniques (Bailey 1995, p. 599 *et seq.*).

We should like to qualify this position a little. It is true that the vast majority of accountants (like the whole population) were obliged to apply without question rules in whose formulation they had not participated, which resulted in a mechanistic training in the rules and a mechanistic application of them. But there also existed an elite of practitioners and teachers who, whether convinced or not of the merits of the system, participated in its constant improvement or at least in attempted improvement. How else does one explain otherwise the numerous articles devoted to a criticism of the system (albeit not its fundamentals) and its improvement?

This elite did, in our view, know the current leading accounting techniques in the West, at least in the areas which could have an impact on communist conceptions, principally therefore in cost control. Monographs devoted to the study of capitalist accounting appeared regularly in the professional journals, and the bibliographies of many works included known works from the West.[10] Certain books show evidence of research of an undeniable quality.[11] Thus the evidence suggests that despite bureaucracy and oppression, thought was not absent as regards the elite. Moreover it is that which explains how they have been able to adapt so rapidly to the 'new' accounting after the fall of communism.

European communist countries

Before World War II, the accounting regulation and literature of the future European communist countries was on the whole marked by Austrian and German influences. Seal, Sucher and Zelenka (1993, p. 11) show that in the future Czechoslovakia before 1939 the only accounting rules were in the Austrian Code of Commerce of 1862 (in the Czech Republic) and the Hungarian Code of Commerce of 1875 (Slovakia). In the same way in Poland, as Krzywda, Bailey and Schroeder (1995, p. 638) note, accounting was regulated by the famous 1934 Commercial Code (*Kodeks Handlowy*) of 'German inspiration'. Hungary applied its 1875 Commercial Code, which, for obvious historical reasons, was similar to that of the Austrian Commercial Code. In Romania the accounting rules before World War II were limited to a few general principles built into the Commercial Code and around 1907 German theories had also strongly influenced accounting thought.

A major characteristic of these Commercial Codes is that they only regulate in a very general way the valuation rules and presentation of financial statements. There were no obligatory accounting charts at this time. It was only with the German occupation that the period 'national' accounting plans would start. Another characteristic is that priority was given, in accordance with German and Austro-Hungarian philosophies of the time, to a legal view of assets accompanied by very prudent valuation rules (see Krzywda *et al.* 1995, p. 650), that is to say a static view of accounting. Of course, despite the application of common fundamentals, there could be quite substantial differences of application between countries.

In due course, after the establishment of communist powers, all these laws would be changed. The countries we have mentioned would all, with more or less rapidity, and often with a little help from their soviet 'big brother', adopt the basic rules of communist accounting such as we have described above. Details of this can be found for Romania in Ciucur *et al.* (1980) and Demestrescu *et al.* (1979), for Czechoslovakia in Benech (1975), for Poland in Jarugowa *et al.* (1979) and for Hungary in Borda (1992) and Piesse (1993). But before the communist period, most countries in East Europe were particularly influenced by German accounting regulation. In most of the countries studied there was after 1939 a twofold influence: that of the Germans in the years 1939–44 and then that of soviet accounting.

If one leaves aside certain nuances, the communist accounting system was to impose, more or less rapidly according to the country, the four principles of classic accounting in a communist economy: material unity, formal unity, regulatory unity and the primacy of classifying costs by function.

Conclusion

Since 1991 rapid changes have taken place in Eastern Europe under the aegis of the state, and these incorporate fundamental concepts of capitalist accounting which reflect in their diversity, all the variants of capitalist accounting. This diversity of concepts seems essentially due to the interplay of foreign influences. It seems to carry with it, subject to changes which are always possible, profound consequences for the economies concerned.

Rapid change

During a discussion in January 1996, the French manager of a major audit firm in an Eastern European country said, referring to the latest legislation such as the requirement to take into account deferred taxation in the accounts of individual companies: 'Poland

and the Czech Republic are in advance of France'. This opinion, intended to be flattering, could be offered in respect of a good number of countries in Eastern Europe. However, practice is no doubt far from being in phase with the regulations and the 'modernism' of these statutes (that is to say its introduction at the level of the most advanced European or international standards) as well as the rapidity with which they have been put in place is striking. There has not been a transition but an accounting revolution in Eastern Europe since 1990.

Changes at the initiative of government

In all the countries of Eastern Europe the accounting revolution has been led by the state which has, in order to implement it, used the instruments traditionally used in those capitalist economies where state regulation reigns: laws, accounting decrees and national accounting plans. Manifestly the private sector is still too weak to accede to power in accounting, at least in the institutional sense. Of course a more detailed analysis is necessary to see what is hidden behind the government. Certainly not the auditors (too recently resuscitated) but very probably the mandarins of the *ancien régime* who have adapted to the new political and economic order.

Changes that incorporate the concepts of capitalist accounting

Communist accounting has had its day: concepts of capital, of assets, of profit or of the scope of regulation or organization of accounting, have all been upset in the countries we are studying in order to introduce, taking account of the variants available, the basic concepts of a capitalist mode of management, i.e. those concepts which reflect the existence of private ownership of the means of production.

Werner Sombart, as we have observed above, has stated that double-entry bookkeeping was to some extent the fundamental sign of capitalism. This opinion can be seen to be very open to debate in the light of the history of the countries of Eastern Europe. If one admits that under the communist reign double-entry bookkeeping existed, one must look elsewhere for the distinguishing mark of capitalism (unless one considers communism a type of state capitalism). In our opinion it is in the concepts of accounting capital and accounting profit that one must look for the traces of capitalism in accounting: it is this truth that has emerged from the new accounting statutes in Eastern Europe.

Changes that reflect the diversity of capitalist regulation

Beyond the core of fundamental concepts that characterize capitalist accounting, there exists a series of variations of these concepts which reflect their adaptation to different kinds of regulation within capitalism. One could say that there are several types of capitalist accounting. This diversity, apparently, is also to be found in Eastern Europe, and to make it evident we shall use here a double set of classification criteria.

We shall first contrast, using terminology borrowed from classical German doctrine, the *static*[12] types of accounting (which give priority to concepts of capital and assets based on legal ownership, and to valuation methods which are oriented towards a rapid expensing of intangible assets and undervaluation of other assets for the sake of the protection of creditors), and the *dynamic* types of accounting (which give priority to concepts of capital and profit oriented towards a measure of the efficiency (rentability) of resources, whatever their legal form, and methods of valuation which largely recognize intangible assets and reject on principle any undervaluation of assets, whether tangible or intangible).

This first point of reference can be applied to the accounting rules for capital, leased assets, depreciation of intangible assets, stocks, short-term investments and debtors and creditors denominated in foreign currencies. This is done in Table 14.1.

Table 14.1 seems to suggest three groups of countries: (1) those where the static concept seems to have been adopted (Hungary and Romania); (2) those where the dynamic concept is strongest (Russia and Bulgaria); and (3) those that hesitate between the two (Poland and the Czech Republic). We shall analyse this after introducing the second set of criteria.

This second set of criteria attempts to ask whether the accounting system recognizes accounting valuation as being different from tax valuation. Here we will base the analysis on the rules given in the accounting statutes in relation to the depreciation of tangible fixed assets and the calculation of the tax charge (in individual company accounts) (Table 14.2).

Poland and the Czech Republic are oriented clearly towards accounting rules being distinct from tax rules, Bulgaria appears uncertain on the point while the other countries, it seems, have a much more tax-oriented approach.

The next criterion is to test whether the accounting has a microeconomic or macroeconomic approach. Two aspects seem decisive in measuring the macroeconomic approach: first, the obligation to prepare a profit and loss account where the revenue is total production, and secondly, a method of classifying expenses by nature which incorporates the distinction of intermediate consumption and value added (Table 14.3).

Table 14.1 seems to show a split between those whose accounting is microeconomic in approach (Hungary, Poland and Russia) and those with a macroeconomic style (Bulgaria, Romania and the Czech Republic).

Table 14.1 Static versus dynamic accounting

Accounting issue	Bulgaria	Hungary	Poland	Romania	Russia	Czech Republic
Capital	Stat	Stat	Dyn	Stat	Stat	Stat
Leased assets	Dyn	Stat	Dyn	Stat	Dyn	Dyn
Depreciation of intangibles	Dyn	Stat	?	Stat	Dyn	Stat
Stock	Dyn	Stat	Stat	Stat	Dyn	Dyn
Foreign currency	Dyn	Stat	Stat	Stat	Dyn	Stat

Note: Stat = static accounting, dyn = dynamic accounting.

Table 14.2 Accounting valuation versus tax valuation

	Bulgaria	Hungary	Poland	Romania	Russia	Czech Republic
Distinction between tax depreciation and accounting depreciation	yes	no	yes	no	no	yes
Tax charge	actual?	actual	deferred	actual	actual	deferred

Table 14.3 Microeconomic versus macroeconomic accounting style

	Bulgaria	Hungary	Poland	Romania	Russia	Czech Republic
Obligation to give total production	yes	no	no	yes	no	yes
Value added	yes	no	no	yes	no	yes

Overall, one can draw the following conclusions from this analysis. Two countries seem clearly marked by an approach to accounting that gives priority to static and fiscal influences: Hungary and Romania. However, whereas Romania has adopted a macroeconomic presentation of figures, Hungary does not seem concerned with it. The other countries are more oriented towards a dynamic concept of accounting giving priority on the whole to figures purged of any tax or static influence. But in the second group there is also a split between the two countries that require a macroeconomic presentation of information (Bulgaria, Czech Republic) and the other countries which seem to do without it (Poland and Russia).

Changes whose diversity is essentially explained by the effect of foreign influences

The fundamental fact dominating the previous analysis is the great diversity of accounting evolution in the countries of Eastern Europe. Despite having come from the same mould, they are now, after a short lapse of time, very different. How can one explain this divergence? Normally the explanation for differences in accounting systems can be found in the diversity of modes of regulation of economic systems. One can, in this respect, distinguish in the heart of the capitalist system seven major types of regulation each of which leads to a particular model of accounting.

These are: regulation by *bankruptcy* (which calls, in principle, for a static view of accounting), by the *stock markets* (which leads to a dynamic view), by the *banks* (which generally is translated into a static view), by *taxation* (which obviously leads to tax-oriented accounting), by *suggested plans* (which leads to the appearance of macro-economic accounting), by *private groups* (leading to group accounting plans at either a national or international level) or finally by a dirigiste state (which encourages the appearance of standardized national plans encompassing management accounting).

One might think therefore that the differences in economic situations and types of regulation would provide an explanation of the evolution of accounting regulation in Eastern Europe between 1990 and 1994. In our view this is not the case. How can one explain, for example, that a country like Russia where privatizations and stock exchange activity are far less prominent than in Hungary ends up with a dynamic kind of accounting, while the authorities in Budapest have opted for static accounting? How does one explain that a country like the Czech Republic where privatizations have taken place at a particularly fast rate, prefers a macroeconomic type of accounting whereas other countries, which are less advanced in their approach to privatization and more conservative, do not feel the need to provide themselves with such an information system?

In fact we think that the influence of types of regulation only makes itself felt in the long term. In the short term other influences can come into play and show themselves to have more explanatory power. It seems in the case of the Eastern European countries we are studying it is strategic alliances and more specifically alliances with foreign partners (whether states or institutions) considered to be most promising (in terms of gaining economic or political advantages) which have had the first word.[13]

An analysis of the accounting legislations shows the borrowing of diverse notions and institutions which do not correspond to needs justified by the current regulation, but which give evidence of a desire to align themselves politically with these countries or institutions. Of course, in certain cases these alignments may be multiple, which gives rise to accounting mixtures that are not necessarily rational in terms of modes of economic regulation.

At the risk of oversimplifying or even worse, of misrepresenting a complex reality, we would suggest on the basis of all the information provided previously a table of fundamental influences which have been exercised and have been accepted in the different countries being studied (Table 14.4).

It seems that two countries have found the source of their inspiration in the accounting traditions of two European nations: these are Romania, the whole of whose legislation is based (Richard 1995b) on French financial accounting (with all its characteristics of static accounting with fiscal and macroeconomic objectives), and Hungary, whose accounting culture is visibly German in inspiration (particularly as concerns terminology, accounting principles, classification of expenses, stock valuation and generally the understatement of assets).

Two other countries have clearly opted for the IASB model. These are Russia and Bulgaria whose statutes, particularly as regards accounting principles, basically reproduce those formulated by the international organization. However, while Bulgaria at the same time called for French expertise at least for reforming its accounting plan,[14] Russia, in calling for UN help with the development of its accounting did not depart from the 'pure' international influence.[15]

Finally, the last two countries, Poland and the Czech Republic, have chosen to play a composite card in allowing several influences to have sway, even if the details of this game have been played out differently.

Poland's strategy is one of flexibility since it allows, in the context of the Fourth Directive, several forms of financial statement, thereby being able to satisfy all of its economic partners, and does not back away from international influence on certain points (for example the question of deferred tax). The 'hesitant' character of the Polish legislation can be explained by this flexibility.

The strategy of the Czech Republic is more complex; as opposed to Poland one finds in this country a French influence in addition to the EU and international influences. In addition, as the Czech Republic imposes on its firms (and therefore their commercial partners) a single model for financial statements (specifically French in origin), this signifies that the possible contradictions inherent in the different sources of inspiration are not, as in Poland, regulated by leaving a free choice of models and principles but appear quite clearly in their

Table 14.4 Country influences

	Bulgaria	*Hungary*	*Poland*	*Romania*	*Russia*	*Czech Republic*
Organization or country	IASC France	EU Germany	IASC EU	France	IASC UN	IASC EU France

juxtaposition. Of course, it is difficult in the context of a work looking from outside to discern the profound reasons for the diversity of foreign influences. It is sufficient here simply to note their existence and their impact.

Profound consequences

A problem with analysing accounting in any country is that one has to put emphasis on the statutes and not on practices and the latter, in former communist states, generally lag behind the accounting regulations, particularly if these are contradicted or constrained by tax rules. However, the accounting regulations constitute a major influence over the evolution of accounting in Eastern Europe. In fact they condition the whole of the education system. As a result there will in the long term be considerable differences in attitudes to accounting and to its practice, depending upon whether accounting specialists were educated from a static or dynamic approach, fiscal or macroeconomic, whether they have learned one system or several and whether their approach is national or international.

All the same, nothing is fixed: the present situation may evolve in the short term under the influence of modifications in international relations (the favoured partners may change) and in the medium term with the effect of economic realities or the impact of types of regulation. One should expect further accounting changes in Eastern Europe.

Notes

1. Sokolov and Kovalev (1993) show that before the 1917 Revolution, there were in Russia no precise rules governing accounting and financial statements. There was an order of 11 May 1899 (related to tax) which gave only 'very general' rules on the preparation of the balance sheet, and these had no practical effect, it seems, as there was 'chaos' in accounting practices which were often marked by an under-estimation of asset values and an opportunist approach to changes of accounting policy.

2. Tchenkov (1973, pp. 5–7) emphasizes that the NEP period saw only the beginnings of regulating the content of the balance sheet and it was only with the arrival of Stalinist policies that the first accounting plans, of 1925 and 1926, marked a real break with earlier periods.

3. Amongst the classics of Russian accounting theory we would cite Sumtsov (1975), Poklad (1963) and Tatur (1968), often cited in other socialist countries (see Jarugowa *et al.* 1979).

4. Higher Council of the National Economy.

5. For a more detailed discussion see Richard (1995a).

6. For further information see Richard (1995a).

7. Liberman and Eidinov (1995, p. 805) insist on this particularity of soviet accounting.

8. The state's right to control the internal management was evident therefore even from the balance sheet.

9. See in particular Scheremet and Tatur (1974).

10. The example of Jarugowa, Malc and Sawicki (1979) would serve to convince on this point.

11. It is always a little dangerous to favour certain examples, but one could point to the quality of the work of Fraas (1969) in Eastern Germany, or Matskevitchious (1977) in

the USSR and Scheremet and Tatur (1974) as far as concerns the analysis of cost and economic analysis.

12. For a reinterpretation of these concepts see Richard (1996).

13. Seal, Sucher and Zelenka (1995, p. 679) 'discover' just as we do contradictions between the types of accounting regulation chosen and the types of regulation planned. But they seem to explain these anomalies as errors or at least iterations, a view that we do not share.

14. The official texts refer in several places to the desire to apply the IASB standards (see in particular National Accounting Standard 6). However, reference is also made to the participation of a national consultant (Gilbert Gélard) and to an expert in the pathfinding programme (G. Rasmussen).

15. Help from the UN is mentioned by Palii (1992) in his commentary on the new accounting plan.

References

Bailey, D. (1995) Accounting in transition in the transitional economy. *European Accounting Review* **4**: 595–623.

Benech, L. (1975) *Bukhgalterskii uchet v Tchekhoslovakskoi sotsialisticheskoi Respublike*. Financi, Moscow.

Borda, M. (1992) Hungary. In D. Alexander and S. Archer (eds) *The European Accounting Guide*. Academic Press, London.

Boross, Z., Clarkson, A.H., Fraser, M. and Weetman, P. (1995) Pressures and conflicts in moving towards harmonization of accounting practice: the Hungarian experience. *European Accounting Review* **4**(4): 713–737.

Ciucur, E., Toiu, A., Ristea, M. and Vilsan, A. (1980) *Contabilitate, Editura didactica si pedagogica*. Editura Economica, Bucaresti.

Demetrescu, C., Possler, L., Puchita, V. and Voica, V. (1979) *Contabilitatea stünta fundamentala si applicativa, scrisul romanete*. Scrisol romanesc, Craiova.

Fraas, G. (1975) *Kostenverursachung, Kostenzurechnung*. Die Wirtschaft, Berlin.

Jarugowa, A., Malc, W. and Sawicki, K. (1979) *Rachunek Kostow*. Panstwowe Wydawnictwo Ekonomiczne, Warsaw.

Krzywda, D., Bailey, D. and Schroeder, M. (1995) A theory of European accounting development applied to accounting change in contemporary Poland. *European Accounting Review* **4**(4): 625–657.

Liberman, L.V. and Eidinov, A.M. (1995) The development of accounting in tsarist Russia and the USSR. *European Accounting Review* **4**(4): 777–807.

Makarov, B.T. (1966) *Teoriya Bykhgalterskogo ucheta*. Financi, Moscow.

Mueller, G.G. (1967) *International Accounting*. Macmillan, New York.

Nikolaeva, S. (1995) *Sostavim otchet vmeste*. Akdi, Moscow.

Novodvorskii, V.D. (1995) *O polojenii financovaja otchetnost predprijatija*, BY no. 7.

Palii, V.F. (1992) *Kommentarii novomu planu chetov bukhgalsterokogo ucheta*. Linf, Moscow.

Piesse, J. (1993) The transition to a new system of accounting: the case of Hungary. *Journal of European Business Education* **2** (2, May).

Poklad, I.I. (1963) *Kurs bukhgalterskogo ucheta*. Gosfinizdat, Moscow.

Richard, J. (1980) Comptabilité et systèmes économiques. Doctoral thesis Université Paris 1.

Richard, J. (1983) Comptabilité pour l'autogestion: la comptabilité des entreprises yougoslaves. Cahiers français no. 210. Documentation Française, Paris.

Richard, J. (1995a) The evolution of accounting chart models in Europe from 1900 to 1945. Some historical elements. *European Accounting Review* **1**(4): 87–124.

Richard, J. (1995b) The evolution of the Romanian and Russian accounting charts after the collapse of the communist system. *European Accounting Review* **2**(4): 305–322.

Richard, J. (1996) Les comptabilités et leurs pratiques. Dalloz (*Vie de l'entreprise*) Paris.

Scheremet, A.D. and Tatur, S.K. (1974) *Kurs analyza ekonomicheskoi dejatelnosti*. Ekonomika, Moscow.

Schmalenbach, E. (1927) *Der Kontenrahmen*, Zeitschrift für Handels–wissenschaftliche Forschung, no. 9.

Schroll, R. (1995) The new accounting system in the Czech Republic. *European Accounting Review* **4**(4): 827–832.

Seal, W., Sucher, P. and Zelenka, I. (1993) Post-socialist transition and the development of an accountancy profession in the Czech Republic (second draft). First draft EIASM workshop on Accountants in Europe: Brussels, December 2–3.

Seal, W., Sucher, P. and Zelenka, I. (1995) The changing organization of Czech accounting. *European Accounting Review* **4**(4): 659–681.

Sokolov, I. and Kovalev, V.V. (1993) Financial statements in Russia at the end of the XIX Century and the beginning of the XX century. *Bukhgaltenskii uchet* **9**: 40–43.

Sombart, W. (1928) *Der moderne Kapitalismus*, 15 Auflage II.

Sumtsov, A.I. (1975) *Teoriya bukhgalterskogo acheta i bukhgalterskii uchet & promishlennosti*. Statistika, Moscow.

Tatur, S.K. (1968) *Choziajstwiennyj rasczot w nowych uslowijach*. Isd Moskowskogo Universitieta, Moskwa.

Tchenkov, C.A. (1973) *Sistema chetov i bukhgalterskii balans predpriyatiya*. Financi, Moscow.

Zakon o Vctovnictve, S. Komentarom a prikladni uctovania, *E. Konspo, 19 Zilina*.

Accounting in the Russian Federation

Tatiana Krylova

Introduction and background

Accounting in Russia has historically been characterized by the dominance of state regulation. In Soviet times accounting was understood as a tool of state control over enterprises, and accountants were appointed by the state as its representative within the enterprise, to monitor the use of the resources allocated to the enterprise by state authorities. There was no professional institute until as recently as 1997 and the accounting profession is only just beginning to influence the development of accounting practices.

Auditing was exercised as another tool of state control, i.e. it was done by state authorities and the results were reported to state authorities. The first independent audit started to evolve as a response to the demands of the first East–West joint venture enterprises in 1988. Joint ventures also presented the first case of exposure of Soviet enterprises to the needs of users of accounting information other than just state authorities. They were the cause of a number of changes in Soviet accounting for joint ventures which eventually led to changes in the Soviet accounting system as a whole.

After the split up of the Soviet Union, and as a result of economic reforms in Russia after 1992, Russian accounting has undergone further changes, initially responding to the needs of foreign investors and the requirements of the International Monetary Fund as one of the conditions of its financial assistance. Over the past decade a number of decrees have been issued outlining the need for and the steps to be taken in reforming accounting in the direction of international accounting. The process was not straightforward and a number of issues had to be resolved including such fundamental ones as the need for reform of Russian companies themselves – at least for those which are not involved in the international financing. The ultimate goal of reform had also to be defined, i.e. what international/foreign system – if any – should be used a target model for Russia.

It seems that a radical change occurred in 1998 when the Russian government issued a decree with a clear statement of the goals of reform. It outlined the needs of investors in a market economy and identified International Accounting Standards as the basis on which accounting will be changing in Russia. At the present stage the accounting system in Russia can be characterized as a transitional one still featuring the requirements of a centrally-administered economy but with an increasingly-felt impact of the principles and rules underlying IAS/IFRS.

Legal and institutional basis of accounting regulation

The legal basis of accounting regulation is outlined by the Accounting Law which was adopted in 1996 and amended in 1998. According to this, general methodological leadership stays with the Russian Government which delegates this duty to particular bodies. The Ministry of Finance is a principal body in charge of accounting regulation in areas other than the banking sector (which is covered by the Central Bank). The legislative framework of accounting regulation in Russia can be best described as shown in Table 15.1.

The Civil Code has the highest legislative authority. It outlines some underlying requirements on providing accounting records and reports by legal entities and provides some broad definitions relevant to accounting and reporting such as statutory capital, market value, net assets, subsidiaries and affiliated companies, etc.

The most important document of the first level is the Accounting Law. It defines the regulatory framework of Russian accounting, its objectives and principles including measurement of assets and liabilities, responsibilities within the organization, requirements for bookkeeping procedures and reporting. The Accounting Law applies to all legal entities based in the Russian Federation, including affiliates and representative offices of foreign companies (if not otherwise specified by international agreements of the Russian Federation).

The Securities and Exchange Committee of Russia provides reporting and disclosure requirements for joint stock companies in addition to those required by the Ministry of Finance. There are two principal documents which outline those requirements, the Securities Market Law of 1996 (with amendments of 1998 and 1999) and the Joint Stock Companies Law of 1995 (with amendments of 1996, 1999 and 2001). Disclosure requirements are developed in relation to prospectuses, quarterly reports of securities' issuers, and reports on material events and actions effected by the company. They also specify requirements on the publication of financial reports by joint stock companies, approval of annual financial statements, audit requirements and rules on availability of the information to

Table 15.1 The legislative framework of Russian accounting regulation

Level	Legislative power	Documents	Responsible bodies
Level I	Compulsory laws	Civil Code, Federal Laws, Government acts, President's decrees	State Duma, Government of Russia, President of Russia
Level II	Compulsory accounting standards	Russian accounting standards (PBU)	Ministry of Finance, Central Bank
Level III	Optional methodological instructions	Chart of Accounts; methodological instructions, guidelines, manuals, interpretations, official letters, etc.	Ministry of Finance, other ministries and agencies, professional and business associations
Level IV	Optional guiding documents of an enterprise	Working documents on accounting policy and procedures of an enterprise	Enterprises

shareholders. There are also more detailed documents issued by the Securities and Exchange Committee explaining specific items to be disclosed. The SEC laws also provide an important point of reference for some definitions crucial for financial reporting such as issued capital, statutory capital, declared capital, treasury stock and other elements of equity capital.

Taxation

In Russia responsibility for taxes lies with the Ministry of Taxes and Duties. Russian Tax legislation is comprised of the Tax Code and a number of federal laws which specify the application of the Tax Code. The Tax Code has two parts. The first part was adopted in 1998. It outlines the general structure and principles of the Russian tax system, such as types of taxes and duties; general taxation rules; definition of a taxpayer; rights, duties and responsibilities of taxpayers; methods of tax control; sanctions for tax evasion. In particular it classifies all Russian taxes as federal taxes, regional taxes (republics, territories and autonomous regions of the Russian Federation) and local taxes.

Part II of the Tax Code was adopted by the State Duma in July 2000 but has already been amended by about a dozen federal laws and it does not yet seem to have reached the end of the process. Part II prescribes principles and rules on specific federal and regional taxes and also defines special tax regimes. In relation to federal taxes, the Code outlines details on value added tax, personal income tax, common social tax, corporate income tax and tax on mineral extraction. Sales tax calculation is explained as part of regional taxes and the agriculture tax constitutes the essence of the chapter on special tax regimes. Part II has a significant effect on the accounting system in Russia.

For a number of decades Russian accounting was basically a set of rules prescribing bookkeeping records for arriving at the tax base for property taxes or income tax. As a result, income shown in accounting books was the difference between the taxable revenues and tax deductible expenses, and the balance sheet assets covered the whole range of taxable property, equipment and current assets. Although a number of efforts have recently been made by the Ministry of Finance to separate tax and accounting as part of the on-going accounting reform, tax legislation still has a significant effect on bookkeeping and financial reporting.

This is due to the fact the that tax authorities are still the major user of financial statements and the demand for a 'fair presentation' of the financial position of an enterprise by Russian investors is still not sufficient to produce enough pressure on companies to present useful financial statements. Where such pressure does exist – mostly coming from foreign investors – normally either the IFRS or some Western country's GAAP (in most cases US GAAP) will be used as a benchmark to produce such information. On one hand, neither incentives nor sanctions exist to ensure that Russian financial reporting rules are followed which might compare with the system of sanctions for misrepresenting the tax base. On the other hand, Russian accounting rules as a system are not yet internally consistent and compliant with fundamental criteria underlying the usefulness of financial reporting for informing financial decisions.

The situation deteriorated in 2001 when Part II of the tax Code was introduced by the Russian government as part of its tax reform. The most significant effect on accounting came from the introduction of Chapter 25 'Income tax of organizations', which requires and provides very specific details on bookkeeping procedures for tax calculations. In particular, it prescribes accounting for taxable revenues and sales, taxable inventories and work-in-progress, finished goods, fixed assets, financial instruments, borrowing costs, etc. It also specifies measurement rules of most of these elements for tax purposes.

Such a development inevitably diminished the importance of accounting and financial reporting, since enterprises could not cope with the two sets of requirements and as a result of much higher pressure in relation to the tax obligations simply started providing financial information based on taxation rules. This also undermined the previous efforts of the Ministry of Finance to introduce the system of tax adjustments which had started to evolve in Russian accounting over the last five years. Such a development is obviously also in contradiction with the Russian government's programme to transform Russian accounting into a system compliant with the IFRS, which was initially stated in the Government decree of 6 March 1998 and later extended in its letter of 13 April 2001.

Interagency committee on accounting reform

Accounting developments have to some extent been influenced by the Interagency Committee on Accounting Reform (IAC) which was created by a government decree in 1998. The very fact of its creation reflected the need for closer coordination of reform among agencies which are directly or indirectly affected by changes in accounting regulation in such areas as taxation, securities regulations, economic policy and price control, education, etc. Although the structure and leadership of the IAC have changed since its inception, the need for coordination has always prevailed. At present the IAC is headed by the Russian Deputy Prime Minister and Minister of Finance. There are also three deputy chairmen representing different aspects of the reform, i.e. the president of the Institute of Professional Accountants, the deputy Minister of Finance and the Deputy Minister of Economic Development and Trade. Other members include senior executives of the Central Bank, Ministry of Education, Ministry of Tax and Duties, Ministry of Justice, Securities and Exchange Committee, and the Antimonopoly policy Committee.

The IAC developed a programme on accounting reform which was approved by the Russian government on 6 March 1998. The programme stated that the main goal of accounting reform is to bring the national accounting system into compliance with the requirements of the market economy and International Financial Reporting Standards. The IAC also produced a plan of action which required development by 2000 of a core set of standards to provide compliance of Russian accounting with the IFRS. However, although creation of the IAC is an important step forward in Russian accounting reform it has been criticized for its lack of proactive efforts on implementation of accounting changes.

Accounting for small companies is governed by the Accounting Law and is further specified by federal laws 'On simplified taxation, accounting and reporting for small businesses' issued on 29 December 1995 and 'On state support of small businesses in Russia' issued on 14 June 1995. Small businesses are allowed to use a simplified chart of accounts and forms of financial reporting.

Accounting standards

Accounting standards are a relatively new development in the Russian accounting system. From the 1920s and until 1994 the principal technical guidance was provided by the uniform Chart of Accounts and the methodological instructions on its use. After the first exposure of Russian enterprises (Soviet enterprises at the time) to market economy accounting in their joint venture structures in 1988, Russia started introducing changes in its accounting system for the joint ventures between centrally planned enterprises and Western companies. The process was substantially facilitated by the involvement of the United Nations experts from the Center on Transnational Corporations in 1989–91. As a result the need to adapt Russian (Soviet) accounting to the different needs of a market economy as opposed to those of a planned economy was accepted by the Russian government.

Transition was accelerated by economic reforms in the country which brought into existence new transactions and activities – such as financial instruments, intangible assets, etc. and new measurement issues. In fact, the beginning of accounting reform could be dated as early as January 1992 when the existing Chart of Accounts was substantially revised, as was the by-law on accounting and reporting procedures. In 1993 Russia officially declared its transition to a new accounting system in accordance with the decree of the Russian government of 12 February 1993 No. 121 'Measures on realization of the Government program on transition of Russian Federation towards internationally accepted accounting and statistic system in accordance with the requirements of market economy'.

At that time it was unclear what particular changes would be introduced, over what period of time and which Western accounting system would be used as a target model for Russia. Initial changes in joint venture accounting were extended to the whole system of Russian accounting through the changes in the Uniform Chart of Accounts. Those included introduction of the accrual principle, accounting for intangible assets, financial investments, bad debts and some others. But what is even more important, the need for a restructuring of the whole legislative framework was stated and in 1994 the Russian Ministry of Finance announced a four-tier structure of accounting regulations. According to this new structure accounting standards (or *polojeniya po buhgalterskomu uchyetu – PBU)* were to become the second level of authoritative documents. Their purpose was to outline the fundamental principles and rules for accounting for specific events, transactions and resources without specific bookkeeping prescriptions, unlike past rules. The first Russian accounting standard (RAS) No. 1 'Accounting policies of the organization' was published by the Russian Ministry of Finance in July 1994 (it was later superseded by a second version in December 1998 No. 60-n which was also partially amended in 1999 by the order of Ministry of Finance No. 107-n.). So far the standards listed in Table 15.2 have been issued.

At the same time another fundamental document was substantially revised to make it more adequate to the new needs of the transitional economy of the Russian Federation – the by-law on accounting and reporting principles and procedures. Before the start of accounting reform this document was one of the major regulations governing the organization and methodology of accounting and reporting in the Soviet Union. Over the past decade it has undergone substantial revisions reflecting the evolution of accounting functions in the transitional economy in Russia. The current version was issued on 29 July 1998 and was amended on 30 December 1999 and 24 March 2000. Basically the document could be seen as a more detailed version of the Accounting Law. The document has the advantage over the Law that it can be amended as soon as changes are required, without going through the legal due process. On the other hand it lacks statutory power for exactly the same reason.

All standards are issued by the Ministry of Finance. Over the last decade there has been a growing involvement of external experts who produce initial drafts for further discussions within the Ministry of Finance. Other bodies involved in technical discussions are the Methodological Council of the Ministry of Finance, the Institute of Professional Accountants and the Working Group of the IAC.

There are a number of documents which have the status of application rules ('methodological instructions') but in reality they govern certain significant areas of accounting and reporting in Russia. These include:

- Methodological recommendations on consolidated accounts (30 December 1996 with amendments 12 May 1999)

- Methodological recommendations on disclosure of income per share information (21 March 2000)

Table 15.2   Russian Accounting Standards as of 1 June 2002

RAS (PBU)	Document number	Issue date	Note
Accounting policies of the organization	PBU 1	9 December 1998, amended 30 December 1999	First version issued on 28 July 1994
Accounting for Construction Contracts	PBU 2	20 December 1994	Being revised
Accounting for assets and liabilities valued in foreign currency	PBU 3	10 January 2000	
Accounting statements* of the organization	PBU 4	6 July 1999	First version issued on February 1996
Accounting for inventories	PBU 5	19 July 2001	First version issued on 15 June 1997, second version issued on 15 June 1998, amended 30 December 1999 and 24 March 2000
Accounting for fixed assets	PBU 6	3 September 1997, amended 24 March 2000	Being revised
Events after the balance sheet date	PBU 7	25 November 1998	
Contingencies	PBU 8	21 November 2001	First version issued on 25 November 1998
Revenues of organization	PBU 9	6 May 1999, amended 30 December 1999	Being revised
Expenses of an organization	PBU 10	6 May 1999, amended 30 December 1999	Being revised
Affiliated parties	PBU 11	13 January 2000	
Segments	PBU 12	27 January 2000	
Intangible assets	PBU 13	16 October 2000	
Government subsidies	PBU 14	16 October 2000	
Accounting for loans and associated costs	PBU 15	2 August 2001	

* In Russian regulations the term 'Accounting statements' is being used rather than 'Financial statements.'

- Order of the Ministry of Finance on publication of annual reports by open joint stock companies (28 December 1996)
- Methodological instructions on accounting for fixed assets (20 July 1998 with amendments of 28 March 2000)
- Instructions on forms of accounting statements (13 January 2000)
- Instructions on preparation and presentation of accounting statements (13 January 2000)
- Methodological instructions on information required for particular items of accounting statements (28 June 2000).

A chart of accounts used to be the principal governing regulation in accounting and reporting in the Soviet Union and later in Russia. Although within the new structure of the legislative framework it has an authority of a Level III pronouncement, i.e. considered a methodological document rather than a normative compulsory regulation, it still plays a dominant role in bookkeeping procedures for the vast majority of Russian accountants.

Before the start of accounting reform in 1992, the Russian accounting system was based on a uniform chart of accounts of 1965. The document was revised substantially in 1990–91 and its new version was enacted starting from 1 January 1992. A number of amendments were introduced over the next 10 years and finally, in 2000, a new significantly revised version of the chart of accounts has been approved and introduced from 1 January 2001 along with the Instruction on its use (Order of Ministry of Finance of 31 October 2000).

The chart of accounts lists the ledger accounts which are to be used by enterprises. Each account has a number, some accounts have sub-accounts. Its current version has 99 accounts which are grouped into eight sections:

- non-current assets
- inventories
- production costs
- finished goods and goods for sale
- cash
- settlements
- capital
- financial results.

There is also a section on off-balance sheet accounts.

The Instruction on the use of the chart of accounts provides a general description of each account, explanations on transactions for which an account can or cannot be used, the links between bookkeeping records. Organizations are allowed to develop their own working chart of accounts based on the chart of accounts and Instruction on its use, which allows them to add additional accounts (upon the agreement with the Ministry of Finance) or introduce new sub-accounts depending on the specific activities of an enterprise.

Although it is stated that the chart of accounts is regarded as a technical document which is governed by principles and rules outlined by the PBUs and other accounting regulations, it is still the case that the chart of accounts has a dominant role in recording business transactions. In addition, while in many cases the Instruction on the use of the chart of accounts goes as far as prescribing the measurement rules for assets and liabilities, none the less a number of frequently occurring transactions are not discussed at all. Although some instructions are not in compliance with the general principles stated in the By-law and PBU No. 1 'Accounting policies of the organization', which have a higher legislative status, in most cases the chart of accounts will in reality be a first point of reference for most practising accountants.

Objectives, assumptions and qualitative characteristics

Objectives, assumptions and qualitative characteristics are outlined in the Accounting Law, By-law, PBU No. 1 'Accounting policy of organization' and BPU 4 'Accounting statements of the organization'. In general they could be summarized as follows:

- *Objectives* of accounting legislation are stated as providing uniformity of accounting procedures; comparable and truthful information on the financial position of an enterprise, its revenues and expenses which is required by users of accounting statements.

- *Objectives* of accounting are stated as providing internal and external users with complete and truthful information on an enterprise's activities and its financial position; the purpose of the use of such information by internal and external users is not specified apart from the objective of having information for control on the legality of enterprise activities and the utilization of its resources and liabilities in accordance with approved norms and budgets.

- *Objectives* of accounting (financial) statements are to provide truthful and complete presentation of the financial position of an organization, its financial results and changes in its financial position.

Table 15.3 lists the assumptions and qualitative characteristics recognized by Russian regulation.

Truthfulness and completeness are considered as overall requirements to be met by financial statements. Truthfulness is defined as compliance with Russian bookkeeping rules rather than a fair presentation of the financial position of an enterprise. However the Accounting Law states that in the case where accounting rules do not allow the entity to present its financial position and financial results truthfully, it can depart from accounting rules but needs to disclose this fact in the notes to the financial statements along with

Table 15.3 Assumptions and qualitative characteristics of Russian accounting

Assumptions and qualitative characteristics	Reference
Accrual basis	By-law, PBU 1
Economic entity	Accounting Law, By-law, PBU 1, PBU 4
Going concern	By-law, BPU 1
Materiality	PBU 1 (only in relation to accounting methods), PBU 4
Truthfulness	Accounting Law, By-law, PBU 4
Substance over form	By-law, PBU 1
Prudence	By-law, PBU 1
Completeness	By-law, PBU 1, PBU 4
Consistency and comparability	Accounting Law, By-law, PBU 1, PBU 4
Timeliness	PBU 1
Rationality (cost-benefit)	By-law, PBU 1
Neutrality	PBU 4

explanations of the reason for such a departure. Otherwise it would be regarded as an obstruction of Russian accounting legislation. The same requirement is further stated in the PBU No. 4 'Accounting statements of the organization'. The possibility to make a departure from Russian bookkeeping rules for the sake of a truthful presentation of financial information is an undoubted step forward since for the first time in Russia it calls for a judgement in accounting practice.

Another important source of information on objectives, assumptions and qualitative characteristics is a document entitled 'Conceptual framework of accounting in a market economy of Russia'. It was approved by the Methodological Council of Russian Ministry of Finance and by the Institute of Professional Accountants on 29 December 1997. This document to a large degree is based on the IFRS framework and contains important definitions of assets, liabilities, equity, revenues and expenses (this is the only document in Russia where assets, liabilities and equity are defined based on their economic substance rather than their role in a production cycle); outlines measurement and recognition criteria as they are defined in the IFRS *Framework*; defines the objectives, assumptions and qualitative characteristics in accordance with the IFRS with the exception of the truthfulness and true and fair view which are not mentioned.

The overall principle of usefulness is introduced in this document with more detailed explanations of specific criteria. Although this document is often cited during doctrinal discussions, it is hardly used in practice since it does not have any authoritative power and also is difficult to understand for most practitioners, due to the lack of additional guidance on the implementation of these requirements and in general due to the lack of any compliance requirements.

Publication and audit

The Accounting Law outlines the requirements for the publication of accounting information. According to this, financial statements should be presented to the owners of the organization and to the statistical bodies in the location where the entity is registered. Quarterly reports should be presented within 30 days of the end of the quarter, and annual reports should be presented within 90 days of the year end.

Open joint stock companies, banks and other financial institutions, insurance companies, stock exchanges, and investment funds are required to publish annual financial statements no later than 1 June of the year following the reporting year.

The Joint Stock Companies Law requires the annual publication of the balance sheet, profit and loss account, prospectus where applicable, announcement of a general shareholders meeting and list of affiliated parties with disclosure of the number and types of shares which they hold.

Public audit is a relatively new development in Russia. It was first introduced in the Soviet Union in 1988 in relation to the joint venture companies between Soviet and Western enterprises. Economic reforms and privatization created a further demand for independent audits. Western audit companies, mainly the Big Four, imported the knowledge and skills required for rendering such services in the first instance, but at the same time Russian audit firms also began to evolve.

For almost a decade, auditing was regulated by the Decree of President issued in 1993 as a temporary regulation in the anticipation of the coming Audit Law. However it took almost 10 years of debates to finally agree on such a law.

At the time of writing the following principal documents govern the public audit in Russia:

- Federal Law 'On audit activities' issued on 7 August 2001, amended 14 December 2001 and 30 December 2001
- Government decree 'On state regulation of audit activities in Russian Federation' issued on 6 February 2002
- Government decree 'On licensing of audit activities' issued on 29 March 2002.

A number of documents supporting a new Audit Law are still being developed. These include a by-law on the accreditation of professional audit associations and a number of regulations on the training and certification of auditors. New audit standards based on International Standards of Audit are being developed as well.

Federal law defines the auditing activities and organizational requirements for audit firms (they should have no less than five auditors, 50% must be Russian citizens which is extended to 75% if a CEO is a foreign citizen), the rights and obligations of auditors, confidentiality requirements, criteria of auditor's independence, insurance requirements and quality control. It outlines certification, qualification and licensing requirements and other aspects of auditing regulation. It also specifies the requirements for a statutory audit.

According to the Audit Law, a statutory audit is required in the following cases:

- for open joint stock companies;
- for insurance companies, financial institutions, stock exchanges, investment funds, certain government non-budgetary funds;
- when annual sales exceed by 500 000 times, or year-end assets exceed by 200 000 times, the legally stated minimum level of wages;
- for certain state enterprises if their sales or assets exceed minimum wage levels as indicated above;
- if required by federal law.

If the State holds not less than 25% of the statutory capital of an organization, the external auditor should be selected through the process of open tender in accordance with procedures regulated by the government.

At present there are approximately 155 professional associations in Russia but most of them are quite small and regional or local; many Russian auditors have not joined any of these associations. The most representative is the Independent Federation of Consultants and Auditors which has 360 audit firms as members. But most of them are small companies. The most powerful is the Institute of Professional Auditors of Russia. It has only 39 firms as members but it is supported by seven out of ten major Russian corporations, which provide financial support to the Institute. Other major associations include the Union of Professional Audit Organizations (37 audit firms), Moscow Audit Chamber and the Audit Chamber of Russia.

Financial reporting

Components of annual reports

Requirements for the annual reports and their content are outlined in PBU No. 4 'Accounting statements of organization' and are specified in the Ministry of Finance order dated 13 January 2000 'Methodological Instructions on Preparation of Accounting. Statements of Organization'. Annual reports of Russian companies consist of the following statements (forms):

- Balance sheet (Form 1)
- Profit and Loss Account (Form 2)
- Statement on Changes in Capital (Form 3)
- Cash Flow Statement (Form 4)
- Appendix to the Balance Sheet (Form 5)
- Statement on Use of Funds Received[1] (Form 6)
- Notes to the Balance Sheet and Profit and Loss Account
- Audit opinion (if applicable)

The *Balance sheet* structure is prescribed by the Ministry of Finance in its PBU 4 as a minimum list of items to be disclosed in the balance sheet (Table 15.4).

From 13 January 2000 Russian companies can develop their own forms of financial statements based on samples provided by the Ministry of Finance which give some more details on items to be disclosed within this structure. Another Ministry of Finance order of 28 June 2000 explains in detail what should be disclosed in each item of the balance sheet including measurement of some of those.

The *Profit and Loss Account* should have the following items:

- Net sales
- Costs of goods sold
- Gross profit from sales

Table 15.4 Structure of the balance sheet of Russian companies

Assets	*Liabilities*
I. Non-current assets	I. Capital and reserves
	1.1. Statutory capital
	1.2. Additional capital
1.1. Intangible assets	1.3. Reserved capital
1.2. Fixed assets	1.4. Undistributed profits (non-covered loss – deducted)
1.3. Profitable investments into tangible assets	
1.4. Financial investments	II. Long-term liabilities
	2.1. Borrowings
	2.2. Other liabilities
II. Current assets	III. Short-term liabilities
2.1. Inventories	
2.2. Value-added tax on purchased goods	3.1. Borrowings
2.3. Receivables	3.2. Payables
2.4. Financial investments	3.3. Deferred income
2.5. Cash	3.4. Reserve on future expenses and payments

- Selling expenses
- Administration and management costs
- Profit from sales
- Interest receivable
- Interest payable
- Income from investments into other organizations
- Other operating income
- Other operating expenses
- Gains
- Losses
- Profit before tax
- Income tax expense
- Profit from ordinary activities
- Extraordinary income
- Extraordinary expenses
- Net income (undistributed profit (non-covered loss)).

More specific requirements on preparing Profit and Loss Account are prescribed in PBU 9 'Revenues of the organization' and PBU 10 'Expenses of the organization'. Technical details on item-by-item preparation are explained in the Ministry of Finance order of 13 January 2000.

The *Statement on changes in capital* provides details on movements in capital items during the year, including statutory capital, additional capital, reserves, undistributed profit, social fund, special purpose financing, reserve on future expenses and payments, valuation reserves. Partnerships and joint stock companies must also provide a section within the Statement on changes in capital giving specific reasons for increases and decreases of capital. The following reasons for capital increases are listed:

Increases due:

- additional issues of shares;
- asset revaluation;
- reorganization (merger, acquisition);
- increase of assets;
- gains which should be credited directly to capital accounts.

Decreases due:

- reduction of par value of shares;
- reduction of number of shares;
- reorganization (merger, acquisition);
- losses which should be debited directly to capital accounts.

The *Cash Flow Statement* has a matrix format where items of cash inflow and cash out-flow are classified as current activities, investing activities and financing activities. It was first introduced in 1996 as a note to the balance sheet and was upgraded to a separate form in 2000 – still as one of the attachments to the balance sheet. Although it is another important step forward in Russian accounting reform, the statement has a number of deficiencies. In particular the emphasis of the presentation is made on the cash inflow and cash outflow items rather than their classification as current, investing and operating activities; classification itself does not comply with the IFRS (for example, financing activities cover short-term investments and short-term borrowings; investment activities include long-term borrowings); comparative data for the previous year are not given.

The *Appendix to the Balance Sheet* requires a number of details explaining the breakdown of, and movements in, major items of the balance sheet such as borrowings, receivables and payables (separate disclosure is required on debtors and creditors which are more than three months' overdue), depreciable assets, financial investments, ordinary expenses and social expenses.

Notes to the Balance Sheet and Profit and Loss Account are required to provide additional explanations on the accounting policy of organizations and provide users with details which are essential for assessment of the real financial position of the organization, its financial results and changes in its financial position. Specific disclosure requirements are specified in PBU No. 4 'Accounting statements of the organization' which are further extended by individual PBUs which deal with specific accounting issues (fixed assets, intangible assets, segment reporting, changes in accounting policy, etc.).

There are no specific requirements on supplementary information such as a management report, directors' report or similar disclosures. However, PBU No. 4 'Accounting statements of the organization' has a separate section outlining possible additional information which might be presented by a company's management if it considered it to be useful for users in their decision-making process. Specifically mentioned are trends in economic indicators of the company's performance, further development of the organization, expected investments, borrowing policy, R&D policy, risk management information and environmental activities.

Measurement and recognition practice

Major differences between Russian PBUs and the IFRS are summarized in Table 15.5.

One of the major issues of Russian accounting is the absence of any legally enforced document on recognition and measurement principles. Assets and liabilities are not defined, the concept of fair value is not used. However Russian legislation prescribes valuation rules in relation to particular types of assets and liabilities.

Valuation rules are generally stated by the Accounting Law. It requires that assets purchased should be measured at total actual acquisition costs; assets acquired otherwise should be measured at market value at the recognition date; assets produced by the organization should be measured at the costs of production. The Law also allows for other valuation methods to be used, but gives no further details. More explanations are given in the by-law which defines actual costs, market value for assets not purchased and costs of production of self-produced assets. The actual acquisition costs include costs of purchase, borrowing costs for purchased assets, commissions and premiums paid, customs, transportation costs, storage costs and delivery costs. The market value of assets granted is defined based on a documentary evidence of the price of this or a similar asset at the recognition date. The costs of production of assets produced by the enterprise include actual costs occurred in the process of production of an asset, such as costs of fixed assets, inventories, labour resources and other costs.

The by-law also outlines specific measurement rules in relation to long-term construction-in-progress, financial investments, fixed assets, intangible assets, inventories,

Table 15.5   International Accounting Standards Checklist

IAS	Russian practice

1. IAS principles are legally required with the exception of usefulness and fair presentation. In practice legal form usually dominates. Application of the rules often results in departure from the principles. Reporting and disclosure rules for equity are different from the IAS. Treasury stock is reported as current assets.

2. In practice the cost of inventories may include overhead and selling expenses and foreign currency exchange differences. Inventories in practice are often not written down to the lower costs. Lower costs are often understood as market value rather than net realizable value.

7. Definitions of operating, investing and financing activities are different from the IAS; cash equivalents are not defined and used; CFS does not allow for comparative data; no requirement on segment cash flow disclosures.

8. The definition of extraordinary items is given by reference to examples such as fires, accidents, etc. which allows for a departure from the IAS. Fundamental errors are not defined; errors are included the in determination of the net profit (loss), separate disclosure, restatement and comparative information are not required. Accounting estimates are not defined and the effect of changes is not required to be disclosed.

10. No differentiation is made between adjusting and non-adjusting events after the balance sheet date; dividends are recognized as an after the balance sheet event without any covenants.

11. Completed contract method is allowed in addition to the percentage-of-completion method. No instructions on immediate recognition as an expense of an expected loss of a contract.

12. No regulation on deferred taxes. Tax loss carry forward is allowed by tax regulation.

14. No requirements on segment cash flow disclosures, segment significant non-cash expenses; reconciliation between the information disclosed for reportable segments and the aggregated information of an enterprise.

15. No regulation.

16. Valuation of assets exchanged differs from the IAS; foreign currency exchange differences are included in the actual costs. Useful life is determined in accordance with the IAS but in practice tax regulation is used as a base both for the useful life and for the depreciation rates.

17. IAS 17 is not in use. Accounting for leased assets is regulated by bookkeeping instructions of 17 February 1997 and does not specify recognition or measurement criteria. Leased assets are not included in the fixed assets on the balance sheet but are disclosed separately in the notes.

18. Some departures from the IAS can be found in revenue definition, lack of clarity in ordinary activities, absence of operating and non-operating revenue definitions, examples are given on operating income, gains and extraordinary income are not in full compliance with the IAS.

19. Not regulated by Russian legislation.

20. Only grants received are recognized as deferred income; grants receivable are recognized at the equity accounts. Grants as financial or fiscal aid are not specified, same as possible cases of their recognition as extraordinary items.

21. Not regulated: translation of financial statements of hyperinflationary subsidiary, treatment of cumulative amount of the exchange differences on the disposal of foreign entity; exchange differences as a result of a severe currency devaluation or depreciation, exchange differences which are related to an enterprise's net investment in a foreign entity, limited disclosures.

22. Not regulated by Russian legislation; some references are made towards goodwill (see IAS 38).

23. Borrowing costs when not capitalized are treated as operating expenses; capitalization of borrowing costs allowed when 'investment property is needed for management purposes of an enterprise'.

24. Narrow definition of related parties linked to a certain percentage of voting power.

26. Not regulated by Russian legislation.

Table 15.5 International Accounting Standards Checklist (*continued*)

IAS	*Russian practice*

27. IFRS 27 is allowed as an alternative for Russian regulation on consolidation – but its application is rare in practice. In alternative Russia regulation a number of departures can be found: obtaining benefits is not a criteria of control (just a power to govern the policies); some exemptions from consolidation are different from those in the IFRS 27 (such as banks); some departures are due to the absence of Russian regulation in relation to business combinations, accounting for investments in associates and financial instruments.

28. No special regulation but some recommendations are outlined in methodological instructions on consolidation; those define associates by 20% threshold; reference to the equity method is not fully consistent with the IFRS.

29. Not regulated by Russian legislation.

30. Regulated by the Central Bank.

31. Not regulated by Russian legislation.

32. Not specifically regulated by Russian legislation.

33. Regulated by methodological instructions. Departures: definition of events which changed a number of ordinary shares outstanding without a corresponding change in resources; restatement requirements (due to absence of regulation on fundamental errors and business combinations) omission of dilutive potential ordinary shares, limited disclosures. No reference to the SIC 24.

34. Same requirements as for the annual reports; includes balance sheet and profit and loss account to be presented monthly and quarterly cumulatively for the current reporting year.

35. No special regulation, requirement to disclose discontinued operations in the notes to the annual report.

36. No special regulation apart from the statement that assets can be devalued in accordance with their market or replacement value. The reduction of value should be debited to the profit or loss of the reporting period or to the revaluation reserve within the limit of previously credited assets revaluation surplus – if applicable.

37. Recognition criteria for provisions do not specify the requirement that a present obligation should be the result of a past event and that it can be legal or constructive; discounting is not required nor some other terms of measurement; specific applications on future operating loss, onerous contracts and restructuring are not mentioned; more emphasis is given to calculations of the probabilities than explanations of best estimates.

38. Some internally generated intellectual property items and brands can be capitalized if an enterprise has an exclusive legal right; some R&D costs and some start-up costs can be capitalized; separability from goodwill is not specified; leased intangibles are not shown on the face of the balance sheet. See also IFRS 22.

39. Not specifically regulated by Russian legislation. References are made to measurement at cost with an option to value at market if lower than cost.

40. Not regulated.

41. Not specifically regulated.

work-in-progress and future period expenses, capital and reserves, payables and receivables, profit and loss. PBU No. 4 states that measurement rules for separate reporting items are set up by related PBUs which in some cases have changed earlier requirements of the by-law. It also outlines that offsetting is not allowed other than in cases specifically prescribed by the legislation; and requires that all amounts in the balance sheet are shown at a residual value with disclosure of all depreciation costs, allowances, etc. in the notes.

Departures from these rules are allowed and should be disclosed, as well as the reasons for the departures and their effect on the financial position and results of an enterprise.

Recognition criteria such as the probable flow of future economic benefits and reliable measurement of an item are not specified as an underlying requirement. Some of these criteria are outlined in individual PBUs in relation to revenues, expenses, fixed assets, intangible assets and contingent provisions.

Financial investments are valued at cost as a general rule. For quoted equity securities, the lower of cost or market value is allowed. Financial investments are disclosed on the face of the balance sheet as equity investments (investments in subsidiaries, investments in associates and investments in other enterprises), debt financial instruments (loans to other companies for a period over 12 months) and other long-term investments. Debt securities are valued at cost and could be amortized over the outstanding period of time. The equity method is not explicitly outlined in Russian legislation. Accounting for associates allows the use of an approach similar to the equity method but it lacks clarity in its concept and application.

Fixed assets are measured at the initial cost of acquisition and depreciated over their useful life. Specific definitions as well as depreciation rules are outlined in PBU No. 6 'Fixed assets'. Specific requirements for the measurement of fixed assets and depreciation rules are also defined by the tax legislation (chapter 25, Tax Code, Part II). Both documents allow the straight-line depreciation method. Accounting regulation also allows the unit of production method of depreciation. In addition it allows the declining balance and the sum-of-years'-digits methods for accelerated depreciation. Tax regulation allows only the declining balance method of these three.

Only fixed assets owned by an enterprise can be recognized in the balance sheet. Leased assets should be recorded in the off-balance sheet account 'Leased fixed assets'. Fixed assets can be revalued once a year in accordance with their replacement value. In the event of an increase in the replacement value compared to the balance sheet value, the surplus is credited to the Additional capital of the organization. In the event of a decrease, the difference is charged to the profit and loss account. The difference can also be charged to the Additional capital as an offset to a previously recognized revaluation surplus.

Intangible assets are measured at the initial costs of acquisition, at the actual costs of production – if generated by the enterprise; at the market value if they are acquired otherwise. Revaluation of intangible assets is not allowed. Intangible assets are amortized over the period of their useful life by the straight-line, declining balance or unit of production method. If the useful life of intangible assets is not determinable it should be stated as 20 years but not exceeding the duration of the enterprise's activities (10 years in accordance with the Tax Code). Capitalization is allowed for externally generated intellectual property if the enterprise has an exclusive legal right, and start-up costs paid by co-founders. Research and development costs may be capitalized if they are completed and/or led to positive results. Intangibles which are owned by an organization are disclosed on the face of the balance sheet; leased intangible assets are disclosed separately in the notes.

Goodwill is defined as the difference between the purchase price of an enterprise and the book value of its assets and liabilities at the date of acquisition. Positive goodwill should be recognized as an asset and amortized over a period of 20 years by the straight-line method. Negative goodwill is recognized as deferred income and should be allocated evenly to operating income.

Inventories are valued at actual cost or at the cost of production if produced by the enterprise. General and administrative expenses are not included in the cost or production costs unless they are directly associated with an inventory item. Inventories obtained otherwise are valued at the market price at the date of recognition. Revaluation of inventories is not allowed. Inventories can be written-off using either the unit cost, weighted average costs, FIFO or LIFO methods. Enterprises can create reserves reflecting the decrease in value of the inventories as a difference between the current market value and the actual value if the latter is higher than the former.

Equity is not defined in Russian legislation. The Civil Code defines statutory capital. Securities legislation outlines the definitions of issued capital, placed capital, treasury stock, declared capital, issue costs, but there are no clear regulations on accounting for all these equity elements. Further details are given in Standards on the issue of shares on creation of a joint stock company, of additional shares and their prospectuses. Some additional accounting treatments are outlined in the by-law, Ministry of Finance order on 'Bookkeeping for securities' (15 January 1997) and in the Chart of Accounts.

There are a number of issues in relation to accounting for equity which need to be addressed:

- Some issues are not addressed by Russian legislation and accounting regulation.

- There are some conflicts on equity definitions between existing legal documents.

- Some of the accounting definitions and interpretations are not in compliance with the IFRS.

- Some generally stated definitions and approaches need detailed explanations to ensure that they are interpreted in compliance with their economic essence and the IFRS.

For example, the following technical issues need to be clarified:

- measurement, recognition and derecognition of the equity items; in particular recognition of additional issues of shares before they can enter the Statutory capital;

- some reserves are still part of equity while they are expenses or liabilities in terms of their economic substance;

- the distinction between profits (losses) as a direct result of economic activities of the enterprise, as opposed to transactions with owners;

- the distinction between gains and losses directly charged to equity based on their source of origin (in Russian accounting additional capital paid in excess of par value is shown together with assets revaluation surplus);

- recognition of and reporting on translation differences;

- termination of the practice where some expenses are written off directly from the retained earnings;

- regulation of transactions with treasury stock;

- special purpose financing (i.e. government grants) classification (should be excluded from equity accounts);

- a number of other issues related to equity disclosures.

Conclusions

Russian accounting is undergoing significant changes. Current developments are influenced by the pressure from the international financial markets, by the increasing pressure from major Russian companies which are looking for external financing and have to deal with different accounting requirements, by increasing awareness of the role of accounting in a market economy. On the other hand, the resources are still lacking to embrace the whole complexity of accounting changes needed to provide adequate information for decision making processes in an economy which is still creating a financial infrastructure.

Russia has announced that starting from financial reports for 2005, all Russian listed companies should produce consolidated accounts as required by the IAS. A new Russian programme on accounting reform has outlined the following regulations to be developed by the end of 2002:

- accounting for income tax;
- financial investments;
- reorganizations;
- accounting for leases;
- discontinued operations;
- interim financial reports;
- accounting for inflation.

Also, a number of discussion papers produced by the recent TACIS project 'Accounting reform in Russia' are being discussed (a programme funded by the EU to provide technical inputs to the Russian accounting regulatory system):

- equity;
- profit, revenues and expenses;
- cash flow statements;
- assets impairment;
- amortization;
- inflation;
- effects of changing prices;
- foreign exchange rates;
- interim financial reporting;
- contingencies.

Discussion papers are supported by detailed explanatory notes on how to implement the proposed changes in the Russian environment.

The further progress of reform will depend on a continued effort of coordination of proposed changes between different regulators in Russia, such as the Ministry of Finance, the Ministry of Economic Development and Trade; Securities and Exchange Commission, the Ministry of Taxes and others. It will also depend on the involvement of the corporate sector and on creating a critical mass of knowledge in the area of finance and accounting.

Notes

1. For non-profit organizations.

16 Accounting needs of developing countries

UNCTAD Secretariat

The lack of a developed accounting infrastructure has been identified by many multilateral agencies (e.g. the World Bank, OECD, UNCTAD) as a major obstacle to economic development.[1] A lack of accountability contributes to financial instability, discourages foreign direct investment and acts as a brake on aid projects. Within a country, a lack of transparency and adequate financial disclosure within local enterprises leads to difficulties in obtaining finance and to a lack of knowledge with which to better manage the enterprise, and ultimately to a loss of competitivity. For governments, lack of transparency and adequate financial disclosure by businesses leads to difficulties in raising tax revenues and in targeting economic development programmes and formulating proper policies. Such a situation may result in counterproductive measures which harm the private sector rather than help it and can lead to the disappearance of resources rather than their creation.

The aim of this study is to review the issue of accounting needs in as wide a range of countries as possible and to attempt to draw from that certain conclusions about how development may be encouraged by improving the accounting infrastructure. The objective of the first part of the report is to identify the nature of the problem, while the second part examines actual accounting rules and practices followed by SMEs in a number of countries, and the third part makes some suggestions for improvements.

Contribution of SMEs to economic development

There are a number of ways in which a government may try to promote economic development. These include attracting foreign direct investment, typically from transnational corporations, and developing parastatal corporations to become indigenous suppliers that can replace imported expertise from transnational corporations. However, as developed countries have come to realize, all large enterprises in the private sector started out as small enterprises, and therefore encouraging indigenous small business is one track which could ultimately lead to indigenous large business.

In addition, in many African countries for example, the majority of the working population is engaged in small business, often at a subsistence level. Small business is a major source of employment, and in helping small business a government opens up the possibility of creating employment. For example Nthejane (1997) reports that in Lesotho there are 125 000 micro-enterprises providing employment for 200 000 people and that about three-quarters of these enterprises are headed by women. There are also approximately 2000 enterprises which employ six or more people, and these have mostly grown from the micro-business sector. However, these SMEs do face considerable obstacles to their evolution. Nthejane says:

> Their owners are generally better educated, more experienced and have better resources than the micro-business operators. However, they still operate in a discriminatory economic environment. These SMEs are excluded from incentives available to large (foreign) industries and subjected to onerous bureaucratic procedures. Almost invariably, SMEs are unable to comply with the cumbersome and complex licensing procedures, import control measures, taxation etc., hence they cannot access the incentives (Nthejane 1997).

There are also similar findings by other researchers.

While these problems may be particularly critical in some African countries, the path of evolution from an informal one-person business to even a small enterprise with several employees is difficult in any country and requires the entrepreneur to develop a range of managerial and administrative skills in addition to those which are being exploited in the manufacturing operation or service which is the motor of the business (International Labour Organization 1997). These skills and the acquisition of knowledge about even basic issues such as taxation, licences, etc., form an immense barrier to the growth of a business and its progression from the informal to the formal sector.

What is an SME?

There is no universally agreed definition of an SME, and there is probably a good reason for this. According to the International Labour Organization, no single definition can capture all the dimensions of 'small' or 'medium' business size. Nor can it expect to reflect the differences between firms, sectors or countries at different levels of development. Most size definitions are based on measures such as number of employees, balance-sheet total or annual turnover. However, none of these measures necessarily travel very well across borders. An annual turnover of less than $100 000 would probably define a micro-business in the USA but could well include a medium-sized company in other economies. According to the Organization for Economic Co-operation and Development, 95% of small or medium-sized enterprises employ less than 100 workers. Even definitions based on employment are subject to the same contextual problems – a company with 100 employees is not considered very large in Switzerland, but there are few companies with more employees in some developing countries.

This study is based on the assumption that size is an important factor in the economic nature of business entities, and that one should identify different economic types because their needs are likely to be different. For the purposes of this study, therefore, the definitions set out below are used.

- *Micro-enterprise*: this refers to a business involving one to five persons (typically a sole trader). Its character would be such that its activities are simple enough to be managed directly on a person-to-person basis, and the scale of the operations means it is unlikely to need or be able to afford to devote significant staff time to accounting. Its operations are likely to concern a single product, service or type of operation. Only basic accounting is needed to record turnover, to control expenses and profitability and, if necessary, to compute profits for tax purposes. It is unlikely to have extensive credit transactions.

- *Small enterprise*: this is taken to mean a business employing 6 to 50 persons. Such a business would probably have several lines of activity and conceivably more than one physical location. It would probably need loan finance and have to report to lenders. Its payroll would potentially be quite large and relatively complex, and it would need management information on turnover and costs analysed by product line. It would potentially do a substantial proportion of its business on credit. It would therefore need a more sophisticated accounting and control system, but probably without having to consider issues such as pensions, provisions, leases and financial instruments. It would probably need a full-time bookkeeper to maintain records and generate information flows to management.

- *Medium-sized enterprise*: this refers to an enterprise employing 51 to 250 employees. Such an enterprise would almost certainly be located on more than one site and involve communication between a number of managers. It would have several product lines, and would do a great deal of business on credit, possibly with export sales and imports. It would require a reasonably sophisticated accounting structure with internal controls and detailed management accounts for different product managers. It would probably have several accounting staff. The economic significance of such a company would probably justify fairly extensive reporting requirements.

These size definitions (in terms of employee numbers) are to an extent arbitrary, and should be interpreted flexibly in the light of actual circumstances in any one country. However, since 95% of all SMEs have less than 100 employees, these boundaries, while arbitrary, capture the target group. The more important issue is to identify the nature of the entity, the complexity of its operations and the need for information to manage the company.

For the purposes of this study, all of the above-mentioned enterprises are considered to be part of the *formal* economy. Entities which keep no accounts and pay no taxes are part of the *informal* economy. While it is an important part of this study to lead to systems which will encourage entities to move into the formal economy, it is not concerned with the informal economy as such. Equally, while the main focus of the study is SMEs, one cannot make proposals concerning accounting for SMEs without taking into consideration the whole gamut of accounting, from the informal sector to listed companies, so that the small company sector is consistent with the economic realities in which it operates and offers systems capable of being expanded into those used by large companies.

Accounting by SMEs

Accounting has a key role to play in any business. At its most basic, accounting is needed to 'keep the score' so that the entrepreneur knows what is happening in the business, how much has been sold, what the costs are, what activities are profitable, whether selling prices leave a suitable margin against cost, etc. Accounting is also critical in managing relationships with the outside world: it records which suppliers money is owed to and which customers money is due from (if credit is given), and also enables the entrepreneur to represent the business to outside interests, particularly potential lenders and the tax authorities.

As a business grows, it needs to seek further financing, investors and trading partners and, particularly where operations may take place across the world through electronic commerce and networking with other small and medium-sized enterprises, it needs an accounting 'passport' – clear financial statements that are prepared on a basis that is understood across the world. Hence, the need for promoting transparency and adequate financial disclosure early on in the developmental phase of SMEs becomes paramount.

Accounting represents an essential tool for the management and evolution of a business, and yet it also poses an immense obstacle for many reasons. While its utility resides in the fact that it 'makes visible' the nature and extent of the business, the entrepreneur may feel that this visibility might be exploited by the state to tax the business or impose licences or other controls. Entrepreneurs are often reluctant to keep adequate accounts because they fear the tax consequences, and yet without taking this step they have no information for managing the company or for enabling lenders to assess the viability of the business and to offer finance for expansion.

In the minds of many if not all small business entrepreneurs, accounting is seen primarily as a tool of taxation. After taxation, its next use is seen as a requirement for raising loan finance. Accounting is frequently perceived as a tool of oppression. Its positive uses in providing a model of the company to enable it to become more profitable and more manageable are generally not understood (perhaps because the business person has no management training) or are underrated.

Another frequent obstacle of this kind is the lack of separation of the business from the owner. In some cultures, the concept of property is fairly fluid, and rigid boundaries between what is personal and what belongs to the family or another group do not necessarily exist. Beyond that, even in cultures where individual property concepts are well established, entrepreneurs often have difficulty in separating their business expenses from their personal expenses, a process which is essential for an evaluation of the business.

Aside from these fairly considerable psychological blocks, there are the problems of how to access accounting for the business. If entrepreneurs are to look after their own accounts, this presumes that they are already literate, and preferably numerate as well, which already excludes a large slice of the entrepreneur population. For the entrepreneur to be trained in accounting supposes that courses are available and that the entrepreneurs can afford to take time away from working to acquire the knowledge (or can be subsidized to do this).

The alternative is for accounting services to be provided from a specialist supplier, which is the solution adopted by many SMEs in developed countries but is rare in developing countries. Here there arises the question of cost and the problem of providing value for money. Entrepreneurs do not see any merit in paying an outside accountant to prepare figures which are used exclusively for tax purposes. Accounting services must be able to demonstrate the management utility of the information. The service provider must be able to offer a wider range of services, including regular management accounting data to measure and improve performance.

Accounting infrastructure

The development of financial reporting is something that occurred as a consequence of the industrial revolution. Accounting is considered a necessary prerequisite for the organization of business. On the other hand, in countries where the prime activity has been agriculture, there has historically been no great need for accounting. In many situations, the accounting regulations that do exist have often been created in an ad hoc manner and have not resulted in a homogeneous accounting environment. This in turn makes the provision of accounting education and accounting services less efficient because of the lack of an organized or uniform approach.

Many developing countries have, of course, some colonial heritage, and this manifests itself most clearly in former French and British colonies. In francophone Africa, many countries use an accounting plan and have detailed accounting requirements for small enterprises, while anglophone countries often have legislation modelled on the UK's 1948 Companies Act. Many commentators have discussed the suitability or lack of suitability of these imports. One possible argument may be that the French system is at least designed for small and medium-sized enterprises, although it requires a fairly elaborate system of accounting for even the smallest kind of enterprise. As a result, this presents a hurdle, discouraging microenterprises in the informal sector from moving to the formal sector. The British system is designed more around the needs of large, listed companies and is to a large degree unsuitable for the vast bulk of SMEs in developing countries.

In many developing countries, subsidiaries of foreign transnational corporations (TNCs) and parastatal organizations are major players in the economy. Subsidiaries of TNCs bring in major investment and generate employment, but they are frequently able to negotiate special deals with the host government which bear on taxation and other reporting issues. In any event, subsidiaries of TNCs are likely to maintain internal records which satisfy the needs of the group's global accounting information system, rather than observing local rules.

In many countries, governments have taken steps to encourage development by setting up enterprises themselves, or sometimes by taking over activities from TNCs. The resulting parastatal organizations cover a wide variety of activities ranging from banking to marketing prime commodities. These parastatal organizations generally escape accounting regulations. They are frequently created by special statute, and their accounting requirements are set out in this statute. However their special status usually means they are not covered by the accounting rules which apply to other companies. In many cases such parastatals have poor accounting systems and report with several years' delay, if at all.

Where small and micro-enterprises form a very large part of the economy, the only rules which affect them are likely to be tax-based rules. It is only in economies with a substantial number of medium-sized companies that indigenous private business is likely to be covered by accounting legislation as such. A number of developing countries are keen to develop stock exchanges, and more recent regulatory activity is often directed to this end, rather than to the needs of the SME sector. Where a stock exchange is the focus, new regulations are typically based on the standards of the International Accounting Standards Board (IASB).

This means that in most developing countries the local accounting rules include a range of different and possibly competing rules; there is a discontinuous patchwork of regulations developed at different times with different objectives. The colonial heritage means that rules may have been imported without any thought for adaptation to local circumstances, and the tendency of regulations to be enacted to meet specific situations as they crop up means that the initial framework has been complicated by a variety of ad hoc measures. The political will to scrap these and start again with a coherent all-embracing approach is often absent, and accounting is low on the list of priorities for government attention.

In countries in transition, the position is different but no less complicated in that the existing systems are not easily adapted to market economy use, but imported systems depend upon being supported by an infrastructure of ethical and professional approaches, support services and concepts which are to a large degree absent. Countries face a puzzling plethora of 'solutions' offered by the West, which will take many years to assimilate and adapt.

Differential reporting

For most of the last 200 years (during which financial reporting as we know it has evolved), it has been taken as axiomatic that there could be only one system of financial reporting for commercial entities. This has been an article of faith, despite the fact that accountants could comfortably believe that the public sector did not need to use accounting which remotely resembled commercial accounting, and that therefore in principle it was not possible to argue that there is only one 'correct' form of accounting. Nevertheless, one of the problems which has been endemic in accounting in developed countries is that, even if some developed countries are beginning to address the issue of differential reporting at home, they continue to export the concept of a single system of financial reporting.

The common position in commercial accounting is that there is no justification for one entity accounting for the same transaction in a different way from another entity. Nevertheless, the fact that the impact would vary between businesses of different sizes is not greatly disputed.

However, the premise that all commercial entities should report under the same framework is probably a key obstacle to the development of useful accounting, because it ignores the fact that, economically and commercially speaking, there is simply no comparison, for example, between the impact of a $10,000 transaction on a one-man business and its impact on a TNC. Let us say that the transaction is a sale. There is no question that it should be accounted for in both cases as a sale transaction. However, economically, the framework is quite different, and accounting should be able to reflect that difference. The argument simply is that, while the basic nature of the transaction does not change, the framework within which it takes place is different, so its consequences may be different, and this should be accepted in designing regulations. Equally, it is perfectly possible, even probable, that the transactions of TNCs are likely to be mostly different in nature and scale from those of the one-man business, and the regulations should not make a 'one size fits all' assumption.

The conviction that accounting rules should be the same for all enterprises is part of the reason for there being a major accounting hurdle to face when a business moves from the informal to the formal sector. The small business is in effect moving in one step from having no accounts to having to follow the same rules as a TNC. Some countries, such as Australia, have recognized this and removed all reporting requirements for small entities. Other countries, including France, Germany and the UK, have at least recognized that in principle the reporting environment for small business is different from that of large business.

However, in developed countries the accounting problem lies not so much in getting companies to keep accounts, since the general level of education is higher and accounting services are more easily obtained, but rather in how to reduce the administrative burden for small companies so that the financial reporting requirements (which are designed for large companies) are not more onerous than they need to be. A recent study by the Canadian Institute of Chartered Accountants (CICA) identifies the problem as follows:

> Given the concept of a single set of generally accepted accounting principles for all enterprises, entities not active on financial markets are required to follow substantially the same accounting standards as publicly listed companies (CICA 1999).

As is the case in Canada, countries with an Anglo-Saxon accounting tradition generally (a) aim their accounting regulation at listed companies and (b) require small companies to follow substantially all the same rules. Recent moves, such as the financial reporting standard for smaller entities in the UK and the Canadian initiative do not, however, deviate from the idea of a single set of accounting measurement rules, but merely provide some alleviation of disclosures for small business.

Continental European countries, on the other hand, face a different problem and have recently started to accept differential reporting. In broad terms, continental European countries aim their base accounting regulation at private companies, with taxation being a major preoccupation. The pressure of international harmonization on the large companies listed on several stock exchanges has meant that countries such as Austria, France, Germany and Italy accept differential reporting – large, internationally listed companies are now allowed to produce group accounts on the basis of international rules rather than domestic rules. Continental European countries accept a disconnection between the reporting needs of smaller, private companies and listed TNCs.

Accounting profession

The stage of development of the accounting profession varies substantially among developing countries. Some of them have a well-developed profession. In others, while the profession is large, it is at an earlier phase of development, and in some the profession is almost non-existent. Nonetheless, the Big Four international accounting firms are present in most developing countries and ensure some degree of service availability.

However, while the provision of highly qualified auditors may be useful for large national companies and other economically significant entities, it is less clear that it is useful to the SME sector. SMEs do not require sophisticated accounting, tax and audit advice, rather they require low-cost, effective accounting and management guidance. Large accounting firms are no doubt able to supply the product, but are trained to a level beyond this and charge accordingly. French *experts comptables* are probably the nearest to a professional body which is able to supply this sort of accounting and management service, but they, certainly in their European form, are as highly trained as the audit firms, and therefore are providing a more sophisticated (and therefore more expensive) product than that required by SMEs in developing countries.

The object of this first part of the report is to set out the area which has to be analysed. It suggests that accounting is one of the major obstacles (but far from the only one) which prevents microenterprises from growing, and makes life difficult for small firms. Lack of accounting is an obstacle both in a management context because the entrepreneur cannot see clearly the income and expenditure of the firm, and in a financing context because the firm cannot borrow or obtain other funds for expansion. Not all microenterprises wish to grow, but the development of a thriving indigenous economy depends upon at least some microenterprises developing into bigger companies. Furthermore, for companies to survive and compete in a globalizing world economy, they need continued access to finance and partners in order to obtain technology and expand their markets. But creditors, investors and partners require financial information which is most effectively generated by a simple harmonized system.

Against this, small business often sees accounting simply as opening a window for the government to start taking some of the profits. Entrepreneurs do not know how to use accounting to improve their business and cannot access affordable accounting services of the kind they need.

Current regulations

A significant part of the work on this study involved collecting information concerning the present state of regulations and problems which are experienced in their application. In the early stages of the research project, the secretariat invited help from ISAR members and others and received offers from people in a number of countries. On the basis of the offers received, material has been put together on the following countries:

- Latin America: Argentina, Brazil;
- Africa: Botswana, Cameroon, Kenya, Morocco;
- Middle East: Lebanon;
- Far East: Malaysia, Singapore;
- Economies in transition: Kazakhstan, Poland.

While it is not suggested that this is a representative sample of economies, it does include a spread of examples from newly industrialized countries to countries in an early stage of development. Historically, the process of development involves moving from an economy which is largely devoted to agriculture through industrialization to the post-industrial phase where the economy is primarily devoted to services.

As already discussed, taxation is a major influence on accounting, since accounting is used for the assessment of profits for taxes. Clearly the extent to which taxation of income is a major input to the national exchequer is likely to influence governments in their approach to its collection.

In many countries, the accounting framework is a mixture of inherited rules derived either from a colonial past or from historical trading links. This basic framework has usually been built on with a series of measures designed to meet local needs, and finally in recent times with the adoption of IASB standards in one form or another. Annex II shows the involvement of the sample countries with International Accounting Standards.

It is clear from the information available that these countries are now focusing their regulatory efforts on IASB standards. As noted before, this may result in a situation where there are unrelated sets of accounting rules operating in the same country, and it would be sensible for some rationalization to take place. Given that the most demanding set of rules is that of the IASB, these should be specified for large or listed entities and parastatals, but this should be accompanied by a lighter regulation (consistent with the approach of international standards) for smaller, private entities.

The incomplete nature of regulation is a problem which often presents itself. Accounting regulation is frequently focused on the needs of larger entities or stock exchanges and there are no rules directed specifically at SMEs. Frequently it is only rules on taxation of profits which directly concern smaller entities. To provide a succinct summary of the present position in the sample countries, a summary table of basic points has been assembled. This information came partly from local offices of Deloitte & Touche and PricewaterhouseCoopers, and partly from volunteer researchers. Five basic questions were asked, the answers to which are set out in Appendix I.

Appendix I is intended to provide a thumbnail sketch of the situation for SMEs. It shows that there are significant differences between countries in their approach, and especially as to whether they regard SMEs as a special category or not. In most cases they do not provide any special framework for SMEs, and to the extent that these escape the rules for larger entities, this is due to informal derogations, rather than conscious policy. Inherited frameworks are clearly influential, with Lebanon and Morocco reflecting past French influences in their modulated approach to small enterprises, and Kenya, Malaysia and Singapore reflecting British refusal to recognize small business as a special category.

Field research

While a survey of regulation is useful, a key aspect of any attempt to research regulation of a particular sector is to ask how the regulated entities experience the existing situation. One of the key aspects of this study was the possibility of doing field research into the experiences of SMEs in respect of the regulatory framework which they face. The planned approach was to conduct a series of interviews with various players in the field: entrepreneurs, government officials and professional advisers. Resources were extremely limited, but the secretariat was very fortunate to be able to obtain some data through the good offices of researchers who were able to meet our research needs while pursuing their own. A synopsis of their findings is provided here. We have preferred not to identify the countries concerned; these are just examples of the kinds of problems which SMEs may face, and are not intended to throw light on the regulation or approach in any specific country, nor can any general conclusion necessarily be drawn from them. The problems identified may or may not be found in any individual jurisdiction.

Country A

The researcher interviewed a number of people, and it was clear that the question of taxation was a major issue. One interviewee remarked that all businesses pay tax at 32.5% of their taxable income and there is no relief for small entities or business start-ups. There is massive tax evasion, partly through corruption and partly through concealment of profits. One interviewee said that the poor quality of the infrastructure, the apparent waste of taxpayers' money and the perceived level of evasion were strong reasons why people resented paying tax. As one person said:

> Unincorporated entities, aid projects and parastatals all produce notoriously unreliable figures. The solution has to be education and greater belief in the system. At the moment the belief is: 'any time I produce good accounts, they just tax me more and I don't see any return'.

Another comment: our tax authority 'is actually quite good at collecting taxes, particularly compared with neighbouring countries, but the problem is that they only go after those already within the net and not those evading.'

One entrepreneur suggested that there should be a period of grace for new companies: 'I would prefer it if new businesses paid nothing for the first two years, then for the tax rate to be graded for another year or so until the business has established itself and then for full rates to apply.'

Another problem faced by business is the need to obtain licences. One successful entrepreneur looked back at his beginnings: 'The whole process was a learning experience in itself and it really needs some form of standardization so that the entrepreneur can go to one place to register his business.' A service provider said:

> The biggest problem here is bribery and corruption and very little gets done unless money is offered. . . . Bureaucracy slows most things down, simple processes can be long and frustrating and it is very difficult to get things in writing from anyone. The collapsing infrastructure, such as the telephone system and the poor roads, makes it more difficult to conduct business.

The country had been the setting for an aid project known as the 'barefoot accountant' project. The idea had been to set up a low-cost service provider, supervised by qualified auditors but staffed largely by technicians, to help small enterprises to produce accounts and meaningful management data. This project encountered a number of problems, first the scepticism of potential clients who 'thought we were from the tax office' and also a lack of separation of the business: 'small business owners do not distinguish between business and personal records, they are often assisted by family members'.

The take-up was low: 'We had a target of 960 small business owners and 2000 were approached, although we ended up with only 55 co-operating in the project'. The service was offered at $8 per month; the entrepreneur was supposed to keep details on income and expenditure, and a technician would spend two hours a month turning that into accounting records and management information. The project found that microenterprises were not prepared to spend the money, which in turn caused a problem with retention of technicians who were paid on the basis of the number of businesses they serviced. From an initial staff of 48 technicians, the project dropped to 20, and the busiest of these had only 7 clients. The response was to move the focus to slightly bigger clients and to a fee base which was negotiated individually.

The project has now ended, but an interviewee said:

> This kind of project could really make a difference to smaller businesses and we are thinking of ways to encourage micro-businesses to take up the service, given our experiences. One way might be to create greater awareness and to try to organize seminars; the main problem with this is getting the entrepreneurs to attend, as many would probably have to close their business. Ideally, if we could get some funding again, we would prefer to offer the service free of charge to entrepreneurs, say for the first year, and then introduce a nominal fee. Hopefully, they will then realize the potential benefits and stay with us. Most donors, however, insist that projects need to be self-sustainable and that if a free service is offered initially, these clients will disappear as soon as fees are introduced.

Country B

In this country the tax system is closely integrated with accounting. All incorporated entities are subject to accounting rules as such, but tax rules also require the provision of some accounts from businesses which are not incorporated. The country operates a system for the taxation of business profits which has size variants. Very small unincorporated business (determined by turnover thresholds) does not need to keep accounts and pays lump sum taxes based on the type of business. Larger unincorporated business must keep sales and purchase journals and an inventory list and is taxed 5% on turnover or 15% on turnover according to type of activity. All larger businesses must keep full accounts.

The researcher found that the average level of education of micro-entrepreneurs was relatively low, and that although they could generally read and write, they had no knowledge of commercial subjects and certainly not accounting. The latter was perceived as being an expensive luxury whose sole function is to cause the business to pay tax. These entrepreneurs were unaware of the tax rules and of their own rights and were a prey to corrupt tax officials. The entrepreneur might typically be approached by a tax official demanding sometimes very high immediate payment, even though the amount and timing were not legally justifiable. The entrepreneur would then pay a bribe, smaller than the amount demanded but perhaps greater than the normal tax, to have the tax official go away. These entrepreneurs need accounting as a protection but do not have the education to run their own accounts and cannot afford to hire a bookkeeper.

Some larger enterprises had a quite different approach to these problems. They again found accounting expensive, but are required to produce full accounts. Some preferred to use unqualified bookkeepers and similar unregulated service providers rather than go to qualified professionals because of the perceived cost of the latter. Such entrepreneurs were criticized by a professional accountant as in fact paying too much tax because neither they nor their advisers knew enough about tax to manage it efficiently.

Other entrepreneurs, on the other hand, appeared to keep several sets of figures – one for bank and finance purposes, one for tax and a third for management. The researcher said that it was not clear that these people understood their own convoluted systems. A professional commented that such people often attempted to reduce their tax by paying bribes to tax officials, but it was not clear that the bribes were less than the tax they would have paid with a proper system and good advice.

Country C

Generally speaking, the informal economy in this country is very large in terms of providing a livelihood for large numbers of people, though not necessarily generating large revenues. The Government has major problems getting people to come within the tax net, and had recently been operating a tax amnesty whereby undeclared profits could be legalized (and penalties would thereafter increase for those not taking advantage of the amnesty). Although entrepreneurs, as elsewhere, see accounting as having only to do with taxation, the amnesty had caused a significant number of enterprises to enter the formal economy.

Accounting service providers considered that only the need to raise finance or the threat of tax penalties would cause small businesses to start producing proper accounts. However, a partner in a Big Four firm said that a number of small clients came to them for advice, particularly when seeking finance, but once the finance had been obtained (or the tax threat dealt with) the client would cease to keep records and would not return. Only pressure from a bank lender would bring the client back later, in a panic. He also noted that many small clients underestimated the cost of the service and subsequently failed to pay the firm's fee.

There is an active sector in the field of 'unqualified' service providers in the area of accounting. These typically provide a wide range of business services and do well with small to medium-sized business clients. The owner of one such business said that many small enterprises failed through lack of adequate accounting information and many simply cannot manage effectively. He cited a case referred to him by a bank where a trader needed finance but had no idea what her gross margin was between buying and selling prices, nor how much was tied up in her stock. It was purely a matter of chance that the business was profitable. He said that the lack of any notion of management meant that such entrepreneurs had no idea of the function of accounting in managing a business, and therefore they could not see any point in it, other than to help the tax authorities. He said that a major part of his job was explaining to clients how accounting helped them improve their business.

This service provider used a standard accounting software package for his clients and said he thought it would be a major improvement if there were uniform software and accounting. He noted that there were three main lenders to small business in his town, and that each one required the financial forecast supporting a loan proposal to be prepared a different way. This increased the cost to the borrower considerably, and this could be avoided with a uniform system where the banks would know that all clients would have the same kind of data, and the banks themselves could base their assessments on that.

The experiences of the three developing countries are similar. Tax evasion and corruption remain major disincentives to accounting. Entrepreneurs have no idea of accounting, management and business. They could therefore not see any point in it, other than to help tax authorities. Thus, there was no demand for accounting services. The result was multiple sets of books – for banks, tax and management purposes which contained information so confusing that it was unusable.

General conclusions

The object of this final part of the report is to identify various courses of action which are open to governments in addressing the provision of help to SMEs in the accounting area.

It deals with the need for help, the kind of regulations which may be useful, and the methods which might be used to deliver this help.

In essence the field research shows that only a very small minority of SME managers in developing countries have any formal bookkeeping capacity, and this poses a considerable obstacle to the growth of their businesses. In the first instance, many entrepreneurs have only the haziest notion of whether their business is really profitable and what their cost structures are. Consequently they are not in a position to improve profitability. Equally they are unable to raise loan finance because they cannot demonstrate the profitability of the business or the assets owned. Finally, they are at risk from a tax perspective because the government has no accurate data on which to make policy decisions, grant tax exemptions, etc., while at the same time they cannot contest excessive assessments.

Looking at the profitability issue first, even when a business works entirely on a cash basis, it is quite difficult to measure costs and profits accurately because expenses may relate to several transactions – a trader buys stocks which are then broken up for sale individually over a period, and there may be expenses such as petrol, vehicle maintenance and similar items which do not relate directly to the product transaction but are part of the business cost. In such circumstances, the entrepreneur needs to have either good training in cost control or an advanced instinct for figures, both of which are rare among SME entrepreneurs.

The absence of any calculation of cost, including allocations, means that the overall profitability of a business is unknown. For a subsistence sole trader, this is not necessarily a problem, but any entrepreneur who wants to develop the business needs this information. Without knowledge of cost structures, the entrepreneur cannot determine which products are the most profitable, or attempt to restrict costs other than in a most general way, or cut out activities which do not make a contribution. The business needs cost information and knowledge of cost behaviour in order to be managed and to be developed.

From an external perspective, there is the issue of accountability and visibility. This impacts both upon the availability of finance and also on government intervention. As far as finance is concerned, commercial lenders need at the very least to have some evidence of the putative borrower's past managerial performance and some forecast of future performance. This means that the entrepreneur must know his existing cost structure and cash flow patterns, as well as be able to prepare forecasts for future projects.

If the bank agrees to a loan, it will then want to be able to monitor the performance of the business and its capacity to repay the debt. Government or aid agency schemes have the same accountability problem – they need to assess the viability of the scheme proposed to them and they need to be able to monitor it subsequently. It is for this reason that the World Bank, for example, issues its own accounting manual and insists upon proper financial reporting from aid projects.

Governments need economic data on SMEs both for managing the economy and for taxation. This is precisely why many owners do not want to undertake an accounting exercise – they perceive the existence of an accounting visibility as leading only to taxation, and they think that opacity protects them from taxation. Up to a point they are not wrong. However, this opacity leaves them open to pressure, either legal or illegal, from tax officials. The secretariat's empirical work shows that corrupt tax officials may use the absence of accounts to extract bribes from owners, and unlike legal tax obligations where accounts are available, there is no ceiling on the bribes. Some regimes allow the tax authorities to levy tax based on an estimate, and put the onus on the tax payer to prove the estimate wrong. Without accounts, the entrepreneur cannot contest the estimate. At the same time, the Government cannot manage the economy and cannot identify SME needs and try to meet them without accurate data on those businesses.

SME accounting system

Based on the accounting needs described above, it is possible to identify several characteristics which an accounting system for SMEs should have.

1 Management utility

One of the difficulties of accounting is that there is a major split between management accounting (generating data for the management of the business) and financial accounting (score-keeping at its basic level to provide information for banks, regulators, shareholders and tax authorities). One reason for the split is that financial accounting is usually regulated on a national basis, whereas there is no regulation whatsoever of management accounting and the same techniques are widely (but not uniformly) used worldwide. Because national rules can vary substantially, little attempt has been made in the past to integrate management accounting with financial accounting. Even the French *plan comptable général,* which included a non-obligatory section on management accounts, is now to lose that element.

A large company does not feel this split because accounting units are usually tasked with both maintaining the accounting database and then exploiting it by producing all manner of reports for both internal and external consumption. However, many small enterprises see accounting as only serving the latter purpose, and do not appreciate the value of management data; if they have accounting records, they often make no attempt to exploit them for management purposes. Some accounting software does try to bridge that gap. In any case, any system should have as a requirement that the data are exploitable for management information.

The kind of management information needed would have to be of sufficient analytical detail to enable the manager to see what contribution[2] is made by each major product or line of business (if there is more than one). This implies some sort of clear information about variable and fixed costs, including depreciation and other allocations.

2 Uniformity

At one level it seems that uniformity may be desirable for efficiency reasons. However, Anglo-Saxon accountants in particular have in the past denounced uniformity as leading to meaningless figures which are incapable of translating the individual nature of the business. This may be so, or it may be an impression for which there is no real justification. Countries such as the UK have found that disclosure (in this case in the income statement) was enhanced by using standard-format financial statements imposed within the EU. Even if freedom of choice were important, it is not clear that the basic principles permit of much freedom – assets cannot suddenly become liabilities, revenues are not expenses, and so on.

On the contrary, freedom of choice may lead to inefficiencies. As previously indicated, one service provider encountered during field research noted that in one major town there were only three banks to which SMEs could look for finance, but each one asked for a different form of cash flow projection. This meant that an entrepreneur had to pay for three different projections when doing the rounds of the banks. This is clearly counterproductive. The existence of a uniform system would lead to very considerable economies. Provision of software, training courses, accounting services, preparation of tax returns, audit, transfer of staff between employers: all benefit from a uniform system. The existence of a uniform system would encourage lending institutions and all who interface with SMEs to train their staff to exploit data prepared in a uniform manner.

At the same time, it has to be recognized that the accounting needs of a simple business are simple, but as the business gets bigger, so does its need for more sophisticated internal information and disclosure to the outside world. The system therefore needs to be able to take in the possibility of a progression from very simple records to more complex systems. The Plan SYSCOA that was recently evolved in francophone Africa is a good example of what one might describe as a 'nested' system which allows for the possibility for micro-enterprises to record only simple cash transactions, while small enterprises move to an accruals-based but simple ledger system which is then capable of being expanded ultimately into full-blown reporting according to international principles.

The United Nations supports International Accounting Standards (IAS) as the basis for good financial reporting by large companies with international listings, and many developing countries also base their national accounting rules on IAS. Government logic in supporting small business is to encourage the evolution of the indigenous economy by helping small business to become larger. It follows that, if this policy is successful, the accounting system for small business must lead to an easy transition to compliance with large company rules and therefore with IAS.

In practice, IAS are applicable to SMEs, because an accruals-based, historical cost system is the basis of most IAS reporting. Where they are unsuitable is that they exclude reporting for tax purposes and they include treatments for many complex transactions that are not undertaken by SMEs. The latter is a practical problem in that an accountant applying IAS needs a far wider knowledge of accounting than a technician operating a simple accruals/historical cost system. An accountant preparing annual reports to IAS standards must obviously be capable of applying them, so the professional costs to the business of applying IAS are high and do not bring any benefits.

Basic accruals-based historical accounting in a simple form is compatible with IAS and therefore suitable as the starting point for small companies, without any need for them formally to apply IAS as such.

3 Tax compatibility

The relationship with tax reporting is more difficult. The larger company has no difficulty, particularly in a computerized system, in maintaining information in such a way as to be able to present 'economic' reports for management and shareholder purposes, as well as fiscal reports for tax authorities. For the smaller companies, this is an inefficiency, since keeping, as it were, two sets of figures, one for tax and one for management, is both costly in terms of accounting time and potentially confusing to the entrepreneur. Therefore records probably need to be kept on a uniform basis, normally consistent with tax requirements, but with reports designed to make clear the tax effects on measurement in a simple way. IAS, of course, do not at this time address how accounting records are maintained, only what principles are applied in the annual financial statements. There therefore seems to be no apparent contradiction with IAS if the database is maintained on a tax-compliant basis in the case of small entities.

The two areas which are most likely to be affected by this are depreciation and provisions. Many tax authorities fix or at least have understandings about depreciation rates which are acceptable to them. If these are above what is economically realistic (and governments often use accelerated depreciation to help business invest) but must appear in the accounting records as deductible, then the business will show artificially high costs in some periods and artificially low ones later. Managers need to be aware of this distortion. Some tax authorities also allow the use of provisions to help preserve the capital base of the company (because that in turn promotes employment), but this also distorts the apparent costs of the business.

At the very smallest end of the spectrum, it is not clear that introducing any accruals accounting system is likely to be cost effective for the entrepreneur. Some simple records are necessary to provide management information and economic data. In French-based systems this is dealt with by allowing very small firms to record only sales and applying a tax regime (subject to turnover limits) based either on a percentage of turnover or on a flat sum.

The suggestion would be, therefore, that an SME framework be introduced. This would be based on compatibility with IAS, but would provide a nested set of rules whereby, as the business grew, it would progress up a ladder of accounting evolution, starting with cash-basis accounts and moving then to simple accruals and ultimately to full IAS. This system recognizes that reducing disclosure requirements from IAS is just not a sufficient solution in a developing economy. The transition from no accounts to full IAS must be as smooth as possible, with no sudden steps in it. The suggested system is:

- microenterprises (maximum 5 people): cash-based records;
- small enterprises (6 to 50 people): accruals-based accounting system using, preferably, a standard chart of accounts with a simplified structure and which also provides for management information;
- medium-sized enterprises (51 to 250 employees): accruals-based accounting system, consistent with IAS, with a more complex chart;
- large unlisted enterprises: largely IAS-compliant accounts;
- large publicly listed enterprises: full IAS accounts.

Small enterprises need only a very simple database, they have few different types of transactions and need only simple summaries. For example, the classic French chart of accounts provides three-digit codes for basic categories of data, such as 210 for tangible fixed assets. In a very simple business no further analysis may be required, but as a business grows and acquires more assets, it can either increase its files by using 211 (say) for buildings, 212 for land, etc., or it can go to four or five digits (2100 for buildings, 2101 for land, etc.). This means that the basic structure of the database (and therefore the accounting system) is the same whatever the size of company (e.g. tangible fixed assets will all have codes starting 21), so once trained a person can understand the accounts of any business, but that a small business need have only a very simple database so that it is easy to enter data into it and produce simple reports.

Notwithstanding other possible approaches, a small enterprise could start out with this very simple system and then move up to the more complex charts as the complexity of the business called for it. Each version of the chart should be consistent with the others, and would lead to a situation where the most complex version provided all the data required for consistent IAS-based annual accounts.

For some economies the principal advantage of this approach would lie in the fact that it provides a certain degree of uniformity, allowing among other things for low costs of training and provision of software, standardized forms, and ease of comprehension on the part of lenders. Another advantage would be that, since the basic level of the system is very simple and uses minimum categories, it poses as few problems as possible for the inexperienced. Nevertheless, the categories are fully consistent with those of larger companies using full IAS and can be easily expanded as the small business grows.

The suggestion is that the chart of accounts should be linked (as is the French chart) to the presentation of financial statements. However, while it is thought to be not cost-effective to have separate figures for tax purposes as opposed to management purposes, a single statement could helpfully provide not only total figures but also some cost analysis where the enterprise has more than one product or type of activity, and some distinction could be made between costs that are allowed for tax and those that are not to help the entrepreneur make the bridge between accounting profit and profit on a tax basis in countries where these are different.

Notes

1. This chapter is a report which was presented to the Inter-governmental report group of international standards of accounhting and reporting in Geneva in July 2000.

2. Contribution is used here in the technical accounting sense, meaning the excess of the revenue from the sale of one (or more) units of a product or service over the variable costs of producing that unit.

References

Canadian Institute of Chartered Accountants (1999) *Financial Reporting by Small Business Enterprises*. CICA, Toronto, Ontario.

International Labour Organization (1997) *General Conditions to Stimulate Job Creation in Small and Medium-Size Enterprises*, Report of an International Labour Organization Conference, 85th Session, Geneva.

Pule Nthejane (1997) The process of policy formation in Lesotho. In J. Franz & P. Oesterdiekoff (eds), *SME Policies and Policy Formulation in SADC countries*. Botswana. Friederich Ebert Stiftung.

Appendix I

Table 16A.1 Sample countries and their involvement with International Accounting Standards

Country	IFAC member	Stock exchange	Accounting requirements – listed domestic companies	Accounting requirements – listed foreign companies	Accounting principles	Legal guidance
Argentina	Yes	Buenos Aires Stock Exchange	Argentine (GAAP)	Argentine GAAP, IAS or their national GAAP with reconciliation to Argentine GAAP	(Local) Consejos Profesionales de Ciencias Economicas on the basis of the 'technical resolutions' of the Federacion de Consejos and those adopted under legal authority, primarily developed by the Comision Nacional de Valores (for listed companies) and specialized industry standards developed by regulatory agencies such as the Central Bank of the Argentine Republic	
Botswana	Yes				IAS are recommended, although not legally required	Securities Commission Law of 1976
Brazil	Yes	Rio De Janeiro and São Paulo Stock Exchanges	Brazilian GAAP	Brazilian GAAP	The Brazilian Institute of Accountants (IBRACON) issues standards	
Kenya	Yes				Institute of Certified Public Accountants of Kenya resolved to adopt IAS commencing 1 January 2000	
Malaysia	Yes	Kuala Lumpur Stock Exchange	IAS or Malaysian GAAP	IAS, Malaysian GAAP, or a reconciliation to Malaysian GAAP of net profit or loss and shareholders' equity	The Malaysian Accounting Standards Board (MASB) sets legally binding financial reporting standards	Financial Reporting Act of 1997 established the MASB

Appendix I

Table 16A.1 Sample countries and their involvement with International Accounting Standards (*continued*)

Country	IFAC member	Stock exchange	Accounting requirements – listed domestic companies	Accounting requirements – listed foreign companies	Accounting principles	Legal guidance
Poland	Yes	Warsaw Stock Exchange	Polish GAAP, but if traded overseas must include a reconciliation to IAS or US GAAP	IAS or US GAAP with a reconciliation to US GAAP	Committee on Accounting Standards, with nine members from different sectors	Accountancy Act of 1994, also requires conformity with EU Directives
Singapore	Yes	Stock Exchange of Singapore	Singaporean GAAP	Singaporean GAAP, IAS (no reconciliation) or US GAAP with reconciliation to Singaporean GAAP	Statements of Accounting Standards (SAS) issued by the Certified Public Accountants of Singapore	

Source: IASB web site (http://www.iasc.org.uk)

Appendix II

Table 16A.2 Accounting regulation in sample countries

Questions asked	Argentina	Cameroon	Kenya	Lebanon	Malaysia	Morocco	Poland
(a) Are there any accounting regulations which cover unincorporated entities, and if so, what is the source of these, and do such entities generally comply?	Accounting standards are mandatory for all companies regardless of size.	Accounting regulations covering all entities, including unincorporated entities, exist.	There are no statutory regulations imposed on accounting for unincorporated entities.	Starting in 1996 all businesses, regardless of size, are required to adopt IAS within three years.	There are no accounting regulations specifically applicable to unincorporated entities.	There are no regulations that specifically apply to this kind of business.	Simplified books, in accordance with the Ministry of Finance Book of Revenues and Costs.
(b) At what size or other threshold does a limited liability company (or other entity) start to have an obligation to have a statutory audit?	All limited liability companies, regardless of size, are subject to statutory audits.	Statutory audit if PLC has more than 10 million CFA in share capital, or 250 million CFA in turnover or more than 50 permanent employees	All companies are required to have a statutory audit.	All limited liability companies to be subject to independent audit. SMEs with profits of over $500 000 submit an audit report with tax filing.	All incorporated limited liability companies are required to have a statutory audit, regardless of their size.	When turnover exceeds 50 million dirhams.	Two out of the following: average employment 50 people; total assets > 1 million euro; net sales > 3 million euro
(c) Are there special accounting rules for incorporated entities with fewer than 50 employees?	No	No	No	No	No	No	No
(d) At what point does a business become liable to pay tax on its profits?	No threshold	No threshold	No threshold	No threshold	No threshold	No threshold	Taxable revenue < US $500
(e) Are there any special tax rules for small businesses?	The Monotributo	No special tax rules	No special tax rules	No reply	No special tax rules	No special tax rules	No special tax rules

Source: Publications of large audit firms

Multinational companies and international capital markets

Wolf Bay and Hans-Georg Bruns

One of the most important functions of external financial reporting is the provision of information on the economic and financial position of a group. Shareholders, potential investors and analysts need to be able to analyse and compare listed companies in order to make investment decisions. Companies have an interest in providing the market with such information as meets market participants' expectations in terms of quantity and quality.

Accounting rules are laid down in national laws and other forms of regulation and are generally compulsory for all companies within a given country but are different from country to country. This situation is not a problem as long as companies and investors restrict their transactions to a single country or a closed economic area. However, increasing internationalization has shown accounting to be a form of baggage that does not travel well. Annual reports compiled in one country can only be understood with difficulty if at all by investors in other countries. A conclusive cross-border comparison of companies usually fails due to different ways of dealing with measurement problems and different emphases in disclosure requirements. Thus barriers are created for companies and investors that lead to costs that are really avoidable.

Internationalization is proceeding at all levels of the world economy, and multinational companies have a considerable interest in being active on international financial markets. However, national differences stand in the way of this, and for many foreign companies a desired presence on the American capital markets has proven to be particularly problematic. It is generally agreed that the most stringent accounting requirements and disclosure rules prevail there. As discussed in Chapter 1, an important aim of current harmonization initiatives in the area of financial reporting is to achieve simplified access to the American capital markets, which is the world's largest and most important financial centre. In this chapter we shall examine why multinational companies are interested in international financial market activity, we shall consider the merits of different markets, and then look at the particular difficulties encountered by Daimler-Benz as a result of its historic decision to become the first German multinational to be listed on the New York Stock Exchange. The authors are executives at Daimler-Benz and debis Financial Services (the group consulting subsidiary).

Advantages and disadvantages of foreign markets

For many large corporations the expansion of their international activities is one of the most important goals if not a condition for continuing success in international competition.

International institutions such as the World Trade Organisation (WTO) aim to support cross-border trade in goods and services by reducing trade barriers. New markets are opened to companies in this way and also as a result of significant changes in world politics, such as the collapse of the Soviet Union. These worldwide changes do also mean, however, that new competitors are pushing their way into established local markets.

Many companies from the industrialized countries are increasingly internationalizing other corporate functions apart from sales. Thus global sourcing of raw materials and components is expanded and – as far as possible – production processes are shifted abroad. These steps not only often allow costs to be reduced substantially but also significantly reduce problems such as dependence on currency movements and import restrictions. Countries are chosen for the redeployment of activities on the basis of their role in product sales or because they offer significant cost advantages. Shifting production abroad enables the production programme to better suit the demands of local customers. Frequently products manufactured in foreign plants are specially made for the local market.

These developments in the markets for goods and factors are paralleled by developments in financial markets. More and more companies are actively engaged in the world's most important capital markets, ranging from holding foreign investment accounts or foreign securities to issuing debt and equity. The decision to establish or expand a presence on a foreign capital market allows a company to extend its position as a global financial player as well as to underline its commitment to that foreign market. This signal is strongest when the shares of the company are quoted on the local stock exchange. These apparently rather abstract aims bring with them a number of concrete advantages that support foreign ventures and listings.

Strategic focus

That the company takes a long-term approach to a particular market is essential for the move to a foreign market, be it the market for its product or the financial sector. The importance of the involvement in the financial market can be grounded in the standing the company enjoys in the product market in that country. The interest in a company's products can be enhanced by a stock listing because the company is signalling that its objectives are not just quick product sales but rather a longer-term tie with this market. The customer on the product market also gains the opportunity to participate financially in the company. However, for the company the attractiveness of the financial centre also plays a significant role. The company may not only considerably expand its financing choices but also have the opportunity to raise capital on more favourable terms than in its home market.

The strategic aim of the company can also be to broaden its investor base and gain investors in those markets in which large portions of its turnover are achieved. In this way the investor structure approaches the turnover structure. Often certain investor groups can only be reached through a foreign listing. In particular, for private investors and small institutional investors the purchase of shares in a foreign country is of little interest because of the transaction costs involved. In addition, certain institutional investors are restricted by law or their statutes to acquiring only domestically traded shares. Of course, a listing in their domestic market also allows all of these investors to follow the evolution of the share price of the foreign company in the currency they are used to.

Degree of recognition

Active engagement on a foreign capital market significantly increases a corporation's visibility. The company's stock exchange disclosures generate increased interest on the part of the financial community, and the financial press devotes particular attention to listed companies, not only by publishing the share price but also through analysis and commentaries as well as interviews with senior management.

Limitations of the national market

The move to a foreign stock exchange can also be motivated by limitations encountered in the national market. Investment in shares is not equally popular in all markets. In the UK the proportion of stocks in private investors' portfolios amounts to 12%; in the USA this is as much as 20%. In Germany privately held shares are merely 6%. This aspect is one of those which has to be taken into account when large capital increases or privatizations are planned. The inclusion of foreign markets can then become a necessity because it cannot be guaranteed that the national capital market can absorb the amounts involved at a good price.

Customer orientation

Finally a listing on a foreign exchange gives the company the opportunity to offer its financial products – and ultimately a company's securities must be regarded as products – on the most appropriate markets. Where particular interest in these products exists, the company should meet this demand. In product markets the need for a customer orientation is self-evident. Because investors should also be regarded as customers, customer orientation should also be the first object of the finance division.

Increasing internationalization of capital markets provides advantages not only for corporations but in the same way for investors because a much greater choice of investment opportunity is offered to them. The availability of new technologies and new communication and information media allow large amounts of capital to be transferred within seconds at almost any time. Via online systems the developments on the most important stock exchanges can be followed in real time. This enables investors to set up portfolios that match their risk reward expectations most closely. A growing trend can be observed, particularly in the USA, for investors to put part of their capital in foreign securities.

In order to participate in international capital markets, however, investors must have sufficient, comparable information on alternative investments. The potential rewards and risks of individual investments can be analysed and evaluated in detail. This is particularly important for the securities of foreign companies: investors will prefer the kind of information that they are accustomed to and understand and that allows a comparison with companies in the home market.

Companies must take account of the conditions set by the market when determining their stance on information. As the supply of securities grows, investors are in a position to avoid those whose quality they cannot judge clearly; if in doubt the capital will be invested elsewhere. Companies are competing for scarce financial resources in the international capital markets: attractive and economically acceptable financing conditions can only be achieved when the information expectations of investors and analysts are met. A policy of openness can have a positive impact for the company because more analysts will be prepared to follow its development on a regular basis. With the larger following in the investment community and the accompanying transparency, further benefits in the capital markets such as lower cost of capital should accrue.

However, companies that wish to increase their presence on foreign capital markets must be aware that they will encounter different information cultures in different countries, which can result in a number of changes concerning disclosure. In this context a comparison with the situation in the physical product market may be helpful. If a company intends to sell its products in a certain country it is only natural that local requirements and regulations are observed, for example as regards safety requirements or technical norms. Vehicle manufacturers do not question that they must equip their products with right hand drive for markets such as Great Britain or Japan, because this conforms to the standard in those countries.

Capital markets are usually very similar to each other except for requirements related to company disclosures and accounting measurements. Investors and analysts in each country are used to their standards and are rarely prepared to accept substantial divergence from these, especially if this amounts to a reduction in the level of information. It will be difficult in the long run for a company to target a foreign capital market and to obtain many special exemptions in order to circumvent local practice. Even when this could be achieved by means of negotiation, it would be judged very critically by investors and analysts. Strongly divergent disclosure practices on the part of the foreign company would prevent investors from fully evaluating the company and comparing it to others. The newcomer would then be perceived as very exotic and would therefore not achieve its original goal.

A company should carefully consider whether it is prepared to conform to the required level of information before seeking a listing on a given market. The requirements of individual foreign markets vary considerably, notwithstanding increasing convergence as a result of the activities of IOSCO (International Organization of Securities Commissions – see Chapter 1). An extension of financial activities onto foreign markets can lead to significant changes and hence additional costs. Consequently, special importance is lent to the careful analysis of a target capital market.

Major capital markets

The decision to have an active involvement in a particular foreign financial centre must be made – as discussed above – in accordance with the company's overall strategic orientation and its specific product strategies. A concentration of many company activities in one country is a strong argument for seeking a stock exchange listing there, even if the exchange is rather small. Generally, though, companies will seek a listing on one of the leading international stock exchanges that can ensure sufficient liquidity due to large trading volumes and has a suitable image and reputation. It can also be presumed that security pricing on such an exchange is subject to correspondingly strict supervision and that prices are not distorted by factors such as widespread insider dealing. On top of this, such markets generally have appropriate economic conditions with relatively low inflation, economic growth and low or no restrictions on capital flows. Furthermore, due to their vast know-how the local financial community is usually very actively and comprehensively involved in these financial markets. The following financial centres could be considered to meet these criteria.

The world's largest and most important exchange is still the New York Stock Exchange (NYSE). Turnover in 2001 amounted to $10,489bn and the market capitalization at the end of the year was $11,027bn. However, turnover in foreign stocks was only $787bn. This is low compared to some other international bourses.

The London Stock Exchange is one of the most international exchanges, witnessed by the fact that in 2001 foreign corporates made up $2,651bn of the total turnover of $4,550bn. By the end of 2001 the market capitalization of the London Stock Exchange amounted to approximately $2,165bn, which makes it the number one exchange in Europe.

The other important European trading centres are Euronext (Paris, Amsterdam and Brussels) with $1,843bn and Frankfurt (Deutsche Borse) with $1,072bn in 2001. Turnover in foreign stocks was $136bn in Frankfurt out of a total of $1,306bn, while on Euronext foreign turnover was $19bn out of $3,180bn.

The third significant trading zone is Asia and here the Tokyo stock exchange is dominant. Measured by market capitalization of $2,264bn, it is the world's third largest exchange (after the NYSE and Nasdaq). However, its value has fallen considerably in recent years. In the late 1980s Tokyo was well ahead of the NYSE. There are few foreign companies listed in Tokyo, these amounted to $0.4bn in turnover only out of a total of $1,660bn in 2001. Apart from Tokyo there are a number of other stock exchanges in the region, such as Hong Kong and Singapore, that are gaining in importance and interest.

Listing requirements

When choosing a stock exchange, its size and relevance to the company's strategic goals form only part of the basis of the decision. The listing requirements set by the market regulators should not be neglected.

In the majority of cases two different contacts must be distinguished, namely the authorities who run the market and the stock exchange regulator. The interests of these two institutions may well conflict. The world's large exchanges are competing with each other and have a strong interest in attracting as many important companies as they can. Therefore they would normally be prepared to make concessions in relation to listing requirements for their favourite candidates. The supervisory bodies that maintain order in the market and safeguard the interests of investors – especially private investors – are in a different position. These authorities insist that investors are adequately informed by foreign companies as well as domestic ones.

The criteria imposed by these two kinds of body can be divided into technical and information specific aspects. Stock exchange managers frequently set size criteria that must be met by companies before being admitted to listing. Amongst others, these are company size measured by turnover, book value or market capitalization, concentration of equity capital, period of listing on the domestic stock exchange and recent developments. Often certain minimum benchmarks must have been exceeded in the last three or four years, although this does not usually present much of a hurdle for global corporations.

The situation is substantially different in terms of the requirements concerning information, especially disclosure rules. An English language version of the annual and interim reports that are usually filed with the respective exchanges and sent to foreign shareholders is virtually compulsory. In addition, investors and stock exchange regulators must be informed immediately of events that might influence stock prices. In the USA and the UK, in particular, this requirement has been general practice for many years.

Besides these general requirements, which are the same on many international stock exchanges, some stock exchange regulators or exchanges demand wider disclosures that may involve compiling voluminous new documents. The situation is seen at its most extreme in the USA where every foreign listed company must file an extensive report, the Form 20-F, with the Securities and Exchange Commission (SEC) on an annual basis. Form 20-F is divided into two large parts. Items 1 to 16 require primarily comments on a number of aspects of the company, such as strategy, products, production, procurement, research, market and competitive situation, environmental protection, legal aspects, development of the company's share price on the most important stock exchanges, and tax issues for US investors as well as a five-year overview of the development of key company ratios. Item 9 is very important. This is the management's discussion and analysis of results of operations and financial condition and requires companies to explain results in detail for the last three years. In each case the company must provide information that the investor or analyst needs to understand the accounts, but which cannot be gleaned from the annual report as such. The second major part of the form 20-F – items 17 and 18 – deals with the financial statements.

If shares are directly offered in the US market as a primary or secondary offering, companies must compile a different document, the form F-1. In content it largely corresponds to form 20-F, but includes additional information relevant for the offering such as size of the stock issue, list of underwriters, planned use of new capital, timeframe of the offer, etc.[1] Another important requirement in the context of an offering is that important corporate contracts that do not relate to the day-to-day business must be filed with the SEC and thus made publicly available.

At the half-year stage an interim report must be filed with the SEC according to form 6-K, including interim financial statements. Reconciliation with US accounting standards is not compulsory but seems appropriate in order to inform national and international investors in the same form. Quarterly reports are not compulsory for foreign companies.

It is essential for reporting to the SEC that the information contained in the respective documents is comprehensive and allows reliable insights into the company's economic situation. American investors in particular rely on the accuracy of the information and do not hesitate to sue for damages in the event of inaccuracies or misinformation. Consequently the information included in form 20-F is checked for the company by lawyers and auditors, whose position is also at risk. Since the underwriters are equally liable for the accuracy of information provided in the context of share offerings, they subject the information contained in forms F-1 or F-3 to an intensive 'due diligence' process, which may involve individual board members at group level. Additionally the SEC reviews the documents critically and demands, where appropriate, further explanations or additional information in the shape of a comment letter from the company.

Price-sensitive information has to be given to the market directly as it arises, outside of the formal reporting framework. It makes sense for a company to compile internal disclosure guidelines which define the context for action – especially for top management – quite narrowly in order to ensure that information is directed to the market in accordance with the requirements between reporting dates. In this context the insider rules effective on different stock exchanges are very relevant because contraventions of these rules generally lead to far-reaching consequences for the company and the persons involved.

Apart from the New York Stock Exchange other international exchanges also have their own requirements. The essential ones are listed in Table 17.1.[2]

When seeking a listing on a foreign stock exchange, companies are often dependent on the support of other parties for meeting listing requirements. To some extent this may even be compulsory. For instance a listing on the NYSE requires a certified public accountant to audit and give an opinion on the annual report according to SEC rules. Contact with the SEC – especially when important documents are submitted – is usually effected by means of a lawyer. Table 17.2 provides an overview of the most important parties involved and their main tasks.

Apart from pure disclosure requirements companies may have to comply with national accounting rules when seeking a foreign listing. The annual report is obviously of prime interest, because only this opens up opportunities for investors in the respective countries to obtain a comprehensive view of the economic and financial situation of the company and its subsidiaries. Individual company accounts are also compulsory in some countries such as Germany but not in other countries such as the USA.

Table 17.1 Key requirements of selected international exchanges

Requirements of stock exchange and regulatory bodies	New York	Tokyo	London	Frankfurt	Paris	Singapore
Application	Original listing application to stock exchange and SEC	Apply to stock exchange, after listing register shares at Ministry of Finance	Apply to stock exchange	Apply to stock exchange exchange regulator	Apply to stock exchange and stock	Apply to stock exchange
Important documents	Form 20-F or form F-1 or form F-3	Securities report	Stock exchange prospectus (listing particulars)	Stock exchange prospectus	Stock exchange prospectus	Stock exchange prospectus (information memorandum)
Key listing steps	Internal audit of information (form 20-F). Due diligence process by underwriter (form F-1, F-3). Disclosure of important contracts of non-current business	After submitting documents one or more of the exchange's extensive questionnaires must be answered	Requirements contained in Yellow Book Prospectus subjected to in-depth verification process by involved lawyers. Disclosure of important contracts of non-current business over last 2 years	Audit of listing conditions, publication of prospectus, file listing request with stock exchange	No intensive audit process	Prospectus based on form 20-F. Questionnaire especially on board members as decision basis of stock exchange committee
Annual commitment	File form 20-F (full year) and form 6-K (half year, with interim report, reconciliation not necessary). Send long-form annual report to all ADS holders	File securities report for full and half year in Japanese, full year report based on short form annual report, interim report necessary	No special requirement	Annual report available at clearing house, interim report published no later than 2 months after end of period	File short form annual report in French, interim report sufficient in English	No special requirements

Note: ADS, Amercian Depositing Share

In the area of accounting, particularly, the requirements differ widely between countries. Several levels can be distinguished.

Mutual and unilateral recognition of accounts

Under mutual recognition the stock exchange regulator in the host country accepts the accounts as they have been compiled for the domestic market. This method, which is easiest for companies, is based on the notion that despite different accounting standards individual accounts are comparable in their quality and accordance with the rules as verified by independent auditors. European stock exchanges follow this practice.[3]

Additional information

A second possibility is for the company to use its home country accounts and provide additional information in the notes or another part of its annual report. For instance, many German companies voluntarily produce segmental reporting that goes beyond the mere segmentation of turnover required by law (para 285 No. 4 HGB) and a cash flow statement.

Table 17.2   Supporting parties for foreign listings

| | Supporting Parties | | |
Exchange	Sponsor	Lawyer	Auditor†
New York*	Investment banks as advisors and organizers of roadshows	Contact with SEC and NYSE, contract negotiation	Auditing of financial statements according to US GAAP
Tokyo	Mediator between exchange and company, support on questionnaire	Translations, produces securities report	Advice on financial report
London	Mediator between exchange and company, produces prospectus	Verification process, incl. correctness of prospectus	Advice on financial report and balance sheet categories
Frankfurt	Bank as advisor and mediator between exchange and company, produces prospectus	Where necessary support company	No essential tasks
Paris	Mediator between exchange and company, produces prospectus	No essential tasks	Advice on financial report, certifies accounting rules
Singapore	Mediator between exchange and company, produces prospectus	Verification process, draws up contract with depositary	Certifies information in prospectus

* Additionally a depositary and a custodian are necessary for a listing on the NYSE and in Singapore. The depositary is responsible for the delivery and collection of American Depositary Shares (ADS) and Singapore Depositary Shares (SDS), respectively, and the administration of dividend payment as well as proxy statements. The shares, on the basis of which ADSs and SDSs are issued, are deposited with the custodian.

† If the audited national accounts can be used, no new comprehensive audit takes place in relation to the stock exchange listing.

This method only makes sense if it involves relatively little information and does not require that published figures are restated under different preconditions.[4] Such a solution is only really practical to meet the requirements of a single foreign bourse. Where the company is faced with the demands of several foreign stock exchanges, there is a high risk that the notes become overloaded with the respective additional information requirements and that a clear and consistent statement on the economic and financial situation of the company can no longer be provided. Multiple additional disclosures may also influence the auditor's opinion.

Exercising treatments options

Conforming with accounting standards predominant on international markets can be achieved by using the options contained in domestic accounting rules. Many German companies apply the revenue-based format of the profit and loss account, in accordance with international practice. Other possibilities arise from refraining from writing off goodwill against reserves and capitalizing and amortizing goodwill against profits instead, avoiding optional provisions and recognizing deferred taxes. Such changes in recognition and measurement rules can have a significant impact on reported earnings. This approach is limited to opportunities where domestic rules leave options which can be exercised in approximating accounting standards of other countries. However, this is not always possible. For instance, foreign currency translation under US GAAP requires unrealized gains to be disclosed. This treatment is diametrically opposed to the German prudence principle and thus it is unacceptable for financial statements prepared in accordance with German and many other European accounting rules.

Adopting different principles

If annual reports based on domestic accounting rules are not recognized in the host country and additional information in the notes and the use of treatment options are not sufficient, the only remaining option is to compile financial statements under the accounting norms of the other country. However, this only makes sense if these accounts are recognized in several countries. Separate accounts for each country cannot be an option for a multinational corporation for reasons of practicality and because of the ambiguity created and the loss of clarity of information.

In most of the alternatives discussed above, conformity with or complete adoption of another system of rules is only appropriate when dealing with a system that is widely used and accepted internationally. The only two are the International Accounting Standards (IAS), issued by the International Accounting Standards Board (IASB) and US accounting rules, US GAAP. IAS are already accepted by the authorities of several countries. Accounts under US GAAP are compulsory for all companies that seek a US listing.[5] In addition, accounts prepared under US GAAP are recognized in most countries around the world. Thus Daimler-Benz was able to rely on the documents compiled for the SEC for its listing in Singapore. The problems associated with differential reporting requirements are discussed in more detail below.

Cost-benefit analysis

The costs of a foreign stock exchange listing are directly related to the demands made by the exchanges and the supervisory authorities. For instance, a listing on the NYSE, due to the complexity of the disclosure requirements and the necessity of reconciling accounts with US GAAP, involves extensive use of lawyers, accountants and other advisors, which results in commensurate expense. On other exchanges, where the listing requirements are less stringent, the costs of these advisors are much lower.

There are also listing fees which are due both for the initial listing and then on an annual basis, and it is necessary to incur costs in the areas of public relations and advertising. It is not only a question of appearing in the appropriate media but also roadshows must be arranged to brief investors and analysts and inform them face to face about the circumstances of the company. In the USA, in particular, successful companies cannot avoid having to arrange for top management to meet the most important investors, present their strategy and answer questions very openly.

All inclusive, a listing on a foreign exchange can require an expenditure of several million dollars – which is why cost–benefit analysis appears sensible. Making such an analysis is difficult, though, because the cost can be accurately measured but the benefits are hard to quantify and it may indeed be impossible to identify all possible effects in such an analysis.

The concrete advantages that can arise from listing on a foreign exchange can be shown by Daimler-Benz's share issue in 1994 when DM3 bn was offered. The issue price was set at DM640, which corresponded to 80% of the market price (DM805) at the time. In the following days the price fell noticeably. On the first day of authorized trading the overall market showed a very negative trend. The Deutsche Aktienindex (DAX) dropped by more than 80 points. Because of this the Daimler-Benz share fell to below DM700. On the same day Daimler-Benz recorded strong demand from the USA and the stock stabilized above DM700. The developments on the foreign market proved to be extremely positive and supportive of the domestic market and turned the share issue into an overall success.

Increases in information disclosure also need to be included in the cost–benefit analysis. Because of the significantly larger disclosure and accounting requirements in some countries – particularly the USA – the company has to provide information to the market which so far has neither been made available to investors in the domestic market nor been published by domestic competitors. This could lead to a view that a foreign listing entails competitive disadvantages.

This danger can, in our opinion, be considered to be relatively low. On the one hand, many companies from countries with more extensive disclosure standards provide this information generally without suffering competitive disadvantage in international markets. On the other hand, investors in the domestic market should react positively and quickly to this development because the additional information provided by the company substantially improves the basis for analysis and decision-making. The more likely outcome will be for this information to be demanded from other companies in the same market.

Independently of local standards in individual countries, international practice increasingly affects demands made on internationally active companies. It can be seen in Germany that many large companies disclose information in their annual reports that is not required by law. How far individual companies conform to market demands also depends on whether the data are available or can be produced in an adequate and cost-effective form within the company. The situation becomes more problematic when the requirements of the market or the foreign authorities contradict national rules. This problem is particularly relevant in relation to accounting rules.

Problems of multiple reporting

As discussed above, the most extensive and restrictive requirements are those for a full listing on the NYSE because, amongst other things, the domestic financial statements need to be reconciled with US GAAP. This can mean compiling a second set of accounts since in most countries accounts according to US GAAP are not recognized for domestic filing purposes. The same applies for financial statements compiled according to IAS. The obligation to reconcile certain report items with another accounting system as well as the publication of two possibly varying earnings numbers are therefore regarded as the largest obstacle to going to Wall Street.[6] This is not necessarily a problem in all European countries; for example, in France, Italy and the UK it does not exist. In Germany a draft law is submitted to allow group accounting according to IAS or US GAAP as an alternative to accounts drawn up under national law.

Above all this situation poses the question as to which earnings number is the correct or better one out of the two published, especially when the results differ widely. From a theoretical perspective neither figure can be regarded as absolutely correct. A more useful measure for market purposes would be economic profit which considers all future net income. Since such a figure cannot be calculated free of subjective interpretation and estimation of future developments, any accounting evaluation can only be an unreliable approximation. Published results can only be evaluated in the context of the underlying system of principles used to determine the measurements. Different rules necessarily lead to different results. For instance it is possible in the UK to value fixed assets above historical cost, while in other countries, such as the USA and Germany, this practice is not permitted. Both approaches can be justified, so it is pointless to draw conclusions about the quality of the competing earnings numbers. National custom plays a not insignificant role. In the past, earnings were more likely to be smoothed in Germany. In the USA such behaviour could be observed as a trend but not in such marked style.

However, it is not in fact so very unusual for German companies to present two earnings figures. Apart from the annual report prepared according to commercial law requirements, many large companies furnish a second results number according to DVFA/SG (German Association for Securities Analysis/Schmalenbach Gesellschaft) guidelines. Here, amongst other things, the attempt is made to exclude those elements included in the commercial accounts that have an irregular character and are thus not relevant to the long-term earnings potential of the company. The intention is to make the accounts of different companies more comparable through this elimination. The calculation of this second earnings number requires data not normally accessible to external users, so only the company itself can accurately calculate the results according to DVFA/SG. The problem is that this number is not at present subject to control by the statutory auditors and is therefore not attested as 'correct' by an independent third party.

After being listed on the NYSE, the experience of Daimler-Benz was that the market can be made to understand and accept two different earnings numbers, but that large variations between the two figures certainly call for an explanation. There is demand for explanation even when the earnings measures are very close overall because dramatic discrepancies in individual items can surface between the two systems. In order to avoid unnecessary discussion, the company should aim to reconcile accounting practice as far as possible. The remaining discrepancies are then explained by fundamental accounting differences that cannot be further approximated in the context of existing regulations. A varying and possibly contradictory use of options in the two sets of accounting principles is difficult to communicate to the market. For Daimler-Benz the situation has been that in Germany the press primarily emphasized the domestic GAAP numbers while elsewhere it was increasingly the US GAAP values. In Germany this problem will be solved if the draft law – allowing group accounts according to international standards as an alternative – comes into effect. However, analysts almost everywhere prefer the scope and depth of information as prepared for the American capital market.

Apart from the external effects of the publication of additional accounting information, there are internal changes which arise for the company as well. The information production process is particularly affected. Apart from the consolidation, the parent company can handle generating the relevant data for the second set of accounts in the initial preparation phase as well. In this way the additional information necessary for the second set of accounts can be collected within the framework of periodic compilation of data from individual subsidiaries. The next step in the reporting process involves assembling this data for domestic reporting, but the data processing for the second financial statements can be performed by existing programmes which may simply need to be expanded by some new modules.

By integrating the second set of accounts into the general accounting process within the parent company, one can also ensure that the relevant know-how about the accounting rules of the other country is built up and continuously updated centrally within the corporation. The second aspect is of key importance because the development of accounting rules in Anglo-Saxon countries is much more fluid than is the case in Germany. Thus the US Financial Accounting Standards Board (FASB) reacts relatively quickly in issuing standards and interpretations that relate to new developments. Only through continuous monitoring of the development of standards can future changes in the rules be recognized in advance and the necessary data collected in a timely fashion.

Comprehensive knowledge of the accounting standards for the second financial statements is also important because the data supplied by corporate entities is tested for content and plausibility. This is not a problem for those subsidiaries that already can or indeed have to report using the secondary rules (e.g. for US subsidiaries of a non-US group that is also listed in the USA). For these companies it would of course be even simpler if they had only to produce one set of accounts without the need to reconcile their numbers with the domestic system of the parent.

After the introductory phase it is well worth considering whether data collection and auditing should be transferred to subsidiary levels in the group. This requires the necessary know-how to be created in these other companies in the meantime and the parent company to pass on changes in accounting rules to individual accounting departments in time. Through this transfer to lower levels in the group, identification with the new accounting systems is further advanced at all levels of the corporation.

While the compilation process calls for consideration of technical accounting aspects, problems of content also arise for corporate management. Many of the decisions made by top management have an impact on and are represented in external reporting. The way in which decisions will be represented in this central source of information for investors has therefore to be included in management decision-making because accounting rules may certainly contain opportunities for optimization of the picture of the company. Where two different accounting systems have to be considered simultaneously, this can lead to contradictory treatment of the same factual circumstances, in which case the optimal arrangement is not easily attainable.

The company must decide in these circumstances which earnings measure it wants to place in the foreground and what aims it pursues with its financial statements in the long term. When representing individual values it must also not be forgotten that users impose their own expectations on the accounting measures and these are shaped not least by their habits and environment. If management strongly leans towards the American accounts this creates a tendency for greater fluctuation of profits. For German investors this means a re-orientation, which in turn requires an intensive communication campaign from the company to enhance the understanding of market participants.

In this context the question of determining the dividend payout must also be considered. The accounts of the parent company serve as the basis for measuring the dividend payout, while the information function clearly stands in the foreground for group accounts.[7] Compiling a second set of group accounts adds an additional dimension. Due to its dominant role within the context of information representation, the group accounts form the basis for investment decisions by investors. Should the group accounts stand in stark contrast to dividends paid, this could strengthen the call, especially on the part of international investors, for dividends to be calculated on the basis of group accounts.

A further problem area can be perceived for the company if the question of internal measures is considered alongside the external results. Since investors evaluate the company on the basis of external group accounts, problems arise for management decision-making if the internal system delivers divergent information in terms of the income statement. Top management frequently receives information in such highly aggregated form that decisions could be made on the same basis as the information that is also made available externally. However, a precondition would be that the figures are compiled free of creative accounting manipulations. Hence it is worth considering whether internal and external systems can be reconciled to the extent that unambiguous signals emanate to management and the market. Only in this environment can it be hoped that investors might receive clear and unambiguous statements.

To illustrate the problems of having two income measures, the following section provides more detail on the experiences of Daimler-Benz AG since it has been listed on the NYSE.

Dual annual reports at Daimler-Benz

With its decision to list on the NYSE on 5 October 1993, Daimler-Benz AG had to reconcile its German accounts with accounting standards accepted in the USA. A restatement of financial data going back to 1990 was also required. The company needed to decide in which form the US requirements were to be complied with.

When compiling the form 20-F statement, foreign companies can choose in terms of accounting between Item 17 or 18, and the latter is further subdivided into Option 1 and 2. Item 17 sets easier requirements because it calls only for accounts according to national rules together with a reconciliation of equity and earnings to US GAAP, a cash flow statement and an overview of movements on equity. Option 1 of Item 18 calls for all additional information required under US GAAP to be included in the notes as well. This includes, for instance, certain information on business segments, details on pension provisions and taxes and market values for securities held and financial instruments. However, values derived from national accounting rules serve as a basis for the notes. Item 18 Option 2 entails complete reporting according to US GAAP, i.e. valuation, presentation (e.g. structure of the balance sheet as well as the income statement) and the notes follow American rules. The reconciliation of equity and earnings is not required in this case.

Each one of these alternatives has its advantages and disadvantages. Thus Item 17 sets the lowest requirements as regards the accounts of foreign companies. On the other hand, it does not – apart from a few exceptions – enable the company to raise fresh capital on the US market. For that the company must prepare accounts in accordance with Item 18. One reason is that the Securities Exchange Act 1934 is the legal basis for listings and trading, whereas direct issues of equity come under the Securities Act 1933, which sets substantially more stringent demands on companies and their financial reporting in wide areas. It does not matter whether Option 1 or 2 of Item 18 is selected. Option 1 carries the advantage that there is much more transparency on where the main differences between national and US GAAP accounts lie. Option 2 facilitates the evaluation of the company for US investors and comparisons with other, especially US-based, companies. Selection of Option 2 also opens up the possibility of reporting only one income figure worldwide, if the foreign company's domestic rules for group accounts allow such a far-reaching approximation of internationally accepted accounting rules.

Daimler-Benz decided in favour of Item 18 Option 1 because selection of Item 17 would not permit future share issues in the USA. Complete adoption of US GAAP (Item 18 Option 2) was not selected as a first step because at that time neither American nor German investors were familiar with the differences in measurement approaches. Here selection of Option 1 created the opportunity to enhance the level of understanding of each other's reporting rules and to contribute to a factual discussion. In 1996, however, Daimler-Benz switched to Option 2 and since then the group accounts are disclosed only on the basis of US GAAP in the annual report.

In the context of the reconciliation under Item 18 Option 1, the capital and retained earnings under the HGB (German commercial code) are reconciled to stockholders' equity and net income according to US GAAP. In order to calculate these, all elements of the financial statements have to be checked for compatibility with US GAAP in the end, and the impact on the results arising from the differences must be ascertained. Tables 17.3 and 17.4 provide an overview of the reconciliation of shareholders' funds and net income for the years 1992 to 1994.[8]

The analysis of stockholders's equity shows very large differences between the two systems for Daimler-Benz. Shareholders' funds of DM18 bn to DM20 bn for the years 1992 to 1994 according to German accounting rules compare with almost 50% higher DM26 bn to DM29.5 bn under US GAAP. The main reason for this is a different way of evaluating the riskiness of transactions, which results in different levels of provisions. This point will be further developed below.

Table 17.3 Reconciliation of stockholders' equity of the Daimler-Benz group to US GAAP for the years 1992 to 1994 (DM mn)

	1994	1993	1992
Stockholders' equity according to HGB	**20 251**	**18 145**	**19 719**
Minority interest	(151)	(561)	(1 228)
Appropriated retained earnings	6 205	5 770	9 931
Long-term contracts	262	207	131
Goodwill and acquisitions	1 978	2 284	1 871
Divestitures and exclusions from consolidation	(652)	—	—
Pension provisions and post-retirement benefits	(2 250)	(1 821)	(1 212)
Foreign currency translation	63	85	(342)
Currency hedging transactions	1 013	381	580
Securities investment	27	—	—
Other valuation differences	(185)	(698)	(1 708)
Deferred taxes	2 874	2 489	(138)
Stockholders' equity according to US GAAP	**29 435**	**26 281**	**27 604**

Table 17.4 Reconciliation of the net income of the Daimler-Benz group with US GAAP for the years 1992 to 1994 (DM mn)

	1994	1993	1992
Group net income according to HGB	**895**	**615**	**1 451**
Minority interest	159	(13)	(33)
Change in appropriated retained earnings	409	(4 262)	774
Long-term contracts	53	78	(57)
Goodwill and acquisitions	(350)	(287)	(76)
Divestitures and exclusions from consolidation	(652)	—	337
Pension provisions and post-retirement benefits	(432)	(624)	96
Foreign currency translation	(22)	(40)	(94)
Currency hedging transactions	633	(225)	(438)
Securities investment	(388)	—	—
Other valuation differences	73	292	88
Deferred taxes	496	2 627	(646)
Effect of accounting changes			
for post-retirement benefits	—	—	(52)
valuation of securities under US GAAP	178	—	—
Group net income according to US GAAP	**1 052**	**(1 839)**	**1 350**

In terms of net income the results were relatively close for 1992 and 1994 while only in 1994 did the US results exceed the HGB results, but a large negative difference arose in 1993. Net income of DM615 million in the German accounts were juxtaposed with a loss of DM1.8 bn in the US reconciliation. This significant discrepancy, which has been constantly cited in the press as an example of the large differences between the accounting systems, is primarily based on the fact that Daimler-Benz decided in 1993 to approximate US standards as far as possible in its domestic accounts. Paradoxically this resulted in commercial accounts approaching tax-based values which often form the basis of measurement under US GAAP, for instance in inventory valuation. By means of this step a clear and unambiguous image of the corporate position was to be transmitted to investors. In 1993 these measures led to positive effects on results in the HGB accounts which had no parallel in the US GAAP report because they had already been accounted for with the switch to US GAAP in 1990.

The minor differences between earnings numbers in the majority of the periods considered is only surprising in so far as it has often been argued that the German system is more conservative by far and that switching to US GAAP should therefore lead to significantly higher reported earnings. Nevertheless the point should not be missed that despite the relative overall agreement of the total values, substantial discrepancies exist in individual areas, the sum of which seems, though, almost to equal out because the discrepancies are not uniform in direction.

US/German accounting differences

One of the largest divergences between German and US accounting rules occurs in the area of provisions, reserves and valuations. The HGB rules on the creation of these items do not correspond to criteria demanded by US GAAP because the German 'Vorsichtsprinzip' (prudence principle) is more far-reaching than the US conservatism principle. The differences that arose here were regarded as similar to appropriated retained earnings or specific reserves. This item and especially the approach to and valuation of provisions highlight the different accounting views. It should be made clear that from a German point of view these funds are not available for distribution as they are treated as liabilities under HGB rules, whereas they are regarded as equity under US GAAP. Thus this item can serve as a bridge between two accounting cultures.

The conditions for creating provisions are significantly more restrictive under US GAAP than German accounting law. Thus US GAAP permits only provisions that entail obligations to third parties. Hence provisions for expenses, for deferred maintenance that is carried out in the first quarter, and for internal costs of the annual general meeting or the annual report are excluded under US GAAP.

A further difference is that the obligation to make a payment must be probable and the amount must be capable of being accurately calculated or estimated by qualified people. Under the more stringent German prudence principle, a potential liability suffices in essence to justify the establishment of a provision. If a range of values for the provision exists, US GAAP requires using the value with the highest probability or, if the probabilities are equally distributed, the lowest value. In Germany the highest value is normally applied.

Differences in provisions also arise in the context of which cost components should be included. For instance, provisions for potential losses from existing orders are generally based on full costs under HGB whereas US GAAP permits only an approach based on direct costs. Other elements contributing to differences are special tax write-offs and general provisions on receivables, neither of which are permitted under US GAAP, and differences in approach to asset valuation, for example in inventories. When reconciling capital in 1992 the cumulative differences in retained earnings amounted to almost DM10 bn, of which almost 80% was made up of provisions. As a result of taking the step of approximating American valuation rules within the German accounts of the group in 1993, this amount has diminished over time and amounted to DM6 bn by the end of 1994.

Goodwill arising from first consolidation is also subject to divergent treatment. In past acquisitions (e.g. AEG, MBB) Daimler-Benz has written off goodwill directly against reserves, as is permitted as one option in the HGB. This is not allowed under US GAAP; goodwill has to be capitalized and amortized over a period not exceeding 40 years. As can be seen from the reconciliation of equity in Table 17.3, the difference in goodwill amounted to roughly DM2 bn from 1992 to 1994.

Substantial differences between the two accounting systems also arose for pension provisions. In Germany pension liabilities are valued according to the partial value method. The amount to be provided for is determined according to actuarial methods and is based on the total pension payments at the time of establishing the provision, reduced by the value of the annuities to be received up to pensionable age. Usually a discount factor of 6% is applied, as prescribed for tax accounts (para 6a Abs 3 S 3 EStG). According to the US Standard SFAS 87 the projected unit credit method is to be used in the USA. Here the cash value of the acquired pension rights of the active and inactive employees and service recipients at the balance sheet date is determined. In contrast to the German method, expected future salary increases must be taken into consideration.

Against this, the market rate of interest in the individual countries in which the respective pension liabilities are entered into is used to discount the liability. On average Daimler-Benz's discount factor moved between 7% and 9% during the years 1992 to 1994 for US purposes. Due to these differences in the valuation of pension liabilities, the equity reconciliation for 1992 featured a higher provision under US GAAP of DM1.2 bn which rose to over DM2.2 bn by 1994. In the case of pension provisions it seems that a less conservative valuation exists in Germany by comparison with the USA, despite the dominant influence of the prudence principle in German accounting.

In this context post-retirement benefits should also be mentioned. These relate in particular to provisions for the obligation to cover health care costs of pensioners in the USA. For US companies the creation of these reserves led to substantial losses in the early 1990s. For Daimler-Benz, however, this had no serious effect, because the social security systems in Germany and most European countries are structured differently from those of the USA.

There were discrepancies in accounting for financial instruments and in foreign currency translation as well. Under US GAAP the prudence principle is violated because not only unrealized losses but also unrealized gains are recognized in foreign currency translation. For instance, outstanding foreign currency items are translated in the balance sheet using the closing rate and any unrealized gains are included in the income statement. Such an approach is not permitted under HGB rules. The additional gain from currency hedging under US GAAP amounted to DM600 mn for 1994 alone.

Including these unrealized gains in the financial statements provides to some extent a better insight into the financial position of the company. Furthermore it limits the possibilities for manipulations by the management if they want to influence the net income by pre-balance sheet transactions. For example, where there is a currency position that has no direct underlying business transactions (open position) this may be closed out early in the market in order to realize potential gains arising from hedging activities.

Deferred taxes are also an important item, where, however, according to both HGB and US GAAP only timing differences are captured, i.e. only differences which impact commercial and tax accounts calculation but at different moments. Deferred taxes result from three sources, namely, discrepancies between commercial tax accounts, elimination processes at group level and from differences between German and American accounting principles.

In the German group accounts tax deferrals arise mainly from consolidation processes that impact earnings. Deferred taxes resulting from single company accounts are calculated following the liability method but are only entered at the value by which consolidated deferred tax liabilities exceed consolidated deferred tax assets. Taxable loss carry-forwards in excess of liabilities do not lead to recognition of deferred tax assets.

In the USA SFAS 109 prescribes setting up deferred taxes according to the liability method for all temporary differences. As in the HGB rules, the effects of eliminations from group accounts consolidation that impact net income are to be included. Deferred taxes emanating from individual company reports are not, however, netted. In the context of ascertaining deferred taxes, future advantages from temporary differences between valuations of tax accounts and group accounts as well as from tax allowable loss carry-forwards are to be taken into account. For recognition of deferred tax assets, which is compulsory in the USA, the company needs to ascertain whether these assets will be fully realizable in the future.

The deferred taxes position can be subjected to significant fluctuation over time. Thus for 1992 Daimler-Benz had deferred tax expenses of around DM650 mn; however, for 1994 it had tax income of nearly DM500 mn. For the year 1993 deferred tax income reached over DM2.6 bn, half of which derived from tax allowable loss carry-forwards.

Long-term contracts did not have much impact at Daimler-Benz. Under German law revenues and expenses are booked according to the realization principle, which is consistently interpreted on a very conservative basis. US principles basically prescribe the percentage of completion method which provides for recognition of profits in line with the degree of completion. In the majority of cases at Daimler-Benz these contracts are designed so as to allow partial settlements. Such milestone contracts are also common in the USA and recognized for financial reporting purposes. Larger differences arose due to adopting the percentage of completion method in the aerospace and satellite businesses. For 1994 the value of long-term contracts amounted to DM50 mn.

Several differences between the two accounting systems also exist in the treatment of leasing. According to German accounting rules leasing contracts which are signed by leasing companies that belong to the group are capitalized by the lessor in the majority of cases. Under US GAAP the treatment of these leasing contracts is largely the same. As opposed to German law, SFAS 13 requires capitalization by the lessee when at the start of the contract the cash value of the future leasing rates and the guaranteed remaining value amount to at least 90% of the purchase cost or of the market value of the lease object. Other divergences between the two accounting systems exist in certain special cases, such as sale and lease-back contracts. The sum of the resulting changes is very low for Daimler-Benz.

Additionally, there are a few elements in the reconciliation that have an impact which arise from particular economic or corporate events and lead to differing treatments in the reconciliation. For instance, in 1994 a leasing company which was fully consolidated under HGB was only included at equity because of the participation of external majority shareholders. However, US GAAP did not recognize this sale because from an economic perspective the rewards and risks are not fully transferred to the new partners. Hence in terms of the reconciliation a profit of around DM650 mn in the German accounts had to be eliminated and allocated pro rata.

Conclusion

Given the existing differences between the two systems which can have a major impact on reported figures, it is desirable to arrive at an accounting system which facilitates access to foreign capital markets for international companies and which can be compulsory in the long term for many states and hence durable. Companies must be in a position to orient themselves in their financial reporting and disclosure along the needs of their most important users. If companies regard the international capital markets as the relevant context for their financing activities and especially for equity capital financing, then they must be able to satisfy the demands of participants in those markets. The liberalization of the domestic market is essential to avoid the global players being prevented from pursuing their goals and being discriminated against in international competition. The multinational corporations must move in the direction of only producing one set of accounts.

An internationally valid and accepted set of rules would need to ensure that companies provide comprehensive, transparent and understandable financial statements for investors and analysts. In addition it must be reliable, i.e. it must allow an accurate insight into the economic circumstances of the reporting company. Compliance with the standards must be audited and attested by independent auditors.

In addition, the adoption of international standards should make it easier for investors to compare reports of companies from different countries. However, it should be emphasized that initially full comparability will be difficult to achieve because country-specific social, cultural, legal and economic structures continue to be reflected in accounts compiled according to international standards. For global players these national idiosyncrasies should diminish in importance with increasing international activity.

The issue of comparability is particularly important when investors directly allocate their capital to companies in different countries as part of their international investment decisions. Then it is essential that the accounts of these companies deliver an information basis that allows detailed comparisons. This question is less problematic, according to Busse von Colbe (1995), if investors initially allocate their capital to countries and only select country-specific companies as a second step. Then national financial statements could be resorted to, to evaluate investment risk and return. Nevertheless international investors would prefer a wider and more familiar basis of information in this situation as well.

Furthermore international standards should be relatively easily implemented by companies, that is the benefits must outweigh the costs. The process of switching to an accounting system that is different for the company definitely leads to additional costs even if these occur only once. A corresponding benefit can be attained if such financial statements are supported worldwide on as broad a basis as possible and unconditionally accepted in all major capital markets. The evolution of IAS with IOSCO discussed in Chapter 1 of this book goes in this direction.

However, the formulation of international accounting standards by the IASB and their recognition by IOSCO is only one of the two necessary steps. The second supporting pillar must be built by individual countries, because if an international standard exists according to which companies are prepared to compile financial statements then this standard should also satisfy national requirements. Otherwise internationally active corporations would continue to be forced to compile two sets of accounts. It is specifically the prevention of these circumstances that is one of the key aims of present activities.

Several alternative solutions can be offered:

1. national rules are adapted to conform to international standards;
2. compulsory adoption of international standards for consolidated accounts;
3. optional adoption of international standards.

The first alternative may be regarded as very time-consuming and tedious. In addition, accounting norms needed for international financial markets would then become compulsory even for those companies whose activities are contained within the domestic market. Therefore strong opposition from small and medium-sized companies and also some large companies could certainly be counted on. A 1995 study conducted amongst large German corporations and German academics showed that 28% of the company representatives have expressed the opinion that German accounting rules should not be changed. (Förschle *et al.* 1995).

The same problem would arise for the second alternative if international accounting rules were fully taken on and made the foundation of group accounts. Even limiting compulsory adoption to part of the population, for example listed companies, would surely not be accepted without resistance. In addition, unlisted companies would be prevented from having access to foreign capital markets.

Thus only the third alternative in which voluntarily compiled financial statements are accepted as an alternative to accounts drawn up under national rules offers a solution. In many countries, for example France, Italy, the Netherlands and the UK, this alternative is already tolerated today. Group accounts prepared in these countries by some companies according to IAS or US GAAP are accepted as equivalents by the authorities. This behaviour is not necessarily a formal right but is tolerated, by the EU as well as national authorities.

In Germany this approach is not possible so far, but there have been some recent changes in this area. The German Ministry of Justice has presented a bill (draft law) according to which the duty to compile financial statements under the accounting requirements of German GAAP may be waived for multinational companies registered in Germany. If certain prerequisites are fulfilled, these companies will instead have the opportunity to prepare their accounts according to IAS or US GAAP. It seems to be obvious that at least some German companies are eager to take advantage of this opportunity, as soon as the bill is approved by parliament. In contrast to group accounts, the individual company accounts could continue to be tightly aligned with the tax rules, or vice versa, via the *Massgeblichkeitsprinzip*. Thus there is no change for the tax authorities. The application of domestic principles such as creditor protection, prudence and conservatism could remain intact for individual company accounts.

For the future it must be assumed that many companies will expand their presence in international capital markets as part of their globalization strategy and will seek listings on the world's most important stock exchanges. A significant obstacle on this path exists in the form of very different accounting rules and the lack of mutual recognition of financial statements across borders. Companies are thus forced to produce a second set of group financial statements based on other accounting rules, such as US GAAP. In order to accommodate the interests of companies but also of investors and analysts, it would be desirable for all parties if international accounting standards existed which are accepted not only in all financial centres but also by respective national authorities.

Notes

1. If several forms 20-F are available, the shortened form F-3 can be used for the offering. Here the most recent form 20-F is referred to so that only updates and details of the offering need be provided.

2. For further details the reader is referred to the literature and the respective publications of the stock exchanges and supervisory bodies.

3. See Stock Exchange Listing Prospectus Directive (80/390/EEC), amended by (82/148/EEC) and (87/345/EEC). Individual European exchanges make additional demands that have to be met by foreign companies. This increases the costs attached to such a step. For this reason attempts are being made to reduce the hurdles for companies with market capitalization of more than 1.5 billion ecus and turnover in excess of 250 million ecus and achieve simplified listings (this is known as the Eurolist project). However, there is a precondition of having already obtained a minimum of three listings.

4. This problem is created by quantitative translations of numbers compiled under national accounting rules into another accounting system. The problem of reconciliation will be dealt with in more depth later.

5. Reconciliation with US GAAP is not necessary for trading via Pink Sheets listings, which is possible with the ADR (American depositary receipt) Level 1 programme.

6. In October 1993 Daimler-Benz was the first German company that listed on the New York Stock Exchange.

7. Many German companies therefore only print shortened versions of the company accounts in their annual reports.

8. Negative values in brackets. For further details see Daimler-Benz form 20-F for 1993 and 1994.

References

Busse von Colbe, W. (1995) *Zur Anpassung der rechnungslegung von Kapitalgesellschaften an internationalen Normen*. BFuP, p. 376.
Förschle et al. (1995) p. 407.

Foreign currency translation

Paul A. Taylor*

With the explosive growth in international trade and financial markets in the last 25 years, multinational enterprises have become dominant. Volvo, the Swedish-based car manufacturer, for example, transacts in numerous currencies including the euro, Danish kronor, Japanese yen and US dollars, and has foreign operations trading in France, Germany, the UK, the USA and many other countries. The decision how best to re-express its foreign currency transactions and financial statements into its reporting currency and how to report the resulting gains and losses is vital; so is accounting for its hedging activities to reduce exposure to large exchange rate fluctuations. This chapter examines:

- basic concepts;
- foreign currency transaction translation;
- foreign currency financial statement translation;
- foreign currency hedge accounting.

The term used in most countries for the re-expression of foreign currency transactions and financial statements is 'foreign currency translation',[1] necessary to allow shareholders or management to monitor the performance of multinational groups. It does not mean actual conversion of one currency into another.

Basic concepts

Exchange rates and exposure

A company holding foreign currency is exposed to changes in exchange rates, which will cause the foreign currency to gain or lose value in terms of domestic currency. Traders quote buy (bid) or sell (ask) rates for a currency. For accounting purposes the average of such quotes at close of trading is often used.

Exchange rates are quoted as either:

- *Direct quotes:* how much home currency to purchase one unit of foreign currency, or
- *Indirect or reverse quotes:* how much foreign currency to purchase one unit of home currency.

The indirect quote is the inverse of the direct quote (Table 18.1).

Table 18.1 Exchange rate quote: local currency Yen (¥), foreign currency £ sterling at 31 March 2001

Type of quote	Exchange rate	Translation method
Direct	179.360 ¥ to the £	Multiply
Indirect	0.005575 £ to the ¥	Divide

Note: 0.005575 = 1.0 / 179.360

Continental European and many other countries use direct quotes. In this chapter this convention will be used as exposure concepts are more easily grasped using it. Foreign currency amounts are translated by multiplying by direct quotes or dividing by indirect quotes. Readers from indirect quote countries (e.g. the UK, and for certain currencies, the USA) should take the inverse of indirect quotes and treat them as direct quotes – so $1.5079 to the £1 becomes £0.6632 to the $1 (= 1 / 1.5079). Most currency trading takes place in spot markets for immediate delivery (in practice two working days). Derivatives markets are discussed later.

Accounting versus economic exposure

The 'home' currency present value of foreign currency investment cash flows changes as expected exchange rates change, termed 'economic exposure'. 'Accounting exposure' refers to exposure of balances and flows arising from *past* transactions or events. These are usually translated either at their original transaction rate (the 'historical rate') or the rate at the current financial statement date (the 'closing rate' or 'current rate'). Deciding which to use for the various balance sheet and profit and loss account items is fundamental. Different proposals and their justifications are explored below.

For example, a US company purchases inventory costing €250 000 (euro) from a French exporter on 31 December and holds it until 31 March. Suppose the exchange rate is 1.0620 $ per € at 31 December, and 1.1380 at 31 March. If the inventory were translated at the original transaction rate (OTR) it would be stated at $265 500 (= €250 000 × 1.0620) at both dates – there would be no accounting exposure. However, if the current rate were used, at 31 December, the translated amount would be $265 500, but by 31 March this would increase to $284 500 (= €250 000 × 1.1380). A foreign currency asset would be exposed when the overseas currency, the euro, strengthened against the dollar, giving an exchange gain of $19,000 (= €250 000 × (1.1380 − 1.0620)). Suppose the equivalent indirect exchange rates for the US company were 0.94162 € per $ at 31 December (= 1 / 1.0620) and 0.87873 (= 1 / 1.1380) at 31 March. Translated amounts would be unchanged at $265 500 (= €250 000 / 0.94162) and $284 500 (= €250 000 / 0.87873). In what follows, in order to be consistent with international standards, the term 'closing rate' is used to mean the spot rate at the balance sheet date (in the USA this is termed the 'current rate').

A shortcut way to determine if there are gains or losses

Foreign currency assets or liabilities translated at the original transaction rate are not subject to accounting exposure, only balances translated at the *closing* rate. Use the following shortcut to determine whether an exchange gain or loss results.

- Treat foreign currency assets as positive (plus) balances and liabilities as negative (minus) ones.

- Strengthening of the *overseas* currency is treated as positive (plus) and its weakening as negative (minus).

- Deduce if there are gains (plus) or losses (minus) on translation by multiplying the sign of assets / liabilities by the sign of overseas currency strengthening / weakening.

In the above case a foreign currency asset balance (plus) was exposed when the *overseas* currency (euros) was strengthening (plus) against the dollar – more dollars are needed to purchase each euro at the year end. The gain can be deduced as 'Gain (plus) = Asset exposed (plus) × Overseas currency strengthening (plus)'. If a liability had been exposed, a loss would have resulted, 'Loss (minus) = Liability exposed (minus) × Overseas currency strengthening (plus)'.

Stages in preparing consolidated financial statements for multinational groups

In Table 18.2 there are three stages in preparing consolidated financial statements for multinational groups. Consider a group where a French parent holds a controlling stake in Danish and other subsidiaries. The Danish subsidiary trades in the USA, Japan and the UK.

Stage 1: the Danish subsidiary translates its dollar, yen and sterling denominated *transactions* into kronor. Its own financial statements are now uniformly measured in kronor.
Stage 2: the kronor financial statements are translated into the reporting currency, euros (€).
Stage 3: these euro denominated financial statements are consolidated with the euro financial statements of the parent and other subsidiaries to produce euro consolidated statements in the reporting currency. The chapter now examines each of the three stages, based on the requirements of International Standards.

Foreign currency transactions

A foreign currency transaction is recorded *initially* in the reporting currency by applying the spot exchange rate at the transaction date. There is much debate about how to report

Table 18.2 Stages of preparing consolidated financial statements for multinationals

Stage	Description	Consequence
1. Transactions	Foreign currency transactions translated by each group member in own statements	Each group member's financial statements are expressed in their *own* (foreign) currency
2. Translation	Each group member's financial statements translated into group reporting currency	All foreign financial statements expressed in group reporting currency
3. Consolidation	All translated statements consolidated	Consolidated financial statements in group reporting currency

such transactions at *subsequent* financial statement dates. Ebbers and McLeay (1996) report considerable national differences. At the date of the survey practices differed over two dimensions, whether:

1. resulting assets and liabilities should be translated at the closing or original transaction rate.

2. exchange gains and losses should be immediately recognized in the income statement or recognition should be deferred.

Balances translated at the closing rate are exposed. Where the closing rate is used to translate all balances, all balances are exposed. This is termed in Anglo-Saxon countries, the *one-transaction* approach or perspective. However, IAS 21, *The Effects of Changes in Foreign Exchange Rates* (1993) and many countries require a *two-transaction* approach. Under IAS 21 assets and liabilities are translated consistent with their measurement basis in the original foreign currency financial statements. Non-monetary items must be translated at the original rate of exchange, and monetary items at the current rate of exchange.[2] Resulting exchange gains and losses must be recognized immediately in the income statement, and the amount of such exchange differences must be disclosed.[3] Revalued non-monetary items are to be translated at the rate at the revaluation date.

In the case of foreign currency or foreign financial instruments, as will be discussed later, the requirements of IAS 39, *Financial Instruments: Recognition and Measurement*, issued in 1999, will determine whether the financial instrument should be measured in foreign currency at fair value, original cost or amortized historical cost. Once this is determined, IAS 21 applies, and in most cases such financial instruments, being monetary items, will be translated at the current exchange rate.[4] IAS 21's requirements are now illustrated before discussing national variants. Fictitious currencies ('louis' and 'nobles') are used below to keep calculations simple to aid intuitive understanding of gains and losses.

Example 18.1 – Foreign currency transactions

Clinton Inc., reporting in dollars ($), purchases inventory for 150 louis on 31 December 2001. The foreign currency payable is paid on 31 December 2002. Exchange rates are as follows:

Date	Direct quote ($ per louis)	Indirect quote (louis per $)
31 December 2001	0.3333	3
31 December 2002	0.5	2

Required

Show how the transaction would be accounted for:

a) under the one transaction approach, and

b) under the two transaction approach.

Solution

One-transaction approach: Both inventory and foreign payables are initially recorded at $50 [i.e. =150 × 0.3333 = 150 / 3] using the original transaction rate. *Both* are adjusted to $75 [i.e. = 150 × 0.5] at 31 December 2002, using the then current rate. The payable is settled by a payment of $75. All balances are 'exposed'. Some argue this approach is inconsistent with historical cost accounting as exchange rates used for non-monetary items reflect events since the transaction date.

Two-transaction approach (IAS 21): Both inventory and foreign payables are initially recorded at $50 [=150 × 0.3333.]. At 31 December 2002 non-monetary items, here inventory, continue to be translated at the original transaction rate, remaining at $50, whereas monetary items, foreign payables, are adjusted to $75 [=150 × 0.5] using the closing rate. Only the liability is exposed. The *overseas* currency is strengthening, giving a loss of $25m reported in the income statement [loss (minus) = liability exposed (minus) × overseas currency strengthening (plus)]. This results from financing a foreign currency liability from the purchase date [rate 0.3333] to the settlement date [rate 0.5] and paying back $75 (when the originally recorded amount was $50). It can be calculated directly as 150 × (0.5 − 0.3333) or as 150 × ($\frac{1}{2} - \frac{1}{3}$). Note that for indirect quotes, the *overseas* currency is strengthening if the rate decreases in value, here from 3 to 2 louis to the $.

If the financial statement date is prior to settlement, the exchange rate at this date is used. Under IAS 21, exchange differences on both settled *and* unsettled transactions are recognized in the income statement. Some countries regard exchange gains on unsettled transactions as unrealized.

National variations – monetary items

Ebbers and McLeay (1996) and European Commission (1995) found considerable national variations from IAS 21's requirements on the translation of monetary items. IAS 21 requires the closing rate to be used and all gains and losses recognized immediately in the income statement – as does SFAS 52 in the USA, which terms accounting for such transactions 'remeasurement', rather than 'translation'.

Short-term monetary items

Table 18.3 summarizes national variations. The most common is to measure foreign currency receivables and payables at the closing rate, but defer the recognition of exchange 'gains'. Widespread practice in Germany is even more conservative, keeping the balances themselves at the historical rate unless the closing rate is more prudent (the imparity principle). Van Hulle (1996, p. 380) reports increasing agreement within the European Union that including positive exchange differences on monetary items in income in *consolidated* financial statements is not contrary to EU Directives. National differences remain on their treatment in individual company statements. Such balance sheet deferred gains are inconsistent with 'asset' and 'liability' definitions in the IASB's and other Anglo-Saxon standard-setters' conceptual framework documents.

> Short-term foreign currency receivables and liabilities are valued at the rate on the balance sheet date. Long-term foreign currency receivables are recorded at the rate prevailing on the acquisition date or at the lower rate on the balance sheet date.

Long-term foreign currency liabilities are recorded at the rate prevailing on the acquisition date or at the higher rate on the balance sheet date. (BASF 1999 Annual Report, p. 62)

Transactions denominated in currencies other than the entity's functional currency [see later] are converted to the functional currency using current exchange rates. Transaction gains are included in income. (ELF Acquitaine 1999 Annual Report, p. 21)

Foreign currency receivables and payables are translated at appropriate year-end current rates and the resulting translation gains and losses are taken into income currently. (Sony Corporation 2000 Annual Report, p. 68)

Long-term monetary items

Some countries have different treatments for exchange differences on long-term monetary items than short-term ones. Some require or allow deferrals of additional types of exchange gains or losses, e.g. Canada, France and the Netherlands. Canada, for example, historically has required deferral of exchange differences on long-term foreign currency debt of fixed maturity, and amortization of such differences over their life. The argument is that exchange differences may reverse over such a long period, but there is little empirical evidence of this. The practice is under review. In France exchange gains and losses on long-term loans can be used to adjust the interest charge. In Japan gains and losses on long-term monetary items are not usually recognized as they are translated at historical rates. They can be adjusted to the closing rate if material, which then becomes the new historical rate.

Example 18.2 shows how to compute exchange gains and losses on foreign currency balances which *change* during the year. The methodology developed is important for an understanding of statement translation which is examined later.

Table 18.3 Translation of unhedged short-term monetary items – national variations

Countries	Rates used for monetary items	Treatment of exchange gains
USA, Australia, Canada, Denmark*, Ireland, Netherlands*, Portugal, UK	As IAS 21 / SFAS 52, all at closing rates	As IAS 21, SFAS 52
Belgium*, France**, Spain, Greece, Italy	As IAS 21, all at closing rates	Losses recognized in income statement, but gains deferred
Germany, Austria	Receivables – lower of historical rate and closing rate (imparity principle) Payables – higher of the two rates	Gains on monetary items not recognized

* authoritative recommendation, ** option to defer gains

Example 18.2 – Changing exposure – the two-transaction approach

At 31 December 2001 a US company has inventory originally purchased on that date for 150 louis, and accounts payable of 210 louis. On 30 June 2002, it purchases further inventory for 60 louis. There were no other transactions affecting these balances during the year. Payables have not been settled.

Exchange rates at	Direct quote ($ per louis)	Indirect quote (louis per $)
31 December 2001	0.3333	3.0
30 June 2002	0.4	2.5
31 December 2002	0.5	2.0

Required

Compute closing balances and exchange gains and losses for the year ended 31 December 2002, consistent with IAS 21's requirements.

Solution

At 30 June 2002 inventory increases from 150 to 210 louis and payables from 210 to 270 louis, and remain at that level. All transactions are initially recorded at original transaction rates. Monetary items (payables) are retranslated at the closing rate, whereas nonmonetary items (inventory) are not. Table 18.4 shows the computation of exchange gains and losses:

Table 18.4   Computation of balances and exchange gains or losses

Balance	Amount exposed in louis	Exchange rate			$ amount
Payables					
Opening liability	(210)	×	0.3333	=	(70)
+ Purchases at orig transaction rate	(60)	×	0.4	=	(24)
= Balance at original transaction rate					(94)
+ Exchange loss		(= residual difference)			(41)
= Closing liability at closing rate	(270)	×	0.5	=	(135)
Exchange loss direct calculation		=	$-210 \times [0.5 - 0.3333] - 60 \times [0.5 - 0.4] = -41$		
Inventory					
Opening asset	150	×	0.3333	=	50
Purchases at orig transaction rate	60	×	0.4	=	24
Balance at original transaction rate					74
+ Exchange gain or loss		(= residual difference)			Nil
= Closing asset remains at OTR	210				74
Exchange difference direct calculation		=	$150 \times [0.3333 - 0.3333] + 60 \times [0.4 - 0.4] = $Nil		

In it, opening balances for payables are translated at the start of year rate [i.e. 0.3333], the original transaction rate for opening inventory. Transactions in the year are initially recorded at their original transaction rate [i.e. 0.4]. At the year-end, the payables closing balance is retranslated at the closing rate [i.e. 0.5]. The translation loss for payables is the difference between opening balance and transactions translated at their respective original transaction rates, and the final balance retranslated at the closing rate. It could be viewed as the amount lost by not settling all transactions immediately. The 'exchange loss direct calculation' line demonstrates why a loss results – because a varying liability balance is exposed when the overseas currency is strengthening – the original liability balance of 210 louis is exposed from when the rate was 0.3333 to when it is 0.5, and the increase of 60 louis is exposed from its transaction date, when the rate was 0.4, to when it is 0.5. Inventory remains at its original transaction rates and is not exposed.

Devaluations

Under tightly specified circumstances, IAS 21 condones using the one-transaction approach after severe devaluations, though the two-transaction approach is still its benchmark approach.

Foreign currency financial statements

Assume now that Stage 1 in Table 18.2 is complete – each subsidiary has translated its own foreign currency transactions. Stage 2 in that table is to re-express each member's financial statements into the group's reporting currency. A number of approaches have been suggested. The most popular are the:

- closing (current) rate approach;
- temporal approach;
- monetary/non-monetary approach;
- current/non current approach.

IAS 21 requires the closing rate approach for foreign group entities, but the temporal approach for foreign operations which are integral to the reporting enterprise's operations. International practice has to a large extent followed this stance. Some countries use the monetary/non-monetary approach for integral operations. Under historical cost accounting temporal and monetary/non-monetary approaches are virtually identical. National variations in these two approaches are discussed later.

Asset and liability translation definitions

Each approach defines differently which foreign currency assets and liabilities are to be translated at the current rate, and which at original transaction ('historical') rates. These are shown in Table 18.5, based on IAS 21's requirements for closing rate and temporal approaches, and are similar to SFAS 52 in the USA.

The closing/current rate approach

This approach predominates worldwide. It is termed the 'current rate' approach in the USA and the 'closing rate' approach in a number of other countries. The latter term is used in this chapter. IAS 21 (1993) requires it for all foreign entities, i.e. foreign operations not integral to the operations of the reporting enterprise. *All* asset and liability balances are translated at rates current at the financial statement date. Nobes (1980) has found it to be the first widely adopted method in Anglo-Saxon countries. The group is characterized as a collection of 'net investments' in autonomous foreign entities transacting in *local* curren- cies. Their individual assets and liabilities are purchased, used and financed in the local currency environment. Therefore gains and losses on assets will offset losses and gains on liabilities, so all should be translated at the current rate. Many argue that closing rate approach gains and losses correlate better with economic exposure than other approaches because a current rate is used for all the foreign entity's assets and liabilities. In addition, it is argued that ratios computed in foreign currency statements (e.g. current assets divided by current liabilities) are more consistently reflected in reporting currency consolidated statements, since all balances are translated at a uniform rate. Opponents counter that multiplying historical costs by current exchange rates produces neither historical nor current costs.

Gains and losses taken direct to equity: IAS 21 requires closing rate gains and losses to be taken direct to equity. Some justify this on the grounds that such gains and losses do not appear in local currency statements. Another justification is the analogy with asset revaluations. In countries where such revaluations are allowed (e.g. the UK) revaluation gains and losses are taken direct to reserves. Thus adjustments to 'net investments' should be similarly treated. But such translation gains and losses are not revaluations per se, because current rates are applied to historical costs. Carsberg (1991, p. 104), however, considers closing rate gains and losses to be genuine gains and losses to be included in income.

Table 18.5 Exchange rates for translating assets and liabilities under historical cost accounting

	Current/ closing rate	Temporal/ monetary/ non-monetary	Monetary/ non-monetary	Current/ non-current
Cash, short-term receivables and payables	C	C*	C*	C
Inventory and short-term investments:				
• at cost	C	H	H	C
• if lower net realizable value	C	R	C	C
Fixed assets				
• at cost	C	H	H	H
• at revaluation	C	R	H	H
Long-term payables and receivables	C	C*	C*	H

Key
C = closing rate, H = original transaction rate, R = fair values using current rate at revaluation date
C* = closing rate under IAS 21 – some national variations

Temporal and monetary/non-monetary approaches

These are very similar to each other under historical cost accounting. What one country calls the 'monetary/non-monetary approach' may be indistinguishable from what another calls the 'temporal approach'. The monetary/non-monetary approach translates monetary assets and liabilities at the closing rate, and non-monetary items at the historical rate. The temporal approach translates items at rates corresponding to their measurement bases in the local financial statements (in the USA this is termed 'remeasurement'). IAS 21 requires its use for foreign operations integral to the operations of the reporting enterprise. 'Temporal' means 'relating to time'. Balances at original transaction prices (e.g. inventories or fixed assets at cost) are translated at original transaction rates, and balances at current prices, at the closing rate (under IAS 21 mainly payables, receivables, loans). Under historical cost accounting this broadly corresponds to the monetary/non-monetary distinction. In addition, items such as inventory written down to net realizable value or revalued fixed assets are translated at the rate at valuation adjustment date.[5] Under current cost accounting the temporal approach would use all current rates, like the closing rate approach.

The temporal approach (Lorenson, 1972) treats transactions of foreign subsidiaries *as if* they are direct transactions of the parent. Suppose a foreign subsidiary purchased inventory. *If* the parent had made the transaction, inventory would subsequently have been translated at the original transaction rate and the payable at the closing rate. If the foreign subsidiary sold merchandise, receivables would be translated at the closing rate, the same basis *as if* the parent had made the sale. Different national attitudes to prudence result in different translation bases for monetary assets and liabilities, discussed later.

Gains and losses treated as income or expense: such treatment is deduced from the 'as if transactions of the reporting enterprise' rationale. Statement translation gains or losses are viewed as if transaction gains and losses and recognized as income or expenses. Certain continental European countries allow deferral of exchange gains under this approach.

Current/non-current approach

A variant of this could be used in Japan prior to April 2000, when new requirements similar to IAS 21 were introduced. Current asset and liability balances are translated at the current rate, and non-current assets and liabilities at the historical rate, including non-current monetary items. In support of this approach it has been argued that over the lives of long-term balances, exchange rates revert to norms. There is little empirical support for this view.

Financial statement translation approaches and accounting exposure

As discussed earlier, only assets or liabilities translated at *current* rates are exposed to exchange rate changes. Each statement translation approach in Table 18.5 defines a different set of assets and liabilities to be translated at the current rate, and thus exposed. The exposure under any approach is the net foreign currency balance resulting from adding together the set of assets and liabilities translated at the current rate under that approach. This aggregate will be an asset balance under some approaches (usually closing rate and current/non-current) but a liability balance under others (usually temporal and monetary/non-monetary).

The aggregate balance exposed

Under the closing rate approach all assets and liabilities are translated at the closing rate, so net assets are exposed. Under the monetary/non-monetary approach, monetary items are exposed – cash plus receivables, less current and non-current liabilities. Fixed assets and inventory at cost are not exposed since they are non-monetary and translated at original transaction rates. The aggregate exposure is therefore a net monetary liability, since short-term monetary assets for most companies are exceeded by long-term monetary liabilities. Under the temporal approach all items which have a *current-dated* measurement basis are exposed – similar to the monetary/non-monetary approach.

A shortcut way to determine if there are gains or losses

The earlier shortcut approach for evaluating gains or losses can be applied here, but now to aggregate balances. For example, under the closing rate approach, the aggregate balance exposed, net assets, is an asset balance. If the *overseas* currency is strengthening, a gain results [Gain (plus) = Asset (plus) × Overseas currency strengthening (plus)]. Under the temporal and monetary/non-monetary approaches, the aggregate balance exposed is a liability and a strengthening overseas currency will result in a loss [minus = minus × plus].

Financial statement effects

The circumstances under which the closing rate approach shows a gain (a strengthening overseas currency) the temporal usually shows a loss, and vice versa! Under the latter gains and losses are included in income, whereas under the former they are not. This will affect reported income volatility and ratios and trends. Suppose an overseas currency is weakening – stocks at the closing rate under the closing rate approach will be reported at a lower amount than if translated at the historical rate under the temporal approach. This would lower the reporting currency current ratio, all other factors being equal. Stock turnover ratio would also be affected. If the overseas currency were strengthening, the opposite might happen. The reader is invited to reflect on such effects.

The relationship-contingent choice of translation approach

The USA was first to mandate foreign currency translation treatments. In 1975, SFAS 8 had required the temporal approach in all circumstances – Canada followed suit. However, SFAS 52 in 1991 made a complete volte-face, requiring the current rate approach (closing rate) unless foreign operations are mere extensions of the reporting enterprise's operations, when the temporal approach is to be used. IAS 21 follows SFAS 52.

IAS 21 requirements

IAS 21 requires, and many national standards require or recommend, that the statement translation approach be based on the nature of the relationship between the reporting enterprise and its foreign operations. Where these are *foreign entities* autonomously operating in local currency environments, the closing rate approach is to be used and exchange gains or losses classified as part of equity. Where a *foreign operation is integral to the reporting enterprise's operations*, the temporal approach is to be used (some countries use the monetary/non-monetary approach) and gains or losses recognized as income or expense.

Classifying foreign operations and entities

IAS 21's basis for distinguishing between 'foreign operations that are integral to the operations of the reporting enterprise' and 'foreign entities' is the immediacy of cash flow effect for the reporting enterprise of exchange rate changes on the foreign operation. Where this derives from individual monetary items, the temporal approach is to be used (i.e. immediate cash flow effect = integral to operations). Where it derives from the enterprise's net investment in a foreign entity, the closing rate approach is to be used. IAS 21 does not explicitly use the terms 'temporal' or 'closing rate approach'. IAS 21 comments that 'a foreign operation that is integral to the operations of the reporting enterprise carries on its business as if it were an extension of the reporting enterprise's operations'. A 'foreign entity' carries out its business functions 'substantially in its local currency'. Table 18.6 shows IAS 21's criteria for indicating that foreign operations should be classified as a foreign entity.

SFAS 52 has similar requirements, based on a 'functional currency' concept (Revsine, 1984). This is the currency of the primary economic environment within which the entity operates 'normally that is, the currency of the environment in which the entity generates and expends cash'. The temporal approach is required only where the functional currency of the foreign enterprise is the parent's, and the current rate approach (closing rate) where the functional currency is that of the place of location. SFAS 52 uses the term 'translation' for the current rate approach, and 'remeasurement' for the temporal approach. Under the current rate approach group entities are deemed to have multiple functional currencies, and under the temporal approach a single functional currency. Nearly all countries have distinguishing criteria similar to IAS 21.

If there is a change in classification of a foreign operation, IAS 21 requires the appropriate new approach to be applied from the date of reclassification. It requires disclosures reflecting the nature and reasons for the change, impact on shareholder equity and net profit or loss for prior periods, and restated comparatives.

National variations

Superficially there is greater international agreement on financial statement translation than transaction translation.[6] Most countries have regulations or authoritative pronouncements which prescribe the relationship contingent approach, resulting in the dominance of the closing rate in practice. Some use the monetary/non-monetary approach for integral foreign operations. Some adapt the treatment for gains or losses on monetary items under temporal or monetary/non-monetary approaches as for transaction translation e.g. Spain, and option-

Table 18.6 Indications of 'foreign entity' rather than 'integral foreign operation'

Relationship with reporting enterprise	*Nature of controlled foreign operation's activities*
Autonomy	Significant autonomy from reporting enterprise
Intra-group transactions	Not a high proportion of transactions with reporting entity
Product/service costs	Labour, materials, components primarily paid/settled in local currency
Sales	Mainly other than in reporting currency
Immediacy	Reporting enterprise cash flows insulated from such day-to-day activities

ally in Germany. Germany requires consistency between subsidiaries, but has no prescribed approach. A variant of the current/non-current approach was allowed in Japan, but the closing rate approach is also popular. Many large multinationals follow IAS or US GAAP in their consolidated accounts and national requirements in their individual company accounts.

> All asset and liability accounts of foreign subsidiaries and affiliates are translated into Japanese yen at appropriate year-end current rates and all income and expense accounts are translated at rates that approximate those rates prevailing at the time of the transactions. The resulting translation adjustments are accumulated as a component of accumulated other comprehensive income. (Sony Corporation 2000 Annual Report, p. 68)

Closing rate approach – further matters

IAS 21 and SFAS 52 require separate disclosure of net exchange differences classified as equity for the period and a reconciliation with opening and closing amounts. On disposal of a foreign entity, they require such cumulative translation differences taken direct to equity to be recognized in the income statement in the same period as any gain or loss on disposal. In the UK, Australia and Spain accounting practice is to leave such gains and losses in equity at such disposals.

Income and cash flow statements

Income statements

Table 18.7 summarizes IAS 21's requirements. Not all countries use an average rate under the closing rate approach – in the UK average or closing rates are permitted, and closing rates are preferred in France. Some countries, e.g. Germany, translate income and expenses at the average rate, but include the aggregate difference between using this and the closing rate as an income or expense. Under the closing rate approach, using the average rate is consistent with the net investment rationale, to reflect the exposure of the net investment; using the closing rate is consistent with the translation objective to preserve original currency relationships (e.g. debtors divided by sales).

Cash flow statements

IAS 7 and SFAS 95 in the USA require cash flows to be translated at original transaction rates or approximations thereto. The UK requires, somewhat illogically, translation at the rate used to translate the profit and loss account.

Table 18.7   Income statement translation per IAS 21

Translation approach	Rate for income statement items
Closing rate • foreign entities	At transaction rate giving rise to them. In practice average rate used, including for cost of goods sold and depreciation.
Temporal • operations integral to reporting enterprise	At transaction rate giving rise to them, approximated by weighted-average rates if fluctuations do not make them unreliable. Original transaction rates for depreciation and cost of sales (consistent with corresponding fixed assets and inventory rates).

Choice of exchange rates

Where multiple rates exist, IAS 21 does not give guidance. SFAS 52 requires for transactions, the settlement rate at its initial recording date, and subsequently for receivables and payables, the settlement rate at the current financial statement date. Under the closing rate statement approach the dividend remittance rate is to be used if there are no unusual circumstances. The rationale for the temporal approach implies using rates analogous to transactions. SSAP 20 in the UK recommends the mean of buying and selling spot rates under the closing rate.

Example 18.3 – Translation of foreign currency financial statements

Mezzanotte SpA is the long-time Mediterranean subsidiary of Sleepless Inc. Its financial statements in its local currency of 'nobles' are as follows. The reporting currency of the parent is dollars ($):0

Balance Sheets at 30 June (nobles millions)

	2002	2001
Fixed assets (net)	1 220	1 200
Inventory / Stock (cost)	800	400
Receivables / Debtors	800	300
Cash	100	140
	2 920	2 040
Current payables	600	240
Long-term payables	980	800
Capital stock / Share capital	440	440
Retained earnings	900	560
	2 920	2 040

Income statement – year ended 30 June 2002

	Nobles (millions)	Nobles (millions)
Sales		4 000
Cost of sales		2 200
Gross profit		1 800
Depreciation	260	
Other expenses	1 100	
		(1 360)
Operating profit		440
Interest payable		(60)
Net profit		380
Dividends		(40)
Retained profit		340

Notes

(a) Exchange rates were as follows:

Transaction date	Direct quote ($ per noble)
Opening fixed assets / capital stock issue	0.90
Original transaction rate for opening inventory	0.87
30 June 2001	0.83
Original transaction rate for cost of sales	0.81
Original transaction rate for fixed asset purchases and loan issue	0.74
Average rate for all other transactions during year including dividends	0.77
Original transaction rate for closing inventory	0.71
30 June 2002	0.67

(b) Depreciation is calculated on opening fixed assets for the year, not on additions.

(c) *Transaction details*

Movement on fixed assets:	*Nobles (millions)*
Opening net book amount	1 200
Purchases	280
Depreciation	(260)
Closing net book amount	1 220

Required

(a) Translate opening and closing balance sheets and the income statement of Mezzanotte SpA into dollars ($) under closing rate and temporal approaches. Calculate the gain or loss on translation.

(b) Explain why the translation difference under each approach is a gain or loss.

Solution

Table 18.8 shows the translation process using the exchange rates required by IAS 21.

1. *Balance sheets:* under the closing rate approach all balance sheet balances are translated at the closing rate at the relevant financial statement date (i.e. 0.83 or 0.67). Under the temporal approach, fixed assets and inventory are translated at their original transaction rates, and all other balances at current rates.

2. *Income statements:* under the closing rate approach, all items are translated at the average rate (0.77); under the temporal approach depreciation and cost of goods sold are translated at original transaction rates corresponding to the rates used for fixed assets and inventory in the balance sheet.

3. *Gain or loss on translation:* assuming no capital stock issues, etc., this is calculated as the difference between translated income (obtained by adding translated revenues, expenses, dividends, etc.) and the change in balance sheet translated equity (closing translated balance sheet equity minus opening translated equity). The translation gain is an income statement item under the temporal approach, whereas under the closing rate approach the translation loss would be taken direct to equity, and classified separately as part of the 'cumulative translation adjustment'.

Table 18.8 Translation of foreign currency financial statements

Opening balance sheet in millions

Description	Closing rate approach			Temporal approach		
	nobles	*rate*	*$*	*nobles*	*rate*	*$*
Fixed assets	1 200	× 0.83	= 996.0	1 200	× 0.90	= 1 080.0
Inventory	400	0.83	332.0	400	0.87	348.0
Accounts receivable	300	0.83	249.0	300	0.83	249.0
Cash	140	0.83	116.2	140	0.83	116.2
Accounts payable	(240)	0.83	(199.2)	(240)	0.83	(199.2)
Long-term loans / payables	(800)	0.83	(664.0)	(800)	0.83	(664.0)
Equity	(1 000)	0.83	(830.0)	(1 000)	Mixed	(930.0)

Closing balance sheet in millions

Description	Closing rate approach			Temporal approach		
	nobles	*rate*	*$*	*nobles*	*rate*	*$*
Fixed assets	1 220	0.67	817.4	940 @ 0.90		1 053.2
				280 @ 0.74		
Inventory	800	0.67	536.0	800	0.71	568.0
Accounts receivable	800	0.67	536.0	800	0.67	536.0
Cash	100	0.67	67.0	100	0.67	67.0
Accounts payable	(600)	0.67	(402.0)	(600)	0.67	(402.0)
Long-term loans / payables	(980)	0.67	(656.6)	(980)	0.67	(656.6)
Equity	(1 340)	0.67	(897.8)	(1 340)	Mixed	(1 165.6)

Income statement in millions

Description	Closing rate approach			Temporal approach		
	nobles	*rate*	*$*	*nobles*	*rate*	*$*
Sales	4 000	0.77	3 080.0	4 000	0.77	3 080.0
Cost of goods sold	(2 200)	0.77	(1 694.0)	(2 200)	0.81	(1 782.0)
Depreciation	(260)	0.77	(200.2)	(260)	0.90	(234.0)
Other expenses	(1 100)	0.77	(847.0)	(1 100)	0.77	(847.0)
Interest expense	(60)	0.77	(46.2)	(60)	0.77	(46.2)
Dividends	(40)	0.77	(30.8)	(40)	0.77	(30.8)
						140.0
Temporal exchange gain to income statement					**Gain**	**95.6**
Translated retained earnings			261.8			235.6
Closing rate translation loss to equity	**Loss**		**(194.0)**			
*Translated balance sheet equity change**			67.8			235.6

* obtained from translated balance sheet (above): Closing rate = 897.8 − 830 Temporal = 1165.6 − 930.0

Understanding the translation exchange gain or loss

To understand the nature of the translation exchange gain or loss an overall view of Mezzanotte's local currency transactions and financial statements is needed. To do this the following additional assumptions about Mezzanotte's transactions are necessary: Assume interest, fixed asset purchases and dividends were all paid in cash. All other transactions were on credit. Purchases of inventory were 2600 million nobles, cash from receivables 3500 million nobles and cash payments to accounts payable 2240 million nobles.

Mezzanotte's local currency transactions and financial statements are summarized in Table 18.9. In the table, its opening balance sheet is shown in the top line and closing balance sheet in the bottom line. Each transaction is shown on a separate line with debits being positive entries and credits negative ones. Transactions are analysed into those affecting the income statement, and other transactions. For example, sales are a debit (positive) to the receivables column, and a credit (negative) to the income statement/equity column. Depreciation is a debit to the income statement/equity column, and a credit to the (net) fixed asset column, etc. Each column contains the same information as a 'T' account. The table has been set up so that the first four columns relate to monetary items, the next two to non-monetary items, and equity is the final column.

Closing rate approach

In Table 18.8 we computed a statement translation exchange loss of $194 million under the closing rate approach by taking the difference between the translated income statement and the balance sheet change in translated equity. How does this relate to the concept of accounting exposure? Consider first the closing rate approach. Earlier it was demonstrated that net assets exposure is the aggregate exposure under the closing rate approach. Which transactions change that exposure? In Table 18.9 'net assets' is the sum of all columns except the equity column – indicated by the 'net assets exposed' bracket over the top of the table. Transactions which affect net asset exposure are those which do not cancel to zero when we add these six columns. For example the transaction line for 'received from customers' adds to zero if we add all amounts within the six 'net assets' columns (i.e. cash and receivables columns cancel). However, sales, cost of goods sold and depreciation (the income statement entries) do not add to zero across the net asset columns because each one has one entry in the *equity* column. The reader can check that the transactions which affect net assets in aggregate are therefore sales, cost of sales, depreciation, other expenses, interest expense and dividends. Those that do not are: purchase of inventory, receipts from customers, payments to suppliers, fixed asset purchase and loan issue.

Opening net assets (the sum of opening balances for cash, receivables, payables, long-term payables, inventory and fixed assets) is exposed from when the exchange rate was 0.83 to when it is 0.67. Transactions for the year which change net assets, are exposed from when the average rate was 0.77 to the closing date rate of 0.67. Using the methodology of exposure discussed earlier in Table 18.4, the top part of Table 18.10 shows how the aggregate exchange loss of $194 million is derived (arising from both opening balance and transaction exposures). An exchange loss occurs because a changing net asset balance is exposed when the *overseas* currency, nobles, is weakening [Loss (minus) = Asset (plus) × Overseas currency weakening (minus)].

Temporal approach

How does the temporal exchange gain of $95.6 million relate to the concept of accounting exposure? Monetary/current-dated balances are the aggregate exposure under the temporal approach, indicated by the 'net monetary/current dated liabilities exposed' bracket over

Table 18.9 Transactions summary for Mezzanotte in nobles (millions)

Closing rate →
Temporal →

| Description | | Net assets exposed | Net monetary/current-dated liabilities exposed | | Not exposed | | Equity (residual) |
	Cash	Receivables	Current payables	Long-term payables	Inventory	Fixed assets	Equity = capital stock + retained earnings
Opening balance sheet	140	300	(240)	(800)	400	1 200	(1 000)
Income statement:							
Sales		4 000					(4 000)
Cost of sales					(2 200)		2 200
Depreciation						(260)	260
Other expenses	(1 100)						1 100
Interest paid	(60)						60
Dividends paid	(40)						40
Other transactions:							
Purchases of inventory			(2 600)		2 600		
Received from customers	3 500	(3 500)					
Payments to suppliers	(2 240)		2 240				
Fixed asset purchases	(280)					280	
Loan issue	180			(180)			
Closing balance sheet	100	800	(600)	(980)	800	1 220	(1 340)

the top of first four columns of Table 18.9 – cash, receivables, payables and loans. What transactions affect temporal approach exposure? – those transaction lines which do not cancel to zero when the first four columns are added. These are *purchases* of inventory and *purchases* of fixed assets, as only *one* side of the transaction entry is inside the four exposed columns. They do *not* include cost of goods sold and depreciation expense, as *neither* entry affects the four columns. Neither do they include payments to suppliers and receipts from customers, which cancel as *both* entries are inside the four columns.

The bottom part of Table 18.10 lists those transactions which affect temporal exposure. Opening and closing balances (the sum of cash, receivables, payables and long-term payables) are in aggregate net *liability* balances. Fixed asset *purchases* are exposed from the original rate at the transaction date (0.74) to the year end (0.67). An exchange gain occurs because a changing net liability balance is exposed when the *overseas* currency is weakening (plus = minus × minus).

Table 18.10 Explanation of exchange gains and losses

Exchange gain on	Aggregate amount exposed		Exposure period end	original	Gain or (loss)
Closing rate	Net assets				
Opening balance	1 000				
	[= 140+300+400+1,200–240–800]	×	0.67 –	0.83 =	(160.0)
Sales	4 000	×	0.67 –	0.77 =	(400.0)
COGS	(2 200)	×	0.67 –	0.77 =	220.0
Depreciation	(260)	×	0.67 –	0.77 =	26.0
Other expenses	(1 100)	×	0.67 –	0.77 =	110.0
Interest	(60)	×	0.67 –	0.77 =	6.0
Dividends	(40)	×	0.67 –	0.77 =	4.0
	1 340				
	[= 100+800+800+1 220–600–980]		*Aggregate loss*		(194.0)

Temporal	Net current-dated valuation items (liability)		Exposure period end	original	Gain or (loss)
Opening balance	(600)				
	[= 140+300–240–800]	×	0.67 –	0.83 =	96.0
Sales	4 000	×	0.67 –	0.77 =	(400.0)
Purchases	(2 600)	×	0.67 –	0.77 =	260.0
Other expenses	(1 100)	×	0.67 –	0.77 =	110.0
Interest	(60)	×	0.67 –	0.77 =	6.0
Dividends	(40)	×	0.67 –	0.77 =	4.0
Fixed asset purchase	(280)	×	0.67 –	0.74 =	19.6
	(680)				
	[=100+800–600–980]		*Aggregate gain*		95.6

Cash flow statement translation and other notes to the accounts

Translating the cash and fixed asset column transactions in Table 18.9 provides the basis for the consolidated cash flow statement, and for consolidated fixed asset movement notes to the accounts (see Taylor 1996, pp. 316–324).

Consolidating translated statements

Readers with no prior knowledge of consolidation procedures can omit this section without loss of continuity. Table 18.2 listed three overall stages in multinational consolidation: (1) transaction translation, (2) statement translation, and (3) consolidation of translated statements. Stage 3 is now examined. It includes similar issues to domestic consolidation: the split of pre- and post acquisition profits, determination of goodwill, etc. However, the distinctive features which apply to multinational consolidation relate to (a) the exchange rates to use in determining goodwill and (b) the analysis of post-acquisition equity into two parts – the first relating to cumulative exchange gains or losses since acquisition under closing rate statement translation, and the residual which relates to translated post-acquisition profits. Only the closing rate approach is examined in Stage 3.

The translation of equity is the same as the translation of net assets [since equity = net assets]. Since we are dealing with consolidated balance sheets, the timeframe for exposure is from the *date of acquisition* of the foreign subsidiary to the current financial statements date. Example 18.2 examined the translation of a single account balance over a year. The principles in translating equity, itself just an accounting balance, are identical. As before, (1) the opening balance is exposed from the *opening* date to the current date, and (2) the transactions affecting equity are exposed from the *transaction* date to the current date. The opening balance date is *the date of acquisition* rather than the start of the year. The term *'cumulative translation adjustment'* is therefore used to reflect this normally greater timescale. In the single accounting balance case we can determine the gain or loss on equity by taking the difference between the sum of translated opening balances plus translated transactions, and the closing balance translated at the closing rate. Under the closing rate approach we are evaluating the (cumulative) exposure of net assets [=equity] since acquisition. Therefore these gains and losses are *post-acquisition* gains and losses. The steps are summarized as:

Step (i) Translate the opening balance of equity at the rate at the date of acquisition.

Step (ii) Translate 'transactions' (anything that changes equity – in our simple Example 18.4, retained earnings for each year since acquisition) at the relevant average transaction rate(s) for that year.

Step (iii) Determine the gain or loss on 'exposure' of equity as the difference between these translated amounts in (i) and (ii) and the closing balance translated at the rate at the current balance sheet date.

Example 18.4 – Translation and consolidation of foreign currency equity balances

Sleepless Inc. acquired a 100% interest in Mezzanotte SpA on 30 June 2001. Mezzanotte Spa's capital stock (share capital) and retained profits at that date are shown below in millions of nobles, with changes since that date. Sleepless Inc. has no other subsidiaries.

Equity in Mezzanotte	Nobles (millions)	Exchange rate (direct quote)
Capital stock (shares) at 30 June 2001	440	0.90
Retained profits at 30 June 2001	360	0.90
Equity at 30 June 2001	800	0.90
Profits retained in year to 30 June 2002	200	0.85
Equity at 30 June 2002	1 000	0.83

Required

At 30 June 2002:

(a) Under the closing rate method show how Mezzanotte's translated equity should be translated to meet IAS 21's requirements. Assume the income statement for 2002 was translated at a uniform average rate of 0.85.

(b) Assume Mezzanotte was acquired by Sleepless Inc. for $1000 million, and that Sleepless Inc.'s own retained earnings in its current balance sheet are $750m. Calculate consolidated balance sheet figures for the cost of goodwill ignoring amortization, consolidated retained earnings and the cumulative translation adjustment.

In Table 18.11 the three steps are shown:

Step (i), opening equity at acquisition is translated at the acquisition rate [720 = 800 × 0.90].

Step (ii), changes in equity (i.e. retained profits) are translated at average transaction rates [170 = 200 × 0.85].

Step (iii), the cumulative exchange loss of $60m is the difference between the sum of these amounts and the closing balance translated at the closing rate [830 = 1000 × 0.83]. The layout is similar to the translation of payables in Table 18.4 earlier, and the cumulative translation loss is explained in a similar fashion.

Table 18.11 Translation of equity

Details	Amount exposed in louis DR/(CR)	Exchange rate used for translation	$ amount
Equity of subsidiary			
Opening balance rate at date of acquisition	(800)	× 0.90 =	(720)
Change in equity (retained earnings) 2002 at average rate for 2002	(200)	× 0.85 =	(170)
Closing balance at original transaction rates			(890)
Cumulative translation adjustment since acquisition	—	(= residual difference)	60 ←
Closing balance at closing rate at end of 2002	(1 000)	× 0.83 =	(830)
Cumulative translation loss direct calculation		− 800 × [0.83−0.90] − 200 × [0.83−0.85] = + 60 ←	

The above figures form the basis for the consolidation of the translated statements (Stage 3) as follows:

I. *Goodwill at acquisition* – Equity at acquisition of $720m [= 800 × 0.90] is cancelled against Sleepless's investment of $1000m, to deduce goodwill cost at acquisition of $280m.

II. *Post acquisition changes:*

(a) *Translated post-acquisition retained profits* are obtained by combining Mezzanotte's translated post-acquisition profits of $170m with Sleepless's retained profits of $750m to get consolidated retained profits of $920m.

(b) *Cumulative translation adjustment* – this is the amount of the post-acquisition change in equity which relates to the foreign currency exposure of net assets since acquisition (under the closing rate approach). It is a loss, a debit balance of $60m. Net assets/equity have been exposed since the acquisition date and the overseas currency has been consistently weakening.

Further refinement – goodwill translation

IAS 21 allows goodwill to be treated either as:

1. a *reporting* currency balance (e.g. as in Australia, Sweden and the UK), or
2. a *foreign* currency balance (the required treatment by SFAS 52 in the USA).

As a reporting currency balance: the reporting currency balance alternative has been used in the above example where goodwill cost has been anchored at acquisition at the reporting currency amount of $280m. If it were amortized over a 10 year period it would be amortized at $28m per annum.

As a foreign currency balance: if goodwill were a foreign currency balance, the parent's investment at acquisition would be equivalent to 1111m nobles [= 1000/0.90]. Therefore goodwill would be calculated as 311.11 nobles [= 1111 − 800] at acquisition. At acquisition translated goodwill cost would still be $280m [= 311.1 × 0.90], but at 30 June 2000 its cost would be *retranslated* at $258.13 [= 311.1 × 0.83]. Amortization would therefore need to be updated each year.

Under the reporting currency alternative for goodwill, net assets are exposed, whereas under the foreign currency alternative, net assets *and* goodwill are exposed. For reasons beyond the scope of the current text it can be demonstrated that the foreign currency alternative is more consistent with the net investment rationale.[7]

Other matters

Disclosures

In addition to disclosures discussed earlier, IAS 21 also encourages disclosure of an enterprise's foreign currency risk management policy. SFAS 52 requires a more detailed analysis of reserve movements caused by exchange differences (e.g. showing effects of hedges, inter-company balances, taxation and sales or disposals).

Hyperinflationary economies

The closing rate approach faces particular problems for foreign entities in hyperinflationary economies. Rapidly depreciating exchange rates applied to fixed original costs creates the so-called 'disappearing assets' syndrome. Under current cost accounting this would be off-set by increases in current values but not under historical cost accounting. Internationally, two alternatives have been proposed:

(a) Closing rate translation of price-level adjusted historical costs using a local inflation index. This is required by IAS 29, *Financial Reporting in Hyperinflationary Economies*. Income and expense items are to be translated at the closing rate. France and the UK, for example, tend to use this approach.

(b) The temporal approach, required, for example, by SFAS 52 and in Canada.

Alternative (a) is consistent with an autonomous foreign entity perspective. Alternative (b) uses the parent's own currency as 'store' of value, which seems inconsistent with the multiple functional currency rationale for the closing rate approach – the relationship between movements in the foreign and reporting currencies is used as a proxy for an inflation index. Hyperinflationary economies are defined as where the *cumulative* exchange rate exceeds 100% over a three-year period, equivalent to an annual compound growth rate of 26%. Volvo uses the temporal/monetary/non-monetary approach for such subsidiaries.

> Financial statements of subsidiaries operating in highly inflationary economies are translated to Swedish kronor using the monetary method. Monetary items in the balance sheet are translated at year-end rates and non-monetary balance sheet items and corresponding income statement items are translated at rates in effect at the time of acquisition (historical rates). Other income statement items are translated at average rates. Translation differences are credited to, or charged against, income in the year in which they arise. (Volvo Annual Report 2000, p. 54)

Accounting for foreign currency risk management and hedging

Hedging is a major task in multinational treasury management. Foreign currency financial instruments such as forward contracts, futures, options, currency and interest rate swaps are often used to reduce exposure to foreign currency risk. Such foreign currency *hedging instruments* are readily marketable, very volatile in price, and can be used for *both* hedging and speculation. In their hedging/insurance use, their price changes offset those of the underlying foreign currency *hedged item* as shown in Table 18.12. The cost of such hedging instruments is related to the amount of 'insurance' required. Without particular hedge accounting rules, gains and losses on hedging instruments may be reported either:

1. in different parts of the financial statements, or

2. in different periods

to the underlying hedged position.

Hedge accounting is subsumed within the larger area of accounting for financial instruments, an area undergoing radical change. The FASB in the USA has consistently led the field in this area and has issued a number of accounting standards.[8] In June 1998, the FASB issued the standard with the most implications for accounting for foreign currency aspects,

SFAS 133, *Accounting for Derivative Instruments and Certain Hedging Activities*, now, as amended by SFAS 138, required for fiscal years beginning after June 2000. The IASB took advantage of such standards to produce more codified treatments in IAS 32, *Financial Instruments: Disclosure and Presentation*, in 1998, and in March 1999, IAS 39, *Financial Instruments: Recognition and Measurement*, effective for financial years beginning after 1 January 2001. In this area disclosure standards had preceded the more difficult area of measurement standards. Other national standard-setters have also been active in the area, particularly in the disclosure area.

It is likely that even these standards will be viewed as transitional steps towards a more comprehensive treatment. In December 2000, a Joint Working Group of International Standard Setters[9] produced a more far-reaching 'Draft Standard and Basis for Conclusions on Financial Instruments and Similar Items', proposing that financial instruments be measured at fair value and most special hedging accounting approaches be discontinued. This is discussed later. The treatments in SFAS 133 and SFAS 39 are likely to be required for some time, and are examined here. Because of the focus of this chapter, accounting for financial instruments will only be discussed insofar as it affects foreign exchange risk management and hedging.

Foreign exchange risk management and hedging

Much foreign currency hedging and speculative activity takes place through forward contracts, futures and options markets, rather than spot markets.

Forward exchange contracts and futures

A forward contract is a price agreed *now* for future delivery. For example, on 9 January 2002, in the USA, the spot rate for £ STG was 1.4399 dollars to the pound. The three-month forward rate for April delivery was 1.4321 dollars to the pound – the amount to be paid in three months to receive delivery of £1 STG at that time. Forward rates are also quoted, for example on the London Stock Exchange, as premiums or discounts on the spot rate (here a discount of $0.0078 = \$1.4321 - \$1.4399$). These reflect the time value of money and differentials between home and overseas interest rates. Suppose a US enterprise with a £100 million foreign currency payable due in three-months enters a three month forward contract to pay $143.21 million for delivery of £100 million in June. This predetermines the price of pounds for future delivery. The amount to be delivered is termed the *notional principal* of the contract.

A forward contract usually costs nothing to enter into other than transaction costs, since the forward rate is set so that there is no expected net gain to either party. Its value can subsequently go up or down. One month later in February, pounds for April delivery (now a two-month forward exchange contract) may become more expensive than the January

Table 18.12 Effects of hedging

Scenario	Hedged item/ underlying position	+	Hedging instrument	=	Net hedged position
1. Loss on hedged item	Loss	+	Gain	=	Offset
2. Gain on hedged item	Gain	+	Loss	=	Offset

price, so the existing contract becomes valuable. If pounds become cheaper, the contract may have a negative value. Changes in value of the forward contract will offset changes in the foreign currency payable.

When payable and forward contract mature, the payable is settled at the spot rate. The forward contract is either sold or settled. It has a maturity value equal to the difference between the maturity date spot price and the contract price. This is received by its holder or, if negative, paid out. The net effect of both transactions is as if the company had settled the payable at the forward contract price.

Foreign currency futures can be viewed as tradable forward contracts with standardized features and slightly different institutional arrangements, e.g. daily settlements.

Example 18.5 – Hedging using forward exchange contracts

Privet Inc. purchases land for 500 million thalers on 1 April 2002, payment to be made on 31 December 2002. To hedge against exchange rate movements, Privet Inc. enters into a forward exchange contract on 1 April to purchase 500 million thalers on 31 December 2002 at a forward exchange rate of 0.39 dollars to the thaler (direct quote). The spot rate at 1 April was 0.38, and at 31 December 2002 is 0.45.

Required
Assuming the forward contract is settled on a net basis at maturity, discuss the cash effects for Privet of the above arrangements.

Solution
The cost of the forward contract at April 1 is zero. The forward price for 500 million thalers is $195 million [= 0.39 × 500].[10] Given the settlement spot rate at 31 December is 0.45, the sequence of events will be:

1. Privet will receive $30 million dollars from the other party, the forward contract value at 31 December 2002. This reflects that the contract enables Privet to purchase 500 million thalers, $30 million cheaper than the current spot rate – for $195 instead of $225 million [= 500 × 0.45].

2. Privet will settle the 500 million thalers foreign currency payable at the spot rate price of $225 million.

3. Privet's net outlay will be $195 million, equivalent to the forward contracted price.

Directional insurance – options

Forward contracts reduce earnings volatility by predetermining a future price. This fixed price could turn out to be expensive compared with spot prices at the date of delivery. Many treasurers therefore prefer to buy foreign currency options, which insure against unfavourable exchange rate movements whilst allowing companies to take advantage of favourable ones. A US treasurer with a three month £100 million foreign currency payable, worried that sterling will strengthen, might purchase a call option, i.e. an option to buy £100 million at a predetermined exchange rate, the *exercise price*, in three months (an option to sell is called a 'put' option). Unlike the forward contract, the option will be exercised only if exchange rate movements are unfavourable, but let lapse if they are favourable. Directional insurance is more expensive.

Speculation vs. hedging

Foreign currency derivatives are purchased for speculative as well as offsetting purposes. Worldwide accounting practice is generally settling on using current values for derivatives, with gains or losses taken to income. Historical cost is unhelpful since the initial cost of a forward contract is approximately zero, and option costs are usually a fraction of the underlying share prices. Price changes of such derivatives can be very large.

Use of derivatives

Guay and Kothari (2001) find that in a random sample of 234 large non-financial sector US firms that larger firms tend to use derivatives. Of 143 derivative users, 124 had positions in foreign exchange (FX) forwards and futures, whilst only 33 firms had FX swaps and only 27 FX options. However, the notional principals of FX swap and option contracts were about three and a half times those of FX forward and futures contracts. Surprisingly they find that dollar exposure of derivatives was smaller than they had expected, but still significant. Makar, De Bruin and Huffman (1999) find that large US firms' FX derivative use increased with the level of foreign currency exposure. They also find that FX derivative use seemed to be an alternative risk management strategy to geographic diversification. For given levels of FX exposure, the lower the level of geographic diversification the higher the use of FX derivatives and vice versa.

Hedge accounting

Hedge accounting problems only arise where hedging instruments are accounted for on a different basis to hedged items and so their income statement effects do not offset. Under GAAP such different accounting bases are quite common:

- *Measurement differences:* in many countries derivatives (widely used as hedging instruments) are measured at market value, whereas many hedged items, such as non-derivative financial instruments, are measured at cost.
- *Recognition differences:* hedged items may comprise contractual commitments and anticipated future transactions, which are not recognized currently in financial statements whereas the hedging instruments are.

Examples of *measurement differences* are apparent, for example, in IAS 39's classifications and various accounting treatments of financial instruments shown in Table 18.13. The IASB with IAS 39 brings some order to accounting for financial instruments, but recognizes currently there is no acceptance for a uniform basis for accounting for such instruments. Accounting for all financial instruments at fair value with all gains and losses being reported immediately in income would be currently too radical a proposal. The alternative, historical cost for all instruments, would result in many derivative financial instruments being reported at low original costs (for example, options) or no original costs (forward contracts). Large and possibly negative movements in fair values of such instruments would not be reported.

Hedge accounting and the use of derivative and non-derivative hedging instruments

Hedge accounting is normally only available when derivatives are used as hedging instruments. However in the case of hedging *foreign currency* risks, IAS 39 permits hedge accounting where non-derivative hedging instruments are used. SFAS 133 restricts hedge accounting where non-derivative financial instruments are used to a smaller subset of hedging foreign currency risks: (1) hedging net investments in foreign entities or (2) fair value hedges of foreign currency firm contractual commitments. Both are discussed later.

The requirements of IAS 39, *Financial Instruments: Recognition and Measurement*, should be applied first to determine whether the foreign currency financial instrument or financial instrument held by a foreign entity should be measured in fair value, original cost or amortized historical cost. Then IAS 21's requirements should be applied and, since most financial instruments are monetary items, they should be translated at the current rate of exchange (but see footnote 4).

IAS 39 and SFAS 133 both consider three hedging classifications, shown in Table 18.14 and explored below with respect to foreign currency hedges:

1. Fair value hedges
2. Cash flow hedges.
3. Hedges of net investments in foreign entities.

Fair value hedges

Fair value hedges are defined by IAS 39 as hedges of exposure to changes in the value of assets or liabilities currently recognized in the financial statements. The need for specific hedge accounting requirements arises because of *measurement differences* in the bases used to account for the hedged item and for the hedging instrument.

Table 18.13 IAS 39 Classification of financial instruments

Classification	*Measurement basis*
Financial instrument assets	
1. For trading (held for generating short-term profit)	Fair value. All changes to be recognized in income statement. Includes all positively valued derivatives not held for hedging purposes.
2. Originated loans and receivables	Historical cost or historical amortized cost basis
3. Intended to be held to maturity	Historical cost or historical amortized cost basis
4. Available-for-sale (instruments not falling into 1, 2 or 3 above)	Fair value. All changes either recognized in income statement or as a component of equity until sold or disposed of.
Financial instrument liabilities	
1. For trading (held for generating short-term profit)	Fair value. All changes to be recognized in income statement. Includes all negatively valued derivatives not held for hedging purposes.
2. Other	Historical amortized cost basis

For example, the fair value of a long-term fixed rate loan payable originated by a company will fluctuate with changes in market interest rates. The company may choose to insulate itself against such fair value fluctuations by engaging in an interest rate swap of variable rate for fixed rate payments. Assume the loan is 100% effectively hedged. Normally the hedged item, the loan, would be accounted for at historical amortized cost whereas the hedging instrument, the swap, a derivative, would be accounted for at fair value with its gains or losses being taken to the income statement. IAS 39's hedge accounting requirements would require remeasuring the loan from cost to fair value and to take its gains and losses to the income statement as well so as to offset the income statement effects of the swap. Fair value hedge accounting 'accelerates' the measurement of profits on the hedged item to coincide with the profit measurement basis of the hedging instrument.

Specific hedge accounting is usually not necessary for hedged derivative or non-derivative foreign currency *monetary* balances because IAS 21 already requires all such monetary balances to be translated at the closing rate with gains or losses to be taken to the income statement. There will rarely be perfect offset in the case of hedged monetary balances because they are usually recorded at non-discounted face value, whereas the fair value of hedging derivatives is determined on a present value basis. The hedged item and

Table 18.14   IAS 39 Classification and treatment of hedging relationships

Type of hedge	Underlying position hedged	Hedge accounting treatment
Fair value hedge	Asset or liability currently recognized in the financial statements	Fair value gain or loss on hedging instrument recognized as profit or loss. Carrying value of hedged item is adjusted for gain or loss attributable to the hedged risk, which is recognized in net profit or loss.
Cash flow hedge	Future cash flows (e.g. because of future contractual commitments or anticipated future transactions)	Gain or loss on hedging instrument recognized (and 'stored') in equity, not as profit or loss, providing hedge is effective. If contractual commitment or future transaction results in asset or liability, this 'stored' gain or loss adjusts its initial amount. Otherwise it is recognized in net profit or loss in same period as hedged firm commitment or future transaction affects net profit or loss.
Hedge of a net investment in a foreign entity	(Closing rate) net investment in a foreign entity.	Gain or loss on effective hedging instrument recognized (and 'stored') in equity, not as profit or loss. On disposal of net investment, gain or loss on the hedging instrument transferred from equity and utilized in determining gain or loss on disposal of net investment.

hedging instrument would normally be separately accounted for. Under SFAS 133 foreign currency hedging of firm contractual commitments is also treated as a fair value hedge. This will be examined below.

Cash flow hedges

Foreign currency cash flow hedges, hedges of anticipated future foreign currency cash flows, are regarded as giving rise to *recognition differences* since the underlying transactions are not yet recognized under GAAP. The *hedging instrument* (for example a foreign currency forward, futures or option contract) will be measured on a fair value basis with its fair value changes being recognized. However, until the hedged item, the future transaction, is itself recognized under GAAP such fair value changes need to be 'stored' somewhere temporarily. IAS 39 and SFAS 133 require gains and losses on the hedging instrument in cash flow hedges to be recognized/'stored' as part of equity, but *not* as profit or loss.

However, there are differences between IAS 39 and SFAS 133 in:

(a) their respective definitions of which hedged foreign currency transactions can be treated as cash flow hedges. Both standards require hedges of anticipated foreign currency transactions (such as anticipated foreign currency sales or purchases) to be so classified. However, whereas IAS 39 treats hedges of firm foreign currency contractual commitments (e.g. to purchase fixed assets or inventory) as cash flow hedges, SFAS 133 treats them as fair value hedges.

(b) the treatment of how, in cash flow hedges, the 'stored' gains and losses on the hedging instruments are to be utilized when the underlying hedged transaction takes place. Under IAS 39, when the forecast transaction results in the recognition of an asset or liability, the stored/deferred amount is used to adjust the initial measurement of the asset or liability. Under SFAS 133 the gains and losses remain as part of equity and are amortized to income direct from there to offset the amortization/utilization of the hedged item. Whilst the balance sheet presentation will be different, the income statement effect will therefore be very similar.

The difference between the two standards on the hedging of firm contractual commitments derives from their stance on using hedge accounting principles to amend the normal recognition principles for assets and liabilities under GAAP. A firm contractual commitment is a present, not a future transaction. Both IAS 39 and SFAS 133 accept that such firm contractual commitments therefore lead to assets or liabilities being created (i.e. the ability to buy or sell at a contracted amount cheaper or more expensive than the market price) which are not recognized under current GAAP.

IAS 39 takes the normal GAAP position as predominant to justify treating hedges of such firm contractual commitments as cash flow hedges so that this overriding non-recognition rule is not violated. SFAS 133, on the other hand, treats such hedges as fair value hedges, and in so doing allows the acceleration of recognition of the fair value of the firm commitment, but only to the extent of valuing the element of its total value which is effectively hedged. It is therefore only the recognition of a component of the total fair value of the firm commitment. The acceleration principle of fair value hedging therefore overrides the normal GAAP principle that firm commitments are not recognized.

Example 18.6 – Cash flow hedging of an anticipated future transaction (IAS 39 and SFAS 133 cash flow hedge) or a foreign currency firm commitment (IAS 39 only, cash flow hedge)

Consider the following two alternatives:

(a) On 1 April 2002, Privet Inc. decides it will need to purchase a fixed asset on 31 December 2002 for 500 million thalers. This will be essential because it is essential to a major project to introduce a new product line starting early in 2003. The fixed asset will only be delivered when payment is made on 31 December 2002. Privet's year-end is 30 June.

(b) The facts are in (a), except that on 1 April 2002, Privet Inc. signs a contract to take delivery of the fixed asset on 31 December 2002 for 500 million thalers. Payment is to be made under the contract on 31 December 2002.

Assume that in either case, in order to hedge against movements in foreign exchange rates, Privet Inc. enters into an over-the-counter (OTC) foreign currency forward contract on 1 April to purchase 500 million thalers on 31 December 2002 at a forward exchange rate of 0.39 dollars to the thaler. At 30 June 2002 the forward contract to receive at 31 December, 500 million thalers for $195 million, had a positive market value of $7 million.[11] At 30 December it had a positive market value of $30 million. Spot exchange rates are as follows:

Date	Spot rate [$ to the thaler]
1 April	0.38
30 June	0.40
30 December	0.45
31 December	0.45

Solution

In case (a) the hedge is of a forecasted transaction, and in case (b) it is of an unrecognized firm commitment. We will assume that in both cases the hedge has been identified as an effective hedge (see the next section), which means in case (a) that the future transaction must have been deemed 'highly probable'. This seems likely as the enterprise seems commercially committed if not contractually committed. IAS 39 would allow both cases to be accounted for as cash flow hedges. SFAS 133 would also allow this for the anticipated transaction, but would require the hedged firm commitment to be accounted for as a fair value hedge – see later. Simplifying assumptions are made above to enable emphasis of the core accounting principles involved:

- the payment date coincides with delivery of the asset[12] and
- the forward contract matures at the same date.

Cash flow hedge – the anticipated transaction under both standards, the firm commitment under IAS 39

At 1 April, the forward contract (the hedging instrument) has a zero initial fair value (the forward price is calculated determined to give a zero initial contract value). Under IAS 39 and SFAS 133 the foreign currency forward contract hedging instrument will be recorded at fair value and gains and losses on its fair value 'stored' as part of equity and *not* recognized immediately in net profit or loss (under SFAS 133 it would be classified as 'other comprehensive income').

At 30 June year end – T accounts

Asset – Forward contract at fair value		Equity – Forward contract hedging gain	
30 June Contract gain	7	30 June Contract gain	7

At 30 December immediately prior to asset purchase

Asset – Forward contract at fair value		Equity – Forward contract hedging gain	
30 Dec Contract gain	30	30 June Contract gain	7
		30 Dec Further contract gain	23
			30

At 31 December at date of asset purchase

Under IAS 39 the hedging gain on the forward contract of $30 million [225 − 195] would be used to adjust the initial cost of the fixed asset of $225 million to the hedged price of $195 million. SFAS 133 would not permit the adjustment of the initial cost. The hedging gains and losses would be 'realized'/amortized in the income statement direct from equity, offsetting depreciation on the fixed asset unadjusted cost.

Asset – Forward contract at fair value			Equity – Forward contract hedging gain		
30 Dec Contract gain	30			30 Dec Contract gain	30
		31 Dec Cash	30	31 Dec Land price adj	30

Asset – Cash			Asset – Fixed Asset [at hedged cost]		
31 Dec Forward contract	30	31 Dec Currency for land	225	31 Dec Spot purchase	225	31 Dec Asset price adj	30
			195		**195**

Fair value hedge – firm commitment under SFAS 133

The positive fair value exposure of the foreign currency forward contract, here a financial asset, is used to proxy for the value of the hedged component of the negative fair value exposure of the fixed asset firm commitment. Both are recognized at the same time and gains on one offset losses on the other, as follows:

At 30 December immediately prior to asset purchase

Asset:

FX payable forward contract		Fixed asset purchase forward contract	
30 June Contract gain	7	30 June accelerated recognition	7
30 Dec Further contract gain	23	30 Dec accelerated recognition	23
	30		**30**

Income statement			
30 June Fixed asset firm commitment 'accelerated' recognition	7	30 June FX forward contract gain	7
30 Dec Fixed asset firm commitment 'accelerated' recognition	23	30 Dec FX forward contract gain	23
	30		**30**

Hedge of a net investment in a foreign entity

Under the closing rate approach gains and losses on statement translation exposure, on the net investment (= net assets), are recognized directly as part of equity (the cumulative translation adjustment, analogous to 'revaluation' gains and losses as discussed earlier). Suppose a parent company were to hedge the foreign currency net investment in a sub-. sidiary (asset) by using a non-derivative, by raising a foreign currency loan (liability) in a currency the same as or highly correlated with the subsidiary. Without specific hedge accounting requirements, *translation* gains and losses on the net investment (the hedged asset, under the closing rate statement translation approach) would be reported directly in equity, whereas what would be offsetting *transaction* losses or gains on the *parent's* foreign currency loan (the hedging liability) would be recognized in the parent's own income statement. So, as an exception to the normal two-transaction approach where all transaction gains and losses are recognized in the income statement, IAS 21 allows foreign currency *transaction* losses or gains on loans hedging net investments in foreign entities to be taken *direct* to equity.

Disposal of a net investment in a foreign entity

Such losses and gains on hedges of net investments which have been taken direct to equity must under IAS 21 be recognized in the income statement when hedged net investments are disposed of. However, such a practice of 'recycling' such losses and gains to the income on disposal is not followed, for example, in the UK and Australia.

Inclusion of intra-group balances in the net investment balance

IAS 21 allows monetary items receivable or payable by, for example, the parent to a subsidiary classified as a 'foreign entity' to be treated as part of the net investment.

As stated earlier, both IAS 39 and SFAS 133 allow hedge accounting where non-derivatives are used to hedge net investments. This is consistent with earlier foreign currency translation standards such as IAS 21 and SFAS 52 in the USA, and other national standards which contain similar 'hedging' dispensations (e.g. SSAP 20 in the UK, and European Commission 1995, p. 20).

Example 18.8 – Hedging net investments with foreign currency loans

Suppose in Example 18.3, Sleepless Inc. had taken out at 31 December 2000 a loan of 800 million nobles to finance its 100% net investment in Mezzanotte SpA, which it continues to hold. Explain how the exchange gains or losses on the loan for the year ended 31 December 2002 would be treated under IAS 21's hedging requirements.

Solution

Sleepless Inc.'s exchange gain (plus = minus × minus) on the loan would be $128 million [= − 800 × (0.67 − 0.83)] as the liability was held for the whole year when the overseas exchange rate was weakening. In Example 18.3 the closing rate exchange loss on Mezzanotte SpA (the net investment) for the year was $194m. If the two transactions were not linked, the $128 million exchange gain on the loan would be Sleepless Inc.'s *transaction* gain and appear in its and the consolidated income statement. The $194 million *statement translation* loss would be taken direct to equity. Under IAS 21's hedging provisions, the two would be offset in equity and only the net figure of $66 million [= 194 − 128] would be the change in the cumulative translation adjustment balance for the year. If the gain on the loan were greater than the 'net investment' loss, the balance would be dealt with in the income statement. IAS 39's requirements as to what constitutes an allowable (i.e. effective) hedge are now discussed.

Identifying an effective hedge

In all three categories of hedge accounting requirements (fair value hedges, cash flow hedges and hedges of net investments in foreign entities) IAS 39 and similar national standards such as SFAS 133 have criteria for determining whether hedges are effective. Such criteria help deter preparers from 'identifying' false hedges to take advantage of creative accounting possibilities. If hedges are not deemed effective, hedge accounting is not allowed and when hedges become ineffective, hedge accounting must be terminated immediately. In order to qualify for hedge accounting under IAS 39 the following conditions must be met:

- *Intention:* at the inception of the hedge the hedging relationship and its purpose within the enterprise's overall risk management strategy has to be formally documented and designated.

- *Effectiveness:* the hedge must be expected to be highly effective *and* its effectiveness must be reliably measurable, monitored and shown to have been highly effective over the financial period. IAS 39 normally defines 'highly effective', as when actual offset is within the range of 80% to 125%.

- *Degree of certainty:* for cash flow hedges only, hedged forecasted transactions must be highly probable and must present an exposure to variations in cash flows that could ultimately affect reported profit or loss.

Further discussion of these conditions is beyond the scope of the present chapter. Hedge accounting under IAS 39 is normally available for hedging single items or anticipated transactions. However, IAS 39 allows hedge accounting for part of an item or for portfolios of items with similar characteristics where hedging effects do not interact in unusual ways. Some argue (e.g. early IASC exposure drafts and an ASB 1996 Consultation Paper in the UK, 'Derivatives and Other Financial Instruments') that the true effect of hedging can only really be assessed on an overall enterprise basis, since different hedging effects can interact, but both IAS 39 and SFAS 133 side-step this possibility because of difficulties of enforcement.

The criteria for effectiveness of hedging net investments are discussed in IAS 21, but the criteria of IAS 39 must also be applied. Conceptually, Harris (1991, pp. 16–23) argues against the possibility ever of establishing the effectiveness of hedging net investments in foreign entities, commenting 'if a net investment is of an indefinite term, then any hedge is a matching obligation of the same duration . . . [and] it is hard to conceive of many companies having such hedges.' Beaver and Wolfson (1984) argue, based on interest rate parity theory, that the closing rate approach misstates the 'true' cost of foreign currency loans of foreign entities and that the true cost should be the interest charge *net* of currency appreciation or depreciation.[13] Flower (2000) echoes such arguments. The temporal approach achieves this effect for loans since both interest and currency appreciation or depreciation would offset each other in the consolidated income statement. Under the closing rate approach, if subsidiaries were to lend in high interest, depreciating currencies, the high translated interest receivable on these loans would pass through the consolidated income statement, but the *statement translation* exchange losses on such loans will bypass income as part of the consolidated cumulative translation adjustment. There is evidence that Polly Peck in the UK used such methods in its 1989 accounts to make its interest charges look favourable when overall group borrowing was increasing (Gwilliam and Russell 1991, p. 25).

Current developments in accounting for foreign currency financial instruments and hedging

Both IAS 39 and SFAS 133 are regarded as being transitional steps towards a more comprehensive treatment of accounting for financial instruments. In December 2000 a Joint Working Group of International Standard Setters produced a consultation paper entitled, 'Draft Standard and Basis for Conclusions on Financial Instruments and Similar Items'. This more radical and a more unified treatment of the area proposes fair value for virtually all financial instruments. This would remove at a single stroke nearly all existing measurement differences, which create the need for fair value hedge accounting. It would also remove a truly undesirable characteristic of existing hedge accounting standards – that assets and liabilities with identical characteristics are accounted for differently purely according to whether or not they are designated as being hedged. The consultation paper recommends abandonment of specific hedge accounting requirements for hedges of financial instruments – this includes both what are now fair value hedges and hedges of anticipated transactions.[14] The avenues for creative accounting in the area of cash flow hedges (in 'estimating' the timing of when gains and losses on estimated hedged transactions will hit the income statement or even policing whether such anticipated transactions actually exist) explain the lack of enthusiasm of standard-setters for hedge accounting in this area. Firm contractual commitments present less of a problem.[15]

The JWG Group's intention of reducing the incidence of special hedge accounting requirements by changing the reporting basis for financial instruments reflects a wider debate over the advantages or otherwise of hedge accounting to shareholders. Hedging changes the risk profile of a firm, which could clearly benefit managers by making their jobs less risky, but the extent to which it creates shareholder value is less apparent. Some believe that markets reward stability, others that it is better just to report it 'as it is' and let the market make its own judgements.

Disclosures

Disclosure standards nationally and internationally had preceded measurement standards. For example, IAS 32, *Financial Instruments: Disclosure and Presentation*, was issued in 1998, and a variety of international pronouncements, such as FRS 13, *Derivatives and Other Financial Instruments,* issued in 1998 in the UK, and AAS 1033, 'Presentation and Disclosure of Financial Instruments', issued in 1999 in Australia, deal with disclosures relating to financial instruments and risk (e.g. interest rate, credit and market price risks). Later standards tend to take a more coherent but less detailed approach than, for example, earlier US GAAP pronouncements, which established many of the parameters of the debate.

Relating to foreign currency risk exposure, IAS 32 requires, for example, disclosures for hedges of anticipated future transactions, a description of such transactions including expected timing, a description of the hedging instruments, and the amount of deferred or unrecognized gains and losses with expected timing of recognition as income or expense (para 91). It also requires disclosures of any other deferred or unrecognized gains and losses on hedging instruments (para 94). Certain national standards are more specific and extensive than international standards in many areas and require greater narrative disclosures.

> *Currency Risk (extracts):* . . . Such risks may be naturally hedged, as when a receivable in a given currency is matched, for example, between Group companies, by one or more payables in the same amount, and having an equivalent term, in the same currency. They may also be hedged using derivative financial instruments. All currency risks arising on financial transactions, including interest, are generally fully hedged. The instruments used are mainly currency swaps, interest and principal currency swaps and forward exchange contracts. The level of hedging is regularly reviewed. At the end of 2000, the situation was as follows:

€ million	31 Dec 2000	31 Dec 1999
Primary asset instruments exposed to currency risk	2 813	2 774
Primary liability instruments exposed to currency risk	2 159	913
Amount naturally hedged	(1 102)	(784)
Amount hedged through derivative financial instruments	(2 205)	(2 220)
Residual unhedged currency exposure	1 665	683

(Bayer Annual Report 2000, p. 74)

Overview and future directions

The overall translation approach for statements

Translating foreign currency financial statements raises fundamental questions on the objectives of financial reporting. Flower (2000) from a stewardship perspective makes a strong case for the temporal approach, whereas Carsberg (1991) argues from an economic decision-making perspective for the closing rate approach. Many current controversies would disappear under current cost accounting. The temporal approach would then use all current rates. Many hedge accounting problems would also disappear. However, a focus on stewardship generally supports historical cost for prudence and creditor protection reasons.

The temporal approach is most consistent with a pure historical cost valuation basis and the view of a group as a single economic entity. However, it shows 'losses' when many users would expect 'gains' and vice versa. The closing rate approach can be seen as a crude adjustment of historical cost translated balances towards current values, but the approach needs special dispensations to work in extreme circumstances such as hyperinflationary economies. Opponents of its multi-centred view of a group argue that if foreign entities are so autonomous, they should instead not be consolidated but be accounted for under the equity approach (Van Colbe 1993). IAS 21's relationship contingent approach seems to link the appropriate use of both temporal and closing rate approaches to underlying circumstances. In practice it operates more as an endorsement of the closing rate approach. It is easy to forget that its precursor, SFAS 52, in the USA, overthrew the exclusive use of the temporal approach by a single vote in the FASB.

The usefulness of translated figures

How useful are translated figures to investors, analysts and management? This is difficult to assess. Finance theorists (e.g. Sercu and Uppal 1995) assert that the only purpose of translation approaches is to aid prediction of cash flows and risk. We know little about how analysts or investors process information into share prices. Castanias and Griffin (1986) found that divergence in analysts' earnings forecasts increased following the initial adoption of SFAS 52. Chen, Comisky and Mulford (1990) in a later study, suggest this might merely have reflected a learning effect.

Are different translation approaches viewed as cosmetic adjustments which have no substantive impact on share prices? Some studies have examined whether the stock market reacts to unnecessary costs when managements hedge merely to massage reported accounting numbers. The closing rate approach is said to lead to less spurious hedging costs since it is more correlated with economic exposure. Studies looked for cost reductions when such spurious hedges were unwound when the US changed from temporal to current rate approaches. The stock market was hypothesized to react by pushing up share prices as spurious costs were no longer incurred. Ziebart and Kim (1987) claim to have found empirical evidence to support this view, but, Garlicki, Fabozzi and Fonfeder's study (1987) found the view unsupported. See Houston (1989) for a review of such work.

Do closing rate approaches allow tighter management of multinational enterprises because they produce accounting numbers more consistent with the local currency financial statements used to appraise and motivate managers? Many ways are used to motivate managers, and there is no reason why internal performance measures, particularly at mid-management levels should have to correspond to group overall external financial accounting policies.

Recent developments

Recent US and international accounting standards in the area of financial instruments and hedging have brought some much needed structure to the measurement and recognition of foreign currency financial instruments and their use in hedging as well as disclosure and presentation of such matters. However, these could well be only a transitional phase. It is very possible that, eventually, standards internationally could require fair valuation for almost all financial instruments and may abolish hedge accounting dispensations. This would be evidence of the supremacy of the balance sheet primacy perspective underlying most current conceptual frameworks over the matching and income statement primacy perspective. It is difficult to foresee when this may happen, or indeed to be sure that such radical proposals will command universal acceptance given attitudes to prudence and realization in many countries. The increasing authority of the IASB and the adoption of its standards by EU companies by 2005 will surely lend weight to such proposals.

Notes

*   Thanks to Gabi Ebbers, Pelham Gore, John O'Hanlon, T.S. Ho, Stuart McLeay, Ken Peasnell, Bernard Raffournier, staff of standard-setting bodies, students at Lancaster University and the University of Melbourne, and editors for assistance and comments on earlier drafts. Any errors remaining are my responsibility.

1. The term 'translation' is used in a more specialized sense in the USA, discussed later.

2. In some countries, monetary assets are not measured at current amounts, e.g. Germany. See later.

3. There are national differences and many countries recognize losses immediately, but defer gains.

4. Non-monetary foreign currency financial instruments, such as an investment in an equity security, should be translated at the current rate, if they are carried at fair value

and historical rate if not. IAS 39's hedge accounting requirements, as discussed later, may apply if such items are hedged.

5. Purchasing power parity arguments that changes in exchange rates reflect inflation price level differentials support the treatment of 'real' assets under the temporal approach. Carsberg (1991, p. 103) comments that 'an unrecorded increase in the current cost of fixed assets . . . [under historical cost accounting] may be offset by the failure to recognise the effect on the value of the assets of a fall in the value of the foreign currency'.

6. Unlike its position on transaction translation discussed earlier, the European Commission Accounting Advisory Forum (European Commission 1995) considers that neither deferral or non-recognition of net positive translation differences arising from *statement* translation of foreign operations are necessary, since in Europe *consolidated* accounts are not normally subject to capital maintenance and taxation legal requirements.

7. See Taylor (1996, p. 85).

8. Such as SFAS 105, 'Disclosure of Information about Financial Instruments with Off-Balance-Sheet Risk and Financial Instruments with Concentrations of Credit Risk', in 1990, SFAS 107, 'Disclosures about Fair Value of Financial Instruments', 1991, SFAS 115, 'Accounting for Certain Investments in Debt and Equity Securities', in 1993, SFAS 119, 'Disclosure about Derivative Financial Instruments and Fair Value of Financial Instruments', in 1994 (superseded), SFAS 125, 'Accounting for Transfers and Servicing of Financial Assets and Extinguishments of Liabilities', in 1996.

9. Comprising representatives or members of accounting standard-setters or professional organizations in Australia, Canada, France, Germany, Japan, New Zealand, five Nordic countries, the UK, the USA and the IASB. The views taken are not official views of the standard-setting bodies represented.

10. The 9-month forward rate of 0.39 is consistent with the initial spot rate of 0.38 and, for example, 9-month interest rates in the home country of 6%, and in the foreign country of 3.282%.

11. This would be consistent say with a six-month forward rate of 0.4047 dollars to the thaler if the six-month domestic rate of interest were 5%. This forward rate implies that under a new forward contract at 30 June, the forward price at 31 December for 500 million thalers will be $202.35 million [= 0.4047 × 500 million]. The current contract entered into on 1 April enables the purchase of 500 million thalers for $195 million on 31 December, so its present value will be $\frac{202.35 - 195}{1.05} = \$7$ million.

12. If a foreign currency payable arose at delivery to be paid later than the asset acquisition date, only the hedging gain at the asset acquisition date would be adjusted against the initial asset amount. Later gains or losses on the forward contract would be offset against losses or gains on the foreign currency payable.

13. Based on a theoretical relationship termed the 'Fisher' effect, that the change in exchange rate between two countries should be exactly counterbalanced by the interest rate differential between them. This effect does not hold well empirically in practice.

14. It does not consider hedges of future commitments for non-financial items.

15. In its 1994 discussion paper to prevent the abuse of hedge accounting for anticipated transactions, the ASB in the UK had aired the possibility of confining its use to commercially committed transactions,where it is infeasible for the business to withdraw. This may be more rigorous than basing hedge accounting on 'high probability' of occurrence.

References

Beaver, W. and Wolfson, M. (1984) Foreign currency translation gains and losses: what effect do they have and what do they mean?, *Financial Analysts Journal*.

Carsberg, B. (1991) FAS 52 – Measuring the performance of foreign operations, in J.H. Stern and D.H. Chew (eds) *New Developments in International Finance*, Blackwell, Oxford.

Chen, A.Y.S., Comisky, E.E. and Mulford, C.W. (1990) Foreign currency translation and analyst forecast dispersion: examining the effects of SFAS No 52, *Journal of Accounting and Public Policy*, Winter: 239–256.

Ebbers, G. and McLeay, S. (1996) Regulating the unregulated: the case of foreign currency reporting in Europe, Unpublished paper, University of Wales, Bangor.

European Commission Accounting Advisory Forum (1995) *Paper on the Accounting Advisory Forum Foreign Currency Translation*, European Commission.

Flower, J. (2000) Foreign currency translation, Chapter 15 in C. Nobes and R. Parker (eds) *Comparative International Accounting*, 6th edition, Prentice-Hall.

Garlicki T.D., Fabozzi F.J. and Fonfeder (1987) *Financial Management*, Autumn: 36–44.

Guay, W.R. and Kothari, S.P. (2001) How much do firms hedge with derivatives?, Accounting Research Network, *Financial Accounting Abstracts*, Working Paper Series, March.

Gwilliam D. and Russell T. (1991) Polly Peck – where were the analysts? *Accountancy*, January: 25.

Harris, T.S. (1991) Foreign currency transactions and translation, in Choi F. D. S. (ed.), *Handbook of International Accounting*, Wiley, Chichester, Chapter 16.

Houston, C.O.H. (1989) Foreign currency translation research: a review and synthesis, *Journal of Accounting Literature* **8**: 25–48.

Lorenson, L. (1972) Reporting foreign operations of US Companies in US Dollars, *Accounting Research* Study No. 12, AICPA, New York.

Makar, S.D., DeBruin, J. and Huffman, S.P. (1999) The management of foreign currency risk: derivatives use and the natural hedge of geographic diversification, *Accounting and Business Research,* Summer: 229–237.

Nobes, C.W. (1980) A review of the translation debate, *Accounting and Business Research,* 10: 421–31.

Revsine, L. (1984) The rationale underlying the functional currency choice, *The Accounting Review*, LIX: 505–514.

Sercu P. and Uppal R. (1995) *International Financial Markets and the Firm*, South Western Publishing / Chapman and Hall, London.

Taylor, P.A. (1996) Foreign currency translation, in Taylor P.A., *Consolidated Financial Reporting,* Paul Chapman Publishing, London, Chapter 11.

Van Colbe (1993) Foreign currency translation, in Gray, S.J., Coenenberg, A.G. and Gordon, P.D. (eds) *International Group Accounting – Issues in European Harmonisation*, 2nd edn, Routledge.

Van Hulle, K. (1996) Prudence: a principle or an attitude?, *The European Accounting Review,* 5: 375–382.

Ziebart, D.A. and Kim, D.H. (1987) An examination of the market reactions associated with SFAS No. 8 and SFAS No. 52, *The Accounting Review*, **62**(2): 343–357.

Further Reading

Adams, J.B. and Montesi, C.J. (1995) *Major Issues Relating to Hedge Accounting,* Special Report, Financial Accounting Series No 154–B, October 1995, Financial Accounting Standards Board, International Accounting Standards Board.

Castanias, R.P. and Griffin, P.A. (1986) The effects of foreign currency translation accounting on security analysts' forecasts, *Managerial and Decision Economics*, **7**: 3–10.

Demirag, R. S. (1987) A review of the objectives of foreign currency translation, *The International Journal of Accounting,* Spring: 69–85.

Joint Working Group of Accounting Standard Setters (2000) *Financial Instruments and Other Items,* International Accounting Standards Board.

Nobes, C. W. (2000), GAAP 2000 – *A Survey of National Accounting Rules in 53 Countries,* Arthur Andersen, BDO, Deloitte Touche Tohmatsu, Ernst & Young International, Grant Thornton, PriceWaterhouse Cooper.

Ordelheide, D. (ed.) (2001) *Transnational Accounting,* 2nd edn, Volumes 1, 2 and 3, Palgrave Macmillan, Basingstoke.

Patz, D. (1977) A price parity theory of translation, *Accounting and Business Research*, **8**: 29, 14–24.

Taylor, P.A. (1985) The foreign currency translation approach: a matrix funds flow analysis, *The British Accounting Review*, Spring: 3–20.

Wilson, A., Davies, M., Curtis, M. and Wilkinson-Riddle, G. (2001) *UK & International GAAP – Generally Accepted Accounting Practice in the United Kingdom and Under International Standards* 7th edn, Ernst & Young/Tolley.

Segmental reporting

Axel Haller

Introduction

The diversification of companies into different business sectors is one of the predominant characteristics of today's business world. This means that the financial statements of multi-product companies such as Siemens, Nabisco or Procter & Gamble cannot be used by analysts to evaluate the performance and position of the company in relation to other entities operating in the same areas, because the individual set of activities of each group is different. On top of that, the aggregated financial information of such multi-dimensional entities does not enable the users to relate this information to the different socio-economic environments in which the diversified entity is operating. However, the volatility of the group's results is significantly affected by factors attributable to the environment in which the entity operates, in addition to company-specific internal factors, such as the quality of the management, the organization and control of production and other processes in the company. This means that the future prospects of an enterprise depend to an extent on the business sector and the geographical area the enterprise is engaged in. If, therefore, the objective of the financial statements is to provide useful information for economic purposes, users must be able to evaluate the performance and prospects of a company in the context of the different markets in which it is operating.

Rates of profitability, opportunities for growth, and degrees of risk may vary greatly between different areas of a group's activities. The set of diverse business areas in which a company works and its relative position compared to its competitors are major strategic factors for the future prospects of a company. These different areas of activity are usually called segments. According to the general definition proposed by the Organization for Economic Cooperation and Development (OECD), a segment 'is to be understood in general terms as a distinguishable component of a diversified entity or group of entities, engaged in operations which are more closely related to each other than to those of the rest of the entity or group' (OECD 1990, p. 8). The segmentation of an entity into different distinguishable components of business activities is not exclusively a phenomenon of groups but can occur within single legal entities. However, almost all of the large multinational enterprises are combinations of several, often many, legal entities, which report the economic situation for the group as a whole through consolidated financial statements. For this reason the issue of segmental reporting is often regarded as the 'counterpoint to consolidated information in that it involves the disaggregation of the consolidated financial statements' (Radebaugh and Gray 2002, p. 196).

In other words, while consolidated accounts provide an economic summary, they frequently need then to be disaggregated into economically distinct segments to permit a better understanding of the different businesses involved. With the increasing globalization of markets and the accompanying growth of multinational companies, it follows that the consolidated financial statements become more highly aggregated and the presentation of segmented information as an integral part of financial statements becomes more necessary to provide useful information for economic decisions.

Reasons for segmental reports

The disclosure of disaggregated information by segments provides the users of financial reports with a tool to identify and analyse the opportunities and risks that diversified companies face. Understanding these is a key to appraising the performance and potential of an entity as a whole, which is the ultimate objective of all financial statement users. The size and degree of uncertainty of future cash flows, which are of most interest to investors, are affected by the economic prospects the entity has in its various segments. Those prospects are directly related to the economic situations in the different industry sectors and geographical markets where the group is active. Segmental reporting helps investors to make better informed decisions because it allows them to combine company-specific information with external industry and country-specific information. This helps them to estimate the impact that changes in significant components of a business may have on the entity as a whole. For example, if a French company has 25% of its sales in the US pharmaceuticals business, a forecast depression of the US economy needs to be factored into estimates of the following year's expected profits. Segment information provides investors with a better information base from which to assess the amount of future cash flows of an entity and the uncertainties associated with those cash flows.

This explanation no doubt reveals clearly that the topic of segmental reporting has emerged and has been developed in the American accounting model where decision usefulness is the central objective of financial reporting. The position taken in the US conceptual framework (see Chapter 3) is that useful information is that which helps to evaluate the amount and variability of future cash flows to investors and creditors. In accounting models where the computation of the distributable income of individual companies is the predominant objective, mostly continental European countries following German/French models, segmental reporting has never been regarded as an important issue. This is why in those countries only rudimentary regulations covering the disclosure of disaggregated data have existed until today. The financial statements of the single legal entities have for a long time been the predominant set of financial statements. The consolidated accounts, for which the disaggregation of data is usually the most relevant, have only just started to become more important in those countries, as accounting becomes internationalized.

While segment information is useful for forecasts, it is also, of course, relevant to the evaluation of an entity's past performance and the deployment of resources between different segments. This gives shareholders and other stakeholders an insight into management's decisions in the past and its effectiveness and efficiency in fulfilling its function of stewardship. This stewardship aspect of financial reporting is something of a bridging factor between different accounting models, because it is included in all of them (see Chapters 3–6).

There is strong empirical evidence that disaggregated data disclosed by companies has a significant information content for users of financial statements. Market-based studies, predictive ability tests as well as surveys with analysts and other financial reporting users mostly show that segment data enhances decisions. Users emphasize that for a diversified company it is more effective to project earnings or cash flows on a segment-by-segment basis than on the basis of the company as a whole. Segment data provides the basis for a more refined evaluation and estimation of a company's future development than would otherwise be possible from published information (for details of the wide range of empirical studies and surveys on segmental reporting see Mohr 1983; Prodhan 1986; Boersema and Weelden 1992, pp. 39–41; Pacter 1993, pp. 131–202). In recent years it is investors and analysts who have in particular regarded segmental reporting as very useful for their assessments of companies' prospects and have therefore increasingly demanded the disclosure of appropriate segmented information (Boersema and Weelden 1992, pp. 13–32; Pacter 1994, pp. 53–54; Knoops *et al.* 1996, pp. 12–13).

While in the past the argument has been advanced that the costs of providing disaggregated data exceed the benefits, practical experience has tended to prove the opposite. Today the benefits of segmental reporting are mostly regarded as being higher than the related costs. There are two types of costs which may be distinguished in this context (Boersema and Weelden 1992, pp. 32–39). First, there are the direct costs of compiling, processing and scheduling the segmented data. Those are generally no longer seen as significant, because diversified companies generate and use disaggregated information for internal planning and control purposes and usually therefore already compile and organize their accounting data internally in a segmented manner. Even if this is not the case or if the information used internally is not in a form that can be used for external reporting purposes, in the days of computerized information systems it seems unlikely that the marginal cost of data generation does play a significant role. A real additional component of direct costs is additional audit fees, because reliability considerations suggest that segmental data should be subject to audit (and must be when segment information is included in the notes). These costs should not, though, be extreme. Despite these arguments, direct costs are a major reason for the exemption of small companies from segmental disclosure requirements.

The indirect cost arising from the disclosure of disaggregated data, which is often referred to by multinationals as a reason for their reluctance to make such disclosures, is that of a potential competitive disadvantage. But if one looks closely at this argument, it becomes obvious that the contrary is the case. If every entity provides the same segmented information, then there is no competitive disadvantage but rather an aid which is helpful in competing in the market for the scarce resource of capital. The provision of decision-useful information is an advantage for the national economy as a whole. A disadvantage only occurs if companies are treated in a different way, that is if there are some companies who are obliged to make such disclosures and others who can omit them. This is still the situation in the international context since there are countries with quite precise and rigid segmental reporting obligations (e.g. USA, Australia, UK) and others with few or undemanding requirements (see below).

It should also be borne in mind that large, diversified entities reporting on a segmented basis probably disclose far less information and are far more difficult to compare than smaller corporations operating in just one business area. These unsegmented entities disclose much more information about their single business than do multi-segmented entities in their segmental reports. The absence of a requirement to report segmented data would result in a significant competitive disadvantage for non-diversified companies. Therefore segmental reporting also has a positive effect on competition in this respect.

Another aspect which may be considered to weaken the competitive disadvantage argument is the fact that segmental reporting only shows the results of the company on different markets and not the reasons for achieving these results. For example, a segment disclosure may make it obvious that a company has a higher rate of return in a specific segment than its competitors. The reasons for the higher profitability, which could be better production control, higher quality, better marketing or many other factors, are not disclosed.

None the less the potential competitive disadvantage has resulted in a position where several pronouncements contain clauses that allow companies not to report specific segments or to omit the whole segmental report if the disclosure of the disaggregated information is seriously prejudicial to the interests of the reporting entity (e.g. UK SSAP 25; art. 286, para 2 German Commercial Code). However, this perception of disclosure entailing a negative competitive effect has been given less and less attention by accounting opinion in general.

The usefulness of the disclosure of segmented data for capital market purposes is indicated by the fact that all countries which are related to the US or the British accounting models have issued standards that require such information as compulsory components of annual financial statements long before countries with other accounting models have started to do so. In addition, diversified multinational companies based in countries with other accounting models usually report on disaggregated bases, in order to satisfy the expectations and demands of international users of their financial statements, such as investment analysts.

Development of national and international standards of segment reporting

The first national regulation concerning segment reporting was developed in the USA. Accounting Principles Board (APB) Opinion No.2, issued in 1967, contained a recommendation to provide segmented data for products or product groups in the annual report. Three years later this disclosure was made obligatory for listed companies by the Securities and Exchange Commission (SEC).

Then in 1976 the FASB (which had replaced the APB) developed the first comprehensive national standard, SFAS 14. This standard required information on both business and geographic segments and specified the kind of disclosure. This standard subsequently served as model for a number of standards in other countries (e.g. standards in Australia and Canada as well as those of the IASC, see Sims 1989).

Intergovernmental organizations have also been active in this area. The UN's Center for Transnational Corporations (whose accounting works is now done by the UN Intergovernmental Working Group of Experts on International Standards of Accounting and Reporting: ISAR – see Chapter One) formed an accounting group in the early 1970s to address this issue. During its deliberations, the UN group tried to put an emphasis on the disaggregation of information concerning geographic regions in which multinationals are active. The object was to 'motivate' multinationals that are active in exploiting natural resources or in manufacturing in developing countries to publish country by country information about their investments and the economic success of these investments. This clearly had political implications for the relationships between host governments and foreign investors but the UN group had no means of mandating the disclosures it sought.

The UN initiative did however call forth a similar initiative from the Organization for Economic Co-operation and Development (OECD). It produced its own recommendations, much more rooted in corporate practice. Its 1976 non-compulsory guideline was used by some companies based in countries with little national legislation concerning segment reporting.

Probably more significant on the international scene was International Accounting Standard No. 14 (IAS 14) which was approved by the IASC in 1981 and which was relatively similar to SFAS 14. IAS 14 served as model not only for companies that wanted to present themselves internationally with their annual report, but also for some national standard-setters in newly industrializing countries and developing countries in writing their national standards.

The national and international regulations concerning segment reporting which had been developed up to the end of the 1980s were all more or less based upon SFAS 14 (e.g. AAS 16 in Australia, SSAP 25 in the UK as well as SAS 23 in Singapore). They differed in content and degree of detail, but were very similar as concerns the concept of a segment report (for further information about the content of the standards see Pacter 1993; Haller and Park 1994).

By comparison with these, the regulations on the disclosure of segmented data contained in the Fourth and Seventh EC Directives lagged behind considerably. These only required the publication of segment sales revenues according to fields of activities and geographic regions. They also granted companies the right to omit the disclosure of information if the management believes that the disclosure would probably cause negative effects for the company or its subsidiaries. This very basic regulation has been one reason why the standards of segment reporting in EU member states (apart from the UK and Ireland) have been far below the requirements of international standard-setters and practices in other countries. This can be interpreted as a consequence of the lack of interest in the decision usefulness of financial reports which was shown in Continental Europe.

However, even in Continental European countries, such as Germany, segment reporting has, since the end of the 1970s, been a field where companies have 'voluntarily' disclosed more than was legally required. Global companies based in Continental Europe have tried to satisfy the information expectations of international users by publishing segment reports according to IAS 14 or the OECD recommendation. Segment reports have been seen to be a useful instrument for investor relations (see Gray and Roberts 1989, Haller and Park 1994a; Knoops et al. 1996).

New generation

After growing criticism on SFAS 14 from the users of segment reports, the FASB decided at the beginning of the 1990s to develop a new standard. It set out on a joint project with the Canadian standard-setter (Canadian Institute of Chartered Accountants, CICA) which started with research reports from both Canada (Boersema and Weelden 1992) and the USA (Pacter 1993).

Some months later the IASC also started to redraft its IAS 14. This was due to the fact that IAS 14 was included in the so-called 'core standards', which the International Organisation of Securities Commissions (IOSCO) required to be revised (see Chapter 1). The IASC joined the joint Canadian/American project in 1995. This was expected to help with resources and lead to comparable standards. However, despite these efforts and the fact that the revision of IAS 14 was started after having conducted more research that came to the same conclusions (Pacter 1994), the three institutions could not find a consensus.

While FASB (SFAS 131) and the CICA (Sec. 1700 CICA Handbook) passed uniform standards in June 1997, IASC published one month later its revised IAS 14 which pursued a different concept of segment reporting. It is a matter of opinion as to how far this difference is justified by rational and conceptual reasons as it is by strategic or political considerations. Undoubtedly, the conception chosen by the FASB and the CICA had been subject to severe debates in the USA and in Canada. So it could be seen as a chance for the IASC to publish its own 'different' standards in order to prove its institutional and professional independence. This could have been considered as a significant objective at the time when IOSCO accreditation was close.

SFAS 131 and the revised IAS 14 are now the major and most influential standards for segment reporting. They serve as a model for national standards all over the world. This is the case, for example, with the German standard DRS 3, adopted by the German Accounting Standards Board and published by the Federal Ministry of Justice in May 2000. This follows the FASB and IASC standards and tries to combine the content of both. Table 19.1 summarizes the chronology of major standards for segment reporting up to May 2000.

Table 19.1 Chronology of the development of selected major pronouncements about segment reporting

Date	Standard
1967	USA, APB Statement No. 2
1970	USA, SEC
1976	USA, FASB, SFAS 14: Financial Reporting for Segments of a Business Enterprise
1976	OECD, Guidelines for Multinational Enterprises (revised 1988)
1977	UN, International Standards of Accounting and Reporting for Transnational Corporations (revised 1989 and 1995)
1978	EU Fourth Directive (Art 43, para. 1, Nr. 8)
1981	IASC, IAS 14: Reporting Financial Information by Segment
1983	EU Seventh Directive (Art 34, Nr. 8)
1990	OECD, Segmented Financial Information
1994	UN, Conclusions on Accounting and Reporting by Transnational Corporations
1997	USA, FASB, SFAS 131, Disclosures about Segments of an Enterprise and Related Information
1997	IASC, IAS 14 (revised): Segment Reporting

Major issues in the preparation of segment reports

The following sections discuss the central steps and problems which arise while preparing segment reports and which therefore are dealt with in standards on segmental reporting. The standards referred to are the revised IAS 14 and SFAS 131, as they have already shaped (and will shape in future) developments in the area of the disclosure of segment data.

Objectives of segment reporting

The standards clearly state that segment reporting is an indispensable tool for improving the usefulness of information in annual reports. With disaggregated data, the user of annual reports should be better able to assess the economic situation of a diversified company and therefore to assess the future performance (the amount, quality and probability of future cash flows) of an enterprise.

As the definition and identification of segments should be determined by the situation of the individual enterprise, the information is subjective and enterprise specific. Consequently, inter-company comparability – which is normally seen as a major objective of regulation – is not particularly privileged in these standards. This is an area where the two standards also differ. While FASB accepts a lack of inter-company comparability in its approach, the regulations of IAS 14 try to assure a minimum level of comparability.

Obligation to publish segment information

The standards need to specify what type of enterprises should follow them. The very basic regulations of the EU directives, and national rules based on them, refer to incorporated business (usually limited to medium-sized or large companies) or they refer to corporate groups. While the old version of IAS 14 referred to companies that issued securities as well as to economically significant entities, the new version (as well as SFAS 131) of the standard is limited to companies whose equity and debt securities are publicly traded and to enterprises that are in the process of issuing equity or debt securities in public securities markets.

Neither IAS 14 nor SFAS 131 contain any clause allowing a preparer to escape publication on any grounds. This demonstrates that the accent is put on the information interests of the users of the annual report and not on the interest of the companies in not disclosing information useful to competitors.

Concepts of segment reporting

There are two basic concepts as to how segment information should be measured: the *autonomous entity approach* and the *disaggregation approach* (see OECD 1990, pp. 18–19). According to the autonomous entity approach the segmented information is treated as an approximation of the financial statements which would have been prepared by the individual segments if they were operating as independent entities. On the other hand, according to the disaggregation approach, the segments are considered as an integral part of the enterprise, and the objective is therefore just to achieve a division of aggregated data.

The two approaches can lead to different segment measurements, especially if there is a high degree of interdependency between the activities of the segments. A simple example will illustrate this: supposing two segments of a group are sharing the same physical property and legal structure for marketing in a particular country, and are achieving cost savings as a result. This cost sharing might not be available were they operating as autonomous units. Using a disaggregation approach, costs that have been caused by the two segments are to be allocated to these two segments according to their consumption of the resources. Using the autonomous entity approach, the real costs are ignored, and the full costs which would have been incurred if each segment were an independent company would be measured. Consequently, in this example, group costs would be overstated and lower segment results would be reported.

The autonomous entity approach improves the external comparability of the segment since it can be compared with a similar independent company, or with a similar segment belonging to another group. However, it suffers from the major disadvantage that it introduces notional values into the report and these are obviously very difficult to verify objectively. It also makes it very difficult to establish a clear and understandable relationship between the data disclosed in the segment report and that disclosed elsewhere in the annual report. In consequence, there is an international consensus (explicitly stated in SFAS 131) that segment reports should be based on the view of segments as integrated parts of the enterprise. This means that the disaggregation approach is applied.

Relationship to internal reporting

Standard-setters also have two possible approaches in relation to the group's own internal reporting system. On the one hand, the form and content of the segment report could be defined independently of the internal structure of the enterprise, in order to provide reports from all groups which are comparable for external users. On the other hand the segment report could decide to make the internal structure and reporting system visible to external users.

The first approach was the one pursued by the first wave of segment reporting rules, but the FASB decided to move to the second approach in SFAS 131. The basis for this is the idea that the most valuable information for decision-making is likely to be that used by management, so this should also be provided for investors. Therefore, the new segment reports should reflect as their main characteristic the internal organization of reporting and control, on which the central decision-making authority bases its decisions (SFAS 131.4).

The main conceptual difference between SFAS 131 and IAS 14 lies in the degree of rigidity of the application of what is called the *management approach*. While the FASB applied this approach as a general overriding concept for all elements of segment reporting, IASC applied it to the identification of reportable segments, without using it to determine the scope, amount and definition of the segment data to be disclosed.

Determination of segments

General principles

The central challenge while splitting up a company into segments (either for internal or external purposes) is the determination of the individual segments. In this context generally three questions have to be answered:

1. What are sensible criteria on which to distinguish between segments?
2. How can individual segments be identified?
3. To what extent can individual segments be combined to a reportable segment?

Definition of segments

An appropriate definition of a segment would be its relevance for decision making. If the determination of segments is to contribute to better economic decisions – which is an explicitly stated goal of external financial reporting as a whole and which is also a prerequisite for the effectiveness of internal management – it cannot be done in an arbitrary way. As decision-making can be characterized as a trade-off between risks and opportunities, the most useful determination of segments seems to be the one that can most realistically represent the market risks and opportunities of a company within a specific business area. Internationally, the most economically sensible approach of determining segments seems to be the one that groups areas of activities that have similar risks and opportunities (called the *risks and rewards approach*).

The most significant dimensions that are used in practice are the following:

- type of product or service;
- geographical regions;
- customer or supplier groups;
- legal entities (i.e. single companies) of a corporate group.

Segmentation according to the products and services offered by a company is called *segmentation by industry or business*. This dimension is particularly useful because the structure and economic conditions relating to a particular kind of industry are a key driver of opportunities and risks, and therefore a major determinant of current and future cash flows for almost all types of enterprises.

Segmentation by geographical regions splits up accounting information in the different geographic areas a company is engaged in. This dimension also provides important information about the opportunities and risks companies face because those depend on the socio-economic environment in each physical market in which the company works. Those conditions vary widely from location to location, and will impact upon questions such as political risk, foreign exchange risk, and taxation, as well as rate of growth of different economies and current position in the economic cycle.

There are two possible approaches. On the one hand, the segment can be defined as the location where the product or the service is produced (*origin of sales*) and on the other hand as the location of the customers (*destination of sales*). The first is rather relevant for the company's cost profile while the second is the decisive parameter for the sales. Both, however, are decisive for the overall success of a company.

Also a *segmentation by customer groups* (e.g. wholesale and retail, private or corporate customers) or suppliers (special raw materials, mass raw products) can be seen as representing another aspect of the risk structure of a company if those characteristics cause particular dependencies or competitive advantages of the company due to the business sector the company is in.

Segmentation by legal entities is only useful in order to generate sensible information about the relationship of risks and opportunities in a group, if each of the entities is not diversified but represents one of the three dimensions of segmentation mentioned above. Preparing a segment report based upon legal entities within the annual report would mean reversing the consolidation entries used in preparing the group accounts.

Indentification of segments

Having decided what is the nature of the segment one wishes to capture, the next issue is to distinguish those elements within the group. Given the aim of improving the information base for decision making, a segment should be a distinguishable component of an enterprise whose activities are very homogenous as regards its contribution to overall profitability and their exposure to risk/opportunities (*segment homogeneity*). Moreover this component should be different in this respect from others on the same segmentation dimension (*segment heterogeneity*).

The definition of the characteristics to assess segment homogeneity is decisive to the information value and the usefulness of the segment report. Therefore, all the different standards impose concrete criteria for the determination of the segment homogeneity and heterogeneity, respectively.

However, the definition of segments involves a good deal of interpretation. For instance car manufactures like Volkswagen might ask themselves if it is necessary to publish segment reports for specific lines of business, because all business activities are related to the manufacturing of cars. They will find themselves breaking out different segments of the car market.

Combination of segments

As in other areas of corporate reporting (internal as well as external) the phenomenon of information overload has to be considered. This means that the marginal benefit from additional information can decrease or can even be negative. The number of reportable segments should not be too high. Segments that are relatively insignificant in terms of the overall economic risk and return might not be disclosed individually but be combined with other insignificant segments.

The above explained three central issues in determining a reportable segment apply for all segmentations of an enterprise, for internal as well as external purposes. Internally, the company obviously decides for itself if and how an internal structure has to be set up for the purposes of reporting, management and control. These internal structures often result from historical developments, the less organic growth through acquisitions or specific beliefs of strong executives, which therefore do not always match with the economic idea of segmentation.

Content of relevant standards

Traditionally, standards on segment reporting have prescribed the two following dimensions: industry segments and geographical segments (e.g. SFAS 14, IAS 14, OECD 1976 and 1990, UN 1977, 1988 and 1994, Fourth and Seventh EC directive and national regulations in Europe and other countries like Australia and Japan). Other kinds of segment have not been deemed useful.

For the purpose of better inter-company comparison of industry segments, official industry classifications like the *Standard Industrial Classification (SIC)* of the USA or the international version, the *Standard Industrial Classification of all Economic Activities (ISIC)*, have been put forward as a possible basis for identifying segments, however such general classifications do not take into account the internal circumstances of the enterprise.

SFAS 131 has abandoned any pre-selection of the segment dimensions. The approach is wholly based on the way that management organizes the segments within the enterprise for making operating decisions and assessing performance. This means that the identification of segments should match with those chosen for internal management purposes. The reason for this is the assumption that, since the internal segmentation has been arrived at to facilitate the decision processes of management, it would also be useful for external users' decisions. Consequently the FASB defines an operating segment quite broadly as a component of an enterprise that engages in business activities from which it potentially earns revenues and expenses and for which discrete financial information is available which is used by the chief operating decision maker on a regular basis to make decisions about the allocation of resources and to assess performance.

Those components of an enterprise which have primarily administrative or management functions and do not generate profits or positive cash flows cannot be treated as operating segments (SFAS 131.10). The main advantage of the consistent implementation of the management approach is that the organization, structure and the strategic orientation of the management of an enterprise can be assessed and analysed from outside. The FASB presumes that management follows attempts to mirror the structure of the risk and return pattern of the group's activities in its internal segmentation. Even if this is not the case, the externally reported segmentation has nevertheless to match the internal one. Even if the enterprise mixes the traditional segmentation dimensions (like business segments and geographical segments), the internal approach must still be adopted for external reporting.

This is one of the major differences compared to the IASC approach. IAS 14 also requires that the external report matches with the internal one, but only as long as these are based on business or geographical segment dimensions. The IASC presumed that those two dimensions of segmentation best reveal the pattern of risk and return related to the enterprise's activities and is therefore the most commonly used segmentation in enterprises

(IAS 14.9 and IAS 14.27). If an enterprise's internal reporting and control structure for central management are based neither on business segments nor on geographical segments, the management should take into account the internal reporting structure on the next level of the enterprise's organizational hierarchy. If the definition of segments according to business or geographical areas is not applied on any organizational level, IAS 14 requires the segmentation for external reporting purposes should deviate from the internal structure.

This shows that the IASC has ranked the risk and reward approach ultimately higher than the management approach. That is the reason why this approach is called a *management approach with a risk and reward safety net*. The major reason for this approach was that the use of uniform segmentation dimensions was deemed to allow a better comparison between companies, although the comparability of segment data is generally quite restricted due to the general subjectivity of the segment determination process and the specificities of the companies.

According to IAS 14.9, determining the activities to be included in the same segment is based on factors such as the nature of the products or services, the nature of the production processes, the type of class of customer for the products or services and the methods used to distribute the products or provide the services, etc.

As far as geographical segments are concerned, IAS 14 allows either a segmentation following the location of assets (which means location of an enterprise's production or distribution) or the location of its customers (which means the location where the enterprise's products are sold or services are rendered), depending on which aspect best reflects the structure of risks and returns of the business. The determination of geographical segments depends mainly on external parameters, which determine the production and sales conditions and the connected economic risk. Beside the similarity of the general political and economic conditions, the standard mentions other factors which have to be taken into account for the homogeneity or heterogeneity assessment: relationships between operations in different geographical areas, proximity of operations, special risks associated with operating in a particular area, exchange control regulations and underlying currency risks.

In order to reduce the number of reported segments, both IAS 14 and SFAS 131 allow the combining of internally determined operating segments which are substantially similar. A segment has only to be reported separately if its activities have a significant impact on the risk and return potential of the whole enterprise. A segment is seen as having a significant impact, if either the revenue, result or the assets of the segment are greater than 10% of the respective amount of all segments. It is important for the assessment to analyse how far a segment exceeds one of these limits over the long term. Amounts which result from intersegment transactions, have to be taken into account in the application of the 10% criterion for the segment revenue and the segment result. Segments which are not judged as significant may be combined into a separately reportable segment which has a majority of similar economic characteristics, or it may be included in the segment report as a reconciling category. The components aggregated in this category obviously do not fulfil the criteria of homogeneity or heterogeneity concerning products, service or properties of specific geographical regions, but solely in terms of insignificance for the assessment of the risk and return situation of the enterprise.

As a significant set of reported segments is essential for the usefulness of these reports, SFAS 131 and IAS 14 both include a rule concerning the minimum number of reported segments. This should prevent a situation where the number of reported segments is very low and a major portion of the enterprise's activities is aggregated in the reconciling category. If the total of external revenue attributable to reportable segments constitutes less than 75% of consolidated revenue, additional segments have to be identified as reportable segments (even if they do not pass the 10% thresholds), until the explicitly reported segments represent at least 75% of the group revenue.

Neither IAS 14 nor SFAS 131 define a concrete minimum or maximum number of reportable segments, although SFAS 131 notes that more than ten reported segments could put in question the usefulness of the segment report. It is a decision of management to determine an optimum which is most appropriate to mirror the economic situation and prospects of the company. Major general determinants of the quantity of segments are principles such as comprehensibility and clarity as well as reliability and representational faithfulness (drawn from the conceptual framework). The use of a large number of segments leads the possibility of information overload and exaggerates the problem of allocation of joint assets or joint expenses which is likely to grow with the number of segments. An increasing number of segments makes the allocation of those items to individual segments more and more arbitrary (see later).

The question of identification of reportable segments also bears on the treatment of *vertically integrated business segments*, i.e. those which earn the majority of their revenues from transactions with other segments of the enterprise. As in most cases those segments share the economic situation of their distribution segments which deliver the final products to the market, and therefore have similar risk/return profiles, it is sensible not to report those segments separately but to combine them with the sales segments. Only if vertical integration of business activities is typical for an industry (e.g. oil or gas) is it thought desirable to report the stages of product development as separate segments.

However, while IAS 14.35 states that reportable segments should be those which earn the majority of revenue from sales to external customers, SFAS 131 is silent about the handling of vertically integrated segments. This is a logical effect of the management approach, because the internal treatment determines the external reporting. It is important to take into account that the requirement of segment autonomy is primarily related to business and not geographical segments, as the production- or service-related, geographically-specific risks always exist, independently of the fact that the production is sent or the service is rendered to internal or external customers.

Segment data

The usefulness of a segment report also depends very much on the type and amount of data disclosed per segment. Although the segmentation of the whole balance sheet and the income statement has been suggested in the literature (e.g. Ijiri 1995), and has a lot of information potential, this implies a considerable allocation problem for items which are involved in several segments, which increases the subjectivity and potentially the arbitrariness of the data in the segment report. This is how standards have typically required the disaggregated disclosure of only specific elements of the balance sheet and income statement.

The first standards on segment reporting required the same data for both business and geographical segments. The second generation standards differentiate the data according to the relevance of each segmentation dimension for the economic situation of the enterprise. IAS 14 distinguishes between a *primary* and a *secondary reporting format* (also called *two-tier segmentation*). The primary format should be used for the segmentation dimension which most represents the dominant source and nature of the enterprise risks and returns and which therefore has the primary impact on the economic situation and development of the enterprise. According to the standard, the choice between business segments and geographical segments as primary reporting format should be based on the internal organization of the enterprise and its internal reporting system, because this usually depicts best the sources and nature of risks and returns.

In cases where the internal management and reporting structure is based neither on business segmentation nor on geographical segmentation, the management has to decide which of both segmentation dimensions represent most appropriately the risk and return profile of the enterprise, in order to be able to undertake the classification in the primary and secondary reporting format for the external segment report. If both segmentation dimensions seem to have an identical influence on the enterprise or if the internal reporting system takes both dimensions equally into account, business segments have to be chosen as primary and the geographical segmentation as the secondary segment reporting format according to IAS 14.27.

SFAS 131 does not use the terms primary and secondary format, as it only focuses on the segmentation used for internal reporting to the chief operating decision maker of an enterprise. It talks about *operating segments*. In addition to the disclosures for operating segments, an enterprise also has to present so-called 'enterprise-wide disclosures' covering revenues from external customers for each product (service) or each group of similar products (services) and revenues and long-lived tangible and intangible assets related to the enterprise's country of domicile and to all foreign countries in total in which the enterprise has transactions.

The data which should be disclosed for the primary and secondary segment reporting format under IAS 14 and for the operating segments under SFAS 131 are explained below and summarized in Table 19.2.

Consistent with the management approach, SFAS 131 specifies that the data to be disclosed per operating segment depends in quantity and content on the data which are used for internal management, control and reporting purposes. The only obligatory disclosure for each segment is the measure of profit or loss (*segment result*) reviewed internally by the chief operating decision maker. All the other revenue components in the column 'operating segment' of Table 19.2 and which are marked by 'X' have only to be disclosed per segment, if they are part of this internally used segment result. In the simplest case, if segments are managed on the basis of pure sales figures, than sales are the only data per segment which have to be disclosed in the external segment report according to US GAAP, as sales do not include any of the items mentioned in SFAS 131.27. If segments are internally managed on the basis of a net income figure per segment, all components marked with 'X' have to be disclosed for this segment. The disclosure of segment assets (and the connected investments) is only required if the value of assets is used internally – apart from the result – in managing the enterprise.

Table 19.2 Overview of the information required in segment reports according to IAS 14 and SFAS 131

| | IAS 14 | | SFAS 131 | |
	Primary Segment	Secondary Segment	Operating Segment	Further Information
Segment revenues	X			
Segment revenues with external customers	X	X	X[1]	X (for each product-orientated and geographical segment)

Table 19.2 Overview of the information required in segment reports according to IAS 14 and SFAS 131 (*continued*)

	IAS 14 Primary Segment	Secondary Segment	SFAS 131 Operating Segment	Further Information
Segment revenues from transactions with other segments	X		X[1]	
Segment result	X		X	
Segment assets	X	X	X[2]	X (for each geographical segment)
Segment liabilities	X			
Costs to acquire non-current tangible and intangible segment assets	X	X	X[1]	
Depreciation and amortization of segment assets	X		X[1]	
Significant non-cash expenses	X		X[1]	
Investments accounted for under the equity method	X		X[1]	
Profit or loss from investments accounted for under the equity method	X		X[1]	
Interest income and expenses			X[1]	
Extraordinary income and expenses			X[1]	
Unusual income and expenses			X[1]	
Tax earnings and expenses			X[1]	
Reconciliation between segment data and aggregated data disclosed in other financial statements	X		X	
Notes on:				
• intersegment transfer prices	X		X	
• composition of the reported segments	X	X	X	
• determination of the segment data			X	
• changes in accounting policies adopted for segment reporting	X	X	X	
• major customers			X	
• segments not separately reported with more than 10% of revenues from transactions with external customers	X			

1 Information is only required if the marked components are part of the disclosed segment result or segment asset value.

2 Disclosure of segment assets is only required if those assets are internally reported to the chief operating decision maker for decision purposes.

In contrast to SFAS 131, IAS 14 prescribes exactly which data have to be disclosed for the primary and secondary segment reporting formats and gives minimum components. *Segment revenue* not only includes sales, but also other revenues from operating activities. In principle, these are net revenues, which implies that revenue impairments and sales taxes have to be deducted. The following items are specifically excluded from segment revenues: extraordinary items, interest or dividend income (unless the segment operations are primarily financial), gains on sales of investments or gains on extinguishment of debt (unless the segment operations are primarily financial). Revenues which result from transactions with other segments have to be included in segment revenues and also disclosed separately, measured on the basis of the transfer prices actually used, which has to be specified.

The *segment result* is defined as the difference between segment revenues and expenses and can be interpreted as segment-specific income from operations. Segment expenses are expenses resulting from the operating activities of a segment and which can be directly or on a reasonable basis allocated to this segment. The determination of a segment's expenses is directly matched with its revenues. Segment expenses may not include: extraordinary items, interest expenses, losses on sales of investments or losses on extinguishment of debt, share of losses of associates, joint ventures, or other investments accounted for under the equity method, income taxes and general administrative expenses, head-office expenses, and other expenses which relate to the enterprise as a whole. Similarly, the interpretation of the segment result as a segment specific performance measure implies that non-periodic gains and losses, i.e. gains and losses from the sale of tangible or intangible assets or revaluations of assets may not be regarded as components of segment result. The standard also states that the segment result has to be determined before any adjustment for minority interests.

Segment assets are all assets which are employed by a segment in its operating activities and which can be allocated directly or on a reasonable basis to the segment. Therefore this includes all current and non-current fixed tangible and intangible assets (including investments accounted for under the equity method and goodwill), which are necessary to produce the segment revenues. Tax receivables or deferred tax assets and financial assets (excluding the case of financial institutions) are not treated as segment assets. Segment assets are measured at the same values at which they are included in the consolidated balance sheet.

Segment liabilities are all liabilities that result from the operating activities of a segment and that can be allocated directly or on a reasonable basis to a segment. If the segment result includes interest expenses, the interest-bearing liabilities have to be included in the segment liabilities. Following the IASC liability definition, segment liabilities also include provisions allocable to the segment. Income tax liabilities may not be included.

All the other items and information shown in Table 19.2, although explicitly required, are not further defined in the standard. According to IAS 14 an enterprise that discloses a cash flow figure per segment (as they are encouraged to do) need not also disclose amortization and depreciation expenses or the total amount of other significant non-cash expenses. The standard encourages the companies to disclose the nature and amount of any items included in segment revenue and segment expenses which are qualified to be relevant to explain the performance of each reportable segment.

Allocation of aggregated data to individual segments

Segment reporting has to deal with the problem of making allocations of aggregate consolidated figures, since assets may well be used or expenses engaged jointly by more than one segment. The handling of such joint components in segment reporting can, as with the allocation of costs in management accounting, be solved in three different ways. First, items which are not directly attributable to only one segment could be excluded totally from the disaggregation process. At the other extreme, all such items could be allocated, even if this is only possible on an arbitrary basis. Thirdly, the most reasonable approach is to restrain the allocation of joint items to those which can be allocated to individual segments on a reasonable basis. This means using appropriate allocation bases which are derived from objectively measurable cause and effect relationships. However, even with these, this allocation involves a considerable amount of subjectivity.

IAS 14 refers to the compromise approach, using cause and effect relationships. The allocation has to be done on a basis of reasonable, objective, justifiable criteria. According to the management approach this should basically be done the same way as it is done for internal management and reporting purposes, as long as this allows a reasonable allocation. However, if an internal allocation is considered as not suitable for external purposes, the joint components should be allocated differently for external reporting.

In order to allow the calculation of a return on investment ratio for each individual segment, the segment result and the segment assets should be interdependent, i.e. the numerator and denominator defined in a way which is consistent. That is why the standard requires that joint assets and related expenses should be allocated to both the business segments and geographical segments. Depreciation, energy, maintenance costs and other costs of a jointly used building for example have to be allocated to the segments proportionately with the asset.

As far as SFAS 131 is concerned, the implementation of the management approach means there is no requirement concerning consistency between earnings and the assets attributed to one particular segment. Similarly, there is no requirement concerning the allocation of joint items. The treatment of data in the external segment reports has to be the same as in the internal reporting system. The standard assumes that an efficient internal system will be coherent in these respects.

Expenses, assets and liabilities which are not directly allocated to segments should be part of the reconciliation between the items included in the reported segments and the aggregate totals in the consolidated financial statements. Those items which should not be allocated to individual segments are, amongst others, expenses which relate to the whole enterprise and not to particular segments, such as head office expenses or expenses of the centralized R&D department.

Relationship with group accounting principles

The FASB and IASB standards differ significantly in their approach to consistency of accounting principles as between the segments and the published group figures. The management approach in SFAS 131 requires that the data disclosed in the published report has to coincide with the data used in the internal report. It could therefore happen that a segment report uses data which does not comply with the principles used in the group accounts. This might happen, for instance, through selective application of a full fair value approach or the use of inflation adjusted values, or the use of different national rules. However, there are few differences in the measurement approaches as between management and financial accounting in US practice, major deviations are unlikely to be encountered in reality.

IAS 14, on the other hand, has dropped the management approach in this respect and requires (as the older standards of segment reporting did) that the disaggregated data must follow the same accounting policies as for the group financial statements. The term *symmetry* is quite often also applied in this context.

Reconciliation with group data

The information content of a segment report suffers considerably if there is no link between the segmented data and the data disclosed in the other financial statements of the enterprise. That is why all the standards on segment reporting require that the sum of the segment results and the segment revenues have to be reconciled with the corresponding aggregated values in the published group income statement. Similarly, the sum of the segment assets and liabilities have to reconciled with the asset and liabilities of the group balance sheet. Reconciliation differences arise from different causes. One is the fact that segment data often include amounts which result from inter-segment transactions which are eliminated in the aggregated statements. Another major difference is the elements (expenses, assets, liabilities, etc.) which concern the enterprise as a whole and which cannot be allocated to individual segments. Furthermore, they also can result from differences in the definitions of segment items and the related items in the balance sheet or income statement (for example the difference between the segment revenue and the ordinary income of the income statement, which differ in the components included).

The only concrete requirement in IAS 14 and SFAS 131 relating to this is that segment revenues should include revenues which result from transactions with other segments. Those revenues have to be disclosed separately to allow the user of the report to assess the level of integration of the individual segments. This implies that inter-segment transactions are not eliminated at the segment levels but in the reconciliation between the disaggregated and the aggregated data.

According to the management approach, the scope of the consolidation procedures carried out in a segment report following US-GAAP depends on the procedures applied to calculate segment items for internal reporting purposes. As a result of the application of the management approach and the usage of internally generated data for external purposes, the reconciling amounts disclosed in reports presented on the basis of SFAS 131, can generally be expected to be higher than those presented under IAS 14. That is why the FASB requires that the individual components of the reconciliation difference for each segmented item have to be explained, so that the users of the report have a clear view over the relationship between the aggregated and disaggregated data.

Data for other than primary or operating segments

Some segment-specific data may be required not only for the primary or operating segments, but also for others, however in less detail. IAS 14 prescribes two segmentation dimensions, business and geographical. The main detail goes in the approach chosen by the company as its primary segments, leaving the alternative approach to be the so-called *secondary reporting format*. For this, basically the same measurement criteria and principles are applied, the standard only requires the segment revenues from external customers, the segment assets, and the total cost incurred to acquire non-current tangible and intangible segment assets, if the threshold of significance of 10% of the respective group totals are exceeded.

If the primary reporting format for reporting segment information is geographical segments that are based on location of assets (origin of sales), and if these locations are different to those of the customers (destination of sales), then the segment revenues of each customer-based geographical segment has also to be presented (subject to the significance thresholds). Inversely, if the primary segmentation is based on the location of the customers, the secondary reporting format should additionally present the segment tangible and intangible fixed assets by geographical segments based on the location of assets.

This minimum information about the segment revenues, segment assets and segment investments for all secondary segments implies that every designated segment contains comparable data concerning these three categories, independently of the individual enterprise's choice of business or geographical segmentation as primary or secondary reporting format. To guarantee this was an important aim the IASC wanted to achieve with IAS 14.

Although the identification of segments is derived from the internal reporting structure the FASB, in its standard, has set up minimum information requirements about products and services and the geographic areas of an enterprise's activities, which are called '*enterprise-wide disclosures*'. Here the importance of the business sector as well as geographical data evaluation of the enterprise is recognized. If the operating segments are not based on products and services, SFAS 131 requires that at least the revenues from external customers have to be reported based on this segmentation criterion. If the operating segments do not reflect different geographical regions, the standard requires disclosure of at least the segment revenues from external customers as well as the value of long-lived assets (excluding some designated types of asset) attributed to the enterprise's country of domicile, and that related to all foreign countries in total from which the enterprise derives revenues or in which it holds assets. If particular revenues or assets in foreign countries are regarded as material, these revenues and/or assets should be disclosed separately. SFAS 131 is silent about the identification of segments and leaves this therefore to management's discretion. However, unlike the data disclosed in the operating segments, the data of the enterprise-wide disclosure has to be based on the accounting policies used to prepare the enterprise's general-purpose financial statements. An enterprise has the right not to make these enterprise-wide disclosures if it is impractical to generate appropriate disaggregated data, i.e. it would cause costs which were too high.

Supplementary information

The segment report can only fulfil its information objective if the quantitative data is accompanied by qualitative and verbal explanations. The most six important categories of supplementary information according to IAS 14 and/or SFAS 131 are discussed in the following subsections.

Description of the composition of reported segments

The rather subjective nature of the choice of segments can be mediated by some discussion of their nature and the reasons for their choice. These supplementary explanations are required by IAS 14.81 and SFAS 131.26. The latter, because of its focus on enterprise specific segmentation, demands more detailed information about the criteria used for the definition of the reportable segments of a particular enterprise.

Disclosure of the basis of inter-segment transfer prices

The prices used for transactions between segments within the enterprise have an impact on the revenues of the selling segment as well as the expenses of the buying segment, and the profitability of both. Consequently the basis the enterprise actually used for its transfer prices is a required disclosure under both standards. The basis can be market price (most often encountered), cost recovery prices or market prices subject to a certain discount.

Information about changes in accounting policies and lack of consistency

The segment report should be presented in a consistent manner. This should allow reasonable comparisons of the data disclosed in different time periods and between similar segments of different companies, what are significant characteristics in terms of the information value of the reports. Any deviation from consistency should be explained and (if possible) its quantitative effect should be calculated. If such deviations occur, the prior period segment information, which is disclosed for comparative purposes, should be restated unless it is impracticable to do so. If an enterprise changes the identification of its segments and it does not restate prior period segment information on the new basis, due to impracticability, then the enterprise should report segment data for both the old and the new bases of segmentation.

Typical deviations from consistency might be, for example, when transfer prices have been changed, when the allocation of revenues, expenses, assets or liabilities has changed or when the enterprise changed accounting policies in its general purpose financial statements which have influence on the data of the segment report.

Explanation of disclosed segment data

Because of the possible differences between the accounting regulations that apply to the segment report and those that apply to other parts of the annual report – as can occur if SFAS 131 is used – it is necessary to explain how the disclosed segment data are defined and measured in order to facilitate understanding of the reconciliation amounts. SFAS 131 explicitly requires further explanations on the following points: differences between the measurements of the reportable segment results and the enterprise's consolidated income (before taxes, extraordinary items, discontinued operations, and the cumulative effect of changes in accounting principles); differences between the measurements of segment assets and the consolidated assets; changes from prior periods in the measurement methods used to determine reported segment profit or loss and the effect of those changes as well as the nature and effect of any asymmetrical allocations to segments.

Major customers

According to US GAAP (but not to IAS) an enterprise has to provide information about the extent of its reliance on its major customers. If 10% or more of all revenues of an enterprise are the result of transactions with a single external customer, this is considered a major dependency (note that in this context customer is not defined as a single enterprise, but as the whole group of which a customer company is part). In such a case the enterprise has to reveal its dependency, disclose the total amount of revenues from this customer and indicate in which segments these revenues have been earned. The amount of revenues allocated to each segment and the identity of the customer are not required to be disclosed.

Specific information on mainly integrated segments

According to IAS 14 (but not to SFAS 131), an enterprise has to identify segments which earn a majority of their revenues from sales to other segments and which therefore are not reported as individual segments separately but combined with other segments ('integrated segments'), but whose revenues with external clients account for at least 10% of the group revenues. Additionally, the amounts of revenue from sales of such a segment to external customers as well as from internal sales to other segments have to be explicitly disclosed.

Form and layout of the segment report

Neither IAS 14 nor SFAS 131 require a specific layout, but they both illustrate in their appendices examples of tabular layouts of the segmented information. Table 19.3 shows the example given in the appendix to IAS 14.

In order to improve the comparability of the data, comparative figures for the previous year should also be disclosed, even if a particular segment has not been reported in the prior period due to lacking significance. The disclosure of data of more than one prior period is not required under IAS 14. According to SFAS 131 the segment reports should include as many prior years as the general purpose financial statements.

A combination of the data of two segmentation dimensions in a matrix form, that, for example, indicates the results of industry segment A in the market of geographical area III, offers very detailed information, however it also embodies the latent danger of an information overload and therefore a decline in understandability. Additionally a *matrix presentation* increases the problem of allocating items correctly to the specific segments because two dimensions have to be considered simultaneously. Nevertheless some companies do publish a segment report in the form of a matrix, as illustrated in Table 19.4 by the segment report in the annual report of 1998 of Cadbury Schweppes, which is based on the British segment reporting standard (SSAP 25). Such a form of presentation is not required (but also not prohibited) in either IAS 14 or SFAS 131.

Segment data as a part of interim reporting

Before SFAS 131 there was no national or international standard which regulated the presentation of disaggregated data in interim reports. Segment reporting was a feature only of annual reports. SFAS 131 now requires that each interim report (quarterly or half-yearly) should include the presentation of segment revenues, inter-segment revenues as well as segment results, on the same basis as the annual figures. The total of the segment results has to be reconciled with the result (before taxes and extraordinary items, discontinued operations and the cumulative effect of changes in accounting principles) of the whole enterprise shown in the income statement of the interim period. If there have been major changes in the segment assets compared to those disclosed in the last annual report, in the identification or composition of the segments or in the method used to determine the segment results during the course of the interim period, this has to be explained in the report.

IAS 14 is silent about the disclosure of segment data in interim reports. However IAS 34 (the standard that regulates interim reporting) requires that the notes of an interim report have to include segment revenue and results for business segments or geographical segments, whichever is the enterprise's primary basis of segment reporting on the same basis as the segment report in the annual report.

Obviously both standards (IAS 14 and SFAS 131) require less segment information to be presented in interim reports. But they refer to the same basis and policies of segmentation and the same definitions of segment items which are used for the segment report included in the annual report.

Consequences of the management approach

Due to the fact that the IASC – despite of its efforts together with the FASB and the Accounting Standards Board of the Canadian Institute of Chartered Accountants to

Table 19.3 Example of a segment report of IAS 14, business segments

	Paper products 20×2	20×1	Office products 20×2	20×1	Publishing 20×2	20×1	Other operations 20×2	20×1	Eliminations 20×2	20×1	Consolidated 20×2	20×1
Revenue												
External sales	55	50	20	17	19	16	7	7			101	90
Inter-segment sales	15	10	10	14	2	4	2	2	(29)	(30)		
Total revenue	70	60	30	31	21	20	9	9	(29)	(30)	101	90
Result												
Segment result	20	17	9	7	2	1	0	0	(1)	(1)	30	24
Unallocated corporate expenses											(7)	(9)
Operating profit											23	15
Interest expense											(4)	(4)
Interest income											2	3
Share of net profits of associates	6	5					2	2			8	7
Income taxes											(7)	(4)
Profit from ordinary activities											22	17
Extraordinary loss: uninsured earthquake damage to factory											—	(3)
Net profit											22	14
Other information												
Segment assets	54	50	34	30	10	10	10	9			108	99
Investment in equity method associates	20	16					12	10			32	26
Unallocated corporate assets											35	30
Consolidated total assets											175	155
Segment liabilities	25	15	8	11	8	8	1	1			42	35
Unallocated corporate liabilities											40	55
Consolidated total liabilities											82	90
Capital expenditure	12	10	3	5	5	5	4	3				
Depreciation	9	7	9	7	5	3	3	4				
Non-cash expenses other than depreciation	8	2	7	3	2	2	2	1				

Source: IAS 14, Appendix

achieve uniform standards – did not accept the management approach as an overall concept in the same way as it is embodied in SFAS 131, it is necessary to think about the advantages and disadvantages of an adoption of this concept and to consider the reasons for the IASC rejection. The management approach causes effects largely on two levels: that of the enterprise preparing the segment report, and that of the users of the report, which are considered primarily to be the investors.

For the management of the enterprise the most obvious advantage of a consistent application of the management approach is that this avoids an additional workload: time consuming data transformations and additional analysis are not necessary. Although, in times where information technology is widely used in accounting, the potential to reduce costs of data storing or transporting are almost negligible, the major advantage can be found in the way of generating the data, ensuring its quality and its informational value as well as in the speed and efficiency with which reports are prepared.[1] The allocation of jointly used assets to individual segments and the related problem of splitting up the data (finding and defining reasonable indicators of cause and effect relationships) has to be solved only once.

Due to the fact that the same data and information are used for internal as well as for external purposes, they are usually judged to be more meaningful, and this generates a higher motivation among the employees who prepare the segment report and reinforces the acceptance of this task. Last but not least, the identification of the management of each segment with the published results is considerably higher, if the results correspond to internal performance measurements. Overall it is reasonable to assume that the management approach leads to a faster and more efficient preparation of the report, while guaranteeing the good quality of the data disclosed.

Table 19.4 Segment report for the period 1998 of Cadbury Schweppes

1998	Total	United Kingdom	Europe	America	Pacific	Africa and Others
	£m	£m	£m	£m	£m	£m
Sales						
Beverages	1 937	55	346	1 250	201	85
Confectionery	2 169	948	453	265	304	199
	4 106	1 003	799	1 515	505	284
Trading Profit						
Beverages	362	(12)	38	301	21	14
Confectionery	280	134	23	43	58	22
	642	122	61	344	79	36
Operating Assets						
Beverages	260	(38)	59	172	47	20
Confectionery	1 002	366	218	107	178	133
	1 262	328	277	279	225	153
Trading Margin %						
Beverages	18.7	(21.8)	11.0	24.1	10.4	16.5
Confectionery	12.9	14.1	5.1	16.2	19.1	11.1
	15.6	12.2	7.6	22.7	15.6	12.7

Besides this very positive effect of more efficient and more up-to-date data being presented, the major advantage of the management approach for the investors lies in the insight into the organizational, management and control structure of the enterprise as well as in the performance measure which is primarily used by the management. This enhances the transparency of the report and is an important piece of information with regard to the objective of enterprise reporting which is to display the activities of the enterprise to help investors forecast future developments. As a consequence the investors have the opportunity to judge the management, not only on the basis of reported results but also on the basis of the rationality and quality of the organizational and management system applied, as far as that information is disclosed in the segment report. In addition it is easier for the investors to analyse the consequences of management decisions specifically for each segment and therefore judge the performance of the management on a disaggregated basis.

As a disadvantage, the adoption of the company specific internal structures and data for external reporting reduces considerably the possibility of making quantitative comparisons with the corresponding data of other enterprises. Although – as discussed above – a completely satisfactory level of comparability can never be reached due to the specific segment identifications of each enterprise, the degree of comparability is higher if there are externally defined segmentation dimensions and segment definitions as well as definitions of the items disclosed as in IAS 14, and this is not the case if the management approach is used strictly as specified in SFAS 131. Furthermore the overall impact of the management approach implemented in SFAS 131 also implies that the data disclosed in the segment report have not necessarily to be determined on the basis of the accounting policies and principles applied in the general purpose financial statements.

Another limit to the comparability of the segment data is that the definitions and measurement methods applied to the disclosed items (such as segment assets or segment result) can differ within one report from segment to segment or do not have to be in a sensible relationship. This can prevent users of the segment report from making reasonable input–output comparisons (such as rates of return) per segment. It is quite unlikely that this happens in practice because of the negative signalling effect and the limited effectiveness for management and control purposes this might have, although it is possible. The lack of comparability also reduces the usefulness of a segment report for benchmarking an enterprise with regard to the segments of its major competitors or other benchmark enterprises (see Fey and Mujkanovic 1999, p. 263).

In addition, even time series comparability turns out to be reduced because of the management approach. This arises as a result of frequent changes in the organizational structure of the management and internal reporting system. These are generated quite regularly today as a consequence of an increased rate of mergers and reorganizations and automatically cause inconsistencies in segment reporting. Although the negative impact of such changes on the information value of the reports is limited through the requirement to adapt the disclosed prior-period data to the new organizational structure, it is questionable whether this is really successful, taking into account the difficulties which an organizational change causes for accounting in general. In any case the adjustments of the prior-period data generate a considerable workload for the enterprise, and therefore probably reduce the efficiency gains of the management approach.

Another potential limiting factor of the decision usefulness of the segment report is the fact that one of the major characteristics of a sensible identification of segments – a homogeneity of the segments with regard to their risk and return profile – is not explicitly required in the management approach of SFAS 131. The internal report and control structure may have been influenced by the way the enterprise has grown and the interactions between managers rather than as an economically coherent view of the enterprise. This can result in segments where their definition and identification is not based on homogeneous market opportunities and threads (Ordelheide and Stubenrath 1998, p. 285). The consistent adoption of the internal corporate structure is at this point for the FASB a more important objective in the definition of segments than homogeneity of risk and return. However the FASB refers to this criterion of homogeneity in relation to the issue of deciding which of the internally determined segments might be combined into reportable segments.

The focus on internally used accounting data, which is inherent to the management approach, should not, however, lead to very significant deviations from the data determined in the annual report in US enterprises, because of the traditional close linkage between internal and external determination of results in American accounting. Any reconciliation difference can be expected to be in most cases relatively small. If there are non-congruent and independent internal and external systems of income calculation, which can still be the case in other countries, for instance in Germany (despite developments in most of the larger groups), there can be very significant differences, which cause considerable reconciliation amounts which have to be further explained to the users. The more the internal data and measures differ from those in the general purpose financial statements, the more important is the function of reconciliation and the thorough explanation of the reconciliation amounts. If the explanations are very comprehensive and detailed, this can even be seen as another advantage of the management approach, because the disclosure of the reconciliation amounts allows the addressees to analyse and judge those.

Conclusion

The presentation of disaggregated data within the framework of a segment report is today regarded as a major instrument for providing information useful for decision making for the users of financial reports of global diversified enterprises. The two 'competing' approaches and models of how to design and define such a report, which are represented by the two most influential standards, the IAS 14 and the SFAS 131, mirror and illustrate the overall conflict between the qualitative characteristics of financial reporting, such as relevance, reliability and comparability.

The approach followed by SFAS 131, to match the structure and content of external reporting with the internal management and control system, focuses primarily on relevance, because the individual circumstances of an enterprise are shown realistically and the users get a direct insight into the way the enterprise is managed. However, this approach diminishes reliability as it leaves considerable degrees of freedom in design and judgement to the management of the reporting enterprise. Furthermore the comparability between different enterprises is considerably restricted. Reliability and comparability might have been better achieved by very general, strict and detailed norms which have to be applied similarly by all enterprises. Those standards on the other hand would not allow the creation of a realistic picture of the individual situation of a specific enterprise. While SFAS 131 has gone a quite considerable way with the concrete application of the management approach, IAS 14 tries to find a greater balance between the qualitative characteristics and therefore put more weight on reliability and comparability.

However, as matter of fact, due to individual identification of segments, different degrees of segmental integration and allocations of joint-items, segment reporting generally suffers under a lack of comparability, which cannot be addressed by particular norms without losing a considerable degree of usefulness of the information disclosed.

This is the reason why – even in applying relatively detailed standards – the quality and usefulness of published information in segment reporting depends (much more than in other fields of accounting) on the attitude and willingness of the management to give a realistic insight in the economic situation of the enterprise. Deficits in the quality of the quantitative information of the report can be eliminated by providing additional narrative information, which can help to explain the specific decisions of management with regard to the definition and identification of the segments and the definitions of the disclosed segment data.

The standards on segmental reporting described in this chapter may be criticized for the reason that they focus (according to their underlying conceptual frameworks) exclusively on the information needs of investors. The idea discussed in earlier periods of providing segment information which is useful for other stakeholders has been totally dropped. For example, the intention of less developed countries to get insights through geographically segmented reports in the social and economical impact of the activities of multinational companies on their societies, which the UN proposed 20 years ago, has not been included in SFAS 131 or in IAS 14. Equally, the information interests of the governments (for example to facilitate national statistic and accounting purposes) or of the employees (information on productivity or localizations of specific plants, etc.) has not been taken into account in the current standards.

Note

1. The FASB also mentions this advantage explicitly (SFAS 131.4).

References

Boersema, J. and Weelden, S. (1992) *Financial Reporting for Segments*. Canadian Institute of Chartered Accountants (ed.), Toronto.

Fey, G. and Mujkanovic, R. (1999) Segmentberichterstattung im internationalen Umfeld. *Die Betriebswirtschaft*, **59** (2): 261–275.

Gray, S. and Roberts, C. (1989) Voluntary information disclosure and the British multinationals: corporate perceptions of costs and benefits. In A. Hopwood, (ed.) *International Pressures of Accounting for Change*. Prentice Hall, Hemel Hempstead, pp. 116–139.

Haller, A. and Park, P. (1994) Grundsätze ordnungsmäßiger Segmentberichterstattung. *Zeitschrift für betriebswirtschaftliche Forschung*, **46** (6): 499–524.

Haller, A. and Park, P. (1994a) Regulation and practice of segmental reporting in Germany. *European Accounting Review*, **3** (3): 563–580.

Ijiri, Y. (1995) Segment statements and informativeness measures: managing capital vs. managing resource. *Accounting Horizon*, **3**: 55–67.

Knoops, C., Bank, J. and Happée, R. (1996) *Segmental reporting in the Netherlands: regulations, empirical results and perceptions of management and financial analysts*. Unpublished paper, presented at the 19th annual meeting of the European Accounting Association, Bergen.

Mohr, R. (1983) The segmental reporting issue: a review of empirical research. *Journal of Accounting Literature*, **2**: 39–71.

OECD (1990) *Segmented Financial Information*. Paris, OECD.

Pacter, P. (1993) *Reporting Disaggregated Information*. FASB (ed.), Norwalk, Connecticut.

Pacter, P. (1994*) Reporting Financial Information by Segment – Background Issues Paper*. IASC (ed.), London.

Prodhan, B. (1986) *Multinational Accounting: Segment Disclosure and Risk*. Croom Helm, London.

Radebaugh, L. and Gray, S. (2002) *International Accounting and Multinational Enterprises*, 5th edn. Wiley, New York.

Sims, M. (1989) The development of authoritative pronouncements on segment reporting. *Accounting History* 19–28.

Further Reading

Accounting Standards Committee (1990) *SSAP 25: Segmental Reporting.* London.

Adler, H., Düring, W. and Schmaltz K. (1995) *Rechnungslegung und Prüfung der Unternehmen*, 6th edn. volume 2. Revised by Forster, K.-H. *et al.*, Schäffer-Poeschel, Stuttgart.

American Institute of Certified Public Accountants (1994) *Improving Business Reporting – a Customer Focus.* Comprehensive report of the Special Committee on Financial Reporting, New York.

American Institute of Certified Public Accountants/Accounting Principles Board (1967) *APB Statement No. 2, Disclosure of Supplemental Financial Information by Diversified Companies.* New York.

Association for Investment Management and Research (1993) *Financial Reporting in the 1990s and Beyond.* Charlottesville.

Baumann, K.-H. (1987) Die Segment-Berichterstattung im Rahmen der externen Finanzpublizität. In H. Havermann, (ed.) *Bilanz- und Konzernrecht.* IDW-Verlag, Düsseldorf, pp. 1–23.

Bernards, O. (1995) Segmentberichterstattung in den Geschäftsberichten deutscher Unternehmen – theoretische und empirische Ergebnisse. *Deutsches Steuerrecht*: 1363–1368.

Böcking, H.-J. (1999) Segmentberichterstattung – Ein Baustein zur Kontrolle und Transparenz im Unternehmensbereich. In D. Dörner, D. Menold, and N. Pfitzer, (eds) *Reform des Aktienrechts, der Rechnungslegung und Prüfung.* Schäffer-Poeschel, Stuttgart, pp. 509–538.

Böcking, H.-J. and Benecke, B. (1998) Neue Vorschriften zur Segmentberichterstattung nach IAS und US-GAAP unter dem Aspekt des Business Reporting. *Die Wirtschaftsprüfung*, **51** (3) 92–107.

Business Accounting Deliberation Council (1988) *Opinion on the Disclosure of Segment Information*, Tokyo.

Canadian Institute of Chartered Accountants (1979) *Section 1700: Segmented Information.* The Accounting Research Committee (ed.), Toronto.

Canadian Institute of Chartered Accountants (1997) *Section 1700 (revised): Reporting Disaggregated Information about a Business Enterprise.* Accounting Standards Board (ed.), Toronto.

Emmanuel, C. and Garrod, N. (1987) On the segment identification issues. *Accounting and Business Research* **17** (Summer): 235–240.

Emmanuel, C. and Garrod, N. (1994) Segmental reporting in the UK – How does SSAP 25 stand up to international comparison? *European Accounting Review*, **3** (3): 547–562.

Emmanuel, C. and Gray, S. (1978) Segmental disclosure by multibusiness multinational companies: a proposal. *Accounting and Business Research* 169–177.

FASB (1976) *Financial Reporting for Segments of a Business Enterprise; SFAS No. 14.* Stamford, Connecticut.

FASB (1997) *Disclosures about Segments of an Enterprise and Related Information, SFAS 131.* Norwalk, Connecticut.

Gray, S. (1981) Segmental or disaggregated financial statements. In T. Lee, (ed.) *Developments in Financial Reporting.* Allan, Oxford, pp. 27–56.

Gray, S. and Radebaugh, L. (1984) International segment disclosures by US and UK multinational enterprises: a descriptive study. *Journal of Accounting Research* (Spring): 351–360.

Haller, A. (2002): IAS 14 – Segmentberichterstattung (Reporting financial information by segments). In J. Baetge, D. Dörner, H. Kleekämper, and P. Wollmert, (eds) *Rechnungslegung nach International Accounting Standards (IAS),* 2nd edn. Schäffer-Poeschel, Stuttgart.

Haller, A. and Park, P. (1999) Segmentberichterstattung auf Basis des 'Management Approach' – Inhalt und Konsequenzen. *Kostenrechnungs-Praxis*, special edn. 3: 59–66.

IASC (1981) *IAS 14: Reporting Financial Information by Segment.* London.

IASC (1997) *IAS 14 (revised): Segment Reporting.* London.

Langenbucher G. (1999) Segmentberichterstattung als Ergänzung der Rechnungslegung. In K. Küting, and G. Langenbucher, (eds) *Internationale Rechnungslegung.* Schäffer-Poeschel, Stuttgart, pp. 157–180.

Nichols, N. and Street, D. (1999) Segment information: What early adopters reported. *Journal of Accountancy*, **1**: 38–41.

OECD (1976) *Declaration by the Governments of OECD Member Countries and Decisions of the OECD Council on Guidelines for Multinational Enterprises.* Paris.

OECD (1988) *Multinational Enterprises and Disclosure of Information: Clarification of the OECD Guidelines.* Paris.

Ordelheide, D. and Stubenrath, M. (2000) Segmentberichterstattung. In W. Ballwieser, (ed.) *US-Amerikanische Rechnungslegung*, 4th edn. Schäffer-Poeschel, Stuttgart, pp. 379–405.

Pejic, P. (1997) *Segmentberichterstattung im externen Jahresabschluß.* Gabler, Wiesbaden.

United Nations (1977) *International Standards of Accounting and Reporting for Transnational Corporations.* Commission on Transnational Corporations (ed.), New York.

United Nations (1989) *International Accounting and Reporting Issues: 1988.* UN Centre on Transnational Corporations (ed.), Geneva.

United Nations (1995) *International Accounting and Reporting Issues: 1994.* UN Centre on Transnational Corporations (ed.), Geneva.

The audit of multinationals

Marco Rochat and Peter Walton

The multinational company poses particular problems in terms of its audit. At a technical level, the auditor is reporting on the consolidated financial statements as opposed to those of the individual companies which make up the group. But at the same time, the viability of the consolidated statements depends directly on that of the underlying statements on which it is based. This means that the auditor who prepares a report on the group statements is in effect giving an opinion on those of all the companies in the group. However, those companies will be sited in many different countries, maintaining accounting records and preparing statements according to different accounting regimes, and being audited, perhaps by many different firms of auditors, according to different auditing and professional standards. In this chapter we shall look at the issues raised by the specifically international nature of the task and the solutions which are currently used, and then go on to review the procedures for the audit of the consolidated accounts of a multinational.

The management structure of a multinational company depends a great deal upon the nature of its operations, the diversity of its products and often upon history, since a multinational has usually grown partly through organic development and partly through acquisitions (Table 20.1).

Essentially a multinational can be seen as a collection of more or less autonomous operating units under a more or less distant central control. The issue of the degree of central control is widely debated in the management literature (e.g. see Mintzberg 1979) and impacts upon the choices made in terms of management reporting and financial accounting systems.

However, for audit and some financial reporting purposes, each subsidiary is an autonomous unit which has filing and other legal obligations in the country in which it is based, which relate to the national regulatory framework. In this context it is not very practical to have the company audited by a firm from the multinational's home country. There are operational difficulties such as the need to be aware of local accounting, dividend distribution, taxation and auditing regulations, quite apart from the potential legal problems of the audit firm being licensed in the host country. Consequently the multinational, and the auditors of its consolidated statements, find themselves obliged to consider to what extent the nature of the audit provided corresponds to what is required by the multinational for its consolidated statements, and to what extent the accounting measurements are suitable for inclusion.

Table 20.1 The growth of Nestlé

1867	Farine Lactée Henri Nestlé founded
	Mergers and acquisitions:
1905	Anglo-Swiss Condensed Milk Co
1929	Peter-Cailler-Kohler Chocolats Suisses
1947	Potages Jules Maggi
1960	Crosse & Blackwell
1961	Locatelli
1962	Findus
1969	Vittel
1970	Libby
1971	Thomy
1973	Stouffer
1977	Alcon
1978	Chambourcy
1985	Hills Brothers
1985	Carnation
1986	Herta
1988	Buitoni
1988	Rowntree
1992	Perrier
1993	Fintalgel
1994	Alpo
1997	San Pellegrino
1998	Spillers Petfoods
2001	Ralston Purina

Source: Nestlé annual reports.

National differences in accounting

The consequences for the multinational of facing a multiplicity of accounting regimes are addressed from different points of view in Chapters 17 and 21. Here we will look at the problem simply as it affects the financial reporting of individual subsidiaries. Essentially the multinational faces a situation where the production of its consolidated accounts requires, in principle, that the same accounting policies be applied to all subsidiaries, whether these policies are those of the parent, the IASB, US GAAP or some other basis. This means that virtually all foreign subsidiaries have to produce two sets of figures: one according to local GAAP which are required for national filing and taxation purposes, and a second according to the policies adopted for the consolidated accounts.

There are several ways for the multinational to handle this problem. One way, often chosen by US multinationals, is to have uniform accounting procedures throughout the group, usually based upon parent company GAAP. The major advantage of this is that the consolidated accounts relate directly to the reporting systems of the subsidiaries. All managers are using common performance measurement yardsticks, both in terms of annual performance and, usually, the monthly management reporting system. This in turn makes it easier to have standard internal control and internal audit systems, and also makes life easier for the group auditors. Financial controllers can be moved around the group easily without any substantial retraining.

Under this sort of approach each subsidiary then restates its figures locally for national tax and filing purposes. Often the restatement would be carried out with the help of the local auditor, since the necessary detailed knowledge may not be available within the company, depending upon the size of the local operation.

The reverse of this approach is to allow each subsidiary to be more or less autonomous in its accounting. Where this is the case, the subsidiary prepares accounts as a quasi-independent company, according to local accounting rules. These accounts are then passed to group headquarters for consolidation, and the central accounting function has to have restatement routines available to adjust the accounts to a uniform basis. This requires that headquarters has staff who follow the evolution of accounting principles in countries where major subsidiaries are located, and that they have sufficient detail in each set of figures to make the necessary adjustments. These adjustments would be subject to scrutiny by the group auditor.

This kind of system has the related disadvantages that uniform internal control and audit procedures cannot be applied, and accounting staff cannot be moved easily around the group. Against that, there is the major advantage that when a major acquisition is made, the acquiring group does not have to accept the very substantial costs of changing the systems in the new subsidiary. These costs are both visible, in terms of technical studies, new software, changing over accumulated data, staff training, etc., and invisible in terms of management's alienation and loss of confidence in the measurements.

The balance of costs and benefits depends upon the company and indeed the management culture at the centre. Typically a company with a small number of large subsidiaries may not find uniform systems necessary, while a company with many smaller operations may benefit from these. Sometimes the situation is fudged with subsidiaries being encouraged to align their systems progressively on the centre, while remaining within the bounds of local GAAP. In such cases one sometimes sees the following notes (for tangible fixed assets) in the annual report

> The (depreciation) rates used overseas are not materially different from the rates used above, but they vary according to local conditions and requirements.
>
> (Cadbury Schweppes annual report)

Burlaud, Messina and Walton (1996) reporting on the depreciation policies of British and French groups observed that depreciation in subsidiaries is often not restated to a uniform basis.

National differences in audit

The group audit depends upon the accounts of each subsidiary having been audited effectively and on more or less the same basis. However, there are many national differences in audit and these concern both the scope and objects of the audit and also the training and duties of the auditor (Trolliet 1994). Historically the audit developed as a means of investors (principals) reassuring themselves as to the management of their wealth by their agents. In nineteenth-century company law the auditor was often a shareholder. In developed economies there has been an evolution towards the audit of a public company being carried out by an independent professional who has the necessary competences to express an opinion on the accounts. However, this evolution has taken place in different ways, leading to a situation where the audit task is understood differently in different countries.

In Anglo-Saxon countries the auditor is generally understood to be giving an opinion to the effect that the financial statements adequately represent the economic position of the company. The US audit report (see below) says that the financial statements 'fairly represent' the situation of the company, while the EC directives call for the auditor to confirm that the accounts give a 'true and fair view'. However, countries with a strong Roman law tradition interpret that fairly narrowly (e.g. see Ordelheide 1993). In Germany in particular, the auditor is primarily confirming that the accounts have respected accounting rules. In many cases this will not necessarily have a dramatic impact, but occasionally there will be a situation where, although the accounts are perhaps correctly drawn up, there are other circumstances which need to be known to interpret them. For example, there is the case of a French group which had a South American subsidiary that was making oil rigs. The subsidiary had a lucrative contract with a client and reported strong profits, without any mention in the audited accounts of the fact that the client was having financial difficulties (and ultimately went into liquidation).

The duties and obligations of the auditor may also be different. In general the auditor, in order to give a worthwhile opinion, is expected to be totally independent of the client, and for that matter the state. In many countries the auditor is, though, free to sell other services. In the UK companies are now obliged to report in the notes to the accounts how much they pay to their auditors for non-audit services, and this is frequently as much again as the audit fee. Recent changes to US disclosures have revealed ratios as high as five to one between non-audit and audit fees.

These auditors say independence is a state of mind, and ethical requirements ensure that no client represents a significant proportion of turnover. In addition, the audit engagement is on a year-to-year basis. Critics say that this puts the auditor in a difficult position vis-à-vis the clients. In France the auditor (nor theoretically any associated entity within the same network) may not provide any services except audit to an audit client. This is also the case in Germany. In both France (six years) and Italy (three years) the audit engagement is for a fixed period, which is intended to bolster the auditor's freedom.

The question of relations with the state is also delicate. French auditors are required to report any legal infractions to the public prosecutor, and also have a duty, where there is some question of the client's going concern status, to initiate discussions with the board of directors and ultimately the courts. The auditors of banks are in a particularly sensitive position in terms of the potential conflicts between their responsibilities to the shareholders and those to the bank regulators and depositors. In former centrally planned economies the auditors were seen as a form of state economic surveillance, and as these countries move towards market economies, the creation of a viable, independent, commercial audit service is difficult. They have a problem, for example, in separating the function of the auditor as independent economic reporter from that of checker of tax returns for the state. In some countries the state delivers a licence to audit, whereas in others it is private sector professional bodies that both license and monitor auditors.

International audit firms

The wide national variations in accounting rules, taxation and auditing create a problem for multinationals in achieving both control of subsidiaries and viable consolidated accounts. The solution which they have mostly chosen is to engage a single audit firm which can meet their needs worldwide, and whose organization more or less parallels their own. There are now four major firms ('The Big Four') which operate in this way and are able to offer a worldwide service. These are networks based essentially on amalgamations of US and UK accounting firms which have taken place successively in the last 25 years.

They are not generally groups with a single centralized control like their clients, but rather networks of fairly large national practices which offer both a national service and an international service, with some shared training facilities, procedures and manuals and quality control. When a multinational headquartered in (say) Detroit engages the US national firm as auditor, all its foreign subsidiaries are audited by foreign national offices of the audit firm. In this way the client need only address the local office, and all foreign subsidiaries are taken care of automatically. The local office does not need to have many staff, since local staff are used all over the world. The situation has evolved now to a point where the audit firm may well be both bigger and better known internationally than its client. This means that any company trying to expand or bring its shares to the stock exchanges has a major incentive to use a Big Four auditor, whose seal of approval will carry substantial weight in the markets. Nearly all the world's major multinationals use Big Four audit firms.

This is not to suggest that there are no other firms working worldwide. There are other networks with substantial cross-border business. However, the brand effect of the Big Four is very powerful. The second tier tend to provide referral services for each other when national clients have a major foreign operation, rather than provide a worldwide service to multinationals. In addition, belonging to an international network provides a means for the medium-sized firm to distinguish itself from competitors.

For the time being the audit profession remains one which is organized nationally, with international business done through exchanges with national offices in other countries. The Big Four move some of their staff from country to country, but this is usually to service international clients and there will always be a significant number of partners who have the national professional qualification in each major office. Consequently while they service multinational companies, a large part of the work is performed by national offices for national subsidiaries and there is very little cross-border work where staff in one country service a client in another.

The professional licensing and qualification structures militate against the transfer of staff between offices. In practically all countries the partners or shareholders in an audit firm have to hold national audit qualifications, so any international parent/national subsidiary structure, similar to a multinational, is not possible, and partners cannot easily transfer from one country to another.

The latter is mitigated to some extent by 'mutual recognition' of professional qualifications. Typically such agreements allow an auditor qualified in country A to acquire the professional qualification in country B by taking special examinations which deal only with local law. This has been the case in the EU for several years and there are also bilateral agreements between countries such as the USA and Canada, and Australia and New Zealand. However, professional bodies in individual countries are generally very reluctant to enter into mutual recognition agreements, partly because they fear dilution of professional standards, and partly because one of the reasons such organizations exist at all is to protect the national market for their members' services, so opening up the market to foreign competition is fundamentally unattractive.

The governance of the big international audit firms is a subject which has received a lot of attention in recent years. As indicated, the national licensing structure usually means that a parent/subsidiary relationship is not possible. Instead the firms operate as networks where each national office is autonomous, but signs an agreement to cover use of the brand name, revenue sharing, cost sharing and quality standards. In such circumstances the direct intervention of a controlling international management is virtually impossible.

> However, here in the US, the (Securities and Exchange) Commission staff continues to have difficulty in gaining access to foreign auditors' work papers on a timely basis when there is a question about the propriety of the financial reporting done by a foreign filer or a foreign subsidiary of a US company. The US (audit) firm almost invariably argues the foreign portion of the audit was done solely by a foreign affiliate of the firm that they have no control over, even though both market themselves to the public using the same brand name, and cannot require that the work papers be produced to those in the US requesting them.
>
> *Source*: Lynn E. Turner, former chief accountant of the US Securities and Exchange Commission. Extract from a speech made to the American Accounting Association, 12 August 2001.

A recent issue in this connection is the use by national offices of the international brand when signing audit reports on financial statements which have been prepared and audited to local standards. This problem was highlighted by Rahman (1997) who analysed the financial crisis in South East Asia. He came to the conclusion that companies based in that area had published financial statements, audited by the local member of a Big Four network, but not using international standards of disclosure and measurement. Foreign investors had been reassured by the auditor's name and had not realized that the accounts were prepared according to local rules. The subsequent currency crisis brought about a realization that, amongst other things, related party transactions and foreign currency borrowing had not been revealed and the level of risk was much higher than the investors had been made aware.

Since then, a number of prominent commentators, including the World Bank, have suggested that it is misleading to use an international audit brand and not do an audit to international standards. The profession has reacted, at an international level in a number of ways. The Big Four, together with the two largest mid-tier networks (Grant Thornton and BDO), have set up a big firm liaison committee to address such issues and now produce an annual survey (*GAAP 2001* was the most recent) which monitors convergence on IFRS.

National professional bodies are represented at an international level by the International Federation of Accountants (IFAC). IFAC has been working to improve the quality of audit in a number of ways. Since its creation in 1977, the organization has produced audit standards (see below) as well as providing guidance on ethics and education. In 2000 it changed its structure to include a separate division, the Forum of Firms, which represents international audit firms. Membership of the Forum is voluntary, but member firms have to agree to apply IFAC quality control norms throughout the world and submit to investigation by a disciplinary committee if necessary. The Forum has an executive committee, the Transnational Audit Committee. In theory this new structure should lead to a heightened awareness that the demands of the international capital markets are for a uniform standard of financial reporting and auditing. However, it will be a number of years before the new mechanisms are working effectively.

International standards

As has been discussed in Chapter 1 and Chapter 17, many multinationals have chosen to use either IASB standards or US GAAP for their worldwide consolidated accounts, and we shall not reiterate the arguments here. However, we will address the question of audit standards. There is probably not the same degree of variability in audit standards between (developed) countries as there is in accounting, not least because the economic consequences are not the same. There are, though, differences, as we have discussed earlier. As with accounting, the way round this is to specify audits based on international audit standards.

IFAC has a committee which produces International Standards of Auditing (ISAs) which may be used for international audits and which are also used by national audit regulation bodies as a benchmark. This committee was known as the International Auditing Practices Committee, but in 2002 changed its name to the International Auditing and Assurance Standards Board (IAASB). Its standards are shown in Table 20.2.

In 2001 the committee set up a working party whose aim is to have the IAASB's standards endorsed by the International Organisation of Securities Commissions (IOSCO) as being the minimum for companies listed on foreign exchanges. Such endorsement would put ISAs on the same footing as IFRS in relation to stock exchanges.

As with international accounting standards, the international auditing standards provide a benchmark set of practices capable of enhancing the value of financial information in the international markets. In addition, the guidelines provide a useful input into the development of national guidelines in countries where the profession is relatively small or in a state of evolution.

We have carried out our audit according to international auditing standards and standards recognised by the profession in Switzerland.

Source: Extract from KPMG audit report of Nestlé Group

Performing a group audit

The rest of the chapter is devoted to an analysis of the audit of the consolidated statements of a multinational company. By their nature, multi-location group audits represent greater complexity in their planning, execution and control than most simple company audits. As a result key audit procedures such as strategic planning, risk assessment, issuance of clear instructions and defined and agreed-upon reporting procedures are absolutely indispensable ingredients for the proper performance of multi-location (group) audit engagements.

While the thrust of this chapter is the group audit, the following gives a brief summary of the basic approach to individual company audit applied by an auditor. Thereafter subsequent sections concentrate on the group audit aspects.

Key aspects of an audit

It should be noted that a modern approach views every audit as a customized professional service, valuable to the management of the client company as well as to the traditional users of financial statements. The approach and methods are intended to address the needs and concerns of both management and the users of the financial statements, and require an understanding of the client's business, the nature of its transactions and its information, accounting and control systems. Financial statements on which the auditor reports summarize the results of business activity, and a thorough understanding of that activity is fundamental to the professional assessment of the financial statements.

Judgement pervades every aspect of the auditors' work, because absolute certainty is no more obtainable in auditing financial statements than it is in preparing them. The auditor must apply judgement constantly in assessing the reasonableness of the many decisions

Table 20.2 International Standards on Auditing (ISAs) and International Auditing Practice Statements (IAPSs)

	Preface to International Standards on Auditing and Related Services
	Glossary of Terms
100	Assurance engagements
120	Framework of International Standards on Auditing
200	Objective and General Principles Governing an Audit of Financial Statements
210	Terms of Audit Engagements
220	Quality Control for Audit Work
230	Documentation
240	Fraud and Error
250	Consideration of Laws and Regulations in an Audit of Financial Statements
260	Communications of Audit Matters with Those Charged with Governance
300	Planning
310	Knowledge of the Business
320	Audit Materiality
400	Risk Assessments and Internal Control
401	Auditing in a Computer Information Systems Environment
402	Audit Considerations Relating to Entities Using Service Organisations
500	Audit Evidence
501	Audit Evidence – Additional Considerations for Specific Items
510	Initial Engagements – Opening Balances
520	Analytical Procedures
530	Audit Sampling and Other Selective Testing Procedures
540	Auditing of Accounting Estimates
550	Related Parties
560	Subsequent Events
570	Going Concern
580	Management Representations
600	Using the Work of Another Auditor
700	The Auditor's Report on Financial Statements
710	Comparatives
720	Other Information in Documents Containing Audited Financial Statements
800	The Auditor's Report on Special Purpose Audit Engagements
810	The Examination of Prospective Financial Information
910	Engagements to Review Financial Statements
920	Engagements to Perform Agreed-upon Procedures Regarding Financial Information
930	Engagements to Compile Financial Information
1000	Inter-Bank Confirmation Procedures
1001	CIS Environments – Stand-alone Microcomputers
1002	CIS Environments – On-line Computer Systems
1003	CIS Environments – Database Systems
1004	The Relationship Between Bank Supervisors and External Auditors
1005	The Special Considerations in the Audit of Small Entities
1006	The Audit of International Commercial Banks
1007	Communications with Management
1008	Risk Assessments and Internal Control – CIS Characteristics and Considerations

Table 20.2 International Standards on Auditing (ISAs) and International Auditing Practice Statements (IAPSs) (*continued*)

1009	Computer-assisted Audit Techniques
1010	The Consideration of Environmental Matters in the Audit of Financial Statements
1011	Implications for Management and Auditors of the Year 2000 Issue
1012	The Audit of Derivative Financial Instruments

and estimates that underlie the client's financial statements and in evaluating audit evidence which is persuasive rather than conclusive.

The auditors' primary concern is not with individual transactions and balances as such but with the financial statements as a whole. The audit does not begin with an examination of individual transactions or documents. Rather it begins by taking an overview of the company's business, how it is organized, how its major operating units function and how its transactions are directed, controlled and recorded. This approach enables the auditor to focus quickly on those aspects of the business that significantly affect the financial statements and thereby reduce his effort on other aspects. For example, the company may have different kinds of activity, or its profits may be largely earned in one particular area, or it may have high economic risk exposures (foreign currency losses, long-term contract losses, etc.) in specific parts of the company. An understanding of the nature of the company's activities and organization provides the basis for assessing risk and for determining the audit strategy.

To apply this 'top-down' approach in an efficient manner, the auditor will divide the audit into manageable parts, often business units, reflecting the way the client is organized. The auditor also divides the business unit financial statements into suitable parts. For each component the auditor considers the underlying assertions (i.e. revenues, expenses, assets, liabilities, etc.), risks and possible controls. Audit procedures are then chosen with a view to obtaining sufficient evidence to support the assertions underlying the component.

The nature, extent and timing of the audit procedures the auditor performs to gain evidence to support the assertions is driven by his assessment of the risk that assertions may be invalidated by error or irregularity and the efficiency, as well as the effectiveness, of alternative audit procedures. For example, a profit generated on a single long-term contract where the company's client has not yet paid any money for the work would suggest a check on both the calculation of the costs and proportional profits recognized in the company's accounts and a confirmation that the client agrees the amount outstanding and has the resources to pay. On the other hand, the existence of a factory which the company has owned for years and in which it manufactures its main product does not require extensive investigation.

Within the audit firm, each audit client is the responsibility of a partner in the firm (known as the engagement partner). The audit of an individual company will be carried out under the detailed supervision of a manager (a 'senior') who has probably completed his professional examinations, who is assisted by other staff ('juniors') who are at varying stages in their professional training and carry out much of the detailed work on the client's premises. The audit will be carried out in compliance with the professional auditing standards which apply in the country where the client is located.

Audit cycle

Although the sequence of steps in which a specific audit takes place may vary from audit to audit, each audit involves three essential phases – planning, execution and completion. The three phases portray the audit as having a finite starting and ending point. In practice, there is a cycle to recurring audits: the completion of one year's audit naturally leads to and provides input for the planning phase of the following year's audit. The knowledge gained from the audit each year accumulates and contributes to ensuing audits.

Clients operate in different businesses, are exposed to different risks and have differing information, accounting and control systems. Accordingly, it is necessary to plan the approach to the audit in advance to address the specific risks and problem areas for that particular client. The planning phase involves a series of stages. First, the auditor develops the audit strategy for the audit as a whole. Then he or she performs more detailed planning for individual components to determine the specific procedures to be performed. Finally he or she prepares audit programmes. Generally this is done with reference to the auditor's files concerning previous audits and in discussion with the internal audit unit (if there is one) and financial management of the company concerned.

The execution phase puts the audit plan into action. It entails performing the planned audit procedures to obtain audit evidence. The purpose of the execution phase is to obtain sufficient audit satisfaction on which to base the audit report, i.e. to have sufficient assurance that the financial statements reflect the underlying records and give a fair representation of the company's position. Audit satisfaction is obtained by performing substantive audit procedures or by obtaining sufficient evidence to support reliance on controls.

Companies of any size should have internal control procedures to help ensure the accuracy of their accounting function and prevent fraud. Such controls are usually based on the principle of separation of functions, that is that purchases, for example, are authorized by someone distant from the payment procedure, and that payment requires authorization by someone distant from the purchasing and cheque validation procedure. This kind of approach is difficult in small companies because of the low volume of transactions, and the number of stages in processing has been reduced by sophisticated systems. Larger companies may well have an internal audit unit which is responsible for installing such controls and checking that they are effective. The external auditor has to form an opinion as to the viability of the controls (sometimes referred to as the 'control environment'), since that will determine whether verification of individual transactions ('substantive checking') is necessary in order to have an opinion as to the accuracy of the company's financial records.

The execution phase will frequently be divided into one or more interim or pre-final visits carried out before the client's year-end and a final visit carried out after the year-end. For small, independent companies the audit often follows on the year-end, but companies of any size usually need to finalize their annual accounts as soon as possible after the year-end. Consequently it is appropriate to carry out some audit work prior to the year-end. Groups of companies in particular have the problem that they have to consolidate the accounts of many subsidiaries and that the audit of these needs to be substantially complete before the consolidation process can start. Large, public companies often try to announce their estimated profit for the year within three months of the year-end, and they can only do this with any certainty if they have already completed draft accounts. The time constraints produced by the need to report draft annual figures to the financial markets can cause considerable pressure for audit firms, and it is desirable to identify potential problems as early as possible.

As part of the completion phase, the engagement partner and senior members of the audit team critically review the work performed. The objective of the review is to ensure that the audit plan has been effectively implemented and to conclude whether the audit findings have been correctly evaluated and whether the audit objectives have been met.

Part of this process may involve negotiating with company management in the event that there are assertions which the auditor does not feel have been supported, and which therefore need adjustment, or where the auditor disagrees with the accounting solution that has been found for a particular problem. This is a process that is usually resolved satisfactorily but has the potential to lead to qualification of the accounts. The auditor will usually prepare a 'management letter', once the audit is completed, to report in detail to the company management on any weaknesses observed in the systems or other areas needing attention. This is a standard part of the audit engagement but this report is not communicated to shareholders. In subsequent audits the auditor will usually check what action has been taken in the weak areas identified.

In addition, it is necessary to step back from the detail and perform an overall review of the financial statements. This review, in conjunction with the conclusions already drawn from the detailed audit work, should provide a proper basis for the audit report. It should focus on the areas of major significance or risk in order to confirm that they have been dealt with adequately both in the audit work and in the financial statements.

Group audit

Moving on to the group audit of a multinational company, the external audit firm has to report on the fair presentation of the consolidated financial statements of a multinational company and its subsidiaries. This may be in accordance with local accounting principles but, as discussed, increasingly is in accordance with International Accounting Standards. At the same time, the audit must be conducted in line with auditing standards, and those appropriate may well be the International Standards of Auditing. The consolidated financial statements are the ones the group will in general use for the purposes of raising finance, reporting to shareholders, etc. It is generally these statements that attract the greatest risk of subsequent litigation if the client runs into difficulties.

The group auditor has an obligation to express an opinion on the group consolidated financial statements and is responsible for establishing the overall group audit plan tailored to the requirements of the individual multinational and for determining the scope of the audit work to be performed throughout the group worldwide. The group audit partner (based at the 'principal office', which is normally in the same location as the client group's headquarters) should establish the overall audit plan and should oversee its satisfactory completion. This does not imply that the principal audit partner assumes responsibility for work assigned to supporting offices (other offices of the same firm worldwide who are involved in auditing parts of the group), particularly in other countries, but does contemplate an overview of their work, including visits to the client's important locations as necessary to be familiar with local operations and conditions, and to be satisfied with the work carried out.

Multinational companies frequently have an audit committee (companies issuing securities in the USA and therefore registered with the SEC are required to have such a committee). This usually consists of non-executive board members who may also invite senior company executives concerned with the accounting and internal control functions to attend. The idea, which is American in origin, is that audit and control problems may be discussed more easily in the absence of senior operating management. Both senior and junior financial management may not wish to jeopardize their position in the company by openly criticizing procedures. The presence of outside directors should in theory also prevent negative audit findings being sidelined subsequently. The group auditor will therefore often work with the members of the audit committee, rather than the board of directors.

To have a sound basis on which to plan a group audit and to issue clear instructions to supporting offices, the principal audit partner should have an understanding of

- the group's management structure and philosophy;
- group management's expectations;
- the group's significant business activities in each of its locations;
- geographical, political and other environmental factors which affect operations significantly;
- any factors which give rise to significant risk;
- statutory requirements, minority interests, loan agreement provisions or other circumstances which may require a local examination of greater scope than the principal office might otherwise require.

The knowledge needed for effective planning may be obtained in a number of ways. These include discussions with management in the client company, visits to client locations and the communication of information by supporting offices. It is the responsibility of the principal office, when requesting work of a supporting office, to issue written instructions that clearly describe the work to be done, the required form of reporting and the reporting deadlines. The instructions should also identify the partner and manager responsible for coordination of the group audit and provide any other pertinent information.

Before finalizing deadlines with parent company management, the principal office should ensure that they are consistent with those given to subsidiaries by the parent company. It is also advisable to notify supporting offices, especially smaller offices, of the desired deadlines as soon as possible so that problems, if any, in meeting the deadlines can be identified and addressed.

The principal office may become aware of matters that should be considered by subsidiary management in preparing statutory or other reports that will be publicly available and by supporting offices in reporting on them. Parent company management should be requested to inform the subsidiary of such matters. Failing this, the principal office should take other steps to ensure that the supporting office does not issue a report that would be inappropriate in the circumstances known to the principal office.

The group auditor assumes all responsibility for coordinating the work of local auditors to the extent necessary for the audit of the group accounts. Accordingly, he or she will issue detailed group audit instructions to the local auditors. The group auditor should monitor the performance of the local auditors and review the timely receipt of their reports and other material.

Audit strategy

The group auditor will plan the audit from a top-down perspective designed to:

- update the auditor's specific and detailed understanding of the group's operational philosophy, organizational culture and corporate objectives,
- review and update his or her understanding of the management and organizational structure and ways in which management plans, conducts and controls operations.

Extensive partner and manager participation in the planning process ensures the use of proper judgement and experience in the development and execution of the audit plan. The audit strategy is based on meetings with management and is subject to revision in response to changes in the group's control structure and operating environment.

The primary concern of the group auditor is not with individual transactions and balances but with the financial statements taken as a whole. The audit is planned and performed to obtain reasonable, but not absolute, assurance that the financial statements are free from material mis-statement. The audit strategy is designed to address audit objectives related to the completeness, authenticity and fair and consistent presentation of the financial statements.

The principal components of the group audit strategy will include:

- *Consideration of inherent risks*; that is, the susceptibility of the financial statements to material error or irregularity, before recognizing the effectiveness of control systems (for example, is the profit measure heavily dependent upon the valuation of year-end inventory and work in progress?).

- *Consideration of the control environment* and the extent to which this affects the control risk; that is, the possibility that the control systems may fail to prevent or detect material error or irregularity (is the efficacy of controls checked regularly? are there frequent changes of personnel in sensitive areas?).

- *Division of the group into business units* (offices) and consideration of the audit scope to apply to each unit, the inherent risks considered to apply and materiality.

- *Analysis of the financial statement components* and consideration of the inherent risk associated with each component.

During planning, the group auditor identifies the significant audit risks attached to the engagement. Exercising his/her professional judgement, s/he selects audit procedures that s/he believes can reduce risk to an acceptable level in relation to the consolidated financial statements taken as a whole. Audit risk is defined by professional standards as the combination of:

- *Inherent risk* (the susceptibility of the financial statements to material errors or irregularities, before recognizing the effectiveness of the control systems).

- *Control risk* (the risk that the control systems may fail to prevent or detect material error on a timely basis).

- *Detection risk* (the risk that audit procedures may fail to uncover material error or irregularity, if it exists).

The group auditor considers risks arising from the nature of the client's operations, the expenditures, the financing plan and other pertinent factors. S/he isolates the sources of information, the transactions and other areas of audit interest that have the greatest, or the least, potential for material errors or irregularities. For each component, s/he identifies and assesses the specific risks associated with it and stops at the stage where further detailed analysis will not result in a more effective audit. The group auditor's objective is to reduce those risks to an acceptably low level.

Audit scope

Multi-location audits commonly involve varying the scope of work either among or within business units (i.e. having a different range of audit tasks in different parts of the company). The audit scope to be applied by the local auditors is based upon materiality and audit risk assessment criteria as evaluated by the group auditor. This audit scope setting process might need changing if during the audit process it becomes apparent that the actual situation and/or key data are significantly different.

The scope of auditing procedures to be applied at a unit within the client group is also based upon a number of other considerations such as:

- the candour and integrity of corporate and local management;
- operating, management and financial control systems;
- the auditor's knowledge of the group's business conditions and changes in operations;
- new requirements of the relevant regulatory bodies;
- cumulative audit findings of prior audits, including areas qualitatively and quantitatively material and matters susceptible to subjective judgements;
- planned rotation of audit emphasis to maintain the effectiveness and efficiency of the audit.

The audit scope will be set so as to enable the group auditor to express an opinion upon the consolidated financial statements. Accordingly, savings can be obtained by reductions in the scope of the work performed at certain selected locations which are of lesser significance to the group's financial position and which do not require a full scope examination for local statutory purposes. The group auditor therefore establishes different audit scope levels with different levels of audit work to be conducted by the supporting offices for group consolidation purposes. The following are various possibilities open to the principal office for modifying the audit scope of a business unit:

- provide the supporting office with a planning memorandum and detailed audit programmes, including scope decisions, for all or certain audit areas;
- request the supporting office to perform an audit, either of certain accounts or of the financial statements as a whole, with scope restrictions related to materiality limits set by the principal office;
- request the supporting office to perform such work as it considers necessary on certain accounts, functions, etc.;
- provide specific guidelines for a review (as opposed to an audit) of the business unit's financial statements;
- request certain audit procedures, such as observation of inventory counts or circularization of accounts receivable.

As a rule the group auditor keeps in mind that, at least at a consolidated level, every component of the consolidated financial statements is to be adequately covered by the various audit procedures applied at every location. Wherever the group audit approach involves limited procedures and/or rotation of emphasis, the group auditor should be satisfied that the management understands the limitations of the audit.

The supporting office (normally a national partnership within the same network in another country) is responsible for completing the work requested by the group auditor and in accordance with the time, format and other requirements as stipulated in the group audit instructions. In addition, the local auditor is responsible for the audit of the local financial statements in accordance with the local country laws.

The group auditor issues his group audit instructions to the supporting offices. This document specifies the audit work to be done by the local auditors on the consolidation schedules. The usual contents of group audit instructions are as follows:

- objectives of the examination;
- description of the business unit (e.g. subsidiary) to be examined;
- timing of the work;
- scope of the work;
- accounting and auditing issues;
- reporting on work;
- non-audit services;
- fees;
- names of key personnel at the principal (instructing) office;
- copies of most recent annual report and any relevant internal audit reports, minutes and other documents.

Working with unrelated audit firms

Multinational groups sometimes utilize a number of unrelated external audit firms in their various subsidiaries. The group auditor may be asked, in issuing audit opinions on a group's consolidated accounts, to utilize and rely upon the work of other external auditors concerning *material* subsidiaries and components of the group. This is clearly a delicate area and it presents the group auditor not only with audit coverage issues (i.e. is the work of the other auditor reliable and adequate for my purposes?) but also with some genuine logistical and organizational problems. The International Auditing Standard dealing with this says:

> The principal auditor should qualify his report or disclaim an opinion when he concludes, based on his procedures, that he cannot use the work of the other auditor and has not been able to perform sufficient additional procedures with respect to the financial statements of the component reported on by the other auditor (ISA 5, para 11).

The group auditor should be satisfied with the professional reputation and independence of the other auditors. To reach this position, the following have to be considered:

- making inquiries about the professional reputation and standing of the other auditors;
- inquiring whether the other auditors are familiar with applicable accounting principles, auditing standards and requirements of regulatory agencies, and will report in accordance with them;
- notifying the other auditors that coordination with them will be necessary to achieve a proper review of matters affecting the consolidation of the financial statements;
- making inquiries about the independence of the other auditors;
- notifying the other auditors in advance that the group auditor will be relying on and, where applicable, referring to their reports.

Where the group auditor assumes sole responsibility for the group report, an additional element of caution is advisable, particularly if the part audited by other auditors is only marginally immaterial. It may be necessary to undertake one or more of the following procedures, especially if the minimum procedures discussed above are inconclusive:

- visiting the other auditors to discuss the audit procedures followed and the results;
- reviewing the other auditors' work programmes;
- reviewing the other auditors' working papers, including their evaluation of internal controls and their conclusions as to other significant aspects of the audit;
- requesting completion of an audit questionnaire where it is accepted practice to do so;
- reviewing the tax accounts in cases where the other auditors are examining part of the group tax return.

Consideration should also be given to:

- participating in discussions about the accounts with management of subsidiaries audited by the other auditors;
- making supplementary tests of accounts audited by the other auditors.

Before undertaking these additional procedures, the group auditor should consider the need to inform parent and/or subsidiary management of his or her plans.

Where the group auditor is not satisfied with the other auditors' competence s/he cannot simply dismiss or ignore this fact by referring to divided audit responsibility in their report on the group accounts. In such circumstances the group auditor should carry out additional procedures to obtain satisfaction about the other auditors' work. In the event that, in the final analysis, s/he is unable to obtain satisfaction regarding the reliability of the other auditors' report and work s/he should qualify the report accordingly.

Audit of consolidation and year-end process

The group auditor should carry out an audit of the consolidation process, and this would comprise:

1. Verification that the correct subsidiary accounts have been properly consolidated.
2. The audit of the consolidation eliminations and corrections.
3. Evaluation of the audit adjustments reported by supporting offices.
4. Final analytical review of the consolidated financial statements by the group auditor.

The group auditor reviews the audit reports and memoranda on examination of the supporting offices. The group auditor relates the contents of these reports to his observations arrived at as part of his analytical review work and the financial reviews done by the company. In appropriate cases the group auditor requests additional information.

The consolidation process requires certain eliminations (such as inter-company items, unrealized profits on stocks) as well as certain consolidation entries (such as provisions in appropriate cases, depreciation of goodwill, etc.). It can be further complicated through different percentages of participation in group companies, different accounting dates, foreign currency treatments (such as hyperinflation) and acquisitions and disposals during the year. Minority interests in the group profits and group assets have to be calculated. Also the calculation of the tax effects of consolidation entries can be difficult.

Apart from the consolidation of the balance sheet and the income statement numbers, the group auditor will also carry out consolidation audit work on the notes to the accounts, including tests on the adequacy of disclosures.

In order to cover the period between the receipt of the reports of the supporting auditors and the final signing date of the audit report on the group accounts, the group auditor will carry out certain 'subsequent events' procedures. These procedures are aimed to ensure that no new facts or events have taken place after the submission of individual company reports which would require amendments or disclosure in the group accounts.

The group auditor ensures through the completion of appropriate disclosure checklists and further by reference to the law, statutes and accounting standards that the group accounts comply with the legal and other reporting requirements, such as those of foreign stock exchanges. The group auditor ensures that any deficiencies and shortcomings are corrected.

The group auditor accumulates the results of his own audit work and those of the supporting offices and discusses these with group management (or the audit committee) for appropriate follow-up or corrections. The group auditor evaluates what the cumulative effect, if any, of all the unadjusted corrections and uncertainties will have on his audit opinion on the consolidated accounts.

At the end of the process the auditor will also report to the audit committee on the adequacy of internal controls and any other matters which it is felt require attention. In recent years the directors' responsibilities for the preparation of the annual report have been increasingly emphasized and in some jurisdictions this has led to a position where the directors are obliged to state in the annual report that in their view the internal control system is adequate.

Conclusion

The group audit involves attestation of the validity of the most visible financial statements produced by a multinational group. The group auditor is not obliged to audit the statements of group subsidiaries as such, but the group statements depend, obviously, on the accuracy of the component parts, and therefore the relationship between the group auditor and those auditing subsidiaries is crucial to the risk of mis-statement or error. The preparation of the group accounts and therefore also their audit involves meticulous planning and careful coordination of a very tight timetable in order to produce reliable figures rapidly. This has to be done within a controlled budget.

The successful group audit calls for a clear identification of the areas of the audit which have the greatest inherent risk and a coordination of resources in order to obtain the maximum certainty in the most effective manner. Clear communication between local auditors and the group auditor of accounting information but also other information about potential economic problems and similar hazards are essential. This communication and planning should be a continuing cycle which leads naturally from one year's audit to the next and a systematic reduction of risk through growth of knowledge.

The external group audit has an important role to play for the multinational. As far as the financial markets are concerned, the auditors' report is a guarantee of the reliability of the financial statements, and these financial statements underpin the company's ability to raise money and to generate capital gains for existing shareholders. Given the variability of audit around the world, the group audit provides an assurance that even the most far-flung subsidiary has been checked adequately. The importance to the markets of this assurance of uniformity of quality is what explains the rise of the Big Four global accounting networks. Internally, the audit also provides a useful tool to management by confirming that control systems are working properly and by identifying potential problems.

References

Burlaud, A., Messina, M. and Walton, P.J. (1996) Depreciation: concepts and practices in France and the UK. *European Accounting Review* **5**(2): 299–316.

Mintzberg, H. (1979) *The Structuring of Organizations*. Prentice-Hall, Englewood Cliffs, NJ.

Ordelheide, D. (1993) True and fair view: a European and a German perspective. *European Accounting Review* **2**(1): 81–90.

Trolliet, C. (1994) *L'Exercice de la Profession Comptable dans la CEE*. Editions Comptables Malesherbes, Paris.

Walton, P. (1996) Accountancy professionals in the global classroom. *Accountancy* international edition, December, pp. 54–55.

Further Reading

Arens, A.A. and Loebbecke, J.K. (1994) *Auditing: an Integrated Approach*, 6th edn. Prentice-Hall, Englewood Cliffs, NJ.

Needles, B.E. (ed.) (1985) *Comparative International Auditing Standards*. American Accounting Association, Sarasota, Florida.

Sherer, M. and Turley S. (1991) *Current Issues in Auditing*. Paul Chapman Publishing, London.

Simunic, D.A. (2001) Statutory Auditing. In M. Warner (ed.) *International Encyclopedia of Business and Management*, 2nd edn. Thomson Learning, London.

Woolf, E. (1994) *Auditing Today*. Prentice-Hall, Englewood Cliffs, NJ.

Appendix: Engagement Timetable

Summarized below is the outline of the audit process and the approximate timing involved. The bold line for each activity depicts the timeframe for the activity in question, but is not intended to illustrate the time actually spent.

ABC Group – Engagement Timetable

ACTIVITY	20X1					20X2					
Planning											
● Strategic plan development	—										
● Accumulation of fee information	—										
● Audit strategy memorandum		—	—								
● Agreement of audit strategy with Audit Committee				—							
● Issuance of audit instructions				—							
Interim audit											
● Branches/subsidiaries			—	—	—						
● Head office				—							
Final audit											
● Branches/subsidiaries						—	—				
● Head office							—				
● Consolidated accounts							—				
● Draft report to the Audit Committee								—			
● Final audit report								—			
● Internal control memorandum to management									—	—	
● Letter on internal controls to the Audit Committee											—

21 Accounting differences and financial statement analysis

Bernard Raffournier and Peter Walton

The practice of financial statement analysis in an international context, i.e. using financial statements prepared in different countries, poses special problems due to the lack of comparability of the methods of valuation and presentation used by the preparers. The origins of these differences have been discussed in previous chapters and we will here concentrate on their impact on financial statement analysis. In fact professional users of financial statements (brokers, investment institutions, etc.) find these problems with analysis a major obstacle to investment since, apart from anything else this makes it difficult for them to use standardized decision models which depend on accounting inputs. Research by Choi and Levich (1991) showed, by way of example, that 50% of investors interviewed in New York, London and Tokyo did not invest in foreign stocks largely as a result of not being able to analyse their accounts. The problem is experienced not only by investors but by companies wishing to attract investment (as is discussed in Chapter 17). They are able to address it by voluntarily aligning their accounting policies with IASB or US rules. For example, Deutsche Bank opted to produce consolidated accounts according to IAS, citing, amongst other advantages, that the international investment community would then be able to analyse the accounts more easily and value the company more appropriately.

For the moment such companies remain the exception and analysis in an international context remains a difficult exercise. By way of illustration, the debt/equity ratio is one of the most frequently calculated analytical ratios but different accounting policies make cross-border comparisons fragile:

- Debt (number influenced by: classification of some debt as short-term, capitalization of finance leases, exclusion of financing subsidiaries from consolidated accounts, provisions and in particular pension provisions).

- Equity (number influenced by: revaluation of fixed assets, write-off of goodwill against reserves, use of provisions and excessive depreciation to reduce profits and build hidden reserves, treatment of minority interests).

In addition to the ways in which the accounting policies affect the ratio, this particular ratio is subject to the fact that different countries see the optimal mix between debt and equity quite differently from one another.

Attempts have been made in the past, notably by the European Federation of Financial Analysts Societies (EFFAS), to devise standard analytical approaches for use in international analysis but we do not propose to follow that route. In our view, the reasons for undertaking analysis may be many and varied, and the analyst is better advised to look very closely at the individual companies under review rather than use any standard rules of thumb. Those who want the famous 'quick and dirty' methods beloved of some financial houses will have to look elsewhere; we think international analysis should be slow and careful!

Before looking at the main accounting differences and their consequences for analysis, we think it is worth looking at the actual practice of financial analysis because the diversity of national economic and social environments which affects accounting also affects analytical methodology.

Different approaches to analysis

Although analysts nearly always use the same tools (comparison of ratios through time and space), financial analysis is far from being a universal technique. There is a variety of analytical approaches which corresponds to the variety of accounting approaches. We can, therefore, conveniently adopt the same approach as in accounting and recognize an Anglo-Saxon method and a continental European method.

The Anglo-Saxon approach is, of course, oriented towards the capital markets. It concerns itself generally with the point of view of an investor who is interested essentially in the risk and return on an investment. Based on a theoretical model where the value of an asset is the present value of future cash flows, the accent is placed on the prediction of cash flows and estimates of the level of risk of the business.

Great importance is placed on the earnings per share ratio, based on its presumed correlation with cash flows. In order to enhance the predictive ability of this ratio it is necessary to eliminate the effects of events which are not part of the normal activity of the company. Consequently stress is laid on distinguishing between ordinary and extraordinary activities, and also operations which are being disposed of. By way of example, the British analysts[1] have produced their own very detailed standard for calculating this ratio, finding the official definition not to their liking (see Chapter 6 on the UK).

The investment is generally seen in the context of the management of a portfolio, rather than as a long-term investment. The forecasting horizon is therefore relatively near, given the liquidity of the market, which allows shares to be sold at any time. This is not to say that there are not some investment funds which hold for the long term, or indeed some which value on the basis of dividend streams.

Finance theory would suggest that the market is efficient, that is to say that the share price impounds all the information available. The efficiency of the market also presumes that companies cannot affect the share price through accounting manipulations because the financial statements are only one of the sources of information available to investors. Having said that, it is far from clear that investors are never taken in by creative accounting. Equally brokers are usually on the lookout for shares that are undervalued (or indeed overvalued), and will often attempt to sell shares to investors on the basis of revised profit estimates or revised risk assessments which suggest that the share is undervalued by the market at a given moment (or advise them to sell where they believe the share is overvalued).

The continental European approach differs in many ways from this (e.g. see Colasse 2001). It is first more all-embracing because it is not limited to an assessment of risk and return. It tries rather to carry out a full diagnosis which includes other aspects such as the long-term financial stability of the company. This approach is less that of the portfolio manager, concerned with the profitability and liquidity of the investment, than that of the investor concerned about the long-term life of the business. It corresponds more to that of other stakeholders in the business, especially employees.

The question of financial stability takes on particular importance in the light of the long-term nature of the study. This approach gives a special prominence to the idea of working capital, despite the consolidation of the financial markets which has caused the distinction between long-term and short-term finance to lose much of its former importance.

The analysis of performance is not limited to financial profitability, but rather extends to economic viability. The business is considered as a wealth-creating entity and emphasis is placed on the calculation of wealth generated and its division between the different factors of production (suppliers of capital and labour). The concern for longevity and financial stability leads to a preoccupation also with maintaining productive capacity and with cash flow generated from operations. The analysis of the profits is therefore often accompanied (particularly in France and Germany) by an analysis of the development of value added and its distribution. Some German companies supply a statement of value added (Haller 1997) in addition to the usual statements (balance sheet, profit and loss account and notes).

The continental European approach gives much less importance to stock exchange information than does its Anglo-Saxon equivalent, because, amongst other things, it is practised in countries where the market for shares is less developed and does not constitute the principal source of financing for companies. Belief in the efficiency of the markets is much less usual. Accounting figures are also treated with caution because the investors in these countries know what influence taxation has and understand the biased view of the company provoked by an excessive concern for prudence and the possibility of manipulating the published results through certain accounting practices (hidden reserves in German-speaking countries).

At the risk of generalizing, we can say that the Anglo-Saxon analyst and the continental European analyst do not look at the issuer with the same eyes. The qualities that would lead to a positive investment decision are different, and expectations about the nature of the accounting information being offered are different. Consequently the sort of ratios calculated are different, which means that in international analysis the impact of different accounting policies falls differently, depending upon who is doing the analysis. Having made that point, it should also be noted that just as accounting for large companies is becoming more and more internationalized and homogeneous, so are financial analysis techniques, and capital market-oriented methodologies are increasingly being used by continental European analysts.

The place of financial ratios

The rest of this chapter focuses on the impact that different measurement and recognition policies may have on inputs to accounting ratios. However, one should not forget that ratios and accounting numbers generally are only part of the process of evaluating a company.

The first issue is that, of course, accounting numbers are not the only input into the assessment of a company's prospects. Analysts use many other factors, mostly economic, about the state of the economies where the company trades, the state of the industry, etc., to help predict future performance. An example of this is given in Walton (1994) who cites Moody's, the credit rating agency, which examines the following questions when giving a credit rating to a bond issue:

Industry

Company

Capital structure

Sovereign risk

Bond instrument

Financial flexibility

Capital expenditure

Internal cash flow

Competitors

Use of debt capacity

Customers

Management risk appetite

Moody's talk to company management – and indeed most large companies now have an active policy of seeking out analysts and presenting the company in 'roadshows'. Since a firm like Moody's provides ratings for all large companies, they talk to all the competing managements too, and therefore have a broad picture of competition and patterns of development. Moody's offer the following 'rating pyramid' which illustrates how they approach the rating decision:

Sovereign macroeconomic analysis:
↓
Regulatory environment
(national and global)
↓
Competitive trends
in sector
↓
Market position
↓
Quantitative analysis:
financial statements
past performance
future projections
↓
Qualitative analysis:
management
strategic direction
financial
flexibility
↓
Rating

Clearly the analysis of the individual company statements play an important role, and so also does comparison within the industry sector, but financial accounting numbers are not the only input to the decision process.

Another general point to make about ratios is that there are no 'magic' ratios which somehow encapsulate all that is important to understand about the position of a particular company. First, ratios can only be interpreted on a comparative basis: comparing one company with another in the same sector (cross-sectional analysis), and comparing the same company over time (time-series analysis). Time-series comparisons are particularly important because they show the *trends* in a management's behaviour and these are important for predicting the future.

Secondly, while the Anglo-Saxon financial press tends to fix upon single numbers, and in particular earnings per share, this is extremely crude information which is frequently misinterpreted. Such a single number can be profoundly influenced by a particular set of circumstances, by a chance event and up to a point by management manipulations. In any event the return on an investment can never be evaluated independently of the risk associated with the underlying activity.

An analyst must always answer the question: is this company likely to give an adequate rate of return in the future, in relation to the perceived riskiness of the activity and the current price of the company's securities. This process involves considering all aspects which bear upon the return (within the financial statements: sales, operating costs, financing costs, availability of cash flow to finance growth, management's ability to improve profitability), the riskiness of the company (within the financial statements: gearing, adequacy of working capital, management of finance, etc.).

Stickney (1990) writes of the financial statements as 'score sheets' of a firm's business activities which measure these and present them 'in a form that interested parties can understand'. He illustrates the areas to be understood as shown in Figure 21.1.

The analyst must try to understand the company, and use the financial statements to gain as much insight as possible.

Factors that generate differences

In this section we review those factors that influence the accounting numbers presented by individual companies, and therefore the inputs into the analytical models used by capital market intermediaries and inevitably their perceptions of the company.

Presentation of financial statements

The information given in financial statements has always been much more plentiful in the Anglo-Saxon countries. British and American companies have for many years published

Figure 21.1 Understanding financial statements

fairly extensive 'notes to the accounts' while their European counterparts have long been satisfied with the publication of just a balance sheet and profit and loss account with a minimum of additional information. This difference is due primarily to the financial markets which play a much more important role in the Anglo-Saxon world and the concern for transparency which has usually been displayed by the accounting regulators in those countries.

As a consequence of the internationalization of business, national differences have tended to disappear in favour of an alignment on more complete sets of information. The majority of the largest companies in the industrialized world now produce comparable accounting information, whatever their legal obligations may be. National regulations are themselves becoming harmonized under the influence of international standards and above all of efforts between states. The Fourth Directive has thus imposed on continental European companies the obligation to prepare notes which form part of the financial statements and which, in addition to certain compulsory items, are supposed to contain all the information necessary to understand the balance sheet and income statement. In this sense the work of the international analyst is becoming simpler, but nevertheless there remain significant differences in the presentation of financial data, not only in the statements but also in the notes.

The balance sheet can be presented either horizontally (column of assets accompanied by a column of liabilities and equity)[2] or vertically (assets then liabilities then equity). The first presentation places emphasis on the relationship between resources (liabilities and equity) and their uses (assets). It illustrates the balance sheet equation that sources of finance equals uses of finance. As such it is typical of an approach which considers the enterprise as a pool of resources and favours the calculation of major financing relationships, particularly working capital. It is not therefore surprising that this is the presentation favoured by countries in the Franco-German tradition. In France this presentation is required by the Plan Comptable Général.

It is a linguistic curiosity that whereas French and German have single words for each side of the balance sheet (assets = Actif or Aktiva, financing = Passif or Passiva), English has no single word for the financing side, always splitting this between equity and liabilities (the latter word has, furthermore, a pejorative connotation in English). Some would argue there is also a conceptual split which is evidenced in balance sheet presentation. The vertical presentation places emphasis on equity and its residual nature which derives from the formulation 'assets less liabilities equals equity'. It considers the business more as capital invested by the owners than as a pool of resources. The vertical approach is used by nearly all British companies, although it is only used by a minority of US companies.

In the balance sheet assets are classified according to their liquidity and debt according to maturity. The order of classification establishes some relationship between assets and debts of a long-term nature. This classification by increasing liquidity and shortening maturity leads to the presentation first of fixed assets and permanent capital. Combined with a horizontal presentation, this also brings out working capital. This is the required presentation in Belgium and France for individual company accounts. There is, however, no automatic connection between a horizontal presentation and classification in ascending liquidity and decreasing maturity. This order of liquidity is used in the UK, even though a vertical presentation is preferred, while the reverse order is used in horizontal balance sheets in the USA.

The order of presentation is theoretically a secondary consideration because the differences are transparent. However, there are some nuances. The continental European balance sheet includes deferred charges and deferred credits as a separate heading at the bottom of the asset side and financing side respectively. These are rarely shown separately in the vertical balance sheet and tend to disappear into other headings. Deferred charges such as prepayments will appear under 'sundry debtors' as a current asset but the heading may also include expenses related to asset purchases to be written off over five years (which in some jurisdictions would be added to the carrying value of the related asset) or share issuance charges (written off against share premium in other jurisdictions). These are, though, rarely substantial items.

Similarly, there is the delicate question of the classification of any short-term element of long-term debtors and creditors. There are two opposing views: some accountants think that any portion of medium- and long-term debtors and creditors which is due in less than one year should be reclassified as short-term assets and liabilities in strict application of the classification of balance sheet items by maturity (this is the case in the UK and USA). Others give priority to the nature of the debtor or creditor and oppose these regular reclassifications and prefer that the information about the portion due in less than one year should simply be given in the notes. The financial analyst needs to pay attention to the policy pursued by the company or risk having an incorrect view of its financing, working capital and liquidity.

The income statement can also be presented in different ways. Both the horizontal format (revenues and expenses in columns) and the vertical format (single column with revenues followed by expenses) are both found. However, it is in the classification of expenses that a more obvious difference resides. Analysis of expenses by nature (raw materials, depreciation, staff costs, taxation, etc.) is generally found in the countries that have a legal concept of accounting (Germany, France, Spain, Italy, etc.); the analysis by function (cost of sales, distribution cost, administration, etc.), which reflects a management accounting approach, is traditional in Anglo-Saxon countries where financial accounting and management accounting are less distant from each other. The information provided is different but is equally useful, so it is difficult to say which presentation is the more desirable (a point of view reflected by IAS 1, on the presentation of financial statements). There is nothing, of course, preventing companies from giving a second analysis in the notes, as the IASB suggests.

Another difference is in the turnover figure. There is a tradition in continental Europe for showing production rather than sales, with a corresponding transfer to or from the balance sheet for the amount by which sales and production differ.

In many countries there is no requirement to prepare a financing statement. Most large companies do, however, prepare one in some form or other. Two main models are found. The older model is based on the notion of working capital (the excess of long-term finance over the investment in fixed assets, or, if one prefers, the excess of current assets over current liabilities). This model focuses on that portion of long-term financing which is devoted to financing the company's trading cycle (stocks, debtors, etc.). It is based on the idea that there is a relationship between the period of the financing and the length of life of the use to which it is put, or expressed more precisely, on the hypothesis that the permanent production capacity (buildings, plant, machinery, etc.) should be financed by long-term instruments (equity, long- and medium-term debt). This model relates to a preoccupation with financial equilibrium and is therefore more in line with the continental European than the Anglo-Saxon concept of accounting and is often found in Germany. It is also the model proposed by the French Plan Comptable Général, and one finds examples also in many Spanish and Italian companies. However, even in these countries this model is starting to be replaced by the cash flow statement.

The cash flow statement is the model used in the Anglo-Saxon countries. It is the one preferred by the IASB. The basis of it is the company's treasury, defined as cash and cash equivalents (highly liquid short-term investments). The object of the statement is to set out the monetary flows that have occurred during the financial year. This approach relates very well to the Anglo-Saxon idea that the essential object of financial reporting is to facilitate forecasts of future cash flows (an objective which is formally set out by both the FASB conceptual framework and that of the IASB). The cash flows are generally classified into three types: operating cash flows, investing cash flows and financing. Given that the nature of the accounting system is to concentrate on economic transactions and not inflows and outflows of cash (i.e. accruals accounting), this can pose problems. This is why the cash flows can normally be calculated either directly or through a reconstitution based on the reported net profit to which are added back depreciation and provisions. While Australia and Japan require the use of the direct method, it is only recommended in other countries.

Methods of financing

Financing habits differ considerably between countries. It is generally known that in Japan and Germany, and indeed widely in continental Europe, bank lending is the main form of financing for companies, whereas in Anglo-Saxon countries share issue is much more common. This makes international comparisons difficult. One cannot really compare the debt/equity ratio of a Japanese or German company with that of an American or British business. Equally one cannot expect that a German or Japanese company would have an interest cover ratio equivalent to that of an Anglo-Saxon company of similar quality.

These differences in financial behaviour are also manifest in the dividend distribution policy. It is generally accepted that Anglo-Saxon companies pay higher dividends than their German or Japanese equivalents. A pay-out ratio of 4% (of capital) would therefore seem low in the USA but satisfactory or even generous in a German or Swiss context.

Commercial practices are also a source of important differences. In continental Europe credit given by companies to each other plays an essential role in financing the business, because practically all transactions are on credit. Trade credit currently runs for at least 60 days in some countries such as France (and indeed runs for so long in some Eastern European economies that companies are reluctant to recognize sales transactions on an accruals basis because they risk paying income tax before the client has settled – if they ever do). In the USA, on the other hand, most transactions are paid in cash with the business cycle financed largely by bank lending. A comparison of average credit periods given by suppliers or to debtors is rarely useful when comparing companies from different countries.

Law and taxation

The influence of law and taxation is the aspect which most clearly distinguishes between accounting systems. The two extremes are the German system and the Anglo-Saxon one. The former is characterized by the legal nature of the accounting rules and the alignment of accounting on tax requirements. On the other hand, the Anglo-Saxon model is one where the authority of accounting standards derives from practice and accounting is, with few exceptions, totally independent of taxation. The accounting of most countries is found between these two extremes. Overall one could say that the countries with a Roman law system (France, Italy, Spain, etc.) and Japan tend towards the German model. The relative influence of the two models has a major impact on the interpretation which can be done on accounts.

In countries where the accounting rules are fixed by law, the presentation of financial statements is generally more uniform. As far as the state is concerned this uniformity facilitates tax assessment and the use of the data for statistical purposes. In France, for example, political and economic considerations have apparently strongly influenced the shape of successive accounting plans.

However, the fact that the accounting rules are based in law provides some disadvantages. In the first place the law cannot foresee all the particular cases which may arise and the same rules are applied blindly without regard to the special circumstances of this company or that. The accounting rules also change less rapidly as economic circumstances develop, since a statute takes much more time to change than a professional rule. Finally, however exact the statute may be, it may not cover some situations, thereby leaving companies free to make their own interpretation which naturally reflects their particular interests and does not necessarily translate the economic situation of the company accurately. This is particularly evident in Switzerland where the absence of precise legal rules allows many businesses to use accounting principles that have been rejected at an international level (creation of hidden reserves, unjustified changes of accounting policies, etc.). Generally speaking, the inclusion of accounting rules in statutes operates against the portrayal of a true and fair view because it encourages preparers and auditors to pay more attention to conformity with the law than to conformity with the real financial position of the company.

In countries that follow the German model, accounting choices are heavily influenced by tax considerations. In order to minimize tax, companies generally prefer using estimates and methods that reduce the profit. Depreciation generally corresponds to the maximum allowed by the tax authorities and provisions and write-downs are generally exaggerated. In the Anglo-Saxon countries where the accounting treatment of a transaction does not determine its tax treatment, the opposite is true: companies can aim to report a flattering result which satisfies shareholders without carrying a penalty in tax terms. All other things being equal, one should therefore expect that the profitability of an American or British company would be clearly greater than that of a German company.

The influence of taxation can also lead to putting into the accounts some transactions which have no economic justification because in some cases the tax authorities tie a tax benefit to a particular accounting entry. An example of this is the French case where the tax rules for a long time gave companies the right to deduct from their taxable profit an allowance for the maintenance of stocks. This allowance was tied to the creation of a specific provision in the books. The effect of taxation may, though, be isolated in a particular way, as is the case in France and Italy for the creation of provisions whose origin is purely fiscal. In France and Spain the balance sheet part of excess depreciation is shown as part of equity. In Germany a part of excess depreciation may be shown in the balance sheet as a 'special reserve with equity portion'. Despite these arrangements there is no doubt that a close relationship between fiscal and financial accounting severely diminishes the usefulness of financial analysis.

It should, however, be remembered that fiscal considerations only have a role to play in accounts that are destined as an input to tax assessment, which in most cases means the individual company statements. In many countries companies that prepare consolidated statements may eliminate tax considerations from the group accounts. However, this is not always condoned, particularly where the regulations say that the consolidated accounts should be prepared on the same basis as those of the parent company, as in the USA, or where, as in Germany, group accounts may be on a different basis from the parent company but must conform with German law. In any event it is not generally clear from the notes to the accounts whether the group accounts have been restated in order to eliminate tax effects, which makes analysis problematical. Some companies in particular do not bother to restate depreciation in subsidiaries and simply say in the notes that depreciation rates in foreign subsidiaries follow local custom. It is then quite impossible for the analyst to make even a guess about what mix of policies has been followed.

Main problems in financial statement analysis

Despite all the efforts made in the direction of international harmonization (the creation of International Accounting Standards, the EC directives, etc.) the variety of valuation methods and of presentations of data is such that practically every financial statement heading is subject to differences between countries. This part of the chapter is not aiming to bring all these out – that task is virtually impossible – but to draw attention to the main differences which can have a significant effect on the evaluation of the performance and of the financial position of a business from an analysis of the published financial statements.

Scope of consolidation

In principle all companies controlled by the parent should be fully consolidated. This principle, however, does not ensure homogeneity in the scope of consolidation because the concept of control is not the same in each country. There are two main approaches.

In the USA it is considered that the parent must have the majority of votes in order for control to be established. Only companies in which the parent is the majority shareholder are therefore consolidated. Owning 49% of the votes is not considered by the Americans to allow control, whatever the degree of dispersion of the balance of the votes. Minority stakes are accounted for by the equity method if the investor company has 'significant influence', and accounted for at cost otherwise. Significant influence is assumed to exist where the investor has at least 20% of the voting rights.

The IASB and most other countries have a wider conception of control. They admit the possibility of de facto control independently of the voting rights. This control might be the result of the company's statutes, or an agreement between shareholders, or holding the majority of votes within the board of directors or having the power to appoint or dismiss the majority of board members. This concept is used in Australia and in most European countries. French law, for example, formally recognizes that control may exist where the investor has 40% of the votes and there are no other significant blocks of votes.

Under normal circumstances a consolidation of an American group should be more restricted in scope than that of a European group. However, the real consequences are probably more limited because control is in general accompanied by holding a majority of votes – control with a minority holding is finally fairly rare. One of the reasons for the control rule is to reduce the possibilities of using associated companies as a vehicle for off balance sheet financing. Where the 50% rule applies, it is worth looking closely at the activities of associates. The financial analyst should also pay attention to variations in the companies included in a consolidation, particularly where US rules are followed, because it is only necessary to drop the shareholding to below 50% to avoid having to consolidate a subsidiary in poor health.

Some industrial and commercial groups have a financial subsidiary (bank, leasing company, etc.). Sometimes, as in Japanese *keiretsu*, it is considered to be a normal part of a group structure that there should be a 'house bank' (e.g. Sumitomo Bank). Sometimes it is to enable very large companies to 'disintermediate' – to have direct access to the inter-bank financial markets without paying fees to an independent bank (e.g. BP has an in-house bank). Sometimes it is a question of providing consumer credit to customers in order to sell the products manufactured by the group (e.g. General Electric or General Motors in the USA). These companies are often excluded from consolidation because of the special nature of their activities. This practice is legitimate to the extent that the inclusion of such companies, with their different balance sheet structure, would confuse the picture of the group as a whole and falsify ratios to an extent. Unfortunately some heavily indebted groups have taken advantage of this possibility to hide the extent of their indebtedness. All that was necessary was to create a specialized company to which were transferred all the group's debts and sufficient assets to pay the interest. Given its exclusively financial nature, the subsidiary could then be excluded from consolidation and the debts would disappear from the group balance sheet, although most countries require a summary of the accounts of a subsidiary which has been excluded on these grounds to be disclosed in the notes.

Such abuses have led the US authorities and the IASB and the UK no longer to accept this reason for excluding a subsidiary from consolidation. Indeed the US standard (SFAS 96) permits no exclusions of subsidiaries under any circumstances. However, most countries (Germany, Spain, France, Italy, the Netherlands, etc.) still allow it. Subsidiaries which are being held for disposal may also be excluded in most countries, and this provides an opportunity to withdraw a loss-making subsidiary from the consolidated figures without actually selling it, although presumably the auditors would ask questions if it remained unsold for too long. In order to have a full picture of indebtedness and company activity the analyst should look carefully at the scope of the consolidation and in particular any changes to this and the methods used for reporting on financing subsidiaries. The Enron case and the use of special purpose entities (SPEs) to exclude some activities from consolidation demonstrates the difficulty of defining the scope of consolidation and the nature of this potential loophole.

Revaluation of assets

Although historical cost remains the dominant practice, revaluation of assets in general and fixed assets in particular is permitted by international standards. IAS 16 accepts, in fact, as an alternative allowed treatment, that tangible fixed assets can be carried at valuation, as also does the Fourth Directive. National regulation in this area is very diverse. There are three clear groups of countries:

(a) those that allow revaluation, sometimes with conditions attached: Australia, Belgium, France, the Netherlands, the UK;

(b) those that allow this only from time to time, at moments fixed by law: Spain, Italy, Japan;

(c) those that forbid any revaluation: Germany, the USA.

Amongst the countries in group (a) the regularity of revaluations depends on their tax treatment because most companies do not take up this option if that induces a tax liability. One finds such practices more commonly therefore in the countries where the taxable profit is not automatically linked to accounting profit (the Netherlands, the UK). In France loss-making companies sometimes revalue to preserve a loss carry-forward which would otherwise be lost, but otherwise revaluation is only practised in the consolidated accounts because any revaluation surplus appearing in the individual accounts is taxable.

Revaluation of assets has the effect of improving the information available to the analyst by providing a more current valuation of the business assets. Its disadvantages, though, are not negligible. In the first place the practice makes it difficult to compare between companies that revalue their assets and those that remain faithful to pure historical cost.[3] Time-series comparison of the balance sheet of the individual company is also complicated by revaluations within the period under review. The analyst depends on the degree of disclosure in the notes to enable the revaluation to be stripped out if necessary.

The analyst should also beware of the inherent subjectivity of valuations, especially when these are carried out by the firm itself. Revaluing assets is often a solution of last recourse used by companies in difficulties to inflate their equity and thus increase their debt capacity. Rupert Murdoch's News Corporation is famously reported to have escaped having problems with restrictive debt covenants in the recession at the beginning of the 1990s by relying on Australian accounting rules to revalue its newspaper titles and other intangibles. Revaluation is also sometimes used by companies that fear an attempted takeover, on the basis that the increase in net asset value makes the takeover offer seem less attractive. Rank Hovis McDougall in the UK were the first company to recognize self-created brands in their balance sheet (not without controversy) following a takeover bid which they defeated. That did not in fact stop them being taken over by a different predator later.

It should not be forgotten that any revaluation of depreciable assets normally will cause a subsequent increase in depreciation charges, based on the new carrying value. Subsequent profits are therefore reduced which has, for the analyst, the problem of making comparisons difficult with companies that use pure historical cost. However, the depreciation effect usually causes companies only to revalue non-depreciable assets (land or perhaps brands) or, as has not been unknown in the UK, to charge the excess depreciation (i.e. above historical cost) directly against the revaluation reserve.

Depreciation and provisions

In theory systematic depreciation and special write-downs of assets should reflect the real loss of value of assets. The life of the asset for depreciation purposes should be chosen solely as a function of the expected use of the asset. Write-offs should only be made when there is a real drop in value of the asset. The influence of taxation and a particular view of accounting mean that these principles are far from being observed everywhere (for example, see the discussion of Daimler-Benz's policies in Chapter 17).

In the countries where the accounting statements are the basis of the calculation of taxation, businesses will evidently consider the fiscal implications of their accounting decisions. They will generally seek to reduce taxes by making the most use of all the possibilities open to them. Depreciation is therefore based on methods and periods accepted by the tax authorities, even if that means that the charge is greater than what is economically justified. Non-depreciable assets, and in particular stocks and trade debtors, are similarly valued in an extremely prudent manner which manifests itself in the creation of generous provisions. For the same reasons businesses in these countries will tend to anticipate accounting for certain expenses or to overestimate potential liabilities by creating relatively large provisions. In general it should be anticipated that German, French, Spanish and Italian companies apply depreciation rates and make provisions which are higher than those of their Anglo-Saxon equivalents, because an expense must appear in the accounts if it is to be accepted for tax purposes.[4] In the UK depreciation rates for tax purposes are fixed by the government and applied irrespective of the company's accounting policies, which means that British businesses have every reason to understate depreciation. Accounting for provisions in shareholder accounts helps persuade the tax authorities of their validity, but the British tax authorities are not sympathetic towards general provisions for anticipated liabilities, requiring that any provision allowed for tax must be capable of being calculated with a high degree of accuracy. There is therefore little reason for British companies to use general provisions.

As tax is usually calculated on the accounts of the individual company and not the group, nothing prevents depreciation and provisions being restated in the consolidated accounts, as discussed above.

This tendency to overstate depreciation and provisions is reinforced by the basic conception of accountancy in some countries. In Germany the accounting rules are informed by a desire to protect creditors and ensure a long life for the company. While the true and fair view is officially recognized as the objective of accounting, this is largely a secondary consideration which is considered to apply to the notes rather than the balance sheet. The result is an extremely prudent valuation of equity whose objective is to ensure that the capital is not distributed to the shareholders. The overstatement of depreciation and provisions is not condemned but to a certain extent encouraged. In Germany the introduction of the European directives has had a little effect on this tendency but it is also current practice in other countries that follow the Germanic traditions. In Switzerland, for example, the creation of hidden reserves is expressly authorized by the law. However, the large companies there tend nowadays not to use this facility, at least in their consolidated accounts, and prefer to align their policies on international accounting standards.

This represents a considerable problem in cross-border comparisons and there is no solution for it. Analysts should check depreciation policies in the notes, but these are often disclosed in a very vague way, such as 'machinery is depreciated on a straight-line basis over periods varying between 3 and 25 years', making little real comparison or adjustment possible. Where it is possible to calculate the depreciation charge for the year as a percentage of turnover, this may be a worthwhile barometer. As regards provisions, the analyst should compare the opening and closing balance sheet amounts (i.e. current balance sheet and previous year comparative) to calculate net movement in the year, and also reconcile this with any figures provided in the cash flow statement for the calculation of operating cash flows by the indirect method, if there is such a statement.

Leasing

Leasing can be classified as falling into two categories: operating leases (or simple hires) and financial leases. The latter covers all those contracts which transfer to the lessee all of the risks and rewards inherent in the leased asset. These contracts generally have the following characteristics: they run for the whole life of the asset, the present value of the lease rentals is equivalent to the value of the asset at the time the contract is signed, there is a transfer of title to the lessee or an option for this on the expiry of the lease. Contracts such as hire purchase agreements or rentals with an option to purchase fall into this category.

The accounting treatment of financial leases is often cited as an illustration of the difference between the two types of accounting systems. For those with an essentially legalistic view of the accounts, an asset cannot appear in the balance sheet unless it is owned by the company, whatever the circumstances under which the company has use of it. On the other hand, those with an essentially economic view of the accounts prefer that substance is given priority over form and the asset should be accounted for by the company which assumes the risks of its ownership, even if it does not legally own the asset. According to these, then, the asset should appear in the balance sheet of the lessee.

Here one comes across the traditional dividing line between Anglo-Saxon countries, which take an essentially economic view of accounts, and the continental European countries, which have a more legally oriented view of accounting. With the former, the leased asset is found in the balance sheet of the lessee, while with the latter it is found in the balance sheet of the lessor. In France, for example, the accounting regulations forbid the capitalization of leased assets, at least as far as individual company accounts are concerned. In Anglo-Saxon countries the asset must be accounted for in the lessee's balance sheet. The Spanish regulations have an interesting variant to attempt to bridge between the two systems: the asset is accounted for in the balance sheet of the lessor, but the lessee recognizes as an intangible asset the right to use the leased asset. In Germany the situation is rather fluid. Ordelheide and Pfaff (1994) say that the criteria are not dissimilar to IAS 17, but the overall effect is that 'as a general rule, leased assets are shown in the lessor's balance sheet' but the lessee must show commitments under leasing contracts in the notes.

The split between the two systems may be emphasized in that the Anglo-Saxon countries are now looking at the possibility of introducing a rule requiring capitalization of all leased assets, whatever the length of the lease. This is largely being done to combat non-compliance with existing rules for accounting for leased assets. Leasing companies have increasingly responded to the accounting rules by drawing up leases which deliberately avoided the criteria for capitalization, such as renewable short-term leases, etc.

For the financial analyst it is clear that the Anglo-Saxon solution is preferable. From a financial point of view, a lease can be seen as simply an alternative to a loan (with the advantage that in many countries it remains off balance sheet). The lessee finds himself in the same position as if the asset had been purchased with a loan. The lease rentals cover the reimbursement of the loan together with financial costs. The rentals are loan repayment annuities.

Accounting for the asset in the balance sheet of the lessor means that the assets used by the lessee are not properly reflected in the lessee's financial statements and nor are the lessee's financial commitments revealed. Taken to an extreme, a business that finances all its productive capacity with leases would have a balance sheet with no fixed assets and no long-term debt. In this situation an understanding of the true financial position of the company and its debt requires that the balance sheet is restated. Theoretically this involves adding the market value of leased assets to the balance sheet as well as the present value of future rentals, calculated at market rates. Most jurisdictions where capitalization of leases is not practised require disclosure of outstanding lease rental commitments, which allows the analyst to approximate the adjustment by adding the present value of the future lease rentals to both sides of the balance sheet.

Accounting for goodwill

The way in which goodwill is accounted for is certainly one of the subjects that has created the most discussion. It is very significant for the financial analyst because the policy used by a company has a direct effect on the perceived performance of the group and its apparent financial position. Goodwill is the difference between the cost of the shares in the subsidiary and the fair value of the net assets acquired. The interpretation of this excess is difficult. Some see it as the price paid to acquire intangible assets whose nature makes it impractical for them to be separately recognized in the fair value calculation (e.g. client loyalty, technical knowledge, etc.). Some see it as an anticipation of future revenues to be earned from the shareholding, others as simply evidence that the purchaser has paid too much for the acquisition. Others point out that the price paid to acquire shares represents an estimate of the present value of future receipts from the investment. As such it has nothing to do with the value of the individual assets which form the business acquired and has no relevance to the consolidation process, except that the substitution of individual assets for the overall investment leaves a hole in the balance sheet which accountants find inconvenient. The polemics that surround the accounting treatment are a function of the lack of agreement as to what it represents.

Some accountants, living in a world of economic rationality, think that the payment of goodwill represents the acquisition of a benefit, whether this is due to intangibles or to some anticipation of future growth. In these circumstances the goodwill has the characteristics of an asset and should therefore be capitalized in the balance sheet and subsequently be amortized over its useful life. However, others take the view that, given the vague nature of goodwill, this solution results in recognizing a fictitious asset. They prefer that goodwill should be written off immediately by deducting it from equity at the time of acquisition. This solution is also preferred by those who see goodwill as an acquisition premium, paid to induce the original shareholders to sell their asset.

The two solutions produce quite different effects on the consolidated accounts. Capitalization of goodwill leads to a reduction of profits in future periods as a result of the amortization charge. Write-off against reserves avoids this disadvantage but gives an increase in the debt/equity ratio. It seems on the whole that companies consider the profit effect more significant than equity and in the countries where this is possible, most of them choose to deduct goodwill from reserves. Clearly any approach to performance evaluation and analysis of financial structure requires that the method of accounting for goodwill is examined.

Restating those accounts where goodwill is written off to reserves is the normal approach, but this is made difficult where goodwill has been written off in several years and has simply disappeared from the accounts. Some companies, aware of this problem, leave a cumulative goodwill figure as a negative item in equity in order essentially to enable users to restate the balance sheet for the purposes of calculating the financial position. In any event, capitalization of goodwill does not of itself ensure comparability between companies because of the differences in amortization periods used. In theory goodwill should be written off over its useful life, but its vague nature makes any objective estimate impossible. In practice amortization periods applied vary enormously, even within the same group, which makes cross-sectional comparisons very difficult.

A further variant is that goodwill is a residual figure and a company that wishes to lessen its impact has the option of overvaluing the underlying assets whose fair value is deducted in arriving at the goodwill value. If goodwill is normally capitalized and amortized, there will only be a saving of goodwill amortization if assets that are revalued have a useful life longer than goodwill (e.g. buildings) or are not depreciable (e.g. land). However, the revaluation of land is fairly limited and the ideal solution is to recognize other assets that are not depreciable. Commercial brands have played this role. The lack of precision which surrounds intangible assets permits of the argument that they are not depreciable, and indeed some companies say that current advertising expenditure maintains the value of the brand and depreciation would be a double charge. Some companies have profited from the lack of regulation to attribute a very high value to the brands of companies which they bought and thereby diminish goodwill. This practice comes up against IAS 38 which specifies that all intangible assets (including brands) should be amortized.

In 2001, the FASB decided that goodwill should not be systematically depreciated but simply impaired when necessary, in response to which the IASB announced its intention to adopt the same position. This change will have a considerable impact on the equity and profitability of firms, especially for those with an intensive acquisition policy. Moreover, because the fair value of goodwill cannot be estimated with a high level of reliability, firms will have considerable discretion in determining the amount and timing of these impairments. This will enable them to manage their earnings more easily.

In general, accounting rules for intangible assets are likely to change in as much as business practice, particularly in consumer sectors, pays an increasing importance to brands and other intangibles as key assets rather than production capacity. This is calling into question a traditional dismissal of intangibles as 'soft' assets whose existence and value are both difficult to determine. In the USA the new rules widen the range of intangibles to be recognized in an acquisition.

Deferred taxation

The matching principle requires that taxation should be accounted for in the same period as the transactions which gave rise to the tax liability, even if its payment is made in a subsequent period or has been anticipated. Each time that the taxation of income or the deduction of expenses for tax takes place in a period other than that in which the income or expense was accounted for, this results in a corresponding deferred or anticipated tax item. The significance of these items depends on the closeness of the relationship between tax rules and financial accounting.

In the countries where tax is aligned on accounting (Germany, Japan and to a lesser extent France, Italy and Spain) there are few sources of deferred taxation and consequently little importance is placed on this. Deferred taxation rarely appears in the financial statements of individual companies and even in consolidated statements the figures are modest. On the other hand, in Anglo-Saxon countries, which are characterized by a considerable independence between the accounting rules and the tax rules in key areas such as depreciation, the regulations for deferred tax are quite specific and the amounts concerned can be considerable.

The rules for accounting for deferred tax are articulated around two axes. The first axis concerns which differences should be accounted for. One group prefers a global calculation which includes all temporary differences, while the other excludes recurring differences or those which will only reverse in the long run. The international trend is towards full provision.

Another difference should be pointed out. This concerns the particular timing difference which arises from tax losses which can be carried forward. A loss in one financial period is generally deductible from profits in future periods, at least for a limited time. Any loss therefore creates a potential future tax saving which will not be realized unless the company creates sufficient profits to absorb the loss within the time limit allowed. Given the uncertainty inherent in this, accounting standards generally provide special rules for the treatment of tax losses carried forward. However, in the USA these are treated just like other timing differences.

The second axis concerns the treatment of the balance of deferred taxes in subsequent accounting periods. The two main methods are that of an unchanging amount (deferral method) and that of a variable amount (liability method). The first considers that the calculation of the amount of tax when the provision is created is definitive; the balance is not therefore changed should there be a subsequent change in the tax rules. Under the liability method, on the other hand, the balance of the provision is adjusted for any later changes. After a long period of hesitation marked by several changes of opinion, the Anglo-Saxon countries seem to be settling on the liability method. The rules are likely to evolve further as IASB and FASB converge their standards.

Capitalized expenses

Certain expenses produce their effects over several financial years. It is therefore logical to spread them over those years so that the rhythm of recognition of the expense coincides more or less with the revenues generated by it. This procedure is only applied, of course, to costs whose effects are not immediate such as research and development or borrowing costs.

In some industry sectors vast sums of money are devoted to the research and development of products or manufacturing processes. To the extent that these costs represent potential future revenue it is legitimate to capitalize them, which is why most countries, with the exception of the USA and Germany, accept this. The uncertainty inherent in this kind of activity requires, though, that prudence is used to avoid capitalizing assets which turn out to be fictitious. This is why regulations generally allow only development costs to be capitalized. Fundamental and applied research costs are expensed as incurred. The conditions under which capitalization takes place are also very strict. Usually the project must have a good chance of being realized and of being a commercial success.

In practice one usually finds a great deal of similarity in accounting principles within the same business sector. In Switzerland, for example, no large pharmaceutical or chemical enterprise capitalizes its development costs, enormous though these are. One might suppose that the capitalization of these costs would be seen by the financial markets as a signal of difficulties. In Japan, on the other hand, the capitalization of development costs is normal practice.

Certain assets, such as factories, can take a particularly long time to construct and require substantial financing. The inclusion of the cost of equity financing in the carrying value of the asset has always been rejected. However, some consider that there is nothing against the inclusion of borrowing costs, on the basis that these are not fundamentally different from other construction costs. Others are opposed to this on the basis that it means that the same asset would have a different accounting value depending upon whether it had been financed by equity or debt. In most countries the regulators have not found it necessary to take a view on this and have left the choice in the hands of the businesses, while limiting the capitalization of interest to those assets whose construction or whose stock period (e.g. whisky) is particularly long. Only in the USA is interest capitalization compulsory.

Once capitalized, the interest will be reflected in future depreciation charges. Capitalization therefore has the effect of transforming a financial expense into an operating expense. The analyst may be led into underestimating borrowing costs as a result of this, and should examine the notes carefully.

Transactions in foreign currencies

The way in which transactions in foreign currencies are accounted for is a source of many variations which upset the analysis of the financial statements of companies with substantial foreign activities.

The first problem is the treatment of unrealized exchange gains and losses at balance sheet date. All regulations require that debtors and creditors denominated in foreign currencies should be recalculated using the rates current at balance sheet date, but how this is reflected in the accounts is not the same at all. In the Anglo-Saxon countries there is a tendency to restate the balance sheet amounts and take the differences, positive and negative, to the profit and loss account. Other countries, including France and Germany, consider that the prudence principle prohibits the recognition of unrealized gains. France restates the balance sheet figure but carries the unrealized gain as a deferred credit. Germany does not restate long-term debtors or creditors where this represents an unrealized exchange gain but may restate short-term items. This solution leads to a classic undervaluation of profits since unrealized losses are recognized but not unrealized gains.

The statements of foreign subsidiaries can also be translated in several ways. The methods set out in IAS 21 (closing rate and temporal methods) are not the only ones. One sometimes comes across the monetary/non-monetary method, which consists of converting the monetary elements at the closing rate and the non-monetary at the historical rate. Each method is also applied with many variants with the result that the range of choice is finally very wide. Even where the methods are relatively well codified, the rules of application are not always followed. It seems clear, in fact, that most companies use only the closing rate method, even though this is supposed to apply only to autonomous subsidiaries. Ultimately this is perhaps less important than that the method chosen should be applied consistently.

The issue of how to account for exchange differences arising from translation is a lot more difficult. Given that these differences can sometimes be very large, the choice of passing them through the income statement or taking them directly to equity can have a major impact on the evaluation of the performance and the financial position of the business. In theory the rules are very precise: a translation difference arising from the application of the closing rate method is taken directly to equity, while that arising from the temporal method flows through the income statement. But these principles are not always respected and the analyst must be vigilant and consider whether the treatment used has not been adopted with the object of manipulating the external evaluation. It is easy to see that companies must be tempted to put positive differences in the income statement and negative ones in equity, as the Polly Peck case in the UK has shown.[5]

Extraordinary and exceptional items

One of the most important objects of analysis is to determine the group's capacity to generate profits, that is to work out its long-term profitability. In many countries the structure of the income statement aims to help in this objective by setting apart those transactions and events which are not expected to occur regularly. The revenue and expenses of the business are often displayed with a distinction between ordinary/extraordinary or current/exceptional, as the case may be. These two types of classification are not necessarily equivalent, and indeed there is a good deal of confusion in practice as to what is implied.

The arrangement current/exceptional is generally used in continental European countries. It is based on the frequency with which events take place and contrasts those which happen regularly with those which do not. However, a normal event such as the failure of a large client might well be considered as exceptional if the amount lost was greater than the normal losses of this type to which the company was accustomed.

The distinction ordinary/extraordinary used in Anglo-Saxon countries is oriented more round the nature of the transaction or event. It contrasts transactions that are part of the company's normal activities with those that have a different origin. It is not necessarily the regularity of the event that determines its classification but its nature (although an extraordinary event that happens every year would appear no longer to be extraordinary). By contrast with the first case, the write-off of a client account could in no sense be considered to be extraordinary, whatever the value, because it relates to the normal trading activities of the company. Extraordinary elements are therefore relatively rare; IAS 8 cites earthquakes as an example. At the same time the analyst who wishes to identify unusual transactions is not frustrated. The business, while respecting the ordinary/extraordinary distinction, should isolate unusual transactions that are part of normal business and identify them as exceptional.

In general this is a thorny issue. Historically extraordinary items have been excluded, in Anglo-Saxon countries, from the calculation of the ever-important earnings per share ratio. This has meant that listed companies who want their share price to rise have every interest in flowing expenses through the extraordinary category and profits through ordinary. In the UK this has led in turn to a redefinition of extraordinary items as being extremely rare and unlikely ever to be repeated, while matters such as reorganization provisions and asset disposals are definitively treated as 'ordinary' but potentially 'exceptional'. In France the same transactions would fall into the non-current category (but which also uses the label exceptional). The IASB has removed the extraordinary category from the income statement. Analysts are advised to read the relevant part of the UK chapter (Chapter 6) on this subject, but in general they should view these distinctions as being at least open to question. They should inform themselves (from the notes) of the nature of any transaction being classified as non-regular and form their own view.

Changes in accounting principles

The comparability of financial statements in a time-series requires that the accounting principles used should not be changed, or at least that in the event of change the effects of the change should be clearly indicated so that the user can make any adjustments that are necessary.

It is important to distinguish between a change of accounting *principle* and a change in accounting *estimates*. The latter concern calculations where in the absence of precise information figures have been based on estimates. This is the case in particular for the economic life of assets and the amount of provisions. These estimates should be reviewed from time to time (in theory every year) and changed if it transpires that they are no longer valid.

Changes in accounting principles (e.g. method of depreciation, stock valuation method, etc.) are much more strictly regulated. IAS 8 allows them only in two cases: (a) if a statute or an accounting standard requires them, or (b) if they will lead to a more appropriate (truer and fairer) presentation of the transactions or events that make up the financial statements.

While the consistency principle is nowadays more or less universally accepted the rule is not necessarily applied in a very rigid manner. In countries where hidden reserves are usual (Germany, Switzerland) changes in estimates and accounting principles are normal practice since it is precisely these changes that enable companies to hide their profits. In Germany consistency is taken to apply to valuation rules and statement formats, but not to recognition principles. In the countries where accounting practices are aligned on taxation (Germany, and Japan in particular but to a lesser extent Spain, Italy and France) a change in the tax rules is generally sufficient to justify a change in accounting principles.

Changes of estimates differ from changes of principle not only in their accounting treatment but also in the disclosure necessary. A change in estimates affects only the current financial year and perhaps future years, but past years are not brought into question. However, a change of accounting principle must be applied retrospectively, which implies that the financial statements from past years must also be changed. The effects of the change on past years can be dealt with in two ways. IAS 8 suggests that the net effect is recognized in the value of opening equity and that where comparative figures are given in the accounts, these should be recalculated.

But this approach comes up against the principle of inviolability of the opening balance sheet which is adhered to in most continental European countries, where no change is permitted to a balance sheet which has been voted on by the shareholders. This is why IAS 8 also provides, as an allowed alternative treatment, that the net effect of the adjustment to previous financial years should flow through the current period income statement and that the comparative figures are not adjusted. In this case the consequences of the change of method should be presented separately, for example in another column of comparatives.

Here too actual practice is often far from the regulators' ideal. Outside the Anglo-Saxon world it is rare for the company to give all the necessary information. In the countries where hidden reserves are allowed, changes of estimate or changes of method are rarely indicated because this disclosure would take away the secret nature of the reserve. Otherwise companies limit themselves to noting the change and, in the better instances, showing its effect on major balance sheet categories. However, in Germany, where figures from previous periods cannot be changed, neither the effects of change nor comparative figures are disclosed. Generally speaking it is often very difficult for the analyst to appreciate fully what are the real effects of these changes.

Conclusion

The analyst's job is far from easy in the best of circumstances since the companies may be trying to hide unpalatable facts or to put a spin on them so that they are interpreted in a particular way, although increasingly tough disclosure rules make this possibility more remote than it once might have been. In an international context the analyst's task becomes even more difficult because of the need to have some knowledge of the different accounting rules and their impact upon ratios.

In this chapter we have tried to highlight those areas of accounting policies that are capable of having the most effect in the calculation of classic ratios and other analytical tools. We do not believe that there is any magical single method that will give the international analyst the right answers. We think there is no substitute for painstaking examination, above all of the notes to the accounts and the discussion of company accounting policies. When evaluating a particular company we recommend that the analyst check the background rules of the home country by reference to the chapter in this book, to see which financial statement items need the most scrutiny or potentially restatement for the purposes of cross-border comparisons.

Notes

1. The Institute of Investment Management and Research (IIMR).

2. A 'horizontal' balance sheet might also be set out vertically on the page with a list of assets followed by a list of liabilities and equity, so physically appearing as a single vertical column rather than two columns side by side. This is not the issue. The important question is whether the balance sheet presents total assets and total financing, or whether it presents assets less debt equals equity.

3. UK companies that revalue fixed assets often use the term 'modified historical cost' to describe their accounting base.

4. In France and Italy depreciation charges which are considered to be greater than what is economically justified are shown separately in the balance sheet, which avoids understatement of the related assets.

5. A listed UK company which had deposits in Turkish pounds which were depreciating rapidly. The high rate of interest proposed in such countries gave an apparently high rate of return, and was taken into profit, while the diminution of value of the investments was taken into equity.

References

Choi, F. and Levich, R. (1991) Behavioural effects of international accounting diversity. *Accounting Horizons* **5**(2): 1–130.

Colasse, B. (2001) *L'analyse financière de l'entreprise*. Repères/Editions La Découverte, Paris.

Haller, A. (1997) *Wertschöpfungsrechnung*. Schäffer Poeschel Verlag, Stuttgart.

Ordelheide, D. and Pfaff, D. (1994) *European Financial Reporting – Germany*. Routledge, London.

Stickney, C.P. (1990) *Financial Statement Analysis, a Strategic Perspective*, 2nd edn. Dryden Press, Fort Worth.

Walton, P. (2000) *Financial Statement Analysis*. Thomson Learning, London.

Further Reading

Samuels, J., Brayshaw, R. and Craner, J. (1995) *Financial Statement Analysis in Europe*. Chapman Hall, London.

White, G., Sondhi, A. and Fried, D. (1994) *The Analysis and Use of Financial Statements*. John Wiley & Sons, New York.

Index